Also by Rolf Knight

A Very Ordinary Life
Stump Ranch Chronicles
A Man of Our Times (with Maya Koizumi)
Work Camps and Company Towns in Canada and the U.S.
Indians at Work
Along the No. 20 Line

Traces of Magma

An annotated bibliography of left literature

Rolf Knight

Draegerman
Vancouver, British Columbia
Canada

Canadian Cataloguing in Publication Data
Knight, Rolf
Traces of Magma
ISBN 0-86491-034-7
1. Annotated bibliography
2. Left wing literature, 20th century comparative

Draegerman
139 South Glynde
Burnaby, British Columbia, V5B 3J3
Canada

CONTENTS

Introduction iii

North America, Britain and the Dominions
    Great Britain 1
    Ireland 16
    Canada 21
    United States 35
    Australia and New Zealand 62

Latin America and the Caribbean
    Mexico 68
    Central America 73
    Dominican Republic 78
    Puerto Rico 79
    Cuba 80
    Colombia 86
    Venezuela 88
    Ecuador 89
    Bolivia 92
    Peru 95
    Chile 98
    Argentina 101
    Uruguay 102
    Paraguay 105
    Brazil 106
    Caribbean 110

Europe: Western
    France 115
    Spain 121
    Portugal 130
    Italy 135
    Germany 142
    Austria 154
    Netherlands and Flanders 156
    Scandinavia
        Denmark 158
        Iceland 161
        Norway 163
        Sweden 165
        Finland 170

Europe: East, Central and Balkans
    U.S.S.R. 174
    Poland 194
    Czechoslovakia 200
    Hungary 206
    Rumania 212
    Bulgaria 215
    Yugoslavia 218
    Albania 222
    Greece 224

Middle East and North Africa
    Turkey 229
    Iran 235

                Israel 238
                Palestine/Palestinian 241
                Lebanon, Syria, Iraq 244
                Egypt 246
                North Africa and Sudan 250

Africa
                Ethiopia and Somalia 254
                Francophone Africa 258
                Nigeria and Ghana 262
                Central and East Africa 265
                Union of South Africa 269
                Other South African 273
                Mozambique and Angola 275

India and South East Asia
                India 278
                Pakistan 291
                Sri Lanka, Burma, Thailand 292
                Viet Nam 294
                Malaya 297
                Indonesia 299
                Philippines 302

East Asia
                China 306
                Korea 315
                Japan 318

Bibliographic Sources 329

Authors' Index 349

INTRODUCTION

This is basically an annotated bibliography of left wing novels about the lives of working people during the 20th century. It includes some collections of poetry, drama and short stories as well as a smattering of non-fictional material such as oral and life histories, but mainly it is a compendium of novels. It includes more than 3,000 titles originally in some 50 languages by circa 1,500 authors from over 90 countries. It is not a survey limited to socialist realist or narrowly proletarian novels of the 1930s, although representatives of that literature are certainly included.

Bibliographers do not normally attempt a compilation of works as wide ranging as those presented here. The main purpose of this bibliography is to provide an introduction to left fiction for lay readers. It is intended for those who, for whatever reason, have become interested in what this literature has to say about events, forces and people throughout the world during the course of one moderately long lifetime. It is for those who probably have only a vague notion of which authors and titles exist and where to begin.

The bibliography adopts a broad and common sense understanding of what constitutes "left" literature. A programmatic definition would not materially ellucidate the titles. I have cast a wide net. Suffice it to say that a basic feature of virtually all the works is a gross disparity between existing social conditions and the author's vision of more equitable arrangements. Wide ranging or highly circumscribed in focus, moulded in a variety of historic, political and literary forms, this writing entails demands for social justice for the disinherited sectors of humanity. Most of the titles cited attempt to be honest and sympathetic accounts of working people, which in itself distinguishes them from most other literature. Whether through lyrical storytelling, bitter protest or subtle implication these works propose a fundamental reordering of the power over peoples' lives and destinies. In all their variety, they are voices for the party of humanity.

The themes found in the novels cited are almost as varied as the experiences of working people during the course of the present century. They portray the multiple forms and many faceted strictures of caste and class, as well as the strategies which people evolve to circumvent or oppose such exactions. They deal with the contending claims of new understandings and the pull of older values, they depict the bonds of narrow loyalties and widening allegiances which may broaden the horizons of once isolated people. They treat with the corrosive effects of social disenfranchisement but also with tenacious hope and the resurrection of struggles for social justice from the most unpromising of conditions. The themes deal with the costs of wars "just" and unjust, with militancy and quiescent cultural resistance. They picture the workings of social institutions in particular societies through the understandings, personal relationships and manifold responses of ordinary people enmeshed in them.

As literature, the works usually pursue the broader processes in operation through the experiences and emotions of a relatively limited number of characters. While not always captured in the annotations, the themes of hardships and struggle are typically alloyed with accounts of private joys, of collective achievements and personal pride wrung from the most diverse situations. Despite the tenor of some of the comments here, the body of this literature is not overwhelmingly or exclusively concerned with the themes of "struggle, struggle, toil and trouble".

There are inherent limitations which a bibliography such as this encounters. One must accept that it is impossible to provide anything like an exhaustive survey of left wing novels on the scope dealt with. The partial and somewhat subjective selection entailed is not purely arbitrary. It attempts to sample the various themes, authors and traditions in the literature from different periods and countries. No single person would subscribe to all contending views presented.

A more serious limitation is that the left literature of some countries has only by exception survived a censorship of silence to enter sources accessible to the compiler. One has to use and choose from what is available. This is not a select survey of eminent authors and celebrated novels as such. Don't be surprised to find the work of renowned writers such as Elias Canetti, Margil Batwood, Raja Rao and other literary luminaries absent here. The absence of any particular work or author does not imply any derogation. As literature per se some of the material excluded may be greater than some of the desperate chronicles which have found a place here.

The left wing fiction surveyed includes the work of many of the greatest authors of the 20th century. But it hardly needs saying that not all the items cited are works of great art. There are other reasons for their importance. One may have critical qualms about features of certain works and yet find them of considerable value. In principle, each title should be considered on its own merits and regardless of an author's reputation or anonymity. All in all, many of even the lesser known titles presented here embody greater literary merit than we are usually led to believe.

Different writers with their own particular passions and styles touch responsive chords in different readers. Given differing temperaments, degrees of familiarity and tastes, who is to say which treatment of a topic is most moving or illuminating for any single reader.

Readers will find certain real and specious gaps in coverage which ideally might be remedied. Only two things are sure about their responses: first, almost everyone will take umbrage that some of their favourite authors and works have been left out while others they heartily dislike have been included and, second, interested readers should discover a swath of fascinating material previously unknown to them. They should realize that it is not merely a question of what might have been added but rather which titles included one would delete in order to make space for additional entries. Everyone will have their own prime candidates for exclusion.

The unabashedly documentary aspect of much of the material surveyed here is sometimes of as great an importance as the purely literary value of the books --although normally the titles are a mixture of both. Given this concern with social documentation, what is the reason for concentrating on novels and other fiction, forms often dismissed by serious intellectuals of right and left alike? The contention here is that there is no simple distinction between the validity of "objective" accounts and that of some kinds of "fiction". Many of these novels are based upon an extensive firsthand knowledge and a complex grasp of the events and forces described. Often the fictional works are the only ones which deal with the everyday lives of ordinary people caught up in and acting to transform the particular conditions around them.

Of equal importance, novels and other fictional work do capture many people's interest more effectively than analogous formal studies. Fiction can have a moving as well as an illuminating quality which engages the reader. Of course, one must admit that some scholarly accounts are as excitingly written as the best novels and that much allegedly realistic fiction--some left wing novels among them--may be worse than useless as social chronicles. None of this should be taken to imply that even the most cogent novels are a substitute for more systematic studies. But if the realm of literature should not be taken for actual history, neither should most schoolbook histories or public affairs documentaries.

The emphasis on novels rather than on other kinds of fictional literature derives from the premise that the novel is seemingly the most general and accessible form of left fictional literature. The novel does appear to be a particularly suitable vehicle for social documentation and those stemming from other societies do seem to survive translation better than do most other kinds of writing. More than any other format, novels are likely to be translated and be potentially available in bookstores and libraries.

While I have made a special effort to locate English language editions of the novels cited I have not hesitated to include seemingly untranslated works. Although the main readership of this bibliography will be those whose native language is English, I would presume that at least some multilingual readers will also peruse it. But there is a more fundamental reason for including works untranslated into English. The rationale is that of any literary survey--to introduce readers to the range of authors, titles and topics in the corpus of the literature discussed. Comparable surveys of national literatures are typically written for those unable to read the works in the original languages. Even if the overwhelming majority of readers cannot peruse novels about Bombay textile workers in Marathi, or accounts of the lives of Egyptian peasants in Arabic, etc., this bibliography may provide a sample of the themes dealt with in the progressive literature of those peoples. In this regard, it should have worth as an introductory survey regardless of which titles cited the user actually does read.

Included here is a selection of poetry and drama where the author or the work is too important to go unmentioned. Even the most megalomanic bibliographer should know better than to mess with poets or to imply that one is able to annotate their works. Yet in some countries poetry was/is so central to the progressive literary tradition that it would do violence to the picture not to mention it. The works of poets like Hugh MacDiarmid, Pablo Neruda, Jannis Ritsos, Nazim Hikmet and others just cannot be left out. Similarly, the smattering of drama listed here, ranging from a broad sample of workers' theatre pieces to the work of Berthold Brecht. They are the merest handful, only suggesting the richness of that genre. But the power of both drama and poetry depends on its presentation. Drama is meant to be seen and poetry is meant to be heard.

The bibliography also contains a small number of non-fictional work such as oral and life history, the occasional memoir, examples of a genre once called "reportage" and yet more diverse items. Such accounts typically have a personal quality which gives them an appeal not dissimilar to novels. They are cited here when they touch on some topic of especial interest which would otherwise remain unmentioned. One format little represented is the short story. While some volumes of collected stories are listed, there are usually no entries of single stories--or indeed any items which appeared only in unbound folio form. This does to some extent distort the picture of left literature in certain countries, where such work was long restricted to forms which could be accommodated in small journals, union newspapers and so forth. The exclusion of this material is largely a question of accessibility. No matter how seminal or evocative a piece of writing, if it has not been issued in book form it is effectively unavailable.

There is a considerable disparity in the volume and the nature of work from the various countries dealt with. Quite expectably, more left literature was produced in some countries than in others. In some regions such writing has only recently begun to emerge while elsewhere there have been marked shifts in the trajectory of this literature over the past three generations. Needless to say, these differences and changes do not stem merely from mercurial literary fashions but flow, however distortedly, from the social and political realities in those countries at various times.

Literature of course does not fully or exactly reflect the actual experiences of any particular nation or group. It is a selective mirror of the backgrounds, interests and perspectives of the extant authors. There can be some extraordinary gaps. For instance, the multi-generational experiences of African miners, dockers, factory workers and others are only rarely central in novels by most African authors. What constitutes a progressive stance is of course relative to the contending forces in any particular country at a given time. Where I have found little in the way of working class literature I have tended to include some titles whose concerns mainly reflect the aspirations of a reformist sector of the middle class.

As might be expected, the predominant themes and topics of left wing novels vary by country and period. For instance, the swath of books about the lives and struggles of the peasantry throughout eastern and southern Europe during the first half of the 20th century have few analogues in British literature, which in turn has a rich body of work about the long established culture of industrial workers. Similarly, the literature of popular armed struggle against assorted neo-colonial and anachronistic ruling classes in Latin America is absent in the left writing of the United States, which instead was especially strong on strike novels. Cuban novels dealing with the assorted hopes, setbacks, achievements and distortions involved in attempting to carry forward a socialist revolution do not appear in fiction from countries which have not experienced such transformations. These are merely a few gross examples of the differing thematic emphases found in the various national literatures.

The titles in the various national sections do not always represent the comparative extensiveness or paucity of left literature of those countries. In attempting to provide a sample of such writing from as many regions as feasible the bibliography may underrepresent some particularly extensive literature to include lesser known traditions. Considering the expected readership, there is an extensive coverage of some English language material. For Canada, with its near total absence of left novels in English, I have included a selection of oral history, biography and other work which elsewhere are treated as tangential to the main thrust of the bibliography.

Although the bibliography presents a broad cross section of the heterogeneous topics and themes in left literature, the selection is not necessarily representative of their relative preponderance. In fact, I have tended to limit citations of work about some of the more recurrent topics (such as American strike novels or Soviet socialist construction literature) in order to include examples of less frequently treated themes. The focus is on novels which provide a progressive social critique of whichever society they happen to emerge from. In addition, there is a special effort to include titles by authors who stemmed from or were part of the working class and peasant worlds about which they wrote. Despite its stress on heterogeneity the bibliography does survey the extant authors and titles with some semblance of balance and representatives of all the major genres of left literature are cited.

The entries in the body of the bibliography are usually quite straight forward and once the reader gains some familiarity with them the annotations should be largely self-explanatory. However, some brief comment may be in order to introduce the format and clarify what the annotations do and don't indicate about the works listed.

The basic ordering of authors and titles here is by country, not by the original language of the work or the nationality of the author. More precisely, the works are entered under the country in which the work is set. For instance, the semi-autobiographic novels about the Spanish working class during the interwar years by the "English" writer Ralph Bates are found in the section on Spain, not Great Britain. Alternately, Ferreira de Castro's various novels about Brazil and Portugal are separately listed in the section for those two countries. (There are a few exceptions, the logic of which may be evident in the citations themselves.) This is a pragmatic scheme intended to aid readers in locating titles about particular countries. While some of the accounts involve events in a number of countries there is typically one predominant locale. And, as it turns out, the overwhelming majority of novels about any given nation were written by nationals of that land. This is mainly inherent in the body of the literature itself and involves no premise that only members of a particular group can meaningfully portray the lives and responses of that people.

Where of relevance, the sub-national or linguistic derivation of the work cited is mentioned in the annotation itself; for instance, Bosnian, Serbian or Croatian writing in Yugoslavia. A comparable distinction sometimes noted in the annotation is the language in which the work was originally written. This is of considerable importance in multinational, multilingual states. For India, by example, annotations indicate whether the title is in Hindi, Punjabi, Malayalam or one of the other half dozen major Indian languages. For a few countries, such as Canada and Czechoslovakia, I have followed the normal procedure of listing the literature of the two major languages separately. Authors and titles in the various sections are cited alphabetically regardless of which linguistic sub-traditions they may stem from.

In a few instances I have provided very condensed biographic notes about a particular author in the annotation of one of his or her major titles. These are intended to suggest something of the authors' times as well as their personal backgrounds and will hopefully serve as a reminder that the themes dealt with did not just arise from writers' fertile imaginations. It would be desirable to have an appendix providing biographic sketches of all the authors cited. Their lives were sometimes every bit as remarkable as their writing.

The names of the authors and the titles of works have been transliterated from their native language into English approximations where necessary. Frequently there are only inexact and unstandardized analogues in English to approximate the script and phonemes of Greek, Arabic, Amharic and so forth. One therefore finds the names of authors and titles variously transliterated in different sources. For instance, one Greek novelist is alternately transposed into English as Dimitros Chadtzis or Dhimitris Hadzis. Similar problems arise in the transliteration of titles from their original languages into English script. I have normally reproduced those versions presented in the sources, occasionally indicating variant spellings in brackets. Normally, the authors' "pen names", i.e., as appearing on publications, are those cited in this bibliography. Their "real" names are sometimes listed in brackets.

Variation in the translation of titles is possibly a more obvious matter; there may be no exact equivalents between English and the original language or the title may revolve around an ideomatic meaning. For instance, Vilhelm Moberg's novel entitled Raskens alludes to a supposedly uniquely Swedish aspect of farm tenant-landlord relations. Where a work has actually been translated into English one can merely list that title, otherwise one must choose between the alternative provisional translations assigned by different reviewers. For example, Denji Kuroshima's Bososeru Shigai is variously transposed as "Armed City", "Beseiged City", or "Conquered City", all of which entail some important differences in English. Where critical I have noted alternate editions and titles of a given work in the body of the annotation.

The reader will note that most accents, diacritics and other notations of pronunciation have been excised in the citation of titles and names. This seemingly cavelier step, possibly most evident in Spanish and French spellings, is taken in the interests of practicality and consistency. The array of diacritics normally used in the 50 odd languages included here is enormous and quite impossible to reproduce en toto.

As to the form of citation, authors are normally listed alphabetically by surname(s) in each national section. The first title of a work is that of the original language and the following date that of the initial publication. The bracketed title following the main entry is an English translation of the original. Where the bracketed English title is underlined this indicates an actual English language edition of the work. The following date is that of the English edition. Consider what is denoted by one bibliographic entry, in this case a well known work by an eminent Turkish novelist.

YASHAR KEMAL (Yasar Kemal GOKCELI)
Ince Memed, 1955 (Memed My Hawk, 1961)

The above indicates that the author's name, under which he published and is normally cited is Yashar Kemal. His "real" name is in brackets, Yasar Kemal Gokceli. Ince Memed is the original title of the work in Turkish (transliterated into English script) and it was initially published in 1955. The following bracketed title, Memed My Hawk, is the title of the English language edition, which first appeared in 1961. A more literal translation of Ince Memed might be "(Thin Memed)" and if there were no actual English edition this translation of the original title would follow in brackets. For instance, a later work by Yashar Kemal, Kuslar Da Gitti, 1973 (The Birds Too Are Gone), lists the Turkish title and original date of publication with an English translation of the title in brackets. It indicates that no English language edition exists to date or, more accurately, none was found. Such entries are then followed by the descriptive annotations.

This is an incomplete bibliographic record in that it does not mention translations of a work into other than English. Some of the titles here have appeared in a variety of editions in two dozen and more different languages. A range of other sometimes useful bibliographic data, such as where and by which publishing house(s) the work was issued are also excluded. Furthermore, I have annotated only a few of the more important and representative works of any particular author, occasionally appending some unannotated titles. There is no attempt to present a complete listing of the works of even the most eminent writers, which in some cases would run to thirty and more volumes. To do so would necessarily exclude mention of other authors entirely and the intent here is to introduce as wide a range of work as feasible. Anyone intrigued by the work of a particular author or the comprehensive publication records of a given title may make their own search. The appended Bibliographic Sources may serve as a further guide.

While it would be desirable for the compiler to have a first hand familiarity with all the titles considered for inclusion, a bibliography such as this must resort to secondary accounts for most of the works cited. Both the sheer bulk of the material and its inaccessibility to any single editor requires that. Usually I have consulted at least two separate sources for each title. Disparities in reviews are partly circumvented if one sets aside their evaluations of philosophic intent and "pure literary merit" and so forth and instead restricts oneself to the comparatively objective features of topic and content in the works discussed.

A difficulty facing all annotation is how one can meaningfully summarize the subject matter of a work, to say nothing of its imagry and style, in the few sentences or paragraph which one has available. An annotation cannot be a precis summary of a work. Some titles seem to allow for fairly concise treatment while others almost defy meaningful brief description. Ironically, the more complex and subtle a work the less possible it usually is to do it justice in annotation. Providing a somewhat fuller description or appending some subjective evocation such as "excellent" or "outstanding" does not substantially change this limitation.

Limitations imposed by space may result in the descriptions taking on a code-like quality in annotation. A spurious repetitiveness sneaks in, a tendency for works to seem more similar than they actually are. Of course, it would be unrealistic not to find a certain recurrence and convergence in novels which deal with the real world--especially where they deal with similar protagonists, in a particular country during the same period. The body of literature about the lives of British miners during the interwar years might be an instance. There are so many facets and so many possible approaches to most of these themes that the accounts never cover exactly the same ground. Their treatment is as wide ranging and heterdox as the varied concerns and insights of the authors themselves.

Although no general classification of the subject matter of the titles is possible, certain kinds of descriptive information is recurrently provided in most annotations. The citations state what form of work the title is, they outline its topic or theme and specify the region and period in which it is set. Annotations of novels sometimes include such descriptive qualifiers as "surrealist", "proletarian", "naturalistic", "neo-realist" and yet other terms. In the context of particular literary traditions these "stylistic" denotations once had special meanings. They may still convey something of the qualitative aspects of the work, although the general reader is forwarned not to read extraneous meanings into them.

The annotations detail the particular regional and historic settings of the titles. These are as specific as the works themselves. They range from the thoughts and actions of an Italian-American construction worker in Manhattan in late 1938 during the last hours of his life to the lives of Andalusian migrant workers in Madrid during the 1960s to the "collective" experiences of the Punjabi peasantry from the first decade of the century to the emergence of an independent India. Such particulars are not merely notations of geography or chronology. For most of the works the details of social setting are of utmost importance. Chronicling the background and conditions of daily life are fundamental features of these novels and not merely the stage on which the "real" story unfolds.

Frequently a particular event or set of events is central in a novel with a work revolving around the British General Strike of 1926, the Bolivian miners' rising of 1952 or the Israeli occupation of Palestine in 1967, for instance. These are useful pegs to hang an annotation on but it should be understood that novels revolving around such events are not necessarily limited to them. Alternately, works may deal with the aggregate conditions and developments in which the protagonists are involved throughout a historic period(s), with no single event being exclusively central. For instance, a trilogy novel may deal with the experiences of German working class families from before W.W.I to the early 1950s. Brief notations can only superficially convey the scope of the more wide ranging novels. What readers will take from the descriptions will depend partly on what they already know about the topics.

The annotations usually indicate the particular classes, groups, occupational or other social strata on which a work may focus--Peruvian Indian mineworkers, agricultural labourers on the manorial estates of Hungary, women and child textile workers in Japan, and so forth. Even though the novels normally interweave the actions of various strata they generally pivot around the lives of a specific sector

of the working class or peasantry. Such class designations should not be taken
to denote an allegorical treatment.
     Whatever their viewpoint and focus, the works cited are usually free of
hagiographic caricatures about the working class. They treat with the flaws and
failings, the misconceptions, debilitating fantasies and narrow chauvinism which
many working people around the world have been heir to--as well as their strengths
and decency. They recognize that a certain section of the working class, be they
lumpen or not, may be irredeemably committed to the defense of its own serfdom.
Despite the phraseology which crops up in some of the annotations, these novels
do not typically embody the pat ideologies against which the reader may have been
warned.
     Of course, what constitutes being cliched or mundane resides in the eye (or
some other part of the anatomy) of the beholder as much as in a novel itself.
For some, the merest suggestion that there are such phenomena as classes,
exploitation and class struggle--or even an objective social reality--is anethema.
Any work dealing with such themes in however an honest or subtle a manner is
dismissed inter alia as "ideological"--meaning spurious. For others the near
endless intricacies, the manifold traditions, daily heroism, dreams and sometimes
triumphs of working people are just hopelessly boring. One has to face the fact
that no literary work can stimulate interest where none exists. You can lead a
horse to water but you can't make it think.
     A wide range of work sometimes from contending ideological tendencies is
presented here. An exasperating oversimplification is often involved in labelling
authors and works with stock political designations. The annotations here probably
unwisely do at times contain descriptive qualifiers such as "populist", "communist",
"socialist" and so forth. "Unwisely" not because those terms are meaningless or
inconsequential but unwisely because there is no real way of briefly describing
what those perspectives actually represented to distinct writers in various
countries during different periods. Usually I have noted such designations only
where the author presents it as a central aspect of the work itself.
     One will be misled if one mistakes the current stereotypes of the various
political persuasions for their changing reality over time. There is often more
complexity in these allegiances than either detractors or proponents admit.

NORTH AMERICA, BRITAIN AND THE DOMINIONS

Great Britain
Ireland
Canada
United States
Australia and New Zealand

GREAT BRITAIN

ALLEN, Jim

Days of Hope, 1975
A novel of a British working class youth who is initially violently opposed to the
British pacifist intellectuals during W.W.I but who becomes gradually radicalized
by that conflict and especially in the depression ridden years immediately after.
Some good accounts of the hidden history of desperate working class militancy in
Northern England at the beginning of the 1920s, in particular the military
suppression of near-starving Durham coal miners, the hunger marches and the events
leading to the general strike of 1926. Marred by the author's sectarian portrayal
of virtually every prominent labour leader of that period as either a fool or an
opportunist.

ALLEN, Walter

Blind Man's Ditch, 1939
A novel of the despair of a recently "radicalized" unemployed middle class youth
who finds no viable solutions forthcoming during a decade of depression except-
the looming war. Allen later became one of the leading British literary
historians whose influential survey The English Novel (1962) fails to mention a
single left-wing novel.

All in a Lifetime, 1959
An often moving novel of the reminiscences of a former skilled craftsman looking
back over more than 60 years of his life from the 1890s to mid 1950s. It
illuminates the skein of British working class intellectuals and the culture of
reading, debates, politics, music, etc. which developed from the late 19th
century around a utopian socialist framework. A compelling aspect of the novel
is the theme that the hero's own adult children have become part of the "master"
class, who neither share nor understand the values he continues to hold.

ARMSTRONG, Thomas

King Cotton, 1947
A historical novel of the Lancashire region during the 1860s when it was the
centre of the world's textile industry. Traces the lives of all those involved
in that industry from the plantations of the American south to the cotton docks
of Liverpool, the businesses and homes of the owners, but dealing particularly
with the working and domestic lives of the masses of English men, women and
children toiling their lives away in the region's cotton mills.

The Crothers of Bankdam, 1956
A historical novel of the Yorkshire region; a chronicle of crofters, workers and
entrepreneurs during the mid 19th century and the transformation of a farming
region into one of the early industrial zones of England.

BALL, F.C.

One of the Damned, 1958
The reminiscences of a house painter in the Hastings (city) building trades union
during the 40 years after Robert Tressell's 1911 working class account, The
Ragged Trousered Philanthropists. An account of how people and conditions have
and haven't changed, as seen partly through Ball's difficulties in trying to save
some of Tressell's decorative painting in Hastings from the descendants of
Rushton, Slyme and Co.

Also Tressell of Mugsborough, 1951.

BARKE, James

Major Operation, 1936
A novel which revolves around a small coal merchant in Glasgow during the 1930s
who, after a major illness, finds himself bankrupt, impoverished and adrift, cut
off from both his own past and the working class. Deals with his relations with
a wide ranging Scottish communist organizer. Captures something of the turbulence
as well as despair of depression-ridden Glasgow.

Land of the Leal, 1939
A novel about two generations of poor Scottish crofters from the late 1870s to
late 1930s, the continuing appeal of Robert Burns' radical liberalism, slipping
into cautious conservatism during W.W.I, but the militancy of children forced
into the Glasgow slums in 1930s and re-discovering the best as well as the flaws
in their parents' traditions.

Also The World His Pillow, 1933 (a novel).

BENNY, Mark

Charity Main: a coal field chronicle, 1980 (original 1934)
A semi-autobiographical chronicle of the traditions of North British industrial
workers and the indignities imposed upon them by unemployment and all variety of
government and business officialdom during the early 1930s.

BERTRAM, Anthony

Men Adrift, 1935
A novel portraying the personal chaos and hopelessness (mixed with amorphous
rebellion) which, as much as poverty, overwhelmed unemployed British workers
during the depression.

BLATCHFORD, Robert

Merrie England, 1896
A didactic account of how most English workers lived in the degraded natural
environments and penal colony-like quarters in late Victorian England. Ironically
played against the then predominant hoopla about "British progress" and suggesting
that conditions were worse for working class than in pre-industrial times. A work
once known throughout the English-speaking labour world.

BLUMENFELD, Simon

Jew Boy, 1935
A crude but powerful first novel set in the Jewish working class district of
Stepney Green in East Side London during the early 1930s. Of variably warm and
difficult lives led in the deepening economic crisis but mainly about the rise of
British fascism led by Sir Oswald Mosley's British Union of Fascists who begin to
attack the Jewish population of the area. After police and government prove
uninterested in or incapable of halting the assaults, Jewish workers and a broad
range of non-Jewish militants forge a self defense organization which physically
drives the fascists out of the district and off the streets. Based on actual
happenings and presented from a left working class perspective intended to
counter the then current "progressive" ethnic chauvinism.

Phineas Kahn, 1937
A richly detailed novel of the lives of a Jewish shopkeeper's family of Blumenfeld's
parents' generation, their immigration from Galicia before W.W.I and their quarter
century lived in the Stepney Green district of London. It chronicles not only
their personal lives and events in that neighbourhood but also their participation
in reading and culture in general (not merely Yiddish culture). The broader
cultural aspects of sections of the European working class was often dismissed
by even progressive writers.

Also Doctor of the Lost, 1938, They Won't Let You Live, 1939
Two other novels set in depression Britain and colored by the looming fascism and
approaching war in Europe. After which Blumenfeld gave up writing.

BRECHT, Bertold

A Penny for the Poor, 1936
A play set in late Victorian London, peopled by characters from John Gay's Beggar's Opera. "An outrageous satire of intrigue and villainy which uproariously reduces capitalism to sheer extravagant scoundrelism." Written while Brecht a refugee in Britain.

BRIERLY, Walter

Means Test Man, 1936
A novelized account of a week in the life of an unemployed Derbyshire miner; a cry of outrage at being thrown aside by industry and degraded by the calculated humiliations inflicted by the means test investigations recurrently made of those receiving the dole. Retains the bone deep sense of being a part of a working class community.

Sandwichman, 1937
A novel of a sandwichboard-man walking the streets of London, a job that doesn't support or even feed him. A living advertisement of the failure of British capitalism which has created both the desperate misery and also men who will accept such a job without revolting.

BURNET, John

Useful Toil, 1974
A collection of brief autobiographies and oral histories of working people from mid 19th century to the 1920s, focused on the varied and changing cultures of British working class.

COLEMAN, Terry

The Railway Navvies, 1965
A popular history of the backgrounds, work and lives of four generations of migratory Irish-British railway construction workers who cut the grades and laid the steel for Britain's rail and industrial complex from 1840s to W.W.I. An account of lives very different from the usual picture of Victorian and Edwardian society.

COMMON, Jack

Kiddar's Luck and the Ampersand, 1976 (original 1936)
Two autobiographical novelas about a working class childhood and young manhood during the 1920s and early 1930s in Heaton (Newcastle Tyneside); documents of school terrors, anger, inter-class views, relations with family and friends. An undoctored memoir with the warts and inannities retained.

COMMON, Jack (ed.)

Seven Shifts, 1980 (original 1938)
A collection of stories and sketches about British working class life in the 1930s by a group of worker-writers.

COOBMES, B.L.

These Poor Hands, 1939
Another once influential autobiographical chronicle of British working class life from W.W.I through the depression.

DASH, Jack

Good Morning Brothers!, 1967
A semi-autobiographical account of an East London dockworker and militant shop steward from childhood in W.W.I to the early 1960s; rich in detail of family, neighbourhood and changes in working class life and conceptions. Revolving around the struggles to gain some control over the mechanization and job loss involved in modernizing London docks in the years after W.W.II. Also touches on the internal

struggles to mobilize support for the Canadian Seamens Union faced with a
coordinated assault at the beginning of the cold war.

DELANY, Shelagh

A Taste of Honey, 1958
A simple and moving play about a teenage working class girl who, though shy, sets
out to live on her own for the first time. The unformed and surprising joys of
life despite the emptiness of her jobs, the discovery of a certain personal
freedom and the real if understated tragedy of becoming pregnant and trapped. A
really remarkable work written by a then 18 year old girl.

DOHERTY, Len

A Miner's Sons, 1955, The Man Beneath, 1958
Two novels of a mine union militant in a north country mine village from the 1930s
to the 1950s. The Man Beneath is a stream of consciousness reminiscence of a
miner trapped underground in a cave in. Miner's Sons attempts to capture the
changes and continuity of a rank and file activist's feelings about decades of
struggle and the shifting interests of younger miners.

EDWARDS, K.

The Mutiny at Invergorden, 1937
A brief memoir of the "mutiny" of the sailors of the British Atlantic fleet based
at Invergorden in fall of 1931 in response to massive pay cuts. Might be
compared with G.E. Manwaring's (1937) The Floating Republic, a popular history of
the mutiny of the British fleet during the French revolution.

ENGELBRECHT, H.D. and HANIGER, F.C.

Merchants of Death, 1934
A once internationally renowned expose of the manipulations of the armaments
industries in Europe and America, their agents, deals and influence in political
decisions of war and peace, from before W.W.I to 1930s. Some fascinating
documentation of the cannibalistic roles of arms industries in W.W.I. A
journalistic history of the early "military-industrial" complex.

EVANS, George Ewart

Ask the Fellows Who Cut the Hay, 1956, The Horse in the Furrow, 1960, The Pattern
Under the Plough, 1966, The Farm and the Village, 1969, Where Beards Wag All,
1970, The Days That We Have Seen, 1975
Six volumes of social history of East Anglian farm workers, drawn largely from
recorded oral accounts. Richly detailed descriptions of the actual lives, culture
and views of the village and farm working class of the region from the last
quarter of the 19th century to circa 1920. The contributors' accounts provide
strikingly different, often combative, counter pieces to the Thomas Hardian
portraits of bucolic quaintness and acceptance of one's lot. Evans' work has been
deeply influential among the last generation of British social historians.

FOX, Ralph

The Novel and the People, 1937
A posthumously published "literary history" of the European novel from the 16th
to 20th centuries to the extent that it expresses popular strivings; by an
extraordinarily prolific Marxist journalist, literary critic and biographer who
fell in the Spanish Civil War.

FOX, Richard

Smokey Crusade, 1938
An autobiography of a rank and file socialist in the British trade union movement,
from factory work in pre W.W.I London, organizing anti-war (W.W.I) meetings in
working class districts, imprisonment and return to union organizing in the 1920s.
Accounts of the 1926 General Strike, the devastating effects of its collapse, and
the very slow re-emergence of working class militancy in the 1930s.

FRASER, Ronald

Work, Volume I, 1968, Volume II, 1969
Two volumes of oral reportage about working in a wide array of jobs in the UK
during the 1960s, of British working men and women, native-born and immigrant,
old and young. Astutely compiled by the author of the superb oral history, Blood
of Spain.

GALLACHER, William

Revolt on the Clyde, 1936
A memoir of a trade union leader and later Communist Party MP; deals with the
militancy of the union movement in the Clydeside shipyards which during W.W.I
established "control over" working conditions in the industry through their
Workers Councils.

GARRETT, George

Liverpool, 1921-1922, 1934
A booklet memoir of the depression-wracked Liverpool working class (especially
dockside) districts during the early twenties; the hunger marches, mass demonstrations and protests and their suppression by police and military. By a
Liverpool Irish seaman-writer who rose to brief prominence in 1930s through his
prolific short stories in small left journals.

GIBBON, Leo Grassic

Sunset Song, 1932, Cloud Howe, 1933, Gray Granite, 1934
A novel trilogy collectively known as A Scots Quair; widely held to be the finest
example of British socialist fiction to date. There is no way to adequately
describe it in a brief annotation, but in outline the trilogy deals with the
lifetime of a lowland Scotch crofter's daughter and the microcosm of the European
world in change over the last three centuries as caught in the corners of her
small world and experienced through her packed, if narrowly bounded, life between
the 1890s and 1930s. From the residual quasi-feudal relations of Scotch
landlordlings and tenants to the contentions of international monopoly capital.
The second thread in the trilogy is the life of her son, from the atavistic
patriotism of W.W.I through the Labourism and defeats of 1920s, the deeping class
conflict and the rise of home grown fascism in Scotland of the early 1930s, during
which time the son becomes a communist militant. An unromantic picture of the
flaws and failings of the main characters and the frequent ignorance which,
however, does not alter the need for a socialist transformation. A many-layered
work written in Scots dialect.

GREENWOOD, Walter

Love on the Dole, 1933
A novel of a Manchester worker's family during 1928-1931, being mainly the account
of a young factory worker who is just beginning to build his own life when he is
laid off. It chronicles his increasing hopelessness of ever finding a job again,
his crumbling world and relations with family and friends, his psychological
states as he finally goes on the dole and the full measure of administered
degradation is heaped upon him. It captures the spitefullness of middle class
England and the purposeful humiliation which more than anything else outraged the
unemployed. Probably the most widely read working class novel of depression
England.

There Was a Time, 1967
A nostalgic but informative account of Greenwood's childhood in a decaying
tenement district of a small industrial town (Salforth) during the first dozen
years of this century. Emphasizes the mutual support of friends and neighbours
in ethnographic detail and describes the overwhelming class and economic
restrictions which disallow most of them ever leading secure or full lives.

HALWARD, Leslie

To Tea on Sunday, 1935
A collection of sketches and stories of mainly young men and women, mostly still

marginally employed, who after four years of a depression which has shattered their propsects are just then beginning to make a break with their previous visions of propriety and order. The ties of the "respectable" working class and lower middle class to now lost positions, and their hardly radical reassessment of what is in store for them. Also Gus and Ida, 1939, a novel.

HAMILTON, Patrick

Twenty Thousand Streets Under the Sky, 1935
Comprised of the three short novelas Midnight Bell, The Siege of Pleasure and The Plains of Cement; centred on the habitues of a small pub near Euston Station, London, at the end of the 1920s and revolving around the lives of a declasse set of lower middle class commercial travellers, staff and hangers on. The stagnant but still human world of a failed British Babbittry.

Hangover Square, 1974 (original 1941)
A somewhat surrealist novel of the final decay of the types met in Twenty Thousand Streets. Revolves around a menage de trois of the lumpen bourgeoisie in London on the eve of W.W.II, their hatreds, violence and self-destruction; their conflicts with the life style of their former class, but especially about underlying attraction to the psychology of fascism.

HANLEY, James

The Furys, 1935
A novel of a Liverpool Irish seaman's family during the early 1930s, the trapped, socially restrictive, religiously oppressive and destructive treadmill existence which the father dreams to escape by returning to sea. Portrayed through the eyes of the son, just beginning to enter adulthood and determined to escape his parents' and neighbours' lives in his own way, but without success. "Liverpool not as a free and easy seaport town where material poverty was compensated for by communal solidarity, but as a...nightmare."

The Secret Journey, 1936
A sequel to The Furys, in which we see that family caught in the coils of hopelessness drive each other to despair. A mixture of insight, sympathy and derogation of British working class by a prolific seaman-writer.

A Woman in the Sky, 1973
A simple and sensitive novel set in a block of London Council flats during the early 1970s; revolves around the death of one of two elderly women who have been roommates and the effects on a handful of friends and neighbours. Death and the attempts of the aged to live out their lives in ever narrowing possibilities.

Also Drift, 1930, a novela.

HEINEMAN, Margot

The Adventurers, 1960
A novel of the strains of "advancement" from and commitment to British working class in 1950s. It counterposes a miner's son who manages to acquire a college education and uses it to become a ruthless opportunist to a lower middle class intellectual who commits himself to the struggles of Welsh niners, retaining the egalitarian visions of communism despite the shock of the revelations about Stalin and the suppression of the 1956 Hungarian rising.

HESLOP, Harry

Under the Sway of Coal, 1925 (reprinted in 1929 as The Gate of a Strange Field)
One of the first proletarian novels from Britain; written by a north country coal miner and union militant and dealing with the traditions, lives and struggles of those coal mine communities over the previous generations but set in the desperately depressed 1920s. Treats with the Hunger March of 1922 and the use of the British army to occupy some of the mine villages at the time. Written with crude authenticity and anger.

Last Cage Down, 1935
A somewhat more doctrinaire "proletarian" novel about the life of a Durham miner
(a "natural leader" naturally) and his resistance to the exploitation and murderous
working conditions in the infamous Frampton Collieries. His gradual evolution from
an emotional anarchist to a communist union leader. Gives detailed descriptions
of work in the north British mines of the times and the carryover of mid 19th
century pre-socialist miners' traditions and lodges in social life.

Also Goaf, 1934, another British miner's novel, and Journey Beyond, 1930, a novel
of the impact of the first year of the depression on an unemployed white collar
employee.

HOBSBAWN, Eric J.

Primitive Rebels, 1959
A superb popular history of the pre-socialist/pre-union forms of egalitarian
struggle (mainly in southern Europe) with two chapters, "The Labour Sects" and
"Ritual in Social Movements", which deal with conditions in mid 19th century
Britain. Primitive Rebels, and much of Hobsbawn's other work, is a model of
readable and compelling historical writing. Also see his Labouring Men, 1964,
mainly a survey of British working class social history in late 19th and early
20th centuries. Everything by Hobsbawn is worth reading.

HOBSBAWN, E.J. (with George RUDE)

Captain Swing, 1968
A brilliant popular history of the wide spread revolt of British agricultural
workers during 1830-1834. Accounts of the protest marches, underground
organizing and pressures on agricultural employers (including machine wrecking)
and of the massive military and civil suppression which largely crushed it.
Describes the spread of the proto-union movement to artizans and recreates the
world from which the "Tolpuddle Martyrs" of the British labour movement sprang.

JACKSON, Thomas A.

Solo Trumpet, 1953
The autobiography of a ubiquitous working class orator, writer and participant in
assorted left-socialist organizations and political campaigns in Britain from the
turn of the century to the 1940s (and thereby also a memoir of the minority stream
of Independent Labour Party activism over that period).

JAMESON, Storm

None Turn Back, 1936
A novel which portrays the workings of the Labour Party and allied union leaders
during the 1926 general strike; their temporizing and acceptance of the
established order as compared to the spontaneous upsurge of solidarity and self
reliance which that struggle liberates in masses of politically and socially
diverse working people. In the course of that struggle ordinary people take on
new qualities and their inner desires for a different world comes to the surface.
Part of a novel trilogy which includes Company Parade, 1934 and Love in Winter,
1935, and treats with the fortunes and trajectory of various sections of the
British working class and Labour Party from the end of W.W.I to the depression.

Here Comes a Candle, 1938
A collage of scenes from Soho, then still an inner city London slum and not a
nightclub quarter; ranging from preachers to prostitutes.

JONES, Glyn

The Blue Bed, 1938
A collection of stories by a Welsh working class radical, the longest being an
account of the Jack Frost "rebellion" during the Chartist era which mixes history,
fiction and surrealist use of folk myths. Other stories deal with Welsh
working people past and present in a vein sometimes outraged and sometimes
grotesquely humourous.

Also The Nine Days Wonder, 1937 and Times Like These, 1936, two novels of working class life and struggles in Wales from the mid 1920s to mid 1930s. Lyrical and sardonic in parts.

JONES, Lewis

Cwmardy, 1937
Subtitled "The story of a Welsh mining valley", it is a novelized social history of the strains of working class militancy and everyday lives and work among Welsh miners of the Rhondda from late 1890s to 1921. A powerfully authentic account drawn from the reminiscences of Jones' family and fellow miners, it focuses on the military suppression of the miners' strike in 1910 and the various trajectories from Labour Partyism to militant syndicalism which evolve. Of the Boer War, W.W.I and the responses to the Russian revolution in what was one of the citadels of the "British" left (and of its social and cultural bases). Ends with the main character becoming a communist activist. Said to be one of the most impressive proletarian novels of Britain in 1930s.

We Live, 1939
A sequel to Cwmardy, carrying the hero and his fellow miners from 1921 and the post war depression through the devastating General Strike of 1926 (which ended as a campaign of starvation against the miners). Ends with the departure of the protagonist to join the International Brigades in the Spanish Civil War, where he is killed.

KIBBLEWHITE, Liz and RIGBY, Andy

Fascism in Aberdeen: street politics in the 1930s, 1975
One of the "People's History" booklets which appeared in vast array in the UK during the 1970s and covered an extraordinary range of topics and places. Kibblewhite and Rigby deal with the demonstrations and clashes between Scottish workers in Aberdeen against the home grown fascist movement during the early 1930s. It "reminds us that (fascism) in Britain, in the 1930s, like the National Front today, rested on a broad base of royalism and imperialism, the Union Jack a more potent symbol than the swastika."

LAMBERT, David

No Time for Sleeping, 1957
A novel set on the Glasgow Clydeside during the 1930s, the relations between communist militants and other workers, the poverty and desperation as well as the political upsurge which breaks with the memories of past defeats. Revolves around a Scotch working girl who is drawn into the mass struggles of the time.

He Must So Live, 1954
A novel "sequel" to No Time for Sleeping, also set in Glasgow of 1930s. Both of Lambert's novels evince a retrospective balance but no apologetics.

LINDSAY, Jack

1649: A Novel of a Year, 1938
A historical novel of the forces, the ideologies and interests in contention at the end of the English civil war in 1649. Focuses on the Cromwellian army, especially the "revolutionary" Leveller elements in it, and the social milieu from which they sprang. Suggests the future trajectory of the defeated and victorious forces. Lindsay's work helped resurrect the historical novel as a vehicle for contemporary commentary.

Betrayed Spring, 1953
A novel of working class Britain in 1945-1947 seen through the families, friends and work mates of three returned British soldiers scattered from London to the Tyneside. The initial promise raised by the election of the first Labour government in 1945 and the gradually deepening frustrations as "nationalization" and other reforms fail to markedly improve the lives of British working people.

Rising Tide, 1954
A novel of British waterfront workers and seamen, their work, families, daily lives

--the memories of the 1930s, W.W.II and the recent hopes for a Labour government pervading their present. Revolves around the deepening reaction in the British Labour Party as it enrolls in the Anglo-American cold war. Centres on the struggles in Britain to support the Canadian Seamens Union strike of 1949 and internal conflicts in the British labour movement as domestic struggles of the cold war are played out.

Moment of Choice, 1955
The last of the quasi-trilogy which includes the two above works. A novel set in the Yorkshire industrial region which counterposes the paths of the aspirant and established bourgeoise with that of members of the disparate and fragmenting regional working class during 1950-1951. Revolves partly around frustrated attempts to mobilize British workers against the British government's support of America in the Korean War. Of the growing political apathy and alienation which infect British working people during that and the next decade.

All on the Never-Never, 1961, The Way the Ball Bounces, 1962
Two novels about British working people during the late 1950s, where class realities and conflicts continue but have been papered over by the aspirations of an American consumer society. Also Lost Birthright,1939 and Choice of Time, 1964, two novels about the radical Chartist tradition (Lost) and British incorporation into the American raj a century later (Choice).

LONDON, Jack

The People of the Abyss, 1903
A journalistic account of life and conditions in the East London slums of 1902; the tenements, work houses, penny stock peddlers, half starved children and permanently unemployed workers in the capital of the then greatest empire in the free world. Written in London's muck-raking, purple prose style.

McARTHUR, A. and LONG, H.K.

No Mean City, 1935
A journalistic narrative which portrays the violence, drunkenness, degradation engendered in the worst of the Glasgow slums in the 1930s. Yet captures some of the evanescent vitality of that world and the capacities and drive of its inhabitants when opportunity permits. Written in Glasgow dialect by a former Glasgow worker and later reporter.

MacDIARMID, Hugh

Collected Poems, 1962
A major collection of the poems by the greatest revolutionary socialist poet of Great Britain (Scotland) of this century. MacDiarmid manages to capture the past and keep fresh the continuing traditions of working class socialism regardless of the changing ideological fashions of British literature. Localist and written in Scotch dialect as much of it is, his poetry exudes a universal relevance.

MITCHELL, Hannah

The Hard Way Up, 1977
A rediscovered biography of a rank and file activist (1871-1956) in the Independent Labour movement from the turn of the century to 1930s. Deals with the lives of working women and their difficulties within the established union movement as well as under capitalism, from an early working class feminist viewpoint.

MORRIS, William

Three Works of William Morris, 1968
Includes the two novelas The Dream of John Ball (original 1886), an evocation of the hidden revolutionary tradition of the English people portrayed in a dream-like return to the Peasant Rising of 1381, and News From Nowhere (original 1890), a utopian leap into a future socialist Britain. Morris, a leading proponent of the revival of craftsmanship and folk arts, was probably the most eminent voice of revolutionary utopianism in England during the late Victorian era. The definitive work on Morris is E.P. Thompson's (1955) William Morris, Romantic to Revolutionary.

MORRISON, Arthur

A Child of Jago, 1896, The Hole in the Wall, 1902
Two quasi-documentary portraits of the lumpen proletariat and petty criminal life
in the Wapping district of London at the turn of the century. R. Samuel's East End
Underworld, 1981, is a life history revising much in these "Cockney school" accounts.

PHELAN, Jim

Ten-A-Penny People, 1938
A semi-autobiographical collage novel which begins with a Liverpool Irish youth
who is driven by his father to work on the docks, the brutality of his family life
and his escape to sea where his shipmates become his first real family, educating
him with Jack London books and so forth. The style changes as he matures and
leaves the ship to work in an endless series of temporary jobs throughout the UK.
Gives a mosaic of parallel experiences by acquaintances and interweaves dialogue,
description, pop culture and cliches, snatches of ironic poetry, political events,
and working class folk history.

The Name's Phelan, 1948
A memoir of an Irish Liverpool writer; runaway from a farm village to the Dublin
slums at age ten, a seaman before W.W.I, member of IRA and prisoner, long-time
convict, as well as being a migratory worker in America, the UK and Europe.
Particularly interesting in accounts of comparable people and experiences which
Phelan ran across in his lifetime. All rather different from the more usual
picture of an established, localized British working class.

PEOPLES' AUTOBIOGRAPHY OF HACKNEY

Working Lives, Volume 1, 1890 to 1945, 1974, Volume 2, 1945 to 1977, 1978
Two collections of oral history of working people's lives in an old East London
district from the late Victorian period to present. Now running to over 50 titles,
the Hackney series is comprised of booklets dealing with individual lives,
industries, historic periods and specific events over the last 90 years in the
Hackney district. The "Peoples' Autobiography of Hackney" was one of the first
and most extensive of the working class local histories which flourished in
Britain during the 1970s.

PRESTON, Richard

End of Cornwall, 1938
A novel whose background is the poverty of depression-struck Cornwall, a region
already badly depressed for a half century before 1930. Revolves around an
attempt to get a depleted and closed down tin mine in operation on a handcraft
basis and similar endeavours in the anachronistic fishing industry. Of an
economically stripped region with its recent overlay of artists and middle class
vacationers. Done in the format of a murder thriller.

RUTHERFORD, Mark (William Hale)

The Autobiography of Mark Rutherford, 1976 (original 1881)
A fictional autobiography of a British artizan-intellectual who comes of age
during the last phase of Chartist militancy in the 1840s, his commitment to the
equalitarian-democratic ideals of that movement through the seemingly endless
night of mid-Victorian capitalism and British imperialism. A document of the
underground current of radical republicanism.

The Revolution in Tanners Lane, 1976 (original 1893)
A novel which is a thematic prelude to Autobiography of Mark Rutherford; set in
the period 1814-1834 and about the radical republicanism of a London printer, the
proto-class struggle which culminates in the Peterloo massacre and of flight to
evade arrest. Portrays the following twenty years of the protagonist's life and
of his despair as former comrades and members of his once radical Independent
Church sink into a cautious conservatism. Again, the story of an individual's
attempt to keep the radical-democratic spirit alive, at least in himself, during
a period of working class somnolence. Ends with the first stirrings of socialism
in Britain.

RYAN, Patrick

How I Won the War, 1963
A broad spoof of the memoirs of British W.W.II generals; being a self-congratulatory reminiscence of an imperviously stupid and hidebound young lower middle
class lieutenant who remains blind to the sensible contempt of his men. His
enthusiastic pursual of "hilariously" idiotic orders gets most of his men killed,
but leaves the lieutenant unscathed and completely unchanged at the end of the
war, thereby ensuring his post-war success as a rising businessman. Flawed by
an unhealthy dose of unsatiric British racism.

SAMUEL, Raphael (ed.)

Miners, Quarrymen and Saltworkers, 1977
A collection of scholarly but readable accounts about the working and domestic
lives, the traditions of British workers in small industrial towns and villages
from 1860s to 1920s. Also see his (1971) Village Life and Labour, in the same
vein but focused on the traditions of farm workers and those in village handicraft
industries of that period.

SILLITOE, Alan

Saturday Night and Sunday Morning, 1958
Sillitoe's first well known novel; of a mindlessly rebellious and destructive
young worker in a Nottingham bicycle factory of mid 1950s who at times shows
perceptive insight into the malarkey they are being fed but who ultimately is a
caricature of the boozing, skirt-chasing, lumpenized protagonist in vogue among
British "authors of working class origin" during the 1950s.

The Loneliness of the Long Distance Runner, 1959
A novel revolving around a juvenile inmate of a Borstal school who has a simmering
distrust of all authority. Relates how his rebelliousness has landed him in
reform school but deals mainly with the all pervasive system of humiliations and
gradated restrictions which are intended to break the inmates' spirits and which
the majority of prisoners do come to incorporate. Culminates in the hero's
rejection of an opportunity to "better himself" within the confines of the school
when he throws a long distance race in a competition with a public school team
arranged by the warden. Allegorical parallel between Borstal school and British
society of the late 1950s.

Key to the Door, 1962
A chronicle of the family background of a protagonist such as in Saturday Night.
Character delineations range back and forth from the 1950s to the 1890s and
portray the alloy of magnamity and vicious authoritarianism, of Victorian
pettiness and chauvinism mixed with visions of justice, of abject servility and
rebelliousness represented in the heterogeneous family members.

SLATER, Montagu

Domesday, 1933
A play about the triumph of a home grown fascism in Britain sometime in the mid
1940s. Written at a time when British fascism was near its zenith, Domesday
attempted to indicate what the roots of the movement were, who would support and
oppose it, who would suffer and who benefit and what in general the consequences
would be.

Cock Robin, 1934
A once well known play which revolves around the murder of an old utopian
socialist soapbox speaker by a gang of British fascist thugs in early 1930s and
the attempt by one of the right wing leaders to make political hay out of the
incident.

Stay Down Miner, 1936
A reportage account of the underground sitdown strikes in South Wales collieries
in 1935. The conditions which led up to this desperate action, the miners'
families and heterogeneity of those involved. Also produced as a successful play
the same year.

SMITH, Herbert

A Field of Folk, 1958
A novel of the daily lives and ongoing travails of eking out a living from factory
work and wresting some joy from living in a west London industrial suburb during
the mid 1950s. Some astute portraits of the understated emotions and dialogue of
British working people, but also conveys a sense of somulence and the difficulties
in maintaining working class political activity just barely ticking over.

SOMMERFELD, John

May Day, 1936
A collective novel which presents a collage of parallel events in cinematographic
style to capture the locale, people and class culture in a long established working
class district of Thameside London during the preparations for a May Day during
the mid 1930s. A vivid and lyrical work.

TRESSELL, Robert

The Ragged Trousered Philanthropists, 1968 (original 1911)
The pioneer working class novel of Britain; written by and about one year in the
life of a socialist house painter in the provincial town of Hastings (Muggsborough)
circa 1910. A slow moving but cumulatively powerful account of the daily rounds
of work, the thwarted satisfactions of not being allowed to do a good job and the
constant fears of being laid off. Portrays the enslaving effects which the fear
of unemployment has on the hero and his fellow workers, their differing natures
and how they generally gull themselves into supporting their own exploitation
(i.e., they are the ragged trousered philanthropists). All this mixed with
variety-hall satire leavened with a hatred of bosses, washed in the blood of the
lamb preachers and working class stool pigeons who waft through the scenes. Given
at times to period piece sermonizing, the book however remains an evocatively
real account of Tressell's Britain.

WALSH, Jane

Not Like This, 1953
A reminiscence of the travails and special hardships of British working women in
the late 1920s and how unemployed women during the hungry thirties were virtually
disregarded by relief agencies, who as often as not added insult to injury through
the humiliations they imposed. Set around the Lancashire textile mills and told
by a militant working class woman. Of the protests, hunger marches, varied
socialist politics of time but also of the more personal and neighbourly
strategies of survival.

WARNER, Sylvia Townsend

Summer Will Show, 1936
A novel revolving around the qualms, attraction and social difficulties of
recently radicalized middle class individuals drawn to the essentially working
class British communist movement by the depression and the threat of fascism
during the 1930s.

WATERHOUSE, Keith

Billy Liar, 1959
A satiric novel of the romanticization of working class life in contemporary
Britain. Set in a Yorkshire industrial town of mid 1950s, it counterposes the
deadend jobs, intellectual vacuity and stagnant social life of a young, apolitic
factory worker, his hackneyed and escapist fantasies as well as his sardonic
comments about supposedly "folksy" traditions.

WATERMAN, Ray

A Family of Shopkeepers, 1972
A roman-de-clef of an East End London Jewish family in the 1920s and 1930s, laced
with "warm and wonderful" nostalgia but also recapturing some of the once
extensive left wing cultural activities, such as the Yiddish Workers' Theatre
groups.

WESKER, Arnold

Chicken Soup With Barley, 1958
A play about growing up in a "poor but vital" East London district during the late
1930s and 1940s, the warmth of family life and the communality of class feelings
giving way to the seeming anomie of working class existence in the 1950s. Argues
for the once rich cultural interests and traditions which existed among working
people. Two other plays in a similar vein are (1958) Roots and (1960) I'm Talking
About Jerusalem.

WILLIAMS, David·

John Frost, 1939
A historical novel about South Wales miners in the 1830s and 1840s; the various
streams of the Chartist movement ranging from thoroughly secular radicals to
working class preachers, but who in their fundamental loyalties are not so
different. Their struggles to oppose the deepening dispossession and exploitation
of Welsh people during the inception of the industrial revolution there.

WILLIAMS, Raymond

Border Country, 1960
A novel revolving around the disillusionment and fall of a once militant railway
union leader after the collapse of the General Strike of 1926 and the abandonment
of the striking miners by the Trades Union Council. Proceeds from the 1920s to
mid 1950s and realistically details the "hero's" progressive alienation from his
seemingly defeated co-unionists and his decision to become a small contractor (in
which he succeeds in exact proportion to his decline into cynicism and avarice).

WILSON, Amrit

Finding a Voice: Asian Women in Britain, 1978
Accounts of the experiences of Asian immigrant, working class women in Britain
from the 1950s to 1970s, their strivings for personal liberation in a world of
new opportunities and new oppression. From a feminist viewpoint.

BRITISH CHILDREN'S HISTORICAL NOVELS

BURTON, Hester

Castors Away, 1962, Time of Trial, 1963, No Beat of Drum, 1966
A novel trilogy set in England during and shortly after the Napoleonic wars;
beginning with a typical "patriotic pluck" story (Castors Away) of a drummer boy
at the battle of Trafalgar who naively portrays the serf-like conditions in the
British navy. The trilogy ends with (No Beat of Drum) the increasing agitation
and hunger at the end of the wars as seen by an adolescent apprentice, and the
developments culminating in and following the 1817 Peterloo massacre, in which
British troops cut down demonstrating English workers.

CARTER, Peter

The Black Lamp, 1966
A more mature novel of the Peterloo massacre and the republicanism, desperation
and hunger among increasing numbers of English craft workers. The turmoil and
underground political culture of an impoverished class as seen through the eyes
of a fifteen year old weaver's apprentice.

COPPARD, Audrey

Nancy of Nottingham, 1975
A children's novel about the milieu of the so-called Luddite (or "machine
wreckers") resistance to the spread of early factory capitalism around Nottingham
in 1820s. Revolves around a teenaged brother and sister adopted into a family of
pro-Luddite handweavers, the secret debates about the strategies of opposing

factory system and a good deal on the nature of underground communication and opposition (when free enterprise employers had the gallows in their stock of negotiating techniques).

CORDELL, Alexander

The White Cockade, 1970, Witches' Sabbath, 1971
Two novels set in Ireland in the 1790s. White Cockade portrays the brutal oppression, poverty and hunger of the Irish natives under British colonialism and the underground preparations for the 1798 rising. Witches' Sabbath deals with the 1798 rising itself, the most massive and bloody in Irish history, and the long drawn out repression following its defeat as witnessed by two adolescents.

HARNETT, Cynthia

The Great House, 1949, The Wool Pack, 1951, Ring Out Bow Bells, 1953, The Load of the Unicorn, 1959
Four novels set in late Tudor and early Stuart England and focused on various locales with their differing sets of industries and people. Said to be among the best researched of children's novels, they provide detailed and illustrated accounts of the physical settings, technology and daily lives of a cross section of typical working children, women and men during an era when English capitalism was still contesting strong remnants of feudalism. An indication of conditions in other parts of Europe and elsewhere are sometimes interwoven through the agency of trade and traders of regional goods. All of this is worked in through effective narratives.

HUNTER, Mollie

The Ghosts of Glencoe, 1955
A novel of children living in the violence of the decaying Scottish clan system as well as the spreading English colonial control of Highlands at the end of the 1600s.

A Pistol in Greenyards, 1965
A novel of the Highland clearances in late 1700s by Scottish lords and English capitalists; the removal of the Gaelic inhabitants or their reduction to marginal crofters. The confustion, betrayal and unavailing resistance as seen through the eyes of children of the victims. John Prebble's (1966) Glencoe, (1961) Culloden and (1963) The Highland Clearances are more adult popular histories of those developments.

LEESON, Bob

Maroon Boy, 1975, Bess, 1976
Two children's novels set around Portsmouth from 1588 to 1628; Maroon Boy being an account of a runaway boy scrounging a living in a major port of Elizabethan England. Bess being the story of an adolescent farm girl and her young womanhood, a strong yeowoman character who inherits the family farm and "runs it" herself --with hired labour.

White Horse, 1977
The last of the quasi-trilogy begun with Maroon Boy; a novel of the English Civil War of 1640s as seen through the eyes of children participants.

The Cimaroons, 1979
A children's novel of a "republic" of escaped slaves in the Caribbean during the late 1700s.

LINDSAY, Jack

Men of Forty-Eight, 1948
A novel of the traditions of the Chartist movement and their final recrudescence in agitations throughout England in 1848, the year of the revolutionary upsurge throughout continental Europe.

It is somewhat misleading to list this and Lindsay's similar works as "children's literature", in that they deal with the hidden history of everyday life of ordinary people, readable by adults as well as interested children.

Civil War in England, 1954
A popular history of English civil war of the 1640s, concentrating on the nature of the communitarian "Digger" faction in Cromwell's army.

Nine Day's Hero--Wat Tyler, 1964
A novelized biography of the life and times of Wat Tyler, a "working class" leader in the English Peasant Rising of 1381.

PRICE, Susan

Twopence a Tub, 1972
A novel of women and child mine labour and their lives in a Black County coal mine village of 1850s.

TREASE, Geoffrey

Bows Against Barons, 1934
A children's novel of escaped serfs and Robin Hood-like social bandits against feudal barons. Chapayev in merry old England of 1300s.

Comrades of the Charter, 1938
A novel of Welsh farm workers and artisans involved in the Chartist movement of 1830s and 1840s; the secret meetings, struggles against rent collectors, employers and police, the demonstrations and hunger marches, and Guild radicalism as seen through the eyes of children participants.

Cue for Treason, 1940
A novel set in 16th century England, the intrigues of feudal lords and dying struggles of feudalism against advancing capitalism. Allusions to the appeal of fascism to sections of British ruling class in late 1930s.

Thunder of Valmy, 1960
A children's novel of the French revolution, revolving around the first major victory of French Republican forces against Royalist and external White armies at the battle of Valmy. Engages the reader's sympathies with the French revolution and intended as a counter to the reactionary sentiments peddled in the Scarlet Pimpernel and endless similar "classics".

Follow My Black Plume, 1963, A Thousand for Sicily, 1964
Two novels about Garibaldi's liberation army in southern Italy during mid 19th century. The millenial struggle to overthrow an anachronistic autocracy which fails in that it only results in the hegemony of Italian capitalism--in a fairly typical children's adventure plot.

The White Nights of St. Petersburg, 1967
A novel set in Petrograd during 1917-1918; being a sympathetic account of the conditions and forces underlying the Russian revolution as seen through the eyes of children who gradually come to sympathize with the revolutionary forces.

TREECE, Henry

The Eagles Have Flown, 1946
A children's novel of Celtic England circa 100 A.D. under spreading Roman colonization.

The Children's Crusade, 1948
A story of the chaos and wretchedness of 13th century England and France from which the juvenile poor were dragooned into a religious crusade against the Turks (most of them winding up sold into slavery by the Crusaders before ever reaching the Holy Land). A counter to the Victorian children's literature of chivalry, Ivanhoes and armed quests.

IRELAND

BEHAN, Brendan

Borstal Boy, 1958
A semi-autobiographical reminiscence of Behan's Belfast background and IRA
traditions which got him into a harebrained plot to blow up a British battleship
at age 17. Memoirs of late adolescence and yearnings in a Borstal school prison
during W.W.II.

Confessions of an Irish Rebel, 1965
A lyrical, exaggerated account of the culture and psychology of Irish resistance
as inherited by a boyo like Behan. Sometimes tongue in cheek, sometimes incisive
commentary.

BREEN, Dan

My Fight for Irish Freedom, 1958
Autobiography of one of best known guerrilla commanders of Irish Republican Army
(Tipperary Flying Column) in the war of Irish independence and Irish Civil War.
Also the political battles against the rightist Free State government.

CONNOLLY, James

Labour in Irish History, 1910
A short popular history of the role and real interests of Irish labour and
peasantry usually hidden in accounts of the "Great Events" of Irish history over
the last 400 years. By the founder of Marxian socialist movement in Ireland.

CORKERY, Daniel

The Hounds of Banba, 1920
Collection of stories about civilian life and guerrilla struggle in Ireland from
1916-1920 by a Cork Republican editor. Said to catch the reality of everyday life
better than most.

Also A Munster Twilight, 1916; collected short stories.

DEVLIN, Bernadette

The Price of My Soul, 1969
A political autobiography and astute analysis of the nature, misconceptions and
changes necessary in Ulster if its communities are to cease oppressing each other
and themselves. By the former 22 year old MP from Belfast Bogside, mainstay of
the Irish Socialist Republic Party.

FIGGIS, Darrell

The Return of the Hero, 1923
A chilling account of the brutality and bloodletting by the Irish Free State forces
against their IRA opponents during and after the Irish Civil War; also of the
blacklisting of IRA supporters and the ferocity of a frightened Irish middle class
in countriside.

Recollections of the Irish War, 1927
A dispassionately sad account of the various tendencies and phases of the Anglo-
Irish War of Independence.

JACKSON, T.A.

Ireland Her Own, 1947
A popular if schematic "Marxist" history of the heterogeneous but unending
struggles for Irish independence over four centuries.

LARKIN, Emmet

James Larkin, Irish Labour Leader, 1876-1947, 1965
A biography of the Irish left-labour leader, organizer of the Transport Workers
Union and Dublin General Strike of 1913; also of the first 25 years of the modern
Irish labour movement and one of its founders.

McGAHERN, John

The Barracks, 1963
A novel revolving around the life of a police constable and his wife in a small
Irish town; an examination of the social restrictions and self-imposed repression,
the authoritarianism of contemporary rural Ireland.

Nightlines, 1970
Collection of short stories about "modern" but no less stagnant rural Ireland of
late 1960s.

MACKEN, Walter

Seek the Fair Land, 1959
A historical novel of the Cromwellian invasion and subjugation of Ireland in mid
17th century.

The Silent People, 1962
A historical novel of the Irish Famine of 1840s and 1850s.

The Scorching Wind, 1964
A novel of the struggle for Irish independence from 1911 to 1920s. The focus in
all of Macken's novels is the common people, their persistence, striving and basic
decency despite the cultural superstitions and institutionalized ignorance under
which they contend.

Rain on the Wind, 1950, The Bogman, 1952
Two novels set in the author's Galway, being a recreation of a rural Ireland which
had largely disappeared by 1950.

O'BRIEN, Nora Connolly

Portrait of a Rebel Father, 1935
A biography of James Connolly by his daughter.

O'CASEY, Sean

I Knock at the Door, Pictures in the Hallway, Drums Under the Window, Inishfallen
Fare Thee Well, The Rose and the Crown, Sunset and Evening Star, 1963
O'Casey's six volume autobiography (originally written between 1935 and 1953)
which charts his life and times from an abysmally poor and superstition-ridden
Protestant family in the slums of Dublin in the late 1880s to his emergence as
a leading Irish playwright, and the harassment which drove him into exile in
Britain. Impossible to describe adequately, the volumes mix melodrama, luminescent
portraiture of social conditions, egocentric trivia, brilliantly sardonic prose-
poetry railing at the philistinism and serfdom of ruler and ruled in Ireland and
Britain, and more. I Knock at the Door is a reminiscence of near fatal poverty
as a child and youth of Dublin slums from late 1880s to circa 1909; Pictures in
the Hallway deals with the explosive emergence of working class struggle in
Dublin from 1909 to 1914 and the general strike in which O'Casey played a
role; Drums Under the Window recounts the flawed hopes, desperation and
miscalculated opportunism intermixed in the forces which led to the Easter Rising
and the beginning of the Anglo-Irish war. The remaining three
volumes are of a more restricted interest, Inishfallen being of O'Casey's
emergence as a major Irish playwright in the 1920s and of the forces of Irish
reaction which drove him into exile after 1926. Rose and Crown and Sunset and
Evening Star deal with his increasingly iconoclastic feuds and work in Britain
from 1930s to 1953. While lacking the verve of the initial volumes they do
include some "literary" analyses of sacred cows (such as George Orwell's
posturings) which still make refreshing reading today.

The Shadow of a Gunman, 1923, Juno and the Paycock, 1924, The Plough and the Stars, 1926
Three of O'Casey's best known early plays set mainly during the final period of armed struggle for Irish independence and amid the counter revolutionary period following the end of the Irish Civil War. These made O'Casey an internationally renowned playwright but also got him driven out of Catholic Ireland.

O'CRIOMHTAIN, Tomas

An T'Oileanach, 1929
A life history transcribed and translated from the Gaelic; of life in a peasant-fishermen hamlet on a small western island during the late 19th and early 20th centuries. Documents the Celtic village society.

O'DONNELL, Peader

Islanders, 1927
A novel of how the weight of Irish history has become crystallized in the neo-colonial culture of the 1920s, in particular about the unarticulated class differences between small peasants and landless workers and the emergent Irish farmer-landlord elements which have become the local bosses after the end of the war of independence.

Adrigoole, 1929
A documentary novel of a peasant family in Donegal which supports and hides Republican partizans during the Irish Civil War and thereby becomes the target of local notables who send the father to jail in a frame up. Local merchants strip the family of all its possessions so that the survivors actually starve to death. Based on an actual event in mid 1920s Irish Free State.

The Knife, 1930
A novel of the distrust and hatred between Catholic and Protestant poor in Ulster in 1930, its centuries-old history and the ongoing social and psychological dynamics reinforcing those divisions, to the joy of many priests, pastors and local rulers.

The Gates Flew Open, 1936
An account of O'Donnell's participation in the Irish Civil War but mainly his prison experiences in the hands of Free State forces; describing his desperate jail break and escape. Told in a surprisingly restrained and objective manner, it treats the IRA as the inheritors of the past Irish struggles for justice (O'Donnell himself was a member of the Irish Socialist Republican party and an activist for the Irish contingent in the International Brigades in Spain).

There Will Be Another Day, 1963
An autobiography which if somewhat mellowed reaffirms his views and commitments to struggling humanity in Ireland and throughout the world over the past half century.

Also Storm, 1922, Wrack, 1931, Proud Island, 1975; additional novels about Irish history and struggles, mainly during the 20th century.

O'FLAHERTY, Liam

The Informer, 1925
A somewhat melodramatic novela adapted into an internationally famous play; revolves about the nature of a former IRA soldier during the Anglo-Irish war who turns police informer. But more basically, it deals with the unheroic and petty opportunism and hatreds which emerge with the seemingly endless underground war.

Skerrett, 1932
A novel of a teacher who struggles against backwardness and clerical reaction to bring some "modern" and secular knowledge to children on Aran Island in the period 1877-1902, interwoven with a sensitive account of the last Celtic Ireland. A tribute to one of O'Flaherty's boyhood teachers.

The Assassin, 1933
A reportage account of the background and rise to power of a general in the

conservative Cosgrove Free State government of 1920s; the openly fascist
sympathies of one General Kevin O'Higgins and his hopes of establishing a clerico-
fascist regime in Ireland patterned after Il Duce's Italy in early 1930s.

Famine, 1937
The first volume of a novel trilogy, being a minutely detailed account of the Irish
Famine of the 1840s which documents the utter desperation of the mass of peasantry,
the complete indifference of the Anglo-Irish ruling class, but underlines the
voraciously hypocritical and ruthlessly speculative role of the Irish middle class
and land holders who are characterized with bitter hatred. Of how the Irish
bourgeoisie and Church and peasant docility deepen the calamity.

Land, 1946
A historical novel of the Irish land struggles of the 1860s and 1870s, the
resurrection of Irish nationalism and the failed Fenian rising of 1870s.

Insurrection, 1950
The final volume of the trilogy, which portrays the conditions and ferment in
Ireland in first decades of the 20th century, culminating in the Easter Rising of
1916.

Spring Sowing, 1924, The Tent, 1926, The Mountain Tavern, 1929
Three collections of short stories mainly of Irish countrisides, from good local
colour sketches to exasperated caricatures; people and daily life in Irish Free
State of 1920s.

Thy Neighbour's Wife, 1923, The Black Soul, 1924, The Martyr, 1927, Mrs. Gilhooly,
1928, Two Years, 1930, The Puritan, 1931, Shame the Devil, 1932
Other novels about aspects of Irish society during the interwar years.

O'MALLEY, Ernest

On Another Man's Wounds, 1935
A novel of the Irish War of Independence (1916-1921) by a former IRA partizan and
later leader of Irish contingent in International Brigades during the Spanish Civil
War.

Army Without Banners, 1937
A memoir of Irish Republican Army from 1916 to end of Civil War; one of the most
authentic and most frequently cited accounts.

O'NEIL, Brian

Easter Week, 1939
A composite social portrait of the various sectors of Irish society, their lives,
background, political views and heterogeneous responses to the events of Easter 1916.

PLUNKETT, James

Strumpet City, 1969
An epic historical novel of the Irish labour movement set largely in Dublin in the
years before W.W.I; "focus on the labour movement, Irish socialism, and the
experience of the urban working class...as industrializing Ireland tries to come
to terms with the significance of a new culture." An outstanding work.

The Trusting and the Maimed, 1959
A collection of stories dealing with the lives of Irish working people, labour
unions and socialist movement from late 1930s through W.W.II. By a leading Irish
labour unionist.

The Risen People, 1958
A play about the 1913 General Strike in Dublin and the ripple of effects it had
throughout Ireland and Great Britain.

RYAN, Desmond

Remembering Sion, 1934, The Sword of Light, 1939
Two historical novels of the inchoate class conflicts sometimes obscured by the

struggles for Irish independence over the last century. By a left labour disciple of James Connolly.

URIS, Leon

Trinity, 1976
A huge, best selling American novel set in Northern Ireland mainly during the 1900-1914 period. The class conflicts between rich, poor and poorer, as well as those between Catholic and Protestant, in Ulster as developed from three centuries of colonial oppression and resistance. Undoubtedly Uris' most progressive work which, however, does not escape the ethnic chauvinist stereotypes which have made his other writings so popular.

CANADA

ACORN, Milton

Jackpine Sonnets, 1977; More Poems for People, 1972; I've Tasted My Blood, 1969
Three collections of poetry (which defy annotation) ranging from themes about love
and work, to the sellout of Canadian culture and history, to solidarity with anti-
imperialist struggles around the world. By the leading Canadian left nationalist
poet, Maritimer and one-time carpenter.

ALLAN, Ted and GORDON, Sydney

The Scalpel, The Sword: The Story of Norman Bethune, 1952
A biography of Norman Bethune, the iconoclastic Canadian communist doctor who rose
to international prominence through his development of a front line blood
transfusion service in the Spanish Civil War and through his medical work for and
death with the Chinese Red Army during the late 1930s. Also see Ted Allen, This
Time a Better Earth, 1939, a novel of the experiences, feelings and understandings
of a Canadian volunteer engaged on the margins of the Spanish Civil War.

BAIRD, Irene

Waste Heritage, 1939
A novel revolving around the lives of unemployed men and women in Vancouver (with
attendant love story) during the mid 1930s. The hunger marches, demonstrations,
police assaults and the gradually rising anger and politicization of the central
character. It was the single "quasi-proletarian" novel to appear in Canada during
the 1930s; a sometimes naive but powerful work.

BERGREN, Myrtle

Tough Timber: the loggers of BC, their story, 1966
A collection of reworked reminiscences of loggers who organized the International
Woodworkers of America in BC during the 1930s, particularly those of Hjalmar
Bergren. Concentrates on the period 1934-1946, and provides accounts of the
social and community background to the union struggles. It ends with the ouster
of the original militants from the I.W.A. in the anti-communist purges which
devastated US and Canadian unions during the late 1940s.

BOWEN, Lynne (ed.)

Boss Whistle, 1982
Subtitled "The Coal Miners of Vancouver Island Remember", being largely an oral
history of the lives and times of one of the most militant sections of the
Canadian working class and dealing mainly with the period 1900-1930s. Three central
chapters treat with the Great Coal Strike of 1912-1914. Includes material gathered
by Myrtle Bergren.

BROADFOOT, Barry

Ten Lost Years, 1973
The best known of Broadfoot's oral histories; somewhat bowdlerized by the
exclusion of virtually all political activity, it is nevertheless a wide ranging
resurrection of memories and experiences by ordinary Canadians during the Great
Depression. One of the first Canadian books to bring home the stupidities, the
human waste and the daily minor heroism involved in surviving that decade.

Six War Years, 1975
A sequel to Ten Lost Years, dealing with memories and experiences of Canadians
during the 1939-1945 war years and (unintentionally or otherwise) showing the
speed with which the lessons of the previous decade were forgotten and replaced
by a sometimes muted, sometimes vicious patriotism.

Days of Sorrow, Years of Shame, 1978
An oral history of the internment of the Japanese Canadian population during
1942-1946. Using old and new interviews with Japanese Canadians, it is a wide
ranging account of their everyday lives, hopes, losses, fears and views. It
does not consider the previous struggles and class divisions within the Japanese
Canadian community. See Ken Adachi's (1976) The Enemy That Never Was for a more
historical background.

CAMERON, Silver Donald

The Education of Everett Richardson, 1978
A reportage account of the failed struggle to organize Nova Scotia fishermen and
cannery workers into an effective union by the United Fishermen and Allied Workers
in 1970-71; of the strike which followed and the canners' mobilization of courts,
injunctions, company unions and local press against the fishermen. Told partly
through the story of one Nova Scotia fishermens' leader who was eventually
jailed for union activity and who gradually comes to realize what sort of "justice
and fair play" we can expect.

CARTER, Dyson

Fatherless Sons, 1955
A novel set in a Sudbury-like smelter town during the initial years of the cold
war and Korean War, with flashbacks to W.W.II and the 1930s. It revolves around
the infighting and travails in the Mine, Mill and Smelterworkers Union. One of
the rare proletarian novels published in Canada but with characters serving mainly
as a vehicle for the hero's denunciation of Canadian cold war politics.

CLARKE, Austin

The Meeting Point, 1967, Storm of Fortune, 1973
Two novels which deal with the experiences of immigrant poor Barbadians in
Canada of the late 1960s. In particular, of a black woman who works as a maid
in the house of an upper middle class Jewish family in Montreal and of the serf-
like and racist way she is treated.

DAVIS, Brian (ed.)

The Poetry of the Canadian People, 1720-1920, 1976
A collection of protest, radical democratic and labour poetry mainly from the
mid 19th to early 20th centuries and drawn from such journals as the Colonial
Advocate, Ontario Workman, and Western Labour News. A left nationalist
selection with considerable period-piece charm.

DURKIN, Douglas

The Heart of Cherry McBain, 1919
A "love and adventure" novel with working class sympathies. Set around a railway
construction camp on the Saskatchewan border early in W.W.I with some
descriptions of work and living conditions of the migrant proletariat during
that era.

The Magpie, 1923
A novel set in Winnipeg at the end of W.W.I and during the Winnipeg General Strike.
An angry commentary on the deepening reaction, class repression and a fairly
good portrayal of the social upheaval of that strike. Done with a rare sympathy
(among published Canadian authors) for the strikers and some biting caricatures
of the purveyors of Board of Trade patriotism.

FRASER, Dawn (David Frank and Don MacGilvary, eds.)

Echoes From Labour's Wars, 1976 (original 1926)
A collection of poems and prose accounts about the struggles of Cape Breton
miners, especially during the bitter 1921 coal strike and the occupation of the

mines and coal towns by the Canadian army. Written by a left worker-poet of the
1920s with an updated introduction by Frank and MacGilvary surveying the economic-
political forces in the region at the time.

GARNER, Hugh

Cabbagetown, 1968 (original 1950)
A novel of a group of youths (and of their parents and neighbours) growing up in
an infamous inner city slum of Toronto between 1928 to 1937. Despite occasional
melodrama and some juvenile political caricatures, the work is one of the few
authentically proletarian novels in Canada.

Storm Below, 1957
A novel of four days below the decks on a Corvette on convoy duty in the North
Atlantic during W.W.II. Not a war story in the usual sense, it captures the
feelings and thoughts of Canadian sailors who are as much embroiled in the
personal and caste/class conflicts of shipboard society as in the broader war.

Silence on the Shore, 1962
A novel revolving around the flaws and blindness but fundamental decency of the
poor trapped in urban slums of Canada during the golden age of "prosperity",
with anunliterary hatred of the forces which keep them there. Garner was always
a strange amalgam of pro-working class radical and "know nothing".

GRAY, James

The Winter Years, 1966
Reminiscences of becoming and being a member of the unemployed and on the dole
in Winnipeg during the depression.
Some incisive though hardly radical comments on the social psychology
isolating the unemployed and dissipating their anger. It recaptures some of
the bitterness about the humiliations heaped upon the unemployed by those
slightly better off. By a later journalist and prolific author of popular histories.

HARDY, George

Those Stormy Years, 1956
An extraordinary autobiography of a member of an epochal generation, only a part
of which deals with Canada. Born in 1884, Hardy was a British labourer with
strong union loyalties but little political consciousness who came to Canada in
circa 1902, worked his way west through a succession of jobs and conflicts to
arrive in BC during the burgeoning socialist upsurge in the decade before W.W.I
It presents one of the rare personal accounts of that movement in BC as well as
what was entailed in organizing a Teamsters union in Victoria, BC and leading it
into the I.W.W. during one of the most militant periods of class conflict in this
province. The remaining three-quarters of the memoir deals with Hardy's
experiences as a union organizer in Australia, his imprisonment in the US during
the suppression of the I.W.W., his involvement in the founding of the C.P. USA
and three years spent in China during the mid 1920s before returning to an
industrial backwater in Britain during the 1930s.

HOAR, Victor

The Mackenzie-Papineau Battalion: Canadian participation in the Spanish Civil
War, 1969
An informal history of the Canadian unit of the International Brigades fighting
for the Spanish Republic; partly a campaign history but including the personal
experiences of the volunteers in depression Canada
which brought them to fight against fascism in Spain.

HUTCHINSON, Sidney

Depression Stories, 1976
Crudely authentic reminiscences of riding the rods, jungling up and scratching a
living from a roster of jobs ranging from washing gold to logging during the
depression decade in the Kootenay region of BC (a senescent mining district which

for three generations was a refuge area for all variety of North American dissidents). Captures something of the culture of the western resource proletariat of that generation and remnants of earlier native radicalism.

INTERNATIONAL LONGSHORE AND WAREHOUSEMEN'S UNION, LOCAL 500 (Ben Swankey, ed.)
Man Along the Shore: the story of the Vancouver waterfront, 1975
An outstanding collection of oral history, being an unvarnished set of memoirs of and by Vancouver longshoremen from circa 1900 to the late 1950s. Documents the hardships, pride of work, compromises and humiliations, union struggles, achievements, defeats, danger, on the job social lives, etc. of three generations of West Coast longshoremen.

IRVINE, William

Farmers in Politics, 1920
In part an overview of then recent "populist" farmers' movements in Canada and the northern US and in part a political program to mobilize a progressive farmers movement. In retrospect, a visionary if anachronistic document of the last phase of small farmers populism which on the Canadian prairies still had another generation of life left. For a biography of Irving, his work and times see Antony Madrios' (1979) William Irvine, Prairie Radical.

KNIGHT, Rolf

A Very Ordinary Life, 1974
A life history of an immigrant working class woman from girlhood in the pre-W.W.I Berlin tenements, through the upheavals of the following decade and emigration to Canada in the late 1920s. Recounts a dozen depression years spent throughout western Canada working with her husband at anything from washing gold to cooking in logging camps. Of living with institutionalized anti-German racism during W.W.II and after, of the life of a camp worker's family, the drama and trivia of major social changes as seen from below, of encroaching old age in Vancouver during the 1960s. It relates something of the previous culture of German socialist workers (and by implication contests the popular Canadian image of immigrants as awe-struck peasants) and touches on the working class conscious culture existing in British Columbia of the recent past. Filled with an array of realistically complex and contradictory situations and people, the account suggests some of the extraordinary experiences and qualities of many other ordinary lives.

Stump Ranch Chronicles, 1977
A compendium of two brief life histories of men who were both farmers and resource workers in Western Canada from 1912 to the mid 1970s. It touches on the immigrant experiences and their rapid incorporation into the Canadian "frontier" regions of their times, with some remarkable reminiscences of life and work in railway construction gangs, logging, hand mining, fishing, etc. as well as their years homesteading and farming. The appendix consists of a translated diary of Peace River homesteading during the late 1920s and early 1930s and paints a rather sobering picture of that life. Their stories also are a document of the populist-socialist sentiments once more common throughout the farm regions of Western Canada.

Indians at Work, an informal history of native Indian labour in British Columbia, 1858-1930, 1978
A massive descriptive account of native Indian wage workers throughout the major resource industries of BC and as "independent" commercial producers from the initial European settlement to the beginning of the great depression. Separate chapters treat with the trajectory of the various industries and Indian workers in them: commercial fishing and cannery work, logging and sawmilling, shipping and transport, farming and ranching, mining, service enterprises, etc. A comparative chapter surveys analogous developments of Indian worker-entrepreneurs in other regions of Canada while an extensive appendix provides the social context leading up to and accompanying Indian wage labour. An epilogue suggests the course of developments since 1930 (in lieu of an intended second volume). The study attempts to counter both the indigenous "garden of eden"

romances and the view that native Indians were exclusively helpless victims of
Canadian industrial society, somehow culturally unable to deal with the world of
wage labour. Native Indians here are treated as an (admittedly distinct) part
of the emerging British Columbia working class. It draws on more than 300
primary and secondary sources and provides extensive footnotes.

Along the No. 20 Line, reminiscences of the Vancouver waterfront, 1980
A combined social geography and oral history of the intermixed industrial and
residential districts of the Vancouver waterfront threaded along the No. 20
streetcar line during the 1940s. The first part describes the various components;
the loggers' quarter, the coolie cabins and pensioners, the boats and docks
linking the city to the resource coast, the rail yards, etc. as remembered by a
thirteen year old. The second part is comprised of eight accounts by men and
women, most a generation older and already working in the varied industries along
the waterfront during that decade. A final section outlines the folk history
of labour struggles throughout and changes in that prosaic yet cosmopolitan
district of working class Vancouver.

KNIGHT, Rolf and KOIZUMI, Maya

A Man of Our Times, 1976
Subtitled "The life history of a Japanese-Canadian fisherman", it is the story of
a Japanese immigrant to Canada in 1910 and of his 60 years in a variety of jobs
from oar-powered to modern fishing, in logging, and in factories. A "modern"
and well educated man before his arrival in BC, Ruichi Yoshida's story is
somewhat different from standard ethnic history in that it recounts his and his
comrades long struggles not only against racism but also against the class
exploitation within the Japanese community. It contains some unique accounts of
the Japanese Camp and Millworkers Union from the W.W.I to W.W.II period, a
heterogeneously socialist organization for which Yoshida was an organizer and
editor. Also a somewhat surprising account of life in the internment camps
during W.W.II as not significantly worse than the conditions under which Japanese
Canadian resource workers had previously lived. An appendix provides a capsule
history of the Japanese Canadian labour movement and the thrust of anti-oriental
legislation in BC from the 1890s to the 1940s.

KRAMER, Ken

Black Powder, 1981
A play about the strike of Estevan, Saskatchewan coal miners in 1931 which
culminated in the massacre of a number of demonstrating strikers by the RCMP. A
dramatization of a once hidden part of Canadian labour history resurrected through
research into court and royal commission reports.

LIVERSEDGE, Ronald (Victor Hoar, ed.)

Recollections of the On-to-Ottawa Trek, 1973 (original 1960)
A richly detailed memoir of the conditions and struggles which led up to the Trek
to Ottawa in the summer of 1935, in which a contingent of ultimately more than a
thousand organized unemployed rode freight trains heading for the national
capital to demand a program of public works. Ends with the armed assault on the
trekkers by the RCMP in Regina, a bench mark of Canadian working class history.
Told from the point of view of a Communist party participant, the editor has
added police statements and trial records to provide "balance" for the 1973
edition. Also see Shields and Swankey (1979), Work and Wages.

LIVESAY, Dorothy

Left Hand, Right Hand, 1977
Reminiscences of the left intellectual scene during the 1930s and Livesay's
changing political activities and associations to the early 1970s. Livesay
retains a continuity with the left intellectual traditions of the 1930s, as
recently confirmed by a series of redbaiting attacks on her by right-wing emigres
within the so-called "Canadian Writers Union". Also see Livesay's excellent

reportage piece on the Corbin mine strike of the mid 1930s in Donna Phillips (ed.) (1979), Voices of Discord.

LYSENKO, Vera

Men in Sheepskin Coats, 1947
A memoir-novel of the initial wave of Ukranian homesteaders and workers in the Prairie region from the late 1890s to late 1930s. Drawn partly from reminiscences it is one of the first and still one of the most authentic accounts of what was then an exploited ethnic minority. Woven around a family chronicle, it counters once prevalent ethnic stereotypes to give a progressive and believable portrait of one immigrant world.

McEWAN, Paul

Miners and Steelworkers, 1978
A popular history of the militant labour struggles in the once substantial heavy industry and mines of the Maritime region during the first half of this century. Focussed on the decades between the eve of W.W.I and the beginning of W.W.II.

MACKENZIE, Kenneth

Living Rough, 1936
Memoirs of an English seaman and jack-of-all-trades, it includes a section about working on Great Lakes shipping and elsewhere in Canada during the late 1920s and 1930s. Unseen.

MacPHERSON, C.B.

Democracy in Alberta, 1953
A very readable scholarly study of the ideological roots, the social bases and appeal of the original Social Credit movement in Alberta. Also of the ideological analogues in the Technocracy, Moral Rearmament, Kibbo Kift and other right-wing know-nothing movements in Canada and England. One of the few analyses of the ideological bases of grass roots reaction in Canada.

MADRIOS, Anthony

William Irvine: The life of a prairie radical, 1979
A biography of the radical populist-socialist organizer of farmers movements on the Prairies from W.W.I on, involved in the founding of the Cooperative movement and the Canadian Farmers Union, and one of the left organizers of the Cooperative Commonwealth Federation in early 1930s; a CCF activist until the demise of that party in 1961. As such, Irvine's biography is also partly a history of small farmers radicalism in Canada and its attempted alliances with fraternal sectors.

MALOFF, Peter and SUKHOREV, V.A.

Tanya, 1975
A quietly moving novel of a Doukhobor woman from her youth in Russia to emigration to Canada at the turn of the century. The sects and swirling confusion of life first on a Prairie communal farm and then in the radical pacifist and Christian communitarian Doukhobor settlements of the Kootenays during the first half of this century.

MARLYN, John

Under the Ribs of Death, 1957
A roman d'clef set in North Winnipeg in 1920s and 1930s; about the son of Austro-Hungarian immigrants who is ashamed of his parents lives and is embarrassed by the general contempt of the non-British population. Deals with the son's attempts to make himself over in the image of his Riverview employers (in which he largely succeeds), only to realize how shallow and contemptible a person he has become by joining with the exploiters. Written in a muted but sometimes compelling manner.

MASTERS, D.G.

The Winnipeg General Strike, 1950
A historical monograph of the Winnipeg general strike of 1919, which employers and
the provincial and federal governments treated as an attempt to establish Soviet
Power in Canada and requiring military suppression by the RCMP. Deals with the
conjoined rise of the One Big Union and the sympathy strikes throughout Western
Canada at that time. A scholarly and possibly dated treatment but one of the few
sympathetic accounts of radical Canadian labour history to appear during the cold
war period.

MONTERO, Gloria

Billy Higgins Rides the Freights, 1982
A children's novel about a thirteen year old who is set adrift during the mid 1930s,
becomes involved in the Relief Camp Workers strike in Vancouver of 1935 and winds
up on the Trek-to-Ottawa (!) rubbing shoulders with the actual leaders such as
Art Evans and Red Walsh. Some of the forgotten lessons of that period and their
current relevance underlined for young readers.

MOORE, Brian

The Luck of Ginger Coffey, 1960
A novel about a bemused aspirant reporter who with his family has emigrated from
Ulster to Montreal in the late 1940s; a tragi-comic account of his Horatio Alger
visions as he is exploited and gulled by the paper's editor. The gradual
disintegration of his family through his strivings to resuscitate his middle class
professional image of himself. Some biting details of the untrammeled free
enterprising in the still ununionized Montreal newspaper world and the hero's
fearful disengagement from those attempting to bring union security to the industry.

MOWATT, Farley

People of the Deer, 1951, The Desperate People, 1958
Two thinly researched and sometimes rather romantic, but immensely powerful protest
accounts of the starvation conditions and government indifference which were
decimating the Caribou Eskimo population of the Keewatin interior by the late 1940s
and early 1950s. Very widely read at the time, these two volumes are among the few
Canadian protest novels which can legitimately claim to have played a major role
in changing conditions depicted.

And No Bird Sang, 1978
An understated and moving reminiscence of Mowatt's understandings and feelings as
a young private in the Canadian Army during the Italian campaign in W.W.II.
Juxtaposes his own and Canada's British Tory heritage, the contemporary sentiments
against fascism and his evolving horror of the indiscriminate death and sufferings
inflicted in even a "just war". It is probably Mowatt's finest work to date and
is a welcome relief from the endless stream of self righteous and war-loving
memoirs of Canadian military men which have appeared over the last 30 years.

Mowatt is also the author of more that two dozen other novels which range from
historical adventures to dog stories, from anti-hunting tales to travelogues. He
is probably the most widely translated Canadian author of the post W.W.II period.

OSTENSO, Martha

Wild Geese, 1925
A novel of the isolation and restrictions of frontier farm life in the interlake
region of Manitoba during the early 1920s as experienced by an independent young
woman beginning to feel her sexual and personal desires. Both the theme of female
sexuality and the denigration of farm life were daring topics in the time and it
intimates the feelings of those waves of youths beginning to leave the farms en
masse. Written in a somewhat period piece style but a breath of fresh air when
compared to the analogous tomes of Philip Grove.

PEOPLE'S HISTORY COLLECTIVE

The People's History of Cape Breton, 1972
A booklet-sized popular history of union and allied struggles in the industrial
and coal mining region of Nova Scotia, the citadel of left-wing militancy in the
Maritimes. Some fascinating glimpses of people and events largely unknown outside
the region, mainly from the turn of the century to the end of the 1930s.

PHILLIPS, Donna (ed.)

Voices of Discord: Canadian short stories from the 1930s, 1979
Twenty-six "proletarian" stories and reportage pieces by largely unknown Canadian
authors extracted from the journals Masses and New Frontier of early to mid 1930s.
A number of these accounts are a long ways removed from the usual pleading for
"fair play" and have a growl of real hatred of Canadian capitalism. Phillips'
volume seems to be the only compilation which has actually resurrected some of that
stream of virtually anonymous and often excellent radical writing which for sixty
years appeared in a scattering of small journals.

POTROBENKO, Helen

No Streets of Gold, a social history of Ukranians in Alberta, 1977
An outstanding amalgam of social history, reminiscences and translated oral
accounts of Ukranian working men and women throughout Alberta (and elsewhere in
Western Canada) from circa 1900 to the mid 1940s--in mine towns, work camps, cities
and especially on marginal homesteads. Interwoven are the author's memoirs of
growing up in one such homestead area under still depression-like conditions
during the 1940s and early 1950s. A multi-stranded, vibrant account of the
domestic tensions and external oppression of variously progressive working class
Ukranians of the immigrant generation.

RYAN, Toby

Stage Left, Canadian theatre in the thirties, 1982
A reminiscence of the Workers' Theatre movement in Canada during the mid and late
1930s; personal accounts by some of the surviving participants, the drama of
staging performances (including the frequent police closures as well as logistics)
and the audiences' responses. Recreates the socio-political conditions of
depression Canada as the context of the plays performed.

SHARP, Paul

Agrarian Revolt in Western Canada, 1948
A popular history of the varied farmers, populist and cooperative movement on the
Canadian prairies--their social bases, goals and strategies--from about the turn
of the century to the early 1930s. From a US New Deal perspective.

SHARPE, Errol

A People's History of Prince Edward Island, 1975
An informal history of the varied popular resistance to the squirearchical rulers
of the island province; deals largely with the 19th century and with actions
cloaked in the ideology of so-called "red Toryism". The democratic nationalist
tradition in one of the most traditional of Canadian provinces.

SINCLAIR, Bertrand

Poor Man's Rock, 1920
A novel of marginal salmon fishermen in southern BC waters during and shortly after
W.W.I; the struggles between canners, incipient fishermen's unions, the inter-
ethnic conflicts and of assorted travails. Packed with details of the locale and
specifics of the fishing industry but marred by an anti-orientalism which was
prevalent at the time and by the author's romantic individualism. Sinclair was
both a working fisherman and a very prolific author of partly realistic, partly
escapist adventure tales set in the resource industries of Western Canada. His
works are possibly of greater interest as resource material for social historians
than to readers of progressive working class novels.

SMITH, A.E.

All My Life, 1949
An autobiography of a once famous (or notorious) Methodist minister reared in the social gospel of the pre W.W.I era who was converted to socialism during his involvement in the Winnipeg general strike and its aftermath. He became a Communist supporter and was active throughout Western Canada in the 1920s and the head of the Canadian branch of the Labour Defense League during the endless union struggles and jailings of the 1930s.

STEEVES, Dorothy

The Compassionate Rebel: Ernest Winch and his times, 1960
A biography, sometimes verging on hagiography, of a renowned working class socialist leader in BC from the pre W.W.I era to his death in 1957. The social context of the early Socialist Party of Canada, the union organizing and anti-war actions during the Great War which almost got him lynched, the anti-racist struggles of the 1920s and the expectations for a mass left party in the founding of the Cooperative Commonwealth Federation during the 1930s. Alludes to Winch's and other left CCF resistance to the continual drift of that party to the right and ultimately with his retreat to personal, socially alemeorative legislation in BC.

SWANKEY, Ben and SHEILS, Jean Evans

Work and Wages, 1977
A "semi-documentary" biography of the life and times of Arthur Evans, the primary organizer of the 1935 On-to-Ottawa Trek. Of his previous life as a migratory worker and I.W.W. activist in the US and Canada during the W.W.I period,, the struggles and defeats of attempts to organize western Canadian resource workers in the 1920s, the initial campaigns to defend the unemployed during the 1930s. An extensive treatment of the background and events of the On-to-Ottawa Trek and the trials after it was smashed. Deals with Evans' later attempts to ressurect the Mine, Mill, Smelter Workers Union in the B.C. interior company towns, of anti-eviction actions in Vancouver, jail and his work at washing gold and odd jobs to support his family until his death in 1944.

WALLACE, J.S.

The Night is Ended, 1942, The Collected Poems of Joe Wallace, 1981
Two collections of poetry by the leading communist poet in Canada from the 1920s to the early 1950s. They cover a very wide range of themes from love to revolution, about Canada and events throughout the world.

WARRIOR, Clyde M.

Quitting Time, 1978
A slim collection of poems mainly about contemporary work in the woods, life and society by a brilliant B.C. logger poet. They entail a sometimes sardonic Brechtian fire and insight which is truly extraordinary. Also see Howard White's The Men There Were Then, 1982, poems revolving around the myths, language, humour of B.C. resource workers of the recent past.

WRIGHT, Richard and ENDRES, Robin (eds.)

Eight Men Speak and Other Plays From the Workers Theatre Movement, 1978
A collection of Canadian Workers Theatre plays from the 1930s. Eight Men Speak (Oscar Ryan et al, originally 1934) revolves around the Canadian Communist Party leaders imprisoned by the R.B. Bennett tory regime during the early 1930s. Touches on the prisoners' backgrounds but mainly presents their views about the tasks facing Canadian left with the worldwide rise of fascism. Widely performed throughout Canada as part of agitation to free these political prisoners, when it was illegal to publicly discuss the views broached here.

ZWELLING, Marc

The Strikebreakers, 1972
A reportage work of the organized strikebreaking companies which emerged in
Ontario during the late 1960s and early 1970s. Drawn from evidence presented to
a commission of inquiry established by the Ontario Federation of Labour, it
contains all of the ingredients of the American proletarian novels of the 1930s
--the hoodlum goon squads utilized by some of the most "respectable" companies in
Ontario, the political connections which allow this and the blind eye or actual
support proffered strikebreakers by police and courts. A model of the kind of
reportage writing which could be done in contemporary Canada.

QUEBEC

AMES, Herbert B.

The City Below the Hill, 1972 (original 1898)
A journalist's investigation of social conditions in a working class quarter of
Montreal during the late 1890s, based on surveys and interviews. An interesting
piece of social history written in the vein of "how the other half lives".

BESSETTE, Gerard

La Bagarre (The Conflict), 1958
A novel about a young Quebec worker and part time student in Montreal during the
mid 1950s who becomes involved in the strike of his fellow street car cleaners
and takes up a leading role. Revolves around the tensions between a quasi-
intellectual as a kind of outsider and his fellow workers, who have their
reservations about him. Also deals with his own inner contradictions about
aspirations of upward mobility and opposition to the system of exploitation he has
always known. Some good portraits of life in Montreal working class slums of
period.

Les Pedagogues (The Teachers), 1961
A novel of a professor of education in a Quebec teachers' college who has just
become reinstated after the 1949 teachers' strike when he runs up against the
opposition of the church and a pliant Department of Education minister who block the
hiring of a Polish professor (because he is a non church goer). Various forays
to gain support from teachers and potential allies against the intervention of
church and state lead to his own imminent dismissal and he leaves to become an
organizer of a new Quebec Teachers Union with the support of the Textile Workers
Union, in which the protagonist of La Bagarre is now a leading figure.

Le Libraire (The Bookseller), 1960, L'Incubation (Incubation), 1965
Two novels about the underlying structural conflicts and hostilities in Quebec of
the late 1950s and early 1960s, but tracing the pessimistic existentialism and
alienation of the main characters.

BLAIS, Marie-Claire

Une Saison Dans la Vie d'Emmanuel (A Season in the Life of Emmanuel), 1965
A novel of the degrading and soul destroying penury of rural Quebec, the callous
fatalism and obscurantism fostered by the church and the smug pomposity of the
middle class squirearchy. A pessimistic feminist view which nevertheless touches
on undercurrents of tenderness and love among kinswomen which sometimes make that
life bearable. Revolves around a family of poor farmers
during the indefinite but seemingly unchanging recent past.

Les Manuscrits de Pauline Archange (The Manuscripts of Pauline Archange), 1969
A uniformly grim and black account of the 19th century-like poverty, mortality
and brutalized lives of family and friends of a French Canadian school girl in the
slums of Quebec City during the 1930s and early 1940s. Of the pathological

servility and oppression imposed by that society and its incorporation by the
oppressed themselves. Alternates between a sometimes derogatory "tremendismo" to
sometimes telling insight by one of the most prolific and most honored of Quebec
writers of present generation.

DUMAS, Evelyn

The Bitter Thirties in Quebec, 1975 (Dans Le Sommeil de Nos Os, 1971)
A popular history of strikes and other working class struggles in the supposedly
somnolent Quebec of 1930s. Describes now little known militancy and class-
cultural aspects of Quebec working people (French, English and immigrant) in the
major cities and in industrial towns a generation before "The Quiet Revolution".
Frequently cited as a historical measure against which some of the earlier social
novels might be compared.

FENNARIO, David

On the Job, 1976
A play set in the shipping room of a Montreal dress factory on Christmas Eve 1975,
as French and English Canadian workers in sweatshop jobs stumble over the misread
lessons of their world and lives--angry, exploited, humiliated but riven by
fantasies and enervating cynicism. The battle not joined. May leave viewers with
the uncanny feeling that they've worked with some of the characters.

Balconville, 1978
A play set in a Montreal mixed working class district and revolving around some of
the same themes as On the Job; deals with the "domestic" lives of young workers
(French, English and other) but with flickerings of understanding and opposition
to the system which oppresses them.

Also Without a Parachute, 1972, Nothing to Lose, 1977
Two further plays on the above themes.

FERRON, Jacques

Cotnoir (Cotnoir), 1962
A novel which intertwines two stories: one of a Dr. Cotnoir, a Quebecoise doctor
who practices exclusively in the impoverished Ville Jacques Cartier district of
Quebec City and who treats the physical and psychological scars of his patients.
He comes to see the daily struggles, tribulations and tenacity of Quebec working
people, men and women, as infinitely more heroic than the peripathetic and much
balleyhooed revolts of Quebec middle classes (from 1837 on). The other story
revolves around a prematurely aged worker-patient whose defeats have led him into
self destructive passages of insantiy, but who pulls himself together after
Cotnoir's death. Told through the narration of another young doctor who takes
over Cotnoir's practice and comes to similar views. Insightful and sympathetic
without being patronizing. In part a tribute to Ferron's predecessor in medical
practice on the Gaspe during the late 1940s. Ferron's own work as a doctor among
the poor in Ville Jacques Cartier is itself memorialized in Vallieres' White
Niggers of America.

GELINAS, Pierre

Les Vivants, Les Morts et Les Autres (The Living, the Dead and the Others), 1959
A novel of the radicalization of a young Quebecoise intellectual between 1950 and
1955 as he works with labour unions and left-wing working class groupings in the
battles against the Duplesis regime and its supporters. Ranges from a lumber
worker strike in the Abitibi region to struggles in Quebec City, the bitter strike
of Dominion Textile workers in Montreal in 1952 and the use of Montreal police
goon squads under a particularly notorious officer to smash it. Also of the
successful strike against the French Canadian owned Dupuis Brothers department
stores in Montreal. Some good accounts of Quebec working class life during the
period and its internal contradictions of support for reactionary ethnic
nationalism and emerging struggle for own class interests. Interweaves some of
the salient features of the international scene, the deepening cold war reaction,

the opposition to Canadian involvement in the US-Korean War. Touches on the
hero's break with the Communist party in 1956 after revelation of Stalin's crimes,
yet leaving with the feeling that the people and causes he had been working with
in Quebec were something to be proud of.

GRAVEL, Pierre

A Perte de Temps (Lost Time), 1971
A novel of the social and political situation in Quebec in 1970; it suggests that
only events such as the declaration of martial law during the October crisis will
stir Quebecoise out of their relapse into apathy.

HEWITT, Marsha and MACKAY, Claire

One Proud Summer, 1982
A children's novel revolving around the experiences of a teenaged French Canadian
mill girl working in the 19th century-like conditions of the Quebec textile
factories during the mid 1940s; her account of the bitter organization strike at
Valley Field led by Ken Rowley and Madeleine Parent in 1947. A good interweaving
of labour history and feminist fiction.

LABERGE, Albert

Bitter Bread, 1970 (La Scouine, 1918)
The story of an old peasant woman whose life has been lived in the poverty
and repressed society of rural Quebec of the late 19th and early 20th centuries,
a life sustained by loaves of sourdough bread. An acrid tribute to her querulous
grasping for life in that environment. It was an early contention against the
glorification of rural life being touted by the church and nationalist Quebec
writers. In a somewhat similar vein one might mention Ringuet's (Philip Panneton)
(1938) Trente Arpentes (Thirty Acres, 1964) which, while not working class or
radical, is held to be one of the classics of Quebec social realist novels. It
deals with the stagnant habitant farmlets along the Lower St. Lawrence during the
1930s, the hardly miserable but traditional fixity of life and its economic
unviability--ending with the departure of the hero to find work in the US
industrial towns.

LAMOUREUX, Henri

L'Affrontement (The Battle), 1976
A novel set in Quebec of the early 1970s; deals with the constant industrial
accidents and fatalities in one Quebecoise-owned factory as part of the broader
system of exploitation. The growing militancy of union struggles leading to a
bitter strike and the incorporation of new and the falling away of old supporters
as the nature of the battle evolves. By a Quebecoise worker-writer.

Les Meilleurs d'Entre Nous (The Best Among Us), 1979
Another novel describing the life, tribulation, joys and varied resistance within
a working class neighbourhood of Montreal of the mid 1970s. It includes some
individuals who have left behind their middle class backgrounds to work in
factories and enter the rounds of citizens' group activism in a Quebec seemingly
in ferment.

LEMELIN, Roger

Au Pied de la Pente Douce, 1944 (The Town Below, 1948)
A family chronicle of traditional French Canadian working class life in an old
parish in the "lower town" of Quebec City during the mid to late 1930s. Recounts
the pinch-penny penury, the everpresent insecurity of unemployment and the "warm"
but self-isolating life revolving around an extended family (the kind of "head-in-
the-sand" personalism which more than apathy or revolt mark their reaction to the
depression and clouds of war). Alludes to political events and labour struggles
as a background to daily lives along with the reliance on the church and "one's
betters" for guidance. A quizzical account which later Quebecoise writers
bitterly denounced as a stereotype.

Les Plouffe (The Plouffe Family), 1948
A novel revolving around the Plouffe family from 1938 to 1940 in a similar parish as that in The Town Below. The continuing story of inward looking family life among traditionalist Quebec working people, who look toward church-led social groups and the demogogery of the Union Nationale at the same time they oppose "big capitalists" and are adamantly against Canada's entry into what they see as another "foreign war". Ends with the dissolution of the family (and to a certain extent that way of life) with entry into W.W.II.

NISH, Cameron (ed.)

Quebec in the Duplesis Era, 1970
A collection of essays about Quebec society from the mid 1930s to late 1950s when it was dominated by a clerico-comprador autocracy held together by Premier Duplesis. Details the mechanisms of blatant political and social repression which might have made Huey Long envious. Of the traditional ethnic and lower middle class fears which sustained this regime but also the subsurface disintegration and changes in Quebec society from the late 1940s on.

PARIZEAU, Alice

Les Militants (The Militants), 1974
A novel which sympathetically portrays the nature of and reasons for the militant struggle for Quebec independence during the late 1960s and early 1970s; of FLQ sympathizers, activists and others.

RENAUD, Jacques

Le Casse (The Broken), 1964
A novel of the Montreal lumpen proletariat, written in Joual dialect and imbued with the "tremendismo" which some Quebecoise authors used to belabour Quebec society of the 1960s. Begins with the murder of a young hoodlum by his rival, recreates their world of anarchic violence and callousness and broadens out to portray the decaying physical and social environs of the Montreal poor (or at least the Quebec intellectuals' view of them). The hopelessness of escape or even getting a decent job and the quality of feeling trapped by the time one is ten years old.

RICHARD, Jean-Jules

Le Feu Dans L'Amiante (The Fire in Asbestos), 1956
A remarkable documentary novel of Quebec in the late 1940s, early 1950s. Deals with the historic strike of workers at Asbestos Corporation's Thetford Mines in 1949, from the point of view of the French Canadian strikers and based directly on actual events. How a common industrial dispute was converted into a bitter and open class struggle by the rapacity and arrogance of the industrial and political bosses; and the surprising tenacity of the strikers and their allies who shook the foundations of traditional Quebec. Some powerful accounts of the mass firings, of clashes between strikers and scabs, of the use of Provincial Police as armed occupying forces in the company mine town and their aggressive assaults on strikers and their families. Treats the knee-jerk support given to the foreign owned Asbestos Corporation by Duplesis, and the mobilization of his assembly, press, courts and police, and of the division in the church on the matter, requiring the intervention of the Pope on the side of Duplesis. The French Canadian workers, their families and supporters are the central figures and heroes of the book, hardly the defeated characters of some other novels.

Ville Rouge (Rouge Town), 1948
A collection of short stories about small town Quebec society during W.W.II and in the years immediately after. In part, accounts of how the Duplesis regime is/was a kind of confederation of local bourgeoise interests and how it either buys off or victimizes individuals opposed to its policies.

ROY, Gabrielle

Bonheur D'Occasion, 1945 (The Tin Flute, 1948)
A novel which purports to portray the sombre and straightened lives of a variety
of poor French Canadian working people living in the tight packed and inward
looking St. Henri district (between the rail yards) of Montreal from the late
1930s to early 1940s. Focused on the members of one family, particularly a young
woman working as a waitress in a greasy spoon cafe and of her co-workers and
customers. Touches on the fine grained intraclass distinctions, the flatness and
stagnancy of social life and the apolitic and personally limited responses to some
of the major historical events of their times. The Tin Flute is probably the most
widely read French Canadian novel in English Canada and is widely accepted as a
pioneer work in Quebec social realist writing. A sympathetic account of the Quebec
urban poor despite Roy's patronizing attitude toward her characters.

RYAN, Oscar

Soon to be Born, 1980
An unabashedly proletarian novel set in Montreal of 1939 and dealing with the lives
and backgrounds of a number of intertwined Jewish, French, Irish and English
Canadian working people from W.W.I on. Portrays their everyday lives and concerns
and touches on the trajectories of now largely forgotten struggles in Canada and
abroad during the interwar years. Includes a diary-like account of an organizing
trip across Canada in the early 1930s by a young communist from Montreal which
includes some brilliantly told "tall tale" allegories in the tradition of the early
soap box orators. Despite the overworked use of a central villain, the novel is in
places comparable to the impassioned prose-poetry of Sean O'Casey.

THERIAULT, Yves

Les Vendeurs du Temple (The Compradores of the Temple), 1951
A novel focussed on the role of the higher Catholic clergy in Quebec as they were
involved in sustaining the political corruption and repression of the Duplesis
regime during the late 1940s.

VALLIERES, Pierre

Negres Blancs d'Amerique, 1967 (The White Niggers of America, 1971)
A semi-autobiographical commentary on Vallieres youth in the working class slums
of Montreal during the 1950s and of his parents' trek through various self-
defeating undertakings and jobs since the 1930s. An outraged and in some ways
derogatory diatribe against family, neighbours and Quebecoise working people who,
though angry and personally combative, allow themselves to be gulled by church
and state and exploited by "The English" capitalists. Widely read among student
"activists" of the period.

VILLENEUVE, Paul

Johnny Bugalow (Johnny Bugalow), 1974
A novel of two generations of Quebecoise workers, farmers and petite bourgoise
being rooked and gulled by all and sundry. Shifts back and forth from the anti-
hero's activities in the Quebec Liberation Movement of 1963 and the experiences
of his father a generation earlier who after a youth in a depressed Quebec
industrial town attempts homesteading in the much balleyhooed Abitibi region
during the late 1930s, where he encounters deadening isolation and even greater
poverty. Rounds on his return to the social decay and marginal jobs of the
Montreal slums during the 1950s and of another son whose sporadic employment in
northern construction camps also provides little hope for betterment.
Portrays   the amorphous anger and violence in sections of Quebec society by 1970.

UNITED STATES

AGEE, James

Let Us Now Praise Famous Men, 1938
A famous reportage account of Agee's stay with four impoverished and near
starving white tenant farm families in the hills of Georgia during the mid 1930s.
It mixes compassion and an outrage at the active disinterest in rural poor by
State authorities. Flawed by a certain patronizing voyeurism, but photos by
Walker Evans are now classics.

ALGREN, Nelson

Someone in Boots, 1935
A novel of the bleak and self-destructive life of a young Texas drifter
(definitely not a 'migratory worker') wandering around the US in mid 1930s in
search of work and whatever thrills he can drum up. By chance he comes in
contact with a group of progressives in Chicago and is brought into the margins
of political activity, which provides the only hope of giving some meaning to his
life. But he breaks with this new life when an old Texas buddy reviles him for
associating with Reds and Blacks. A story of the underlying strength of the
racist and reactionary values in American lumpen culture.

Never Come Morning, 1942
A novel revolving around immigrant Polish working class families in Chicago of the
1930s and the decline of some members of the second generation into petty
criminals on the one hand and into labour activists on the other. Focuses on the
brutalization which transforms sometimes the most rebellious and courageous of
the unemployed youths into criminals.

The Man With the Golden Arm, 1949
A novel of marginal people trapped in the drug culture of late 1940s, with visions
of the American dream converted into increasingly deeper degradation. See also
A Walk on the Wild Side, 1956, a comparable novel set in 1950s.

ALLSOP, Kenneth

Hard Travellin', The story of the migrant worker, 1972
A very readable informal social history of the lives and times of US migratory
workers (mainly those linked to riding the freights) from the late 1860s to 1930s.
Also a brief but seminal outline of American industry and the railroads as well as
the changing responses and attitudes toward migrant workers over that period.

AMERINGER, Oscar

If You Don't Weaken, 1940
A moving memoir of the populist-socialist movement in the American midwest
--especially of the radical farmers of Oklahoma--from before W.W.I to the late
1920s. It deals with the ways in which the once powerful and vital native
American left of that region was split, hamstrung and crushed during and after
W.W.I. A catalogue of the economic, judicial, military and ideological means at
the disposal of the American State and how the region became transformed into an
ultra-conservative wasteland with even its progressive history submerged.

ARNOW, Harriette Simpson

The Dollmaker, 1954
A massive and almost ethnographically detailed novel of a family of tenant farmers
from a declining Kentucky hill region, the strictures and also joys of that life,

and their unwilling migration to Detroit to work in the war industries of the early 1940s. Sometimes melodramatic, but often perceptive accounts of the mixed viciousness, desperation and humanity they find among their neighbours in close-packed housing tracts. Accounts of working class racism and know-nothing patriotism, of the journey from being poor to becoming impoverished, and conditions in which tenacity, decency and good hearted innocence are no armour against dissolution.

ASHEIGH, Charles

Rambling Kid, 1930
A novelized autobiography of a youth from East End London who immigrated to the US, from 1913 to the early 1920s. Some good accounts of rambling around America with migrant workers, wobbly bindle stiffs, soap boxing socialists. Sketches of actual rank and file I.W.W. organizers marred by occasional melodrama.

ATTAWAY, William

Blood on the Forge, 1941
A proletarian novel of the migration of black families from worked out southern farms to the steel mills of Pennsylvania during the 1930s.

BARAKA, Amiri (Le Roi Jones)

The Motion of History, 1976
A play which depicts aspects of American history from the 18th century to present, emphasizing cases of unity between black and white workers which dramatize the class roots of oppression. It contains some biting critiques of drug culture, American bohemias, "Eastern" and home grown forms of religious escapism and the ways in which poor southern whites and blacks have been played off against each other. Baraka-Jones has here dispensed with his previous separatist black nationalism.

BEALS, Carleton

Glass Houses, 1932
A reportage novel of the ideological functions and mechanisms of control in the US newspaper industry, told through the story of a reporter who gradually becomes radicalized during the 1920s and whose attempts to portray events as he sees them ultimately lead to his being fired and blacklisted. Beals himself was one of the most prolific and most widely read independent left-wing journalists during the 1920s and 1930s. His reportage books delved into many corners of the rising American Empire; his most widely translated journalistic work being (1928) With Sandino in Nicaragua.

Black River, 1934
A novel of the intrigues of a US oil company, their agents within the American government and their comprador allies in Mexico during the early 1930s. Revolves around the US oil company's attempt to create a semi-autonomous enclave around Mexico's oil producing zone.

BELL, Thomas

Out of this Furnace, 1934
A novel of the conditions in the eastern US steel mills of early 1930s and the initial attempts by rank and file militants of the Steel Workers Organizing Committee to reorganize unions in an industry which had smashed them after the 1919 steel strike. The steel corporations were possibly the most lawless and powerful anti-union forces in America of the 1930s.

All Brides are Beautiful, 1936
A novel of two years in the life of a newly married couple in the Bronx during the mid 1930s. An evocative portrait of a working class neighbourhood and the varieties of people and understandings of work in the small factories and sweat shops around New York, and of unemployment. An understated treatment of strikes and political struggles which are largely peripheral phenomena until the couple are gradually drawn into them. Dialogue said to be handled with great skill.

BESSIE, Alva

Men in Battle, 1939
A novel of US volunteers in the International Brigades during the Spanish Civil
War and what brought those Americans to Spain.

Bread and a Stone, 1941
A novel of depression America, of how the press cynically glosses over and
distorts the reality of the times and of the growth of native proto-fascism. A
bitter denunciation of the hypocrisy involved in the American right and press'
cloaking themselves in "patriotism and democracy" when gearing up for US entry
into W.W.II.

The Un Americans, 1957
A documentary novel of the forces, aims and techniques of repression mounted by the
House Un American Activities Committee and its multifoliate allies throughout
America from the late 1940s to mid 1950s. A much needed reminder that the wave
of reaction was not just the work of a few buffoons like Senator Joe McCarthy and
that it was not ultimately concerned with Communism.

BINNS, Archie

The Laurels Are Cut Down, 1937
A novel touching on the social history of the Puget Sound region of Washington
State, from a resource workers area in the 1880s through the deepening
consolidation of capital and attendent class struggles and with the triumph of
conservatism at the end of W.W.I. Also treats with the American army's intervention in support of the White armies around Vladivostock during the Russian
revolution as experienced by two brothers and the deathly silence and stoney
disinterest back in America when they try to explain what they have seen.

Sea in the Forest, 1953
A popular history of the Puget Sound area, especially in the years 1900 to 1920s.
Cursory but readable accounts of the resource worker-settlers, the early utopian
communities and the various progressive strains which were once a part of that
region's society.

The Timber Beast, 1949
A novel of loggers in Washington State from W.W.I to the 1920s.

BIZZEL, W.B.

The Green Rising, 1926
A novel of the so-called Green Corn Rising of radical farmers in Oklahoma in 1917
against both the US entry into W.W.I and the accelerated conversion of the small
farmers into tenants. Flows from the previous generation of populist and
socialist mass organization in Oklahoma and a last hurrah of radical native
American farmers in the region. Flawed by a rather melodramatic love story.
(Also see entries under Oscar Ameringer, Charles Bush, and William Cunningham.)

BLOOR, Ella Reeve

We Are Many, 1940
An autobiography of Ma Bloor, a latter-day Mother Jones figure who was a ubiquitous
organizer of aid to strikers and participant in working class struggles from the
Michigan copper mines of 1913 to the unemployed of New York during the late 1930s.

BODENHEIM, Maxwell

Ninth Avenue, 1927
Collage novel of people and life in Lower West Side of New York in 1920s; the end
of immigration but a still massive immigrant enclave ghetto with all its poverty
and vitality.

Slow Vision, 1934
A rambling collage "novel" of the dissolution of American society during the first
three years of depression, and an attack on the Roosevelt New Deal policy which,
especially in its first year, was a program to restore the status ante quo.

BONOSKY, Philip

Burning Valley, 1953
A novel of the psychological conflict between ethnic and conservative Catholic
loyalties and the appeal of radical commitment in a youth growing up in a coal
mining town of eastern US during the late 1930s and 1940s.

BOYD, Thomas

Through the Wheat, 1933
A bitterly anti-war novel of an American soldier in W.W.I who afterwards comes to
see the Wilsonian rhetoric ("making the world safe for democracy") as merely the
propaganda of expanding American imperialism.

In Time of Peace, 1935
A sequel to Through the Wheat in which the returned soldier becomes a reporter
during the shakey and class restricted "prosperity" of Calvin Coolidge's
America; the hidden poverty and repression of labour in the late 1920s, with the
reporter's growing understanding of US society and the reborn working class
struggles during the early 1930s.

BRISSENDEN, Paul F.

The I.W.W., Its First Fifty Years, 1957
One of the best informal histories of the I.W.W. from 1905 to 1925, by a left
labour reporter and participant in the US syndicalist movement of the time.
Captures something of the vision and passion of the I.W.W. as well as providing
an overview of the major developments and events.

BRODY, Catherine

Nobody Starves, 1932
A novel set among working people in Flint, Michigan at the beginning of the
depression; the overnight poverty into which many are cast, the immediately
heightened exploitation they face but also the continuing apoliticism and chamber
of commerce rhetoric still dominant among them. Hints at the underlying anger,
hidden ferment which would later emerge in the sitdown strikes.

BROWN, Lloyd

Iron City, 1951
A novel of the differing backgrounds and experiences which have led three black
men to become Communists during the 1930s. Told in flashbacks from prison just
prior to December 1941, their attempts to continue political activity in prison
and the parallel of life in prison and their former "freedom" outside the walls.

BURKE, Fielding (Olive Tilford Dargan)

Call Home the Heart, 1932
A novel which documents the lives of southern hill people, their migration to the
textile mills from worked out farms in the 1920s, the initial steps of unionization
and the Gastonia textile strike of 1929. By a southern left-wing writer.

A Stone Came Rolling, 1935
A novel about the struggles of southern tenant farmers as well as the initial
attempts to unionize the mill towns of Carolina under a regime of native
autocracy; culminates in a stream-of-consciousness account of a bloodily
suppressed mill strike in the early 1930s.

BUSH, Charles C.

The Green Corn Rising, 1932
A brief history of the 1917 rising of Oklahoma socialist farmers against the US
entry into W.W.I. An almost ludicrous fiasco from an organizational standpoint
but remarkable for its intent. A carefully hidden history reconstructed from
Department of War files.

CAHAN, Abraham

The Rise of David Levinsky, 1917
A novel of the transformation of the child of a poor Jewish immigrant family, his gradual acculturation to American business culture, his conjoined success and increasing brutalization as he comes to exploit immigrant Jews and others during the W.W.I era.

CALDWELL, Erskine

Some American People, 1935
Reportage accounts of the poverty, social collapse and outright starvation existing among remaining sharecroppers and others driven into a desperate migratory search for work in the southern US during the mid depression. Especially reviles the Georgia state authorities' refusal to even recognize the existence of a problem. Caldwell was better known as an extremely prolific author of "local colour" novels (such as Tobacco Road and God's Little Acre) and was himself raised on an impoverished Georgia hill farm under conditions comparable to those he described.

You Have Seen Their Faces, 1937
Combined reportage and photo collection portraying the lives of southern hill people during the depths of the depression and intended to mobilize Federal aid and intervention against "States Rights" authorities.

Say, Is This the U.S.A.?, 1941
A collection of sketches and stories of people in the US middle south during the late 1930s; the land emptied and the hopes of recent progressive movements abandoned in a pervading feeling of defeat.

CALMER, Alan

Labor Agitator! The story of Albert P. Parsons, 1937
A biography of the best known of the Haymarket martyrs of 1886; focuses on Parsons' years as a migrant worker, printer, editor and mine union organizer in the US south and a recruiter for the Working Man's Party, the first Marxist party in US. Outlines the trajectory of American labour in that first industrial generation, the evolving amalgam of native and imported political traditions from radical republicanism to early anarchism and Marxism.

CALVERTON, V.F.

Where Angels Dared Tread, 1932
A vibrant account of the millenial visions and experiences of the various utopian socialist communities established in America during the 19th and early 20th centuries. By one of the leading figures of the literary left during the 1920s.

CANTWELL, Robert

The Land of Plenty, 1934
A novel dealing with the daily lives and work of men in a Hoquiam, Washington sawmill in the late 1920s. Drawn partly from the author's experience, it treats the lingering heritage of the now dispersed I.W.W. in the region but is mainly an account of the workers' rising anger at their humiliation which, as much as any exploitation, generates a spontaneous strike that then evolves into a major confrontation between a newly organized woodworkers union and the local lumber companies. One of the most influential proletarian novels of the early 1930s.

CAUDILL, Harry

Night Comes to the Cumberlands, 1962
A popular social history of the Kentucky coal mining regions (in particular the Cumberland region) from the early 19th century to circa 1960; the boom and bust resource extraction by the coal companies, life in the coal camps and company towns, the long history of violent struggle to establish and maintain unions against the system of gun thugs and county sheriffs, and of the frequent betrayal of miners by the United Mine Workers leadership. An account which is both radical and conservative in parts.

CHAPLIN, Ralph

Wobbly, The Rough and Tumble Story of an American Radical, 1948
An autobiography by a leading I.W.W. writer and poet; some excellent accounts of
family life, work and migratory labour in US industrial west circa 1900-1915, and
inside accounts of the struggle by and within the I.W.W., circa 1910-1920. A
sobering and saddening epilogue shows the sort of psychological defeat and escape
which almost two decades of harassment and imprisonment produced in Chaplin and
some other I.W.W. leaders.

COLEMAN, McAlister

Men and Coal, 1943
A popular history of coal miners lives and struggles in the US during the late
19th century to the 1930s.

COLEMAN, McAlister and RAUSHENBUSH, H.S.

Red Neck, 1936
A novel of the struggles to organize coal miners in West Virginia during 1910-1914;
the labour wars and pitched battles involved. By a miner and union organizer;
provides good descriptions of everyday life and work as well as confrontations.

COLMAN, Louis

Lumber, 1931
A novel of small town lumber autocracy set against the tradition of union
militancy of loggers and sawmill workers around Aberdeen, Washington at the
beginning of the depression. A militant heritage of an earlier decade
reemerges during the semi-organized strike which evolves.

COLTON, Samuel (ed.)

Sagas of Struggle; a Labour Anthology, 1951
A collection of popular history and memoirs of participants in labour-farmer
struggles in the US over the previous four decades. Includes an account ("To Rise
Together") about the Negro-white alliances in the socialist farmers' movement
in American midwest during W.W.I by Oscar Ameringer.

CONROY, Jack

The Disinherited, 1933
A semi-autobiographical account of the wanderings of a young man raised in the
Missouri coal mine camps of the 1920s, his brief taste of a modest prosperity
ended by the 1929 collapse, but mainly of his travels through midwest and middle
south US doing every kind of job available; work mates, stupidities, racism,
daily struggle to survive, and the growing anger of the unemployed. See also
A World to Win, 1935 (novel).

CONROY, Jack and JOHNSON, Curt (eds.)

Writers in Revolt, The Anvil Anthology, 1933-1940, 1973
A collection of short stories, poetry, drama pieces and extracts from the work of
some fifty worker-writers originally published in the radical Missouri journal,
Anvil. Contains many of the protest themes of depression America by authors who
became well known and others who remained in obscurity.

CUNNINGHAM, William

The Green Corn Rebellion, 1935
A novel dealing with the rising of farmers under the aegis of the local Socialist
Party in eastern Oklahoma in August 1917 ("Green Corn" being the code word for
the rising). It is portrayed as their final desperate step to prevent the
destruction of dissident small farmers. A realistic treatment of everyday life
and problems on the declining farms and a telling account of the massive arrests
and following repression, after which the base of progressive organization in the
region is crushed.

Pretty Boy, 1936
A novel of "Pretty Boy" Floyd, an Oklahoma outlaw of the early 1930s who acquired a national reputation as a kind of "social bandit" and is treated as such in the novel. It touches on the social basis of that mythology in the past history of farmers "radicalism" which had been crushed and the mass expulsion of tenant farmers and their conversion into "Okies" then just beginning in Oklahoma.

CURRAN, Dale

A House on a Street, 1934
A novel of the gradual radicalization of members of the lower middle class in the day to day events, ideas and struggles of the 1930s in a small northern city.

DAVIES, Rebecca Harding

Life in the Iron Mills, 1972 (original 1861)
On the spot reportage-novel about wives and families of Pennsylvania steel workers during the early industrial period in the US. Now reissued as a "feminist classic".

DEMBY, William

Beetle Creek, 1950
A novel of a black youth in a declining Appalachian mine town and his deepening isolation from everyone and everything as his hopes are battered by the everyday brutality of American life.

DENBY, Charles

Indignant Heart, A Black Worker's Journal, 1979
Autobiography of a left black American worker in the automobile plants of Detroit, 1943 through the McCarthy reaction of the 1950s to the freedom marches and civil rights movement of the mid 1960s; recounted as a rank and file organizer of a "militant" faction in the Auto Workers Union.

DIDONATO, Pietro

Christ in Concrete, 1979 (original 1939)
A widely read "proletarian" novel about the lives and work of Italian and other construction workers in New York of the 1930s; culminates in one of the most horrendous accounts of a fatal industrial accident yet written. A semi-poetic, powerful but not especially radical work written by a New York Italian construction worker who wrote no other.

DORR, Rheta Childe

A Woman of Fifty, 1924
An autobiography of middle class American woman and her evolution into an activist in the American Socialist Party before and during W.W.I.

DOS PASSOS, John

The 42nd Parallel, 1930, 1919, 1932, The Big Money, 1936, Manhattan Transfer, 1937
A tetrology combined in the volume U.S.A. (1941); an epic overview of America during W.W.I and the early 1920s. Deals with the changing fortunes and attitudes of W.W.I veterans, bohemians, middle class, businessmen, immigrants, oppressed workers and I.W.W., in context of times. Documents the destruction of the earlier native US radicalism during the W.W.I years and the consolidation of American reaction by the mid 1920s. Ranging across the USA, it is a work using stream-of-consciousness news reels, newspaper headlines and more standard novel techniques.

DOUGLAS, Jack

Veterans on the March, 1934
A reportage account of the Bonus March on Washington in the summer of 1932 by unemployed veterans which was smashed by troops and tanks directed by General Douglas McArthur and Colonel Dwight Eisenhower; a collage of events and of individuals involved.

DREISER, Theodore (et al)

Harlan Miners Speak, 1932
A report of a commission of inquiry into the armed terrorism launched against
union miners in the Kentucky coal fields of early 1930s. It includes chapters
by Drieser, Dos Passos,Sherwood Anderson and other writers and alludes to the
history of battles between miners and a cabal of regional coal owners, sheriffs,
judges, and private gunmen. "Bloody Harlan" county was long a byword for union
resistance to naked free enterprise.

ENGSTRAND, Stuart

The Tomato Field, 1937
A novel which begins as the story of the interpersonal difficulties of a young
married couple who operate a small market farm but which broadens into a tale of
the fight of farmers against the regional canning company which controls their
market.

Spring, 1940, 1942
A novel detailing the slowly waning depression conditions, the limbo of the
American left and the soon to be reborn war-prosperity patriotism.

FARRELL, James T.

Young Lonigan, a boyhood in the Chicago streets, 1932, The Young Manhood of Studs
Lonigan, 1934, Judgement Day, 1935, A World I Never Made, 1936
A novel tetrology combined in the volume Studs Lonigan (1948) about first and
second generation Irish Americans in a working class district of South Chicago
during the 1920s and early 1930s, in particular the life of Studs Lonigan, a
member of a lower middle class family rapidly declining into lumpen, and his/their
incorporation of a racist and reactionary ideology which supports the forces which
oppress them. A study of angry servility and the cultural bases of proto-fascism.

Tommy Gallagher's Crusade, 1938
A sardonic novel which caricatures the nationally known radio priest Father
Coughlin and his defense of Franco, fascism, God, and order against the forces of
unionism, liberalism, Bolshevism and other anti-American ideologies.

No Star is Lost, 1938, Father and Son, 1940
Two of Farrel's circa two dozen novels, here dealing with members of the more
typical (as compared to Studs Lonigan) sections of the American working class
during the depression.

My Days of Anger, 1943
A reminiscence of Farrel's involvement in various factions of the sectarian left
during the 1930s and the ferocious denunciations and infighting among them.

FAST, Howard

The Last Frontier, 1941
A novel of the rising power of corporate capitalism, the conjoined expansion yet
increasing desperation of small farmers in western America between the 1870s and
1890s and the emergence of class conflict in the frontier farm areas. Set mainly
in Oklahoma Territory (Indian Territory), it treats with the deported Indian
populations and the early white farmers, the railroads, the rise of militant
populist parties and their defeat, ending with the spread of the socialist
organization in the region. One of the best of Fast's novels.

The American, 1946
A novel revolving around John Peter Altgeld, the last progressive Governor of
Illinois in 1894, an already anachronistic remnant of radical republicanism.
Deals with the mounting ruling class reaction and the deepening working class
militancy, with the Haymarket martyrs, the Pullman and A.R.U. strikes and
Eugene Debs all making appearances.

Clarkton, 1947
A novel of a strike in a company town of western Massachusetts shortly after
W.W.II. A realistic account of working class caution and bemusement, of union

weakness in a small town and of the gathering forces of capitalism preparing to turn back the clock and retake whatever gains had been made over the previous decade.

Silas Timberman, 1954
A novel of the political purges, cowardice and run-for-cover wisdom which moulds the concerns and intellectual life of a small American university during the cold war of early 1950s. One of the few radical novels about North American academic world.

Spartacus, 1951
Fast's most famous novel; an American progressive's rendering of the oft recounted tale of the Spartacus slave revolt against the Roman Empire in 73-71 B.C.

The Unvanquished, 1942, Citizen Tom Paine, 1943, April Morning, 1949, The Proud and the Free, 1950
Four "historical" novels dealing with aspects of the American War of Independence. The Unvanquished treats with the hard core national liberation soldiers in the Continental Army during the darkest days of that struggle; Citizen Tom Paine is a eulogy of the radical British propagandist for the "American Revolution" and of the international support for the Republican experiment; April Morning deals with the first day of fighting between British troops and Lexington (Mass.) militia; The Proud and the Free recounts the mutiny of a Pennsylvania regiment near the end of the war against the creeping autocracy threatening to impose itself on the new republic. The exemplify the American "patriotic left" genre.

FLYNN, Elizabeth Gurley

I Speak My Own Piece, 1950
A somewhat schematic autobiographical memoir by the famed I.W.W. organizer and spokeswoman from circa 1910 on and her later role in founding the C.P. USA. Once known as "the Joan of Arc of the American working class", she was probably one of the internationally best known Americans of her time.

FORSETH, Matthea

The Color of Ripening, 1949
A novel of a family of Norwegian American loggers in Washington State from before W.W.I to the early 1940s. Touches on the once widespread and varied streams of radicalism in the region, its gradual decay into American conservatism during and after the undeclared class war in which the I.W.W. is crushed, and the re-emergence of union activity during the 1930s. This is all woven through the more typical story line of a two generational family chronicle.

FOSTER, William

Pages from a Worker's Life, 1970 (original 1939)
Reminiscences of the sometime leader of the C.P. USA; the first third of the volume consists of vibrant accounts of work and life as a member of the migratory American working class from circa 1890 to W.W.I and the heterogeneous threads of indigenous radicalism which were a part of Foster's youth. The latter part of the book entails rather doctrinaire reminiscences of party programs as relating to labour struggles from early to late 1920s.

FRANK, Waldo

The Death and Birth of David Markand, 1934
A frantic novel of American capitalism of the 1920s and its collapse, as mirrored in the experiences of a young business executive who, in a way, becomes more human after his financial bankruptcy and forced readjustment during the early 1930s.

City Block, 1926
A collage novel of daily lives and intertwined desires among the inhabitants of a heterogeneous city block in an eastern US city during the mid 1920s.

FREEDMAN, David

Mendel Marantz - Housewife, 1926
A collection of stories about an aspirantly middle class Jewish housewife in the
Bronx during the mid 1920s; a sardonic account of the incorporation of children
of immigrants into the know-nothingism and chauvinism of the Calvin Coolidge era.

FREEMAN, Joseph

An American Testament, 1936
A memoir of coming of age just before and during W.W.I and a testament to the last
remnants of progressive middle class in western America. Freeman was a major
translator of Soviet literature and Testament was a rather influential book in its
time.

Never Call Retreat, 1943
A sequel to American Testament written after Freeman broke with the C.P. USA but
free from the rancour and recantation usual in such works. It reaffirms a
commitment to the multifaceted and changing struggle for justice in America.

FUCHS, Daniel

Summer in Williamsburg, 1934, Homage to Blenholt, 1936, Low Company, 1937
A novel trilogy collectively known as The Williamsburg Trilogy; about day to day
life in a Jewish working class neighbourhood of Brooklyn in the 1930s. The first
immigrant generation along with the native born eking out a living in a variety
of marginal jobs and a continuation of age-old poverty transferred to the New
World, where only petty criminals seem to get ahead. A sensitive, almost
despairing account of the daily compromises and humiliations, the hopeless
travails of a man in his mid twenties (and of his relatives and friends) who
gradually comes to the not very radical conclusion that he must make himself over
into a more ruthless and dishonest person in order to share in the American dream.

GAINES, Ernest

The Autobiography of Miss Jane Pittman, 1971
A novel written as a life history of a 105 year old southern black woman, with the
civil rights movement of the 1950s as a backdrop. Recounts a working childhood
at the end of the plantation slavery period, a following period of peonage for
"freed" blacks, a brief time of relative freedom and marriage replaced by the
deepening repression and racist terror from the 1890s to W.W.I but the
recrudescence of struggle in the 1930s. A retelling of black history in the US
south as seen through the experiences of one woman.

GILES, Barbara

The Gentle Bush, 1947
A family chronicle of a declining Louisiana plantation family and their shifting
alliances with poor Cajun farmers and tenants during anachronistic struggles
against "outside" land corporations during the 1920s and 30s.

GLASGOW, Ellen

Barren Ground, 1927, Vein of Iron, 1935
Two of the better known titles of a fifteen volume chronicle of a North Carolina
family reaching from the American Revolution to 1940. Barren Ground and Vein of
Iron deal with the period 1900 to 1932, the rise of some family members through
the industrialization of a senescent agricultural region and the decline of others.
The final division of native white population into capitalists and a southern
proletariat.

GOLD, Michael

Jews Without Money, 1930
A semi-autobiographical novel of childhood in the Jewish Lower East Side of New
York during the first decade of this century. A somewhat nostalgic but sympathetic
portrait of the generation of immigrant Jewish poor who through hard work,

sacrifice and frugality remained in poverty. Also see Michael Folsom's (ed.)
Mike Gold, a literary anthology (1972), a collection of stories, fulminations and
reviews, both incisive and dogmatic. Gold was the most vociferous doyen of
"proletarian literature" in the US during the 1930s.

GOODMAN, Henry (ed.)

The New Country, 1961
An anthology of 60 short stories translated from Yiddish; about immigration to
and Jewish working class life in America from the 1890s to 1930s. From Lower
East Side sweat shops to Dakota ranches, of radical and traditional strains in
Jewish working class experiences. Refreshingly free from the
current ethnic chauvinism.

GRAHAM, Margaret (Grace McDonald)

Swing Shift, 1951
A novel based on the life of a militant railway union organizer through the first
half of the century and the occupational culture of railway workers. It
interweaves a social and economic history of railroads in American industrial
developments from the 1880s to 1930s in a readable manner as well.

HALDEMAN-JULIUS, Emanuel and Anna Marcet

Dust, 1926
A novel by the publisher of the once immensely important "Little Blue Books"
series. This entry mainly of interest to historians of American working class
self-education.

HALLGREN, M.A. (ed.)

Seeds of Revolt, 1933
A collection of short stories by a number of worker-writers and providing first
hand accounts of conditions across depression struck America and the incipient
class revolts of the early 1930s.

HALPER, Albert

Union Square, 1933
A collage novel of a cross-section of people living around or passing through Union
Square in Lower Manhattan during 1931. Workers, unemployed, small shop keepers,
businessmen, young and old. Counterposes the philosophizing of two radicals
living in the area with the vastly more complex and contradictory social reality
around them.

The Foundry, 1934
A novel set around an electrotype foundry in Chicago, the plant company itself
becoming a main character which changes, forms and destroys the lives of employees
as the "demands of business" require.

The Chute, 1937
A novel set in a mail order house operating under a system of quotas and speed up;
conveys the seeming rule of machinery over workers and describes the attempts of
employees to modify and ultimately sabotage the operations of the plant as a
primitive kind of retaliation bound to fail when not linked to more organized
means of resistance.

HARRISON, Charles

Generals Die in Bed, 1931
An anti-war novel of a naive American soldier in W.W.I who gradually discovers
what the American war effort is for, and his disillusionment as the US evolves
into the type of society he set out to oppose.

A Child is Born, 1932
A sequel to Generals Die in Bed, set in the mid 1920s about another US veteran
who begins to see the disparities of the real America around him for the first
time.

HAVINGHURST, Walter

Pier 17, 1935
A "collective" novel about a longshore strike and waterfront workers in Seattle
and Portland during the mid 1930s.

HAYWOOD, William D.

Bill Haywood's Book, 1929
A remarkable autobiography by one of the greatest labour leaders in the US during
the 1905-1920 period; head of the I.W.W. at its peak and long time activist in the
Western Federation of Miners during the Labour Wars in the American west. Haywood
evokes the culture of working class militancy at its height in the American west
but conveys some of the less savory aspects and mythology of that milieu as well.

HEDGES, Marion Harrison

Dan Minturn, 1927
A novel set in Minneapolis of the mid 1920s, still then a staging area for migrant
workers and base of mass socialist support. It tells of a working class political
activist and socialist who unexpectedly is elected a state legislator and who
initially intends to use his vote to benefit workers but who through
compromises and political deals rapidly declines into being an opportunist. An
often retold story saved from being hackneyed by Hedges' crudely authentic and
deft juxtaposing of the responses of the legislator's former comrades with those
of his new colleagues. An intriguing novel of one of the last regions of Socialist
Party political power in the US, written by a veteran union leader and editor of
a labour newspaper.

HELLMAN, Lillian

Three: An Unfinished Woman; Pentimento; Scoundrel Time, 1979
A collection of three semi-autobiographic reminiscences by a once renowned left-
liberal playwright; ranging from "Julia" (about an American in the anti-fascist
Austrian underground) to the near universal surrender of American progressives
during the McCarthy era, during which Hellman was one of the few vocal opponents,
for which she was thereafter blacklisted.

HERBST, Josephine

Pity Is Not Enough, 1933, The Executioner Waits, 1934, Rope of Gold, 1939
A novel trilogy dealing with the evolution of corporate capitalism in America and
resistance to it through the three generational family chronicle. Pity Is Not
Enough begins with events in Reconstruction Georgia, the alliances made between
the old autocracy and the new financiers and on through the railway land deals
and assorted looting by the new robber barons in the midwest, culminating in the
Populist upsurge and its defeat in 1896. Executioner Waits follows the varied
fortunes of family members from 1900 to 1929, the springtime of American
imperialism, the labour wars, the growing strength of the socialist movement
(native born and immigrant) and its suppression during and after W.W.I. The
consolidation of free enterprise red in tooth and claw during the 1920s and its
seeming collapse in 1929. Rope of Gold carries the story to the third generation,
now inexorably divided between working class members and those who have managed
to hold on to wealth; the desperation of the early 1930s and into the resurgent
left and union movement which follow. Ends with the sit down strikes and mass
campaigns of the C.I.O. in 1937.

HOLBROOK, Stewart

Holy Old Mackinaw, 1964 (original 1939)
Subtitled "A Natural History of the American Lumberjack", an often romantic but
readable introduction to the social history of American loggers from Maine to the
Pacific Northwest in the 19th and 20th centuries. One of the few popular studies

of industrial camp workers, its central failing is the general exclusion of the rich heritage of political and union struggles among loggers during the 20th century (which Holbrook had very good reason to be aware of).

HUGHES, Langston

The Big Sea, 1940
An autobiography of the leading progressive Black/Negro poet in America during the 1920s and 1930s. A cosmopolitan and ironic account of a wide range of events and experiences in the US and Europe. Hughes was long a seaman as well as being a major poet.   Also see The Weary Blues (1926), a collection of poetry.

IRWIN, Theodore

Strange Passage, 1935
A novel about two immigrant Americans who are brought together on a train filled with fellow deportees during the mid 1920s; flashbacks and dialogue recount what brought them to America, their lives and hopes and the struggles for justice which led to their deportation.

JOHNS, Orrick

Time of Our Lives, 1937
A reminiscence of the radical democratic tradition in western America during his father's generation and Johns' youth in the early 20th century. The deepening US imperialism and the massive suppression of all shades of radicalism during and after W.W.I which led left liberals like Johns to support of the C.P. USA.

JOHNSON, Josephine

Jordanstown, 1937
A somewhat archetypal strike novel revolving around a young writer searching for some purpose in his life who becomes involved in a southern textile strike during the early 1930s. In the course of describing the strike we are taken through the region and the backgrounds of people who in different ways are engaged in that struggle.

JONES, Mary Harris

The Autobiography of Mother Jones, 1972 (original 1925)
The autobiography of a legendary working class orator and agitator during the labour wars of the 1870s to W.W.I. Known throughout the US in her day, this account focuses on the bitter and sometimes armed class struggle in the mid western mining camps and Appalachia coal regions. Marred by unnecessary self-congratulatory rhetoric.

KAHN, Kathy

Hillbilly Women, 1972
Eighteen fragmentary life histories of working class women from the rural-industrial regions of southern Appalachia, touching on events from the mid 1930s to the early 1970s. Done with insight, sensitivity and appreciation by a young civil rights movement activist.

KERN, Alfred

Made in U.S.A., 1967
A novel about second generation steel workers in the Pittsburgh area, their mixture of class consciousness and apoliticism, combativeness and cynicism. Deals with rank and file battles against unsafe working conditions and against corruption and company compradores in the union leadership during the 1960s.

KORNBLUH, Joyce (ed.)

Rebel Voices - An I.W.W. Anthology, 1964
A social history and composite biography of the Industrial Workers of the World, its times, battlegrounds and supporters in US and Canada mainly from 1905 to early

1920s. As seen through the songs, humour, diaries, trial statements, newspaper articles, posters, etc. of its rank and file and spokesmen and women. A magnificent book.

KROMER, Tom

Waiting for Nothing, 1930
A diary-like account of being "on the bum" during the first and possibly worst year of the depression, written by an unemployed young worker who never wrote again. No adventure and little radicalism present but a powerful composite picture of the calculated humiliations and degradations forced on migratory unemployed by those who fearfully clung to some sort of income.

LANE, Winthrop

Civil War in West Virginia, 1971 (original 1921)
A reportage account of the armed battles in West Virginia mining regions during 1920-21, with passing allusions to the previous 40 years of struggle there. Also provides a picture of life in the company towns and coal camps. The 1971 edition gives a list and bibliography of the socialist organizations and press which once existed there.

LANG, Harry

'62, Biography of a Union, 1940
A popular history of the then 30-year life of a militant New York garment workers union revealed through the eyes of its members; their lives merging with union, personal and broader social and political concerns.

LANHAM, Edwin

The Stricklands, 1939
A novel dealing with the attempts to organize tenant farmers unions in the middle south during the 1930s and the (even for the US) extraordinary violence launched against them.

LAWRENCE, Josephine

If I Had Four Apples, 1934
A simple and "apolitic" novel whose story essentially is the bottomless capacity of the US lower middle class for self-deception. The declining fortunes of a white collar foreman during the depression who keeps dishing up the same baloney (to himself and others) about his confidence in the essential soundness of the American system as he and his family wend their way into destitution, always looking for someone a little worse off than themselves to feel superior to.

LE CRONE, Donald

Coxey's Army, 1929
An informal history of Coxey's Army, a protest campaign which attempted to move an army of unemployed from throughout the US to Washington, D.C. during the 1894 depression. Some good descriptions of the conditions, the varied backgrounds and strains of protest and the actual trek of thousands of unemployed who rode the rods headed for the capitol. An event which left a deep impression on some later organizers of the unemployed. Also see Donald McMurray's (1929) Coxey's Army, a study of the industrial army movement of 1894.

LeSUEUR, Meridel

North Star Country, 1945
A popular social history of Minnesota emphasizing the mass populist, socialist and farmer-labour movements which were a power in that state between the 1890s to 1930s. Also of the recrudescence of working class "self-aid" in the form of rent strikes and unemployed working women's organization, etc. in Minnesota during the 1930s.

LEVIN, Meyer

The Old Bunch, 1937
A novel of a group of second generation Jewish American businessmen who wrap
themselves in American patriotism during W.W.I and early 1920s, decrying and
opposing the then widespread left traditions of the working class Jews. And how
they lose their money in the collapse of the crooked financial empire of Samuel
Insull (who is much like them) at the end of the 1920s.

Citizens, 1940
A novel of the massacre of 38 men and women during the Memorial Day picnic held by
striking steel workers on the outskirts of Chicago in 1937. Tells of the shootings
by company detectives and city police in a bitterly laconic style; of police and
judicial venality, the bought and paid for newspapers and politicians and the
sweep of events in one of the more bitterly contested phases of organizing the
C.I.O.

LEVY, Melvin

The Last Pioneers, 1934
A novel dealing with the transition of Seattle from a progressive working class and
loggers town, the class struggles and government suppression of union and radical
groups during and after W.W.I, the triumph of middle class conservatism in the
1920s. The resource workers as the pioneers who have been supplanted.

LEWIS, Sinclair

Babbitt, 1924
A novel about the businessmen rulers of middle America during the early 1920s and
revolving about the life and culture of a middle aged real estate broker, his
class and family in a midwestern town. Its recreation of the jargon, ideology,
deadly know-nothingism and grubby boosterism made it Lewis' greatest novel. Satire
verging on ethnography. Also see Main Street (1922), a somewhat more crude novel
of the same theme set during W.W.I in a Gopher Prairie aspiring to become a
Zenith City.

Elmer Gantry, 1925
A novel of a revivalist preacher and all-round con man during the religious
crusades of early 1920s. A compelling portrait of middle America's initial tryst
with Christian fascism. The anti hero's partly cynical and sycophantic dealings
with Billy Sunday and Aimee Semple McPherson bible thumpers and "Community Leaders"
engaged in the suppression of whatever remaining dissent makes for a chillingly
contemporary theme.

The Man Who Knew Coolidge, 1928
A broad farce of the jargon and ideology of middle America during the regime of
Calvin Coolidge, done as an almost surrealistic caricature.

LONDON, Jack

Martin Eden, 1910
A fictionalized quasi-"autobiography" of London's life and times as part of the
western American working class, from childhood poverty in San Fransicso of the
early 1890s. But mainly of his every changing jobs, situations and people met
during the following dozen years (setting and characters in his other novels).
The theme is the hero's climb out of poverty through writing only to find his
success ashes in his mouth, since it isolates him from all that has made him what
he is. London was one of the best known writers of his time,
a uniquely American radical who in addition to endless
short stores produced some 40 odd novels between 1900 and 1915. They range from
the most cloying adventure tales to others which combine accounts of
tne itinerate western American working class mixed with
"socialist" philosophizing but touched by an unhealthy dose of social darwinism.

The Iron Heel, 1908
An apocalyptic "novel" about the establishment of a long-lived regime of fascism
in America as portrayed (some centuries later) through a rediscovered diary of
one of the early underground resistance leaders. The heroes, heroines and
political strategies are modelled after the Russian Social Revolutionaries of the
time. The account begins with the deepening class struggles of the early 20th
century, follows the decision of American plutocracy and its supporters to opt for
a caste-like fascist society, and is particularly chilling in the descriptions of
means used to separate and crush the various revolts raised against it. The
events and the footnotes (supplied by a supposed 22nd century editor) provide a
sardonic left socialist critique of the various populist, parliamentary,
syndicalist and other reformist responses to capitalism. Although badly marred
by London's self-congratulatory rhetoric it was an internationally translated
and read work in its time.

LUMPKIN, Grace

To Make My Bread, 1932
A novel of the Gastonia textile strike in South Carolina at the end of the 1920s,
an extremely bitter conflict which brought out the underlying quasi-fascist nature
of the American south (an unbroken chain of vigelantism continuing to the present
Greensboro, N.C. massacre). The novel treats with the
strike as the culmination of thirty years of southern industrialization and the
emergence of a southern proletariat.

A Sign of Cain, 1935
A novel of the economic underpinnings of segregation and Jim Crow laws in the US
south of the time, and the terrorism utilized to keep whites as well as blacks in
line. By a southern writer.

LYND, Alice and Staughton (eds.)

Rank and File, personal histories of working class organizers, 1977
Oral accounts of 22 American rank and file union militants, documenting the
continuities and changes in views and struggles from the 1930s to 1970s. It
emphasizes the "basic organic solidarity" among union activists, men and women,
black and white, and despite a wide range of political beliefs, most of which
could not be termed radical.

McCOY, Horace

They Shoot Horses, Don't They?, 1935
A novel set in a Hollywood marathon dance competition, in which it turns out that
despite all the illusory hopes, cut-throat competition and exhausting strivings
there is no prize for "winners". An allegory of US capitalism made into a movie
in 1970s.

McHENRY, Beth and MYERS, Fred

Home is the Sailor, 1948
A semi-biographical novel of a left-wing seaman/organizer; well written and a
detailed account of the times, figures and work in US shipping during the 1930s
and 1940s on the US east coast.

McKAY, Claude

Home to Harlem, 1928
A semi-biographical novel which documents the various threads of the Harlem
Renaissance of 1920s, the emergence of a black intelligensia drawing from US and
Caribbean blacks, their hetergeneous views and interests.

A Long Way From Home, 1937
An autobiography covering experiences on four continents of an emigre Jamaican
black nationalist who, during the 1920s and 1930s, was lionized as a progressive
black writer.

McWILLIAMS, Carey

Factories in the Fields, 1939
A combination of reportage, history and reworked oral accounts of 50 years of
corporate farming and farm labour in California; of the growers political power,
the many attempts to organize migrant farm workers and of the means used to
suppress them. Discusses that industrial plantocracy as the roots of right-wing
republicanism in California.

Brothers Under the Skin, 1951
A journalistic history of the anti-oriental campaigns in the US (mainly
California), including accounts of the immigrant Japanese and Chinese working
class and their struggles. McWilliams was an author in the tradition of the early
muckrakers; he wrote a stream of books about structural injustices in US through
the first half of this century.

MAILER, Norman

The Naked and the Dead, 1948
A novel revolving around a company of American soldiers in the South Pacific
during W.W.II who are a microcosm of the ethnic and class hierarchy and conflicts
in America itself. Even the lowliest dogfaces are generally a conservative lot
despite being aware of their own oppression. It is essentially an account of the
triumph of American imperialist ideology, despite the come-uppance delivered by
the men to one particularly autocratic commander.

Barbary Shore, 1951
A novel of a US progressive who came of age at the end of the 1930s and of his
isolation and alienation in the post W.W.II period with the breakup of the
organizations and causes which had lent emotional sustenance to his life.

MALKIEL, Theresa

Diary of a Shirtwaist Worker, 1910
An actual diary of a woman garment worker and socialist organizer in New York
during the first decade of the century; the horrendous and exploitative
conditions which led to the first massive union drive among women workers, the
following bitter strikes and the brutal attempts to suppress them. The slightly
reworked experiences, feelings, thoughts and actions of a participant.

MALTZ, Albert

The Way Things Are, 1938
A collection of short stories about the migratory unemployed in depression
America; city street corner scenes, letters home, looking for work, etc. Done
with sensitivity and insight.

The Underground Stream, 1940
A novel which revolves around the evolving ruthlessness of a failed businessman
who becomes a personnel director of a Detroit auto plant. Focuses on his
fashioning of a proto-fascist organization which is based on professional
strike-breaking but also directed at suppressing minority groups and radicals as
initial steps to gaining political power. Counterposed are the actions of a
communist union organizer who is intended as the inheritor of the American
"revolutionary" tradition. Some good accounts of the massive armies of private
police and company vigilantes mobilized by leading industrialists during that
period. But one has the sneaking suspicion that the proto-fascists are much more
in the main stream of the American tradition than any democratic-radical heritage.

MILLER, Arthur

Death of a Salesman, 1949
A play about an aging travelling salesman on the edge of losing his job because
he is no longer in step with sales fashions. Deals with his growing realization
that his life has been wasted in following the maxims of American Babbittry.

The Crucible, 1951
A play of the original witch burning movement in Salem, Massachusetts during the late 1600s, as an analogy to the "McCarthy" period then in full swing in 1950s America. An adept allusion to the class and ideological bases of the earlier witch hunt hysteria as a means of repressing dissidents.

The View From the Bridge, 1957
A semi-autobiographical novel of the generation of variously progressive American intellectuals who came of age in the late 1930s and during W.W.II and of the assaults launched by the revitalized American right both before and during the McCarthy years. Of the endless betrayals, humiliations, blacklisting and related fruits of Americanism.

MILLER, Max

The Beginning of a Mortal, 1933
A luminescent reminiscence of a boy growing up in the sawmill town of Everett, Washington during the pre W.W.I period, the social environment, people and class struggles of the industrial frontier.

No Matter What Happens, 1949
A personal reminiscence of the high water mark of radicalism in the Pacific Northwest and the Everett massacre of I.W.W. supporters in 1916 to which Miller was a witness. More generally, a rallying call to maintain the heterogeneous heritage of American radicalism against post W.W.II forces of reaction.

Shinny on Your Own Side, 1958
A quiet, sometimes sardonic, reminiscence of the causes, characters and quarrels among American radicals from the W.W.I era to the early 1950s.

MOORHOUSE, Hopkins

Deep Furrows, 1918
A document of the Cooperative movement on the American plains during the W.W.I era, the responses of small farmers who were being forced out of that way of life. An influential work both in the western US and on the Canadian prairies during the following decade.

MOTLEY, Willard

Knock on Any Door, 1947
A novel of semi-delinquent youths from a midwestern city slum whose criminality is pictured as mainly an inept pursuit of the American dream. Revolves around the "victimization" of one youth and his individualistic rebellion leading to prison and a criminal life, as counterposed to a friend who manages to break free by linking himself with collective struggle through the labour movement.

We Fished All Night, 1951
A novel of the dislocated lives of three W.W.II veterans, their realization that the dreams they had of a refurbished New Deal in America have failed. Culminates in the collapse of the last mass Progressive party led by Henry Wallace in 1948.

MURDOCH, Angus

Boom Copper, 1954
A reportage "novel" dealing with the conditions around the copper mines of upper Michigan and the massive working class battles there in 1913.

NEARING, Scott

Free Born, 1932
A novel about a northern black industrial worker who witnesses a lynching and gradually shifts from a purposefully self-interest stance to militancy.

Dollar Diplomacy, 1926
A popularly written but scholarly expose of the rule of private corporate interests over American foreign policy, especially in Latin America over the previous generation (a more shocking expose then than today). This title is a reminder of

the more than two dozen comparable books by Nearing, a liberal professor of political science who was blacklisted from teaching because of his pacifist sentiments during W.W.I but went on to become the leading critic of US foreign policies and adventures during the 1920s and 1930s.

NEUGASS, James

Rain of Ashes, 1949
One of six novels of working class life in 1940s America. A worker-writer who fought in the Spanish Civil War, returned to America to become a refugee in his own country and died in an industrial accident in 1949.

NEWHOUSE, Edward

You Can't Sleep Here, 1934
A novel about the changes undergone by a laidoff newspaper reporter as he becomes a figure in the unemployed scenes which he once reported and as he feels the effects of media propaganda. Describes the day to day strategies of survival and the way in which authorities go out of their way to humiliate and separate unemployed from those still working. Some good accounts of the hunger marches and demonstrations in New York during the early depression.

NICHOLS, John

The Milagro Beanfield War, 1974, The Magic Journey, 1979
Two tragi-comic novels revolving around the tenacious resistance and hidden understandings, if also the self-destructive bickering and egoism, of Mexican American peasant ranchers and impoverished workers in the mountain communities of northern New Mexico during the 1960s and 1970s. Of their rearguard struggles (normally quite conservative) against the old but ever tightening noose of expropriation and exploitation effected by American land barons manipulating Federal agencies, state real estate and mafiaprise politicians and their assortment of collaborators, hoodlums and state police foremen. The Milagro Beanfield War specifically relates events which emerge in the early 1970s when an angry but quite anti-social handyman/farmer taps "illegal" irrigation water, lost in the previous generation to corporate growers in the lowlands, into his subsistence plot and thereby ressurrects a near miraculous but plausible chain of events which result in halting the construction of a dam which would have doomed the community. The Magic Journey is a broader portrait in a similar vein which ranges from the 1930s to the 1970s, touching on those who have left, remained in or returned to the dying Mexican American hamlets. Treats such processes as the consolidation of American corporate capitalism, its various colonial wars and even the Cuban revolution seen through the experiences of the "villagers" and woven around the allegorical "Miracle of the Dynamite Shrine".

Nichols is one of the major radical novelists to emerge in America during the last generation. His writing is crafted around allegorical caricature, incisive detail, and deft bitter humour which, despite some Hollywood exaggeration, manages to convey the nature of contemporary free enterprise in the US.

O'CONNOR, Harvey

Empire in Oil, 1935
A reportage account of the nature of the American oil industry from the turn of the century to the 1930s, dealing particularly with their support of coups and US military intervention in Latin America but also with their purchase of judges, politicians and gunmen somewhat earlier in America. O'Connor, along with Carleton Beals, was one of the most prolific and wide ranging left-wing journalists from the 1920s to the beginning of the 1950s. Also see Mellon's Millions (1933), a study of the Mellon banking family as a portrait of the long entrenched ruling class in the US. It follows a then thirty year tradition of muckraking exposes possibly best exemplified by Matthew Josephson's The Robber Barons (1934).

Revolution in Seattle, 1965
A popular history and reminiscence of the Seattle general strike of 1919 and of the character of working class Washington State during that period. This was the event which radicalized O'Connor, then a young reporter in that city.

ODETS, Clifford

Waiting for Lefty, 1934
A play dealing with an attempt to organize and carry through a strike of New York taxi drivers in 1934; of the endless (and presently still prevailing) forms of exploitation, the taxi companies' use of vindictive lady reporters, scabs and police which ultimately break the strike. Very widely performed in the Workers Theatre movement through the US and abroad in the 1930s.

O'ROURKE, William (ed.)

On the Job, 1977
A collection of some 20 short stories and reportage pieces of work and life on the job in contemporary USA.

PAGE, Myra

The Gathering Storm, 1932
A novel of the movement of mountain people from their worked out hill farms to the burgeoning factories of American south in the 1920s, their "proletarianization" and their bitter union struggles. Also of the use of the KKK and similar organizations against southern white working class.

With Sun in our Blood, 1950
A proletarian strike novel set in the late 1940s.

PARKER, Edwin

Timber, 1963
A novel of the Washington State lumber industry during W.W.I; loggers, sawmill workers, I.W.W. and homeguards, local bosses; culminating in the Everett Massacre of 1916. Based upon interviews with some 50 surviving participants.

PERSON, Carl E.

The Lizard's Trail, 1969 (original 1918)
Subtitled "a story of the Illinois Central and Harriman Line strikes of 1911-1915", being a documentary account of the lives of railworkers in Chicago and Ohio as well as a critical strike. Treats with the differences between conservative and militant union members and the triumph of the "bread crumbs and butter" unionism, only partly due to its support by rail companies.

POOLE, Ernest

The Harbour, 1915
A novel which describes the port of New York and the then rising militancy of dockworkers and seamen organizers through the experiences of a middle class youth who becomes a part of that world. A general dock strike evolves and is defeated, the blacklisted workers scattering and others returning to work under wage cuts and a company union while the "hero" returns to his class, but now changed into a committed socialist writer. Contains some good descriptions of day to day life of New York dockworkers and their families and the means which employers use to corrupt or eliminate potential union leaders.

The Voice of the Street, 1918, Danger, 1925
Two muckraking novelas about deepening reaction of US during and after W.W.I and of the use which employers made of the anti-foreigner/anti-red hysteria.

The Bridge, 1940
Poole's autobiography, reminiscences of the ups and downs of a radical writer during the 1920s and 1930s when many of the not so distant struggles and figures he chronicled had already been forgotten.

RAPER, Arthur and REID, Ira

Sharecroppers All, 1941
A popular sociological account of sharecroppers throughout the US south, their lives and histories with some mention of the bitterly suppressed attempts at

organization in the 1930s. Their massive expulsion and virtual disappearance from
the land by 1940.

REDDING, J. Saunders

Stranger and Alone, 1950
A novel of a Negro opportunist who wheedles his way up the ladder in a southern
segregated school district to become a puppet superintendent under a Jim Crow
controller. A Horatio Alger story in reverse, of defeatism rewarded. By a black
author.

ROGOFF, Harry

An East Side Epic, the life and work of Meyer London, 1930
A biography of a local folk hero and Jewish left socialist leader in the Lower
East Side of New York from 1890s to 1920. Also a social history of the district
during that period.

ROLLINS, William Jr.

The Shadow Before, 1934
A proletarian novel dealing with the events of the Gastonia textile strike but
using surrealist techniques to capture the surroundings, sounds, dialogues,
thoughts, feelings and newspaper fantasies emerging from that conflict.

ROSENFELD, Morris

Songs From the Ghetto, 1898
A translation of Rosenfeld's original Yiddish socialist poetry and songs dealing
with the sweatshops, tenements and exploitation of Jewish working class in East
End London and Lower East Side New York in the 1880s and 1890s. As a representative of that once rich tradition of Jewish vision of social justice and
socialism Rosenfeld's songs (along with David Edelshtat's "Shnel Loffn Di Reder")
continued to be sung into the 1930s.

ROSENGARTEN, Theodore (ed.)

All God's Dangers, 1974
A life history of a black sharecropper in Alabama from the turn of the century to
1950s, including an abortive attempt to organize for the Southern Tenant Farmers
and Sharecroppers Union in the 1930s, leading to a shootout with sheriffs and
vigilantes. Also an extensive account of what it took for a Negro militant to
survive a decade and a half imprisonment on a chain gang.

ROTH, Henry

Call It Sleep, 1962 (original 1934)
A novel of the childhood terrors of a Jewish immigrant child in Lower East Side of
New York in circa 1910. Long dismissed, it is now considered a masterpiece in
the handling of dialect and childhood reminiscence.

SAXTON, Alexander

The Great Midland, 1948
A novel set around the Chicago marshalling yards of an intercontinental railroad
between the years 1912-1941, it captures the drastically changing times, the
lives and the shifting relationships of a number of rail workers, their friends
and families. Involves a variety of radical traditions of blacks and whites,
native and immigrant, and the personal tensions and conflicting loyalties of one
man and his evolution into a communist. Written with knowledge of the work and
the complexity of the lives of people depicted.

SCOTT, Leroy

The Walking Delegate, 1922 (original 1905)
An important early socialist novel which deals with the struggle within a New York
local of the Iron Workers Union between a corrupt comprador leadership (which is

also extremely shrewd and tough and attuned to workers' weaknesses) and rank and file union militants who are attempting to turn the union into a more combative organization to defend its own members and other workers. A detailed knowledge of union politics and company tactics along with a fine portrait of the then current social scene.

SEAVER, Edwin

The Company, 1930
A novel of the degeneration of the supposedly once independent American middle class into a class of fearfully conformist and sycophantic toadies to the corporate business world during the 1920s.

Between the Hammer and the Anvil, 1937
A sort of sequel to The Company; set around a university campus of the early 1930s, it surveys the cautious "radicalization" of a few teachers and students but the underlying conformism and heightened servility of the majority of students and faculty who have even the slightest hope of keeping a foot on the social ladder.

SHACKELFORD, Laurel and WEINBERG, Bill

Our Appalachia, an oral history, 1977
A collection of oral histories of farmers, mill workers, miners, small storekeepers, mothers and others in the Appalachia region from the early part of the century to the present.

SHAW, Irwin

Sailor Off the Bremen, 1941
A collection of short stories which portray the continuing confusion of young US workers and unemployed at the end of the depression and on the eve of W.W.II. Conveys the feeling that the process of radicalization during the previous decade has failed to become more than skin deep, with the underlying layers of political apathy and illusion re-emerging unscathed.

SINCLAIR, Upton

The Jungle, 1906
A novel of the Chicago meat packing industry at the time, a jungle of exploitation, degradation, poverty and unsafe conditions for the immigrant and native born workers involved. The work rapidly became an international classic of socialist literature and was translated into most of the major languages of the world. During the following generation Sinclair was the most prolific progressive writer in America (apart from a brief and soon recanted support for Wilsonian "New Democracy" in W.W.I). Sinclair's more than forty titles are typically novelized social reportage of conditions in some sector of American society, centred around a major event, based upon considerable research and presented from a radical reformist viewpoint.

Jimmie Higgins, 1919
A novel of a rank and file American union activist, not especially brilliant or charismatic or heroic but tenaciously decent and loyal to his class and union, the fundament of all union militancy. It is set in the years immediately before and during America's entry into W.W.I and treats with the confusions, factions, betrayals and suppression of various components of the American labour movement.

100% - The Story of a Patriot, 1921
A bitterly sardonic novel of the background and ideology of one minor leader of the host of right-wing vigilante organizations which brought the US to the brink of its own form of fascism during the early 1920s. Conveys the hodge-podge ideology and booze-befogged jargon of this armed Babbittry; also of the assaults on militant unions, radicals, non-whites, immigrants and dissenters in general.

The Brass Check, 1922
A muckraking novel of the propaganda ground out by the US newspaper industry, the support of reaction at home and American imperial adventures abroad and the means

used by editors to keep their reporters in line. Also treats the cover-up of
massive unemployment and employment swindles in US. (George Seldes' (1938) You
Can't Print That returns to the same theme, in particular of the stringently
censored press coverage of misery and revolt in depression America.)

Singing Jailbirds, 1924
A brief account of the hundreds of I.W.W. political prisoners jailed in California
and the Pacific Northwest during and after W.W.I, victims of a judicial system as
repressive and arbitrary as any dictatorship.

King Coal, 1926
A novel of the US coal industry in the mid 1920s which still employed over a
million workers in some of the most horrendous working conditions in the country.
Treats some of the final battles of the Labour Wars in the US, mainly in the
midwestern and eastern coal regions, where "J.L. Lewis Peacemakers" confronted
company sheriffs. Of coal barons, immigrant and native born miners and the
incessant infighting within a fragmenting union movement.

Oil, 1927
A rather romantic novel about a ruthless independent oil man and his cannibalization
by fellow entrepreneurs, but mainly about the "radicalization" of his son who
fruitlessly contends with the plethora of repressive agencies in 1920s America.

Boston, 1928
A novel of how an entrenched section of the US ruling class determined upon and
carried through the execution of two philosophical anarchists (Sacco and Vansetti)
in Boston during the mid 1920s as an object lesson to American radicals in general.
The outrage is not so much that two innocent men are unjustly executed but that
the whole complex of supposed civil rights and legalities of American democracy
are powerless to protect individuals should the ruling class decide to eliminate
them.

King Midas, 1930
A novel of the banking industry in the US from the late 19th century on and its
consolidation as the supreme financial power in the country. Focuses on the
schemes and supra-governmental powers of the House of Morgan but includes the
doings of lesser financial luminaries. Counterposes the indifference to and
capacity of the great banking houses to even profit from a depression with the
disastrous effects of their manipulations on a host of workers, farmers and small
business people.

The Fliver King, 1937
A novel of the life and times of a Henry Ford-like industrialist, his maundering
visions of a paternalistic industrial serfdom, his role in establishing a nation-
wide system of labour spies and company police forces during the 1920s and his
support of homegrown fascist organizations in the mid 1930s. Counterposed are
the lives and struggles of two generations of auto workers culminating in the
factory occupations and sitdown strikes in the Fordlandia plants in 1937.

Little Steel, 1938
A novel of the particularly bloody attempts to organize workers at Republic Steel
during the late 1930s; with the history of the political connections, Judge
Gary-like associates and anti-union strategies of that company reaching back
through a previous generation.

Also see Manassas, 1925, A Captain of Industry, 1928, Mountain City, 1931,
Dragon's Teeth, 1940; four more of Sinclair's better known novels along the lines
of the above.

SMEDLEY, Agnes

Daughter of Earth, 1938
Smedley's novelized autobiography, from her girlhood travails in the "man's world"
of Rocky Mountain industrial towns before W.W.I to her radical political activities
among immigrant left circles on the US east coast during the Palmer raids of the
early 1920s. Smedley later became an indefatigable journalist for the
revolutionary left in Asia. Daughter re-issued in 1973 as a "feminist classic".

SMITH, Wessel

F.O.B. Detroit, 1938
A novel of workers on the car assembly lines of Detroit, their backgrounds ranging from displaced hill farmers to ex-craftsmen with skills now made obsolescent by mechanization. The novel treats with the cultural and personal as well as the economic bases for the emerging union militancy during the hard-fought union organizing battles of the later 1930s.

SPIVAK, John

Georgia Nigger, 1933
A novel revolving around a Georgia lynching and one of the early black proletarian novels of the 1930s. Foreword by Langston Hughes.

STAVIS, Barrie

The Man Who Never Died, 1951
A popular biography of Joe Hill, the best known of the I.W.W. songwriters and martyrs. His life and times in the labour struggles of the American west.

STEELE, James

The Conveyor, 1935
A novel of the evolution of the auto industry in the Great Lake states during the 1920s and early 1930s, drawn from the author's own experiences and research into labour history. Begins at the end of W.W.I with many of the workers in the expanding industry drawn from southern and senescent industrial regions, the emerging "perfection" of the assembly line system and the ever-tightening labour discipline and speed up on the job. A good treatment of the system of company police and anti-union spies which was developed by auto and other big industries and of the very gradual and often round about changes among auto workers as they became a body which could sustain a union to challenge the forces ranged against them.

STEINBECK, John

In Dubious Battle, 1936
A novel dealing with a bitterly contested strike of migratory farm workers led by communist organizers on California plantations during the mid 1930s. Some good descriptions of the reactionary small town citizenry of the California farm belt which the author knew so well.

Grapes of Wrath, 1939
Probably the epic novel of depression America, no brief annotation can outline this work. It revolves around the expulsion of poor and tenant farmers from Oklahoma during the mid 1930s,   personified by the flight of the Joad family as they become a part of the stream of Oakies swirling through the Hoovervilles, roadside jungles and fearfull small towns of middle America to become migratory harvest workers on the corporate farms of California. Also made into one of the greatest movies ever produced by the American film industry. Incredibly, Steinbeck ended his life as a defender of American reaction at home and imperialism abroad.

STEVENSON, Philip (Lars Lawrence)

Morning, Noon and Night, 1954, Out of the Dust, 1956, Hoax, 1957
A novel trilogy following the fortunes of a number of American working people from the 1930s through W.W.II to the mid 1950s. Treats with the seeming discontinuity and inapplicability of lessons learned and visions held in each decade for what comes next. Yet also of the fundamental realities of working class life which often change less than one is led to believe.

STRIBLING, T.S.

The Sound Wagon, 1940
An astute novel which in part portrays the overnight return of cautious conservatism and Little Orphan Annie patriotism among a broad cross section of

ordinary people in Detroit at the end of the depression. Of how even partial economic recovery largely obliterates what lessons and visions had been slowly acquired over the previous decade.

TAYLOR, Paul S. and LANGE, Dorthea

An American Exodus, 1939
A combined reportage account and photo album of the flight of displaced farmers from the midwest and middle south, expelled by drought and foreclosure during the mid 1930s. Done for the Farm Security Administration, many of the photos have become the visual images of the great depression in the US.

TERKEL, Studs

Hard Times, 1969
A collection of oral accounts dealing with a cross section of American experiences in the great depression; ranges from reminiscences of armed farmers occupations, anti-eviction actions and union militancy counterposed to reminiscences of little affected middle class worlds and all manner of know-nothingism. Often moving, especially in that it is played against general ignorance of those times among most of the members of a slightly younger generation. Terkel himself is a product of the New Deal and one of its few remaining proponents.

Working, 1972
A collection of oral accounts dealing with the working lives and attitudes to work of a broad cross section of Americans from corporate managers through a host of petty hustlers to some industrial workers during the late 1960s, with glimpses of those lives over the previous generation. It is a depressing portrait of the cynicism and alienation surrounding those working lives and of the endless petty status differences which so many cling to.

Also Division Street, America, 1967, an unintentionally depressing oral history of Chicagoans in the mid 1960s.

TERRILL, Tom and HIRSCH, Jerrold (eds.)

These Are Our Lives, 1975 (original 1939)
A selection of thirty-five life histories of southern farmers, rural workers and tenants. A few of the circa one thousand life histories collected by the Federal Southeastern Writers Project during the late 1930s and reaching from the late 19th century.

Such As Us: Southern Voices of the Thirties, 1978
A further selection of life histories of southern workers, farmers and others drawn from the Southeastern Writers Project files and focused on experiences before and during the depression.

TULLY, Jim

Circus Parade, 1924, Shadows of Men, 1927
Two collections of stories mainly about itinerant workers throughout the US in the 1920s; riding the rods, panhandling, the fluctuating jobs and the random violence dispensed by representatives of authority and even by members of the more established working class. Told with an anarchic contempt for established American society of the time.

Beggars of Life, 1926
Tully's autobiography.

TIPPET, Tom

Horse Shoe Bottoms, 1935
A novel of Illinois miners during the 1870s to late 1890s by a miner-writer native to that region. An authentic if at times crude account of work and life moved by an at times chauvinistic but indigenous working class militancy.

VORSE, Mary Heaton

A Footnote to Folly, 1918
A reportage account of the lives of immigrant workers and their families in the
iron ore mines of upper Michigan, of the bitter union struggles by the I.W.W. and
others to organize unions in the face of company police and anti-foreigner
sentiments.

Men and Steel, 1920
A reportage account about the US steel strike of 1919. It became one of the most
critical defeats of US labour during the decade and signalled the beginning of a
broad assault upon labour unions in general.

Strike, 1930
An influential proletarian novel dealing with the deepening exploitation and
desperation of textile workers in the US south during the 1920s and culminating
in the Gastonia strike of 1929. As distinct from some other accounts of that
conflict, Vorse brought the experience of fifteen years of labour reporting
to her work.

WALKER, Charles R.

American City, a rank and file history, 1937
A "biography" of Minneapolis, Minnesota, focussed on the daily lives and understandings of working people in that city, part of the national economic and
political system but their continuing strain of Farmer-Labour radicalism.

WALLIS, Keene

Bughouse Square, 1922
A volume of poetry about characters in a rooming house largely inhabited by
migratory resource workers in the Pacific Northwest of the period.

WEATHERWAX, Clara

Marching, Marching, 1935
A picaresque proletarian novel of labour in Washington State from the 1920s to the
early depression years but focused on an Aberdeen sawmill strike in 1934. Accounts
of fruit pickers, loggers, stevedores and sawmill workers and catch-as-catch-can
beach combers. Title taken from the first line of poem/song, Bread and Roses.

WHITE, Walter Francis

Flight, 1927, The Fire in the Flint, 1930
Two reminiscence novels of the varied but fundamentally common experiences of
blacks in the US in the 1920s. By one of the first progressive black writers.

WITTKE, Carl

We Who Built America, 1939
Accounts of immigrant workers in America from the 1890s to the 1930s. Includes
accounts by oriental and Mexican as well as a wide range of European immigrants,
and uses an "oral history" format.

WOLFERT, Ira

Tucker's People, 1940
A novel of an inveterate lumpen enterpriser who begins his career as a company
goon and strikebreaker and rises to become a petty and later more prominent
racketeer in 1930s Chicago. The theme explores the parallels between the growth
of Tucker's policy racket and the course of business in the US over the previous
forty years; the growing corporate technical efficiency yet increasing human

wastage, the spreading involvement of gangster alliances and a suitable proportion of profits spent on political protection, but also of the conflicts which lead to ever-increasing violence.

WRIGHT, Richard

Uncle Tom's Children, 1938
Four separate stories of US blacks in the depression era; from the acceptance of traditional caste oppression or flight to urban ghettos, to an account of personal self-defense and ending with a story of a militant and successful hunger march by blacks and whites in the American south during the early 1930s.

Native Son, 1940
An autobiographical novel of growing up black in America during the late 1920s and 1930s, his deepening awareness of the scope of oppression, his rejection of his family's passivity and his transitory alliance with the broader left.

YGLESIAS, Jose

A Wake in Ybor City, 1966
A novel which begins with a wake in the old Cuban section of Tampa, Florida during the early 1960s and which evolves as an evocation of Yglesias' grandparents' generation who were immigrant cigar-makers and part of the socialist culture of reading and debate, union activism and social vision from the 1890s to 1930s. Gradually unfolds that almost forgotten past through the initially puzzled naivety of Yglesias' son (a not very radical "radical" of the 1960s). Yglesias himself was one of the best American journalists of the 1960s. Wake in Ybor City is an often magnificent book.

Also see The Goodbye Land, 1960, a reportage novel of Latin American culture and peoples in the American southwest over the previous generation, and An Orderly Life, 1962, an autobiography.

AUSTRALIA AND NEW ZEALAND

CALTHORPE, Mena

The Dyehouse, 1961
A novel of men and women factory workers, their lives and families, and of working
class struggles in post W.W.II Australia in the context of US cultural and
political penetration.

CASEY, Gavin

It's Harder for Girls, 1942, Birds of a Feather, 1943
Two collections of short stories set in and around the Kalgoorlie mining region;
some astute accounts of the work and domestic lives, humour mixed with a sombre
reality and individual acts of resistance by working people to the bosses during
the 1930s.

Also Snowball, 1958, a novel.

CATO, Nancy

Brown Sugar, 1974
A family chronicle of the descendants of New Hebrides Islanders captured in
"blackbirding" slave raids during the 1860s and 1870s and shipped to Queensland
sugar plantations to work as bound labour. Also touches on the other Melanesian,
Polynesian and Australian aborigines swept into peonage of Australian plantations
up to the beginning of the 20th century. Based on extensive research and carrying
the story through the varied personal histories of the descendants in Australian
society of the 1960s.

CUSACK, Dymphna

Say No to Death, 1951, Southern Steel, 1953
Two Australian working class novels set during and in post W.W.II period.

CUSACK, Dymphna and JAMES, Florence

Come in Spinner, 1951
A novel of civilian working class life in Sydney during W.W.II; published by
Australian Left Book Club.

DAY, Alf S.

The Democrat, 1896
An early populist play of the "radical 1890s" in Australia, set among a group of
political prisoners in a Melbourne jail.

DYSON, Edward

Fact'ry 'Ands, 1906
A novel of the first generations of Australians forced off land into the packed
tenements and new factories of Melbourne at the turn of the century. Marred by a
"local colour" style, it has some good descriptions of the sweatshop and rather
"unfrontier-like" conditions of urban workers in sunny Australia and the bitterness
and anger which fueled the upsurge of socialist and syndicalist organization and
support during the following decade.

FORREST, David

The Hollow Woodheap, 1962
A satiric novel of the myths and realities of Australian society during the late
1950s. Touches on the Australian variant of the "drug store cowboy" imagery in
what has become a largely urban and suburban nation.

Also The Last Blue Sea, 1959, a novel.

FURPHY, Joseph

Such is Life, 1903
A sardonic collage of scenes and plots woven together around the theme of the mind-numbing colonialism of the small town bourgeoisie and the hidden and open class struggles emerging in Australian society at around the turn of the century. Juxtaposes the "rebelliousness" which is merely a fetish of Australian self-image with some real conflicts between Australian workers and bosses. Done in a quasi-journalistic style by one of the most read populist writers of the period.

HARDY, Frank

Power Without Glory, 1950
A muckraking novel about bribery and political corruption in post W.W.II Victoria municipal government, which was sufficiently close to the bone to trigger judicial suppression. A detailed account of the rise of a city boss in the New Australia.

The Four Legged Lottery, 1958
A collection of short stories about everyday life, provincialness and vision, squabbles and hopes of ordinary people in urban Australia of late 1950s.

Also The Hard Way, 1961, autobiography.

HERBERT, Xavier

Capricornia, 1938
A rather romantic but widely cited novel of the treatment of aborigines in Northern Australia from initial white settlement of a region in 1904 to the consolidation of a provincial Australian society in mid 1930s. Woven around the lives of two generations of a mixed aborigine-white family, the changing character of social restrictions, racism and opportunities. Their advance into the margins of the lower middle class but still haunted by echoes of a lost world.

HEWETT, Dorothy

Bobbin Up, 1959
A novel of work and life in an Australian textile factory; women workers, unions, politics and the continuing class struggle in contemporary Australia.

LAMBERT, Eric

Twenty Thousand Thieves, 1951
A muckraking novel portraying the use of Australian troops as colonial cannon fodder in North African campaign of W.W.II. Fodder knows best.

Watermen, 1955
A novel of an attempt to establish a fishermen's coop in a small upcoast town and the internal and external problems which arise.

LAWSON, Henry

While the Billy Boils, 1970
A collection of eighty-odd stories originally written during the first decade of the century by a prolific populist journalist, a cross between O'Henry and Jack London. Describes the lives of Australian resource workers, impoverished farmers and squatters, and the city working class in Sydney.

MANN, Leonard

Mountain Flat, 1939
A novel of social and class divisions, hatreds and friendships, in a small rural community, and a feeling of unchallengeable provincialness.

The Go Getter, 1942
An ironic novel of a young Australian Babbitt, a salesman living in a Melbourne working class district during the 1930s depression. Juxtaposes accounts of

unemployment and relief work with the protagonist's "go-getter" rhetoric but also his deepening realization that his and others' fates are beyond their individual control.

Also Andrea Caslin, 1959, a novel.

MARSHALL, Alan

How Beautiful are Thy Feet, 1949
A much praised, rather subtle and humourous proletarian novel of the work and lives of a group of Australian boot factory employees during the depression.

MARTIN, David

The Young Wife, 1962
A novel of Greek Cypriot immigrants in Melbourne during the early 1950s; revolves around a young woman trapped in a repressive marriage and life. A powerful and tragic portrait of one immigrant world.

MORRISON, John

The Creeping City, 1949
A reportage novel about the urban boom and blight of post war Sydney, the spread of suburbs and the dissolution of the old working class city districts.

Port of Call, 1950
A collage novel about the lives of seamen and dock workers in Melbourne.

Twenty-Three, 1962
Collection of short stories about lives of waterside workers in post W.W.II Australia.

PALMER, Vance

Golconda, 1948, Seed Time, 1957, The Big Fellow, 1959
A novel trilogy which charts the rise of a young miner to union organizer to opportunist political leader in the Australian Labour Party. A social tapestry of the contradictory forces and psychological dynamics of bread and butter unionism and working class philistinism in Australia from late 1920s to post W.W.II. Also a richly detailed study of Queensland labour movement and a sympathetic account of the slowly dying ideals of the hero as he becomes a careerist.

Separate Lives, 1931, Sea and Spinifex, 1934, Let the Birds Fly, 1955
Three collections of short stories dealing with the daily lives of a wide range of ordinary Australians; their dreams and basic decency, the changing and unchanging class and social forces in Australia over a generation.

The Legend of the Nineties, 1954
A survey of the radical populist and socialist literature in Australia of the 1890s, the causes and social forces in contention and their transformation into largely innocuous myths by the 1950s.

Also The Passage, 1930, a novel.

PRICHARD, Katherine Susannah

The Pioneers, 1915
A novel of poor farmers and squatters gradually failing on the marginal lands they gradually lose to large landholders; an account which countered the then current Australian myth of yeoman farmers and success through hard work.

Black Opal, 1921
A novel of opal miners in New South Wales during W.W.I. The first of Prichard's left novels about working people throughout Australia.

Working Bullocks, 1926
A novel of timber workers in the Karri forests of Western Australia; their daily lives and social world, the unemployment, migratory work and exploitation. Deals

with the sporadic but growing consciousness of being part of a broader working class and culminates in a widespread strike after W.W.I.

Coonardoo, 1929
A somewhat romantic protest novel of aborigine-white relations on a Western Australian cattle station of the 1920s; a sort of Australian Laughing Boy.

Haxby Circus, 1930
A picaresque novel of a circus travelling through small town Australia; a vehicle for portraying the backside of the outback communities.

The Roaring Nineties, 1946, Golden Miles, 1948, Winged Seeds, 1950
An epic novel trilogy which chronicles the lives and conditions of Australian gold miners (and by implication other resource workers) from the 1890s to 1940s. Roaring Nineties deals with the final gold rush boom of 1890s to 1900 and the emergence of a proletarian consciousness by the end of this period. Golden Miles covers the period 1900 to circa 1930, the upsurge of I.W.W. syndicalism and working class socialism in the pre W.W.I period and the patriotic reaction and regression following that war. Winged Seeds chronicles the extraordinary hardships of working people in depression struck Australia, the hardened socialist and union movement which re-emerged, into W.W.II and ending with the initial but much contested introduction of cold war conservatism in late 1940s. The trilogy at the same time chronicles the evolution of Australian capitalism from local owner-operators to national companies which ultimately become part of multi-national financial complexes, with the parallel responses of Australian union organization over almost 60 years. A rich tapestry of characters, scenes, daily lives of miners and their families over three generations and the changing world of which they are a part. Prichard's greatest work.

Also Kiss on the Lips, 1932, a collection of short stories; Intimate Strangers, 1937, a feminist anti-war novel set in W.W.I Australia; Subtle Flame, 1967, a novel.

RONAN, Tom

Moleskin Midas, 1956
A novel about destruction of the populist strain in rural Australian society and the entrenched conservatism of the surviving farmers during the W.W.II period; their corrosive influence on Australian politics and society.

RUDD, Steele

On Our Selection, 1899
Collected stories of Australian homesteaders on marginal plots (selections) who, for all their toil and endurance, build on sand and ultimately lose all. In a sense, stories of the end of the small farmers' frontier.

STEAD, Christina

Seven Poor Men of Sydney, 1934
A stream of consciousness novel about the emotions, thoughts and lives of seven men (not mainly of the working class) who are defeated as much by their anomie as by the poverty of urban Australia during the early depression.

STIVENS, Dal

Jimmy Brockett, 1951
A novel of the wheeling and dealing and rise of a self-made Australian robber baron, a particularly rapacious enterpriser of the 1920s to 1940s, and how he got where he did.

STONE, Louis

Jonah, 1911
A romantic novel of working class life in cities of Edwardian Australia; the huddled sweatshops, exploitation and cramped lives as background to a typical love story.

TENNANT, Kylie

Tiburon, 1935
A semi-autobiographical novel of the unemployed in a New South Wales country town during the early 1930s.

The Battlers, 1941
A sequel to Tiburon, set in the later 1930s during which the unemployed gradually come to see their condition as caused by economic-political forces and interests and not as due to personal failings. Touches on the mass demonstrations and strikes of the period.

Foveaux, 1939
A novel revolving about the financial interests and politics behind a slum housing project in Sydney during the 1930s.

VICKERS, F.B.

The Mirage, 1955
A realistic protest novel about the treatment of Australian aborigines during this century; but mainly about conditions in post W.W.II period.

WALLACE, J.W.

Social Shadows, 1896
A play which was one of the forerunners of the Workers' Theatre drama in Australia; ranges from the London Dock strike of the period to the colonial snobocracy in Melbourne; from a populist socialist perspective.

WATTEN, Judah

The Tracks We Travel, 1950
A collection of short stories recounting life in the working class districts of Sydney during the late 1930s.

Alien Son, 1952
An evocative series of vignettes of recently arrived immigrants; Jewish family and boy adjusting to and growing up in Australia during the late depression years.

Time of Conflict, 1961
A proletarian novel set in depression Australia and dealing with the migrations and growing class and political consciousness of a young Australian worker. An effective portrayal of the indecision, myths, individualism and his deepening involvement in organized struggle.

Also The Unbending, 1954, Shares in Murder, 1957, two novels.

NEW ZEALAND

DAVIN, Dan

For the Rest of Our Lives, 1947
A novel of the human destruction experienced by three members of New Zealand Expeditionary Force in the Middle East during W.W.II and of the neo-colonial interests they gradually perceive behind their sacrifices.

DEVANNY, Jean

The Butcher Shop, 1926
A period piece novel portraying the continuing Edwardian class structure of New Zealand society in the 1920s, especially the delusions and self-restrictions involved in "respectable tradesmen's" lives.

HYDE, Robin (Iris Wilkinson)

Passport to Hell, 1936, Nor the Years Condemn, 1938
Two biographical novels of an Indian-Spanish New Zealander who escapes from a

reform school, works around the country and goes to sea, becomes a soldier and "hero" in W.W.I, is court martialled. And of his return to an impoverished and drab existence in New Zealand in the 1920s and 1930s.

Wednesday's Children, 1937
A novelized portrait of Auckland's poor in the early 1930s.

LEE, John A.

Children of the Poor, 1934, The Hunted, 1936
Two bitter semi-autobiographical novels of children of poor who become wards of the state and inmates of what in effect were work houses during the first decade of the 20th century. The Hunted tells of the author's escape from a work house-reformatory and living on the run as an adolescent in pre W.W.I New Zealand.

Civilian Into Soldier, 1937
Another semi-autobiographical novel which deals with the savagery which "well bred" genteel Kiwi soldiers soon developed during W.W.I. By a later left Labour MP.

MULGAN, John

Man Alone, 1939
An angry novel of a New Zealand migrant worker who can't stand the traditions of his country, who drifts through jobs in city and countryside, gets involved in the Auckland unemployed riots of mid 1930s and goes off to fight in the Spanish Civil War. One of the only proletarian novels from New Zealand.

PARK, Ruth

A Harp in the South, 1948
A very popular, nostalgic novel set in an Auckland working class district during W.W.I. Being a sort of New Zealand version of A Tree Grows in Brooklyn.

PEARSON, Bill

Coal Flat, 1963
A portrait of provincial town life in New Zealand during the 1950s; informal sociology in novel form.

LATIN AMERICA AND THE CARIBBEAN

Mexico

Central America

Dominican Republic

Puerto Rico

Cuba

Colombia

Venezuela

Ecuador

Bolivia

Peru

Chile

Argentina

Uruguay

Paraguay

Brazil

Caribbean

MEXICO

ALMANZA, Hector Raul

Huelga Blanca, 1950 (White Strike)
A novel dealing with Mexican bracero workers migrating to US corporate farms during the late 1940s, the conjoined exploitation by Mexican recruiters and government officials as well as by the US employers.

Candelaria de los Patos, 1952 (Candelaria de los Patos)
A novel of the lives of inhabitants of an impoverished slum district in Mexico City, conveying a feeling of pervasive helplessness.

Pesca Brava, 1960 (Courageous Catch)
A novel about the lives and struggles of Mexican peasant-fishermen in the 1950s.

ANDA, Jose Guadalupe de

Juan del Riel, 1943 (Juan of the Rails)
A somewhat melodramatic novel about an upper class youth drawn to the working class after the Mexican revolution. Set mainly in the late 1920s and 1930s. The "revolutionary" Mexican governments prove to be concerned with the workers only to the extent that the unions can be used to further the political interests of the new bureaucrat-capitalists. Deals with the suppression of militant labour unions and the incorporation of others into the government-controlled CROM in 1930s. Plotted around the life and death of the protagonist, who becomes a dissident union organizer and railway worker.

Los Cristeros: La Guerra Santa en los Altos, 1937 (The Cristeros: Holy War in the High Country), Los Bragados, 1942 (The Ill Disposed)
Two reportage "novels" dealing with the nature and the bases of the counter revolutionary holy war launched by the Mexican Catholic hierarchy against the Mexican government (because of its secular reforms separating church and state) and fought by the church's most reactionary supporters, the Cristeros, against former revolutionary peasantry between 1926 and 1929. Bragados is a sequel dealing with the resurgence of reactionary terrorism by the Cristeros in 1934 to 1938 against the social reforms and anticipated "socialism" initiated by the Cardenas government.

BATES, Ralph

The Fields of Paradise, 1940
A novel set in Mexico during the late 1930s; about the revolt of a peasant village against the local caudillo and his pistoleros who rule the region as if there had never been a Mexican revolution. A complex treatment of the characters and forces involved, "ending" in a partial but significant political victory by the villagers unlike the defeat their Spanish brothers had just suffered. Also see Bates' outstanding novels about the Spanish peasantry and working class during the 1920s and 1930s.

CASTELLANOS, Rosario

Los Convidados de Augusto, 1964 (Guests in August)
A collection of stories and character studies mainly about the restricted lives of women "from respectable families" living in a provincial Mexican town (of Chiapas), entombed by the social strictures and their own acceptance of them. The dead hand of traditional bourgeoise Mexican society portrayed by a veteran social realist author.

CORONA ROJAS, Benigno

La Barriada, 1948 (The Quarter)
A collage novel of the lives of slum dwellers in Mexico City during the late 1940s; written as a naturalistic "slice of life" account.

FUENTES, Carlos

La Region Mas Transparente, 1958 (Where the Air is Clear, 1960)
A novel revolving about the reminiscences of an aging ex-general which ranges
from 1910 to 1951; of his peon childhood and youth, the upheavals and chaos of the
revolution and especially of the endless false starts and betrayal of social
renovation by opportunists and the new ruling class in the generation following
the revolution. Yet, despite the poverty and desperation in which so many Mexicans
continue to live, a view that something was gained, some unretractable promise of
social justice has been made and that the most reactionary powers and traditional
ideologies in Mexican past have been shattered.

La Muerte de Artemio Cruz, 1962 (The Death of Artemio Cruz, 1966)
A novel of the life of Mexican multi-millionaire, how he rose to power during and
after the Mexican revolution by taking over the holdings of the old landed families
and defending the interests of the new capitalists like himself through his
newspapers. A more pessimistic account than La Region, it is told in flashbacks
during the last days of the dying protagonist and emphasizes the total venality
and ruthless stupidity of the Mexican ruling class.

GUERRERO, Jesus R.

Los Olvidados, 1944 (The Forgotten)
A collage novel of the lives of the poor and semi-employed peddlers, cripples,
their families and children, etc. wandering through the slums of Mexico City
during the early 1940s. Made into a powerful film by Luis Bunuel.

GUZMAN, Martin Luis

La Sombra del Caudillo, 1929 (Shadow of the Caudillo)
A thinly fictionalized account of the inner workings of personal cliques around
the Mexican presidency and in the Partido Revolucionario Institucional during the
1920s. Narrates the backgrounds and lives of some of the actual political leaders,
the operation of a system in which power brokers not only contend for their own
gain but also for that of their supporting chiefs against the offers of other
aspirant bosses. So that even the residue of their one time commitment to social
reform comes to naught. Told partly from Guzman's own experiences in the inner
circles of power during that period and skewed by a technocratic-elitist vision
of social reform.

El Hombre y Sus Armas, 1938 (The Man and His Weapons), Panoramas Politicas, 1939
(Political Panoramas), La Causa del Pobre, 1940 (The Cause of the Poor),
Adversidades de Bien, 1958 (Adversities of Righteousness)
A four volume popular history of the Mexican revolution, from its seedbed before
1910 to the end of major social reform in 1940.

LEWIS, Oscar

Pedro Martínez, 1964
A massive and detailed life history of Pedro Martinez, a poor Zapotec peasant
farmer raised in pre-revolutionary Tepotzlan; a member of the Zapitista forces
during the Mexican revolution, a quizzical peasant activist in the sometimes very
bloody struggles within his village during the changing factions of the 1920s,
as well as more usual accounts of wife and family and domestic life from youth to
old age, still as peasant and sometime migrant worker. An astute account which
captures the alloyed cultural conservatism and revolutionary nature of one of a
host of comparable peasants. Also provides a fine grained political history and
chronology of events in Tepotzlan from before 1910 to the 1950s which documents
the ongoing impetus of national and even international forces within a seemingly
sleepy peasant village over a half century. A remarkable work which no brief
annotation can do justice to.

As a background to Pedro Martinez one might look at Lewis' Life in a Mexican Village
- Tepotzlan Restudied (1951) which is probably the most fine grained, comprehensive
and all round best anthropological account of a Latin American peasant village yet
done--from agriculture to politics, traditional colonial Zapotec culture to 1940s
modernisms. A superb counter to the still prevalent romances about such worlds.

Five Families, 1959
A brief and very readable collection of edited oral histories about the daily lives
of five Mexican families in the mid 1950s, with synoptic historical backgrounds
of their lives. Includes a fragment of the account by Pedro Martinez, as well as
two accounts by families of the submarginal proletariat and petty peddler class
in Mexico City, an introduction to the Sanchez families, and an account from a
member of the upper middle class.

The Children of Sanchez, 1962
A massive oral history of the lives of the various members of the multiple families
of one Sanchez, a Mexico City worker introduced in Five Families. They constitute
a sort of cross section of the range of goals, lives, views of the Mexican urban
working class (though none of them are particularly radical or politically active).
It portrays many of the typical day to day responses, triumphs and worries of
urban working people not yet a proletariat. A Death in the Family (1966) expands
on the contrastive and sometimes contradictory experiences of members of the
Sanchez family, unearthing some hidden emotions and views on the death of a family
member. Emphasizes the psychological layers and complexity involved in seemingly
simple lives.

LOPEZ Y FUENTES, Gregorio

Campamento, 1931 (Encampment)
A descriptive collage of the men and women of the Mexican revolution on the march
in an encampment during one night in 1914. Flashbacks, monologues, verbatim
transcripts which portray the ignorance, hope, idealism, rage. A magnificent and
terrible slice of the forces in the Mexican revolutionary camp, of the foot
soldiers whose sacrifices we know will later be betrayed.

Tierra, 1932 (Land)
A collage novel; a series of portraits of the agrarian problem in Mexico 1910-1920;
haciendas and exploited peons, priests and landlords, powerless peasants. The
central theme is the Zapata rebellion and the Army of the South, his defeat and
the Zapata legend sustained. Of the later emergence of radical peasant organization
which may eventually institute the goals of the old Zapatistas.

Mi General, 1934 (My General)
A bitter satire on the mediocrity and delusions of grandeur of ex-revolutionary
generals who support whoever can continue to guarantee their villas and stipends.
Sardonic accounts of their banal nostalgia and bumbling self-glorification.

El Indio, 1935 (The Indian)
A novel about an Indian community conned into revealing the location of a nearby
ore body, and how they are rapidly overwhelmed by the "economic development" which
follows, with its attendent roster of entrepreneurs, and are finally pushed out of
their former lands.

Huasteca, 1939 (Huasteca)
A novel of the rise and fall of a Mexican entrepreneur who fronts for US oil
companies in Vera Cruz region. Of the exploitation of local oil workers and the
do nothing nationalist rhetoric of the Mexican government.

Los Peregrinos Inmoviles, 1944 (The Imobile Migrants)
Novel of a southern Mexican Indian village freed from peonage by the revolution,
whose people set out to recover their original lands. Directed by folk memories
and legends, they travel through the region, are exploited and tricked, and find
that nothing has really changed.

Milpa, Potrero y Monte, 1951 (Cornfield, Pasture and Scrubland)
A series of sketches about rural workers, landless peasants, migrant braceros,
cowboys, mountain Indian groups who have all been defrauded; depicted through the
wanderings and experiences of three peasant sons of a former Zapatista who leave
their home when the father dies.

MAGDALENO, Mauricio

Campo Celís, 1935 (Estate Celis)
Novel of a Mexican peasant, one Bernardo Celis, whose hunger to acquire more and

more land is released by the chaos and opportunism during and after the Mexican revolution, so that he ends up as a minor hacienda owner, exploiting his former neighbours with a special rapacity and insight.

El Resplandor, 1937 (The Splendour)
A novel set in 1920s and 1930s; a village of Otomi Indians in southern Mexico who have lost their lands to a hacienda and decide to send an adopted Mestizo boy to be educated so that he may help them win back their lands. They distrust all non-Indians and will have no dealings with the Agrarian Reform Commissions. Their siezure of hacienda lands leads to a shootout with hacienda guards and local police, which while unsuccessful destroys the alliance of hacienda and regional politicians and results in the entry of representatives of the national power structure in the form of the returning educated village son and a new "Indian" governor of the state. In the end the hacienda and village lands wind up in the hands of new Indian and Mestizo owners, with the Indian peasants no further ahead.

MANCISIDOR, Jose

La Asonada, 1931 (The Mob)
An outstanding Marxist interpretation of the Mexican revolution in novel form. Deals with the various class elements and heterogeneous regional peasant strains which underlay that upheaval, their endless manipulation and betrayal during and after the fighting, the clerical armed counter revolution, and the widespread apathy and cynicism which set in with the triumph of the new ruling class of ex-revolutionary caudillos.

En La Rosa de los Vientos, 1941 (In the Rose of the Winds)
A novel set in Vera Cruz during the Mexican revolution, the incursion of Woodrow Wilson Democracy in the form of invasion by US Marines in 1914, the incorporation of middle class students into the revolutionary forces because of their anti-imperialist sentiments. Also in same vein, La Ciudad Roja, 1932 (Red City), taking events into the 1920s.

Frontera Junto Al Mar, 1953 (Frontier Conjoined to the Sea)
A novel of the second phase of the Mexican revolution (circa 1914-1917), the struggles to overthrow the reactionary and comprador dictator Huerta and the battles against the American Army Expeditionary forces sent into northern Mexico to "maintain the peace". Revolving around the life of an anarchist leader with flashbacks to Mexico before 1910.

El Alba en las Cimas, 1956 (Dawn on the Peaks)
A novel of the Mexican expropriation of American oil holdings in late 1930s, the first such step by any Latin American country, and the attempts and strategies of US corporations to topple the Cardenas regime and recoup their holdings.

MUÑOZ, Rafael

Si Me Han De Matar Mañana, 1934 (If They Should Kill Me Tomorrow)
A set of short stories and sketches by a former reporter and soldier; dealing with the blind destructiveness unleashed in the Mexican revolution, unchecked and undirected by any clear cut class, ideological or party control. Title taken from an evocative line in a Zapatista marching song.

ORTIZ HERNAN, Gustavo

Chimenas, 1937
A novel of an ordinary soldier, his family, friends and neighbours during the aftermath of the Mexican revolution; their deepening bitterness over how little improvements in life have occurred after so much sacrifice.

PONIATOWSKA, Elena

La Noche de Tlatelolco, 1971 (Night of Tlatelolco)
A documentary account of the massacre of some hundreds of Mexican University students by military police in a suburb of Mexico City during the fall of 1968. The background of student activism and their demonstration against the diversion and looting of massive government funds in the Olympics fair rather than used for

social development projects. An oft cited account of what was the most visible and blatant case of Mexican government repression during tne 1960s.

REVUELTAS, Jose

Los Muros de Agua, 1941 (Walls of Water)
An autobiographical novel of the author's imprisonment for political activity during the Cardenas period; sketches of prison life in the political prison camp of Islas Marias, his own feelings and reflections about Mexico under a supposedly left-nationalist government.

El Luto Humano, 1943 (The Human Wake)
An epic novel of Mexico mainly during the Cardenas era (1934-1940), the generals and new politico-capitalists of the ruling party, of the remnants of the old ruling class, of Indian and other peasants, of fruitless reforms and strikes, of urban workers. The kaleidoscope of tensions, struggles, hopes, despairs and illusions of Mexico during its New Deal period. Revueltas' masterpiece. Also Los Dias Terrenales, 1949 (Earthy Days) and El Apando, 1969 (The Pilferer), two novels of Mexico in tne generation since 1940, the seeming dissipation of the left and hopes for basic social change.

SALAZAR MALLEN, Ruben

Camino de Perfeccion, 1937 (Road of Perfection), Soledad, 1944 (Solitude), Paramo, 1945 (Upland)
Three novels touching on the lives of urban proletariat and rural working class in Mexico; documentary realism with sometimes lyrical descriptions of the conditions in various regions of the country at the time.

Oja de Agua, 1949 (Eye of Water)
A novel of a feared and hated local Mexican cacique (landlord cum political boss) who remains entrenched after a generation of institutionalized social "revolution" in Mexico of the 1940s. Also La Iniciacion, 1966 (The Initiation), a comparable novel set a generation later in urban Mexico.

Viva Mexico, 1968
A novel which revolves around an actual case in which a family disintegrates through attempting to bring a notorious gunman, protected by judiciary and police, to trial for assassinating the father. The blatant and well known nature of the case is treated as an indictment of all of Mexican society, both of those who are in power and those who allow such forces to remain in power.

TRAVEN, Bruno

La Carreta, 1930 (The Carreta, 1966)
The first of a six volume series of novels which follow the lives of Indian and Mestizo protagonists in southern Mexico and Chiapas from the final years of the Diaz regime through the Mexican revolution to mid 1920s. Distorted by Traven's sometimes Zane Grey-like plots and tremendismo, they also contain detailed accounts of conditions of labour, social life and peonage, as well as the streams of resistance which finally break out in open revolt. The series includes (1931-1939) Government, Sun Creation, The March to Caobaland, The Rebellion of the Hanged and The General From the Jungles, all available in recent reprints.
Also his The Cotton Pickers, 1976, a novel of migrant agricultural workers in central Mexico during the mid 1920s as told by an American Wobbly.

YANEZ, Augustin

Ojerosa y Pintada, 1960 (Bleary-Eyed and Blotched)
A "slice of life" portrait of Mexico City in 1960 as seen through twenty-four hours in the life of a taxi driver as he moves through city locales, from slums to government residences, from Indian peasant marketers and urban workers to bootlickers and front men of the powerful. A city and its inhabitants. A little known work by an author better known for psychoanalytic philosophizing about the "deep structure" of the Mexican society.

CENTRAL AMERICA

GUATAMALA

AREVALO, Juan J.

The Shark and the Sardines, 1964
A book length allegorical essay which comments on the destructive role of the US in small Central American republics like Guatemala, particularly relating CIA involvement in the overthrow of the mildly reformist Arbenez government.

ASTURIAS, Miguel Angel

El Señor Presidente, 1946 (El Señor Presidente, 1964)
Novel of an "old style" Central American dictatorship (the reign of Manuel Estrada Cabrera) in Quatemala which, with American backing, turns the clock backward to reimpose colonial institutions such as forced labour and neo-serfdom among Indian peasantry. The general decline of the literate classes into terrorized, sychophantic lackeys.

Hombres de Maíz, 1949 (Men of Maiz, 1966)
A Novel Prize winning novel, being a combination of realism and surrealism which treats with the long history of Indian oppression and their hidden inner worlds as seen through the Quiche Indians' views of land, spirits, myths, etc. In Asturias hands this is not the currently fashionable and obscurantist "Fourth World" spirituality theme.

Viento Fuerte, 1950 (Strong Wind, 1965)
A novel of an American couple who are disgusted with US exploitation of Quatemala and who attempt to work with Indian peasants to establish a cooperative but naturally fail due to their own naivety, Indian distrust and external government hostility.

El Papa Verde, 1954 (The Green Pope, 1965)
A novel of the rise and astute rapacity of a US owner-operator of a banana plantation who, with the connivance of a venal Quatemalan government, expels local peasants and old landlords from their lands. Some deft sketches of the cynical public relations program of "hemispherico-prosperity" which is trotted out.

Weekend in Quatemala, 1956
A group of stories drawn together in novel form, dealing with the invasion of the CIA organized army of Castillo Armas in 1954 to overthrow the shortlived reform government of Arbenz. Treats with the lost hopes, the failures to resist, and the killings and repression which followed the right wing restoration. Bitter sketches of the US investors, reporters, "Latin American experts" and other creatures who flooded into Quatemala after the coup.

Los Ojos de los Enterrados, 1960 (The Eyes of the Interred, 1966)
A novel set during the Ubico dictatorship of 1931-1944, dealing with the rise of organized and increasingly militant workers, both urban and rural, who oppose both the Ubico dictatorship and the US embassy which sustains it. A mixture of folk tale and myth, the title drawn from the Maya aphorism that "only when injustice is overcome can the dead close their eyes". The last volume of a trilogy which includes The Green Pope and Strong Wind.

CASTILLO, Otto Rene

Vamos Patria a Caminar/Let's Go, 1971
A slim bilingual collection of poetry about the deepening, near psychotic repression by Guatemalan oligarchy and its supporters in the mid 1960s, and of the moral and psychological considerations leading some to join the resistance despite everything. Castillo died in a FAR guerrilla detachment in 1967.

GALEANO, Eduardo

Guatemala; Occupied Country, 1969
A major journalistic history of Guatemala under the institutionalized terror of
assorted Guatemal Vichy "governments". Deals with the 1953 CIA invasion on, but
focuses on conditions in the 1960s and the growth of insurgency.

MONTEFORTE TOLEDO, Mario

Donde Acaban Los Caminos, 1953 (Where the Roads End, 1964)
A novel of a love affair between a Quatemalan doctor and an Indian woman, detailing
the pressures brought against them by both the Indian and white communities in
that caste ridden society. The romance is used as a means to dissect the
sociology of Quatemala, with the heroine finally saying a curse on all ethnic
patriotisms and looking for something more worthy of loyalty.

Una Manera de Morir, 1957 (A Manner of Dying)
A complex proletarian novel by a former indigenista writer, it narrates the
disillusionment of a communist peasant organizer with the temporizing of the
Arbenz government and its failure to institute the promised reforms and to lead
its mass support in resistance to the CIA/Armas invasion. Told in the aftermath
of the bloody right wing restoration, it also deals with the fear and despair of
the left, and of attempts to sustain some kind of meaningful social action in the
deepening night of neo-fascism.

Cuentos de Derrota y Esperanza, 1962 (Stories of Defeat and Hope)
Collection of short stories of Quatemala, of defeat and hopes under the heel of
increasingly genocidal neo-colonial regime.

EL SALVADOR

CAYETANO CARPIO, Salvador

La Capucha, 1978 (The Hood)
An account of the system of repression of political and especially class opponents
of the military regime which ruled El Salvador during the 1960s and 1970s.
La Capucha is an instrument of torture and Cayetano Carpio is one of the surviving
leaders of the Farabundo Marti Liberation Movement from the mid 1960s. In part he
describes his own torture at the hands of the military in early 1970s.

LINDO, Hugo

Justicia, Señor Gobernador, 1960 (Justice, Mister Governor)
A bitterly humourous novel about a middle aged, liberal magistrate who begins to
take the rhetoric about "justice" seriously; his attempts to bring some local
bosses to account and to defend other poor people bring him into sharp conflict
with the Salvadorean political and judicial system, and the magistrate is
ultimately committed to an insane asylum.

NORTH, Liisa

Bitter Grounds, The Roots of Revolt in El Salvador, 1982
A booklet political history of the most recent struggles against the military and
allied butchery of Salvadorean peasantry and poor, outlining some of the major
forces, events and background. Also see Thomas Anderson's 1971 Matanza, a US cold
war historian's view, but one which provides extensive documentation of the
voracity of El Salvador's oligarchy and the bloodbath they perpetrated on that
country's peasantry in 1932.

HONDURAS

AMAYA AMADOR, Ramon

Prision Verde, 1957 (Green Prison)
A reportage novel of social stagnation and somnolence in the banana plantation

regions of Honduran north coast, a US corporate enclave largely removed from Honduran control.

Construcciones, 1962 (Constructions)
A social novel of problems of urban workers and poor in the sprawling but unindustrialized capital of Tegucigalpa.

CARIAS REYES, Marcos

La Heredad, 1931 (The Inheritance)
A novel dressed in local colour form but being a diatribe on the absurdities and evils of banana republicanism in Honduras.

Also Germinal, 1936, a collection of stories.

MEJIA NIETO, Arturo

El Tunco, 1932 (Thumbless)
A novel of the stagnancy, illiteracy and miserable poverty of the Honduran countryside hidden behind what seem to be colourful folkways. Also Zapatos Viejos, 1930, a similar type of novel.

NICARAGUA

ALDARACA, Bridget, BAKER, Edward, RODRIGUEZ, Ileana, ZIMMERMAN, Marc

Nicaragua in Revolution/Nicaragua en Revolucion, 1980
A bilingual collection of Nicraguan poetry about the struggles against American imperialism and its local tyrants from 1898 through the 1920s to the triumph of the Sandinista revolution in 1979. Compiled into four historic periods and providing background data on the events as well as biographical material of the thirty-eight contributors.

CARDENAL, Ernesto

Zero Hour and Other Documentary Poems, 1980
A collection of poems about the oppression of Nicaraguan poor and their revolt; from the original Sandino of 1920s to the Sandinista revolution which overthrew the Somoza dictatorship. By a Nicaraguan Catholic priest and Marxist.

RANDALL, Margaret

Sandino's Daughters, 1981
A collection of interviews with mainly young Nicaraguan women who actively participated in the Sandinista struggles to oust the Somoza dictatorship during the 1970s. An instructive and often moving feminist account.

ROBLETO, Hernan

Sangre del Tropico, 1930 (Blood of the Tropics)
A somewhat melodramatic novel of the US military occupation of Nicaragua in the late 1920s and the Conservative-Liberal civil war. The social context of exploitation in plantations and mines by national and foreign capitalists as the basis of civil war and an account of the background of the Sandino forces.

Los Estrangulados, 1936 (The Strangled)
A sequel to Sangre del Tropico which carries the history of US occupation of Nicaragua into the 1930s, the assassination of Sandino and the dispersal of his forces. Of how the US Marine Corp establishes the Nicaraguan National Guard and the Samoza dynasty to preserve US interests after their withdrawal.

TIJERINO, Doris and RANDALL, Margaret

Inside the Nicaraguan Revolution, 1978 (Somos Milliones)
An autobiographical reminiscence of the youth and young womanhood of a member of a rural middle class family who gradually becomes involved in the student and then revolutionary struggles against the dictatorship. Contains some moving tributes

to her fallen comrades and in general a picture of underground struggle before
the mass insurrection which toppled the Somoza regime. A valuable left-nationalist
account, but with little treatment of the lives of working people and peasants as
part of that struggle.

COSTA RICA

DOBLES, Fabian

Ese Que Llaman Pueblo, 1942 (This They Call a People)
A novel about the sordid conditions of life of workers in Costa Rican banana
plantations during the 1930s.

El Sitio de las Abras, 1950 (The Site of the Burning)
Novel about three generations of villagers in a remote jungle region who try to
shake off the control of a large landlord and of their attempts to regain lost
lands through the transformation of traditional village organizations into a rural
labour union.

Los Leños Violentos, 1962 (The Violent Blockheads)
A novel of the continuing poverty and powerlessness of the Costa Rican masses after
the much hailed "democratic" revolution of late 1940s. By a veteran Marxist
writer.

Also En El San Juan Hay Tiburon, 1967 (There's No Shark in San Juan), a novel.

FALLAS, Carlos Luis

Mamita Yunai, 1941
One of the best known Costa Rican novels, dealing with the pervasive presence of
the US United Fruit Company in the country. In a series of flashbacks, it treats
with the youth of a Costa Rican from an Indian-Mestizo village which is
incorporated into the United Fruit empire in the early 1920s; the exploitation,
indignities and expected servility which gradually becomes part of the villagers
lives. Of the protagonist's growing rebellion against this regime, first
individually then as a labour organizer, his imprisonment and flight. The second
part of the book deals with the openly fraudulent elections in which the Company
installs its Costa Rican allies in power.

Gentes y Gentecillas, 1947 (People and Rabble)
Another novel along the lines of Mamita Yunai, carrying the picture of local
corruption and degradation into a somewhat later period and on the national scale.

Marcos Ramirez, 1952 (Marcos Ramirez)
A semi-autobiographical novel of Falles' peasant family and his own youth in the
1920s and 1930s as plantation worker, cobbler, truck driver, labour leader,
political prisoner, and internationally known writer.

LYRA, Carmen (Maria Isabel Carvajal)

Los Cuentos de Mi Tia Panchita, 1920 (Stories of My Aunt Panchita)
Collection of satirical and indignant stories of rural Costa Rican society told
in local dialect as contemporary folk tales.

Also En Una Silla de Ruedas, 1918 (In a Wheelchair), a novel about a vital and
progressive Costa Rican teacher who returns to her hometown and is overwhelmed
by the decaying social restrictions which are imposed on "respectable women" in
that provincial society.

PANAMA

BELEÑO, Joaquin

Luna Verde, 1951 (Green Moon)
A collage account of the US Canal Zone in the 1940s, written in the form of a
diary by a Panamanian student; the rampant racism, the social degradation and

classic colonial sociology of the Canal Zone.   Also describes the left-nationalist struggles against US imperialism there.

CAJAR ESCALA, Jose

El Cabecilla, 1944 (The Ringleader)
A documentary novel of the exploitation and manipulation of the peasants of the northern La Laguna area by political bosses, which led to a millenial religous rising by peasants in 1940 crushed by the National Guard.

CANDANEDO, Cesar

Los Clandestinos, 1957 (The Illegals)
A novel of illegal Colombian workers in the jungle work camps of Darien province in the late 1940s; how they are recruited and the serf-like conditions which prevail. Panamanian landowners and capitalists working hand in glove with a bought and paid for police and political administration.

GUTIERREZ, Joaquin

Puerto Limon, 1950 (Port Lemon)
A novel about the political dealings of the United Fruit Company when faced with an economic and anti-imperialist strike by its plantation workers on the Panamanian frontier. Treats with the alliance of foreign corporation and national compradores as they confront working class demands. One of the best known of Panamanian novels.

Manglar, 1946 (The Mangroves)
Novel about the return of a teacher to the small town where she grew up, reminiscences of girlhood aspirations and reflections of the oppressive social restrictions now seen through the eyes of a woman.

JURADO, Ramon

Desertores, 1952 (Deserters)
A novel about Victoriano Lorenzo, a peasant Liberal guerrilla leader during the "1,000 Days" civil war at the turn of the century when Panama was then still part of Colombia. The supposedly apolitic and apathetic Panamanian peasantry join in revolt but the leaders of the Liberal party betray Lorenzo to the Conservative army because they fear the trajectory of a peasant rising which seems to be passing beyond their control. A parallel to the events in Colombia during the early 1950s.

Also San Cristobal, 1947, a novel about Panamanian sugar caneworkers during the W.W.II period when unionism confronts a neo-colonial plantation system.

OZORES, Renato

La Calle Oscura, 1955 (The Dark Street)
A social novel set among the inhabitants of a tenement house in a poor but cosmopolitan section of the inner core of Panama City in the 1950s.

DOMINICAN REPUBLIC

LAGUERRE, Enrique

El Laberinto, 1959 (The Labyrinth)
A novel about the rise of Trujillo from a poor rural youth to become a policeman
and then commander of National Guard under the US occupation of the Dominican
Republic in 1920s and 1930s, and his evolution into the most ruthless and
avarious dictator in the Caribbean during the post W.W.II period. Account of how
the old ruling class families of Dominican Republic are totally cowed, of the role
of US pro-consuls, of failed attempts to overthrow Trujillo and of the survivors
of those plots.

MARRERO ARISTY, Ramon

Over, 1939
An autobiographical novel about the serf-like existence of Haitian cane workers
in the Dominican Republic and their powerlessness against the exactions of the
plantation managers and the National Guard which acts as a private army for the
wealthy.

Balsie, 1938 (Balsie)
A collection of stories about everyday life in western Dominican Republic during
the consolidation of the Trujillo dictatorship and following the massacre of
thousands of Haitian landless workers there. The seemingly unchanging, slave-like
conditions through which small personal joys and beauty are intertwined.

MOSCOSO PUELLO, Francisco

Cañas y Bueyes, 1936 (Cane and Oxen)
A rather nostalgic novel of the supposed lives of sugar cane workers and the old
plantation oligarchy in the regime ancien of Dominican Republic before the rise of
Trujillo.

READ, Horacio

Los Civilizadores, 1924 (The Civilizers)
A bitterly ironic novel of the first years of the US occupation of the Dominican
Republic; the US administrators, missionaries, investors and Marine Corps rhetoric
about bringing order and civilization to the country.

De La Sombra, 1959 (From the Shade), Cerca de Noche, 1965 (Near to Night)
Two powerful novels about the last bloody years of the Trujillo dictatorship, and
of the installation of his successors by US intervention, with a portrait of the
murderous ambassador, Ellsworth Bunker.

REQUENA, Andres

Los Enemigos de la Tierra, 1942 (Enemies of the Land)
Novel of the poverty and oppression of the Dominican peasantry, their search for
work and migration to Santo Domingo and the unemployment which drives them back
to the countryside; none of their daily heroism leading to any improvement in life.

Cementario Sin Cruces, 1949 (Cemetary Without Crosses)
A documentary novel of the Dominican Republic as a cemetary without crosses to
mark the victims' of Trujillo's police terror. Revolves around the failure of a
guerrilla group to topple the regime in mid 1940s, and of the psychopathologic
mass repression which follows.

PUERTO RICO

ARRIVI, Francisco

Mascara Portorriqueña, 1938-1956 (Puerto Rican Masquerade)
The general title of a novel trilogy about two generations of a poor black Puerto Rican family, from life in the slums of San Juan to a different but even more bitter condition in New York during the 1940s and 1950. Of the multi-faceted skein of racial and class oppression, of how people are caught in it and its consequences.

GONZALEZ, Jose Luis

Paisa, 1950 (Countryman)
A novela about a family's flight from hunger and poverty in rural Puerto Rico in the early 1940s to a possibly more abject impoverishment, trapped in a system of racial discrimination, deculturalization and semi-employment in New York. Constructed around flashbacks during the course of a robbery.

En el Otro Lado, 1954 (On the Other Side)
Collected short stories of Puerto Rican immigrants in the US and others returned to Puerto Rico; most unwilling to accept their lives in America yet unable to make a living in Puerto Rico.

IGLESEAS, Cesar Andreu

Los Derrotados, 1956 (The Defeated)
A novel of the backgrounds and motives of a group of Puerto Rican nationalists who launched an armed attack on the US Senate in the early 1950s, and how they deal with their defeat.

Una Gota de Tiempo, 1958 (A Drop of Time)
A collage novel of the lives of a number of Puerto Ricans during a twenty-four hour period in the mid 1950s; revolves around the creeping social and cultural incorporation of Puerto Rico and its people into the American empire.

LAGUERRE, Enrique

La Llamarada, 1935 (The Blaze)
A powerful novel of sugar cane workers, peasants and their communities in the first two decades of this century; the struggles against the old and new ruling class which emerge after American annexation of Puerto Rico.

Solar Montoya, 1940 (Montoya's Plot)
A novel of the tenant farmers and small peasantry on and around the Puerto Rican coffee haciendas during and shortly after W.W.I.

La Resaca, 1949 (The Surf), Los Dedos de Mano, 1951 (Fingers of a Hand), La Cieba en el Tiesto, 1956 (The Potted Cieba)
A novel trilogy of the struggles of Puerto Rican people for independence from Spain during 1870-1910 (La Resaca); the resistance to incorporation into the American empire, 1910-1930 (Los Dedos de Mano); and the class and union struggles during the 1930s depression (La Cieba en el Tiestro). Involves three generations of a Puerto Rican family, the last winding up as immigrants in the US caught up with other workers in the depth of the depression there.

MINTZ, Sidney (ed.)

Worker in the Cane, 1960
An outstanding life history of a Puerto Rican sugar cane worker, boyhood to late middle age. The rich complex of hopes, insights and failed strivings of a sometimes socialist "rural" worker and the lives of his family and neighbours from the early 1920s to the mid 1950s.

CUBA

AGUILERA MALTA, Demetrio

Una Cruz en la Sierra Maestra, 1960 (A Cross in the Sierra Maestra)
A novel of the Cuban revolution; set in the Sierra Maestra mountains and focussed on one guerrilla engagement but touching on events throughout Cuba in flashbacks. Alludes to the continental nature of the forces in contention through the backgrounds of Latin American volunteers in the July 26 movement and to historic antecedents in the International Brigades of the Spanish Civil War a generation earlier. (Also see his Madrid, Reportaje Novelado de Una Retaguardia Heroica, 1937.)

AGUILILLA, Aracali C. de

Primeros Recuerdos, 1963 (First Memories)
Reminiscences of a peasant girl growing up in a plantation region during the 1920s and her migration to Havana to look for work; life there in an assortment of servant jobs during the 1930s, the turmoil, insecurity, poverty and humiliations and her attempts to wring some happiness from that world.

APARICIO NOGALES, Raul

Frutos del Azote, 1961 (Fruit of the Scourge)
A novel which spans the years 1898-1933 in Cuba through the reminiscences of a man who has witnessed the repeated betrayal of the hopes and struggles of the Cuban people from the War of Independence on. His cynicism is supplanted by anger when he comes to support his son in the revolutionary struggle to oust the Machado dictatorship in 1933.

ARENAL, Humberto

El Tiempo Descendido, 1964 (The Lowered Time)
Collection of short stories about life in Cuba during the final years of Batista; focussed on the question of how revolutionary struggle grows despite all the forces arrayed against it.

BARNET, Miguel

Biografia de un Cimarron, 1968 (Biography of a Cimaroon)
A life history of a "runaway" slave (Cimaroon) who escaped into the mountains and his experience of Cuba from the 1870s to 1950s.

Cancion de Rachel, 1969 (Song of Rachel)
A novel in the form of an autobiography, about a black woman born in the 1890s and reminiscing about her life in relation to "historic periods", especially from Independence to the 1920s, including an account of the Negro rising against peon status in 1912. Done through flashbacks from the Batista period. The serfdom and racism and recurrent resistance, seen through the eyes of a black woman worker and former bar singer.

BUZZI, David

Los Desnudos, 1967 (The Naked Ones)
A panoramic novel of events in Cuba, 1958-1964; the first steps in socialist construction and the responses of a wide variety of people to these changes; from anti-socialist skilled workers to revolutionary sons of corrupt politicians, from rehabilitated juvenile delinquents to actively reactionary peasants. Revolves around the attempts of people to remould themselves so as to become part of a new society in birth and of others who merely strike new poses in order to hang on to as much of the old society as possible.

CABRERA INFANTE, Guillermo

Asi en la Paz Como en la Guerra, 1960 (As In Peace So In War)
A collection of searing sketches about the anonymous heroism of the partizans of
the Cuban revolution and the increasingly pathological terrorism of the Batista
regime from 1952 to 1958.

CARDENAS ACUÑA, Ignacio

Enigma Para un Domingo, 1971 (Enigma on a Sunday)
A "detective novel" which deals with the solution of a murder in 1963 Cuba with
the motives going back to Batista Cuba. A successful treatment of the corruption
of that earlier period with its officially tolerated gangsterism, police and court
venality, the web of ties between business, government, press and criminals.

CARPENTIER, Alejo

Ecue-Yamba-O, 1933 (Ecue-Yamba-O)
An evocation of the continuing vitality of Africanisms and surreptitious slave
culture in the lives of Cuban sugar cane workers during the Machado dictatorship;
mixed with accounts of underground union organizing. To one extent or another
all of Carpentier's novels are surrealistic collages of myth, history, realistic
fiction, and philosophic allusions which defy meaningful brief annotation.

El Reino De Este Mundo, 1946 (The Kingdom of This World, 1957)
A mythic account of the Haitian slave revolt told by a sort of Haitian Til
Eulenspiegel; of the Black spirit transformer who initially raises the revolt and
is executed, through the series of Black Emperors, plantation owners and assorted
rulers, evolving the theme that the struggle is always the same--between the
oppressor and the oppressed.

Los Pasos Perididos, 1956 (The Lost Steps, 1958)
A collage of history and mythology in which 500 years of European and American
Indian experience are combined into a Criollo mythical heritage.

El Siglo de las Luces, 1963 (Explosion in the Cathedral, 1965)
A collage of the history and myths surrounding the slave risings in French and
Spanish Caribbean during the time of the French Revolution; how the attempted
suppression of the Haitian revolution was the betrayal of and death blow to the
revolution in France itself.

El Recurso del Metodo, 1974 (Reasons of State, 1975)
A counterposing of the decadence and petty avaricousness of the French
bourgeoise during W.W.I and the American love affair with "French spirit"; shifts
to the ruthless hypocrisy of the US rulers and their imposition of a pliable Cuban
dictatorship to do its bidding. Also a bitter parody of a 1920s Cuban Presidente,
and the ludicrous pronunciamentos of Woody Wilson's "The New Freedom".

DESNOES, Edmundo

No Hay Problema, 1961 (No Problem!)
A novel about the somnolence and total isolation of much of the Cuban middle class
from the revolution in progress around them during the later Batista years.

Memorias del Subdesarrollo, 1965 (Memories of Underdevelopment)
A novel dealing with the inability of a member of the former upper middle class to
adjust to the socialist reorganization of Cuba; the feelings, interior monologues
and enervated life of one who doesn't oppose the revolution, but who also cannot
give up the parasitic lifestyle of his past.

DIAZ RODRIGUEZ, Jesus

Los Años Duros, 1966 (The Hard Years)
A collection of linked stories about the Cuban revolution and the effects on
surviving revolutionaries, neutrals and Batistianos. Also a reminder to those,
only a few years younger than the revolutionary generation, of just why the hatred
toward the supporters of the former regime exists and why no leeway can be given
to those who may wish to turn back the clock.

FEIJOO, Samuel

Juan Quinquin en Pueblo Mocho, 1964 (Juan Quinquin in Crippletown)
A "story" told in classic folklore style; the life of an archtypical poor peasant
in Las Villas province, working and sacrificing to barely hold his own and never
ever getting a step ahead. The story proceeds quite naturally into a picture of
the local political bosses who panic as apolitic peasants begin to lend support
to the revolutionary forces.

GALLEGOS, Romulo

La Brinza de Paja en el Viento, 1952 (Strawstack in the Wind)
A novel which portrays the struggles in "democratic" (pre-Batista) Cuba during the
late 1940s, particularly of the political use of gangsters to control student
dissent at the University of Habana. By a leading Venezuelan author who was then
in exile in Cuba.

GONZALEZ DE CASCORRO, Raul

Concentracion Publica, 1964 (Mass Meeting)
A panoramic account of the changes being initiated during the first phase of
socialist reorganization in Cuba in 1962. Uses one of the mass mobilization
meetings addressed by Fidel Castro to present a cross section of listeners, their
backgrounds, the variety and degree of change in their lives; in particular about
the new hopes and visions they are coming to hold.

GAROFALO, Jose Miguel

Se Dice Facil, 1968 (Easy to Say)
A collection of six stories depicting different yet converging moments in Cuban
history from 1898 to the Bay of Pigs invasion in 1961. A panorama of Cuban people
from businessmen to black cane workers, it trys to convey the sweep of social
forces in Cuba struggling toward independence and social justice despite internal
and external enemies.

GUILLEN, Nicolas

Motivos de Son, 1930 (Motifs of Song), La Paloma de Vuelo Popular, 1958 (The Dove
of People's Flight), El Diario que a Diario, 1972 (The Daily Journal)
Three collections of poetry by an internationally renouned, prolific and oft exiled
left Cuban poet; they range from his early, somewhat romantic evocation of Cuban
black culture during the Machado dictatorship, through poetry dealing with Cuba
under US/Batista rule and the rising tide of revolt, and lastly a collection of
poems about the human side of attempts to construct socialism after liberation.

HERRERO, Juan Luis

Tigres en el Vedado, 1967 (Tigers in the Surround)
A collection of stories revolving around the horrific repression of Cuban
revolutionaries and sympathizers by the police (especially by the private army of
Senator Masferrer) in late 1950s. Also an unvarnished account of the retribution
dealt out to a band of Masferrer's gunmen at the collapse of the Batista
dictatorship and the initial campaign of the revolutionary militia against the
remnant Batista bands which withdrew into the mountains. Emphasizes the critical
differences between those bands and the previous revolutionary guerrillas yet
capturing the ambiguity of the peasantry during the rapid turnabout of events.

LEWIS, Oscar, LEWIS, Ruth, RIGDON, Susan (eds.)

Neighbours: Living the Revolution, 1977, Four Women: Living the Revolution, 1977
Two huge volumes edited from tape recorded oral accounts of life in Cuba by four
men and women during the late 1960s. They give details of family and daily lives,
the continuation of old schemes and dreams only somewhat changed by the social
revolution going on around them. The accounts are disproportionately weighted
toward an apolitic quasi-lumpen proletariat (which was Lewis' specific topic) and
were criticized as being unrepresentative of the Cuban people as a whole during

this period. While difficult to read because of their unselectivity, these
volumes do raise important questions about any real transition to a socialist
society and probably do document the attitudes of a significant minority during
such transition.

LOPEZ NUSSA, Leonel

Tabaco, 1963 (Tobacco)
A novel set amid the hard pressed small tobacco farmers of Piñar del Rio province
during the 1920s and early 1930s but incorporates events in much of Cuba through
letters from scattered family members. It indirectly but clearly outlines the
incorporation of Cuba into a vassal of US corporations, deals with the control
by the US ambassador of a totally corrupt and violent "Cuban" government, and
describes the mass revolutionary strikes against the Machado dictatorship in 1933.
An understated parallel to the events which twenty-five years later would topple
Batista and the neo-colonial ruling class for good.

MONTENEGRO, Carlos

Hombres Sin Mujer, 1938 (Men Without Women)
Semi-autobiographical prison memoir by a worker-writer and participant in the
struggles against Machado of early 1930s. Mainly an expose of the conditions and
lives of "common criminals" in Cuban prisons in a Hemingway-like style.

Dos Barcos, 1929 (Two Ships)
Collection of tales about Cuban seamen and prison stories.

Los Heroes, 1941 (The Heroes)
Collection of short stories about Cuban workers and lower middle class which touch
on the struggles against the Machado dictatorship during the 1930s.

NAVARRO, Noel

Los Dias de Nuestra Angustia, 1962 (Days of Our Anguish)
A collective novel of the Cuban revolution in the style of Dos Passos; from the
storming of the Moncado barracks in 1952 to the eve of victory in December 1958.
Uses a vast array of characters, places, events and integrating newspaper reports,
radio announcements, ads, snatches of dialogue, biographical and historical
background as well as novelized character description.

Zona de Silencio, 1971 (Silent Zone)
A novel of Cuban communists during the 1930s and 1940s in which their struggles
against Machado and later Cuban regimes are just a part of a vanguard fighting
and organizing throughout Latin America. A redefinition of the roots and context
of the later Cuban revolution.

OLEMA GARCIA, Daura

Maestra Voluntaria, 1962 (Volunteer Teacher)
A documentary novel of the initial educational campaigns in socialist Cuba, in
particular the story of a young woman teacher from an apolitic middle class family
who joins the anti-illiteracy drive in the peasant hamlets during 1961.

ORTEGA, Gregorio

Un de Cal y Otra de Arena, 1957 (One of Lime, the Other of Sand)
Novel of life in Cuba under the government-gangster alliances during the
"democratic" pre-Batista period of 1940s; the all-pervasive venality, the decay
of public services, of the gang wars which serve as politics.

Reportaje de las Visperas, 1967 (Reportage From the Eve)
A novel of the deepening decay of Cuban society and the increasing reliance on
gangsterism and pathologically murderous police terrorism from 1952 to 1956.
Story revolves around the journal of a newspaper reporter who becomes involved
with a textile workers' strike, is arrested and witnesses the tortures. Ends with
assault of workers on a police station to rescue their surviving comrades.

OTERO, Lisandro

La Situacion, 1963 (The Situation)
A novel of two middle class families in Habana on the eve of the coup which
returned Batista to power in 1951; one family rising through its initiative in
currying favour with every passing dictatorship, the other falling through its
support of the ongoing struggles against oppression, foreign and domestic. Treats
with a wide range of sectors in Cuban society and with Cuban history during the
first fifty years of this century.

En Ciudad Semejante, 1970 (In a Similar City)
A panorama of the seven year struggle to overthrow the Batista dictatorship, with
an array of characters drawn from all classes, backgrounds, degrees of commitment
with by no means simple motives or personalities. That account is linked through
family histories with ninety years of Cuban revolutionary history, going back
almost continuously to 1868.

PERERA SOTA, Hilda

Mañana es 26, 1960 (Tomorrow is the 26th)
A novel of a young, middle class supporter of the July 26 movement in Habana
during the last two years of the Cuban revolution. An account of their non-
socialist but social consciousness which leads them to revolutionary sympathy and
the tensions between them and their parents, who have grown cynical about any
possibility of fundamental change and who are fearful of the unbridled terror
exercised by the Batista forces in the name of the middle class.

PIÑEIRO, Abelardo

El Descanso, 1962 (The Rest)
A novel in which the protagonists are almost exclusively members of the Cuban
proletariat; revolves around labour union activities and the use of police and
courts to suppress strikes during the Grau San Martin (1944-1948) and Prio
Socarras (1948-1951) governments. Hardly as horrendous as the revolutionary years
which would follow but underscoring the everyday oppression which the Cuban
workers (as distinct from middle class revolutionaries) have had to deal with in
even the supposedly democratic times. Realistic portrayal of the daily rounds of
working class life during the period.

RODRIGUEZ, Luis Felipe

Marcos Antilla, 1932 (Marcos Antilla)
"A novel of the cane fields", being a series of linked stories about the lives and
exploitation of rural workers, especially sugar cane workers, by Cuban and US
capitalists in the early 1920s.

Cienaga, 1937 (The Swamp)
A once very well known Cuban novel dealing with the plight of Cuban peasants and
cane workers during the mid to late 1920s. Woven around a period piece love and
murder story, "the swamp" is the morass of Cuban society and the processes of rot
which gradually effect all. Also see Como Opinaba Damian Parades, 1916 (In Damian
Parades Opinion), a novela along the above lines.

SARDUY, Severo

Gestos, 1963 (Gestures)
A slice of life account of the Havana underworld and tourist industry run by an
assortment of local and US gangsters during the Batista years; the business-state-
criminal alliances and a panorama of a freed Mafiaprise society then more evolved
in Cuba than elsewhere in the hemisphere.

SERPA, Enrique

La Trampa, 1956 (The Trap)
A novel of the struggle against the Machado dictatorship in the early thirties
during which some of the underground organizations fall into the trap of acting

like personal armies, dispensing their own injustice and developing their own infra-structure of corruption which will blossom when they do come to power.

SOLER PUIG, Jose

Bertillon 166, 1960 (Bertillon 166)
A documentary novel of the Fidelista underground in Santiago city during 1957-58; a collage of urban workers and middle class supporters, of old communists and young romantics, black and white, men, women and all the variety of individuals and motives involved. The title refers to the code word for a fallen comrade and the work captures something of the continuing struggle despite the fear and terror spread by the Masferrer and Batista forces. A believable account not distorted by tidied up hindsight.

El Año de Enero, 1963 (The Year of January)
A novel about Cuban factory workers during the last two years of the Batista dictatorship but mainly about the changes and confrontations in the first two years of revolutionary administration (1959-1960). Revolves around the steps taken to remove the union bosses and labour gangsterism which had become institutionalized among some sections of the labour movement under previous dictatorships. The challenges of social transformation trigger unexpected enthusiasms among some labour leaders and workers and counter revolution among others in a well written account of a little discussed aspect of socialist transformation in Cuba.

El Derrumbe, 1964 (The Collapse)
A novel which attempts to capture the comprador nature of the Cuban bourgeoisie during the 1940s and 1950s through interior monologues. Counterposed is a defense of the sometimes mistaken, partial but real advances made by the Cuban revolution during its initial years.

VITERI, Eugenia

A 90 Millas, Solamente, 1969 (Only 90 Miles)
A novel of a Cuban bourgeoise family which while unsympathetic to Batista fears socialism and goes into exile in Miami. In the land of the free it is unable to hold its own against the new gusano middle class and disintegrates. One son is inveigled into joining the CIA expedition and is killed in the Bay of Pigs invasion of Cuba, other family members find their own paths to degeneration in America. Only the youngest daughter breaks with her family and returns to Cuba to build a new life for herself in an emergent society.

WOODWARD, Miguel Cossio

Sacchario, 1970 (Sacchario)
Novel of one day in the life of a volunteer cane cutter during the 1965 harvest. Flashbacks outline the life of a middle aged, lower middle class man who only vaguely supported the Cuban revolution but who gradually has come to realize the necessity of putting the rampant individualism of the past behind him. The account attempts to capture the infectious and sometimes millenial feelings of solidarity generated during the early years of socialist construction in Cuba.

COLOMBIA

CABALLERO CALDERON, Eduardo

Siervo Sin Tierra, 1954 (Landless Serf)
Novela of a Colombian tenant farmer gulled by the church, plucked by the local caudillos, who sacrifices and saves all his adult life (1925-1950) and manages to buy a small plot of land just before he dies, which his wife has to sell back to a landlord in order to support the family. From tenant farmer to dead tenant farmer in one generation and the hopelessness which surrounds the Colombian peasantry.

GARCIA MARQUEZ, Gabriel

La Hojarasca, 1955 (Dead Leaves)
A novel set in the mythical Atlantic coast town of Macondo in 1928; it proceeds during one hour of a wake held for a local political boss. The interior monologues of the guests paint a picture of a stagnating, corrupt and violent Colombian pueblo between the end of the 1,000 Days civil war in 1903 to 1928. The initial organization of the regional banana workers union and its bloody suppression is a muted background.

La Mala Hora, 1962 (The Bad Hour)
A novel set in Macondo during the amorphous and extremely brutal civil war of the 1950s called "La Violencia". Wall posters circulated by one partizan sympathizer rake up the past and present crimes which have been committed by leading notables during the times of peace. The extraordinary violence of Colombian local conflicts, and the spate of vendettas released by the wall posters suggest that current Colombian society is unsalvageable and must be rebuilt root and branch.

Cien Años de Soledad, 1967 (One Hundred Years of Solitude, 1967)
Garcia Marquez' best known novel, it revolves around a surrealistic "history" of the mythical Atlantic coast town of Macondo over seven generations of boom and bust, brutality and civil wars, endemic corruption and degeneration. A despairing view of Colombian society which some readers may find more given to magical machinations than an account of Colombian peasants or workers. Garcia Marquez won the 1982 Nobel Prize for Literature and is today the most eminent of Latin American authors. All of his titles--many dealing with themes similar to Cien Anos--are available in English translation.

JARAMILLO ARANGO, Rafael

Barrancabermeja, 1934 (Barrancabermeja)
A novel dealing with the miserable working conditions, casualties and exploitation of workers in the Colombian oil fields of the 1930s--with one strike, one tragic love affair, a suicide and some nationalist drum beating thrown in.

MEJIA VALLEJO, Manuel

Al Pie de la Ciudad, 1952 (On the Outskirts of the City)
A semi-documentary account of the backgrounds and lives of "squatters" on the outskirts of Bogota whose houses are destroyed by a police raid. Touches on the responses of slum dwellers in other parts of the city and the callous disinterest of middle class observers who watch the scene of destruction from the overlooking houses.

El Dia Señalado, 1962 (The Appointed Day)
A documentary novel of the personal vendettas which pass for politics and internecine killings in a not unusual Colombian small town during "La Violencia" of the 1950s.

OSORIO LIZARAZO, Jose A.

La Cosecha, 1935 (The Crop)
A novel of the tenant farmers, small coffee growers and rural workers on the edge of despair and desperation, caught in the semi-"feudal" exploitation of peasantry by hacienda owners in depression ridden backlands of Colombia.

El Hombre Bajo la Tierra, 1944 (The Man Below the Earth)
A novel of peasant-miners in the pennyante gold mines and camps of southern Colombia. It touches on the courage and mutual aid between the miners but also the machismo, the subculture of personal violence and danger which helps sustain the horrendous working conditions unchallenged.

El Dia del Odio, 1952 (Day of Hate)
A documentary novel which deals with the urban misery, social decay and economic desperation which lead to the Bogatazo, the spontaneous uprising of the urban poor and working class of Bogota in 1948 (following the assassination of the Liberal populist leader Gaitan). The Conservative repression and the beginings of amorphous civil war which lasted most of the next decade.

El Pantano, 1954 (Quicksand)
Novel of the daily lives of members of the frayed white collar class and of urban workers living lives of trapped hopelessness in the decaying outskirts of Bogota.

SOTO APARICIO, Fernando

La Rebelion de las Ratas, 1962 (Rebellion of the Rats)
A novel of the incursion of a large mining company into a former peasant area and the destructive dislocations it creates. Told through a series of flashbacks by different members of one family whose lives are shattered during a series of confrontations with the mining company and its allies.

URIBE PIEDRAHITA, Cesar

Toa, 1933 (Toa, 1935)
A novel about a Colombian government inspector sent into the Amazonas region in early 1920s to investigate the treatment of Indian rubber gatherers. Suffused with period piece melodrama and assorted inner turmoils, the work nevertheless includes some powerful and detailed accounts of the semi slave-like conditions under which the Indian rubber tappers were held and worked. (An international scandal from the pre-W.W.I period, publicized by Roger Casement, which forced the Colombian government into a PR campaign.) The government inspector comes to realize that he is there just for show, that the conditions are well known to and of no concern to national authorities, who in fact are paid off by the rubber companies.

Mancha de Aciete, 1935 (Oil Slick)
A social protest novel about social and working conditions in the Colombian oil industry, with a nationalist expose of the sell out of national interests to US oil corporations.

ZAPATA OLIVELLA, Manuel

La Calle 10, 1960 (Tenth Street)
An account of the lives of people in an old working class neighbourhood of Bogota during and just after the 1948 rising. Deals with the backgrounds, daily lives and character of an established working class ranging back to the begining of the century. Touches on the anger at the suppression of democratic reform, the underlying caution but simmering rebelliousness. Captures the inherent rejection of ruling class politics and culture.

Cuentos de Muerte y Libertad, 1961 (Tales of Death and Liberty)
Collected short stories of Colombia during "La Violencia".

En Chima Nace Un Santo, 1964 (A Saint is Born in Chima)
A novel of religious fanaticism born from chaos and backwoods poverty. A crippled boy in a mountain village of violence-torn Colombia is proclaimed a miracle worker by desperate peasant followers; their millenial claims bring them into conflict with the regional political bosses whose concern is to crush any alternate source of power. The use of troops to suppress the peasant "prophets" are like a page from a Colombian Os Sertaos.

VENEZUELA

ARRAIZ, Antonio

Puros Hombres, 1938 (True Men)
A documentary novel of political prisoners in a Venezuelan jail during the
Conservative dictatorship of the 1930s; of their backgrounds and what brought
them into opposition.

DIAS SANCHEZ, Ramon

Mene, 1936 (Oil, 1938)
A novel dealing with the effects of the Venezuelan oil boom in a Caribbean coastal
village. A somewhat romantic vision of the bucolic rural past, degraded by the
incursion of the US oil companies which are presented as contemporary
Conquistadores, with all Latin American poor as the new "Indians", and the
Conservative Gomez dictatorship as the contemporary comprador chiefs.

GALLEGOS, Romulo

La Trepadora, 1925 (The Climber)
A novel of peasants and ranchers in the coffee hacienda regions in Venezuela during
the 1920s. By a once very influential "costumbrista" author.

Cantaclaro, 1931 (Cantaclaro, 1936)
A "novel" done in the form of folk ballads and tales sung by a wandering minstrel
in the eastern Llanos (the Sertao of Venezuela) during the 1920s (a region of
bandits, feuding cattle barons, serfs, inchoate violence and a society retaining
the fatal flaws of Latin American history in exaggerated form).

HIMIOB, Nelson

La Carretera, 1938 (The Highway)
A semi-autobiographical novel of student revolutionaries fighting the Vincente
Gomez dictatorship and its US allies in the 1930s as seen through the thoughts
and actions of the survivors imprisoned in La China prison. Said to be one of the
best prison novels of Latin America.

OTERO SILVA, Miguel

Casas Muertos, 1955 (Dead Houses)
A novel of a decaying semi-abandoned small town during the 1940s and told in a
series of flashbacks about the assorted national and local bosses who throughout
the past have only been concerned with enriching themselves, regardless of the
social stagnation this engenders everywhere in the country.

Oficina No. 1, 1961 (Office No. 1)
A novel which takes place in the final days of the Perez Jimenez dictatorship (a
US oil protege who was overthrown through a decade long guerrilla war) and the
advent of a democratic government. A cross section of the various national forces
and classes in play but focussed on the maneuvers and turnabouts by representatives
of the old middle and upper class and their rapid penetration of the new regime.

USLAR PIETRI, Arturo

Un Retrato de Geographia, 1962 (A Portrait of Geography), Estacion de Mascaras,
1964 (Season of Masquerade)
Two volumes of an epic novel about Venezuela in this century; Un Retrato being a
cross section of the country in 1935-36, an interlude between two US supported
Venezuelan dictatorships; Estacion is set in 1948 and the deepening repression of
working class by Jimenez regime.

ECUADOR

AGUILERA MALTA, Demetrio

Don Goyo, 1933 (Don Goyo)
A novel which combines surrealistic allegory and realism; set in an island village
of Negro fishermen near the port city of Quayaquil during the 1920s. It juxtaposes
the folk myths of Don Goyo (an old sage who epitomizes the nature of a passing
pre-capitalist community) and the responses of a young protagonist who is becoming
enmeshed in the working class world of Quayaquil (and who is in a sense the future
of the island fishermen). Suggests the promise of some of the new forces arising
but also the feeling of loss of an earlier and seemingly more "natural" world.

Canal Zone, 1935
A protest novel of the racist humiliations (as well as exploitation) of Negroes
and Mestizos in the Panama Canal Zone under the heel of American colonialism as
symbolic of the treatment of most Latin Americans by the US.

DIAZ YCAZA, Rafael

Los Rostros del Miedo, 1962 (The Faces of Fear)
Novel of poverty stricken government workers in Ecuador and of the objective and
psychological conditions which keep them powerless.

FERNANDEZ, Jorge

Agua, 1936 (Water)
A novel of the conflict between two mestizo peasant villages for irrigation water;
the divisions and feuding which keeps them both powerless and currying the favour
of regional cuadillos. Of the self-defeating stratagems of keeping just a notch
ahead of the poorest of the poor.

GALLEGOS, Geraldo

Salome de Santa Cruz, 1957 (Salome of Santa Cruz)
A documentary novel of the lives of Liberal party guerrillas in Chimborazo province
during the author's youth in the 1920s. Just as a reminder of the deep
pre-socialist traditions of guerrilla struggle in Latin America.

GALLEGOS LARA, Joaquin

Cruces Sobre el Agua, 1946 (Crosses on the Water)
Possibly the greatest of the Ecuadorean proletarian novels; it deals with the
events of November 15, 1922 in Quayaquil, where a general strike was crushed by
the army and the massacre of strikers which followed. The title refers to the
rafts with lighted candles which, in memorial services a generation later, are
placed on the river into which the bodies of the workers were thrown. A tapestry
of the left working class traditions in Ecuador, their continuation through periods
of struggle and of seeming forgetfulness.

GIL GILBERT, E., GALLEGOS LARA, J., AGUILERA MALTA, D. (eds.)

Los Que Se Van, 1930 (Those That Leave)
A collection of stories which were a "shocking" document of Ecuadorean social
reality and which launched social protest writing in that country.

GIL GILBERT, Enrique

Relatos de Emmanuel, 1939 (Tales of Emmanuel)
A novel of the decay and social conflict in the Amazonian frontier region, an area
which for fifty years was touted as the supposed land of opportunity for landless
peasants.

Nuestro Pan, 1942 (Our Bread)
A novel of a group of farmers who attempt to establish a cooperative rice farm in
coastal Ecuador. A detailed account of the day to day satisfactions and problems
involved, but mainly an account of the insuperable power of money lenders,
wholesalers and large landowners. The cooperative falls under the ownership of
a "modern" agribusiness hacendado, most of the farm families drift away, having
lost their land. The four original coop farmers are hired by the new corporate
owners to act as foremen over the migratory farm labour employed in working the
land.

ICAZA, Jorge

Barro de Sierra, 1933 (Clay of the Sierra)
Six stories dealing with different aspects of Ecuadorian social oppression of the
time, rural and urban, of Indian and non-Indian, and of the triumvirate of church,
state and capitalists working as fingers of the same hand. Also accounts of
left wing organizers attempting to mobilize people in economic self defense.

Huasipungo, 1934 (Huasipungo, 1946)
Possibly the best known of Latin American indigenista novels (which converted an
old theme into a proletarian form). Deals with an Indian community in Highland
Ecuador during the 1920s and early 1930s and their struggle to retain their lands
against the expansion of a foreign owned hacienda, the venal courts and the police
seizure of Indian lands which culminates in a bloody battle that destroys the
village and scatters the survivors who become migrant landless labourers, or
Huasipungo.

En Las Calles, 1935 (In the Streets)
A novel about a group of highland peasants forced from their lands when neighbouring
haciendas seize the water rights, their migration to Quito and the daily rounds of
discrimination, unemployment and struggle to survive, leading to individual and
then organized resistance. Also an account of the strategies of repression by the
Ecuadorean ruling class.

Cholos, 1938 (Cholos, 1948)
A novel of mestizo rural workers and foremen sandwiched between large landholders
and Indian peasant labourers; an account of the everyday life of the mestizo
workers and a didactic picture of the "racial" divisions which fetter the poor in
the Ecuadorian countryside.

Huairapamushkas, 1948 (Huairapamushkas, 1954)
A novel of the changing but continuing exploitation of the Highland Indian peasantry
under the emerging small town bourgeoisie who are supplanting the old hacendados
through new balance of political power and with gunmen when necessary.

Seis Veces la Muerte, 1953 (Six Times Death), **Viejos Cuentos**, 1960 (Old Stories)
Two collections of short stories which proclaim that the "old stories" of
exploitation, injustice, repression and smug hypocrisy continue in post W.W.II
Ecuador with only the rhetoric changed.

MATA ORDÓÑEZ, Humberto

Sumag Allpa, 1940
The first volume of the trilogy novel **Sol Amarrado** (Moored Sun); **Sumag Allpa** is
the account of an Ecuadorean Highland Indian who by his middle age has experienced
the roster of exploitation including seizure of Indian lands, debt peonage, forced
labour, and the incursions of priest, police and local politicos. Set mainly in
the 1920s and 1930s.

Sanaguin, 1942
Second volume of the trilogy, which follows the hero of **Sumag Allpa** into the
eastern frontier zone where he works on a sugar cane/alcohol producing
plantation on which the owners attempt to transpose the subjectation of the
Highland regions but are faced with a partly successful revolt by Indian and
mestizo workers led by a white Ecuadorian socialist who afterward goes off to
fight in the Spanish Civil War.

Sal, 1963 (Salt)
The last of the Sol Amarrado trilogy, deals with the now aging survivors of the
previous two volumes, their children and new characters and forces in the changing
process of Indian oppression and resistance in Ecuador during the post W.W.II
period.

NUÑEZ, Sergio

Arbol Que No Da Fruto, 1929 (The Barren Tree)
A novel of the corruption and chaos during the final years of the Moreno dictatorship in Ecuador and the proto-revolutionary resistance among urban workers and
guerrilla struggle in the mountains during 1922.

PAREJA DIEZ-CANSECO, Alfredo

El Muelle, 1933 (The Dock)
A novel of the Quayaquil working class and urban poor. Revolves around the life
of an unemployed seaman and his wife, their past experiences told in flashbacks.
The husband's previous involvement in waterfront unionization in New York leads
to his attempts to organize an Ecuadorean Seamen's Union, a strike evolves and
after its defeat the protagonist is blacklisted.

La Beldaca, 1935 (The Beldaca)
The life history of a tramp steamer and its crew sailing between the small ports
of the Ecuadorean coast; the lives and struggles of the dockworkers, fishermen
and waterside people it touches.

Baldomera, 1938 (Baldomera)
A novel dealing with the quasi-revolutionary strike of Quayaquil workers in
November 1922, of the oppression and poverty from which it grew and of the military
repression which crushed it. This defeat initiates the communist movement in
Ecuador. A powerful and well written account.

Hombres Sin Tiempo, 1941 (Men Without Time)
A semi-autobiographical prison novel; a collage of the "runaway" Indian peons,
con men, teachers, murderers, writers, labour organizers and political subversives
thrown together in a Quito prison during the late 1930s and attempting to survive.

Las Tres Ratas, 1944 (The Three Rats)
A historical novel of the revolutionary traditions of the Liberal Party of Ecuador
and its demise into just another group of office seekers by the 1930s.

La Advertencia, 1956 (The Warning)
The first volume of a trilogy dealing with the backgrounds and lives of activists
in the early socialist movement in Ecuador; from pre W.W.I to 1925.

El Aire y los Recuerdos, 1959 (Wind and Remembrance), Los Poderes Omnimodes, 1964
(All Embracing Powers)
The two volume sequel to La Advertencia, dealing with the resurgent reaction in
Ecuador during the 1930s and the demise of progressive attitudes among most of the
middle class. Carries the history of Ecuadorean working class and left movements
into the 1950s.

ROJAS, Angel

El Exodo de Yangana, 1949 (Exodus From Yangana)
A panorama of Ecuador in the 1940s as seen through the eyes of members of an Indian
community expelled from its lands and travelling through the countryside searching
for work and a place to settle.

SALVADOR, Humberto

Camarada, 1933 (Comrade)
A novel revolving around a working class heroine; it traces the panorama of the
exploitation of Ecuadorean workers but also raises their "self-imposed" repression
(in particular the case of women's oppression) and attacks the philistinism of
Ecuadorean society in general.

Los Trabajadores, 1935 (The Workers)
A proletarian novel which deals with the exploitation of Ecuadorean workers, provides some detailed accounts of attempts to organize unions and the tactics used by ruling class to split off sections of the working class.

Noviembre, 1939 (November)
A novel dealing with the mass repression of the left by the Paez military dictatorship in 1936; of the resurgent reaction and the social stagnation which followed.

BOLIVIA

ARGUEDAS, Alcides

Raza De Bronce, 1965 (original 1919) (Race of Bronze)
The first Bolivian Indigenista novel; set at the turn of the 20th century and relating the journey of a group of highland Indian peasants into the lowland towns to sell their produce and telling of their daily lives and many faceted exploitation as a caste in Bolivian society. An angry, protest work distorted by concepts of racial heredity and culture.

BARBERY, Oscar Justiniano

Zapata, 1963 (Zapata), El Hombre Que Soñaba, 1964 (The Man That Dreamed), El Roto, 1967 (The Broken)
Three novels dealing with the dissipation of opportunities and betrayal of the Bolivian revolution of 1952 which had destroyed the military power of the regime ancien. The succeeding dissention, lack of action and opportunism of "revolutionary" leaders and the following series of counter revolutionary coups and reaction triumphant during the 1960s. But also of the continuing dream of and struggles for social justice among the oppressed.

BARRIOS DE CHUNGARA, Domitila

Let Me Speak. Testimony of Domitila, a woman of the Bolivian mines, 1978
A personal political testimony of the lives of Bolivian working class (of "Indian" miners in particular) under the series of increasingly more fascist military regimes which controlled Bolivia from 1960 on. Told by a woman activist of an Indian miner's family. Also see June Nash, We Eat the Mines and the Mines Eat Us, 1979, an ethnographic account of Bolivian tin miners in the 1970s and their families, using extensive oral accounts and done from an American "neo left" perspective.

BOTELHO GOSALVEZ, Raul

Altiplano, 1945 (High Plain)
Novel of a village of Bolivian Indian peasants who are forced from their lands by repeated drought and who migrate in search of somewhere to re-establish themselves. Told in a documentary style, the conditions and fates they encounter--some going into the mines, others to work in the provincial capital, some becoming migrant agricultural labourers--are a microcosm of the experiences of dispossessed Indian peasants in Bolivia.

CESPEDES, Augusto

Sangre de Mestizos, 1936 (Mestizo Blood)
Nine reportage stories about the Bolivia-Paraguay Chaco war of 1932-35. The needless sufferings of the conscripted Indian soldiers and the stupidity of that war which is described as flowing mainly from the investment interests of the Patino family and allied capitalists.

Metal del Diablo, 1946 (Devil's Metal)
A reportage novel about the Bolivian tin mines from the late 19th century on but mainly of the horrendous living and working conditions in the mining towns during

the 1930s and 1940s. Contrasted to the Roman luxury in which members of the Patino family live as well as the servility of the national government and the Bolivian middle class. Woven around the travails of a number of miners' families to wrest a living from the present and justice in the future.

Also El Dictador Suicida, 1956 (The Dictator Commits Suicide) and El Presidente Colgado, 1966 (The President Left Hanginging), two novels.

JAMES, Daniel (ed.)

The Complete Bolivian Diaries of Che Guevara, 1968
Mainly   the dairy of Guevara during his attempt to establish a guerrilla force in lowland Bolivia, the split with local left leaders and the ultimate destruction of the band. Also contains accounts by some of the survivors and an introductory overview of developments there in 1967.

LARA, Jesus

Repete, 1937 (Repeat)
An anti-militarist novel of the Chaco war of 1932-35 told partly by a journalist and partly through the diary of a dead Quechua conscript. It reviles the officially promulgated patriotism, the pointless deaths and suffering which epitomizes the corrupt nature of Bolivian society.

Surumi, 1943
A novel by a widely translated, Quechua socialist realist writer. Set in Cochabamba province (the primary agricultural zone in the country) and dealing with the oppression and resistance of Quechua peasants against the continuing internal colonialism and "semi-feudal" conditions of the regime ancien of the 1930s. This and all following titles in Quechua are volumes whose texts are actually in Spanish translation.

Yanakuna, 1952
A Quechua novel dealing with the anger and revolt simmering just under the surface of the seemingly unchanging Indian-landlord relations in Bolivia on the eve of the 1952 revolution; land seizures, strikes, driving out of comprador Indian caciques and notables.

Yawarnichij, 1959 (Our Blood)
Possibly Lara's best known novel; describes Quechua peasant communities and haciendas in the highlands after the militarily successful 1952 revolution. The slow and very partial changes which filter into the countryside despite the massive support for land reform and the work of teachers, communists and Quechua miners in forging a militant peasant movement. Ends with the organization of underground cells to continue the struggle when land reform and the social revolution is quashed by the new national middle class. Interwoven are accounts of the centuries long struggle of Quechua peasants against their exploiters.

Sinchikay, 1962
A novel of the attempts of Quechua peasant movement to establish cooperative and collective farm communities in the face of a "land reform" which is geared to foster commercial capitalist farming.

Llalliy Pacha: Tiempo de Vencer, 1965 (Time to Win), Nancahuazu: Sueños, 1969 (Dreams)
Two novels dealing with the attempts by Quechua peasants, miners and workers to continue the 1952 social revolution through their own organizations during the deepening reaction and betrayal of the mid 1950s to early 1960s.

Sujnapura, 1971
A "historical" novel in two volumes (being El Solar y la Gelba and La Derrama) which treat with the effects of the Chaco war on the mainly Indian peasant conscripts, the broader worlds and new ideas they encounter and the initial appreciation of their own power.

Also La Literatura de los Quechuas, 1961 (Literature of the Quechuas), a literary history of modern Quechua writing.

LORA, Guillermo

A History of the Bolivian Labour Movement, 1977
A social and political history of the Bolivian labour movement (an unusually
militant and powerful force in such an underdeveloped country). It is built
around extensive personal biographies of its leaders, rank and file activists and
members over the past fifty years. Labour history with a human face; an acerbic
account by an old Bolivian Trotskyite union leader.

MENDOZA, Jaime

En Las Tierras del Potosi, 1911 (In the Lands of Potosi)
One of the earliest protest novels from Bolivia; dealing with the lives, work and
oppression of Indian workers in the gold mines of Potosi during the first decade
of this century, with allusions to a 300 year history of Indian miners there.

PRADA OROPEZA, Renato

Los Fundadores de Alba, 1969 (Founders of Dawn)
Novel of the life and death of a young seminarian who is appalled by the misery
and hypocrisy he finds in his country and who joins up with a Guevara-like
guerrilla movement. Told through the reminiscences of an Indian peasant who met
him during various stages of his life.

RAMIREZ VELARDE, Fernando

Socavones de Angustia, 1947 (Caverns of Anguish)
A collective novel of Indian peasants striving for a better life, the hopelessness
of their small farmlets and their drift into the mines as wage labour, only to
find that life there is as bad as what they have left behind. Despite all, an
ardent and continuing current of hope for justice remains.

SUAREZ, Gaston

Vigilia Para el Ultimo Viaje, 1962 (Vigil for the Last Journey), El Gesto, 1969
(The Gesture)
Two collective novels about the lives of the urban, non-Indian, working class, of
impoverished sectors of the lower middle class and of other urban poor staggering
under the backwardness imposed by seemingly unshakable military regimes and
gangster businessmen.

PERU

AGUILAR DERPICH, Juan

Oficio? Guerrillero, 1970 (Occupation? Guerrilla)
A novel of a Lima communist organizer captured during the suppression of peasant
guerrillas in the Huancayo region during the mid 1960s; flashbacks to the lives
of Lima slum dwellers and of rural misery which have impelled the protagonist to
enter revolutionary struggle.

ALEGRIA, Ciro

El Mundo es Ancho y Ajena, 1941 (Broad and Alien Is the World, 1951)
One of the best known Indigenista novels of Peru, dealing with the "traditional"
Highland Indian village in mid 1930s whose lands are seized by a neighbouring
hacienda; the initial disbelief and then growing resistance of Indian villagers
against hacendado and his allies in local and national governments. Ends in an
army attack which destroys the village and scatters the survivors to prisons,
forced labour camps or dispersed as migrant workers through the region.

Los Perros Hambrientos, 1938 (The Hungry Dogs)
Novel, a thematic sequel to Broad and Alien, portraying the lives of dispossessed
Indian migrant workers on the coastal plantations and cities during the 1930s.
Treats as well with the comparable lives of mestizo workers there.

ARGUEDAS, Jose Maria

Yawar Fiesta, 1940 (Yawar Fiesta, 1948)
A collection of stories allegedly about Peruvian Highland Indians and their culture
as evidenced in an annual Indian fiesta in 1930s. Alludes to the conjunction of
church, state and all non-Indians in exploiting Indians. The patient if simmering
retention of Indian cultural values from "time immemorial". Highly regarded among
romantics, it embodies many of the themes of "Indianist" writing both in South
and North America. Suffused with racial mysticism, the antithesis of any class
outlook and without the slightest comprehension of comparable histories of working
class-peasant experience or of cooperation and solidarity between Indians and
non-Indians.

Los Rios Profundos, 1958 (Deep Rivers)
An autobiographical novel of growing up in a Quechua highland community as the
orphaned son of a large landowner; learning the face and nature of the caste-
organized colonial society which was Highland Peru in early 1920s.

Todas Las Sangres, 1964 (All Bloods)
Another Indigenista novel set in the late 1940s and 1950s dealing with the
incursion of foreign capital and the "rationalization" of highland haciendas by
corporate technocrats who set about displacing both traditional hacendados and
ousting Indian peasants and labourers by mortgages and machinery.

CONGRAINS MARTIN, Enrique

No Una, Sino Muchas Muertes, 1958 (Not One But Many Deaths)
A slice of life portrait which treats with the humanity of those living in the
barriadas and shanty towns around Lima, but the corrosive social and personal
effects of slum life, which destroys people if not in the first then in the
second generation.

Lima, Hora Cero, 1954 (Lima, Zero Hour)
Collection of short stories on life in the Lima slums and shanty towns.

FALCON, Cesar

Pueblos Sin Dios, 1928 (People Without God)
A sardonic portrait using cinematic techniques of the small mindedness, petty
jealousies and grasping greed of small town merchant-capitalists in Peru of that
period, as being both caused by and a cause of the continuing backwardness and
stagnation of those regions.

El Buen Vecino Sanabria U., 1947 (Sanabria the Good Neighbour)
A bitter farce about a Peruvian comprador president (Manuel Prado) as the darling
of the Grace Line and other US plantation and mining corporations during the
1940s. The title being a play on the "Good Neighbour Policy" of the Roosevelt
era and its deepening penetration of Latin American economies.

Por La Ruta Sin Horizonte, 1961 (The Endless Route)
A novel of the Spanish Civil War, focussing on what that struggle meant to Latin
Americans, epitomizing as it did a century of similar struggles between progressive
and reactionary forces almost everywhere in Latin America.

HUANAY, Julian

El Retoño, 1950 (The Sprout)
A gentle and luminous novela about a 12 year old Peruvian boy from a poor highland
village who decides he must see Lima and runs away. His migration brings him into
contact with a cross section of the Peruvian working and peasant classes. As a
kind of modern day Lazarillo, he encounters tragedies, ignorance, poverty but also
a great deal of kindness among the people--a collage of births, deaths, misfortunes
and hope.

NEIRA, Pablo (Hugo Neyra)

Tierra y Muerte en Cuzco, 1963 (Land and Death in Cuzco)
A reportage account of Peruvian Indian communities engaged in seizing vacant
hacienda lands in the Cuzco region during the early 1960s; touches on the 40 year
history of such struggles which have often involved supportive action by urban,
non-Indian working class organizations.

NEIRA SAMANEZ, Hugo (ed.)

Huillca: Habla Un Campesino Peruano, 1974 (Huillca: A Peruvian Peasant Speaks)
An outstanding oral/life history of a Peruvian Quechua peasant leader, interviewed
in and translated from Quechua. It documents not only his own life but almost
eighty years of struggle by the Indian peasantry of the region--independently,
in alliances with non-Indians and against a variety of situations and forces. All
this is interwoven with accounts of everyday life.

REYNA, Ernesto

El Amauta Atusparia, 1930
A novel serialized in Jose Carlos Mariatequi's journal Amauta; deals with the
Indian peasant uprising in Huaraz of 1925 with flashbacks to an earlier rising
there in 1885. Told as a series of reminiscences which underscore the continuing
exploitation and resistance of Indian peasants and the repression of non-Indian
forces which have attempted to support them.

REYNOSO, Oswaldo

En Octubre No Hay Milagros, 1965 (There Are No Miracles in October)
A novel covering the lives of two families in Lima during one day. Revolves around
the eviction of a working class family juxtaposed to the failed aspirations and
reduced lives of a middle class family as seen through the eyes of an alienated
young college student.

RIOS, Edmundo de los

Los Juegos Verdaderos, 1968 (The True Games)
A novel dealing with the reminiscences and hallucinations of an aged Peruvian
communist organizer dying in prison, his despair and his attempt to make some sense

of his life. Counterposed is a young revolutionary who briefly shares the same
cell, who has been moved by similar reasons and emotions but who, without the long
experience of repression, is disdainful of the other man's despair. Yet through
this the old communist recognizes both himself a generation earlier and also the
continuation of the struggle which has been his life.

SCORZA, Manuel

Rodoble Por Rancas, 1970 (Drums for Rancas, 1977)
A proletarian novel of the web of local, national and international forces arrayed
in the exploitation of Indian peasants and miners in the Cerro de Pasco region of
Highland Peru in the late 1960s, with considerable detail on day to day lives
of peasant/workers and the mechanisms of repression on the local level.

El Jinete Insomne, 1977 (The Sleepless Horseman), Cantar de Agapito Robles, 1977
(To Sing of Agapito Robles)
Two novels which continue the story begun in Drums for Rancas, in which the focus
gradually shifts from the world of Indian villages to the region as a whole during
the waves of land seizures, strikes and armed insurgency, with the accounts taking
on a semi-mythical and ballad-like quality.

La Tumba de Relampago, 1978 (The Tomb of Lightening)
The final volume of the novel tetrology dealing with the Indian peasant struggles
of 1960s which verge on being revolutionary and are finally crushed with military
might. It returns to more realistic and detailed accounts of the complex of events.
Scorza himself was engaged in this peasant mobilization and a leader of the
"Frente Obrero, Campesino Estudantil y Popular". La Tumba may be the finest
volume of this cycle.

VALLEJO, Cesar

El Tungsteno, 1931 (Tungsten)
One of the great   socialist realist novels of Latin America by Peru's leading poet
of the time. An account of the entry and expansion of a large US mining
corporation in the Huanuco region of Peru shortly after W.W.I and its rapid
destruction of traditional society there, both for good and for bad. (There is
little of the usual romanticism about traditional Indian peasant communities here.)
With the incorporation of Indian peasants as miners the outlook and the dialogue
becomes increasingly more proletarian. The novel then shifts to an Indian miner
and labour organizer with a generation of working class experience, his distrust
of traditional church and state "mediators" and also of then current middle class
"Indigenista" intellectuals hovering around to "protect" the Indians. The story
culminates in a strike bloodily suppressed by the National Police who are more or
less at the beck and call of the US mining corporation, but the forces in
contention are more complex and contradictory than in similar strike novels.
Tungsten, of course, is the element added to iron magma to make steel alloys.

Paco Yunque, 1951 (Paco Yunque)
A posthumous novela about an Indian boy growing up in a mixed mestizo-Indian
community during the 1930s, the deadening indignities he faces and the triumph of
retaining one's humanity and vitality under such conditions.

Cesar Vallejo: The Complete Posthumous Poetry, 1978
A beautifully produced collection of Vallejo's last poems, done during the period
of the Spanish Civil War and referring to that confrontation as also embodying
the century-old Latin American struggles for human liberation. Texts in Spanish
and English.

VARGAS LLOSA, Mario

La Ciudad de los Perros, 1958 (Time of the Hero), Casa Verde, 1964 (Green House
or Green Mansion), Conversacion en la Catedral, 1969 (Conversation in the
Cathedral), Captain Pantoja and the Special Service, 1975
Four novels by reputedly one of contemporary Latin America's leading authors.
His "magical surrealism" is said (by literary specialists) to evoke universal
themes in Peruvian contexts. Those interested can go find their own reviews
of these tomes.

CHILE

ALEGRIA, Fernando

The Chilean Spring, 1978
A novel about the multifoliate streams leading to the first socialist government in Chile in 1970, the problems and limits of the Allende regime, but of the upsurge of creative powers among broad sectors of the population. Of the increasing internal and external sabotage and the coup which installs a bloody military autocracy, crushing the lives and hope which had so recently emerged.

CASTRO, Baltasar

Un Hombre por el Camino, 1950 (A Man by the Road), Mi Camarada Padre, 1958 (My Comrade Father)
Two social realist novels about the lives of working people in the copper mines of the Rancagua region from W.W.I to the 1950s; their day to day lives and visionary hopes, their individuality and ongoing struggles passed from generation to generation.

CASTRO, Oscar

Huellas en la Tierra, 1940 (Tracks in the Earth)
A series of sketches about the social conditions of rural poor in the Chilean countryside at the end of the 1930s.

Llampo de Sangre, 1950
A novel of a Chilean copper mining region in which the El Encanto mine itself is one of the main protagonists. The sorrows, joys, work and lives of those who pass into and are moulded by the world of the mine.

COLOANE, Francisco

Cabo de Hornos, 1941 (Cabo de Hornos)
A collection of adventure cum social realist stories of seamen, fishermen and other marine workers from the southern most coasts of Chile.

Tierra del Fuego, 1956 (Tierra del Fuego)
A popular quasi-history of the Tierra del Fuego frontier region of Chile, its geography and peoples--a cross section of their lives, work and backgrounds during the first forty years of this century.

DELANO, Luis Enrique

El Viento del Rencor, 1961 (The Wind of Rancor)
A historical novel of the Conservative-Liberal civil war in turn of the century Chile which ushered in the forces in contention of modern era.

El Rumor de la Batalla, 1964 (Murmur of Battle)
Novel about shock waves sent through Chile by the Spanish Civil War, the divisions into right and left and especially of the traditions of Chilean left resurrected.

DRAGO, Gonzalo

Cobre, 1941 (Copper)
A collection of short stories about the lives of Chilean copper miners during the 1930s.

El Purgatorio, 1951 (Purgatory)
A bitter attack on the Chilean military (prophetic as it turned out), dealing with the dehumanizing procedure used by the military to imbue the conscripts with blind obedience and right wing ideology.

EDWARDS BELLO, Joaquin

El Monstruo, 1912 (The Monster)
A lyrical account of Santiago during its then rapid urbanization and industrialization and of the growth of formless sprawling slums.

La Cuna de Esmeraldo, 1918 (Esmeraldo's Cradle), El Roto, 1920 (The Broken One)
Two novels revolving around the youth and young manhood of a member of the
Santiago lumpen proletariat during W.W.I. Set around a brothel in a rapidly
changing slum area, it details the alloyed callousness and concern, potential
decency but evolving petty criminality of the main character whose various half
hearted attempts to break out of that life are always defeated and who is drawn
back to that life in that it provides whatever warmth he ever experienced.

Valparaiso, La Ciudad de Viento, 1931 (Valparaiso, City of Wind, 1934)
A reportage account of Chile's major port-metropolis, the domain of foreign and
national corporations, with its bourgeoise battening on the labour of workers
both in the city and in the mines, countryside and towns of the region.

En El Viejo Almendral, 1946 (In the Old Almond Grove)
A reminiscence of the social changes and conflicts, the advances and setbacks in
Chilean society as seen through the reminiscences and reflections of the author.

GUZMAN, Nicomedes

Los Hombres Oscuros, 1938 (Dark Men)
An epic novel about the components of the Santiago working class during the 1930s.
Of ex-white collar employees, former artizans and old urban working class, of
former peasants and the new urban workers; their daily lives from youth to old
age, the strategies for daily existence and memories of the working class struggles
which have continued over the previous two generations. Threaded around the
thoughts and actions of a young Marxist labour organizer and his wife.

La Sangre y la Esperanza, 1944 (Blood and Hope)
A sensitive and lyrical novel set in the Mapocho working class district of
Santiago, the daily lives and work and tradition of labour struggles. Focuses on
the personal costs of opposing the Chilean ruling class and the ways in which
people try to stave off despair. Of their hopes/beliefs that the struggle will yet
come to fruition. Seen through the eyes of and narrated by an adolescent boy, son
of a militant street car driver.

Donde Nace el Alba, 1945 (Where Dawn is Born)
A novel with a similar setting and theme as Los Hombres Oscuros but focused more
on the oppressive poverty and more pessimistic as to eventual victory.

La Luz Viene del Mar, 1951 (The Light Comes From the Sea)
A lyrical and realistic novel of life in the nitrate mining region of Iquique of
northern Chile during the 1920s, a locale of proto-revolutionary class confrontations during the first decade of this century.

El Pan Bajo la Bota, 1960 (Bread Under the Boot)
An autobiographical account of Guzman's youth as a worker in Iquique and elsewhere
in Chile during the 1920s and 1930s.

LOMBOY, Reinaldo

Ranquil, 1942 (Ranquil)
A novel set in the first decade of this century when a compliant Chilean government
freed the enterprise of large land owners who then expropriated or otherwise
seized the homesteads of many small farmers, and of the inchoate local risings
which followed.

Ventarron, 1945 (Gust of Wind)
A portrait of the lives of fishermen, miners and other resource workers in the
central coast and mountain region of Chile from the 1920s to 1940s.

MARIN, Juan

Paralelo 53 Sur, 1936 (Parallel 53, South)
A novel of the lives of native Indians and native Chileans in southern most Chile,
their struggles against the elements and against the incursions of corporate
capitalism, from vast sheep haciendas to massive resource extraction companies
which push the original (native and white) inhabitants aside. Culminates in a
frontier working class revolt during W.W.I and early 1920s.

Viento Negro, 1944 (Black Wind)
Novel of conditions in a south Chilean port and coal mining town during the early
1930s; the confrontations between local fascist and communist supporters and the
evolution of a strike by local stevedores against an English coal company into a
citywide general strike, with the eventual entry of the Chilean navy to suppress
it.

NERUDA, Pablo

Selected Poems of Pablo Neruda, 1970 (N. Tarn, ed.)
A massive collection and translation of some of Neruda's most powerful and best
known works--includes part of the Residencia en la Tierra cycle and others written
after 1947.

Residence on Earth/Residencia en la Tierra, 1973 (Don Walsh, ed.)
A collection and translation of a cycle of poems written between 1925 and 1947,
dealing with the popular struggles against repression, colonial and class
oppression in Chile, Latin America and during the Spanish civil war but with
universal applications. By a Nobel Prize winner and one of the greatest left
poets of his lifetime. Texts in Spanish and English and published in memorium to
Neruda's death during the first days of Chilean fascism in September 1973.

SEPULVEDA LEYTON, Carlos

Ahijuna, 1934 (Budding), La Fabrica, 1935 (The Factory), Camarada, 1938 (Comrade)
A trilogy novel; Ahijuna is set in the Matadero district of Santiago and tells of
a youth growing up in a poor working class neighbourhood during the W.W.I period.
La Fabrica is based on Sepulveda's experiences as a teacher in the repressive
Chilean school system of the 1920s, while Camrada deals with a ruthlessly
suppressed teachers' strike in 1930. Although the trilogy revolves around one
protagonist between 1905 and 1930, it is peopled with an array of characters from
all classes in Chilean society of that period. The defeats of the 1920s are
portrayed through the rising hope of later generation that Chilean society can yet
be restructured.

TANGOL, Nicasio

Carbon y Orquideas, 1950 (Coal and Orchids)
A novel about life in the Chilean coal mine camps during the 1930s; a
mixture of lyricism and unmagical realism.

TEITELBOIM, Volodia

Hijo del Salitre, 1952 (Child of the Nitrate)
A novel set amid the nitrate fields of northern Chile and revolving around the
biography of one Elias Lafferte, a regional communist union leader. It deals with
the history, environment and everyday life of flesh and blood working people there.
Includes reminiscences of the Iquique massacre of striking nitrate workers in the
first decade of this century, one of the most horrendous cases of repression in
Chile before the crimes of the present fascist regime. A novelized slice of
Chilean labour and social history.

La Semilla en la Arena, 1957 (The Seed in the Sand)
A sequel to Hijo del Salitre, carrying the lives of a group of working people from
northern Chile forward from W.W.I to W.W.II, through changes, advances and setbacks
but with the continuing struggles of labour as central.

ARGENTINA

ARDILES GRAY, Julio

El Innocente, 1964 (The Innocent)
A novel about migrant farm workers and social unrest in Tucuman province (the plantation zone of northern Argentina) during the 1930s. Focused on the destruction of a boy whose decency and candor are fatal flaws in a frontier capitalist society.

ARRILI, Bernardo

Los Charcos Rojos, 1927 (Red Puddles)
A documentary account of the conflicts between the nascent labour movement and Argentinian capitalists during Arrili's youth, dealing particularly with conditions in the burgeoning meat packing plants around Buenos Aires in the pre W.W.I period. A sort of Argentinian The Jungle.

Mangana (Lariat), Pobres Habra Siempre (There Will Always be the Poor), Protasio Lucero, La Invasion de los Herejes (Invasion of the Heretics), 1927-1942
Documentary novels dealing with the lives of workers, strikes and ideological/ cultural conflicts between protagonists of the Conservatives and Liberals in Argentina from W.W.I to the eve of the Peron period.

BARLETTA, Leonidas

Royal Circo, 1956 (Circus Royal)
A novel about frayed white collar class families in Buenos Aires, their interminable caution, compassion and human potential so thwarted by absurd existences in a stagnating Argentinian society of the 1940s.

De Espaldas a la Luna, 1964 (Back of the Moon)
A more bitter novel of "humble" clerical workers in Buenos Aires between 1916 and 1930, the proto-revolutionary conditions and promise during W.W.I in Buenos Aires and the slide into conservative reaction.

CARNELLI, Maria Luisa

Quiero Trabajo!, 1933 (I Want a Job!)
A montage of newspaper reports, interior monologues, dialogue, scenes protraying the desperation of the working class in depression struck Buenos Aires. Focused on working class women looking for work. Adapted as a Workers' Theatre play.

CASTELNUOVO, Elias

Entre los Muertos, 1925 (Among the Dead), Calvario, 1929 (Calvary), Larvas, 1931 (Larva)
Three collections of stories dealing with the extremes of social decay among the urban poor in Argentina of 1920s; juvenile criminals, pervasive police and social corruption and accounts of a dog-eat-dog world. Verges on "tremendismo".

GALVEZ, Manuel

Nacha Regules, 1919
An influential documentary about the brutality of life in the officially sanctioned brothel districts of Buenos Aires; the strata of thugs, recruiters and bureaucrats allied in this enterprise and the social conditions which bring women into prostitution. Galvez was a prolific "muck-raking" journalist of the period.

GOYANARTE, Juan

La Semilla Que Trae el Viento, 1940 (The Seed Carried by the Wind), La Semilla en la Tierra, 1940 (The Seed in the Earth)
A two volume novel about the wave of Polish immigrants who arrived in Argentina

during the W.W.I period, their varied adjustments to that society over a generation.
An epic account of the emigration which changed Argentina in the first quarter of
the century.

Lago Argentino, 1946 (Lago Argentino, 1964)
A massive novel of frontier settlement and capitalist consolidation in Patagonia
during the first decades of this century. An immigrant entrepreneur goes to
Patagonia to make his fortune, allies himself with and uses assorted immigrant
settlers, workers and Indians whose communities have already been shattered, rises
to local prominence as a hacienda owner until he himself is cut down to size by
resentful members of native-born Argentinian capitalists.

La Quemazon, 1953 (The Conflagration)
A novel dealing with small town politics, labour struggles and strikes in central
Argentina, a region of huge export farms, during the Peron era.

Fin de Semana, 1955 (Weekend)
A satire of a small town speculator who rises to become the owner and doyen of the
local Golf and Country Club set--a Babbit with teeth--and of those types who demure
to him. Set in mid 1950s.

GUIDO, Beatriz

El Incendio y la Visperas, 1964 (End of Day, 1968)
A novel of the impotence of members of the traditional upper classes (with their
caste traditions and alliances) against Peronism. The gradual disintegration of one
such family during the early 1950s under the challenges of a newly emerging middle
class which is even more ruthless than the old rulers.

MANAUTA, Juan Jose

Los Aventados, 1952 (Winnowers), Las Tierras Blancas, 1957 (White Lands), Papa Jose,
1958 (Papa Jose)
Three novels by a militant socialist author; they combine lyrical descriptions of
life and conditions in Entre Rios province, counterpointed with a powerful
defense of the regional peasantry victimized by a variety of political and economic
forces even before the triumph of Argentinian fascism.

Cuentos Para La Dueña Dolorida, 1961 (Stories of the Doleful Mistress)
Collected short stories.

MARTINEZ ESTRADA, Ezequiel

Radiografia de la Pampa, 1933 (X-ray of the Pampas)
An influential reportage history of the incursion of corporate capitalism into the
Pampas; flagrant land thefts, exploitation and police repression of peasantry,
Indians, guachos (cowboy ranchhands) and other workers in the Pampas during the
first thirty years of this century.

MIGUEL, Maria Ester de

Puebloamerica, 1974 (Puebloamerica)
A novel about a Marxist guerrilla group operating in a small town of rural
Argentina in the early 1970s, their backgrounds, hopes, miscalculated strength and
the initial gains they make among some of the population, but also their
complete   destruction when the Argentinian army concentrates against them.

RIVERA, Andres

El Precio, 1957 (The Price), Los Que No Mueran, 1959 (Those That Do Not Die)
Two novels of the lives of Buenos Aires workers in the 1950s; dealing with the
thoroughly corrupt leadership which had taken over the Peronist labour movement,
the suppression or isolation of militant workers who had earlier allied themselves
with the Peronists and of the rampant opportunism and self-seeking of the new
middle class bosses in Argentina.

RODRIGUEZ, Alberto

Donde Haya Dios, 1955 (Where There Is God)
A novel about the systematic destruction of one of the last remaining Indian communities in Mendoza province during the first decade of this century. The Huarpes' farms and villages are made untenable by the diversion of irrigation waters to the spreading Argentinian corporate farms which are able to seize land and water through judicial indifference and official conspiracy.

TIMERMAN, Jacobo

Prisoner Without a Name, Cell Without a Number, 1980
A horrendous but controlled   account of the author's own imprisonment and torture by the Argentina fascists in 1979, and of his fellow surviving prisoners. Timerman was a major left liberal publisher in Argentina, who then left for Israel where his shock is recorded in another book.

URONDO, Francisco

Los Pasos Previos, 1974 (The Previous Steps)
A documentary novel revolving around the initial steps of partizan struggle in Argentina. Begins with the abduction and assassination of a militant labour leader in 1962 by the police and the gradual evolution of groups which feel that armed resistance is the only possible way of toppling the military/ruling class regimes. A detailed account of the specific actions, beliefs and trajectory of a limited number of protagonists in the 1960s to 1973 and their initial successes. Said to be one of the best of this genre. Urondo himself was a member of the Montonero underground and fell in a battle with police in 1978.

VIÑAS, David

Cayo Sobre Su Rostro, 1955 (He Fell On His Face)
A novel about a particularly ruthless army colonel who earns his reputation and initial fortune in the Indian wars and massacres during Argentinian expansion into Patagonia of the late 1870s/1880s. As seen from thirty years later when he has become an esteemed, and totally debauched, elder statesman of the Conservative government in Buenos Aires, pontificating on patriotism, freedom and enterprise.

Los Dueños de la Tierra, 1958 (Owners of the Earth)
The epic novel of Patagonia and the Pampas, being a panorama ranging over three generations. From the seizure of Indian lands and their conversion into huge sheep and cattle ranches in the 1870s but mainly of the struggles of small farmers, guachos and organizations of rural workers against the changing amalgam of landlords and robber barons, and finally of regional workers as part of a nation wide, militant labour movement against corporate capitalism and its state arm. Set in the years 1892, 1917 and 1920, from the repression of Indians to the repression of rural workers.

En La Semana Tragica, 1966 (In the Tragic Week)
A short novel of one week in January 1919, Buenos Aires. Of the General Strike led by anarcho-syndicalists which was the culmination of a generation of agitation and education. The conflict threw the Argentine middle and upper classes into the arms of the reactionaries who smashed the working class organizations with military might and set the clock back for the next twenty years.

Dar La Cara, 1962 (Risk Your Neck)
A novel of Buenos Aires youths and the gathering dusk between the end of the Peron epoch and the fascist regimes which were to follow.

Los Hombres de a Caballo, 1968 (The Horsemen, 1970)
A novel of an Argentinian army unit sent to Peru in the early 1960s to help suppress guerrillas there and as a training mission to combat potential risings in Argentina. Treats with the reflections and interior monologue of a young officer pondering the conversion of the Argentine army from its 19th century self image as "liberators" to being a purely repressive, anti-popular tool of national reaction and foreign exploiters.

URUGUAY

BENEDETTI, Mario

Montevideaños, 1959 (People of Montevideo)
A collage portrait of Montevidean people and their lives, focused mainly on the lower middle class during the late 1950s.

Esta Mañana y Otros Cuentos, 1967 (This Morning and Other Stories)
A collection of short stories about Montevidean life in the 1960s, with a brooding malaise hovering over the misplaced faith of Uruguayan democracy and moderation. The decade before the triumph of fascism.

El Cumpleaños de Juan Angel, 1971 (Juan Angel's Birthdays)
A novela (in free verse) about the life of a young Tupamaro guerrilla in Montevideo, told in flashbacks.

GRANVINA, Alfredo Dante

Fronteras Al Viento, 1951 (Borders of the Wind), El Unico Camino, 1958 (The Only Road), Del Miedo al Orgullo, 1959 (From Fear to Pride)
Three short novels set in a variety of Uruguayan locales during the 1940s and 1950s, all mainly revolving around the stagnation of economy and society and the deceptive Uruguayan self-image of being a Latin American welfare state. A Marxist treatment which prophetically foreshadows the political and class conflicts which were to lead to a ruthless military dictatorship.

Seis Pares de Zapatos, 1964 (Six Pairs of Shoes), Tiempos Arriba, 1965 (High Times)
Two collections of biting and wistful short stories which counterpose the underlying poverty of large sections of Uruguayan population with the dolce vita of the upper middle classes during the early 1960s.

GUTIERREZ, Carlos Mario

Diario de Cuartel, 1971 (Prison Diary)
A collection of poems and sketches smuggled out of prison; experiences and reflections of an Uruguayan journalist and supporter of Tupamaro guerrillas.

PORTA, Eliseo Salvador

Intemperie, 1963 (Intemperate Weather)
A historical novel about the 19th century Uruguayan "liberator" Artigas, a "Marxist" account of the past struggles of national liberation from assorted neo-colonial forces, suggesting that these struggles still continue today in changed form.
Also Con la Raiz al Sol, 1953 (With Roots to the Sun) and Ruta 3, 1956 (Route 3), two collage accounts of Uruguayan life in the countryside and Montevideo in 1950s, intermixing the previous half century of history.

VIANA, Javier de

Yuyos, 1912 (Yuyos), Leña Seca, 1913 (Dry Firewood)
Two collections of naturalistic stories about guachos and ranch workers (the stuff of Uruguayan folk legend) who by then had been reduced to a rural proletariat or sometime bandits wracked by poverty, illness, booze and powerlessness. A somewhat wistful populist account told from experience.

ZAVALA MUNIZ, Justino

La Revolucion de Enero: Apuntes para una Cronica, 1935 (The Revolution of January: Notes for a History)
A chronicle of the civil war between the Colorados (Liberals) and Blancos (Conservatives) in turn of the century Uruguay described as a proto-class struggle

by an old populist politician and writer. It documents the struggles for land, the lives of rural workers and guachos (a class culture in the guise of a sub culture and distorted somewhat by regional and personal loyalties). The social forces and conflicts which ushered in 20th century Uruguay.

PARAGUAY

MARIN CAÑAS, Jose

Infierno Verde, 1935 (Green Hell)
A novel of the devastating Chaco war between Bolivia and Paraguay during the early 1930s. It gives the Paraguayans side through a diary of a soldier but gradually concludes that both the Bolivian and Paraguayan peoples are being used as cannon fodder by their stupidly venal rulers and the guile of foreign corporate interests.

Predro Arnaez, 1942 (Pedro Arnaez)
A novel of a peasant youth who breaks away from the bondage of village society to run away to the city, where he finds a new world opening up to him despite poverty and backwardness.

RIVAROLA MATTO, Jose M.

Follaje en los Ojos, 1952 (Foliage in the Eyes)
A novel of the lives of Yerba Mate collectors; lyrical descriptions of the backland regions and accounts of conditions of the migrant workers.

ROA BASTOS, Augusto

Hijo de Hombre, 1960 (Son of Man)
A "novel" which details the unchanging and seemingly endless forms of exploitation, civil wars and oppressive dictatorships which wracked Paraguay from 1870 to the Chaco war of 1935. With a dollop of religious philosophizing.

Madera Quemada, 1967 (Burnt Wood)
A collection of short stories about the natural beauty of Paraguay overlain by the destruction of its economic, physical and human potentials through generations of rapacious exploitation.

BRAZIL

AMADO, Jorge

Cacau, 1933 (Cacao)
A proletarian novel set in Alagoas state from circa 1900 to W.W.I; about the
extraordinary cacao boom, the unchecked seizures of and battles over potential
cacao lands by planters and their private armies, of the importation and serf-like
exploitation of rural workers (who themselves become caught in the ethos of the
boom) and in general the rapacious sociology of pre-modern gunmen-capitalists
rising to wealth and political power in the region. But mainly about the workers
on whose lives these fortunes were based. The first volume of the Ilheus cycle.

Sergipano, 1938 (The Man From Sergipe)
A novel of one migrant worker drawn into the Cacao region, a Negro from an ex-
slave background, during the first decade of this century. He survives the
bloodshed and travails of the boom period and acquires a small cacao farm himself
--using the same ruthless means as the larger cacao coronels. Much later,
during a bitter struggle between organizing workers and planters, he loses his
farm and life by siding with the class loyalties of his beginings.

Gabriella, Cravo E Canela, 1958 (Gabriella, Clove and Cinnamon, 1962)
A story of Ilheus in the 1920s done in the form of a local colour romance. The
growth of the town from a small port to the centre of the cacao region, the influx
of merchants, speculators, con men and wandering artistes, and the initial
representatives of the national ruling class in the form of a younger son of a
family with connections in the federal banking and political world. This places
him in conflict with the regional planter class and after some intricate twists
and turns the book ends with the "alliance" of the planters under the hegemony of
national financial interests in Ilheus.

Sao Jorge Dos Ilheus, 1945 (St. George of Ilheus, 1954)
A novelized social history of the town of Ilheus and the cacao region of the late
1920s to mid   1930s, in which the former generation of coronels die off and their
descendents and armed gangs lose control over "state" political power (and
effective control over the lands) to the financial power of the national
bourgeoisie.

Also Terras Do Sem Fin, 1943 (The Violent Land, 1952), a novel of the founding
years of the Ilheus cacao boom and the rise of the gunmen-planter class.

Suor, 1934 (Sweat)
A novel set in the old regional capitol of Bahia and dealing with the long
established yet still emerging urban working class there. Revolves around a
decaying tenement in an old neighbourhood and the array of characters in it, from
recently arrived backlands peasants, traditional urban workers and sons and
daughters of black slaves linked by the tenement itself. The folk memory of
chattel slavery (abolished only in 1888) and of wage slavery, of strikes and mass
demonstrations and the panorama of working class life, past and present in Bahia.
The first volume of the Bahia cycle.

Jubiaba, 1936 (Jubiaba)
A novel of a black youth raised in the slums of Bahia, his wanderings and daily
schemes to survive, his "apolitic" but consuming hatred for both his own and all
other oppressors, past and present. It interweaves an account of the Bahian
"black culture" scene and the hero's evolution as a militant labour leader.
Narrated through the eyes of an old, black Candoble cult leader who comes to
realize that political/union struggles are not anti-thetical to the religious
spirit of Candoble.

Seara Vermelha, 1947 (Red Harvest)
A novel set in the Sertao backlands of Bahia state during 1920s; portrays the
drought driven migrants, the fanatic religious cults, Padre Cicero the priest cum

political boss, the 20,000 mile "long march" of the revolutionary Luis Prestes Column through the region,   the bandit gangs (such as Lampiao's) operating in the pay of landholders to suppress peasant revolt. Carries the account through to the children of Sertao migrants and their actions during the Bahia general strike of 1935, alluding to the extraordinary changes in social consciousness in less than a generation.

Capitaes de Areia, 1948 (Beach Waifs), Mar Morto, 1950 (Sea of the Dead)
Two final volumes of the Bahia cycle, lyrical portraits of the lives of black youths and fishermen around the city but given to "Africanist" romanticization.

AMERICO DE ALMEIDA, Jose

A Bagaceira, 1928 (The Bagasse Shed, 1960)
A novel of the stagnant northeast sugar plantation region after the end of 300 years of slavery and planter aristocracy. Set in 1898 and 1915, it revolves around a family of declined plantation owners but describes the influx of starving peasants from the Sertao who clash with the established and only slightly better off plantation workers of the coastal zones. It outlines the seemingly endless jousting of elements of the various classes (mainly against other members of the same class) to gain or hold on to a piece of the declining pie.

Coiteiros, 1935 (The Hideout)
A novel of not at all "social" banditry in the Sertao during the first decades of this century.

AZEVEDO, Aluisio

O Cortico, 1890 (The Tenement), Casa de Pensao, 1894 (Boarding House)
Two collections of stories in novel form set in Rio de Janeiro and Sao Paulo boarding houses and tenements by one of the early naturalist writers of Brazil. Quite audacious at the time in that they deal with the mundane lives of the frayed white collar and the established working class living in genteel squalor in the growing but as yet unindustrialized major cities of Brazil.

BRANDAO, Geraldo

Cafe Amargo, 1966 (Bitter Coffee)
A novel of the decline of a family of coffee fazenda planters in Sao Paulo state between W.W.I and W.W.II as urban-based wealth remoulds local patterns of power and ownership to its own ends. A study of ruling class replacement but also touching upon the changing nature of class conflict.

CALLADO, Antonio

Bar Don Juan, 1971 (Don Juan's Bar, 1973)
A novel of members of the Brazilian underground during the last phases of armed resistance to the Brazilian military dictatorship in the late 1960s. Imbued with intimations of the continental scope of the struggle, but suffused with the defeat of Guevara in Bolivia. It is tailored to the author's view that his Brazilian revolutionaries are mainly egoistic cafe militants who have gotten in over their heads and who in the end are all destroyed, excepting one peasant pistolero.

CASO, Antonio (ed.)

Los Subversivos, 1973 (The Subversives)
A collection of oral accounts of and by surviving Brazilian resistance fighters; dealing with the bases, hopes and defeat of the armed struggle against Brazilian dictatorship in late 1960s. Also see Carlos Marighella, For The Liberation of Brazil, 1971, a collection of essays and writings by the organizer of the partizan resistance which was crushed after a brief flurry of activity. Marighella, a veteran CP leader, fell in that struggle.

CASTRO, Josua de

Death in the Northeast, 1966
A collage of popular sociology, reportage and impassioned political essay which describes the abject poverty of the sub proletariat of Brazil's northeast. Set

mainly among the favela dwellers of Recife, it presents the horrendous figures on nutrition, illness, infant mortality and life expectancy in human terms and outlines the forces driving rural people into cities like Recife. Josua de Castro is the grandson of one of the peasant refugees from the Sertao and became an internationally known director of the University of Brazil's Institute of Nutrition, before he was driven into exile by the 1964 military coup.

Of Men and Crabs, 1970
Reminiscences of growing up around a waterfront shacktown in Recife during the early 1930s; of the joys, beauty and human decency as well as the misery there. Told in the style of an urban folk tale with verve and fantasy but with an unquenched anger at the state agencies' glacial indifference to hunger and poverty.

FERREIRA DE CASTRO, Jose Maria

Emigrantes, 1928 (Emigrants, 1962)
A novel of a Portuguese peasant's immigration to Brazil during the W.W.I period, his journeys and travails in a changing and industrializing Brazil, from the coffee plantations to the rising labour militancy in Sao Paulo and the regional civil wars during the 1920s. One of the classics of modern Portuguese literature.

A Selva, 1930 (The Jungle)
Another novel of a Portuguese immigrant in Brazil during the 1920s; the protagonist, unable to find work in the coastal cities, is recruited to work on one of the rubber plantations of the central Amazon. Ultimately he becomes a storekeeper on the plantation and in this position is able to describe the workings of the slave-like system, the conditions of labour, and debt peonage as well as the dealings of the owner and his foremen. Some bitter accounts of how many of the desperately impoverished workers inform on each other and connive to curry the favour of the fazendero and his henchmen.

FONTES, Amando

Os Corumbas, 1933 (The Corumbas)
A novel which chronicles the lives and declining fortunes of the lower middle class Corumba family who emigrate from a small town to Sao Paulo. It details the social environment, daily lives, the increasingly restricted possibilities and desperation during the early 1930s of the three daughters of the family so that finally it is questionable whether the one who has become a prostitute is any worse off than the one who has found a part-time white collar job.

Rua Do Siriri, 1937 (Siriry Street)
A novel of small town   immigrants and the established city poor in an industrial city near Sao Paulo during the 1930s. About people trapped in an amalgam of authoritarian traditionalism and unbridled Brazilian capitalism. Of their daily struggle for necessities and also for some human joys in which a father comes to accept that his daughter has a right to snatch whatever happiness she can, regardless of what he was brought up to believe.

FRANCA, Oswaldo

Jorge, Um Brasilero, 1967 (The Long Haul, 1980)
A novel in diary form of a long haul truck driver who is a cunning and tough company man, the terror of his co-workers. Set in post-coup Brazil it is a sketch of the type of working class pimp who struck against the Allende government in Chile some years later. Accounts of the corruption, exploitation, the alienation and fearful individualism of some workers in their petty strivings for "favours". Ends with the "hero" being fired by his owner for a minor infraction. A depressingly realistic account.

JULIAO, Francisco

Cambao - The Yoke, 1972
A chronicle of the social background, initial organization and rapid upsurge of the Peasant Leagues in the northeast among the most crushed and supposedly apathetic of Brazil's poor during the early 1960s. An account by the nominal leader of the

Leagues which details the assaults by local landlord gunmen and the massive military suppression of the League after the 1964 coup.

LINS DO REGO, Jose

Plantation Boy, 1966 (Menino de Engenho, 1932, Doidinho, 1933, Bangue, 1934), Dead Fires, 1940 (O Molenque Richardo, 1935, Usina, 1936)
Two semi-autobiographical novels which follow the boyhood and coming of age of a neurotic and decadent son of an old plantation family in the decaying sugar plantation zone of the northeast from circa 1910 to the begining of the 1930s. In no sense working class novels, and debatable as to whether progressive, they are damning portraits of the peonage under which most plantation workers still lived and the unregenerate rottenness of the planter class.

Also Pedra Bonita, 1938 (Wonderous Stone) and Cangacieros, 1953 (Bandits), two novels dealing with the medieval and millenerian nature of the drought stricken Sertao region during the first quarter of this century.

QUEIROS, Rachel de

O Quinze, 1930 (The Year Fifteen)
A partly autobiographical novel of a family of fazenda owners in the coastal northeast and the flood of drought-stricken peasant refugees from the Sertao in 1915 (the most terrible drought year in a century). A naturalistic picture of a disaster-prone region which seems to be fated for catastrophes by history, sociology and nature.

Caminho de Pedras, 1937 (Road of Stone)
A fictional account of a radical labour organizer in the northeast during the 1930s, but largely a psychological study of a middle class intellectual's indecision toward the intertwined stagnation and turmoil of that period.

RAMOS, Gracilano

Sao Bernardo, 1934 (Saint Bernard, 1944)
A novel of northeastern Brazil during the 1920s with the background of peasants fleeing from the Sertao but focused on the petty but extremely violent struggle of two contending landlord families for control of a fazenda. Also see Ramos' novel Caetes, 1938, touching on a similar theme.

Angustia, 1936 (Anguish, 1946)
A novela written in prison revolving around an individual's attempt to sustain his beliefs and overcome the terrors of imprisonment. Might be compared with Memorias do Carcere, 1955 (Prison Memoirs), a posthumously published, more pessimistic actual diary of Ramos' feelings of despair during his imprisonment by the Vargas dictatorship.

Vidas Secas, 1938 (Barren Lives, 1953)
Possibly Ramos' best known novel; of the stagnant yet ruthlessly violent society of small town Alagoas. Deals with the entrenched but declining melange of land-lords, bought judges and politicans, merchants and workers. Of the repression of left wing political and labour organizers who cannot be bought. Written after the defeat of the 1935 General Strike and the imposition of a quasi-fascist dictatorship under Getulio Vargas.

Also Viventes dos Alagoas, 1955 (People of Alagoas), a posthumous collection of sketches and stories about Alagoas state and its people.

RIBEIRO, Joao Ubaldo

Sargeant Getulio, 1978
A stream of consciousness novel which captures the self-induced bestiality, ignorance and mindless brutality of an army seargeant who acts as a gunman for a backlands faction of the regional oligarchy. A chilling portrait of an irredeemable type which continues to provide the enforcement of "law and order" in Brazil at the local level. As in Franca's Long Haul, we find the protagonist/villain himself used and cast aside by his masters at the end.

CARIBBEAN

TRINIDAD

JAMES, C.L.R.

Minty Alley, 1936
A collage of character sketches about the Trinidadian urban poor in 1930s as seen through the eyes of a lower middle class black salesman who comes to live in a Port of Spain slum district. A wistful backward look by a long time expatriate who later became a leading black nationalist literary figure in the Caribbean. See his The Black Jacobins, under Haiti.

LADOO, Harold

No Pain Like This Body, 1972
A short novel of the daily pressures and restrictions which face a rural, East Indian working class family in Trinidad during the 1960s, leading to the emigration of those who can manage to leave.

MENDES, Alfred

Pitch Lake, 1934
A novel about the breakup of a Portuguese small shopkeeper's family, the growing alienation of one of the sons, and the insecure, provincial and money-grubbing demands of that life. A portrait of a caste-like colonial society, the externally and self-imposed social ghettos which constituted Caribbean life in the 1930s.

Black Fauns, 1935
A somewhat romanticized account of the lives of a group of black women and their families living around a slum yard in Port of Spain during the mid 1930s.

NAIPUL, V.S.

The Mystic Masseur, 1957
A novel about growing up in an East Indian lower middle class family in Port of Spain, an enclave of archetypal Victorian colonial society, in late 1930s and early 1940s. Although never radical, Naipul's early works contain sensitive accounts and appreciation of the contradictions and vitality of people in such colonial backwaters.

Miguel Street, 1959
A rather sentimental but readable set of sketches and stories about a series of characters living on a side street of Port of Spain inhabited by the working poor in the 1940s; as seen through the eyes of a young East Indian boy.

A House for Mr. Biswas, 1961
A quasi-biographical novel of the unformed hopes and terrors of a shy yet in a way courageous East Indian petty foreman in rural Trinidad during the 1930s to early 1950s. His wrestling with the pointlessness of his existence and his tenacious if somewhat ludicrous attempts to make something of his life when he lands a job as part-time reporter and salesman for a failing local newspaper in Port of Spain. A revealing (although rather class bound) portrait of what a caste-ridden, declining but peaceful colonial society was like. Naipul's greatest novel.

SELVON, Samuel

A Brighter Sun, 1952
A novel of East Indian sugar cane workers and small peasants in Trinidad of the 1940s; their inner and day-to-day domestic lives, the multi-racial world of rural Trinidad and the inter-ethnic frictions which were a prelude to the conflicts and exodus which followed independence a decade later.

Also An Island is a World, 1956, I Hear Thunder, 1963, and The Plains of Caroni, 1970, three novels on the trajectory of Caribbean society at independence.

WILLIAMS, Eric

Capitalism and Slavery, 1944
A widely read quasi-Marxist popular history of slavery in the Caribbean from the 1500s to the post-emancipation period; the contending interests within the imperial countries and the island planters, the lives and revolts of the slave populations during different periods and the strategies of repression but particularly about the economic forces underlying slavery and abolition. Williams became the first Prime Minister of Trinidad after independence.

JAMAICA

LAMMING, George

In the Castle of My Skin, 1953
A novel which begins as a reminiscence of childhood in a black Jamaican village of the 1930s, situated in a caste-based plantocracy where villagers' lives are little connected with the external world. This gives way to a promising but less secure future; the migration to the cities and the villagers' complete incorporation into a capitalist system. The second part deals with the incipient nationalist and popular movements centering around the organization of labour unions and strikes from the late 1930s to the late 1940s. The turmoil and confrontations of the awakening Jamaican masses, set against the responses of the plantocracy and those of the newly emerging black bourgeoisie. It examines the minor differences in class and personal outlook which determine the varied trajectories of four youths who have grown up together.

Season of Adventure, 1960
A novel which treats with the self-interest and ideology of a native Jamaican bourgeoisie just before, during and after the independence of a "mythical" West Indian island republic. Includes accounts of Vodun and refashioned "black culture" which the new ruling classes encourage as a form of ethnic nationalism and which they attempt to manipulate to demonstrate their own alleged "roots", linking them to "the people". Also of the growing anger and disenchantment of Jamaican peasantry and unemployed toward an old regime under new rulers.

McKAY, Claude

Banana Bottom, 1933
An early Caribbean Negritude novel; of the return of a mission-educated Jamaican girl to her home village of Banana Bottom, a stereotypical "folksy, easy-going, earthy", etc. locale which is supposed to characterize the black soul. Plot revolves about a missionized girl coming to an awareness that this village is more in tune with her personal rhythms than anything else she has encountered. The novel is listed here mainly because it and its author were influential in the Harlem renaissance and in "left wing" circles of the 1930s.

Banjo, 1929
A collage of angry scenes from the lives of Caribbean and other black colonials living and working around the waterfront area of Marseilles in the 1920s; a glorification of the black lumpen proletarian lifestyles they lead as exemplified in the hero. Again, won considerable "left" acclaim except from black activists like W.E.B. DuBois.

MAIS, Roger

The Hills Were Joyful Together, 1953
A novel of the Jamaican working class emerging from peasant and plantation back-grounds, individuals of differing backgrounds and natures living under increasingly similar conditions. Deals with the struggles against entrenched Jamaican capitalists, of the practical goals and varied fantasies of an assortment of characters located in a Kingston slum during the late 1940s. The political activity, imprisonment and death of the most far-seeing of them.

Brother Man, 1954
Another novel along the lines of The Hills, but emphasizing the international
alliances of Jamaican capitalism, its infinite maleability as neo-colonialism,
and the possibility of its being endlessly sustained by whatever bourgeoisie may
arise in an independent Jamaica.

Also Black Lightening, 1955, a novel.

PATTERSON, Orlando

The Children of Sisyphus, 1964
A novel of the vitality and courage of inhabitants of the West Kingston slums on
the eve of Jaimaican independence. Told with Zolaesque detail and revolving about
the web of economic and social disabilities which tend to pull back all who
attempt to break out. "This angry book reverses all the cliches of the Caribbean
scene; for the cliche of liberated sex we are given the massive prostitution
created by poverty; for Cesaire's Afro-Caribbean mysticism, the courageous but
intellectually proposterous Rastafarian cult; for gleaming coral sands Patterson
presents us with the garbage tips over which have sprawled the slums of West
Kingston."

REID, Victor S.

New Day, 1949
A historical novel of the Morant Bay riots of 1865, the forerunner of modern mass
movements in Jamaica; told as the reminiscences of a very old man who on the eve
of the 1944 constitution remembers the events of his childhood. A protest
movement of free black artizans, peasants and poor around Morant Bay proclaimed
"their rights" against the island planters, which the governor purposely
misinterpreted as a "slave revolt" and against which he unleashed a plantocracy
terror. A testimonial to the hidden memories of past struggles of ordinary black
Jamaicans. Written from a socialist perspective.

Sixty-five, 1960
A children's version of New Day.

The Leopard, 1958
A historical novel of an escaped African slave who becomes a leader of Jamaican
Cimaroons in the late 18th century; the roots of black struggle for freedom in
Jamaica.

BARBADOS

CLARKE, Austin

Survivors of the Crossing, 1964
A novel set among Barbadian sugar plantation workers; the poverty and economic
stagnation of a not yet tourist-directed economy. The continuing facade of
subservience and playing dumb in a late colonial society as men dream about
emigration and escape in their rum-shop hopes.

Amongst Thistles and Thorns, 1965
A novel of childhood and youth in rural Barbados by the son of a small shopkeeper,
his emigration to Canada as a young man and the disillusionment he finds as a
worker there. Also see Canadian section for additional titles.

HAITI

BELLEGRADE, Dantes

La Resistance Haitienne, 1930 (The Haitian Resistance)
A brief personal memoir of the resistance to the American (Marine) occupation
government which ruled Haiti between 1916 and 1934; the conditions of the
peasantry and poor during the attempt to establish a consolidated comprador Haitian
ruling class.

CHARLIER, Etienne

Apercu Sur la Formation Historique de la Nation Haitienne, 1948 (Commentary on the Historical Formation of the Haitian Nation)
An analysis of the slave revolt and Haitian wars of independence during the first two decades of the 19th century; the shifting alliances of French planters with American and other slave holding states in the region; the deals between the mulato plantation owners and military autocrats against the ex-slaves who were the bulk of the population. By a Haitian Marxist historian.

DEPESTRE, Rene

Etincelles, 1945 (Sparks)
A collection of poems calling for the liberation of the Haitian people from the yoke of capitalism, foreign and domestic.

Gerbes de Sang, 1946 (Shower of Blood)
A collection of poetry calling for armed revolution as the only way in which Haiti might free itself from misery and enter on the path of socialism.

Minerai Noir, 1956
A collection of poems calling for militancy in tackling Haiti stagnant autocracy; but breaking with Depestre's previous loyalty to the communist party.

ENDORE, Guy

Babouk, 1934 (Babouk, 1934)
A historical novel about the French sugar/slave society and the successful slave revolt and war of independence during the period of the French Revolution and Napoleonic regime. It revolves around one of the leaders of the Haitian revolt and is written in the format of a 1930s "proletarian" novel.

JAMES, C.L.R.

The Black Jacobins, 1963 (original 1938)
A well known popular history of the Haitian wars of independence by a Jamaican writer. A dramatic rendering of the political and military nature of the first successful slave revolt in the Western Hemisphere. Focused mainly on the character of Toussaint L'Ouverture, the major architect of Haitian independence.

LESPES, Anthony

Les Semences de la Colere, 1949 (Seeds of Anger)
A novel about a scheme to colonize an infertile mountain plateau with impoverished Haitian peasants during the mid 1940s; the unreality and callousness of the Haitian bureaucrats involved and the futile travails of landless peasants to make a living in such a locale.

MAGLOIRE, Auguste

Histoire d'Haiti: Les Insurrections, 1935-1937 (The History of Haiti: The Insurrections)
A major history of the Haitian revolts and wars of independence.

ROUMAIN, Jacques

La Proie et L'Ombre, 1930 (The Shadow and the Prey, 1938), La Montagne Ensorcelee, 1931 (The Magic Mountain, 1934)
Two works which plumb Haiti's past and society through myths, surrealism and social realist accounts. La Proie et L'Ombre is a poetic novel and Montagne Ensorcelee a book length prose poem which describe the repeated betrayal and long entrenched poverty of the Haitian peasantry from the independence wars of the early 19th century to the 1920s. Suggests that the poverty of the Haitian masses has been made bearable only through the escape offered by the various Vodun cults, but which ultimately convert real aspirations into dreams. Roumains was the internationally best known Haitian writer from the 1920s to the 1950s and a major spokesman of the Haitian left.

Gouverneurs de la Rosees, 1944 (Masters of the Dew, 1947)
A book length prose poem of a young Haitian peasant who has just returned from a
stint of migratory work in the cane fields of Cuba during the early 1940s; it
touches on the international nature of capitalist exploitation, but centers on
the strength of Africanisms among the Haitian peasantry, a culture which
potentially could be a progressive force in Haitian liberation. Translated by
Langston Hughes.

EUROPE: WESTERN

France
Spain
Portugal
Italy
Germany
Austria
Netherlands and Flanders
Denmark
Iceland
Norway
Sweden
Finland

FRANCE

ARAGON, Louis

Les Cloches de Bale, 1934 (The Bells of Basel, 1936)
The first of a series of four novels dealing with the increasing decadence and
reaction of the French bourgeoisie and the struggles of the French working class
from the first decade of the century to the post W.W.I years. The Bells of Basel
is set in Marseilles of circa 1910, contains a host of characters including a left
socialist woman labour leader modelled after Clara Zetkin. It revolves around the
backroom deals between the Marseilles capitalists, the police, and gangsters who
are used to smash a confederation of militant trade unions there.

Les Beaux Quartiers, 1936 (Residential Quarters, 1938)
The sequel to The Bells of Basel, carrying the account of politics and society in
France on the eve of W.W.I. Details the extent to which the bourgoisie and working
classes have become different and hostile "nations".

Les Voyageurs de l'Imperiale, 1940 (The Century Was Young, 1944)
A step back to the first decade of the century, set among members of the old
merchant aristocracy aboard a luxury train bound on a journey through a Europe
that is soon to disappear, which will give rise to the proto-fascist sentiments
among the middle class during the next generation.

Aurelien, 1944 (Aurelien, 1947)
The last volume of the cycle dealing with the middle class in France during the
1930s and their slide to the right.

Les Communistes, 1949-1951 (The Communists)
The general title of a five volume novel dealing with the collapse of the social
democratic and French humanist traditions during W.W.I, the deepening reaction of
the 1920s, and the mass confrontation between right and left in France through
the 1930s up to the eve of W.W.II. The running account covers only 1939 to July
1940, and the history is dealt with through reminiscences and flashbacks. The
trajectory of characters in the previous novels (see above) as well as new figures
are treated. Although the characters represent class and historic forces, they
are portrayed with believable complexity and individuality.

BARBUSSE, Henri

Under Fire, 1919
The most influential of the French anti-war novels, by the author who during the
1920s formed the "Clarte" movement, a loose network of progressive writers
scattered virtually throughout the world. Subtitled "The Story of a Squad", Under
Fire is the novelized experiences of an established French writer who volunteers
for military service in 1914, witnesses the stupidity and butchery of soldiers
from both sides being used as cannon fodder juxtaposed to the homefront
patriotism and profiteering. A work which gradually and in detail portrays the
generals, politicians and capitalists as the prime enemies of each country's
working class.

BELLANGER, R.

J'ai Vingt Ans, 1937 (I am Twenty)
A documentary novel of French working class life from the last year of W.W.I to
the late 1930s, focussed on the rising tide of war loose in Europe.

BOUTRON, Michel

Hans, 1950 (Hans, 1950)
A novella of a young German P.O.W. working for French farmers around a small
village just after the end of W.W.II, the reluctant but gradual acceptance of
this "enemy" as another human being by many of the French farmers. A somewhat

melodramatic account but progressive in comparison to the rabid ethnic chauvinism of much of the "left intelligensia" of the time.

CARCO, Francis

Rue Pigalle, 1928 (Pigalle Street), Dans La Rue, 1930 (In the Street)
Two of a series of "realistic" crime novels in the tradition of Bruno Traven, revolving around lusts , avarice, conflicts and lives of the lumpen elements in Paris slums during the 1920s.

CESBRON, Gilbert

Pretre-Ouvriers, Les Saints Vont en Enfer, 1952 (Saints in Hell, 1953)
A tract novel of the Catholic worker-priests living and working among the French working class and among North African immigrant workers, mainly in industrial Paris in the late 1940s and early 1950s (before they were dissolved by Pope Pius).

CHAMSONS, Andre

L'Annee des Vaincus, 1934 (Year of the Vanquished)
A novel of the struggle between the working class left and the growing fascist power within French society during the early 1930s.

CURTIS, Jean-Louis

Les Forets de la Nuit, 1947 (The Forests of the Night, 1951)
A documentary account of the varied elements in one French province under German occupation, 1940-1944; those French engaged in business-as-usual, active collaborationists, to underground Resistance workers. The intermingling of daily life and everyday routines and horrendous events.

DABIT, Eugene

Hotel du Nord, 1930 (North Hotel)
A collage account portraying the lives of assorted workers, unemployed and marginal petty bourgeoisie drifting around the urban areas of the industrial northeast of France at the beginning of the great depression. Reminiscent of Orwell's later "Down and Out in Paris and London".

EHRENBURG, Ilya

Zagovor Ravnykh, 1929 (The Conspiracy of Equals, 1930)
A "historical" novel of Francois Graccus Baboeuf, the leader of the Society of Equals which, during the post-revolutionary "Directorate" period in France (of the 1790s), attempted to seize power and return to the ideals of the French Revolution. Focusses on Baboeuf's isolation from his times but also on how his actions foreshadowed the socialist struggles which were to begin a half century later. By a leading Soviet novelist and one time emigre in France.

Padeniye Parizha, 1941 (The Fall of Paris, 1943)
A novel written while a cultural attache in Paris at the beginning of W.W.II; deals mainly with the decay of the French middle class, its growing fear of the French working class and hatred of "alien elements" which lead it into various reactionary fantasies and into sympathy with fascist solutions. Culminates in the military collapse of France and the widespread support of the Vichy regime by the French bourgeoisie.

FREVILLES, Jean (ed.)

Des Ouviers Ecrivent, 1934 (Some Workers Write)
An anthology of reportage, stories and accounts roughly comparable to Proletarian Literature in the U.S. and representing the tradition of French worker-correspondents. Dealing with aspects of working class life in France in the 1920s and early 1930s.

Pain de Brique, 1937 (Bread of Hunger)
A documentary novel of the lives of the French working class and the events leading up to the French General Strike of 1936. Extensive reportage of confrontations in that strike.

GUILLOUX, Louis

La Maison du Peuple, 1927 (The House of the People)
A once influential collective novel about the construction of a "House of the
People" (a combined Labour Temple and socialist cultural centre) in a working
class urban neighbourhood, and a cross section of the lives, understandings and
visions of the French working people effected. Their past and present culture.

Le Sang Noir, 1935 (Black Blood)
A vitriolic novel about the vacillations of the French intelligensia and petty
bourgeoisie in the face of growing fascist militancy in 1930s France. Written
before the United Front policy came into effect.

Also Les Batalles Perdues, 1960 (Lost Battles), a retrospective novel looking back
on the 1930s from a quarter century later and reflecting on the deep rooted
capitalist sentiments even in French working class.

HAMP, Pierre

Maree Fraiche, 1910 (Freshening Tide)
A remarkable early collective novel which deals with the lives of all those who
are involved in a sector of the fish industry and following the flow of fish
caught and unloaded at Boulogne. The lives of fishermen, dockworkers, carters,
fishmongers, wholesalers, retailers, cooks and waiters and the assortment of
people who finally eat the fish, from working class families to habitues of
expensive restaurants.

Le Lin, Le Rail, 1912 (The Railway)
A similar sort of collective account of an industry, in this case about the lives
and surroundings of all the different workers, passengers and others involved in
the operation of passenger and freight runs on one railway line in France during
that period.

Vin de Champagne, 1909 (Wine From Champagne)
A collective novel-documentary of the lives of all classes of people in a wine
grape growing region. By one of the most remarkable left populist writers of the
time.

Le Cantique des Cantiques, 1922 (The Song of Songs)
A collective novel about French women workers in the Paris garment industry, from
sweatshops and "homework" needle trades to the fashion houses and wearers.
Peasant girl migrants, old city families, bosses, luft menschen, wheelers and
wastrels of the social pyramid.

Mineurs et Metiers de Fer, 1932 (Miners and the Iron Trades)
Another collective novel of the people and conditions in the French artizan metal
industries of the period.

Mes Metiers, 1931 (Kitchen Prelude, 1932)
An autobiography of Hamp's working class background in France of 1890s and early
1900s, taking him to his first success as a populist writer.

MacORLAN, Pierre (Pierre Dumarchey)

Chant de L'Equipage, 1918 (The Team Song), Abord de L'Etoile-Matutine, 1920
(On Board the Morning Star, 1924), Quai des Brumes, 1927 (Misty Quay)
Three of a series of crime adventure novellas but involving considerable social
realism; set among the seamen, dockside workers, saloons, prostitutes and petty
criminals of the waterfront areas of different French ports, W.W.I through the
1920s; drawn partly from Dumarchey's own youth.

MAJEROVA, Marie

Namesti Republiky, 1914 (Square of the Republic, 1947)
A Czech writer's autobiographical account of French ruling class Republicanism
masquerading under the cap of liberty in the pre W.W.I years; capitalist and state
oppression imposed in the name of the French Revolution's phraseology. Treats
with the spirited vitality of the Parisian anarchist movement of which Majerova

was a part, but which emerges as totally incapable of organizing or defending the basic interests of French workers from the assaults of State and employers. Set during the waves of mass demonstrations and bread riots in Paris between 1911-1913.

MOTHE, Daniel

Journal d'un Ouvier, 1956-1958, 1959 (A Worker's Diary, 1956-1958)
A novelized journal of an actual union militant and syndicalist working as and among skilled and semi-skilled workers in a Paris metalurgical plant over those two years. Revolves around the headlong flight to consumerism as well as class and political apathy among so many of his fellow workers who see little antithesis to their employers and who are either unmoved by events in Hungary in 1956 or the beginning of the Algerian war of independence in 1958 or even by the emerging struggles of the most exploited sectors of French working class around them. Also Militant Chez Renault, 1965 (A Renault Militant), a later journal of syndicalist aspirations and failure in the Renault factories.

NIZAN, Paul

Antoine Bloye, 1933 (Antoine Bloye, 1973)
An epic novel of the French working class and its transformation into a proletariat with the industrial expansion revolving around the railway construction during the mid to later 19th century.

Les Chiens de Garde, 1935 (The Watchdogs, 1971)
A furious account of the French intelligensia, school teachers, journalists and others who act as secular theologians for the established capitalist order in France. Set in the 1920s and 1930s.

The Trojan Horse, 1937
A novel revolving about the clashes between the left wing working class and pro-fascist forces in France during the early days of the Popular Front government. Deals with the evolution of mass actions but focusses on the character of a declasse intellectual who drifts to the left, becomes embittered by his lack of recognition, and winds up as a right wing terrorist.

Les Conspiration, 1938 (The Conspiracy)
A novel of the trajectory of the French middle class in the 1930s, who, with some exceptions, are described as on a halting but glacial slide to right wing autocracy; by a communist author who opposed the United Front policy, broke with the party after the Hitler-Stalin pact and died on the Western Front in 1940.

PHILIPPES, A.

L'Acier, 1937 (Steel)
A family chronicle novel of French working class life from circa 1912 to the Popular Front period of the mid 1930s.

POULAILLE, Henry

Le Pain Quotiden, 1931 (The Daily Bread)
The first volume of a novel tetrology portraying French working class life over one generation. Le Pain Quotiden being an account of the world and lives of a working class family in the Paris industrial districts at about the turn of the century.

Le Damnes de la Terre, 1935 (The Damned of the Earth)
The second volume, revolving around a carpenter but dealing with the deepening working class struggles and sometimes proto-revolutionary battles in France between 1906 and 1911.

Pain de Soldat, 1937 (Soldier's Bread)
A novel which describes the initial opposition to but temporary dissolution of French working class militancy during its conscription into W.W.I, the decimation of much of a generation in the trenches, 1914-1917.

Les Rescapes, 1939 (The Survivors)
Concludes the tetrology with an account of the brewing apocalyptic bitterness

among ordinary French soldiers in 1917, of the mass mutinies which break out.
Of the French working class responses to the upsurge of revolutionary outbreaks
which course through Europe between 1917 and 1920.

PREVOST, Jean

Les Freres Bouquinquant, 1930 (The Brothers Bouquinquant), Le Sel Sur la Plaie,
1934 (Salt in the Wound)
Two lyrical yet realistic novels of French working class life from about W.W.I to
the early 1930s; by a left student of Simone Weil's urban folk theatre style.

REMY, Tristan

L'Ancien Tonnelier, 1931 (The Old Cooper), Porte de Cligancourt, 1932 (Porte
de Cligancourt)
Two semi-autobiographical novels by a so-called "anarchist-proletarian" author.
Dealing with the lives of the poor, of workers, displaced artizans and street
peddlars; the horrors of W.W.I and poverty of peacetime France in the 1920s
to the beginning of 1930. Porte de Cligancourt set around a market area in Paris.

Le Grande Lutte, 1937 (The Great Struggle)
A documentary novel of the lives of poor and workers in early 1930s but being
mainly a slice-of-life collage of their experiences during the French General
Strike of 1936.

ROMAINS, Jules

Les Hommes de Bonne Volonte, 1932-1947 (Men of Good Will)
The general title of a series of twenty-seven novels which chronicle the social
history of the French middle classes from 1908 to the late 1930s. Portrays the
slide of the French bourgeoisie away from the anti-traditionalist, rationalist
and democratic ideology inherited from the French Revolution toward an unbridled
national chauvinism and reactionary obscurantism. Also touches on the lives of
representatives of other classes. From the final years of the 19th century
as seen in the Agadir Crisis of 1908, the Balkan wars and W.W.I, the reverberations
of the Russian and Central European revolutions in France, the deepening
stagnation of the 1920s and the increasing drift to ideological escapism and
repressive autocracy of the French middle classes during the 1930s.

Verdun, 1973
An English translation of volumes 15 and 16 of Men of Good Will, it portrays the
initial Great Leap Backward of the French middle class, as represented by the
friends and kinspeople of one such family, in the prelude to and during the long
drawn out mutual butchery swirling through the Verdun salient in W.W.I. The
slaughter of a generation and the end of an epoch.

STIL, Andre

Le Premier Choc, 1952 (The First Clash, 1953)
A novel dealing with the lives of French dockworkers around Bordeaux immediately
after W.W.II in which the expected "liberation" turns into a reimposition of the
regime ancien as American army and allied French conservative forces collude
in checking the long pent up working class interests.

The Water Tower, 1954
A sequel to Le Premier Choc, about French dockworkers in 1950 who refuse to handle
arms being shipped to the French army engaged in recolonizing Viet Nam. Outlines
the police and political forces brought to bear against working class left but
also detailing the sources of social and ideological support which existed in
France for such action.

TRIOLET, Elsa

Le Premier Accroc Coute 200 Francs, 1945 (A Fine of Two Hundred Francs, 1947)
Four tales of the French resistance movement in Lyon during the final months of
German occupation in 1944. Details the internal conflicts, ambiguity, opposed

political and personal motives of the underground workers. Recounted from
personal experience by the wife of Louis Aragon.

VAILLAND, Roger

Drole de Jeu, 1945 (A Strange Game)
A frenzied, bitterly ironic and semi-autobiographical novel which chronicles the
chaos of life in the French resistance.

Une Jeune Homme Seul, 1951 (Young Man Alone)
A satiric novel which is a turnabout of the traditional "social ascent" novel, in
which a middle class professional sickened by bourgoisie society strives to and
gradually succeeds in incorporating himself into the working class.

VALLES, Jules

Les Refractaires, 1866 (The Rebels), La Rue, 1866 (The Street)
Two short reportage accounts about the conditions and lives of the working class
and poor of Paris in 1866. Compiled from Valles reports in his newspaper
Le Peuple.

L'Enfant, 1879 (The Child), L'Bachelier, 1881 (The Bachelor), L'Insurge, 1886 (The
Insurgent)
A moving autobiographical trilogy of Valles youth, the evolution of French
capitalism and the stirrings of working class revolt; the author's life as a
radical newspaper editor in Paris in the 1860s and his emergence as a Communard.
Culminating in a bitter and unregenerate defense and account of the Paris Commune
rising of 1870. Portrays its defeat after a three month siege and the mass murder
of Parisian radicals and workers by the army of the French bourgeoisie which
followed.

VAN DER MEERSCH, Maxence

La Maison dans la Dune, 1932 (House on the Dunes)
A naturalist portrait of the poverty, human and physical destruction in the
industrial black belt of French Flanders in 1920s. Alludes to the little changed
misery there painted by Van Gough a half century earlier.

Quand Les Sirenes Se Taisent, 1933 (When Sirens are Silent)
A protest novel of the daily lives, work and exploitation of men and women in the
industrial North East of France leading to a textile workers strike in early 1930s.
Told from a sort of Christian Socialist viewpoint.

Le Peche du Monde, 1934 (The Sin of the World)
A novel revolving around the children of those living in poverty and degradation
in a decaying North Eastern French industrial town of the 1930s.

VERHAEREN, Emile

Les Visages de la Vie, 1899 (Images From Life)
A collection of poetry which evokes the squalor but energy of the lives of coal
miners and mill workers in the Franco-Belgian Black belt during the 1890s and
the upsurge of millenial socialism among them.

ZOLA, Emile

Germinal, 1885 (Germinal, 1892)
A massive account of the lives and environment of French coal miners, men and
women, in the northern industrial zone of early 1880s. It portrays their daily
labours and lives, the dangers and penury, the desperate sexuality, the brutality
and visions which arise. Culminates in a bitter, drawn out strike suppressed by
the French army but in which the seeds of a more fundamental revolt and the
precursor of socialist struggles are sown. Marred at times by Zola's views on
the role of heredity and his exaggeration of "brutalized lives", Germinal was the
internationally pre-eminent left protest novel of that generation. It still
retains a remarkable power and has been translated and reissued in virtually
every major language since its first publication.

SPAIN

ACEVEDO, Isidoro

Los Topos, 1930 (The Moles)
A collective novel of Spanish miners during the late 1930s, their daily lives,
backgrounds, hopes and especially everyday work, with the mine itself as a
central character.

ARCONDA, Cesar M.

La Turbina, 1930 (The Turbine)
A collective novel about the initial electrification of a Spanish peasant region
in 1910. Deals with the many sided struggle between the entrenched traditionalism
of the countryside and the agents of social change. See J. Lopez Pacheco's
Central Electrica, 1958, for how this theme is treated a generation later.

Los Pobres Contra Los Ricos, 1933 (The Poor Against the Rich)
A novel of the spontaneous uprisings of impoverished, landless peasants throughout
rural Spain in 1931-32 and their suppression by the Civil Guard; the deepening
desperation of the Spanish poor.

Reparto de Tierras, 1934 (Division of the Land)
An agitational novel dealing with the class struggle between landowners and
landless during the largely symbolic land reform program (initiated by a
Conservative government) which gets out of hand.

Rio Tajo, 1938
A reportage novel of the peasantry along the Tajo River, their sacrifices, advances
and hopes of two years of Republican reforms during the Spanish Civil War.

ARDERIUS, Joaquin

Campesinos, 1931 (Peasants)
A novel of the panopoly of exploitation and oppression borne by Spanish peasants
and the connected forms of social ferment and auto-repression; from the most
abject servility and fanatic support of their oppressors, to apathy, to anarchist
revolts, to organized and considered class struggles. Arderius authored some
dozen other reportage works and social novels.

AVALOS, Fernando

En Plazo, 1961 (On Installment)
A novel about how, for the poor, a seemingly minor difficulty becomes a tragedy.
Describes the multifarious problems which face a Madrid working class family when
the tenement in which they rent rooms is sold for condominiums, their increasing
desperation to find affordable quarters and the fruitless attempts to solve what
initially seems like a minor matter but which eventually creates additional
hardships in all realms of their lives.

BAREA, Arturo

La Forja de un Rebelde, 1944 (The Forging of a Rebel, 1946)
An autobiographical account of the familial political sub-culture of
Barea's middle class childhood in W.W.I Spain which made him and others like him
left wing Republicans rather than Conservatives. First of a trilogy.

La Ruta, 1950 (The Route)
The second volume of the trilogy, a bitterly anti-militarist account of the
Spanish-Moroccan conflict of early 1920s, described as a vicious and inept
colonial war which served as the seedbed for Spanish military caudillos of the
next decade.

La Llama, 1951 (The Call)
The last of the trilogy which describes the various forces allied in defense of
the Spanish Republic as the embodiment of a century of opposition
against traditional Spain; of the Spanish people in arms against the historic
forces of cultural and political oppression.

La Raíz Rota, 1952 (The Broken Root, 1952)
A semi-autobiographical novel of an exile's love and hate of native Spain, of the
attempts of Spanish refugees to start new lives wherever they may be but of the
continuing pull of people, places and struggles that now seem lost forever.

BAROJA, Pio

La Lucha Por La Vida, 1904 (The Struggle for Life), La Busca, 1907 (The Search)
Two novelas which document life in the slum and working class districts of Madrid
during the first decade of the century. They deal with different elements of
that working class and the experiences of the narrator. Baroja's early work was
a combination of Maxim Gorky and Jack London, capturing the street dialogue, anti-
clericalism and growing rebellion against Spanish cultural and political
traditions by workers and peasants. An amalgam of revolutionary and reactionary
sentiments.

Mala Hierba, 1908 (Bad Weed)
A sardonic novela of a young worker who through individual effort, guile and a
strategic marriage "rises" (i.e. degenerates) into the lower middle class, going
from bad to worse in the process.

Aurora Roja, 1910 (Red Dawn, 1925)
A roman d'clef which documents the growth of Anarchist social philosophy and
political organization among the Madrid working class in first decade of the
century, from the viewpoint of a participant/activist.

BATES, Ralph

The Lean Men, 1934
A semi-autobiographical novel of a British communist organizer in Spain during
the late 1920s who helps organize the Barcelona dockworkers. Also recounts the
uncoordinated risings and crushed revolts of 1931.

The Olive Field, 1936
A complex and moving novel set among Andalusian peasants in 1932 and later shifting
to the Asturias miners' rising of 1934. It narrates the lives of Andalusian
peasants and the townspeople they come in contact with, a picture of the
tremendous heterogeneity under a seemingly homogeneous surface; the interweaving
of personal quarrels and temperaments with class politics and how this is quite
misunderstood by labelling them "Anarchists". One of the most remarkable accounts
of the pre-conditions of the Spanish Civil War. Also see his Sierra (1933),
another revolutionary novel of Spain in the 1920s.

BENAVIDES, Manuel D.

Un Hombre de Treinta Años, 1933 (A Man of Thirty Years)
A memoir of the evolving socialist consciousness of a journalist of thirty years
of age set against the panorama of social ferment in Spain at the beginning of
the 1930s.

BLASCO IBANEZ, Vicente

La Barranca, 1898 (The Ravine)
One of the great Spanish naturalist novels; deals with the relations and struggles
between tenant peasantry and landlords on the Vega plain of Valencia at the end
of the 19th century. It revolves around one family of Aragonese tenants who
persist in working lands from which a landlord wants to expel them and culminates
in the landlord's use of a band of gunmen to destroy and burn out the resisting
families.

La Bodega, 1904 (The Store)
A novel along similar lines as La Barranca, dealing with the peasant rising around
Jerez in 1892. Gives a picture of the squalid social conditions and serf-like
subjugation of peasantry counterposed to the opulence of landlords and a near
medieval uprising which broke out. Chronicles the initial rise of Anarchist
influence among the peasantry of southern Spain.

Cañas y Barro, 1902 (Cane and Clay)
A naturalistic novel about the lives of peasant-fishermen and landless labourers
working in the seaside rice growing region near Valencia at the turn of the
century.

CABALLERO BONALD, Jose M.

Dos Dias de Setiembre, 1962 (Two Days in September)
A poetic social realist novel dealing with 48 hours in the lives of a number of
landless rural workers in the grape growing district of Andalusia during the
1950s; about the intricacy of subjectively important status differences among
them and the circuitous courses leading to stasis or opposition to the regime.

CARRANQUE DE RIOS, Andres

Uno, 1932 (One)
An impressionistic novel which contrasts the high flown phraseology of Spanish
intellectuals with the anger and rejection of Spanish society by workers in the
streets. By a self-educated Madrid worker-writer. Also along the same lines,
Cinematografo (1935) (Cinema)

La Vida Difícil, 1934 (A Difficult Life)
A Brechtian novel set among the Madrid lumpen class and satirizing the then
popular romanticization of such lives.

CELA, Camilo Jose

La Familia de Pascual Duarte, 1942 (The Family of Pascual Duarte)
The first, and for a long time the only, social novel to appear in Franco's
Spain. It cautiously chronicles the brutal and mean-spirited life of the rural
lower middle class as embodied by a "rich" peasant family in an Aragonese village,
the citadel of Franco support. Intimates the empty lives of even "the victors".

La Colmena, 1950 (The Beehive)
A slice of life account of the lives of the Madrid poor, unemployed and rural
migrants; interior monologues, daily events, fragments of the background of those
involved, recorded with a believable and powerful fidelity.

CIGES APARICIO, Manuel

Los Vencedores, 1908 (The Victors)
An early "proletarian" novel dealing with the lives, work and exploitation of a
group of Spanish miners at the time, their gradual resolve to organize, the
firings and strike which follow and is broken by police. Involves some
reportage of an actual case.

Los Vencidos, 1910 (The Vanquished)
A sequel to Los Vencedores which follows the lives of the defeated miners, the
families of strikers killed, those in prison, others forced to migrate and others
returning to the mine to work in smouldering or defeated submission.

Marruecos, 1912 (Morocco)
A reportage work lambasting Spanish colonialism in northern Morocco.

Also Villa Vieja, 1914 (Old Village), Cesar o Nada, 1918 (Cesar or Nothing),
El Juez Que Perdio la Conciencia, 1925 (The Judge Who Lost Conscience), three
other novels of somewhat mellowed social criticism, but attacking the traditional
well springs of power and oppression in Spanish society.

DIAS DE MORAL, Jesus

Historia de las Agitaciones Campesinas Andaluzas, 1929 (History of the Andalusian Peasant Resistance)
A chronicle of the varied strands of Andalusian peasant rebellion during the 19th and early 20th centuries. The bases of and gradations from banditry to organized forms of resistance.

DIAZ FERNANDEZ, Jose

El Blocao, 1928 (The Blockhouse)
An autobiographical novel of a Spanish draftee in Morocco during the Abdel Krim Riff rising, a stupid and disastrous colonial campaign which consolidated anti-militarism sentiments among the Spanish working class. Portrays the anti-colonialist, anti-militarist attitudes deepening among the Spanish soldiers but also their personal struggles for survival and the general callousness which develops.

ESPINA, Concha

El Metal de los Muertos, 1920 (Metal of the Dead)
A novel revolving around the oppression of Spanish miners in Asturias and modeled after events in a strike at the foreign owned Rio Tinto mine at the end of W.W.I. Said to be an antecedent of Catholic left outlook.

FERNANDEZ SANTOS, Jesus

Los Bravos, 1954 (The Brave Ones)
A novel set in a small Castillian village composed of tenant farmers and landless labourers cowering under the arbitrary rule of a local landlord-caudillo. Described through the eyes of a young doctor who is powerless in checking the abuses of the landlord and, because of his class position, is even unable to relate to the peasantry. Despite their hatred, the tenants lack any effective form of resistance.

FERRES, Antonio

La Piqueta, 1959 (The Pickaxe)
A novel of a landless Andalusian peasant who goes to Madrid to find work and becomes involved in a battle by homeless squatters to establish a favela-shacktown on the outskirts of the city. The novel takes place during one hour in the attempted land "invasion" and provides a collage of the backgrounds, lives, hopes and characters of the squatters.

Con Los Manos Vacias, 1964 (With Empty Hands)
A novelized account of an actual event in which two poor peasants were jailed for the murder of a man who was still alive; the indifference of the rural officials and judges and the nature of the "judicial" and penal system which refused to release the men even after it has ascertained that no crime had been committed.

Los Vencidos, 1965 (The Vanquished)
A novel set in Madrid during the summer of 1945 with the world wide defeat of then contemporary fascism--except in Spain. Describes the frenzied storm of repression loosed by the Civil Guard and other traditionalist forces in Franco's regime, the imprisonment, execution and terrorization of the surviving leftists in order to impress on the Spanish people just who is in power and what opposition will mean.

FRASER, Ronald

In Hiding: the life of Manuel Cortes, 1972
A life history of an Asturias miner and militant socialist; from the bloody and abortive Asturias rising in 1934, through the desperate battles to defend the Asturias enclave during the Spanish Civil War. But mainly about the following eleven years of underground existence (lasting to 1948) in which Cortes and initially some thousands of others lived as semi-bandit partisans. A frank and detailed account of underground life, its costs, and the changes in those so engaged.

Blood of Spain: An Oral History of the Spanish Civil War, 1979
A massive account of the backgrounds and streams of experience of a host of
Spaniards from many walks of life and political persuasions during the Spanish
Civil War. Based upon oral accounts from some 200 persons, it is a complex
recapitulation of events both chilling and "mundane", of political processes,
policies and individual responses to developments which coursed through Spain.
It both confirms some long held views but also demands a rethinking of all that
was involved, presenting no simple answers. Extremely wide ranging, balanced
but not neutral. It is impossible to adequately describe this work which is
simply the finest piece of oral history on any topic yet produced. Two provisos
are that a full appreciation requires some background knowledge of Spain and
the Spanish Civil War, for which one might suggest Hugh Thomas' The Spanish Civil
War (1966) and Gerald Brennan's The Spanish Labyrinth (1937). Fraser provides no
accounts of the volunteers from fifty odd countries who fought in the International
Brigades. Some of their stories are scattered throughout this bibliography
listed in their countries of origin.

GARCIA HORTELANO, Juan

Tormenta de Verano, 1962 (Summer Storm)
A novel of the late middle age of that generation of bourgeoisie which rose to
wealth and power through connections with the Franco regime. Touches on the
confiscatory seizures of Republicans' belongings, the repression and exploitation
of working class which are translated into profits for this speculator class. But
mainly portrays the parasitic vacuity and endemic perfidy of their lives.
Similarly Manuel Arce's Oficio de Muchachos, 1963 (Kid's Stuff), a novel of the
self centered, cafe alienation of similar middle class youths.

GARCIA LORCA, Frederico

Obras Completas, 1954 (Collected Works)
The four volume collected works of the prominent Andalusian poet and playwright
who was murdered by the Nationalists at the beginning of the Spanish Civil War.
His poetry was not so much radical as it was "romantic", dealing with themes of
personal rebellion, vagrants and gypsies in a folk loric manner. It was Lorca's
imagry of the forces of social oppression and Spanish cultural conservatism
which captured the imagination of broad sections of the Spanish working class,
some of whom committed long passages of Lorca's poetry to memory.

GOYTISOLO, Juan

Juegos de Manos, 1954 (Juggling Act)
A novel of the self-deception, arrogance and hypocrisy of the new generation of
bourgeoisie; revolves around a group of "society youths" who consider themselves
rebels and anarchists and who are planning the assasination of a bureaucrat.
A character study of the new middle class "anarchists" and their relations to
fascist adventurers.

La Resaca, 1958 (The Surf)
The best known volume of the trilogy Mañana Efimero, dealing with sectors of the
Spanish working class and lumpen proletariat during the depth of the Franco
regime, the constantly rejuvenated reaction and the self-defeating division in
the ranks of the oppressed. La Resaca counterposes the trajectory of a number of
youths drawn into self-destructive lumpen activities with two others from the
same background who become involved with the illegal working class movement. The
partly sympathetic, partly derisive attentions of the lumpen ultimately leads to
the arrest of one underground group. Also Fin de Fiesta, 1962 (End of the Fiesta)
and El Circo, 1957 (The Circus).

La Revindicacion de Conde Don Julian, 1970
A bitterly sardonic novel which was written on Goytisolo's emigration from Spain,
being a diatribe against all things which keep Spain the way she is.

GROSSO, Alfonso

Un Cielo Dificilmente Azul, 1961 (A Sky Stubbornly Blue)
A picaresque novel about the experiences of two truck drivers making deliveries
around Spain and of the assorted people and conditions they encounter.

La Zanja, 1962 (The Ditch)
A collective novel of a village of farm workers in the Andalusian sierra during
one day and night. An encapsulated social history of life in the notoriously
backward and impoverished region of latifundia and landless labourers.

Testa de Copo, 1963 (Cotton Head)
Novel of an Italian-Spanish fisherman who is imprisoned on a trumped-up charge and
the system which drives him into becoming a criminal after his release from
prison. The first volume of a trilogy which includes El Capirote (1966) and
A la Izquierda del Sol (1964) (To the Left of the Sun).

El Capirote, 1966 (The Hood)
Covers the final months of the ex-fisherman who is now a migrant farm worker
labouring in the rice fields of Andalusia, dying of T.B., during the Holy Week in
Sevilla--the epitome of everything that is feudal and reactionary in Spain serves
as a backdrop.

GROSSO, Alfonso and LOPEZ SALINAS, Armando

Por El Rio Abajo, 1966 (For the River Below)
A reportage and travel account of the latifundia regions of the Guadalquivir
river valley in lower Andalusia during the 1960s; a journey back into 18th century
social conditions.

IZCARAY, Jesus

Las Ruinas de la Muralla, 1965 (Ruins of the Wall)
A novel of the social forces in Spain during the late Franco period, set around an
allegorical mural dating from Grandee Spain which is falling to pieces through
irremediable decay and neglect. Counterposed is the growing social ferment as
seen by a group of young communists returning from a secret meeting abroad.

LERA, Angel Maria de

Hemos Perdido el Sol, 1963 (We've Lost the Sun)
A novel of Spanish migrants living in West Germany as guest workers. Also Con
La Maleta Al Hombro, 1965 (With a Suitcase on the Shoulder)

Tierra Para Morir, 1965 (Land for Dying)
A novel of the depopulated Spanish villages where the young have fled to the
cities or abroad in order to earn a living and the anachronistic system of land
ownership and squirearchical power which supposedly underly this exodus. Also
La Trampa, 1962 (The Trap).

LOPEZ PACHECO, Jesus

Central Electrica, 1958
A collage novel about the construction of a hydro electric project in northern
Spain during the 1950s; an astute reconsideration of the theme treated in
Arconda's La Turbina. In Central Electrica both the flooded out peasants and the
workers building the dam are seen as bearing the costs of the development which
produces benefits which will not be shared under Franco or any other capitalist
regime in Spain. A well written, lyrical work.

LOPEZ SALINAS , Armando

La Mina, 1960 (The Mine)
A novel which "tells of an Andalusian peasant who moves north to seek a better
life in the coal mines. After much suffering he is killed in an accident caused
not by fate or bad luck, but by management's neglect of safety precautions".
Despite the simplicity of the theme, Lopez Salinas succeeds in capturing the
resilience and vitality of working class life; his characters retain their humour,
patience yet combativeness. Suffused with both realism and optimism.

Año Tras Año, 1962 (Year After Year)
A novel dealing with the multifoliate character, responses and emotions of members
of the Spanish working class during the depth of Franco dictatorship from 1939
to 1955. Portrays the seemingly all-encompassing defeat and the treatment of
working people as a conquered colony realistically and astutely. The despair and
escapism of some but also the irrepressible spirit of resistance--sub-political
and primitive initially in the forms of non-cooperation, playing dumb, boycotts
--and the slowly reemerging organized opposition. Ends with the capture and
imprisonment of one left wing worker who over the years has been able to rebuild
a skeletal underground union which by then is strong enough to sustain the loss
of its leaders and continue to grow. Done with a deftness that makes the work
possibly the finest left wing Spanish novel of the post war generation.

MARSE, Juan

Encerrados Con Un Sol Jugete, 1960 (Shutup With a Single Plaything)
A novel of the lives of two generations of Spaniards conquered by the Franco-
Nationalist forces, the older generation silent and unable of seeing past the
defeats of the civil war and bloody repression which followed yet with the memory,
past visions and hope for a better society, and a younger generation who are as
much class prisoners as their parents but who without experience of mass struggles
drift into patterns of personal alienation and escape. Yet as they mature and
start families of their own the full import of their oppression comes home to
them and their continuity with the lives and struggles of their parents emerges.

Este Cara de la Luna, 1962 (This Face of the Moon)
A novel which analyses the middle aged children of the Franco middle class; their
play at being a lost generation, of journalist poseurs, cafe existentialists and
other bored self-styled "rebels" who in fact are only a purposeless lumpen
bourgeoisie.

MODESTO, Juan

Soy del Quinto Regimento, 1969 (I Am Of the Fifth Regiment)
A memoir of the "Fifth Regiment", an army corp composed mainly of militant Spanish
workers which was one of the main shock units of the Republican army during the
civil war. Also a memoir of its commander.

MORA, Fernando

Venus Rebelde, 1908 (Rebel Venus), La Noche de San Jose, 1911 (The Night of San
Jose), A Orillas del Manzanares, 1917 (Shores of the Manzanares), El Otro Barrio,
1918 (The Other Neighbourhood), La Peliculera, 1923 (The Movie Show)
A few of many novelas by a prolific author who documented the world of the Madrid
social democratic working and lower middle classes in the first quarter of the
century; accounts of the quiet heroism of their daily lives, personal loyalties
and an embattled faith in science, reason and culture.

NIETO, Ramon

La Fiebre, 1959 (The Fever)
A novel revolving around an archetypal representative of the small town
bourgoisie, the backbone of Franco support. Develops during a trip through the
countryside in the course of which the protagonist reminisces about his life and
that of his class, especially during the crucial years of 1930-35 when the die of
social reaction was cast.

La Patria y el Pan, 1962 (Fatherland and Bread)
A novel of the daily lives of Madrid favela dwellers, largely emigres from the
Andalusian latifundia. The daily courage and initiative required in order to
survive but also the very modest improvements in their lives which lead many to
feel that the city, however alien, offers greater hope of livelihood and
anonymity (if not dignity) compared to the feudal conditions they have left.
Counterposed are the limitations which ensure that few will ever escape the
poverty which surrounds them.

Sol Amargo, 1961 (Bitter Sun, La Tierra, 1959 (The Land), Via Muerta, 1967 (Dead End), three additional social realist novels about Spain in the late 1950s and 1960s.

PAYNE, Robert

The Song of the Peasant, 1939
A novel which describes a corner of the Spanish Civil War in a small Catalonian village. The tensions and differences between anarchists and communists, fishermen and stone masons, joined together in the struggle against fascism. The initial victories, sacrifices and the long bitter retreats culminating in the destruction of the village as the Nationalists sweep through Catalonia in late 1938.

PINILLOS, Lopez

Los Enemigos, 1908 (The Enemies)
A novel of the more than partly successful resistance of the Spanish clergy and traditionalist sectors in one rural region to the electrification of the area; their estimations of what broader effects may result from modernization and the pseudo-humble but cunning opposition they mount to any wider benefits which follow it.

PITT-RIVERS, Julian

The People of the Sierra, 1954
An ethnography of a village of poor peasants, landless workers and shepherds in mountain Andalusia during the early 1950s. Suggests that the history of past struggles and millenial hopes have not so much been forgotten as overlaid with the feelings of defeat.

QUEVADO, Nino

Las Noches Sin Estrellas, 1961 (Nights Without Stars)
A semi-documentary novel about a band of partisans operating in the Pyrenees during the last phase of guerrilla struggle at the end of W.W.II. Their initial support but gradual attrition as the Franco forces concentrate troops in the area and the outside world writes them off. Based on both research and personal experience.

QUINTO, Jose Maria de

Las Calles y los Hombres, 1957 (Streets and Men)
A collection of nine long stories, each one documenting a different facet of the repression which coursed through Franco Spain in the years immediately after W.W.II.

RODERO, Juan Jose

El Sol No Sale Para Todos, 1966 (The Sun Does Not Rise For All)
A novel of the never ending penury which was/is the lot of employed white collar workers in Spain, the financial insecurity where even a minor illness or layoff plunge family into poverty and the impossibility of realizing even the most modest hopes. Threaded around the emigration of a young Spanish woman to Germany where she lives an almost equally penurious existence as a guest worker.

ROMERO, Luis

Los Otros, 1956 (The Others)
A novel which begins with an unsuccessful payroll robbery by a desperate unemployed worker; as we follow his attempts to hide out in different locales of Barcelona we gradually come to realize the scope and depth of the exploitation which triggers this sort of crime by individuals who are not criminals.

El Cacique, 1963 (The Chief)
A novel which takes place during the wake for a village political boss, with a gradual revelation of the range of injustices, corruption and vicious swindles

he and his cohorts, who have come to mourn him, have been engaged in. A capsule
survey of the venality of the real government of the Spanish countryside.

SENDER, Ramon J.

Iman, 1930 (Iman)
A novel about Riff rising in Spanish Morocco during the early 1920s and the defeat
of the Spanish army there. From the viewpoint of increasingly anti-colonial and
anti-militarist Spanish conscripts.

O.P.: Los Terminos del Presagio, 1931 (O.P.: The Terms of the Omen)
Accounts of political prisoners, common and uncommon criminals, warders and penal
policies encountered by Sender while incarcerated in the Modelo prison of Madrid
during the Primo de Rivera dictatorship of the early 1930s. Sketched with black
humour and bitter irony.

Siete Domingos Rojos, 1932 (Seven Red Sundays, 1936)
A narrative of a working class Anarchist uprising in Madrid during the 1920s;
a critical yet sympathetic attempt to understand the psychological and
philosophical strains in Spanish anarchism of the time.

Viaje a la Aldea del Crimen, 1934 (Journey to the Hamlet of the Crime)
A documentary account of the Casas Viejas uprising in a small Andalusian peasant
village of that year. Deals with the feudal conditions, the poverty and the
utopian-libertarian views of the peasant militants. The massacre by the Civil
Guard which followed made the "Casas Viejas Incident" notorious throughout Spain.

Contra-ataque, 1938 (Counterattack, 1938)
A desperate agitational novel intended to mobilize support at home and abroad for
the Spanish Republic; dealing with the sacrifices already made in defending the
Republic and the necessity of mounting a counterattack against the steadily more
powerful forces of international reaction as represented by Franco in Spain.

Mosen Millan; Requiem por un campesino Español, 1953 (Mosen Millan; Requium for
a Spanish peasant)
Novel of a Republican peasant in a small Pyrenees village, his reminiscences on
the eve of his execution by local fascists who count on the support of the Spanish
church and traditional conservative elements more than on any "foreign" ideology.
The unending right wing terror during the 1940s.

La Jornada, 1942-1963 (The Journey)
The general title of a series of autobiographical volumes dealing with Spain of
the early 1920s to 1940. Reprinted in three volumes under the title Cronica del
Alba, 1966 (Chronical of Dawn)

SOLIS, Ramon

Ajena Crece La Hierba, 1962 (The Forage Grows Foreign)
A novel in the form of reminiscences by a Spanish migratory worker in the sugar
beet farms of France; about what conditions were/are like in his home village,
what forces made him and hundreds of thousands of others like him leave their
country to become the poorest paid workers abroad. Also accounts of the wonders
of French "civilization" they encounter as immigrant farm labourers.

SUEIRO, Daniel

La Criba, 1961 (The Screen)
A novel of the daily indignities and penury which is the lot of Madrid white collar
workers, their existence on the margins of genteel poverty which neither second
jobs nor determined striving can much improve. Also Toda La Semana, 1964 (All the
Week), a novel.

PORTUGAL

BRAGA, Mario

Nevoeiro, 1944 (Mist), Serranos, 1948 (Mountain People)
Two social realist novels describing the deadend stagnation and narrowness of
life in peasant regions of northern Portugal from 1930s to W.W.II.

BRANDÃO, Raul

O Pobre De Pedir, 1931 (The Poor Man of Pedir, 1974)
A novel about the lives of poverty stricken peasants in the Porto region of
northern Portugal during the 1920s, the long declining fortunes of peasant farming
and the pityless all-encompassing striving to hold on to and acquire additional
land. The individualistic strategems and pennyante economies which take up and
sap so much of their lives, but ultimately do not defend them against being
overwhelmed by more capitalized commercial agriculture.

BARRENO, Maria, HORTA, Maria, VELHO DA COSTA, Maria

The Three Marias, New Portuguese Letters, 1973
A collection of monologues in the form of fictional letters, poems and belles
lettres written by three Portuguese middle class women and relating such things
as female sexuality, anti-clericalism and the strictures of life under the
decrepid Salazar regime. That this quite personalist and inocuous volume could
raise a furore in Portugal shows how anachronistic the society had become by the
early 1970s.

CABRAL, Alexandre

Fonte de Telha, 1949 (Shingle Spring)
A documentary novel of the 17th century wretchedness and poverty which enfolds
the life of families in a small fishing village near Lisbon during the late 1940s.

Margen Norte, 1961 (Northside)
A novel set in a middle class residential district of Lisbon during the late
1950s, of the drifting, self-inhibited and pointless life of the petit bourgeoise
protagonist, an allegorical product of the generation long Salazar regime. Also
see Cabral's Angolan writings.

FERREIRA DE CASTRO, Jose Maria

Emigrantes, 1928 (Emigrants, 1962)
One of the internationally best known Portuguese novels; an account of one
experience of the endemic Portuguese outmigration during this century. About a
young Portuguese peasant and his family on the edge of poverty in pre W.W.I period
and the husband's emigration to Brazil to make his fortune. Much of the book
deals with his long stay in Brazil and follows the immigrant workers through work
on the coffee estates of Sao Paulo State, labour in the Sao Paulo city industries
during the whirlwind of labour militancy following W.W.I, the regional civil war
of the early 1920s and finally the emigrant's return to Portugal, twelve years
older, almost as poor as when he left and without a home or family. Also see A
Selva, 1930 (The Jungle) in the Brazil section.

Eternidade, 1933 (Eternity), Terra Fria, 1934 (Cold Uplands), A Tempestade, 1940
(The Storm), A la E a Neve, 1947 (Wool and Snow)
A tetrology of novels which follow an impoverished Portuguese shepherd from the
northern hill country through the depression years and on the margins of an
anachronistic, backward rural society and into a different but no less grim
life as an urban factory worker during Portugal's mini industrial boom in W.W.II.

FERREIRA, Vergilio

O Caminho Fica Longe, 1944 (Its a Long Way from the Road), Vagao J, 1946 (Box Car)
Two neo-realist novels about Portuguese peasants, small towns people and migrant
workers in cities; the poverty, backwardness and stifling political autocracy of
late 1930s and the W.W.II years.

Mudanca, 1950 (Change)
A despairing novel which describes the increasing anachronism of Portuguese society
and the lack of any significant change after the defeat of fascism in Europe; the
work marks Ferreira's shift to existentialism.

FONSECA, Manuel de

Rosa Dos Ventos, 1940 (Compass Rose)
An early collection of socialist poetry dealing largely with the hard conditions
on the peasant farms and the mediocrity of life in small towns of the Alentejo
region during the late 1930s.

Aldeia Nova, 1941 (New Village)
A book of stories portraying the stagnant and miserable conditions in peasant
regions during Salazar's "New Order", as seen through the eyes of a group of
children. Also Cerromaior, 1943, a documentary novel of life in a small
provincial town of the early 1940s.

Seara de Vento, 1958 (Crop of Wind)
Another neo-realist novel of the systematic oppression and cultural restrictions
in Portugal (which is widely supported by the poor themselves) and which
bring all efforts of reform to naught.

NAMORA, Fernando

Casa de Malta, 1945 (Tramp's House)
The first of Namora's neo-realistic novels, dealing with social conditions in rural
Portugal during the early 1940s.

Minas de Sao Francisco, 1946 (The Mines of San Francisco)
A reportage novel of the context and conditions of tungsten mining in Portugal.
Revolves around Namora's medical work among poor peasants and miners in backland
regions.

Retalhos da Vida de Um Medico, 1949 (Mountain Doctor, 1956, 1963)
A semi-autobiographic novel revolving around the life of a middle aged doctor who
is trapped in the stagnant world of the Portuguese rural bourgeoisie during the
depth of the Salazar regime; his loss of hope and incapacity to use his profession
for any significant benefit.

O Homen Disfarcado, 1970 (The Disguised Man)
A novel of a Portuguese intellectual who comes to realize that his fashionable
existentialism is merely a product of his isolation, that the supposedly
"insoluble problems of human existence" are (in part) soluble through action in
common with others.

Os Clandestinos, 1974 (The Underground)
A novel of the past history and present conditions which bring a number of (mainly
petty bourgoise) characters into clandestine resistance to the Salazar regime.
An epic account of past strikes, miners' battles, reminiscences of mass
confrontation in 1917, the Spanish Civil War and into post W.W.II period. Woven
into the family memories of the characters. Being in effect the culture of the
Portuguese left, which mobilizes new individuals in succeeding generations.

NASCIMENTO, Manuel do

Eu Queria Vivir, 1942 (I Want to Live)
A novela of the life and reflections of a former rural school teacher dying in a
charity T.B. sanitorium. In part an allegory of life in Portugal for a left wing
intellectual at the time.

Mineiros, 1944 (Miners)
Written in the late 1930s, it is one of the first proletarian novels in Portugal.
An account of 48 hours in the lives of two Portuguese miners, their work, danger,
tenacity yet seeming hopelessness about social change. An authentic portrait of
Portuguese working class life unmarred by the usual dollops of "local colour".

Also O Aco Mudou de Tempera, 1946 (The Muted Steel of Tempering), another
Portuguese proletarian novel.

OLIVIERA, Carlos de

Casa Na Duna, 1943 (House on the Dunes)
A family portrait dealing with the very marginal position of the new rural
bourgeoisie; barely able to hold on to their middle class status and juxtaposed
to a backgrop in which the traditional rural middle class has declined into not so
genteel poverty.

Alcateia, 1944 (Wolf Pack)
A novel about a band of not very social bandits who are nevertheless composed of
the broken and cast off elements in Portuguese society. Their operations in a
backlands district and their sage estimates of how to practically deal with the
assorted corrupt political bosses, judges, police, businessmen who represent
"law and order" provides a brilliant commentary on the nature of a decaying
authoritarian state. As a parallel plot, the novel follows the son of a rural
bourgeoise family, his growing awareness of the society around him and his move
toward a Marxist viewpoint.

Also Pequenos Burgueses, 1948 (Small Bourgeoise), another neo-realist novel set
among middle class of Portugal of time.

PEREIRA, Jose Pacheco

As Lutas Operarias Contra a Carestia de Vida em Portugal - a Greve Geral de
Novembro de 1918, 1971 (Working Class Struggles Against Inflation in Portugal - The
General Strike of November 1918)
Left wing Portuguese working class history, dealing with the mass demonstrations
and proto-revolutionary General Strike at the end of W.W.I.

PEREIRA GOMES, Soeiro

Esteiros, 1951 (Estuaries)
A novel of peasants and small farmers during the 1940s who are completely powerless
to protect their already marginal incomes and landholdings from the exactions of
the national merchant class. The gradual disintegration of the peasant sector
which is foreshadowed by the collapse of artizanal industries and their workers
in the small towns of Portugal.

PIRES, Jose Cardoso

O Render Dos Herois, 1960 (The Conquering of Heroes)
A historical novel of the 1846 peasant rising in Portugal.

O Hospede de Job, 1963 (Job's Guest)
A novel of a father and son, two poor country people trying to cope with the archaic
class structure and irrationality of Salazar's Portugal in 1960s, pitted against
forces which they can neither deal with nor even understand. Presented through
a triple running account of what the different protagonists believe is happening.

Also O Ango Ancorado, 1958 (The Angel Anchored), Historias de Amor, 1952 (Love
Stories), two collections of social realist short stories about the poor and
working people in post W.W.II Portugal; Historias being banned because of its
allusions to the left underground then organizing itself.

REDOL, Alves

Gloria, Uma Aldeia do Ribatejo, 1938 (Gloria, A Village of the Ribatejo Region)
A documentary reportage work of a "typical" peasant village in the fazenda region
of the South Atlantic coast. The lives, strivings and traditional outlooks of

the part peasant-part rural labourer population during a time of deepening depression and social erosion.

Gaibeus, 1939 (Day Labourers)
The best known of the early social realist novels of Portugal, dealing with impoverished peasants and landless rural workers in the rice growing estates of Southern Portugal during the late 1930s. The notorious exploitation by the large landholders and their mayordomos is presented as only the last link of a chain of exploiters leading back to the National bourgeoisie in Lisbon and abroad. It pictures a poverty-strickened and exploited people which as yet has no class consciousness, where dissatisfaction is still personal and sub-political to be "solved" in personal ways--such as the endemic hopes of younger labourers in the rice fields to escape their "fates" through emigration.

Avierros, 1942, Fanga, 1943, Olhos de Agua, 1944 (Eyes of Water), Uma Fenda Na Muralha, 1945 (A Breach in the Wall), Porto Manso, 1946 (Port Meek), Horizonte Cerrado, 1949 (Closed Horizon), Os Hombres E As Sombras, 1951 (Men and Shadows), Vindima de Sangre, 1953 (Blood Vintage)
A series of novels and novelas comprising the Port Wine Cycle. Written in a popular style and intended for a popular audience, they chronicle the lives and the changing/unchanging social and economic conditions of inhabitants of the grape wine producing region around Douro, a locale where peasants have historically been engaged in production for export. A many faceted account of the lives of the various classes from landless rural labour, yeoman peasantry, fazenderos, artizans and city dockworkers as well as the sections of the rural middle class, from near impoverished petty storekeepers to agents of the national bourgeoise. The novels cover the trajectory of the region and its people during much of the first half of the 20th century, from a penurious independence to an insecure vassalage to the national financial and marketing houses.

O Muro Branco, 1968 (The Blank Wall)
A novel about those elements of the middle peasantry and rural bourgeoisie which have survived the processes of consolidation and bankruptcy to make it into the ranks of the established middle class by the late 1950s. Their devolution into a consumer-oriented, comprador sector which oscillates between purposeless stasis and wild ideological adventurism. Juxtaposed to sections of the Portuguese working class which develop a tenacity and class consciousness which earlier writers attributed to the yeoman peasantry.

Also A Barca dos Sete Lemes, 1958 (The Man With Seven Names, 1964), a novel on post W.W.II social conditions but utilizing allegory and urban folk themes as well as realism.

RIBEIRO, Alfonso

Aldeia, 1943 (Hamlet)
A reportage protest novel about the lives and conditions of the impoverished peasantry in the rocky uplands of Central Portugal.

RIBEIRO, Aquilino

Volframio, 1944 (Tungsten)
An investigative account of the tragic social and economic conditions involved in Tungsten mining in Portugal during the early 1940s.

SANTARENO, Bernardo

Os Marginais E a Revolucao, 1979 (Marginal Lives and Revolution)
A collection of four plays ("Remnants", "The Confession", "Monsanto", "Brief Life in Three Photos") which revile those forces that oppressed and deadened Portugal during the near half century of right wing autocracy which seemed to have been ended by the 1974 "revolution". By a leading Portuguese playwright whose work leans toward 19th century naturalism and working class "costumbrismo".

SILVA, Jose

Memoria de Um Operario, 1971 (Reminiscences of a Worker)
A life history of a Portuguese worker documenting events mainly in the northern
part of the country from the late 1930s to 1960s. Being reminiscences of family
life, neighbours and comrades, work and class struggle.

SOROMENHO, Castro

Terra Morta, 1949 (Dead Lands; published originally in French as Camaxillo)
An influential anti-colonial novel which details the oppression of Africans in
Angola and Mozambique and underlines the way in which colonialism holds Portugal
itself in backwardness. Portrays the exactions of the monopoly trading companies
in Africa, how their profits are used to retain control of Portugal by the Salazar
regime. The sacrifices and costs born by Portuguese peasants and workers (as well
as Africans) in sustaining the colonial profits.

TOJAL, Altino M. do

Sardinhas e Lua, 1971 (Sardines and Periods)
A collection of stories about the smugness, class chauvinism and the psychological
repression (especially in women) among the Portuguese middle class of the 1960s.

ITALY

ALVARO, Carrado

Gente En Aspromonte, 1930 (Revolt in Aspromonte, 1962), Vent' Anni, 1932 (Twenty Years)
Two novels which deal with the poverty and traditional oppression of shepherds, landless peasants and rural workers in Alvaro's native Calabria and how it is sustained under fascist rule. Two of the few protest novels to appear in fascist Italy and for which Alvaro was briefly imprisoned.

La Siepe E L'Orto, 1920 (Edge of the Garden), L'Uomo Nel Labrinte, 1926 (Man in the Labyrinth), L'Annata Alla Finestra, 1929 (A Year in the Window)
Three novels dealing with the backward and unjust conditions endured by peasants and working people in southern Italy during the first quarter of this century and the prospect of violence as a way to correct the grave injustices perpetrated by the ruling class.

Quasi Una Vita, 1959 (Almost a Lifetime)
An autobiography of Alvaro's life and that of southern Italy from before W.W.I through the upheavals following that war, the gradual entry of fascist rule in the region, the bitter 1930s, W.W.II and the success of the regional ruling class in surviving the defeat of Italian fascism little changed.

ARPINO, Giovanni

Un Delitto D'Onore, 1961 (A Crime of Honour, 1963)
A novel set in Sicily at the beginning of the 1960s and exploring the cultural bases of authoritarianism; in particular, the traditional servitude of women as exemplified in the case of abduction of a young woman by a refused suitor and the code that she must then either marry her abductor (or have her family kill him) or face permanent dishonour in the community. Made into a fascinating film.

BACCHELLI, Riccardo

Il Mulino del Po, 1938 (The Mill on the Po, 1950)
A two volume novel dealing with four generations of peasants, landlords and petty entrepreneurs in the Po valley of Northeastern Italy from the mid to the end of the 19th century. A not especially progressive but detailed documentation of the rise of the rural bourgeoisie there through the family history of the owners of a watermill. The emergence of industrial capitalism and the tensions between the traditional rulers and the new capitalist class and in general the backside of the struggles to unify Italy under the hegemony of the capitalists. Also Mondo Vecchio Sempre Nuovo (Nothing New Under the Sun, 1955), the third volume of the trilogy.

Il Diavolo al Ponte Lungo, 1927 (The Devil at the Long Bridge)
A novel of the social conditions in the Emilia region of Italy during the 1870s and the attempts of Bakunin and his followers to establish a revolutionary movement there.

BASSANI, Giorgio

Le Storie Ferraresi, 1962 (Five Stories of Ferrara, 1971)
Stories of the Italian bourgeoisie around the Po Valley town of Ferrara in late 1930s to 1943-45 when the Po region is under control of the Social Fascist State but southern Italy is already "liberated" by Allied armies. Portrays the mean spirited posturing, self-justification of this class, their sole commitment to personal interests and their capacity to change their opinions virtually overnight.

BATTAGLIA, Roberto

Storia Della Resistenza Italiana, 1943-1945, 1964 (History of the Italian Resistance, 1943-1945)
A massive history of the Italian partizan movement during the last years of W.W.II which at its height saw some 100,000 men and women in arms. It alludes to the disarming of the partizan forces by the Anglo-American forces at the end of W.W.II and the conveyance of political power into the hands of the Italian conservatives.

BERNARDI, Carlo

Tre Operai, 1934 (Three Workers)
A documentary novel of the lives of the Naples working class during the early 1930s. It treats with the traditional and new forms of oppression and touches on the mainly non-organized forms of personal resistance to it by working people. It is one of the few such works to appear during the period and was an underground classic.

Siamo Tutti Bambini, 1951 (We Are All Children), Vesuvio E Pane, 1952 (Vesuvius and Bread)
Two documentary novels dealing with the lives of working people and the poor mainly in the Naples region, ranging back and forth from the fascist epoch to the post W.W.II period, commenting on the trajectory of Italian society and the continuity of poverty and powerlessness of the poor under all regimes to date.

CALVINO, Italo

Il Sentiero Dei Nidi Di Ragno, 1947 (The Path to the Spider's Nest, 1957)
A novel set around Genoa in the final year of W.W.II, dealing with the experiences of a boy who gradually comes to support and then join the partizans fighting in the mountains.

L'Entrada en Guerra, 1949 (Declaration of War)
Another social realist novel of ordinary working people in Italy at the beginning of W.W.II.

Giornata Di Uno Scrutatore, 1963 (Diary of an Election Observor)
A collection of essays by a veteran neo realist writer; analyses the extensive changes in Italy since W.W.II and suggests that the once powerful appeals of anti-fascist struggle and class culture no longer hold the same meaning to Italians enmeshed in a consumer society.

CASSOLA, Carlo

Fausto e Anna, 1952 (Fausto and Anna, 1960)
A semi-autobiographical novel set in the final years of W.W.II; a love story which evolves into an account of the anti-fascist partizan struggle in northern Italy during 1944. Also in the same vein, La Ragazza di Bube, 1958 (Bebo's Girl, 1962).

Taglio de Bosco, 1954 (Cutting Down the Woods), La Casa di Via Valadier, 1956 (The House on Valadian Street)
Two collections of stories dealing with the lives of ordinary people in central Italy and in the outskirts of Rome during the late 1940s and early 1950s; portrays both the changes in and continuity of ruling class power on the local level in Italy.

DI LAMPEDUSA, Giuseppe

The Leopard, 1958
A novel in the form of reminiscences by the aging head of a feudal Sicilian land-lord family in the years immediately following the Garibaldi-led insurgency which overthrew the Kingdom of the Two Sicilies. The Leopard is hardly progressive (and certainly not proletarian) but it does provide some incisive characterization of the feudal landlords' incorporation into the new capitalist order; their strategies and their manipulation of the rising bourgeoisie and the new Italian state in efforts to crush the spirit of social revolt among the peasantry released

by Garibaldi. The central theme is the Leopard's maxim that "we have to change, so that things will not change for us."

DOLCI, Danilo

Banditi a Partinico, 1955 (The Outlaws of Partinico)
A reportage work of how the Mafia in western Sicily used bandit gangs to terrorize the emerging left wing peasant organizations during the late 1940s. The linkage of the Mafia with local landlords, the Christian Democrat politicians, the former U.S. occupation forces, all of whom had interests in finding an "extra-governmental" force to suppress popular discontent. By a left Catholic activist.

Verso Un Mondo Vuovo, 1964 (New World in the Making)
Another reportage work about the consolidation of the right wing-gangster alliance in Sicily in the 1950s and early 1960s; the way in which development funds and economic growth has been turned to the benefit of the new bourgeoise and has ousted much of the rural poor. Also Inchiesta a Palermo, 1958 (To Feed the Poor).

JOVINE, Francesco

Terre Del Sacramente, 1950 (The Estate in the Abruzzi, 1952)
An epic novel of the social conditions, history and millenial psychology which underlay a rising of peasants in central Italy living under near medieval serf-like conditions during the early years of this century. Revolves around one Luca Marano, a local peasant who emerges as a leader in the seizure of uncultivated lands. Captures the millenial, quasi-religious and anarchist visions; their hunger for bread and justice.

LEVI, Carlo

Christ Stopped at Eboli, 1947
A novelized account of a poor and isolated Calabrian village in which the author was briefly interned by the fascists in 1934. Portrays the intertwined reality of past and present events and conditions, of history and myth in a peasant society, of superstitions and archaic forms of consciousness of being part of the age-old nation of the poor. Describes the ingrained poverty of people alloyed with their hidden vitality and potential resilience.

Le Parole Sono Pietra, 1955 (Words Are Stones, 1958)
An essay sequel to Eboli, castigating Italian intellectuals and government for doing nothing to effectively improve the lives of people in the decaying peasant villages and dying small towns of the hunger lands.

Tutto Il Miele e Finito, 1964 (All the Honey is Finished)
An elegaic description of an Italian island community, becoming deserted as the land and anachronistic industries fail to support the inhabitants.

LEVI, Giorgina

Il Lingotto: Storia di un Quartiere Operaoi Torino, 1922-1973, 1976 (Lingotto: the history of a Turin Workers' District, 1922-1973)
A massive social and political history using oral and other sources; details the intricate and deep rooted culture of working class socialism in one workers' district of Turin (a major north Italian industrial city) from before W.W.I through the generation-long fascist rule and to the 1970s and the varied post W.W.II Italian phases. The varied and intersecting roots of a separate working class culture and its tenacious survival.

MAROLTA, Giuseppe

A Milano No Fa Fredelo, 1949 (It's Not Cold in Milan)
A collection of whimsical though sometimes perceptive stories about migrants from impoverished Italian south coming to find work in the major industrial city of the north during the late 1940s.

MAXWELL, Gavin

God Preserve Me From My Friends, 1956
A biography of the Sicilian bandit chieftain Salvatore Giuliano who from the mid to the late 1940s was used by the Mafia (and their government allies) to terrorize the left wing peasant movements in Sicily. Giuliano's massacre of a peasant rally near Palermo led to the withdrawal of semi-official protection and his capture and death. An account of intertwined U.S., Mafia and assorted "legitimate" political forces in Sicily. In effect a study of gangsterism as a major element of political power in Italy.

MORAVIA, Alberto

La Romana, 1947 (Woman of Rome, 1954)
A novel of a Roman prostitute during the early 1940s; dealing with the venality and hypocrisy of the late fascist era as the epitome of traditional capitalist exploitation (as experienced by a more or less passive victim of that system and not a glamorous independent businesswoman).

Raconti Romani, 1954 (Roman Tales, 1957)
A collection of interconnected stories about the poor of Rome in the years immediately after W.W.II; their personal sagacity but political cynicism, their basically healthy strivings as compared to the degeneracy of the classes which rule Italy. Moravia's work is at times marred by an excess of Christian humility and philosophizing.

NENNI, Pietro

Ten Years of Tyranny in Italy, 1932
A horatory account of the union and working class movements in Italy during the first decade of fascist rule; counterposing the upsurge of mass actions in the years following W.W.I and the unsystematic yet general destruction (or retreat underground) of socialist organization after 1923. By the leader of the left wing of the Italian Socialist Party.

ORTESE, Anna Maria

Il Mare Non Bagna Napoli, 1953 (The Bay is Not Naples, 1955)
A portrait of the lives of the poor in post war Naples, in which the much vaunted excitement and "human warmth" of crowded tenement districts does not alleviate the ignorance, malnutrition, disease and abysmal poverty.

PAGLIARANI, Elio

Cronache, Ed Altre Posie, 1954 (Chronicles and Other Poems)
A collection of poems chronicling the influx of rural dispossessed into Milan during the early 1950s; their culture shock, lives, search for work and changing hopes.

La Ragazza Carla, 1957 (The Girl Carla)
A novel about the by-products of the initial "consumer society" in Milan during the late 1950s. Revolves around the dissolution of personal loyalties and human dignity in the strivings to "get ahead" and obtain junk possessions which in fact make life no richer than the poverty which the parental generation experienced.

PAOLIERI, Ferdinando

Natio Borgo Selvaggio, 1908 (My Barbarous Native Town)
A collection of sketches in novel form which combine naturalistic detail and satire of the pompous know-nothingism, stagnation and petty self-interest of the

bourgeoise at the turn of the century. All the more biting because the native
town is the famed "cultural centre" of Florence.

PAVESE, Cesare

The Selected Works of Cesare Pavese, 1968
A translation of five novelas by Pavese including The Devil in the Hills, The
House on the Hill, The Beach; set in W.W.II Italy on the eve of defeat
revolving mainly around intellectuals and petty bourgeoisie, rethinking their
previous quiessence under fascism, maundering over their mundane love affairs
and deals, and generally revealing their unchanged class chauvinism and narrow
self interest.

PRATOLINI, Vasco

Il Tappeto Verde, 1941 (The Green Carpet), Via de Magazzini, 1942 (Magazzini Way),
Il Quartiere, 1944 (The Naked Street, 1952), Cronica Familiare, 1947 (Family
Chronicle)
Four short novels which combine lyrical and realistic sketches of the city of
Florence, its surroundings and especially the lives of its ordinary
people. Necessarily cautious before 1944, these documentary novels are among
the most critical works to appear in fascist Italy.   Pratolini was a journalist
from the Florence working class who portrayed the tenacious decency, skepticism
and vitality of many working people even under Mussolini.

Cronache Di Poveri Amanti, 1949 (A Tale of Poor Lovers, 1949)
A massive novel set in the working class suburbs of Florence in the mid 1920s
during the consolidation of fascist power but reaching back to the momentous
class struggles there during and after W.W.I. Touches on the deep working class
culture from which those struggles sprang. Treats with the rise and consolidation
of fascism as the outgrowth of a threatened Italian bourgeoisie; of how the police,
courts and state protect and give a carte blanche to the fascist gangs but
suppress all forms of self-defense by the working class. A subtle and believable
description of the seemingly minor differences in social position, class culture
and personality which gradually set individuals on the side of the fascists or in
opposition.

Una Storia Italiana, 1955-1966 (An Italian History)
The general title of a trilogy which details the changes and continuity in north
Italian working class culture from the 1880s and the transition from anarchist to
socialist trade union struggles, through the mass confrontations between capital
and labour in the first two decades of the 20th century, and deepening
repression and generation-long night of fascism from 1923 to 1944, the continuing
undercurrent of workers' struggles which bursts forth again after W.W.II.

Metello, 1955 (Metello, 1968)
The first volume of the Storia Italiana trilogy, it relates the evolution of the
Florence working class into a proletariat from the pre-industrial anarchistic
vanguard of the early 1880s. Revolves around the life of the title character,
Metello, a peasant youth who becomes a socialist bricklayer and union organizer
in Florence. The growing trade union movement, the early confrontations with
Italian capitalism (also then consolidating itself) carried into the first
decade of the 20th century, when the hero has become a semi-retired master
bricklayer, a social democrat somewhat akin to M. Andersen's Pelle the Conqueror.

Lo Scialo, 1960 (The Waste)
The second volume of the trilogy in which the adult children and grandchildren of
Metello, their friends and comrades of the Florence working class during the
proto-revolutionary upheavals of W.W.I and the early 1920s, the growing power of
reaction, divisions between communists, socialists and other tendencies in the
working class, and the triumph of fascism. Treats with the ongoing underground
opposition until the end of W.W.II.

Allegoria e Derisione, 1966 (Allegory and Derision)
The final novel of the trilogy which continues the tale of working class Florence;
the original generations of socialists now dead but their visions and views still

alive, if somewhat muted. Runs from the last years of W.W.II, the collapse of
fascism and the imposition of Christian Democracy up to 1949.

La Costanza della Ragione, 1964 (Bruno Santini, 1968)
A novel of the north Italian working class which carries their story from 1950
to the late 1960s.

RENDA, F. (ed.)

Il Movimento Contadino Nella Societa Siciliana, 1956 (The Labour Movement in
Sicilian Society)
A social history of the multistranded traditions and backgrounds of the labour
movement in Sicily during the 20th century, relating it to regional culture in
general and to earlier forms of peasant struggle as well as to newly emergent
attitudes and interests. By a leading left scholar of the Sicilian labour
movement and a union activist.

SCIASCIA, Leonardo

La Parrocchie di Regalpetra, 1956 (Salt in the Wound, 1960)
A rather rambling account of an ancient Sicilian village of peasants and salt
quarry workers which has known virtually all forms of oppression from Roman times
on. Told by a rural history teacher who mixes reminiscence, myths, local history
and exasperating 19th century rhetoric and regional patriotism in an account of
the fascist-landlord rule during the 1920s to 1940s and the following Mafia-
government regime, where nothing seems to change but for the worse.

Il Giorno Della Civetta, 1961 (Mafia Vendetta, 1964), A Ciascuno Il Suo, 1964
(A Man's Blessings, 1968)
Two novels detailing the rule and struggle for power of Mafia over Sicilian towns
as it evolved after W.W.II; the unchecked reign of murder and terror and the
corrupt or totally impotent agents of the central government.

SILONE, Ignazio

Fontamara, 1934 (Fontamara, 1935)
A semi-documentary novel of a poor peasant village of mountain Italy during the
early 1930s; details the entry of fascism, the merely minor changes in the
traditional system of exploitation as the local bosses are incorporated into the
"New Order". The lives of three generations of peasants who respond in the age-
old manner of personal circumvention of exactions but who are
now slowly (partly) drawn into contact with the broader, extra-local resistance
to fascism. With some of the villagers (exemplified by the young peasant
narrator) becoming aware of the international and historic forces in conflict,
of which they are a part.

Bread and Wine, 1936
A novel of an Italian socialist emigre, a union leader who returns from exile to
work underground in fascist Italy disguised as a priest in an obscure peasant
village. An account of his gradual appreciation of the necessary caution,
complexity, but ingrained resistance inherent in a peasant society.

SOLDATI, Mario

Supper With the Commendatore, 1950
A somewhat whimsical satire of the views of a totally unreconstructed traditional
political boss in Naples during the post war democracy and the little changed
bases of his power.

STRATI, Saverio

La Teda, 1957 (The Torch), Tibi e Tascia, 1959, Avventure in Citta, 1962
Three novels about the lives of peasants and workers, of the undercurrents and
open class conflicts in Calabria in the post W.W.II period.

TESTORI, Giovanni

Il Segretti Di Milano, 1958 (The Secrets of Milan)
A novel of an extended working class family in Milan during the 1950s; heavy on local colour and interpersonal emotions, it treats the continuity of class exploitation but also the apolitically individualist responses to it.

Il Ponte Della Ghisolfa, 1959
A collection of short stories of Milan working class life.

Il Fabbricone, 1961 (The Big Factory)
A somewhat more political novel of the lives of workers and their families in the industrial outskirts of Milan.

VERGA, Giovanni

The She-Wolf and Other Stories, 1962 (original circa 1890)
A collection of short stories and sketches of Sicilian peasants, village notables, landless workers, tax collectors and the squires of the regime-ancien during the 1880s and 1890s, by the leading Italian naturalist writer of his generation.

The House by the Medlar Tree, 1964 (original 1894)
A novel of a Sicilian fishing village in 1890 as described through the eyes of a number of its inhabitants, a pioneer work of Italian realism, even if suffused with "local colour" themes.

VITTORINI, Elio

Conversazione in Sicilia, 1940 (In Sicily, 1949)
A reportage account (in allegorical form) dealing with the old and new exploiters who battened on the labour and misery of Sicilian peasantry, rural workers and shepherds under the fascist "New Order". Set in the 1935-1937 period, it is one of the most bitter accounts to appear in Italy at the time. Written after Vittorini was released from political internment in the region.

Le Donne di Messina, 1949 (The Women of Messina)
A novel of the lives of women and families in the Sicilian town of Messina, as bitterly squalid, impoverished and oppressed after "the liberation" as before.

A Vittorini Omnibus, 1973
A collection of three works; In Sicily (1940), The Twilight of the Elephant (1945) and The Garibaldina (1948), all dealing with the same region and the same sorts of people under different political regimes in peace and war. Captures the mutability yet tenacity of oppression and the responses to it, from fatalism to resistance.

GERMANY

APITZ, Bruno

Nackt Unter Wölfen, 1958 (Naked Among Wolves, 1962)
A novel-reminiscence of eight years survival in the Nazi concentration camps by a
rank and file German communist. Set in Buchenwald in 1945, it revolves around
the actions of the underground committee to save the lives of a number of prisoners
scheduled for last minute execution. Through flashbacks Apritz sketches the
backgrounds of the prisoners and their struggles against the triumph of the Nazis.
But mainly it is a document of the horror of concentration camp world and the
flickering survival of human decency and resistance even there. It is possibly
the finest of that genre.

BECHER, Johannes

Leviste, 1926 (Leviste)
A proletarian novel which rages at the mass slaughter of working
people in "their" rulers wars (W.W.I). Proposes that the only justifiable war is
one which desposes such cannibals.

Ein Mensch Unsere Zeit, 1930 (A Man of Our Time)
A collection of militant socialist poetry about the lives of working people in
Germany and throughout the world; their differing backgrounds yet similar fates
and the visions of a just society. Becher was mainly a prolific communist poet.

BRECHT, Bertolt

The Three Penny Opera, 1930
Probably Brecht's most widely known play; set in late Victorian London at the
height of British Imperialism. Revolves around the schemes of various characters
of the London lumpen proletariat and the only slightly different ruling class,
and constitutes a biting satire dissecting the myths and cliches of an archetypal
imperialist state. The pseudo grandeur thinly overlaying the accepted violence,
degradation, beggary and the underlying fascism (in the character of Mack the
Knife) in such a milieu. A reworking of John Gay's 18th century British play,
The Beggars' Opera.

St. Joan of the Stockyards, 1934
A play translating Joan of Arc from a bemused proponent of French Royalist
nationalism to a naive Salvation Army missionary among Chicago stockyard workers.
She is used by the American rulers but, in a still bemused fashion, gradually
evolves a dangerous messianism against the bosses. Both Joans are betrayed to
their executioners by the frightened rulers. St. Joan, as well as the following
four plays, might better be considered as German exile literature written in the
U.S.

Mother Courage and Her Children, 1941
A play set during the Thirty Years War in Germany of early 1600s but intended as
a more universal charicature of the petty bourgeoise in war time. Revolves around
a woman peddlar who follows the assorted armies trading with all and sundry
regardless of the despoilation and destruction of those around her, finally
including her own children. Ironically this play was performed in the U.S. as if
it were a tribute to the "courage" of such petty war profiteers.

Der Gute Mensch Von Sezuan, 1940 (The Good Woman of Setzuan, 1961)
A play set in warlord China during the indefinite past which pursues the theme
that man (or woman) cannot be both moral and survive in a society built on greed
and violence, that decency and goodness will only prevail with the establishment
of a society which supports it. Contains sardonic satire of religious sages whose
edicts, if followed, would fessle the hands of the best and allow evil even
greater dominance.

The Life of Galileo, 1947 (Galileo, Galilei)
A play revolving around Galileo's retraction of his heliocentric theory of the
planetary system under threat of heresy charges by the Catholic church, only to
find himself imprisoned for life in a monastry. Revolves around the questions of
the limits of compromise and when one must tell the truth.

The Caucasian Chalk Circle, 1948
A play on the theme of Solomon's verdict on two claimants of a child; that a child
"belongs to" whoever most cares for it and a land to which people will make best
use of it for all concerned.

Die Tage Der Kommune, 1949 (Days of the Commune, 1978)
A play about the Paris Commune of 1870, being one of Brecht's works written after
his return to the G.D.R.

Hauspostille, 1927 (Manuel of Piety, 1958)
A fine collection of Brecht's poetry from the 1920s; touches on human lives which
at times rise above destructive and oppressive social conditions. Brecht's poetry
is matched only by the best passages of his drama.

BREDEL, Willi

Maschinenfabrik N&K, 1930 (Machine Factory N&K, 1934)
A novel of the work, life and political struggles of workers in a North German
heavy machine factory in the 1920s. Written partly from personal experiences by
a remarkable proletarian author and revolutionary activist whose work was widely
translated in the 1930s.

Rosenhofstrasse, 1931 (Rosecourt Street)
A collective novel of the daily lives and militant traditions (socialist and
pre-socialist) of a Hamburg working class district in the late 1920s. Written
while Bredel was imprisoned by the Weimar Republic for "literary high treason".

Die Prüfung, 1934 (The Test)
A semi-autobiographical account of his own and his comrades' responses to
imprisonment in an early Nazi prison camp during 1933. Also a call for a United
Front mobilization against worldwide fascism with a then unusual perception of the
extent to which Nazis' had smashed organized opposition.

Dein Unbekannter Bruder, 1937 (Your Unknown Brother)
A novel about the system of informers and repression established throughout
Germany in the first three years of Nazi rule; the incredible difficulties against
which underground resistance was only barely able to survive.

Verwandte Und Bekannte, 1943-1953 (Relatives and Friends) including Die Väter,
1943 (The Fathers), Die Söhne, 1949 (The Sons), Die Enkel, 1953 (The Grandchildren)
A trilogy novel, an epic chronicle of the lives and struggles of three generations
of the Hamburg working class as represented through the kith and kin of one family.
Runs from the beginning of the century to circa 1950 and is arguably Bredel's
finest work. His own life was more extraordinary than any character in his novels.

CLAUDIUS, Edward

Grüne Oliven Und Nackte Berge, 1945 (Green Olives and Bare Mountains)
A novel of the Spanish Civil War as told from the viewpoint of defeated Spanish
Republicans interned in democratic French prison camps during the first years of
W.W.II.

Gewitter, 1948 (Thunder)
A novel surveying the physical, social and human destruction of Germany during
W.W.II as seen from the ruins and as the inevitable outcome of fascism.

DELIUS, F.C.

Wir Unternehmer, 1966 (We Entrepreneurs)
A "play" in free verse which satirizes and exposes the underlying policies of the
large German corporations and their political agents in the Christian Democratic
Party. Consists of a selective reordering and re-emphasis of statements made at
a 1965 C.D.U./C.S.U. Economic conference which brings home their irreducible

ruling class and property-interested outlook behind the rhetoric about social justice.

DOBLIN, Alfred

Alexanderplatz, Berlin, 1929 (Alexanderplatz, 1933)
A huge, rambling, expressionist novel which intertwines extracts of popular songs, newspaper accounts, official reports, jokes and urban folktales in Berlin dialect, and events and scenes around the Alexanderplatz, Berlin in late 1920s. Woven around the experiences and responses of one Franz Biberkopf, a not too bright, if sometimes cunning, petty criminal who in a sense represents the combined lumpen proletariat and lumpen bourgeoise during the final days of the Weimar Republic.

Trilogie: November 1918, 1949-1950 (November 1918, 1958)
A novel trilogy, more sombre and realistic than but using the same collage techniques as Alexanderplatz. It is a vast fresco which attempts to recreate the social, political and historical events, the daily lives and hopes swirling through Berlin in a single month, November 1918. The doings of major figures and forces, of unknown citizens and mundane occurrences during that proto-revolutionary month at the end of W.W.I. The millenial hopes, the everyday drama of getting a loaf of bread, the initial revolutionary struggles and so forth.

DORST, Tankred

Toller, 1969
A quasi-documentary play about Ernest Toller, the anarchist poet and president of the short-lived Bavarian Soviet Republic in 1919, who during his imprisonment under sentence of death wrote what became internationally translated and performed plays for Workers' Theatre. Of his later refugee life and contemporary relevance.

ENZENBERGER, Hans Magnus

Das Verhör von Habana, 1970 (The Havana Hearings)
A documentary drama piece drawn from testimonies given by captured counter-revolutionary "mercenaries" in Havana after the failed Bay of Pigs invasion of 1961. Treats with the differing backgrounds and ideologies of the "mercenaries", the varied interests they have in wishing to re-establish the status ante quo in Cuba. One of the more successful examples of the concern with Third World topics among progressive West German writers of post Adenauer period.

ENZENBERGER, Hans, R. NITSCHE, K. ROEHLER, W. SCHAFHAUSEN (eds.)

Klassenbuch: Ein Lesebuch zu den Klassenkampfen in Deutschland, 1972-1975 (Class Book: A reader of class struggles in Germany)
A three volume reader of working class social history and class struggles in Germany from 1756 to 1971. A kind of counter history to that normally taught in schools; intended for a general readership and from an independent socialist viewpoint.

GLUCHOWSKI, Bruno

Der Honigkotten, 1965 (The Honey Comb)
A novel of the life of a Ruhr miner from the massive industrial strikes of 1912 to the mid Weimar period of 1925. Touches on the triumph of national chauvinism in sections of the union and socialist movement at beginning of W.W.I and the re-emergence of internationalism and the anti-war activism shortly after the revolutionary upsurge in 1918/1919 and the German civil war in the Ruhr during 1920, French occupation and the re-establishment of German capitalism. Done with retrospective knowledge that much of the tradition of socialist working class struggle will be suppressed and lost in the coming three decades of fascist and corporate rule. One of the few recent West German novels to re-establish a direct link with prewar radical literature.

GRÜNBERG, Karl

Brennende Ruhr, 1930 (Burning Ruhr, 1934)
A novel about the supposedly "inextinguishable proletarian militancy" of workers

in the Ruhr heavy industry-coal mining region, which had been/was a citadel of radical working class militancy during the preceding two generations.

GRUPPE 61

Aus Der Welt Der Arbeit, 1966 (From the World of Work)
An influential collection of stories and reportage pieces about work life and workers lives (including those disabled and retired from their jobs) in specific industries in Germany of the mid 1960s. By members of a group of variously radical worker-writers attempting to portray the reality of everyday life and confront the cloud nine rhetoric about "the end of class". Includes stories by Angelika Mechtel, Bruno Gluchowski, Klaus Everwyn and Mathias Mander.

HABER, Horatius

Kopf Und Arm: Die Denkwurdigen Abenteur des Bauernfahnrich's, Wendel Haeberlin, 1976 (Head and Arm: the thought-provoking adventures of the peasant standard bearer, Wendel Haeberlin)
A sardonic novel based on considerable historic research; deals with the fictional reminiscences of a standard bearer in the peasant levies of Thomas Munzer during the Peasant Wars of 1520s. An allegory on actions and justifications still in vogue today with a Brechtian ending which has salvation attained by betrayal and opportunism. Also see Johann Jacob Grimmelhausen, Simplicius Simplisimus, 1965 (original circa 1640).

HAUPTMANN, Gerhart

Die Weber, 1892 (The Weavers, 1898)
A once world famous play about the economic and social destruction of handloom weavers in the Silesia-Thuringia region of Germany from mid to late 19th century through the growth of factories. Powerful accounts of the famine, machine wrecking movements, mass demonstrations and primitive class revolt which burst forth. The play had a galvanizing effect on left wing artists who produced a spate of accompanying songs, poems, paintings and comparable works. The Weavers was translated, adapted, and performed in Workers' Theatre productions around the world for over 40 years (although Hauptmann himself became quite conservative in his later life).

HEYM, Stephen

The Crusaders, 1950
A semi-autobiographical account of the U.S. occupation of Western Europe and Germany immediately after W.W.II; the mixed sentimentality combined with indifferent callousness, ignorance and calculated blindness of the forces in the countries they occupy resulting in the rapid re-establishment of the status quo ante in Germany. Alludes to comparable processes in France and Italy.

HOCHHUTH, Rolf

Der Stellvertreter, 1963 (The Deputy, 1964)
A massive "semi-documentary" play which deals with the role of the Vatican and Pope Pius XII's support of Italian and German fascism as part of the Church's crusade against communism. But mainly the play revolves around the Pope and Curia's suppression of those elements in the Church which would have it make some stand against the Jewish holocaust. An epilogue in the 1964 Grove Press edition contains some historical documentation by Hochhuth, a Swiss emigre writer. Also see Eric Bentley's (ed.) The Storm Over the Deputy, a collection of editorials and articles in European and U.S. press which attempted to silence the play, along with some spirited defense of the work.

Soldiers, 1968
Another book length play revolving around the endless intricacies of British imperial interests which the Churchill government of 1943 wishes to pursue during and after W.W.II; the fact that the war was something other and more than a struggle of "Democracy against Fascism". A rather complicated play-within-a-play, being the recreation of a play originally staged in Coventry in 1943 restaged 25 years later, involving an actor who was a bomber pilot in the fire storm

destruction of Dresden and with the retrospectively acquired knowledge juxtaposed to the sentiments of the original play.

HOELZ, Max (Max Holz)

From the White Cross to the Red Standard, 1928
The autobiography of a once legendary union leader of Saxony-Thuringian miners who during the early 1920s led underground resistance to Freikorps troops sent in to suppress the left. Discusses his youth in a conservative Catholic miner's family, work in the mines during the late 19th century, the struggles to bring Social Democratic labour unions into a traditionalist region at the turn of the century and his own move into the ranks of the revolutionary proletariat during the course of W.W.I. The account takes him into exile in the Soviet Union in late 1920s, where he died during the Stalinist purges.

KAISER, Georg

Gas, 1920 (Gas)
A widely translated surrealist play about the chaos of 20th century capitalism as seen in the operation of an industrial gas works. It is primarily an indictment of capitalism for its unforgiveable wars. An unqualified left wing pacifism is also the central theme of Kaiser's (1924) Die Bürger Von Calais, a play set in late 19th century France, and (1940) Der Soldat Tanaka, set during the 1905 Russo-Japanese War. Both were performed by Workers' Theatre groups.

Lederköpfe, 1928 (Leatherheads)
Another anti-militarist play set among Herodotus' Greek expeditionary soldiers in Asia Minor during circa 300 B.C. The theme is that history as normally taught lies about class interests and about responses that must have been as divergent in the past as in 1928.

KÖRNER, Wolfgang

Versetzung, 1966 (Transfer)
A novel of the oppressive and vindictive bureaucracy operating in a West German welfare office. It revolves around the growing disgust of a lower level welfare worker who leaks details of the particularly unjust treatment of one case to the press only to find himself transfered to the repugnant "debt collection division" as punishment and the administration quite unaltered by the minor public furor.

KURELLA, Alfred

Rosina, 1938 (Rosina)
A memoir of experiences in the Thaelmann Brigade, the large German refugee unit of the International Brigades during the Spanish Civil War. Kurella also wrote a number of novels describing working class life and struggles in Germany during the 1920s.

LANGE, Anna Marie

Das Wilheminische Berlin, 1967 (Wilhelmian Berlin), Berlin Zur Zeit Bebel und Bismark, 1969 (Berlin in the Time of Bebel and Bismark)
A highly readable two volume social history of Berlin and the Berlin working class from circa 1870 to 1914. The rising industrial city, the old quarters and the vast new working class tenement districts, urban environments, popular songs and humour, public services and disservices, food and domestic life, recreations, the anatomy of work and poverty, and the growing trade union and Social Democratic movement becoming a nation within a nation. Deals mainly with the daily worlds of ordinary working people (including children) but also documents the changing industries and the evolving political culture with the deepening confrontations with employers and state. Bebel and Bismark takes the city to 1900, Wilhelmian Berlin continues the account from 1900 to the summer of 1914. Despite the occasional bow to interpretive dogma, the two volumes are a triumph of scholarly yet popular social history.

LETTAU, Reinhard

Fiende, 1968 (Enemies)
A collection of short stories revolving about the McCarthyist ideology of "enemies foreign and domestic" which had seemingly become institutionalised in West German society and polity during the 1960s.

Taglicher Faschimus, 1971 (Everyday Fascism)
Another collection of stories on the theme of "democratic fascist" underpinnings in contemporary Western (German) society.

MANN, Heinrich

Professor Unrat, 1904 (Small Town Tyrant, 1944)
A sardonic satire of the decline and further fall of a pompous and tyranical school teacher caught in the coils of lust for a tawdry dance hall singer. The original lampoons the hypocrisy of the petit bourgeoise of Germany but was turned into a sloppy melodrama in the film The Blue Angel.

Die Kliene Stadt, 1909 (The Small Town)
A more systematic attack on the social and cultural bases of conservatism and class arrogance in pre W.W.I Germany as seen through the lives of small town bourgeoisie.

Das Kaiserreich, 1918-1925 (The Imperial State)
A novel trilogy consisting of Der Untertan, 1918 (The Subject), Die Armen, 1920 (The Poor), Der Kopf, 1925 (The Chief); they combine documentation, social protest and cuttingly ironic portraits of the lives and thoughts of representatives of the main social forces in W.W.I Germany. Depicts the epoch of Kaiser Wilhelm (1901-1918) as one of headlong ruling class greed, banal stupidity and devouring bureaucracy with the working class emerging as an angry, self-conscious nation within a nation.

MARCHWITZA, Hans

Sturm Auf Essen, 1930 (Storm Over the Ruhr, 1932)
A documentary novel about the lives, work and militancy of the Ruhr miners during the Weimar period; of the Ruhr Red Army which helped defeat the right wing Kapp putsch in 1920, through the strikes, blacklists and struggles against the German coal and metal trusts to the eve of the cataclysm.

Der Rote Ein Mark Roman, 1931 (The Red One-Mark Novel)
A novel of the working class struggles in Germany during the late 1920s written in the format of a one-mark potboiler romance.

Die Kumiaks, 1934 (The Kumiaks)
The first volume of a trilogy about the Kumiak family; being the account of a peasant who leaves the indignities of being a tenant farmer to become a miner in the Ruhr, his difficulties in fitting in among born miners. A lifetime of resistance and struggle from before W.W.I to the mid 1920s, and the defeat of his fellow workers despite all their tenacity, courage and class consciousness.

Die Heimkehr des Kumiaks, 1952 (The Homecoming of the Kumiaks)
The second novel in the trilogy, dealing with the lives of the Kumiak family, their neighbours and comrades from the late 1920s to the triumph of fascism in Germany. In this volume the main protagonist becomes a communist, although this does not change him in any substantial way.

Die Kumiaks und Ihre Kinder, 1959 (The Kumiaks and Their Children)
Carrying the Kumiak story from the first years of Nazi power in 1933/34, of the massive and largely successful repression which gradually stamps out all but a very deeply-buried communist underground (even though the class views of miners remain unchanged). The sufferings of W.W.II and the final defeat of German fascism only to find the country divided with the Ruhr under the control of an American-backed, conservative big business regime.

Roheisen, 1955 (Raw Iron)
A constructionist novel describing the building of a huge iron works project in the G.D.R., treated as a first step in the long awaited birth of a socialist economy, which in some ways evolves in an unanticipated manner.

Meine Jugend, 1947 (My Youth)
A lyrical reminiscence of the wretched conditions and social ferment among Silesian
miners (with their feet in two centuries) during Marchwitza's youth in the
first years of the 20th century.

NACHBAR, Herbert

Der Mond Hat Einen Hof, 1956 (The Moon Has a Hole)
An ironic chronicle of a small fishing port on the Baltic coast; the character
and glacial provincialism of small town society only slowly giving way to the
historic developments around them in early 1950s. Told in regional dialect.

Die Hochzeit Von Länneken, 1960 (The Wedding of Länneken)
Another novel set in a Baltic fishing village during the early years of the German
Democratic Republic; revolving around the gradual and only partial dissolution of
former bourgeoise social attitudes (which are more tenacious than formal power),
as witnessed by the responses to the marriage of a fisherman to the daughter of
one of the former leading families. The development of a fishermen's "cooperative"
and the half hidden contest with entrenched conservatism provide a humourous
portrait of the transformations underway. Also written in regional dialect.

Also Oben Fährt Der Grosse Wagen, 1963 (The Big Wagon Travels Above) and Haus
Unterm Regen, 1965 (House Beneath Rain), two other novels treating with aspects
of life in provincial towns and villages of the G.D.R. during the early 1960s.

NOLL, Dieter

Die Abenteur des Werner Holt, 1960 (The Adventures of Werner Holt)
A novel about a W.W.II version of Good Soldier Sjwek, the chronic malingerer,
non-volunteer and rearguardist as hero.

PETERSEN, Jan

Our Street, 1937
An allegedly documentary novel in diary form dealing with the actions, emotions
and thoughts of members of an underground communist cell in the Charlottenburg
district of Berlin in 1933-1934. Accounts of the police raids, fear and isolation,
daily strategies of survival and hopes for a miracle. Also see Heinz Liepman's
Fires Underground, 1935, a narrative of non-socialist opposition during the first
year of Nazi power. A bitter irony is that by the time these two volumes were
published in London most effective underground activity had already been crushed
in Germany.

PLIEVIER, Theodore

Des Kaisers Kulis, 1930 (The Kaiser's Coolies, 1938)
A biographical novel of the lives of two organizers of the first (1917) mutiny in
the German Fleet based in the North Sea ports. Deeply anti-militarist and anti-
patriotic, it touches on the working class backgrounds of the sailors and the
caste-like conditions of subjugation in the navy which laid the bases for the
mutiny, which at first failed.

Der Kaiser Ging, Die Generale Blieben, 1932 (The Kaiser Went, the Generals
Remained, 1938)
A richly documentary novel of the background to, the characters and events of the
1918 mutiny of the German Navy in the North Sea ports; its spread from the stokers
(the coolies) to the ranks on most of the ships and eventually to the garrisons
and workers in the port cities themselves. This in turn triggered the first
phase of the German Revolution and the end of W.W.I. Some excellent accounts of
the sweep of events in late October-early November of 1918 in which Plievier
participated as a rank and file mutineer. With a prophetic afterword on the
chequered trajectory of the officer class who were only temporarily disarmed and
who soon reappeared in various guises.

Stalingrad, 1946 (Stalingrad, 1952), Moscau, 1952 (Moscow, 1958)
Two somewhat flawed, anti-militarist war novels detailing the sufferings and
deaths of ordinary German soldiers used as cannon fodder on the Russian front

during W.W.II. While Hitler, Nazi leaders and rank and file zealots are woven through the scenes, those predominantly responsible for continuing the slaughter are seen as the traditional German officer corps and the class background they stem from, which is more traditionally conservative than it is Nazi. As distinct from the anti-war novels stemming from W.W.I, very little active opposition on the part of soldiers themselves. Stalingrad was partly written while Plievier was in exile in the Soviet Union.

POPP, Adeheid

Autobiography of a Working Woman, 1912
The autobiography of a woman from an apolitic working class background in Germany of the 1880s. She tells of gradually becoming involved in the trade union movement, her first faltering entry into the Social Democratic party and her evolution as a Social Democratic union activist over the next thirty years.

REISSNER, Larissa

Hamburg at the Barricades, 1977 (original 1926)
A collection of reportage articles about Berlin, the Ruhr and Hamburg working classes in 1923. The desperation and misplaced hopes of the times, the background of past risings and the final struggles of the German revolution and its defeat. Told with compassion and insight by a young Polish-Latvian reporter, a woman whose life and work in some ways paralleled John Reed's. The present volume contains a memorial by Karl Radek and a tribute by Boris Pasternak.

REMARQUE, Erik Maria

Im Westen, Nicht's Neues, 1929 (All's Quiet on the Western Front, 1929)
Probably the most widely translated anti-militarist novel of the interwar years. Deals with the strident patriotism instilled in a group of lower middle class German students at the beginning of W.W.I, their rapid re-education about the real meaning of war on the Western front. Details their isolation from those remaining at home and their total inability to communicate what they have experienced as they are decimated. Certainly not a socialist account, it had considerable impact in its time.

Der Weg Zuruck, 1930 (The Road Back, 1932), Drei Kameraden, 1933 (Three Comrades, 1934)
Two novels dealing with the social collapse of Germany after W.W.I, of the still unconsolidated rightist forces and of the rapacious nature of the new speculator class which arose.

The Black Obelisk, 1962
A novel of the social chaos attendant on the 1923 inflation in a small south German town. Seen through the eyes of a group of declasse but variously progressive friends who are veterans of W.W.I. Their sporadic and fruitless personal resistance to the rise of proto-fascist elements in an unreconstructedly conservative region. Has a powerful afterword dealing with the fates of the main characters as of the mid 1950s.

SCHILLING, Wilfred

Der Angstmacher, 1960 (The Fear Maker)
A semi-documentary novel of the penetration of upper rungs of West German society under Adenauer by former Nazis, their supporters and only slightly changed conservative ideologues who continue to carry out their vendettas against those who opposed them in the past or present. Revolves around a German who helped point out a Nazi war criminal to French authorities in 1946, the network of harassment and arrests which he himself then faces by German government officials, judges, employers, etc. who are carryovers from the fascist past even at the end of the 1950s. West German authorities brought legal action against the author after publication.

SCHLOTTERBECK, Friedrich

The Darker the Night, the Brighter the Stars, 1947
Unaffected reminiscences of a young German worker who was arrested for underground
political activity in 1933 and the succeeding twelve years he survives in
concentration camps and political prisons. The afterword comments on his release
in 1945, finding all of his relatives, friends and former comrades either dead or
scattered.

SEGHERS, Anna (Netty Reiling)

Der Aufstand Der Fischer Von St. Barbara, 1928 (Revolt of the Fishermen of Santa
Barbara, 1930)
A folk tale-like novel of a wandering agitator who mobilizes exploited fishermen
in a Baltic village in a strike against the fishing company. It grows into a
wider social revolt that is finally broken by the intervention of the state. Set
ambiguously in the period before W.W.I, the tale draws on themes and allusions to
previous centuries and celebrates the spirit of social revolt as it is sustained
almost sub-consciously and transmitted from the past to the future.

Die Gefährten, 1932 (The Companions)
A novel about the experiences of a decade (1919-1929) of revolutionary struggle
(and defeat) by a number of working class communists from Poland, Hungary and
Bulgaria who briefly cross paths. Despite everything, the animus of resistance
to oppression is passed on to new generations, not so much through ideological
persuasion but as a personal heritage, an undying quest for social justice.

Die Rettung, 1937 (The Rescue)
A novel dealing with the deepening repression and isolation of the Ruhr coal miners
by the Weimar government between 1929 and 1933. (The miners are treated like a
rebellious "native" group, much like Durham coal miners in Britain a decade
earlier.) Focusses on the thoughts of an elderly miner who is not particularly
bright or revolutionary but who finally joins the communist underground after
1933 because of his hatred of the Nazis, is a failure as an "illegal", but keeps
faith with his class and their traditions.

The Seventh Cross, 1942
A novel set in 1937 and documenting the "other Germany" as encountered by a fleeing
radical worker, the surviving one of seven who have escaped from a concentration
camp. As he makes his way across Germany underground to Holland he is helped
usually by strangers from a wide variety of backgrounds, persons unconnected with
any political party who assert their humanity against the Nazi regime.

Transit, 1943
A semi-autobiographical account of Segher's nightmarish flight from Paris to
Marseilles in 1940, fleeing certain imprisonment by the advancing German army
and faced with the gloating callousness of xenophobic and proto-fascist French
authorities.

Die Toten Blieben Jung, 1949 (The Dead Stay Young, 1950)
A portrait of the lives of a cross section of people in Germany from 1919 to 1945;
people who are at first not drawn into the historic clashes but whose lives are
ultimately all controlled by the outcome of those events. Begins with the first
Spartacist rising in Berlin in January 1919; the cast broadens to include Baltic
landlords, ex-Army officers, industrialists, peasants, white collar employees,
Social Democrat workers, bosses, communist functionaries, militant workers and a
host of others. An epic of a generation by a master storyteller.

Die Entscheidung, 1959 (The Decision)
Intended as a panorama of the changing social fabric of the G.D.R. Emphasizes
the G.D.R.'s more than political separation from West Germany and its claims to
embody the traditions of the German working class and socialist past. Treats
with the ambiguities, opposition and failures of official policies as well as the
achievements.

Steinzeit/Wiederbegegnung; Swei Erzahlungen, 1978 (Stone Time/Reencounter; Two
Tales)
A collection of stories ranging from her own reminiscences of exile in Mexico

during the 1940s to an essay of Viet Nam under American bombardment 30 years later--as currents and eddies of the same river.

Also Auf Den Weg Zur Amerikanischen Botschaft, 1930 (On the Way to the American Embassy, 1930), Der Kopflohn, 1932 (Price on His Head, 1936), Der Ausflug Der Toten Mädchen, 1947 (The Excursion of Dead Girls), three other novels of Europe during the interwar years, of refugees and of the fates of one group of 1920 school girls.

STRITTMAYER, Erwin

Ole Bienkopp, 1963 (Ole Bienkopp)
A gently satiric novel of everyday life in a drab Silesian farm village after the establishment of collective agriculture. The decency and pettiness, the virtues and inanities, etc. of the inhabitants. Deals with the doings of a naive young man, one Ole Bienkopp, who always manages to get himself into trouble with either neighbours or the bureaucracy because of his overimaginative leaps into the blue.

Eine Mauer Fällt, 1953 (One Wall Falls)
A collection of stories about the backgrounds, varying responses and people in Strittmayer's Silesian village during the initial years of socialist reorganization in the G.D.R.

TOLLER, Ernst

Seven Plays, 1935
A translation of seven of Tollers' plays. Includes Masses and Man, The Machine Wreckers, Draw the Fires, Transfiguration, Hoppla, Such is Life, Kinkelman, The Blind Goddess, and Mary Baker Eddy. The Machine Wreckers was probably the most internationally performed proletarian play of his generation. Set in England of 1817 and about the Nottingham handloom weavers' attack on the machinery of capitalism epitomized by the power looms which are starving them to death; the forces in contention in early industrial England. Done with an appreciation of "machine wreckers" then uncommon among left intellectuals and touching a deeply responsive chord among the older working class or members of newly proletarianized classes in developing countries. Draw the Fires, on the other hand, deals with the mutiny of the German sailors in November 1918.

Toller was the internationally best known of the left wing German dramatists of the interwar years (Brecht not excepted). His plays seemed to capture something universal in the experiences of the formative working class left and were translated and performed to audiences of Workers' Theatre groups from Japan to India, Britain, Central Europe and even in the wilds of the U.S.A. during the 1920s and 1930s.

VON DER GRÜN, Max

Männer in Zweifacher Nacht, 1962 (Men in Twofold Night)
A novel about a group of miners caught in a cave-in and those above ground trying to rescue them. Centers around two protagonists who in flashbacks, internal dialogue, etc. reveal their contradictory pride of work and their desire to escape the danger, poor pay and social stigma of being a miner.in West Germany during the late 1950s. With all the talk of "disappearance of class", industrial workers lives are as much removed from the middle class as they always were.

Irrlicht und Feuer, 1963 (Willo-the-Wisp and Fire)
A novel about a Ruhr miner at the beginning of the 1960s who is drawn into active solidarity with his fellow miners in opposing the company's introduction of an unsafe experimental drilling machine. He is not so much politicized as made aware of his insecurity and powerlessness under the existing union-company sweetheart arrangements and leaves to drift through a series of other industrial jobs. He ultimately succumbs to the pervasive alienation of German society and misses the residues of comradeship he found in the mines.

Zwei Briefe an Popischiel, 1968 (Two Letters to Popischiel)
A novel revolving around the strivings of a skilled industrial worker for dignity against the preemptory demands of his employers. Treats his growing resentment

and his rejection of bosses demands but ends with his surrender to them to regain a job he left in an amorphous act of rebellion.

WALLRAFF, Günter

Wir Brauchen Dich, 1966 (We Need You)
A collection of "underground reportage" pieces about the home and on-the-job lives of workers in a range of German industries during 1965-66. They document the alienation, insecurity and often poor working conditions and wages; the continuing oppressiveness of working class life in Germany despite all the mumbo jumbo about "Tripartism", "Co-determination", etc. An influential protest chronicle.

13 Unerwunschte Reportagen, 1969 (13 Unwanted Reports)
Thirteen accounts of the reactionary sentiments and anti-working class policies in a variety of West Germany social institutions during the late 1960s; from Hamburg charitable organizations to pastors in the Reischswehr, of police treatment of dissidents to racism in municipal governments. Most of these are oral accounts collected by Walraff in which the parties convict themselves by their own words. Walraff was jailed for impersonating government officials in the course of his research.

Nachspiele, 1968 (Replays)
A three-part documentary drama which juxtaposes absurdity with reality. Deals with the orchestrated scapegoating of West German students and radicals of 1960s by the press and its handlers, the reactionary nature of the German judiciary and how supposedly "fundamental" civil rights are easily overridden when dealing with left wing dissent, and a juxtapositioning of the public rhetoric about class harmony by employers' organizations with their private statements about how to deal with German workers.

WEINERT, Erich

Schlaflose Nacht in Barcelona, 1938 (Sleepless Night in Barcelona)
A questioning reminiscence novel of experiences in the Spanish Civil War. Weinert was a leading communist poet who also wrote a few proletarian novels during interludes of political exile and prison in the 1920s and 1930s.

WEISKOPF, Franz Karl

Unter Fremden Himmeln, 1949 (Under Foreign Skies)
A semi-documentary novel of German exile writers in the U.S. (and elsewhere) from 1933 to 1945, a stream of which he was a part. Their backgrounds, experiences and their responses to and life in exile.

WEISS, Peter

Die Ermittlung, 1965 (The Inquiry)
A play based on the 1962 Frankfurt trials of German war criminals in charge of the Auschwitz concentration camp during W.W.II. Touches on the nature and atrocities in the camp through the testimony of surviving witnesses but concentrates on the question of responsibility and guilt over and above those who are actually charged. Treats with the arguments of legality and illegitimate state power over individuals with a consideration of how guards, officials and to some extent even prisoners supposedly came to "accept" the regime of the camp.

WERKKREIS 70

Werkkreis Literatur der Arbeitwelt (Working Circle Literature of .the Work World)
A collective designation for a number of documentary novelas, short reportage accounts and agitational booklets about the contemporary lives and conditions of West German workers. Includes Erasmus Schöfer's 1970 Ein Baukran Stürzt Um (A Construction Crane Collapses), T. Rother's 1971 Schrauben Haben Rechtgeschwinde (Screws Have a Right Twist), and 1971 Ihre Aber Trägt das Risiko (But You Bear the Risk) and others. Also street theatre pieces such as Peter Schütt's 1969 Kampnagel Lehrteuch-Arbeiter Wehrteuch (Kampnagel teaches you-Workers defend yourselves).

WOLF, Christa

Der Geteilte Himmel, 1963 (The Divided Sky, 1968)
A novel of a love affair in the G.D.R. between an ambitious engineer bent on his
personal advancement and a young woman of no particular expectations who opposes
many aspects of life in her country but who takes the socialist goals seriously.
It is told from a hospital bed in which the heroine relates her gradual break
with her lover who ultimately emigrates to seek his fortune in West Germany.

Nachdenken Uber Christa T., 1967 (Recollections of Christa T., 1970)
A psychological novel in the form of a school teacher's diary and reminiscences
of the first decade of the G.D.R., being a rather pessimistic account of the
faddism and conformism of too many of her students and colleagues who don and
discard whichever political views happen to be ascendent at any given moment with
disingenious indifference.

WOLF, Friedrich

Zwei An Der Grenze, 1938 (Two at the Frontier)
A novel of left wing German refugees scattered throughout Europe. The nightmarish
quality of being pushed from country to country desperately looking for some
place of asylum. With all the doors closed by countries and officials churning
out rhetoric about democracy during the late 1930s.

Heimkehr Der Sohne, 1944 (Return of the Son)
One of a number of novels which portray the disaster awaiting German soldiers
sent to fight on the Russian front in W.W.II. Juxtaposes the claims of Nazi
propaganda with the recollections of dead, crippled and captured German soldiers.

Burgermeister Anna, 1949 (Mayor Anna, 1951)
A novela dealing with the contradictory emotions and motives of a young woman
mayor of a conservative small town in East Germany during the years immediately
after W.W.II; of her work with, sometimes qualms about and growing appreciation
of Soviet occupation government in attempts to reestablish some sort of a
functioning, denazified local administration.

ZUCKMAYER, Carl

Der Hauptmann Von Kopenick, 1931 (The Corporal of Kopenick, 1934)
Zuckmayer's satiric rendering of an already well known story; of how in 1906 a
petty criminal who is refused a passport acquires an army officer's uniform and
forged papers, commands a detachment of soldiers to take over the town hall of
Kopenick and issues himself a passport. The case was widely dramatized by pre
W.W.I socialists to satirize the conformity to authority of German bureaucracy
and its hangers on.

ZWEIG, Arnold

The Case of Sargeant Grischa, 1927
The first and most widely translated volume of what became a series of novels (the
Grischa cycle) which examines, sector by sector, those forces involved in the
original Grischa case. Specifically, The Case deals with a German sargeant in
Poland near the end of W.W.I who helps some POWs escape, but mainly it is about
the Byzantine intrigues and cross cutting interests which are activated by his
court martial as the case progresses up the chain of military command and into
political spheres of disintegrating Imperial Germany. (Everyone being
uninterested in the fate of Frischa himself, rather in the political effects.)
A bitter and sustained analysis, in novel form, of the workings of the imperial
system, in this case German but with clearly universal implications.

Jungfrau Von 1914, 1930 (Young Woman of 1914), Erzeihung Vor Verdun, 1935
(Education Before Verdun), Erzeihung Eines Konigs, 1937 (Education of a King),
Feurpause, 1954 (Lull in Fire), Die Zeit Ist Reif, 1957 (The Time is Ripe)
Later volumes of the Frischa cycle, dealing with the nature and underpinnings
of the German ruling class, its supporters and opponents before and during
W.W.I; the working class as almost another nation, the seeming destruction of
the old order during W.W.I and the trajectories of the surviving participants
in the Grischa case during the 1920s, as representative of broader social
classes.

AUSTRIA

(von) HORVATH, Odon

Die Bergbahn, 1927 (The Cablecar)
A play dealing with the construction of a cablecar installation to a mountain top resort in Austria during the mid 1920s. The sudden emergence of buried class conflict between workers, engineers and capitalists as the operators try to cut corners and heighten construction risks in order to get the facility ready for the tourist season.

Sladek, Der Schwartz Reichswehrmann, 1928 (Sladek, the 'Black Reichswehr' Man)
A play about a rootless young veteran of W.W.I who drifts into the right wing Black Reichswehr army during the 1920s, his further degeneration in that organization until revulsion turns him into a fellow traveller of left.

Ein Kind Unser Zeit, 1938 (A Child of Our Times)
A novel which in some ways parallels Sladek, but carries events through the 1930s and the defeat and retreat of Austrian working class, the piecemeal triumphs of reaction and the seemingly unstoppable cycle of violence and barbarity which have gripped Europe.

KRAMER, Theodor

Die Gaunerzinke, 1929 (Rouge's Markings), Mit der Ziehharmonika, 1936 (With the Accordian), Die Untere Schenke, 1946 (The Lower Tavern)
Three of a number of lyrical portraits about the declassed and dispossed marginal workers, peddlars, petty smugglers, etc. living in the riverside Waldviertel district on the outskirts of Vienna from the 1920s to the late 1930s--their world, lives, self-delusions and humanity.

KRAUS, Karl

Die Letzten Tage Der Menscheit, 1922 (The Last Days of Mankind)
A huge prose play about the disintegration of Austro-Hungary into violently hostile ethnic groups; the multifaceted militarism and destructiveness unleashed from the first to the last day of W.W.I.

Wolkenkuckucksheim, 1928 (Cloud Cuckoo Land)
A satirical play about the increasingly effete yet bitter middle class of Vienna and their escapist search for an irretrievably lost past. Also Die Dritte Walpurgisnacht, 1952 (The Third Walpurgisnight), an apocalyptic play of the human devastation wrought by fascism before and during W.W.II.

SEGHERS, Anna

Der Weg Durch Februar, 1935 (The Way Through February)
Between late 1932 and throughout 1933 a clerico-conservative dictatorship was established in Austria. Known as "Heimwehr Fascism", after Dolfuss' right wing militia, it was initially directed mainly at the suppression of the working class and still counts as "democratic" in bourgeoise history. At the beginning of 1934 this regime decided to crush the working class parties which still controlled Vienna. Despite the surrender of the Social Democratic leadership the Viennese workers and their self defense organizations rose in revolt--and were crushed in a week of bloody fighting. Segher's novel is possibly the best account of those desperate days and of the national and international events leading up to the Vienna rising. It captures the cross cutting forces in contention and evokes echoes of the Paris Commune of a half century earlier.

TODRIN, Boris

Five Days: Austria, February 12 to 17, 1934, 1976 (original 1936)
A brief reportage account of the Vienna uprising against the consolidation of

Austrian fascism; the politics and the desperate street battles which surged
through the working class districts of the city.

WEISKOPF, Franz Karl

Abscheid Vom Frieden, 1948 (Farewell to Peace), Immitten Des Stromes, 1950 (In the
Middle of the Current), Welt In Wehen, 1955 (World in Decline)
A novel trilogy dealing with the last years of the Austro-Hungarian Empire as
experienced by working people (and assortment of other classes), seen largely
from the vantage point of Prague, the major industrial city of Austro-Hungary.
Abscheid deals with the chaos of the break up of Austro-Hungary as the war
progresses and the struggle between radical working class and the emergent national
ruling classes, particularly in Czechoslovakia. Immitten and Welt describe the
last days of W.W.I and the immediate post war year(s), in which the national
components of the collapsing Austro-Hungarian Empire witness the revolutionary
uprisings by their mixed working classes but the eventual triumph of the
reactionary national bourgeoise everywhere. The new rulers' use of a patchwork
of ethnic hatreds and loyalties and external military aid to impose their control
over the restoration states they inherit.

WOLF, Friedrich

Die Matrosen Von Cattaro, 1930 (The Sailors of Cattaro)
An anti-militarist play which celebrates the mutiny of the sailors of the
Austrian-Hungarian Fleet based in Cattaro (on the Adriatic) in 1917. Became a
widely produced piece of proletarian theatre in the 1930s.

Forisdorf, 1935 (Forisdorf, 1935)
A play widely performed by the Workers' Theatre movement; deals with the Vienna
working class district of Florisdorf, its traditions and experience during 1934.

NETHERLANDS AND FLANDERS

BOON, Louis Paul

De Voorstad Groeit, 1943 (The Suburb Grows), Abel Gholaerts, 1944 (Abel Gholaerts), Vergeten Straat, 1945 (The Forgotten Street)
Three novels which are a collage of the lives of a host of ordinary Flemish people. Written in a naturalistic "camera eye" style and portraying the changing conditions of life in towns and cities during the first four decades of the 20th century. Interlaced with some 19th century "national folk spirit" philosophizing.

De Kapellekensbaan, 1953 (Chapel Road, 1955), Zomer Te Ter-Muren, 1956 (Summer at Ter-Muren), Wapenbroeder, 1955 (Brothers in Arms)
An epic trilogy novel of the social history of Belgian Flanders and Holland from the 1890s to the late 1930s, packed with characters from all classes; outlining the rise and struggles of the labour movement and socialism as a central theme. Incorporates allegorical reworkings of old Rhenish folk tales and figures. Chapel Road in particular is a remarkable account of a usually well hidden Flemish working class.

De Bende Van Jan de Lichte, 1957 (Jan de Lichte's Band)
A historical novel of a social bandit in 18th century Netherlands who attempts to launch a rising of the poor.

Pieter Daens, of how in de negentiende eeuw arbeiders vochten tegen armoede en onrecht, 1971 (Pieter Daens, or how in the nineteenth century the workers fought against poverty and injustice), De Swarte Hand of het Anarchisme in de Negentiende Eeuw in det Industrielstadje Aalst, 1976 (The Black Hand of Anarchy in the Industrial City of Aalst during the Nineteenth Century)
Two agitational plays memorializing the anarcho-syndicalist strains of revolt among the Dutchand Flemish working class during the allegedly quiessant past century and asking where the working class opposition to injustice and conservatism is in contemporary Flanders.

Het Geuzenboek, 1979 (The Beggar's Book)
A play set in Flanders of the early 17th century and memorializing the heritage of Flemish revolt during the national liberation struggles against Spain. Set among the insurrectional Sea Beggars army of the rural and urban poor.

BUYSSE, Cyriel

Het Recht Van Den Sterkste, 1893 (The Law of the Strongest)
An early naturalistic "novel" of the Flemish countryside which attempted to counter the prevalent idyls of rural life as the reservoir of Flemish vitality. Portrays the countryside as a swampland of petty greed, narrow minded religious bigotry, ignorance and mind-numbing conservatism.

DeCOSTER, Charles

Thyl Ulenspiegel, 1867 (Tyl Ulenspiegel, 1944)
The best known version of the Ulenspiegel legend; set during the Dutch-Flemish wars of independence from Spain, culminating in descriptions of Ulenspiegel in the camps of the Sea Beggars anti-feudal struggle. As a transformer figure, Ulenspiegel represents the constantly resurrected and transmuted collective personas of a range of Flemish people. A massive, richly allegorical tale, one of the masterpieces of European folk literature and listed here because of its influence on radical democrat and early socialist readers throughout Europe. Read only in unexpurgated versions.

DEKKER, Eduard Douwes (Multatuli)

Max Havelaar, 1860 (Max Havelaar, 1880)
A classic novel of the Dutch exploitation of Indonesia during the mid 19th century.

Touches on the callous hypocrisy of the Calvinistic Dutch burgerdom at home and abroad but is mainly a semi-autobiographical account of how the colonial administration and the Dutch East Indian planters work hand in glove with rapacious native rulers to press the last drop of blood out of the Javanese peasantry. Revolves around the initial naivety of a young Dutch colonial administrator who uncovers the fabric of exploitation and oppression and who in attempting to "correct" the excesses gradually comes to realize the nature of this colonial system. Sometimes melodramatic, the novel was an influential early anti-colonial work in Europe.

EEKHOUD, Georges

La Nouvelle Carthage, 1898 (The New Carthage, 1917)
A novel about the people of Antwerp; juxtaposes the cosmopolitan sea port of North Europe with somnolent Belgian society. Contrasts the burgeoning bourgeoise of Antwerp with the mainly Flemish ex-peasant workers flocking to the city to find work. A bitter attack on the "urban improvement" schemes which mainly result in displacing marginal workers and poor.

ELSSCHOT, Willem

Lijmen, 1924 (Soft Soap)
A sardonic novela about an advertising executive and his Felix Krull con-man schemes in the Dutch business world of the 1920s.

Het Dwaallicht, 1946 (Willow-the-Wisp)
A novela which follows the experiences of three East Indian sailors in their travels through the dockside area of Antwerp during one night as they try to find a former Dutch shipmate. Alludes to the unshakeable stasis of Belgian society behind this cosmopolitan seaport.

GORTER, Herman

Een Klein Heldendict, 1906 (A Little Heroic Epic)
An epic poem about a youth's hesitations and then support of the 1903 Dutch railway strike, the first major trade union confrontation in that country.

HOLST, Henriette Roland

De Vrouw in Het Woud, 1912 (Woman in the Forest)
An autobiographical account of Holst's break with the increasingly right wing Dutch Socialist Party early in the century, and the isolation of a radical in a society such as Holland. Holst was important in the Dutch and international socialist movements from 1906 until 1927, when she returned to the folds of the church.

MULISH, Harry

Het Stenen Buidsbed, 1959 (The Stone Bridal Bed, 1963)
Sketches of the pomposity and flatness of Dutch life in the 1950s, as more or less good humoured satire.

Bericht Aan De RattenKoning, 1966 (Report on the King Rat, 1968)
A considerably more angry reportage novel of the stagnation of Dutch society; of the Provo-youth demonstrations which briefly shook but didn't change anything in Holland during the mid 1960s.

Wenken Voor De JongsteDag, 1967 (Hints for Doomsday)
A collection of bitterly sardonic sketches, stories, and fantastic reports on the yet deeper tranquility and death-like somnolence of Dutch burgerdom.

SCANDINAVIA

DENMARK

AAKJAER, Jeppe

Vreden Børn, 1904 (Child of Wrath)
A novel which catalogues the exploitation and humiliations which one hired farm
hand encounters in rural Denmark at the turn of the century; of the network of
alliances between wealthy farmers, merchants and government officials who act as
the fingers of one hand when dealing with the demands of rural and other workers.
The hero's gradual conviction that conservatism is hopelessly entrenched in
Denmark and his ultimate emigration.

ABELL, Kjeld

Melodien der Blev Vaek, 1935 (The Melody That Got Lost, 1938)
A play which belabours the narrow minded self-interest of the Danish middle
classes toward the bitter poverty and desperate struggles of Danish workers
during the depression years. Juxtaposes workers' conditions and the endless
capacity of the bourgeoisie to shut out and dismiss anything which disturbs their
smug view of the world. Uses songs and street singers in a bitterly Brechtian
style.

Anna Sophie Hedvig, 1939 (Cousin Anna, 1945)
Another play revolving around the Danish middle class' bottomless complacency and
caution when faced with the rising threat of fascism. The heroine of the title
is an elderly spinster school teacher from a comparable background who comes to
speak out against the growing acceptance of fascism among her friends and kinfolk
as "a return to law and order". A microcosm of the ultimate dividing line between
all forces standing for social justice and those prepared to collaborate with
oppression.

Silkeborg, 1946 (Silkeborg)
A play about the varied responses of different sections of Danish society to
German occupation during W.W.II. Set around a provincial family in the Silkeborg
district of Jutland, it deals with the willingness of many Danes to collaborate
with any force which protects their complacent world, no matter how horrendous the
consequences--and of the resistance which others gradually come to mount. Involves
a forward and backward look at a number of Danes from 1905 and of the cultural
and psychological developments in individuals and classes over thirty-five years
which lead them to make one kind of response rather than another during W.W.II.
A disturbing play which, along with other works, got Abell blacklisted as a
subversive during the cold war years in Denmark.

BECKER, Knuth

Det Daglinge Brød, 1932 (Our Daily Bread, 1938)
The initial volume in the Kai Gotsche series dealing with the youth and first jobs
of a landless worker in a Danish village circa W.W.I, and of the world around him
which gradually comes into focus. The Kai Gotsche series is a nine volume set of
semi-autobiographical novels dealing with Denmark and Scandinavia as experienced
by a migrant Danish worker between W.W.I and the eve of W.W.II, a sweeping
personal epic including Verden Venter, 1934 (The World Waits) and Uroligt Foraar,
1939 (Unsettled Spring).

Et Kors Af Brosten, 1956 (Cross of Cobblestones)
The last of the series, dealing with the late middle age of Kai Gotsche and being
a rounded critique of the continuing class hierarchy and smug conservatism in
Denmark on the eve of W.W.II. The ways in which interlocking church, school,
family life and government officialdom sustain the regime ancien despite the
surface reforms of Social Democratic social policy.

BREGENDAHL, Marie

En Dødsnat, 1912 (A Deadly Night, 1931)
An Ibsen-like novel which combines a lyrical portrayal of "the common people" of
Denmark during the first decade of the 20th century and an overview of their
travails.

Billeder af Sødalsfolkenes Liv, 1923 (Pictures From the Lives of Sødal People)
A reportage novel of the lives of Jutland peasantry.

DITLEVSEN, Tove

Barndommens Gade, 1943 (Street of My Childhood)
A somewhat nostalgic reminiscence of girlhood in a poor working class district of
Copenhagen during the 1920s and early 1930s; an account of everyday life and
concerns in that milieu as understood by a young girl.

Also Dommeren, 1948 (The Judge), a collection of short stories.

GELSTEAD, Otto

Jomfru Gloriant, 1923 (Miss Gloriant)
A collection of poems which combine socialist realist themes with lyrical
tenderness; by one of the leading Danish communist poets of the interwar period.

HANSEN, Martin A.

Paradise Apples, 1953
A collection of short stories by a left agrarian writer about Denmark from the
late 1930s to early 1950s, the somnolence and strains within Danish society in
the grip of a conservative culture which only partly hides the underlying ferment.

HERDAL, Harald

Tirsdag, 1932 (Tuesday), Man Skal Jo Leve, 1934 (We Must Live), Ein Lidt
Almindelinge Historie, 1935 (A Rather Common History), Den Første Verden, 1936
(The First World), En Egn af Landet, 1939 (Somewhere in the Country, 1947),
Tusmørke, 1943 (Twilight), Barndom, 1944 (Childhood), Kvelige Menneske, 1949
(Invincible Mankind)
A series of novels about the Danish working class, especially in Copenhagen, from
W.W.I to W.W.II by a working class communist writer and poet. He "endeavours to
speak for the inarticulate, the impoverished of Copenhagen--the young apprentice,
the working mother, the unemployed workers. It is Herdal's strength to be able
to paint in simple words, vivid pictures from proletarian life...and of his hatred
of social oppressors."

KIRK, Hans

Fiskerne, 1928 (Fishermen)
A novel about a colony of primitive-Christian fishermen and their families in
Jutland; their poverty and striving for a collective, more just live but the
repressive and destructive religious bases on which their community is based. A
rather unique theme by a left socialist writer.

Daglejerne, 1936 (Day Labourers)
A collective novel of the lives of rural day labourers in depression-ridden
Denmark.

De Nye Tider, 1939 (The New Times)
The second volume of the intended trilogy begun with Daglejerne, carrying the
account to the eve of W.W.II. The manuscript for the final volume was lost during
political imprisonment in the 1940s.

Also Skyggespiel, 1953 (Light and Shade), a semi-autobiographical novel, and
Slaven, 1948 (The Slave).

KRISTENSEN, Tom

Vindrosen, 1934 (Compass Rose), Hvader Heta?, 1946 (What is Heta?)
Two collections of short stories about everyday lives and hopes of ordinary Danish

people during the 1930s and under German occupation by one of the leading left wing poets of the period. Also <u>Mellem Krigene</u>, 1948 (Between the Wars) and <u>Til Dags Dato</u>, 1953 (Until the Present Day), two collections of reminiscences and essays about social life and culture in Denmark over the preceding three decades.

NEXO, Martin Andersen

<u>Pelle Erobreren</u>, 1906-1910 (<u>Pelle the Conqueror</u>, 1954)
A four volume novel which made Nexo an internationally known writer. A novelized social history of the Danish working class from the last quarter of the 19th century to circa 1910; the protagonist's childhood in a family of landless rural workers, apprentice to a small town artizan, emigration to Copenhagen to find work, a growing consciousness of the broader world and his entry into the socialist and labour movement during the late 1890s. Pelle emerges as a leader in one of the bitter strikes of that decade, is imprisoned and after release becomes a Social Democrat stalwart pushing for assorted political and cooperative reforms. Throughout are a host of varied characters more and less radical than Pelle. Illuminated with Nexo's faith in the working class, told colloquially and with much tongue-in-cheek irony.

<u>Ditte Menneskebarn</u>, 1917-1921 (<u>Ditte, Child of Man</u>, 1920-22)
A multi-volume novel about the twenty-five years of life of a girl from a poor working class family. A generation younger than Pelle, her life involves greater travail, exploitation and experience than his own. She represents what is best in the working class, her only flaw bing a lack of hatred and distrust for those who rule her world. Done with subtlety which only occasionally descends into melodrama.

<u>Midt I En Jaerntid</u>, 1929 (<u>In God's Country</u>, 1933)
A sardonic and panoramic novel dealing with the cabel of large farmers in Denmark who have enriched themselves through profiteering during W.W.I and the starvation years in Europe which followed and who believe they are God's chosen.

<u>Erindringer</u>, 1932-39 (<u>Under the Open Sky</u>, 1938)
Two volumes of reminiscences about the Denmark of Nexo's youth in the 1890s, his commitment to the Social Democrats until W.W.I and his shift to the Communists thereafter. Also treats with conditions in Denmark and the proletarian literary scene during the depression years.

<u>Morten Hin Røde</u>, 1945 (<u>Morten the Red</u>, 1946)
A novel set in the late 1930s which has as its hero one of the minor figures who appears in <u>Pelle the Conqueror</u>. Morten, a Copenhagen worker, becomes a militant communist and is a counterpoint to the opportunism and do-nothingism of many establishment Social Democrats, as represented by the elder Pelle, on whom Morten occasionally comments.

SCHERFIG, Hans

<u>Frydeholm</u>, 1962 (Frydenholm)
A quasi-documentary novel about the varying responses to Nazi occupation of Denmark in W.W.II, from the forces of collaboration to the communist underground resistance, stressing the personal and cultural rather than class backgrounds which led individuals to one response or another.

<u>Idealister</u>, 1945 (<u>Idealists</u>, 1949)
A sardonic novel satirizing the host of basically escapist "idealist" philosophies and programs, such as psychoanalysis and World Federalism, which spread from America and agitated sections of the Danish and European middle classes in the aftermath of W.W.II.

SKJOLDBORG, Johan

<u>En Stridsmand</u>, 1896 (A Fighter)
A somewhat sentimental protest novel of the conditions of tenant farmers and hired labour in Denmark of the time. Of considerable influence through a wide readership in the Folk high schools.

SØIBERG, Harry

Søkongen, 1926-1930 (The Sea King, 1930)
A novel trilogy which combines romanticism and documentary realism about the lives
of Danish ex-peasants and seamen before, during and after W.W.I. Interwoven with
the reformism which Nexo's writing excoriated.

Also De Levendes Land, 1916-1920 (The Living Land), a novel trilogy of the Danish
peasantry and rural workers before W.W.I.

<h2 style="text-align:center">ICELAND</h2>

HAGALIN, Gudmundur G.

Brennumenn, 1927 (Firebrands)
A novel of the impoverished cotters of Northwest Iceland, emphasizing their
independent rejection of the demands of church and state, and their contempt for
the proprieties of the Icelandic rural middle class. An account of their struggles
just to survive on their frost blasted cots. Drawn partly from Hagalin's own
youth.

Kristrun I Hamravik, 1933
A character study of an old woman living on a "farm" in the subarctic Northwest
region, facing society, nature and God(s) without fear and without compromise.
Hagalin's works were often criticized by the left for glorifying such rugged
individualism, however "rebellious" it might be.

Sturla I Vogum, 1938 (
A two volume novel of an individualistic North country cotter who gradually
develops a broader social consciousness and who, against his own basic character,
comes to cooperate with others in organizing political actions geared to achieving
some social security for poor peasantry as a whole.

Konungurian A Kalfskinni, 1945 (The King of Kalfsskinn)
A novel of the authoritarianism which holds sway over the lives of the inmates of
a senior citizens "home" in a small town under the petty dictatorial rule of the
home's director.

JONASSON UR KOTLUM, Johannes

Hrimhuita Modir, 1937 (Rime White Mother)
A lyrical survey and reinterpretation of Iceland's history and literature from a
socialist viewpoint.

Hart Er I Heimi, 1939 (Woe Is Loose in the World)
A collection of short stories and poems warning of the rising fascism of the
1930s but also condemning the continuing rapaciousness of traditional imperialism,
Britain's in particular. Includes the story Stjornufakur (Star Steed).

Verndarenglarnir, 1943 (Protecting Angels)
A novel of the British-American occupation of Iceland during W.W.II who under the
guise of protection do their best to entrench a conservative regime, treating
Iceland as a protectorate, its people as natives and the indigenous left as
subversives in the Anglo-American domain.

Daudsmannsey, 1949 (Dead Man's Land), Siglingin Mikla, 1950 (The Great Voyage),
Frelsisalfan, 1952 (Continent of Liberty)
A trilogy of historical novels dealing with the terrible, summerless years and
famines of the early 1880s, the desperate migration of ultimately amost a third
of the population to North America and elsewhere, and the collapse of traditional
society in Iceland. Kotlum's greatest prose work.

Eg Lost Sem Eg Sofi, 1932 (I Pretend Sleep), Samt Mun Eg Vaka, 1935 (Yet I Will
Stay Awake)
Two collections of poetry dealing with the seeming collapse of capitalist system
in Iceland in depression-wracked early 1930s and of the author's conversion to
communism as a millenial hope.

JONSSON, Sigurjon

Silkikjolar Og Vadmalsbuxur, 1922 (Silk Gowns and Homespun Pants)
A satiric novel of the pretension and hypocrisy of the emerging Icelandic
bourgeoisie in Reykjavik around W.W.I, trying to ape the European ruling classes.

Glaesimennska, 1924 (Dandyism)
A sequel to Silk Gowns, which carries the satire of the Icelandic middle class
into the Conservative-Nationalist period of the 1920s.

LAXNESS, Halldor Kiljan

Thu Vinvithur Hreini; Fuglinn I Fjörunni, 1932 (Salka Valka, 1936)
A richly detailed two volume novel of the cultural history, personalities and
society of Icelandic fishermen and shoreworkers in a small coastal village who,
with their families, struggle to wrest control of the industry from the Danish
monopoly trading companies; set early in the 20th century.

Sjalfstaett Folk, 1934-35 (Independent People, 1946)
An epic novel of the lives and struggles of the Icelandic peasantry during the
first quarter of the 20th century; the mixed strengths and weaknesses of an
individualism which has sustained resistance to an autocratic church-squirearchy
in the past, but which is quite inadequate for current conditions. The worsening
rural economy with people leaving land for cities and others testing cooperative
and political strategies which will allow them to remain as farmers but also move
them into the 20th century. Won Nobel Prize for Literature.

Ljos Heimsins, 1937-40 (Light of the World, 1969)
A novel revolving around the life of an impoverished worker-teacher during the
early 20th century who dedicates himself to challenging the clerical know-nothingism
and squirearchical reaction of the rural districts by unearthing and writing about
the hidden currents of rebellion and spiritual audacity which have coursed through
ordinary Icelandic people in the past. Touches on the vital spark the teacher
imparts to some other men and women as he himself gradually descends into despair.

Islandsklukkan, 1943 (Island Bell), Hith Ijosa Man, 1944 (The Bright Maid), Eldur
I Kaupinhafn, 1946 (Fire in Copenhagen)
Three historical novels set mainly in 18th and early 19th century Iceland under
Danish colonial rule; the consolidation of the clerico-landlord regime of
subservience and obscurantism and the "defensive" response of ordinary Icelanders
who turn inward. In short, of the foundations of cultural conservatism which had
to be faced in the 20th century.

Atomstöoin,1948 (Atom Station, 1961)
A novel about the U.S.-English occupation of Iceland in W.W.II and how the
Conservative government in power uses these forces to entrench itself. An angry
protest at having American airbases and cold war warriors stationed in Iceland.

Gerpla, 1952 (The Happy Warrior, 1958)
A work set in and written in 12th century saga style; portrays the Icelandic
Vikings as usually impoverished, often Quixotic migrants. It explores the
comparative strengths and flaws of Icelandic, Eskimo and European cultures of that
period and in general provides an unheroic and more life-like account of the
sagas.

Brekkukotsannall, 1957 (The Fish Can Sing, 1966)
A reminiscence about growing up in Iceland towns and countryside during the first
decade of this century.

SIRGURTHDSON, Olafur Johann

Skuggarnir of Baenum, 1936 (Shadows of the Farm), Fjallith Og Draumurinn, 1944
(The Mountain and the Dream), Vorkold Jöro, 1951 (Cold Earth in Spring),
Ganguirkith, 1955 (The Mechanism)
Four titles of a larger series of novels which document the changing structure of
Icelandic society from the decaying rural economy of quasi-colonial Iceland in
the early 20th century, the upsurge of labour and left political struggles in

the 1930s, the Anglo-American protectorate during W.W.II and the semi-urban
capitalist society of post war period. Emphasizes that the earlier generations
of rural and urban working class were able to draw on self-sustaining cultural,
economic and political institutions which have been largely lost.

STEPHANSSON, Stephan G.

A Fert Og Flugi, 1900 (On the Go), Heimleithis, 1917 (Homeward Bound), Andvökur,
1919-1938 (Wakeful Nights, Vols. 1-6)
Three collections of iconoclastically socialist poetry by someone who is now
regarded as one of the greatest Icelandic poets of the 20th century. Stephansson
had no formal education, emigrated to America and then Canada as a youth, spent
most of his mature life on an unsuccessful Alberta homestead as an unrecognized
"scribbler" of anti-clerical, anti-capitalist and anti-militarist poetry. The
international stature and scope of Stephansson's poetry is all the more remarkable
given the context of colonial patriotism in Edwardian Canada. Much of his work
was published posthumously.

TRAUSTI, Jon (Gudmundur Magnusson)

Halla, 1906 (Halla), Leysing, 1907 (Spring Floods), Heidarbylio, 1908 (Mountain
Cot)
A trilogy of historical novels dealing with a generation of impoverished shepherd-
farmers and cotters of the Northwest of Iceland from which Trausti sprang. Halla
deals with the childhood and youth of an illegitimate cotter's son from the 1870s
and into the famine years of 1882-83, when summer failed to come, leading to
starvation and mass emigration. Leysing deals with the attempts of some cotters
to establish a cooperative and their fight against the tenant system. It is told
through the eyes of a sympathetic factor of the decaying Danish trading monopoly
(a sort of Icelandic H.B.C.), who recognizes the exploitation inherent in the
regime but who is caught in it as much as the peasants. Heidarbylio carries the
story into the beginning of the present century, a populist account of the partial
retreat of the main character to his childhood home and to past values of an
isolated individualism during late middle age.

NORWAY

ANKER, Nini Roll

Lille-Anna Og Andre, 1906 (Lille-Anna and the Others)
An early feminist novel of the miserable conditions of women workers in early 20th
century Norway, by an inheritor of Ibsen's radical-democratic tradition.

Det Svake Kjøn, 1915 (The Weaker Sex)
Another feminist novel about how women are taught to repress their own feelings
and interests and a then daring call for sexual liberation; the hypocrisy of
Norwegian society toward women.

Kirchen, 1921 (The Church)
A militantly pacifist attack on the preachers and churches of Europe, and on the
Norwegian Lutheran Church in particular, for their hypocrisy and viciousness in
supporting their respective rulers in the charnal house of W.W.I.

BOJER, Johan

Den Siste Vikings, 1921 (Last of the Vikings, 1923)
A novel dealing with the hand fishermen of the Lofoten islands in northern Norway,
the nature of their work and lives and their final displacement by capitalized
fishing fleets in the first two decades of this century.

Folk Ved Sjøen, 1929 (The Everlasting Struggle, 1934)
A portrait of Norwegian seamen, fishermen and other coastal folk which (despite
some quaint, period piece philosophizing) is a panorama of a modernizing Norway
during and after W.W.I. Full of the foibles, self-deception, decency and hopes of
real people. Also Et Folketog, 1896 (A Procession, 1906), Troens Magt, 1903 (Power
of a Lie, 1910), and Den Store Hunger, 1916 (The Great Hunger, 1918).

BRAATEN, Oskar

Kring Fabrikken, 1910 (Around the Factory)
A documentary novel of the lives of Norwegian factory workers during the wave of
industrialization in the first decade of the century. A proletarian account by
the son of an Oslo factory worker.

Ulveheit, 1919 (The Wolf's Lair), Matilde, 1920 (Matilde)
Two novels which provide a rich and vivid picture of the lives of men, women and
children in a working class tenement district of Oslo during W.W.I.

Den Store Barnedåpen, 1925 (The Big Baptism)
A very popular play of the cultural and political traditions as part of the daily
lives of families, workers and factory girls in Oslo working class district in
early 1920s.

DUUN, Olav

The People of Juvik, 1918-1923
The general title for a six volume series of "agrarian" novels set in the Namdalen
region of north coast Norway; the spread and consolidation of capitalist
production and the traumatic changes in the old social relationships during the
later half of the 19th century, as seen through a family chronicle.

EGGE, Peter

Inde I Fjordene, 1920 (In the Fjords)
A novel of daily lives and deepening social conflicts in a central Norwegian valley
during the 1870s to 1890s as the first steps toward industrialization are taken
and the old ruling class of landed squires, church and government notables is
replaced by capitalists. The initial shifts from a peasant to an urban society.

Hjertet, 1907 (The Heart)
A semi-autobiographical novel along the above theme set in the Trondelag region of
Norway in the late 1890s.

FALKBERGET, Johan

Svarte Fjelde, 1907 (Black Mountains)
An epic novel dealing with the lives of miners and railway workers around the
Kiruna fields of Northeastern Norway. Set in the period 1900 to 1906, it portrays
the hardships of life in the mines but, unlike many comparable works, is pervaded
by the ingrained rebelliousness and joie de vie of its characters, whose lives
and dreams of a better world are hardly grey or gloomy. Falkberget was the son
of a Kiruna miner and worked in the mines himself from age nine to his late
twenties.

Eli Sjursdötter, 1913 (Eli Sjursdötter)
The first of a series of historical social novels about the people and forces in
the northern region of Norway which would ultimately become a frontier resource
district. Eli Sjursdötter is the story of an independent young woman during the
"Northern War" of the early 1700s, in which the frontier peasantry and autonomous
herding peoples are drawn into the semi-feudal political control of the Swedish
state with its much more exploitative and oppressive class relations.

Lisbeth Paa Jarnfjeld, 1915 (Lisbeth of Jarnfjeld)
A sequel to Sjursdötter, dealing with the lingering hostilities between the
remaining mountain peasants (the antecedents of the frontier working class of
later centuries) and the lowland squirearchy and controlled peasant society
during the late 18th century.

Den Fjerde Nattevakt, 1923 (The Fourth Nightwatch)
A historical social novel of the mining-peasant region of Røros during the early
19th century.

De Første Gesseller (The First Journeyman), I Hammerns Tegn (In the Sign of the
Hammer), Tarnvekteren (The Watchman), 1927-1935
A trilogy of historical novels under the general title Christianus Sextus, they
deal with the development of the first mines in the Røros region of northern

Norway and the evolution of a frontier peasant proletariat and culture
throughout the 19th century.

Bread of Night, 1940
Another novel of the evolution of the frontier peasant-industrial worker society
in northern Norway from 18th to early 20th centuries.

GRIEG, Nordahl

Var Aere Og Var Makt, 1935 (Our Honour and Our Glory)
A play revolving around the posturing of Norwegian capitalists in W.W.I,
proclaiming their high principles as they scheme to get the maximum profits out
of Norwegian shipping regardless of the suffering and deaths caused to thousands
of seamen, Norwegian and others.

Nederlaget, 1937 (The Defeat)
A play about the last weeks of the Paris commune done as a parallel to the Spanish
Civil War then raging. Raises the hope that some sparks of humanity and
resistance always remain after the seemingly complete triumph of reaction.

Ung Ma Verden Ennu Voere, 1939 (But the World Must Be Young)
A novel of Norwegians and other volunteers fighting and working for the Republican
forces in the Spanish Civil War, and what brought them there.

KIELLAND, Alexander

Garman et Worse, 1880 (Garmen and Worse)
A novel of the burgeoning Norwegian merchant aristocracy as symbolized by the
Garman and Worse Company, their "scientific" justification of exploitation and
the switchover of local pastors from being watchdogs for the older landed
squirearchy to being praise singers of the new capitalist class.

Sankt Hans Fest, 1886 (St. John's Feast)
Kielland's most frantic and bitter novel, a sardonic account of a demogogic,
opportunist local pastor who consciously tailors himself to serve the interests
of the Norwegian merchants. Also see Sne, 1886 (Snow), along the same lines, and
Arbeidsfolk, 1881 (Working People).

UPPDAL, Kristofer

Dansen Gjenom Skuggeheimen, 1911-1924 (Dance Through the World of Shadows)
The general title of a ten volume series of documentary novels which are in a
sense an overview of Norwegian working class and labour history from the late
19th century to the early 1920s. They touch on the evolution and separation of
the working class from the peasantry, of the culture and psychology as well as
politics of the Norwegian working class, of its various components and interrelationships. Some volumes focus on the frontier working class from the
beginning of the century to W.W.I and give a vivid picture of the increasing
radicalism of the times. Accounts drawn partly from own experiences as a shepherd
boy, migratory farm labourer, railway worker, journalist, seaman and industrial
worker/union organizer.

SWEDEN

ANDERSSON, Dan

Kolar Historier, 1914 (Charcoal Burners Tales, 1948), Kolvaktarens Visor, 1915
(Charcoal Watchers Songs)
A collection of tales (Historier)and lyrical poems (Visor) about charcoal makers
in the northern forests of Sweden during the first decade of the century, the most
isolated and impoverished workers in the country. Drawn from Andersson's own
childhood and youth, these sketches are as much apocalyptic as they are
proletarian and embody the millenial quantity of medieval peasant revolts as much
as socialist struggles.

Det Kallas Vikskepelse, 1916 (It Is Called Superstition), De Tre Hemlosa, 1918
(The Three Homeless Ones), David Ramm's Arv, 1919 (David Ramm's Heritage)
Three brief collections of tales praising the people and folk myths which hovered
around Andersson's forest childhood. A maniac anger and wild alienation which
strikes out against reformism and "scientific socialism" as well as the powers
that be and were.

FRIDEGARD, Jan

Jag, Lars Hard, 1935 (I, Lars Hard), Tak For Himlastegen, 1936 (Thanks for
Heavenly Ladders), Barmhartighet, 1937 (Charity), Har Ar Min Hand, 1942 (Here is
My Hand)
A series of novels revolving around one Lars Hard, a "Statare" (landless, often
contracted farm labourers who were almost a caste of super-exploited workers in
Sweden). Set throughout rural and small town Sweden of 1920s and 1930s, drawing
from Fridegard's own background, the novels present a picture of a lumpen
proletarian; brutal, self-interested, given to mouthing reactionary sentiments.
An intimate and occasionally sympathetic, but mainly sobering reminder of one
product of all-pervasive exploitation. The poor bedeviling the poor and weak.

Opfer, 1937 (Sacrifice), Aran Och Hjalttarna, 1938 (Honour and Heroes), Statister,
1939 (Supernumeraries)
Three semi-autobiographical novels of Statare life in Sweden from W.W.I to the
1930s; not part of the Lars Hard series, and told with greater sympathy and
balance. Some vivid portraits of life and labour among rural poor before the
"welfare" state.

Kvarnbudet, 1944 (Message From the Mill), Kvinnotradet, 1950 (The Female Tree)
Collected short stories of rural life in Sweden and the changes under the
Social Democratic governments of 1930s and 1940s.

Tragudars Land, 1940 (Land of the Wooden Gods), Grynings Folket, 1944 (People of
the Dawn), Offerrök, 1949 (Sacrificial Smoke)
Three historical novels of the lives of serfs, peasants and slaves in late
medieval Sweden, presumably as a historic background to the conditions of rural
workers a half millenium later.

HEDENVIND-ERIKSSON, Gustav

Ur En Fallen Skog, 1910 (From a Felled Forest)
An angry novel of the industrialization of the Norrland region of Sweden under the
aegis of thoroughly Dickensian Swedish capitalists. Details the destruction of
an independent peasantry and their conversion into migratory lumber and camp
workers (rallare) during the late 1890s and early 1900s. The situations are
drawn partly from the author's life as a rallare worker during that period. His
characters are filled with a vigour and rebellious grasp on life which is said to
characterize this section of the emerging Swedish proletariat.

Vid Eli Vagor, 1914 (Beside the Waves of Eli)
The first of a series of linked novels about Swedish camp and construction workers
from the turn of the century to W.W.II. Vid Eli deals with the construction of a
large northern hydro project, a vibrant account of the backgrounds, daily life,
work and the roots of political militancy just beginning to emerge among the
rallare workers.

Orion's Balte, 1924 (Orion's Belt)
Another novel of Swedish rallare workers, set during W.W.I and marked by near
despair emanating from that war and the collapse of international working class
solidarity.

De Forskingrades Arv, 1926 (Heritage of the Dispersed)
A novel of rallare workers before, during and immediately after W.W.I. The
established exploitation seems all pervasive but the old-yet-ever-new hope for a
more just world hovers in the wings, being the most fundamental heritage of the
oppressed.

Det Bevingade Hjulet, 1928 (The Winged Wheel)
A novel which follows a group of Swedish construction workers through Sweden and

elsewhere in Europe in the mid 1920s, their irrepressible appetite for life matched by the absurdity of the system they work under.

Jamtlandska Sagor, 1940 (Jamtland Sagas), Sagorfolket Som Kom Brot, 1942 (Sagafolk Who Disappeared), Jorms Saga, 1948 (Jorm's Saga)
Three quasi folk tale accounts of the radical cultural-political traditions of people in the northern region of Sweden and their progressive incorporation into Swedish society under Social Democratic reforms. An ambiguous reflection on the improving conditions of their lives weighed against the seeming loss of previous vision of and commitment to a reborn world.

JANDEL, Ragnar

De Tappra, 1918 (The Courageous Ones)
A collection of poetry memorializing the Finnish revolution and its struggle against Mannerheim's White Guards. Also Till Karleken, 1917, a collection of revolutionary working class poetry dealing with Sweden.

Dem Tranga Porten, 1924 (The Narrow Way), Den Stilla Aret, 1926 (The Peaceful Year), Barndomstid, 1936 (Childhood)
A mellowed reminiscence of childhood in an artizan family of southern Sweden during the first decade of the century.

KJELLGREN, Josef

Manniskor Kring En Bro, 1935 (People and a Bridge)
A collective novel in which the "main character" is/are all those workers involved in building the Vasterbron bridge in Stockholm.

Smaragden, 1939 (The Emerald)
Another collective novel which portrays the heroism of daily life among the Swedish working class during the 1930s, from earning a living to carrying through a nation-wide general strike. Kjellgren was a seaman-writer during most of his adult life.

KOCH, Martin

Arbetare, 1912 (Workers)
A documentary novel describing the daily hardships, endless rounds of work and penury and the hopes of people in a Stockholm working class district during 1910, in the aftermath of the particularly bitter and defeated General Strike. There are no heroes except the mass of working people and their families themselves, who emerge vibrant and alive despite the grey-grim shadows of that world.

Timmerdalen, 1913 (Timber Valley)
A massive social history of the Norrland region in novel form; from the 1870s to the early 1900s during which time it was converted from a primitive semi-agrarian region to one of the major resource and industrial centres of Sweden. A vivid, many-sided saga of the changes in the peoples lives, the fall and rise of social classes, the intertwining of old traditions and new insights. From the first major labour confrontation in the Sundsvall strike of 1879 to the open class confrontation in the Sandö strikes of 1907.

Guds Vackra Värld, 1916 (God's Beautiful World)
A saga tracing three generations of a family of northern Sweden, from peasant proprietors to desperate unskilled workers in Stockholm during the half century before W.W.I. Their hard work, traditions of independence, honesty and decency leading them into utter poverty by free enterprise unleashed.

LINDMAN, Sara

Gruva, 1968 (Mine)
A reportage work of the 1964 strike of iron ore mine workers in the northern and traditionally militant Kiruna district. Working conditions and miners demands against the private Swedish steel corporation operating the mines; of the bureaucratic and essentially pro-company intervention of the Social Democratic

government against the strikers much as in any other capitalist country.
Belabours the image of the "Swedish model" of Social Democracy through the oral
life histories of a number of miners.

Märta Märta, 1970
A play which is a radical presentation of Swedish working class history over much
of the present century as seen through the eyes and experiences of an elderly
woman. One of the most militant of post war drama pieces.

Also Hjortronlandet, 1955 (Cloudberry Country), a reminiscence novel.

LO-JOHANSSON, Ivar

Godnatt, Jord, 1933 (Good Night Earth)
Lo-Johansson's first novel about the lives and conditions of Statare farm
labourers in the early 20th century. Partly drawn from the author's own background.

Kungsgatan, 1935 (King's Street)
A novel of the trajectory of two Statare who have fled to Stockholm in hopes of a
better life, and the insuperable barriers holding them in poverty and powerlessness.

Statarna, 1936-37 (Statare People)
A panoramic two-volume novel of the lives of Statare throughout Sweden, their
culture, superstitions, self-limitations. Their attempts to escape the caste-like
status in the farming areas and their migration to city slums, during the 1920s
and 1930s.

Also Jord Proletarena, 1941 (Proletarians of the Earth), a collection of short
stories along the lines of Statarna.

Bara En Mor, 1939 (Only a Mother)
A novel dealing with the pettiness, backbiting and mutual harassment which the
exploited impose against each other. Focussed on the rebellious determination of
a young mother to escape the Statare world for her own and her children's sakes.

Traktorn, 1943 (The Tractor)
A collective novel of the spread of mechanization on Swedish farms, the changes
in and rapid displacement of Statare as a class, for good and for bad.

Analfabeten, 1951 (The Illiterate), Gardfarihandlaren, 1953 (The Peddlar)
A two volume autobiography; Statare childhood before W.W.I, contract labour as an
adult illiterate, the liberation of literacy through the Volk High School,
and his life as a worker and writer.

Nederstigen I Dodsriket, 1939 (Descent into the Kingdom of the Dead)
An autobiographical account of the author's experiences as an unskilled immigrant
worker living in the slums of East London at the beginning of the 1930s.

MARTINSON, Harry

Nasslorna Blomma, 1935 (Flowering Nettle, 1939)
Semi-autobiographical novel of growing up in the Swedish urban working class before
W.W.I and of going to sea. The lives, work and militant politics of Swedish
seamen.

MARTINSON, Moa

Ragvakt, 1935 (Rye Watch)
A richly detailed yet lyrical novel of working class lives in Sweden in the first
quarter of the century, focussing especially on the experiences of working
women. Martinson grew up in the Norrland region and worked in factories there
from her early teens to her late thirties, was widowed and remarried the seaman-
writer Harry Martinson and began a career as a writer in her forties.

Mor Gifter Sig, 1936 (Mother Gets Married), Kyrkbrollop, 1938 (Church Wedding),
Kungens Roser, 1939 (The King's Roses)
Three widely read novelas which are reminiscences of childhood and the rounds of
working class lives in the industrial cities of Sweden during the first two decades
of this century. Told with love and humour, as well as an anger at the insecurity,

exploitation and illness which is allowed to hover at the margins of peoples' lives. All the more powerful for being understated.

Drottning Gragyllen, 1937 (Queen Gragyllen), Vägen Under Stjarnorna, 1940 (The Road Under the Stars), Livets Fest, 1949 (Life's Feast)
Three historical novels set in Östergotland province during the 19th century. Realistic accounts of peasant family life interwoven with folk tales and myths, as a picture of what Sweden's modern society sprang from.

MOBERG, Vilhelm

Raskens, 1927
The first of Moberg's documentary novels about the lives and society of the Småland peasantry, an archetypically penurious and stoney peasant region of central Sweden. Set during the mid to late 19th century, Raskens details the hardships, landlord-clerical exactions (the title alludes to the personal duties owed by tenants to their landlords) and dour nature of that world but also celebrates the tenacity and basic social decency of a poor peasantry where the ability to bring forth a crop and humane relationships constitutes a considerable triumph in itself.

Lang Fran Landsvägen, 1929 (Far From the Highway), De Knutna Handerna, 1930 (The Clenched Hands)
Two linked novels dealing with the life of a Småland peasant whose original vitality and hope gradually become sapped in a darkening picture of impoverished cotters, brutalized hired farm hands, rapacious Swedish kulaks, and a hopelessly self-centred clergy and government functionaries. The psychological effects of the unending frugality and imposed penury which deadens human potential in obvious and intricate ways.

Soldat Med Brutet Gevär, 1944 (When I Was a Child, 1948)
An autobiography of childhood and a recreation of the world of the poor Småland peasantry in the first decade of the century.

Utvandrarna, 1946 (The Emigrants, 1951)
A trilogy novel; the English translations being The Emigrants; Unto a Good Land (1954) and Last Letter Home (1956). The epic novel of emigration from mid 19th century Sweden by the first of a wave of ultimately more than a million people fleeing a combination of poverty and social restrictions. Moberg carries the account into the 1890s, completing the lives of the first generation of Swedish immigrants to settle in Wisconsin-Minnesota. One of the great works of Scandinavian literature.

MYRDAL, Jan

Confessions of a Disloyal European, 1968
A reconsideration of Myrdal's own left-intellectual background and of the bases and trajectory of Swedish and European Social Democratic traditions over the previous generation or two. Reflections about the extent to which this is/is not still a progressive force in the world today.

STORM, Fredrik

Rebellerna, 1930 (Rebels), Mit Ungdoms Strider, 1940, Arbetardikt I Kamptid, 1941 (Workers' Poems and Battlesong)
Three collections of revolutionary poetry dealing with the struggles of Swedish working class in the 1930s and allied struggles throughout the world.

SANDEL, Maria

Vid Svältgränsen, 1922 (At Starvation's Boundary Line)
A powerful   collection of stories by a socialist woman author; they include some of the most gripping accounts of the lives and struggles of Swedish working class women of the period.

FINLAND

KAATRA, Kustaa Aadolf

Kynnyksellä, 1903 (On the Threshold, 1976), Elämästä, 1904 (From Life),
Suurlakkokuvia Ym Tyovoenlauluja, 1906 (Scenes From the Great Strike)
Three collections of poems and sketches about the lives and struggles of the
Finnish working class, especially of his fellow industrial workers of the Tampere
region, in the years before and during the 1905 rising. Extremely popular in
their time and part of the repertoire of the Tampere Workers Theatre. An active
Workers Theatre movement flourished in Helsinki and some of the other industrial
towns from circa 1900 to 1918.

Punaiset Ja Valkoiset, 1919 (The Reds and the Whites)
An autobiography of Kaatra's life as a working class poet and dramatist, the
conditions from which the plays grew, their intent and the people around the
"proletarian culture" scene. With a self-criticism of their/his utopianism in
the light of experiences in the civil war and the defeat of the Finnish working
class.

Aiti Ja Poika, 1924 (Mother and Son)
A semi-autobiographical novel dealing mainly with the political and social life
of the Finnish working class and socialist movement from 1900 to 1918.

LEHTIMAKI, Konrad

Rotkoista, 1910 (From the Abyss)
A collection of stories about the misery, drunkenness and amorphous violence of
working class life in Finland during the depression years of the first decade of
the century. Both in background and style, Lehtimaki was "the Maxim Gorky" of
Finland, the best known radical Finnish dramatist of his generation.

Kuolema, 1915 (Death), Syvyydestä, 1916 (From the Depths)
Two collections of anti-war stories and about the nadir of hunger, exploitation,
and disease reached by Finnish workers during the first years of W.W.I.

Jaahyvaisset, 1917 (Farewell)
A play about the proto-revolutionary conditions in Finland during W.W.I, produced
by many Finnish Theatre groups in America during that year. Also
Etuvartiotaistelu, 1917 (The Outpost Battle), a play dealing with the beginings
of the Finnish revolution in Helsinki.

Ylos Helvetista, 1918 (Up From Hell)
A novel of the desperation and strivings of Finnish workers for a better society,
their past suppression and the hopes stirred by the overthrow of the Tsarist
regime in 1917 which seemed to promise a better tomorrow. (Written on the eve of
the White Guard counter-revolution in Finland.)

LEINO, Kasimir (Kasimir Lönnbohm)

Kansalaislaulu, 1889 (Citizen's Song), Työkansan Marssi, 1893 (Workers' March)
Myrskylintu, 1896 (Stormy Petrel)
Three long poems which were enormously popular and set to music to become
revolutionary anthems of the Finnish working class.

LINNA, Väinö

Tuntematon Sotilas, 1954 (The Unknown Soldier, 1963)
A novel about ordinary soldiers in the Finnish army during W.W.II (when it was
allied with the German invasion of Soviet Union). Portrays the skepticism of
draftees toward the rhetoric of national glory and anti-communism dished out by
the Finnish propaganda media, describes the sacrificial battles and the soldiers'
main efforts of just surviving a war which they increasingly grow to believe is
the result of the megalomanic interests of the Finnish bourgeoise. None of this
is told from a Marxian viewpoint and the protagonists are rarely even vaguely
socialist in outlook. The novel was initially excoriated in Finland as treasonous
but is currently held to be the most balanced account yet to appear.

Täälä Pohjantahden Alla, 1959-1961 (Under the Northern Star)
A trilogy novel which spans three generations from the 1880s to 1941; the first
volume dealing with the breakdown of the patriarchal farmstead economy of
northern Finland and the drift into wage labour in the last quarter of the 19th
century, the second volume dealing with the horrendous living conditions of the
industrial working class, the rise of a militant labour movement, and the
revolutionary strikes of 1905 to the civil war of 1918. The last volume carries
the story through the white terror and conservative regime of the 1920s, the
recrudescent labour movement of the early 1930s overwhelmed by the pro-fascist
Finnish ruling class up to the invasion of Soviet Union in 1941 (where Unknown
Soldier begins). Focussed on the working class poor, it includes characters
from the entire spectrum of Finnish society.

PAKKANEN, Toivo

Rautaiset Kädet, 1927 (Hands of Iron), Satama Ja Meri, 1929 (The Harbour and the
Sea), Kuolemattomat, 1931 (The Immortals)
Three collections of stories which describe the lives, varying attitudes,
exploitation but also the satisfactions and pride of a wide range of Finnish
working people during the 1920s and early 1930s. A theme running through the
accounts is the "other nation" quality of their views, an attitude that the world
of the ruling bourgeoisie is an "inconsequential sort of excrescence".

Tientekijat, 1930 (The Roadbuilders)
A novel set in the turn of the century mining boom-town on Gulf of Finland where
Pakkanen grew up; dealing with the lives and adventures of the migrant
construction workers there.

Isänmaan Ranta, 1937 (The Shores of My Country)
A novel of the Finnish working class during the first three decades of this
century, the conditions which formed it, the struggles between right and left
leaderships and the triumph of the revolutionary tendencies between 1905 and 1917,
much to the horror of a union official who foresees the defeat and subjugation
of the organized working class by the Junkers and bourgeoise.

Ne Menneet Vuodet, 1940 (Those Past Years)
A sequel to Shores, dealing with the recrudescent socialist and labour movement
in depression-struck Finland and the once again deepening reaction of the late
1930s.

Also Kauppiaiden Lapset, 1934 (Tradespeople and Their Children) and Tehtaan
Varjossa, 1932 (In the Shadow of the Factory).

Lapsuuteni, 1953 (My Childhood, 1966)
Autobiographical account of growing up in the revolutionary years 1905-1918 as the
son of a worker in a Finnish mining boom town, and an attempt to find a
reconciliation between continuing hostility of Red and White Finland in 1950.

PÄRSSINEN, Hilja

Taistelon Tuoksinassa, 1907 (In the Thick of Battle)
A collection of poems and sketches of the militant Finnish working class; some of
her poems were set to music and sung throughout the left Finnish diaspora.

Musta Virta, 1913 (The Black River), Elämän Harhan, 1917 (Illusion of Life)
Two further collections of revolutionary poems and sketches about Finnish working
women and men, at home and emigres abroad. Widely performed in North American
Finnish communities at the time.

RINTALA, Paavo

Rikas Ja Köyha, 1955 (Rich and Poor)
A novel of Finland in the post W.W.II boom era in which the ex-peasant descendents
of the "Kivi's Brothers" (the Kulak bosses of a famous novel) are still pushing
their poorer "brothers" around, but in urban contexts.

Mummoni Ja Mannerheim, 1960-1962 (Grandma and Mannerheim)
A trilogy novel which sets out to deflate the conservative myth of the 1950s which
portrayed Baron Mannerheim (the White Guard general who crushed the original

workers' government of Finland and led the country into W.W.II on the side of the Nazis) as a sort of Bismarkian saviour "above politics".

Leningradin Kohtalonsinfonia, 1968 (Fate of Leningrad Symphony)
A novel deflating the myth of Mannerheim Finland's allegedly "tragic heroism" in attacking the Soviet Union during W.W.II, comparing the defense of besieged and surrounded Leningrad with the actions of the invading Finnish and German armies.

SAARIKOSKI, Pentti

Mita Tapahtuu, 1962 (What Really Happened?)
A volume of prose poetry which incorporates quotations of official and newspaper reports about events and social processes in Finland and throughout the world during the early 1960s; and then translates such reports into what is really happening.

SALAMA, Hannu

Siinä Nakija, Missa Tekija, 1972 (No Deed Remains Unseen)
A powerful novel of the Finnish Communist underground during W.W.II, their backgrounds, views, losses and resistance against the Finnish military regime and its invasion of Soviet Union.

SALO, Arvo

Lapualaiso Opera, 1966 (Lapua Opera)
A Brechtian play which was part of the revitalized political cabaret theatre in Finland during the 1960s. Deals with the machinations of the Finnish bourgeoisie and military in mid 1930s who press for the establishment of a fascist regime.

SILLANPÄÄ, Franz

Hurskas Kurjus, 1919 (Meek Heritage, 1953)
An epic of the generation of poor peasants born in the last decade of the 19th century who in the next quarter century are pushed off the land, migrate to the cities to become incorporated in the working class, are tumbled along toward revolutionary struggles by the horrendous conditions and are defeated by the Junkers in the Finnish Civil War. Title captures the sometimes sardonic quality of this internationally known work. Won the Nobel Prize for Literature in 1939.

SINKKONEN, Lassi

Sumuruisku, 1963 (The Spray Gun)
A novel dealing with the alienation and distrust inculcated among Finnish workers by two generations of suppression and dictatorship and of how a group of workers in an automobile repair shop gradually learn to trust and support each other in union and on the job.

Sinusta Huomiseen, 1967 (From You to Tomorrow), Meita Kohti, 1968 (Towards Us)
Two collections of poetry in the proletarian tradition, revolving about social and political conditions in contemporary Finland.

TIHLA, Hilda

Leeni, 1907 (Leeni)
A semi-autobiographical novel of a young woman from a backwoods peasant village who migrates to the city and finds a different but equally deep poverty in the working class districts of industrializing Helsinki at the turn of the century. However, she discovers a culture and vitality there which was absent among even the wealthiest peasants. An early working class feminist.

Metsäkylitä, 1908 (From a Backwoods Village)
A collection of short stories about the social and psychological repression, as well as material poverty, of life on the "ruggedly individualistic" peasant farmsteads. Told with humour and sympathy for those who are fleeing the farms to migrate to the city.

Koupas, 1910 (Child), Jumalan Lapsia, 1911 (God's Children), Ihmisia, 1916 (Human Beings)
Three collections of stories revolving around the social ferment of the times; the often anachronistic responses of rural and urban poor. The psychological and social bases of temperance movements, the resurgence of Old Believer millenarianism and the personal qualities which lead a working class woman to become a preacher rather than a socialist activist.

TURTIANINEN, Arvo

Puhetta Porthaninrinne, 1965 (Speech on Porthaninrinne)
A collection of poetry revolving around the concerns of peace, anti-imperialism and self-liberation as they emerged in the 1960s and dealing with events in Europe and the Third World as much as with Finland per se. Some also touch on and memorialize the Finnish working class struggles of the 1930s when Turtianinen first appeared as a proletarian writer.

WILLMAN, Elivira

Kellarikerroksessa, 1907 (In the Basement)
A play which vividly recreates the desperation, daily crises and triumphs of life in the Helsinki tenements, with the magma of socialist revolution rising through them.

Vallankumouksen, 1924 (In the Turmoil of Revolution)
An autobiography from childhood in 1880s to exile after 1918, but mainly of her twenty years (1890s-1918) around the Finnish socialist and labour movements as a dramatist. Recalls her life long advocacy of working class feminism, equality and free unions rather than marriage.

EUROPE: EAST, CENTRAL AND BALKANS

U.S.S.R.
Poland
Czechoslovakia
Hungary
Rumania
Bulgaria
Yugoslavia
Albania
Greece

U.S.S.R.

ABRAMOV, Fydor

Brat'ya I Sestry, 1963 (Brothers and Sisters)
A novel set during W.W.II in a forest village of northern Russia near Arkhangelsk;
a scene dominated by hardship, poverty and almost overwhelming toil which falls
mainly to the remaining women in the village, who meet the situation with tenacity
and even compassion.

Dve Zimy I Tri Leta, 1968 (Two Winters and Three Summers)
A sequel to Brothers and Sisters, set in a similar northern village during the
early 1950s; populated by a host of characters, it is a gradual unfolding of
everyday events into an epic. The continuing poverty, backwardness and isolation
of people in such villages suggests that they are still regarded as second class
citizens by central government bureaucrats during the late Stalin epoch, even
though local party members are self-sacrificing community members. Winner, of the
1975 State prize for literature.

AINI, Sadriddin

Odina, 1924 (Odina)
Reminiscences in the form of a novela, about the Tadjik poor and their initially
confused beliefs about and varied responses to the Russian revolution in which
they are caught up. By a Tadjik worker-writer. Also see his Slaves (1935), a
trilogy novel dealing with the history of the Tadjik people from the early 19th
century to the beginnings of collectization in the region in the 1930s.

AITMATOV, Chingiz

Proshchai, Gul'sary, 1966 (Farewell, Gul'sary, 1970)
A novel of "ingenious socialist realism, which provides a rich and fascinating
account of modern Kirghiz folkways." The two heroes are a veteran Kirghiz
communist peasant and his work horse, Gul'sary, now both weary and aged;
reflections of the twenty-odd years of working together, chronicling the hopes and
altruism, the stupidities and overwork, of old and new communality. Without
despair, it treats the recurrent mismanagement by bureaucrats and exactions of
opportunists whose disastrous effects are not set right by the best efforts of men
and horses. By all accounts a moving work.

Belyi Parokhod, 1970 (The White Steamship, 1972)
A novel of a Kirghis boy growing up in a steppe hamlet during the early 1960s; the
remnants of traditional Kirghiz lore and conditions but basically about the
defenselessness of innocence in a callous world. Revolves around the return of
three mythic deer, long gone from the region, which are the promise of earthly
renewal and of the pressures which are brought upon the boy's grandfather to kill
the deer by a local Kirghiz boss. This minor but seemingly unassailable evil
leads, in a convincingly told account, to the boy's suicide. A prize-winning novel
in the Soviet Union.

AKSYONOV, Vasily (V. Akenov)

Zvezdniy Bilyet, 1961 (Ticket to the Stars)
An angry novela about contemporary (1960) Soviet youth, given to boredom, cynicism,
a fashionable churlishness and individualistic fantasies much like American
teenagers. By a major contemporary Soviet novelist.

ANDREYEV, Leonid

The Seven Who Were Hanged, 1958 (original 1909)
A novel written during the repression which followed the collapse of the 1905
revolution; an evocation of the recuperative power of the Russian revolutionary

movement as symbolized in the heritage left by seven Narodnik revolutionaries who were executed in the 1880s. Andreyev was one of the most influential of the left populist writers at the turn of the century.

AROSEV, Alexander

Korni, 1925 (The Roots)
A semi-autobiographical account of revolutionary intellectuals in the post 1905 Bolshevik underground, and how they and other veteran communists were being superceded by apparatchiks by the mid 1920s.

Dve Povesti, 1924 (Two Stories)
Shornev, 1924)
Two novelas in the form of memoirs by a peasant revolutionary (Terenti Zabytyi) and civil war leader (Nikita Shornev) who are disheartened at the bureaucracy setting in, but proud of the near miracles that their own kind have been able to achieve in bringing the revolution thus far.

BABEL, Isaac

Konarmia, 1926 (Red Cavalry, 1929)
A much translated collection of short stories revolving around the characters and actions of a Red Cossack cavalry detachment fighting against the Polish invasion of 1920-21. The social chaos almost everywhere and an attempt to come to terms with the brutality of a revolution and the amorphous violence it liberates; with the expectation that a better world would emerge from that chaos.

Odesskiye Rasskazy, 1928 (Odessa Tales, 1934)
A collection of short stories of Odessa characters, N.E.P. men, con men and the mosaic of peoples in the Marseilles of the Soviet Union.·

Benya Krick the Gangster and Other Stories, 1948
A collection of short stories, the title story being of a Jewish petty gangster in Odessa from before the revolution who gradually becomes the leader of a Jewish Defense Organization (a phenomena totally distinct from the similarly-named organization of American Zionists today).   In the course of the revolution, Benya Krick becomes an opponent of the kind of ghetto world in which he previously flourished.

BAJALINOW, Kasymaly

Spring in Tienshan, 1932
A semi-autobiographical novel of a Kirghiz "slave woman's" daughter who breaks with her oppressed position ascribed by caste and sex, comes under increasing attack by Kirghiz notables and becomes a communist. A witness to the far from complete but still extraordinary social transformations which had occurred in a decade of revolution and socialist change in a former backwater of the Russian Empire.

BAKLANOV, Grigory

Naugot Hlawnogo Naprawlenia, 1958 (South of the Main Push)
A novel of W.W.II which, atypically, concentrates on the unalloyed miseries and horror of the bloodletting at the front and behind the lines, sufferings without "uplifting" or "heroic" qualities.

Jul' 1941, 1965 (July 1941)
A novel of the first weeks of the German invasion of the U.S.S.R. and the helplessness of the Soviet defense forces, which gradually strengthen despite the dogmatic errors and former purges of the Stalinist regime.

BERGELSON, David

Nokh Alemen, 1913 (When All is Said and Done, 1977)
A lyrical, fast paced and unromantic novel translated from Yiddish; of the stagnating world of Jewish traders in the western Ukraine in about 1910; the degeneration and internal oppression of Stehtl life, its deadening superstitions

and class rule. Generally an antithesis of the stuff which I.B. Singer has woven
into an exotic paradise.

By the Dnieper, 1937
A massive and detailed novel of Jewish small town life and the surrounding rural
society in the Russian Ukraine just before, during and immediately after the
Russian revolution/civil war. Packed with fond and loving memories of that
society but also a recognition of the stagnancy and deadend of the stehtl and the
promise of a new world despite its initial horrors. One of the great novels of
Jewish stehtl life.

BESSAL'KO, Pavel

Kuz'ma Darov, 1920 (Kuz'ma Darov)
A novel of an aging social democrat, worker and revolutionary who in 1917 is a
continuation of a century-long struggle against Tsarism. Evokes his own and a
working class contempt for ideological theoreticians, trusting more the emotional
well springs of revolutionary struggle.

BIBIK, Aleksei

Na Chornoi Polose, 1921 (The Black Zone), K Shirokoi Doroge, 1916 (The Wide Road)
Two linked novels which deal with the deep, rich and varied revolutionary
traditions of Russian workers and intellectuals over two generations as a kind of
culture. Of how the various elements merged during W.W.I, regardless of the
differing positions of political spokesmen, leading to mass support for the 1917
revolution. By a veteran journalist and working class writer.

BUDANTSEV, Sergei

Myatezh, 1923 (Rebellion)
A novel about a social revolutionary (left populist) who becomes a Red Army
commander in the civil war, who opposes the actions of a Cheka commission
investigating ideological heresies among his peasant soldiers and who winds up
forsaken by the troops and attacked by party careerists just making their debut.

Sarancha, 1927 (Locusts)
A novel of the return of a White Army soldier and his family to their home in a
war ravaged region of Turkestan, their life and that of their neighbours during
the initial period of rebuilding, culminating in united efforts to wipe out a
locust plague which threatens the survival of a shattered region.

CHAPYGIN, Alex

Bely Skit, 1915 (The White Hermitage)
A novel of the peasant dissenters, a much oppressed and exiled stream of religious
communitarians (the Old Believers). Set in a corner of the northern forests during
the late 18th century, it attempts to plumb the pre-socialist traditions of
resistance to oppression in Russia, linking it to similar emotions which moved
later political revolutionaries.

Razin Stepan, 1927 (Stepen Razin, 1946)
A novel of the social history of 17th century Russia and the background of the
peasant-cossack uprising led by Sten'ka Razin. Chapygin uses a "contemporary"
reportage in the style of Gorky to capture daily life in the period when a quasi-
slavery was imposed on peasantry through serfdom, and the unleashed fury of a
peasant rising.

Gulyashchie Lyudi, 1935 (Migrant People)
Another massive historical novel of Russian society and people in ferment in the
period before the Sten'ka Razin rising.

CHERNYCHEVSKI, Nikolai

What is to be Done?, 1928 (original 1863)
A period piece novel about the turmoil attending the final years of serfdom in
Russia. Written at the time by a left liberal opponent of the Tsarist regime
imprisoned for political activity, it is one of the first Russian novels to portray

the emerging revolutionaries drawn from the declasse middle class, the nature of Tsarist repression and the yet undirected social ferment of the Russian masses. This novel was extremely influential among three generations of Russian revolutionaries from the Narodnaya Volya to the early Bolsheviks.

CHUKOVSKAYA, Lydia

Opustelyi Dom, 1965 (The Deserted House, 1967)
A novelized memoir dealing with the admosphere of fear, distrust and unreality during the height of the 1937 purges in Leningrad as experienced by a woman who is a loyal Soviet citizen but whose son has been sent to a prison camp. It details the transformation of normally decent people into paranoics, and a well adjusted family into shunned and fearful outcasts.

DOMBROVSKY, Yury

Khranitel' Drevnostei, 1964 (The Custodian of Antiquities, 1970)
A novel which relates the thoughts of a young academic in late 1930s who has joined an archaeological museum in Alma Ata to escape the purge fever in the Russian cities, but finds that the director of the museum, the epitome of a servile careerist, is exclusively concerned in using the museum to follow the twists and turns of official policy on contemporary matters. A sardonic portrait of manipulated scholarship.

DOROSH, Efim

Derevenskii Dnevnik, 1954-1970 (A Village Diary)
The general title of a series of books which are composite accounts of Raigorod, a fictional Kolhoze farm community in central Russia. They deal with recurrent and changing problems, joys, minor triumphs and failures of everyday life on a Soviet collective farm. Describes the events with a calm, compassionate and critical view of what collective farming should be like and as skewed by the complex historical and psychological elements at work in such communities. A central character throughout is a Kolhoze administrator (whose diary it is supposed to be), a pragmatic farmer operating in a milieu of sometimes helpful, sometimes blindly bureaucratic central organizations. A panorama of local people, changes, and the need for a better deal for Kolhoze members.

EHRENBURG, Ilya

Lyubov Zhanny Ney, 1924 (The Love of Jeanne Ney, 1929)
A melodrama about a French artiste and her "tragic" love affair with a Soviet diplomatic attache in Paris which was turned into a Hollywood film of the period. Written while Ehrenburg was an emigre in Paris, it is possibly his most self revealing work.

V Protochnom Pereulke, 1927 (A Street in Moscow, 1933)
A novel of daily life in a Moscow residential district during the late N.E.P. period; the tattered stasis, the seeming entrenchment of a new class of merchant speculators and their growing respectability, the bitter disillusionment of Soviet idealists who fear a creeping return of capitalism.

Ottepel, 1954 (The Thaw, 1955)
A semi-autobiographical novel about the repression and distortions of the recently ended Stalin era. A rather self-serving work which was a precursor to the deStalinization writing.

FADEYEV, Alexander

Razgrom, 1925 (The Nineteen, 1929; also The Route)
One of the most widely known novels of the Russian civil war. About a detachment of Red partizans composed of Siberian peasants and men and women from a mining community, their fighting retreat from Cossack White Guard troops and the supporting Japanese army in central Siberia during 1919-1920. Some descriptions of the lives and traditions of Siberian industrial workers and poor peasants which foster their determined resistance. However, Fadayev's glorification of

toughness bordering on callousness by the partizans underlines a recurrent and questionable aspect of this literature.

Also Razliv, 1923 (The Flood) and Protiv Techeniya, 1924 (Against the Current), two novelas which deal with facets of the mobilization of working class forces during the Russian revolution and the civil war.

Poslednyi Iz Udege, 1934-1936 (The Last of the Udeges, 1938)
A trilogy novel of the Russian Far East from the last years of Tsarist rule and through the revolution and civil war. Revolves around the vastly different yet intersecting lives of an idealistic young bourgeoise who joins the Soviet administration and a member of one of the small tribal groups, the Udeges, who have been crushed and scattered both by the earlier Russian colonialism and by the ravages of civil war; particularly the exactions of Japanese interventionist forces in the early 1920s. Smacks of "Last of the Mochicans" in places.

Molodaya Gvardia, 1945 (The Young Guard, 1946)
A massive documentary novel of the underground resistance to German occupation mounted in the Krasnodan region of the Crimea in 1942-43. Fadeyev emphasized the chaos of the situation and the fact that the partizans there evolved more or less spontaneously and outside the impetus or direction of the established party organizations. A touchy topic at the time.

FEDIN, Konstantin

Goroda I Gody, 1924 (Cities and Years)
A novel about a Russian internee in Germany during W.W.I, the mounting anti-war sentiment he sees around him and his liberation by the Bavarian revolution of 1918. An episodic account of his return to the Volga region through a Soviet Russia in the throes of revolution and wracked by intricate local struggles; a kaleidoscopic portrayal of scenes and events. Counterposed is the account of a German POW in Russia who is freed by the Soviets and his difficult and comparable journey back to Germany, then entering a period of revolution and counter-revolution.

Transvaal, 1927 (Transvaal, 1928)
A collection of short stories revolving around an Estonian Kulak who winds up in the Smolensk region of central Russia at the end of the civil wars who, because of his cunning and boss-like manner, comes to dominate the affairs of a peasant village during the N.E.P. period--despite the changes of the revolution.

Pokhishchenie Evropy, 1935 (The Rape of Europe)
A novel of a Soviet journalist in western Europe during 1933-1935; surveys the deepening support of fascism in the upper middle classes throughout Europe and the dire distress of the ordinary people in Germany, but also in Holland, Switzerland, France and Norway.

Perviye Radosti, 1945 (The First Joys), Neobyknovennoye Leto, 1948 (An Extraordinary Summer), Kostyor, 1961 (The Bonfire)
A novel trilogy of a family of pre-1917 Bolsheviks in a small industrial town of the Volga region from 1910 to the eve of the German invasion in 1941.

FORSH, Olga

Odety Kamnem, 1925 (Clad in Stone; also Iron Clad)
A documentary novel of the Narodnik revolutionaries in Russia of the 1870s and 1880s, a compelling collective portrait of their lives and times (including that of Lenin's older brother). Told by a left populist writer whose life overlapped that period.

Voron, 1931 (The Raven)
A novel of the varied and intersecting left intellectual milieu in Russia before 1917; the fact that the later political distinctions made in the 1920s were not so crucial earlier. Links the literary developments with realities of Russian society before and after the revolution.

Pezwiie Shagi Do Woli, 1953 (The Firstlings of Freedom)
A novel of the revolt against Tsarism in the 1820s by a small group of army officers

and intellectuals inspired by the French Revolution. Forsh was a prolific author of
of left historical novels.

FURMANOV, Dimitri

Chapayev, 1923 (Chapayev, 1931)
A chronicle of a famous but in many ways typical peasant guerrila leader who fought
against the White armies in the Urals and Don region and whose support was so
crucial to the Soviet victory in the civil war. It tells of the largely
"instinctive" attachment of peasant leaders like Chapayev to the Bolsheviks of that
period, of his continuing traditional village outlook and contradictions, and also
of his feel for the exigencies of a partizan struggle which is more reliable than
abstract political theory. Furmanov was a political commisar assigned to
Chapayev's unit in 1919/1920.

GLADKOV, Feodor

Tsement, 1925 (Cement, 1926)
The first and most widely translated novel of socialist reconstruction in the
Soviet Union, it became a model for later works. Deals with the destruction of
civil war in Crimea and with the reconstruction of a destroyed cement plant.
Describes the specifics of work and skills (and the excitement which the
reconstruction entailed). Treats with the contending viewpoints and class carry
overs of skilled workers, professionals, political cadres and peasant workers
--none of whom are all-wise or without both flaws and strengths. Their gradual
coming together in a modus vivendi as they rebuild the cement factory.

Energiya, 1932 (Power)
A sort of sequel to Cement, dealing with the construction of a hydro-electric
project in which the normal differences between the strata in Soviet society
become destructive due to the unbridled power which a managing engineer wields.
The lassitude of party officials and the growing dissentions which build up until
rank and file communists and other workers take control of the project.

Tragediya Lyubashi, 1935 (Lyubasha's Tragedy)
A novela of a Russian peasant girl who goes off to the cities after the civil war
to find a job and becomes a textile worker; an indominable non-party activist
and a stubborn proponent of workers' rights in the face of managerial careerists,
she gets branded as a trouble maker.

Povest O Detstve, 1949 (Tale of Childhood)
A luminescent, largely unideological reminiscence of childhood in a poor peasant-
fishermen's village on the Caspian Sea in the 1890s, done in the style of Gorky.
Also The Wicked Year (1951), the last of the four volume autobiography begun with
Tale of Childhood and ending on the eve of W.W.I.

GODINER, S.N.

Der Mentsh Mit Der Biks, 1928 (The Man With the Gun, 1928, 1932)
A two volume novel said to be one of the best accounts of the civil war in western
Russia. The chaos, the shifting counterrevolutionary forces, daily struggles
to survive and the half-mad psychology which develops among normal people under
these conditions. Told partly from the experiences of a Jewish communist
participant, ranging from Minsk to Lithuania and Polish occupied Ukraine.

GORKY, Maxim (Alessey Maximovich Pyeshkov)

Na Dne, 1902 (The Lower Depths, 1902)
A play which catapulted Gorky to international fame and which was ultimately
translated and performed in languages from Japanese to Malayalam. Set in a Moscow
flophouse tenement at the turn of the century with its changing cast of semi-
employed workers and wanderers, men and women, representatives of a wide range of
rootless people from throughout Russia. A naturalistic depiction of the ferment
at work in the country, using flashbacks and evoking the apocalyptic anger which,
for good and for bad, will soon overwhelm Czarist Russia.

Mat, 1906 (Mother, 1907)
A sometimes stilted, sometimes moving novel which deals with the lives of an aged
woman and her son in a slum district of an industrial city of pre-1905 Russia.
Describes her initial fatalism about the seemingly "natural" brutality of that
world and her gradual change through her son's involvement in revolutionary
activity. After the son's arrest and deportation she moves into underground
political activity herself. Made into one of the Soviet film classics in 1920s
by Pudovkin.

Detstvo, 1913 (My Childhood, 1972), V Lyudakh, 1916 (My Apprenticeship, 1972),
Moi Universitety, 1923 (My Universities, 1972)
A three volume reminiscence of Gorky's childhood to early manhood which is as well
an overview of the ferment, poverty and mixture of backwardness and revolt which
permeated provincial Russia during the 1880s and 1890s. There is no way to
adequately describe these volumes except to say that they are kaleidoscopic and
compelling, mixing blindness and brilliance. Gorky had by then already become
a renowned proletarian writer of international fame. The 1972 Penguin edition is
an inexpensive and attractive version of the trilogy.

(The Artamonov Affair, 1925) (Decadence, 1927)
A bitterly sardonic novel of a know-nothing, ex-peasant who more by chance than
anything else finds himself on the side of the Soviets during the civil war. He
attains some power as a municipal fixer dealing with speculators during the N.E.P.
period and lands a post as a functionary in the local Soviet regime by spouting
whatever policies and phrases are fashionable at a given time, lording it over
real workers in a manner not dissimilar to pre-revolutionary officials.

The Life of Klim Samgin, 1927-1936
A four volume cycle of novels covering three generations of Russian workers,
peasants, intellectuals and others from 1880 to 1932. A vast, rambling epic
beginning with the pre-modern Russia of his earliest works, through the 1905
revolution and its suppression, the 1917 revolution and civil war, N.E.P. period
and the socialist construction period under Stalin. Touching on the contradictions,
mistakes and callousness of workers and communists, as well as their heroism and
epochal transformations. The English translations of these volumes are The Life of
Klim Samgin (1929), Bystander (1930), The Magnet (1931), Other Fires (1933).

GROSSMAN, Vassily

Stepan Kolchugin, 1933 (Stepan Kolchugin)
A novel of the terrible famines which coincided with and were partly due to the
early collectivization drive of farms in the Ukraine of the early 1930s.

Narod Bessmerten, 1943 (The People are Immortal, 1947)
A moving and frank account of the Soviet Union during the first years of W.W.II;
the sacrifices, flawed humanity, nobility and petty hatreds but above all the
horrendous hardships that the people endured. Very little mention of Stalin or
party leaders since it sees The People as the ones who are immortal.

Vsyo Techyot, 1972 (Everything Flows)
Novelized recollections of the paralysis and fear which began with the forced farm
collectivization drives and deepened with the purges of the late 1930s; also a
damning account of the unbridled power intrigues and disregard of
elementary justice by the N.K.V.D. during the post W.W.II period.

GUL, Roman

General Bo, 1927 (General Bo, 1930)
An evocation of and tribute to the armed resistance of the Social Revolutionary
party (left populists) after the collapse of the 1905 revolution, centering on one
Boris Savinkov, a legendary underground leader from the late 19th century until the
eve of W.W.I.

ILF, Ilya and PETROV, Eugeni

Twelve Chairs, 1927 (or Diamonds To Sit On)
An enormously popular spoof of the speculator-entrepreneurs who mushroomed during

the New Economic Policy period. A satire of re-emergence of old-fashioned opportunism and crooks, revolving about one Ostap Bender's schemes to recover chairs which are supposed to contain hidden jewels.

The Little Golden Calf, 1933
Another once very popular satire involving the N.E.P. man, Ostap Bender, his high phrased rhetoric attempting to hide his crooked schemes. Set at the end of N.E.P. period in Soviet Union and including Bender's trip abroad.

ISKANDER, Fasil

Sozvesdie Kozlutura, 1966 (The Goat-Ibex Constellation, 1975)
A satire of the grandiose and credulous boosterism of some government administrators, in this case those who are responsible for collective farms in a district of Georgia. They are taken in by a fabrication that one farm has cross bred a hybrid goat and ibex which lives on next to nothing and has an incredible wool and milk output. Portrays the emulation schemes, band wagon self-glorification statistics on anticipated successes which flow forth until the hoax is uncovered.

IVANOV, Vsevolod

Bronepoyezd N 14-69, 1922 (Armoured Train No. 14-69, 1933)
A novel of the partizan struggle in Siberia, revolving around a multinational detachment of Red guerrillas and their relations with Siberian peasantry as they attempt to cut the military rail link between the White Cossack forces of Semenov from the supporting Japanese Expeditionary army in the trans-Baikal.

(The Iron Division, 1937), Parkhomenko, 1939
Two bio-historical novels of the civil war; Iron Division dealing with the Red Cossack forces struggles against the White and allied Cossack armies in the Don region, Parkhomenko being a biography of a Ukrainian partizan leader and the maelstrom of contending forces in the Ukraine during the civil war.

The Adventures of a Fakir, 1935 (also as Patched Breeches, 1936)
A reminiscence of Ivanov's wanderings and experiences as a boy and young man in Central Asia and Russia, told with humour and gusto. "Vsevolod Ivanov's life (1895-1963) was quite as fantastic as some of his stories, yet not atypical of a sector of the Russian working class of his generation. He was born on the border of Siberia and Turkestan, into an impoverished family. His mother was half Polish and half Mongolian, while his father, the natural son of the Turkestan governor-general, dreamt of a university career (he knew seven oriental languages) but ended up as a casual worker, village teacher and alcoholic. ... Vsevolod as an adolescent ran away from elementary school to perform as a clown in an itinerant circus. He then became a wanderer and was by turns a labourer, sword swallower at county fairs, actor and for a time the travelling fakir Ben Ali Bey. ... In 1917 he joined the Red Army, fought in the south-east and went through all sorts of frightful experiences, was wounded and sent to Moscow for recuperation in 1920, where with the help of Maxim Gorky he joined the proletarian writers of the Serapion Brothers, which formed his writing style."

KATEYEV, Valentine

Rastratchiki, 1926 (The Embezzlers, 1929)
A novela about the disorganization of the N.E.P. period. In particular, about two witless and purposeless petty officials who abscond with the payroll of a cooperative factory and roam around the countryside having a spree, being fleeced but unapprehended. A humourous but damning indictment of the level of social disorganization in Soviet society during the mid 1920s.

Kvadratura Kruga, 1928 (Squaring the Circle, 1932)
A once tremendously popular play spoofing the posturing and bureaucracy of the new/old administrative class, especially on the local and regional level, in the Soviet Union of late 1920s.

Molko, 1930 (Milk)
A novela which castigates the stupidities and excesses arising in the agricultural collectivization drives of the time. Set in a Caucauses dairy region, it deals

with an elderly peasant who has been a supporter of the Soviet cause and a model of what was best in village life. His life is wrecked when he is classified as a Kulak by arbitrary standards despite the objections of local communists.

Vremy, Vperyod, 1932 (Forward, Oh Time, 1934)
A novel about the construction of the new city of Magnitogorsk during the Great Leap Forward of the early 1930s; the psychological dynamics of the main characters and the drama of socialist construction. Written with ironic humour and few of the stereotyped heroes and villains which flawed much of the comparable literature.

Beleyet Parus Odinokiy, 1936 (Peace is Where the Tempest Blows, or Lone White Sail, 1937)
A novel revolving around two Mark Twain-like ten year olds living on the margins of the Black Sea on the outskirts of Odessa shortly after the failure of the 1905 revolution. It portrays the events of that already distant past--the dashed hopes, the deepening reaction, the fears as well as the continuing current of underground activity--as seen through the eyes of the two boys. An outstanding work. Lone White Sail was the first of a tetrology which follows events from W.W.I, the revolution and civil war to the N.E.P. period; Khutorok V Stepi, 1950 (Cottage on the Steppes) through the various phases of the socialist construction period to the eve of W.W.II; Ma Vlast Sovetov, 1951 (For the Power of the Soviets, 1952); while Zimniy Vetyer, 1960 (Winter Wind) charts some of the destructiveness of Stalinism.

KAVERIN, Veniamin (V. Zilberg)

Ispolnenie Zhelany, 1935 (The Fulfillment of Desires, or The Larger View, 1938)
A portrait of a romantic monarchist's fantastic and complete misconception of what is going on around him in the Soviet Union. A gently sardonic novel of human capacity for self-deception and delusion.

KIPNIS, Itsik

Khadoshim Un Teg, 1926 (Months and Days)
Novel of a somewhat simple Jewish worker who lives his life within a Jewish community in a small town surrounded by the carnage of war and revolution and his later stint in the Red Army. The vast historical events of which he becomes a part are told as if they were a mere continuation of his previous personal life. Told with irony and traditional Yiddish humour.

KONETSKY, Victor

Kto Smotrit Na Oblaka, 1967 (Some Look at the Clouds)
A set of ten stories strung together as chapters of a chronicle covering 1942 to 1966 by a seaman-writer. Each chapter deals with a different character and focusses on the various phases of W.W.II, the final Stalin years, the interregnum,   the de-Stalinization period and after. A quality of the decency, tenacity and inner honesty of ordinary people, if also of melancholy and hardened outer selves.

KULBAK, Moshe

Zemelnianer, 1931-1935 (Zemelnianer)
A two-volume novel of the conflicts humourous and sad between the older Jewish generation in small town Russia and their children influenced by the Russian revolution's anti-religiosity and sexual freedoms (which emotionally are more disturbing than class politics in these domestic tensions). No real villains and no didactic answers, only the turmoil and attempts of ordinary men and women to come to terms with the new society in creation.

Benjamin Magidov, 1937 (Benjamin Magidov)
A play about a radical Jewish worker and partizan in the Polish occupied western Ukraine of early 1920s.

LEONOV, Leonid

Barsuki, 1924 (The Badgers, 1946)
Novel revolving around the Tambov peasant revolt against the Bolsheviks at the end of the civil war and focussed on the tactics used to defuse the revolt and bring the peasantry back to Soviet side. Told as a documentary on-the-spot account but combined with some biting peasant folk tales. A remarkable presentation of the anger and frustrations on both sides.

Sot, 1932 (Soviet River, 1936)
A Soviet construction novel about the conflicts between ingrained village traditions, both good and bad, and the social changes due to the building of a huge pulp and paper mill in the North Eastern Russian forests on the banks of the Sot river.

Doroga Na Okean, 1935 (Way to the Ocean, 1944)
An unusual novel which alloys the dreams, reminiscences and utopian visions of a dying old Bolshevik in charge of a section of the Siberian railway. An inter-weaving of the ongoing life and problems around him, of the past events, struggles and unexpected wonders in the people he has known in his own packed life. Of injustices and betrayals but also the visions old and new of what a socialist world will eventually be like, in its infinite human complexity.

Russkiy Lyes, 1953 (Russian Forest)
Part novel, part historical documentary of how the Russian forests have been exploited and despoiled from Tzarist times down through various programs of socialist construction. A novelized survey of the long history of schemes to preserve those forests and use them more rationally, of the individuals behind such conservationist attempts.

LIBEDINSKI, Yuri

Nedelya, 1923 (The Week, 1929)
A novela of one week in a small provincial Russian town during the first year of the revolution; attempts to show how major historic events, national and international, affect life in the town directly or very indirectly, regardless of the obscure and sometimes totally misconstructed understanding of them by local inhabitants.

Rozhdeniya Geroya, 1930 (Birth of a Hero, 1931)
A novel about an old Bolshevik who questions whether the long revolutionary struggles and the sacrifices will end in capitalist restoration in the N.E.P. period. A parallel account traces the rise of a particularly noxious variety of party careerist, described with bitter satire. The story "ends" with the "hero" recommitting himself to the hopes and visions that originally inspired his and earlier generations.

LURYA, Nathan (Noteh Luria)

The Steppe Calls, 1932, 1948
A two volume novel about Jews from former shtetls establishing collective farms in the Don-Volga region during the late 1920s and early 1930s, the difficulties of adjustment to farm life, their qualms and difficulties and achievements. The second volume deals with W.W.II and the years immediately after, with the previous hopes of the now aging previous generation gone, weariness setting in. Counterposed with a hope for and call to build a better life in post war period.

LYASHKO, Nikolai (N. Lyashchenko)

Domennaya Pech', 1924 (Blast Furnace, 1929)
One of the earliest novels dealing with socialist reconstruction. A task force of urban workers is sent to rebuild an iron and steel plant in a peasant region. Descriptions of work, on the job tensions between the two groups and the mixture of traditional and revolutionary motives in play. Blast Furnace was a widely translated and very influential work in the early "Proletarian Culture" movement.

Dyhaniie Holubki, 1929 (Breath of a Dove)
A story of the traditional communitarianism and folk religiosity of a south
Russian peasant village in the 1905 period, the thinly hidden class divisions and
the hostility between peasants and local workers which breaks into open battle
and cannot be papered over.

Sladkaya Katorga, 1950 (Honied Penal Servitude)
A long novel about the revolutionary traditions of pre 1917 Russia by an old
Menshevik writer.

MALASHKIN, Sergei

Luna S Pravoi Storony, 1928 (Moon on the Right Hand Side)
An angry expose of the degeneracy which had set in among some Komsomol groups
during the N.E.P. period.

Pokhod Kolonn, 1931 (The Columns March)
A chronicle of the establishment of Kolkhoz collective farms at that time and a
frank portrayal of peasant resistance to them. Despite mistakes and excesses,
his view is that collectivization in some form was necessary to escape rural
stagnation. By a left populist victim of Stalin's purges.

MALYSHKIN, Aleksandr

Stevastapol, 1929 (Sevastopol)
Novel which attempts to paint a mosaic of the Crimea during the early years of
the revolution (1917-1919) as seen through the eyes of a not especially
revolutionary sailor in the Black Sea Fleet.

Lyudi Iz Zakholustya, 1938 (People From the Sticks)
An account of construction projects and industrialization in the Ural mountains
during the height of the thencurrent second five year plan. Attempts to portray
an entire region undergoing forced draft development as well as the changes which
the projects create in the programs and people themselves.

MUSREPOW, Gabit

The Awakened Land, 1928
A novel about the revolutionary social changes which burst forth from previously
hidden tensions within Kazahk peasant-tribal society during and in the years
immediately after the "Russian" civil war (which also involved protracted
struggles between Kazahk partizans of Whites and Reds).

MUSTAFIN, Gabiden

Karanganda, 1930 (Karaganda)
A novel of Kazahk life on the eve of the revolution and the conflicts within
traditional society which break out in one Kazahk district during the civil war.

NEKRASSOV, Victor

V Okopakh Stalingrada, 1946 (In the Trenches of Stalingrad, 1947)
A massive chronicle of ordinary soldiers with ordinary feelings and capabilities
in the six month battle for Stalingrad, the turning point of W.W.II. One of the
most honest and most believable of the Soviet war accounts.

V Rodnom Gorade, 1954 (In the Home Town)
A novel about the return of a wounded Soviet soldier to a shattered Kiev at end
of W.W.II. The panorama of social, physical and personal desolation and the
strivings of ordinary people for basic necessities and a modicum of human warmth
in often shattered personal lives.

Kira Georghieva, 1959 (Kira Georghieva, 1962)
A powerful anti-Stalinist novel about those scooped up in the various purges
during and after W.W.II. The backgrounds and experiences of those who were
"innocent" as not different from those who were "guilty"; their experiences in
prison camps and the effects on those who survived.

NEVEROV, Alekandr (A.S. Skobelev)

Taskent, Gorod Khlyebniy, 1923 (Tashkent, City of Bread, 1934)
A documentary account in novel form of the famine which gripped the major city of
Soviet Central Asia in 1921, the day-to-day survival strategies of individuals,
the changes in people and institutions, the chaos, the heroic and contemptible
responses of local leaders. Told through the experiences of a wandering,
orphaned peasant lad, the novel evoked powerful emotions of personal experience
among Russian readers of the time.

NIKIFOROV, Georgi

U Fonarya, 1928 (Beside the Street Lamp)
A novel about the discovery of a former bourgeoise working in a factory and how
the investigation of his loyalties to the Soviet regime wreck his life. A
denunciation of the self-serving careerism and hysteria of those who manufacture
"class enemies" everywhere.

V Strechnyi Veter, 1931 (Into the Wind)
A novel which investigates the touchy topic of why the Kulaks seemed to retain
such influence among the peasantry, before and during collectivization. Coming
to the view that their strength lay in championing private peasant land holding
versus the collectivization which most peasants opposed.

Mastera, 1935 (The Master Craftsman)
A novel set in the final decades of Tzarist Russia; the massive proletarianization,
deepening exploitation and growing revolt of all manner of workers. Underlines
the fact that working class revolutionaries were spread throughout the various
political   groupings, from Anarchists to Bolsheviks, and did not make as much
of the ideological differences between them as their leadership did. Deals with
the at first gradual then rapid swing of the rank and file to the Bolsheviks
during the revolution.and holds that the
later (i.e. 1935) attempts to discriminate between individual workers on the
basis of previous political differences is dogmatic and unjust.

NIKITIN, Nikolay

Polyot, 1925 (Flight), Tales of Oboyansk, 1928
One novela (Polyot) and a collection of tales (Oboyansk) about the peoples and
conditions in Arctic Russia just before and during the civil war, in an adventure
story format.

Sevyernaya Avrora, 1950 (Aurora Borealis)
A novel about the British and Allied interventionist army in Murmansk during 1918,
their support of the White army and the struggles of Red partizans.

NILIN, Paulin

Zhestokost, 1959 (Comrade Venka, 1962)
Novel of a young Soviet officer during the civil war who succeeds in convincing
a peasant bandit-guerrilla leader and his followers to come over to the Red army,
only to have a Cheka commission, which knows nothing of the actual case, take the
matter out of his hands, leading to the execution of the prisoner. The excesses
of simple-minded dogmatism in extremely amorphous situations.

(DER) NISTER (Pinhas Kahanowitch)

The Mashber Family, 1939, 1948
Der Nister's masterpiece, a two volume novel which describes the intricacies of a
Jewish shtetl before and during the initial industrialization of the 1870s,
through the rising revolt against Czarism of the 1880s on, W.W.I and the
revolution, socialist construction and social conditions, of the appeal of Hassidic
life as well as of superstitious fanaticism. Revolving around four generations of
the Mashber family.

Of the Fifth Year, 1964
A novel of an overprotected youth from a Hassidic family in central Russia who
runs away to become a worker and gets caught up in the 1905 revolution. Some fine
descriptions of Czarist Russia in the fifth year of the 20th century.

NIZOVOI, Pavel

The Ocean, 1930
A novel of the issues raised and social costs incurred by the industrialization
and collectivization impressed on peasant regions; by a veteran revolutionary
writer and a critical supporter of poor peasantry.

NOVIKOV-PRIBOY, Alexey

Tsushima, 1934 (Tsushima, 1934)
A novelized account drawn partly from experience of the life of sailors in the
Tzarist Black Sea Fleet during the Russo-Japanese war; their backgrounds and
thoughts as the Fleet sails around the world from the Crimea, bound for its
destruction by the Japanese navy in the Straits of Tsushima. This was one of the
sparks which touched off the 1905 revolution and the ships are treated as a
microcosm of Tsarist Russia.

ODULOK, Taeki

Snow People, 1935
A family chronicle of a Yukagir reindeer herding family and their kith and kin in
north eastern Siberia from late Tsarist times to late 1920s. By a Yukagir whose
boyhood was spent as a herder during those years and who eventually became a
deputy in the Supreme Soviet. It details the initially considerable autonomy and
independence of the Yukagir, only coming under the commercial control of Russian
traders after the turn of the century, the revolution (which mainly bypassed that
region) and the initial gradual attempts of Soviet government to bring the Yukagir
into the 20th century. Exemplifies a genre of such writing.

OLESHA, Yuri

Zavist, 1927 (Envy, 1936)
A very popular novel which apparently struck a responsive chord among Russian
readers during the N.E.P. period. It explores the nature and ramifications of
"envy" in its various forms in early Soviet society in a satiric, tongue-in-cheek
fantasy.

Vishnyovaya Kostochka, 1929 (Cherry Stone, 1933)
A collection of short stories about the seemingly unchanged human emotions which
continue to exist in the new Soviet society, modified mainly in the rhetoric in
which they are clothed.

OSTROVSKY, Nikolai

Kak Zakalyalas, 1935 (How the Steel Was Tempered, 1937)
One of the best known and most archetypal of the Stalinist novels, a semi-
autobiographical account of the forging of Bolshevik power through the losses and
mistakes and long drawn out struggle in the Ukraine. The assorted foreign
invasions, White armies, Ukrainian Nationalist and other phases of the revolution
and civil war there. Revolves around the rededication of a badly crippled
ex-peasant Bolshevik to turn around the retreat of the N.E.P. period and help
initiate socialist transformation.

OVECHKIN, Valentin

Rayonniye Budni, 1952 (District Weekdays)
Sketches of the everyday life and problems of Soviet agriculture, the deepening
apathy of farmers and the growing disparity between city and village life.
Castigates the bureaucratic strictures which prevent collective farmers applying
their own practical knowledge and decisions. Also Svoimi Rukami, 1954 (In the
Same District), an extended sequel to District Weekends.

Trudnaya Vyesna, 1956 (A Difficult Spring)
Reportage accounts of the problems raised by Krushev's scheme to open up allegedly
"Virgin Lands", the unreality of the gains listed and the fact that regional
farmers had already long ago tried and known of the limitations of the lands and
techniques to be used.

PANFEROV, Fedor

Bruski, 1929-1936 (Bruski, 1931, And Then the Harvest, 1939)
A massive tetrology "novel" dealing with the arguments for, resistance to, the
mistakes, excesses but ultimate necessity for collectivization of agriculture.
Set in a poor Volga peasant region in the early 1930s, it goes back to the late
19th century rise of the Kulak class and of how their power over the rural areas
was strengthened by the initial reforms and land seizures of early revolutionary
period. Bruski incorporates a great deal of reportage material on the economics
and sociology of peasant farms of the 1930 period, although from a Stalinist
viewpoint which Panferov later rejected.

Volga, Matushka Reka, 1954 (Volga, Mother River)
A novel which bares the hardships and sacrifices of a generation of Soviet
citizens, especially rural people, and a cautious criticism of planners and
bureaucrats who disregarded the material and emotional needs of ordinary citizens
in their adoration of monumental projects.

Reflekcia, 1958 (Reflections)
Partly a sequel to Volga; specifically a return to and reconsideration of the
region he described a quarter century earlier in Bruski. A critical comment on
his own rather pat view of the early collectivization process, the costs involved
and the relative failure of the collective farms in the region to achieve their
expected promise.

PANOVA, Vera

Sputniki, 1947 (Fellow Travellers)
A plotless series of sketches of civilians and soldiers travelling together for
a while on a train in war-torn Soviet Union; an unabashedly anti-war account.

The Factory, 1949
A short novel sketching the sadness, exhaustion and tribulations of the Soviet
people in their attempts to rebuild after the devastation of W.W.II.

Vremena Goda, 1953 (Span of the Year, 1957)
Novel of upper middle class life in Moscow during the early 1950s; of how the son
of one socially responsible, decent family gradually becomes a hooligan (with
some unusual accounts of Moscow underworld life), while the son of a corrupt and
careerist family breaks with this background and leaves the capital to start a
more honest life in the provinces.

Seryozha, 1955 (Seryozha)
A novela of a young boy beginning to discover the world and people around him in
post-Stalinist Russia; widely hailed as a sensitive and human account.

PAUSTOVSKY, Konstantin

Kara Bugaz, 1932 (The Black Gulf, 1946)
A combination of history, local colour, and straightforward reportage of attempts
to extract minerals from an arm of the Caspian Sea in Soviet Asia. Paustovsky had
a talent for blending seemingly disparate themes, from adventure to descriptions
of technology, into very readable wholes. Similarly, see Black Sea, 1936 and
Povyest O Lyesakh, 1948 (The Tale of Forests).

Kolchida, 1934 (Colchis)
Another collage account dealing with people involved in reclaiming a sub-tropical
swampland in the southern Caucauses.

Povest O Zhizni, 1946-1962 (Story of a Life)
A five volume autobiography which is a lyrical journey through five decades of
Russian history (circa 1910-1960), its peoples and its different landscapes.
Includes Distant Years, The Restlessness of Youth, The Beginnings of an Unknown
Century, The Time of Great Expectations, and A Throw to the South.

PILAR, Yury

Chelowiek Ostaietcia Chelowiekom, 1962 (Men Remain Men)
One of the better and balanced accounts of the humiliations and sufferings in
forced labour camps of Stalinist Russia; a much published genre from the late
1950s to mid 1960s.

PILNYAK, Boris (B.A. Vogau)

Golyi God, 1922 (The Naked Year, 1928)
A novel which juxtaposes aspects of the lives of the major classes in Russian
society during the revolutionary chaos of 1918 and presents that year as the
culmination of 200 years of struggle against the Tsarist system. The scenes are
threaded together around the experiences and received folk memory of a
superficially simple Old Believer peasant who views the Russian revolution as
the continuation of an older spirit of resistance to oppression.

Mashiny I Volki, 1926 (Machines and Wolves)
A very un-nostalgic account of an upper Volga peasant village still living in
semi-medieval conditions after the end of the civil war, the arrival of communist
organizers and the historic bases for and strength of peasant primitivism in
resisting all things new.

Volga Vpadayet V Kaspiiskoye Morye, 1930 (The Volga Flows into the Caspian Sea,
1932)
A socialist construction novel of building the first major hydro electric project
on the upper Volga; the problems in overcoming shortages of skills and materials
and the equivocal means of overcoming peasant resistance to a project which they
know will change their lives. Pilnyak defends the necessity of industrialization
and of basic changes in the "tradition rich" peasant villages themselves, if
material and social poverty are to be overcome, but with a realization that
something of value will be lost.

Also Pospewanie Fruktow, 1935 (The Ripening of Fruit), another novel weighing
the   costs and hopes of the Great Leap Forward period of the early 1930s.

PLATONOV, Andrei

Reka Potudan, 1937 (The River Potudan)
A collection of stories which portray the tragedy of many survivors of the Russian
revolution in 1920s and 1930s, cast adrift and not yet able to grasp the new
society. Typically, the story "Takyr", set in the early 1930s and about a
Persian woman kidnapped by Kirghiz in Russian Turkestan at the turn of the century.
Her life as a quasi-slave among the tribal Kirghiz and of the Soviet revolution
which arrives in her late middle age, too late for her but which liberates her
daughter who goes away to school but later is drawn back to the region by some
undefinable loss (in part, the past injustices which can never be made good even
for the survivors). Revolves around the personal and tragic vein which runs
through even liberating social transformations.

POGODIN, Nikolai

Sonet Petrarki, 1957 (Petrarch's Sonnet, 1968)
A novela of an aging communist functionary's love for a young woman, and how they
are mauled by the prudery, gossip and maliciousness of some people and
organizations in the Soviet Union of early 1950s.

ROMANOV, Panteleimon

Rus, 1925, 1926 (Russia)
An epic two volume description of Russia at the eve of W.W.I.

Tovarisch Kislyakov, 1926 (Three Pairs of Silk Stockings, 1931)
A satirical expose of the supposed decadence, corruption and sexual excesses among
avante garde intellectuals and some of the new communist cadres during the late
N.E.P. period. A widely read work in its time. Also see Without Cherry
Blossoms, 1934, another collection of satiric stories on similar themes.

SASSYKBAJEW, Satkyn

The Factory Daughter, 1930
A semi-autobiographical novel of the first generation of Kazahk girls and women
to become industrial workers in the 1920s; the new lives they attempt to lead in
a regional society still dominated by traditional family and social restrictions
but with vistas of new opportunity and liberation (not uncontested) beginning
to open for them.

SCHECTMAN, Elya

Erev, 1962 (On the Eve, 1967)
Novel dealing with Jewish life in turn of century Ukraine, the restrictions on
personal life imposed by ghetto culture and the oppression by Tsarist
government and surrounding anti-semitism. Portrays the divisions within the
Jewish community and within families over the question of allying with broader
forces of anti-Tsarist struggle during the 1905 revolution.

SEMENOV, Sergei

Golod, 1922 (Hunger)
A documentary novel of the famine in revolutionary Petrograd during 1919, by a
Petrograd factory worker.

Typhus, 1923 (Typhus)
A documentary collage of the life histories of people in a Typhus ward in a
Ukrainian city during the civil war.

Natalya Tarpova, 1927 (Natalya Tarpova, 1933)
A psychological novel of the feelings, tensions, strengths and contradictions of
the growing number of working women in urban industries in the late 1920s, as
represented by one Natalya Tarpova. The advances being made despite the
contradictions of the N.E.P. period.

SERAFIMOVICH, Alexander (A.S. Popov)

Gorod V Stepi, 1912 (City in the Steppe)
A novel of the tinder dry social charge hidden under a patina of apparent
stability and orthodoxy in one sleepy provincial city enmeshed in structural
changes on the eve of W.W.I. Written by a colleague of Maxim Gorky's and a
Marxist author from 1890s on.

Zheleznyi Potok, 1924 (The Iron Flood, 1935)
A documentary novel using a cinematographic style to portray the Red cossack
forces under Yepifan Kortyukh during the civil war. Some scenes are said to evoke
comparisons with the Pugachev peasant revolt of two centuries earlier.

SERGE, Victor

The Birth of Our Power, 1931
The best known of Serge's works, dealing with the first chaotic and millenial
years of the Russian revolution. From an old revolutionary family, Serge went to
Soviet Union in early 1919 to work with Anarchists, then Bolsheviks and later
joined Trotsky's Left Opposition, was imprisoned in late 1920s and released to go
into exile in 1930s.

Men in Prison, 1930, Memoirs of a Revolutionary, 1951
Two reminiscence works of Serge's life and times in Soviet Union and Western
Europe from mid 1920s to end of W.W.II.

The Case of Comrade Tulayev, 1945
A novel of the character and wiles of the archetypal opportunist who rose to power
in communist party under Stalin and of the seeming powerlessness of principled
revolutionaries against them in 1930s.

SEYFULLINA, Lydia

Pravonarushiteli, 1921 (The Lawbreakers, 1933)
A novel of the orphans and bands of wandering children created by the civil war

and famines; written in 19th century populist style by a woman of Tartar peasant
extraction who was a teacher, writer and organizer of a network of school-
orphanages.

Virineya, 1923 (Virineya)
A play about a peasant woman in a steppe village of South Russia and her first
steps toward liberation from patriarchal village society at end of civil war.

Peregnoy, 1924 (Humus)
A novela set in a south Volga peasant village during the early years of the Soviet
Union; about the regeneration of some former juvenile delinquents and the
degeneration of some former "good people" into scum.

Tanya, 1934 (Tanya, 1939)
A novel of the lives of children uprooted by the civil war, and also of those
dispersed in the upheavals which accompanied the excesses of the early
collectivization drives in the 1930s. Seen through the eyes of a young girl.

SHELEST, Georgy

Notacia Pro Kolymu, 1958 (Notes of Kolyma)
A diary account of life in the most notorious Siberian region of forced labour
camps during the last days of Stalin. One of the most chilling of such accounts.

SHISHKOV, Vyacheslav

Taiga, 1916 (Taiga)
A documentary novel of the environment and history of the peasantry in the taiga
regions of pre-revolutionary Siberia; Siberia as a place of exile but also a refuge
and breeding ground of the dissidents and revolutionaries.

Vataga, 1924 (The Gang)
A novel of the varied, pre-socialist traditions of dissent among the peasants of
northern forest Russia, as they emerge in the early days of the Russian revolution.
Also Children of Darkness, 1931, a novel along the same lines as Vataga translated
into English.

Emelyan Pugachov, 1938-1945 (Emelyan Pugachov)
A trilogy novel about the life and times of Pugachov and his Ukrainian-Cossack
followers who during the late 18th century led the greatest peasant rising in
Russian history.

SHOLOKOV, Mikhail

Quiet Flows the Don, 1930, The Don Flows Home to the Sea, 1932
Two massive linked novels which follow the trajectory of a host of characters from
a Cossak peasant region on the central Don River from the eve of W.W.I, through
that conflict, the beginnings of the Russian revolution (Quiet Flows the Don) and
the long drawn-out twists of the civil war to circa 1922 (The Don Flows Home).
They portray the background and changes in the lives of Cossak peasants, their
not at all simple and not merely class-based gravitation to Red or White forces,
and the long drawn-out struggles that raged through the countryside. Told largely
from the point of view of a Cossak who becomes a leader of White partizans, by
an author raised in a Cossack peasant village of that period. More of an extended
village novel than one in the tradition of Russian proletarian writing, Sholokov's
two volumes were probably the most widely translated Soviet works of that period.

Virgin Soil Upturned, 1935 (or Seeds of Tomorrow, 1959)
A continuation of the Don saga; set in the same Cossack region during the mid to
late 1920s it details the aftermath of the civil war, the retreat of villagers
into themselves and of the initial attempts of farm collectivization and socialist
reorganization with its multiple mistakes, promise and resistance. Originally
written in 1932 during the height of Stalin's collectivization drive, it is flawed
by a strain of dogmatic rhetoric not found in Sholokov's previous two volumes.

SIMONOV, Konstantin

Dni I Nochi, 1941 (Days and Nights, 1946)
A massive collection of journalist-reportage accounts of ordinary Soviet soldiers

and daily events around the battle of Stalingrad in 1942/43. Said to be among
the more authentic of such accounts.

Zhivye I Mortvye, 1962 (The Living and the Dead, 1962), Soldatami Nye Rozhdayutsya,
1964 (We Are Not Born Soldiers)
Two wide ranging documentary accounts which attempt to set straight the history
of W.W.II in the Soviet Union and underlining the repression by Stalinist toadies
and police, the purges during and after the war, and the systematic distortion
of the events. The theme being that the Soviet Union was saved mainly by the
tenacity and heroism of the ordinary Russian soldiers and citizens.

SIVACHOV, Mikhail

Balakhany, 1926 (Balakhany)
A portrait of the mosaic of workers, from a host of peoples in the Caucauses and
from throughout Russia, working in the Baku region oil industry from the late 19th
century to the 1920s.

SLONIMSKY, Mikhail

Sredny Prospekt, 1927 (Center District)
A novel of the disintegration of the old lower middle class in a down-at-the-
mouth district of Leningrad, counterposed to the rising wealth and self-confidence
of the new speculator class during the N.E.P. period.

Lavrony, 1928 (The Lavrovs)
A semi-autobiographical novel of the decline of one middle class family during
W.W.I and after, with a long account of the hopes and misconceptions of those who
supported the February 1917 revolution against Tsarism.

STEINBERG, Isaac

Spiridonova, 1935
A biography of Maria Spiridonova, one of the heroines of the Social Revolutionary
movement. A young underground member of the Social Revolutionary party in Tambov
province during the repressions which followed the collapse of the 1905 revolution,
Spiridonova manages to assassinate General Luzhenovsky, the most notorious Tsarist
hangman. After capture, torture and a trial, her death sentence is commuted to
life imprisonment because of mass demonstrations throughout Russia and
internationally. Her prison train to Siberia is met everywhere by masses of
peasants and workers so that it becomes a nation-wide demonstration against
Tsarism. Surviving Siberian imprisonment, she is freed by the October revolution
in 1917, only to be arrested by the Cheka some years later and goes into exile
abroad.

SYOMIN, Vitali

Semero V Odnom Dome, 1965 (Seven in One House)
An unvarnished, sympathetic and detailed novel of working class life in early
1960s, of everyday events, gossips, quarrels and friendships at home and at work.
Represented by the life of a 40ish war widow from a peasant background living and
working in a decaying section of an industrial city (Rostov On The Don), her
spunky tenacity which sometimes gets her in trouble with factory managers and
government functionaries.

TOLSTOY, Alexei

Khozhdeniye Po Mukam, 1923-1934 (The Road to Calvary)
A massive tetrology of novels variously translated and issued under the titles
The Road to Calvary (1928),The Sisters, 1918, The Murky Dawn/Ordeal (1936). It is
a chronicle of the lives, maundering visions and illusions, endless political
changes among an array of upper class and minor aristocrat families in Russia
from the eve of W.W.I through the phases of the Russian revolution and civil war.
Tolstoy presents all that one might ever wish to know about the inner lives of
that class and presents a tapestry of the events and forces at work during the
decade 1913-1923.

An aristocrat emigre, Alexei Tolstoy returned to the Soviet Union in the mid 1920s and emerged as a prolific writer and later a literary doyen under Stalin. He is responsible for some of the most god-awful, sycophantic chauvinism of that period, notably his "historical" panegyrics about Peter the Great, 1929-1934 and Ivan the Terrible, 1942.

TRIFONOV, Yuri

Utolenie Zhazhdy, 1963 (The Quenching of Thirst)
A novel which deals with the construction of an irrigation project in Turkemenia in 1957-58 with reminiscences and flashbacks to comparable projects in the 1930s of which the hero's parents were part, and their ultimate persecution in the purges of the late 1930s. The thirst to be quenched requires not only water but justice, guarantees that Stalinism will not return.

VESYOLYI, Arytom (Artem Vesely)

Rossiya Krovyo Omytaya, 1924 (Rivers of Fire)
A novel of Baltic Fleet sailors who had been central in the October revolution, back in the Red Navy in 1922 and angry at the course of the revolution; alludes to the backgrounds and attitudes of similar sailors who were involved in the Kronstad revolt of 1921. Told with sympathy by a one-time anarchist.

Strana Rodnaya, 1926 (Native Land)
A panoramic account of the desperation and ambiguity of peasants of the Saratov and Simbirsk regions who first ally with the Bolsheviks and later revolt against them near the end of the civil war. A Russian peasant version of Sholokov's Don Cossack novels.

Gulyay-Volga, 1930 (Volga Rampage, 1934)
A historical novel of a Siberian bandit-peasant leader of the 17th century who was ultimately inveigled into fighting for the Tsar against the Mongols. Vesely attempts to convey the similarities in isolation, distant repression, independence of the Siberian peasantry both in Yermak's time and in the Russian revolution some 300 years later.

Also Gorkaya Krov (Bitter Blood) and Divkoye Serdtse (The Wild Heart), two story collections from the mid 1920s.

VLADIMOV, Georgi

Bol'shaya Ruda, 1961 (The Ore)
A novela of an abrasive individual who cannot find his footing anywhere, whose wanderings and series of jobs are revealed in flashbacks as he drives a truck in an open pit iron ore mine. His rootlessness is mistaken for alienation or apathy and his striving for participation is only partly recognized after his death in an industrial accident.

Tri Minuty Molchaniya, 1969 (Three Minutes of Silence)
Novel of a seaman on a Soviet trawler operating from a Baltic port; again dealing with a character riven by aggressive surliness but with an underlying desire to be part of something more meaningful.

YAKOVLEV, Aleksandr

Oktyabr, 1923 (October)
A "novel" without plot which presents a collage of events, characters and emotions of an array of Russian citizens in the various districts of Petrograd on the eve of the October revolution.

YAROV, Nicolai

Devyatnadtsatyi God, 1926 (The Year 1919)
A panoramic collage novel of the millenial and also the darkest year of the Russian revolution pictured through the frenzy of activities, plans and the fragmentary reports of successes and defeats throughout the Soviet Union and among the left forces in world as filtering into the Moscow Soviet during 1919.

YEVDOKIMOV, Ivan (Ivan Evdokimov)

Kolokola, 1926 (The Bells)
A panorama of Russian life during 1904-1905; in villages, on great estates, in city slums, in middle class drawing rooms, in factories, underground cells, at mass meetings and finally in the wave of strikes and mass demonstrations which usher in the 1905 revolution. Held to be one of the finest and truest accounts of that period, by a veteran Narodnick writer.

Christiye Prudy, 1927 (Christiye Prudy)
A collective novel of the Moscow Christiye Prudy district during the N.E.P. period.

Poslednyaya Babushka Sz Semigor'ya, 1934 (The Last Old Woman of Semigor'ya)
A courageous and warmly human play about an old peasant woman determined to preserve the way she has lived all of her life and resist entry into a collective farm during the height of the collectivization drives.

ZALYGIN, Sergei

Na Irtyshe, 1964 (On the Irtysh)
A novel which re-examines the methods and costs of collectivization in the 1930s, by an agricultural engineer who witnessed it and who later became a leading writer. Set in a small Siberian village in 1931 it deals with the responses of a peasant farmer and partizan veteran who supports the Soviet regime whole heartedly, who sees the advantages in collectivization but who cannot bring himself to place his family and livelihood in the hands of unreliable and uncontrollable farm administrators who rise and fall through political maneuvers. Nor can he give up his meagre possessions to some collective pool. He is made a scapegoat by those who see him as an obstacle to their own careers, and partly because of his honesty, is gradually ostracised and has to leave the village.

Solyonnaya Pad, 1968 (Salt Valley)
A novel comparable to Irtysh, it re-examines the costs and means used in the Russian civil war. While affirming the absolute necessity of winning that struggle despite all suffering, it rejects some of the trajectories which developed. Specifically, it treats with the leader of a Red partizan detachment who becomes progressively more callous and paranoic toward all those who differ with his deepening dogmaticism. Set during the civil war and in its immediate aftermath.

ZOSHCHENKO, Mikhail

Rasskazy Nazara Ilyicha Gospodina Sinebryukhova, 1922 (The Tales of Nazar Ilich Sinebryukhov)
A wildly satiric account of the experiences and responses of a callow and thoroughly opportunist climber, a corporal of the former Tzarist army who worms his way into the lower echelons of the new Soviet bureaucracy, exchanging one set of cliches and self-righteous rhetoric for another. Written in "Skaz" style (a Runyonesque melange of purple phrases, vulgarities, ad-man grammar) which made Zoshchenko the best read satirist of the 1920s.

Vozvrashchonnaya Molodost, 1933 (Restored Youth, 1934)
A series of short stories strung together as a novel about the doings and inner world of an aging astronomer who mourns a past world (mainly non-existent and of which he was never a part) until he leaps into the clutches of a deliberating young woman. A sort of Russian Blue Angel satire; a series of the most grotesque fantasies and pathetic adventures, culminating in his return home to wife and job no wiser than when we first met him.

The Woman Who Could Not Read and Other Tales, 1940
Another collection of witty, marvellously ironic tales of characters and events in the Soviet Union of mid to late 1920s.

POLAND

ANDRZEJEWSKI, Jerzy

Popiol i Diament, 1948 (Ashes and Diamonds, 1962)
A novel set in the city of Cracow shortly after liberation in 1945, it deals with
the culmination of internal Polish conflicts of the previous generation. Focuses
on a young soldier of the right wing Home Army, his growing awareness of how he
and his dead comrades have been used by a stupid and corrupt Polish ruling class
(those at home and those abroad). A critique of the Polish martyr complex, in
that the "hero" carries out his final orders to assassinate a Polish communist
leader who has just emerged from a concentration camp, although he knows that this
is the final bankruptcy of the Polish right.

BERENT, Waclaw

Ozimina, 1911 (Winter Wheat)
A novel set during one night in Warsaw on the eve of the Russo-Japanese war (1904)
which would end in revolution throughout the Russian empire. It portrays the
social isolation and intellectual deadend of the Polish middle class as seen
through characters at an all night party, who are totally unaware and unconcerned
about the lives and struggles of working people in the streets not far from where
their party is going on.

BOGUSZEWSKA, Helena and KORNACKI, Jerzy

Wisla, 1935 (The Vistula)
A collage novel of the lives of workers who live along or earn their living from
the Vistula river--barge men, fishermen, longshoremen, sand diggers, etc. A
remarkable social document produced by the two leading writers of the "City
Outskirts" (Przedmiescie) group, which tried to capture the collective feelings
of particular districts, streets and groups of working people in Poland.

Jada Wozy Z Cegta, 1936 (The Brick Carts Are Rolling)
A collective novel of small town artizans and semi-industrial workers in
depression Poland; reportage, oral history, novelized sociology.

Polonez, 1936-1939 (Polonaise)
A trilogy documentary novel of the everyday lives of a cross section of working
class, peasantry and impoverished middle class people throughout Poland in the
last three years of the Polish colonels' regime on the eve of W.W.II.

BOROWSKI, Tadeusz

Pozegnanie Marig, 1948 (Farewell to Mary), Kamienny Swiat, 1948 (World of Stone)
Two collections of stories which deal with experiences in Nazi concentration camps
in Poland in which the original personality of even the survivors perish.
Borowski grew up as the son of a Polish worker in the Soviet Union, emigrated to
Polish occupied Galicia and was an underground resistance writer during W.W.II.
Arrested and sent to concentration camps, he survived and again emigrated to
Germany in the late 1940s where he became a supporter of the then illegal German
Communist Party until his suicide in 1951.

Aushwitz Tales, 1961, or This Way For the Gas, Ladies and Gentlemen, 1976
Twelve short stories about Dachau and Aushwitz concentration camps where Borowski
was held during 1943 and 1944. Told in a simple and seemingly naive style about
the people and conditions, the unpredictability and horror so far outstrips moral
standards and political explanations that life verges on the absurd.

BRANDYS, Kazimierz

Drewniany Kon, 1946 (Hobby Horse)
A novel; a sardonic portrait of a sentimental young man of "Polish National Ideals"

confronted by Nazi occupation and responding with endless temporizing. The Polish London government and the nationalist Home Army emerge as a continuation of the Polish home grown reactionaries of the interwar years.

Citizens, 1948
A novel of the first years of socialist reorganization in post war Poland; of the continuing dissention, changes, slowly growing support but also of the entrenched resistance by remnants of the old order. Marred by Stalinist cliches.

Miedzy Wojnami, 1948-1951 (Between the Wars)
A four volume novel of the Greater Poland resurrected by Polish expansionists after W.W.I; of the deepening exploitation and oppression by Polish Pans (landlords) and capitalists, of the radicalization of some Polish workers and intellectuals, of the occupation and repression of Ukrainian Galicia. In short, an overview of Restoration Poland, 1918-1939.

Matka Krolow, 1957 (Sons and Comrades, 1964)
Brandys' best known novel, dealing with the tragedy of a family of Polish working class communists from the 1930s, their struggles against Polish and German fascism to liberation, only to become enmeshed in the Zdanov-Stalin purges of the late 1940s.

BRAUN, Andrzej

Lewanty, 1952 (Lewanty)
One of the better novels about socialist construction and industrial development in post W.W.II Poland. In particular, about the complex problems, shortages, tactics encountered in rebuilding coal production, one of the major bases of Polish industry in a still war shattered country during the late 1940s.

BREZA, Tadeusz

Spizowa Brama, 1960 (The Bronze Gate, 1966)
A historical novel cum reportage piece on the Vatican Curia and its recurrent policy of supporting the regime ancien and status ante quo wherever and whenever it has influence. Focuses on the Vatican during the last ten years of Pope Pius the Twelfth and the tensions between the progressive and reactionary forces within Catholic polity. Alludes to the Polish church's conservative role in all of this.

Urzad, 1961 (The Office)
An expansion of the above theme, focusing on the Holy Office of the Vatican.

BRONIEWSKI, Wladyslaw

Robotnicy, 1923 (Workers), Wiatracki, 1925 (Windmills), Dymy N Ad Miastem, 1927 (Smoke Over the City), Troska I Piesni, 1932 (Worry and Song), Krzy K Ostateczny, 1939 (The Last City)
Five collections of poems about the Polish urban proletariat during the interwar years. By a leading left wing poet of the period.

DABROWSKA, Maria

Ludzie Stamtad: Cykl Opowiesci, 1926 (People From Over Yonder: A Cycle of Tales)
Accounts of turn of the century life in the Polish countryside with a focus on poor peasants, agricultural labourers and similar sectors as the main heroes and heroines. Dabrowska was one of the major populist writers of interwar Poland.

Noce I Dnie, 1932-1934 (Days and Nights)
A four volume novel, one of the epic accounts of rural Polish society from the late 19th century to the establishment of Restoration Poland after W.W.I. A panorama of the cultural, social and economic changes over three generations seen through the lives of a family of ex-peasant miners and another family of much declined Polish petty nobility.

Gwiazda Zaranna, 1953 (Morning Star)
A collection of stories about war devastated lives and towns in Poland at the time but also of the returning vitality emerging in the staggering task of rebuilding.

Na Wsi Wesele, 1955 (A Village Wedding, 1957)
A short novel about the everyday concerns, joys and personal hopes of younger
Poles living in the farming villages after initial collectivization period (soon
to be reversed). A warmly descriptive portrait of human resilience, of
continuities and changes among people who are no longer truly peasants.

FRANKO, Ivan

Zakhar Berkut, 1892 (Zakhar Berkut, 1944)
A historical novel of a 15th century Ukrainian peasant who rises to power and
becomes a lord in the Carpathian region under the Tartars; his struggle against
the church and Polish-Austrian feudal forces in his attempts to liberate the
peasantry under the aegis of more distant overlords but with his best intentions
leading only to greater suffering. Written by an "anarchistic" Galician-Ukrainian
writer who captured the sardonic mistrust and smouldering anger of the peasantry
and whose work was read from the Peace River homesteads of Canada to the oil fields
of Baku.

GALECKI, Stefan (Andrzej Strug)

Ludzie Podziemni, 1908 (Underground People), Dzieje Jednego Pocisku, 1910 (A Story
of One Bomb)
Two short novelas about revolutionary students and workers fighting the Czarist
regime in Poland before and after the 1905 revolution. Galecki was a Polish
Narodnick from the 1890s on, was sent to Siberia for his political activities and
became a member of the underground Polish socialist party at the time described
in the novelas.

Pokolenie Marka Swidy, 1925 (The Generation of Marek Swida)
A semi-autobiographical novel of Galecki's comrades, their struggles against
Czarism, their participation in W.W.I and their increasing horror of that war, and
of the not-so-comic-opera reaction which became established in Restoration Poland.

Mogila Nieznanego Zolnierza, 1922 (The Tomb of the Unknown Soldier), Kluez
Otchlani, 1929 (The Key to the Abyss), Zolty Kryz, 1933 (The Yellow Cross)
Two socialist pacifist novels which recount the horrors of W.W.I in central Europe
as the inherent outgrowth of capitalism in its imperialist phase. The Yellow Cross
(a trilogy itself) deals more with the "betrayal" of earlier ideals in the
expansionist, militarist and reactionary   nationalist regimes of Restoration
Poland of the 1920s.

HLASKO, Marek

Ten Stary Zlodzie, 1958 (This Old Thief), Zapis, 1965 (The Record)
Two novels of the lives of marginal, sometimes semi-lumpenized, people living on
the social fringes of post war Poland during the 1950s and 1960s.

KADEN-BADROWSKI, Julius

Luk, 1919 (Arch)
A muckraking account of the Polish petty nobility and merchant nationalists in the
hopelessly chauvinistic provincial city of Cracow before and during W.W.I.
Romantic escapism and hypocrisy raised to a life style.

General Barcz, 1928 (General Barcz)
A broadly satiric novel about a leading Polish general (Haller) who, with his
cronies, aspires to create an autocratic "New Poland" under a military junta.
Sufficiently realistic to result in charges of slander.

Czarne Skrydla, 1925, 1929 (Black Wings)
A massive two volume novel dealing with the Silesian coal mining region of Poland
suffering under French capitalists, bloodhound Polish managers, bootlicking
Polish politicians and bought-and-paid-for labour officials. Portrays the most
militant Polish miners as approximating the ideals touted by the earlier populist
nationalists. Detailed accounts of the everyday lives of miners and others in the
Silesian mine region during the 1920s.

Mateusz Brigda, 1933 (Mateusz Bridga)
A three volume sequel to Black Wings, which chronicles the corruption,
exploitation and shameless greed of the business politics in Poland by the
beginning of the 1930s. The country's descent into a morass of backwardness and
18th century autocracy.

KONWICKI, Tadeusz

Rojsty, 1956 (Marshes)
A novel of a Polish-Lithuanian youth from a violently anti-communist family who
joins the Home Army in W.W.II and continues in an anti-Soviet underground band
in the marshes of northeast Poland after liberation. A sort of confession of
errors of youth and of the leaders that misled him. Konwicki was an archetypally
"flexible" author, shifting with the dominant political tendencies, writing a
number of Stalinist novels and later re-emerging as a right wing Polish emigre
writer.

KOZIOL, Urszula

Postoje Pamieci, 1965 (Stations of Memory)
Novelized memoirs of a young girl in a peasant village from immediately before
W.W.II to late 1950s. A warm but unromantic reminiscence of hardships, love,
work, family life as well as the religious and ethnic bigotry among villagers.
Portrays the devastation of the war and ends with the migration of rural people
to cities and the transformation of village life into a variant of urban culture
in 1950s.

KRUCZKOWSKI, Leon

Kordian I Cham, 1932 (Kordian and the Plebian)
A re-analysis of Polish history in the form of a historical novel. It juxtaposes
a nobleman "hero" of the 1830 Polish rising to the account of that struggle by a
peasant participant; suggests the totally different hopes, aims and attitudes
of the bulk of the insurgents (that of a peasant revolt) from the romantic
idealism in the ruling class accounts of Polish history. The deep differences
between these two Polands.

Pawie Piora, 1935 (Peacock Feathers)
Another novel which probes the theme of class skewed Polish history.

Sidla, 1937 (Trap)
A gloomy chronicle of the lives of unemployed white collar workers and the
impoverished lower middle class in depression-ridden Poland.

KRZYWICKI, Ludwik (ed.)

Memoirs of Peasants, 1929
A collection of oral history, diaries, personal accounts and social documents
about Polish peasantry from the late 19th century to the late 1920s. Edited from
a left populist point of view, it was a very influential source of reference and
reportorial protest.

Memoirs of the Unemployed, 1934
A companion piece to Peasants, it is a similar collection of oral history,
personal accounts, social documents about the lives of migratory workers and
unemployed, both in rural and in industrial regions during the depression era.
Contains extensive accounts of Polish workers/peasants who had emigrated over the
previous fifteen years in search of work.

KUREK, Jalu

Woda Wyzej, 1935 (Rising Waters), Komornicy, 1939 (Tenant Farmers)
Two documentary novels dealing with the economic and social bankruptcy of a tenant
peasantry (Komornicy) and the dissolution of a broad range of self-employed
artizans and cottage industries in small town Poland through the depression and
the ultimately self-destructive rapacity of Polish rulers.

MENDELSOHN, Ezra

Class Struggle in the Pale, 1969
A brief social history of the background and nature of class differences within
the Jewish villages and urban ghettos of Western Russia, Lithuania, Russian
Poland and Galicia during the last third of the 19th century and to the beginning
of W.W.I. Accounts of how the "traditional" religious and business class was
intertwined and often acted together to check the demands of Jewish workers.
Contains a provocative outline of the upsurge of socialist, anarchist, and
millenial secular culture which emerged among shtetl workers. Of the organizations
within Jewish communities and of those reaching out to broader alliances. Written
from a social democratic viewpoint and quite fascinating.

MORCINEK, Gustaw

Wyrabany Chodnik, 1932 (Account of a Mine Gallery)
A novel of the evolution of labour unions and working class organization among the
Polish coal miners of Silesia between the 1890s and 1920. Deals with the annexed
Silesian region and skewed by a Polish ethnic nationalist outlook.

NALKOWSKA, Zofia

Granica, 1935 (Boundary Line)
A bitter novel about the former "left wing" Polish intellectuals who, after 1918,
rushed to sup at the table set by General Pilsudski. Nalkowska was and remained
an important left populist woman writer from before W.W.I to the late 1940s.

Wezly Zycia, 1948 (Knots of Life)
A major novel about the decaying and increasingly fantasy-prone Polish ruling class,
their assorted toadies and the string of Polish generals presenting themselves
as "saviours of the nation" during the late 1930s. As seen through the eyes of
a family of impoverished middle class Poles who have retained an earlier
progressive outlook and who at the end of W.W.II conclude that "better the devil
than to go with the previous rulers".

NUROWSKA, Maria

Nie Strzelac Do Organisty, 1976 (Don't Shoot the Organ Player)
A collection of short stories about village life in contemporary Poland with the
theme that very little that could be called traditionally "peasant" remains (which
is not for the worst). The language, tastes, activities, sexuality and tensions
are much like those of working people and lower middle class in medium sized
towns. The soil and nature are increasingly a mere backdrop to village life.

RUSINEK, Michael

From the Barricades into the Valley of Starvation, 1956
An autobiographical account of a middle class poet in Polish occupied Slovakia,
opposed to Polish reaction and caught up in the struggle against the Nazi
occupation. But mainly a diary-like account of two years in a series of
concentration camps in central Europe, and the contending elements among the
prisoners.

SCHULZ, Bruno

Sklepy Cynamonowe, 1934 (Cinnamon Stores)
An evocative reminiscence of childhood visions of the world as seen around his
father's store in the Jewish quarter of Drohobycz, an oil field town in Galicia,
during the early years of this century. By a member of the "City Outskirts"
group of writers.

Sanatorium Pod Klepsydra, 1937 (The Sanitorium Under the Sign of the Hourglass)
A Kafkaesque account of absurdities and adventures in a small Polish town in the
late 1930s; the deepening anti-semitism during the final inglorious years of
Restoration Poland.

SCIBOR-RYLSKI, Stefan

Wiengel, 1951 (Coal)
A socialist construction novel dealing with the reopening and expansion of the
Silesian coal mines under the Polish first five year plan.

SIEROSZEWSKI, Waclaw

Yakuty, 1896 (The Yakuts), Ucieczka, 1904 (The Flight), Za Kolem Polarmym, 1926
(Beyond the Polar Circle)
Accounts by a Polish Narodnik sent to Siberian exile for revolutionary activities
in early 1890s; they deal with the lives of Siberian native people (Yakuty), of
the lives, backgrounds, adventures and continuing political activity of political
prisoners there. Sieroszewski was also the author of what became the international
revolutionary anthem Warshavianka.

UNILOWSKI, Zbigniew

Dwadziecia Lat Zycia, 1937 (Twenty Years of Life)
A documentary written in slangy, colloquial Polish; of childhood and youth in a
Warsaw working class district during W.W.I and the 1920s.

WAT, Aleksander

Bezrobotny Lucyfer, 1927 (Lucifer Unemployed)
A collection of satirical short stories about the headlong rush of Polish middle
classes and intelligensia to the most incredible fantasy and faddish degeneracy
in the 1920s.

WITTLIN, Jozef

Sol Ziemi, 1936 (Salt of the Earth, 1939)
An impassioned pacifist and anti-militarist novel in the vein of All Quiet on the
Western Front; set among Polish soldiers and civilians under contending regimes
during W.W.I.

ZALEWSKI, Witold

Tractory Zwiciezom Wiosne, 1949 (Tractors Will Capture the Spring)
A reportage novel of the first attempts of socialist reconstruction and
collectivization of Polish agriculture in the late 1940s (a process partly
reversed a half dozen years later).

ZEROMSKI, Stefan

Forest Echoes, 1913
A historical novel of the 1863 Polish uprising in which an aristocratic Polish
leader is juxtaposed to the peasant forces in the revolt; he comes to recognize
that the reasons why the peasantry joins the rising are totally different than
the self-deluding "ideals" of the landlord nationalists. One volume of the
trilogy Popiely (Ashes, 1928).

Roza, 1909 (The Rose)
A novel of the Polish socialist and middle class insurrectionists during the 1905
revolution which shook Tsarist Russia. Touches on the apathy of the Polish
peasantry who have little preference to the urban "socialists" over the Russian
overlords.

Przedwiosnie, 1925 (Before the Spring)
Novel of a middle class Pole working in Russia during the 1917 revolution, his
mixed fear of and appreciation for the promise of that revolution. Back in
Poland he enlists during the Polish-Soviet war, only to realize that the
preservation of a Poland of stupid Pans, rapacious money lender capitalists and
a beaten down peasantry has been no victory. Novel ends ambiguously with the
hero joining a demonstration of workers in Warsaw but still frightened of
fundamental changes.

CZECHOSLOVAKIA

CZECH

CAPEK, Karel

Obycejny Zivot, 1934 (An Ordinary Life, 1948)
A novel about a quiescent railway clerk in small town Czechoslovakia of 1920s who at middle age discovers previously submerged selves and worlds within himself. An influential and somewhat Kafkaesque investigation of the multifaceted complexity of even seemingly trivial individuals and lives. Also Prvni Parta, 1937 (The First Rescue Party), a somewhat more realistic novel about the lives of Czech miners during the 1930s, emphasizing their complex individuality despite being members of a self conscious class.

CAPEK-CHOD, Karel

Kaspar Len, Mstitel, 1908 (Kaspar Len, Avenger, 1957)
A novel about the gentry rule and anachronistic injustices in rural Moravia during the late Hapsburg period by a Czech populist writer. Also Turbina, 1916 (The Turbine), a naturalistic novel set in W.W.I Moravia.

HASEK, Jaroslav

The Good Soldier Svejk, 1926
A satiric anti-militarist novel dealing with the doings of one Private Svejk, a petty Czech thief who is conscripted into the Austro-Hungarian army in W.W.I but who systematically makes himself so ignorant and obeys orders so literally that he manages to get himself shunted into mindless but safe duties. An exemplification of the theme "to obey but not to comply", a broad farce aimed at the cliches of patriotic duty and honour. Marred by a recurrent Czech ethnic chauvinism, it was the most widely translated Czech novel of the interwar years.

HEYM, Stefan

The Eyes of Reason, 1951
A novel about the communist ascension to power in Czechoslovakia between 1944 and 1948 as the culmination of a generation of struggle. A somewhat stereotyped account by a once well known refugee author who wrote in Germany, America and Czechoslovakia.

HORA, Josef

Hladovy Rok, 1926 (Hungry Year)
A novel about the bedrock misery, the chaos and the emergence of medieval millenialism among the villagers in the backlands of Czechoslovakia during the final years of W.W.I.

HRABAL, Bohumil

Closely Watched Trains, 1962
A bitter-sweet novela about an adolescent boy in a small Czech town during W.W.II, his general naivety and first gropings with sexuality and his almost accidental involvement with the margins of the underground. Touches subtlety on those Czech elements quite prepared to live with fascism if it doesn't disturb their own lives. The novela manages to escape the endemic ethnic chauvinism which infects so many accounts of W.W.II resistance activities.

KARASLAVOV, Georgi

Sporzilov, 1931 (Sporzilov)
A collective proletarian novel of the Sporzilov working class district in Prague during the late 1920s and 1930, where Karaslavov and other left Bulgarian refugees lived as construction workers. Also see Bulgarian section.

KISCH, Egon

Die Drei Kühe, 1938 (The Three Cows)
An account of the Spanish Civil War as experienced by Czech members of the
International Brigades who, with many others, had to flee Czechoslovak democracy
in the 1920s during the repression of left wing militants and ethnic minorities
under the Masaryk regime.

KONRAD, Karel

Rozchod, 1934 (Retribution)
A bitter, sometimes surrealist anti-war novel which reviles past
imperial regimes and their willing subjects for the slaughter of
W.W.I but also reviles the then current military posturings of Czech and other
Central European restoration states.

KRATOCHVIL, Jaroslav

Vesnice, 1924 (Spring Songs)
A collection of sketches and stories about life in Czech villages at about the .
turn of the century, done in a 19th century naturalist style but alluding to the
external and class forces at work underneath the "local colour".

Prameny, 1934 (Sun Ray)
A chronicle of the Czech Legionnaires who served as a counter-revolutionary army
in the Soviet Union during the Russian Civil War and who became the conservative
nationalist force behind the Masaryk Czech Republic during the 1920s.

MAJEROVA, Marie

Nejkrasnejsi Svet, 1923 (The Most Beautiful of the World, 1929)
A documentary novel set in the Czech industrial region and dealing with the lives
of workers in heavy industry during the period of massive capitalist expansion;
about the nature of recently liberated Czech nationalism and its repression of
ethnic minorities within the newly established Czechoslovakia, the rapacity of
the rising Czech bourgeoise and the struggles of a militant working class during
1920-1922.

Sirena, 1935 (The Siren, 1954)
A massive chronicle of three generations of a proletarian family in the Kladno
region and also a social history of the transformation of that region from
agriculture to coal mining and heavy industry. Focuses on the developments
from the final decade of Austro-Hungarian rule, through W.W.I, the industrial
expansion and class struggles during the early Czech Republic and into the
depression era. With a changing cast of foreign and Czech exploiters and the tides
of working class resistance. Possibly the best known work of one of the finest
Czech novelists of the interwar years.

Havirska Balada, 1938 (Ballad of a Miner, 1960)
A sequel to Sirena, dealing with the lives of Czech miners during the depression
era; the rising tide of European fascism but also their rejection of enlisting
in a united front under the Czech bourgeoisie.

Also Panenstvi, 1907 (Virginity), an early feminist novel of a young woman from
a provincial Czech town who refuses to accept the passivity expected of women and
who strikes out to create her own life and loyalties; Namesti Republiky, 1914
(Square of the Republic, 1947), a remarkable novel of the struggles of the
Anarchist-led working class movement in Paris during the decade before W.W.I and
its defeat (see the France section); and Bruno, 1930 (Bruno) and Ma Vlast, 1933
(My Country), two additional novels about the Czech working class and the
trajectory of Czechoslovakia in the years after independence.

MARTINEK, Vojtech

Cerna Zeme, 1954 (original 1926-1932) (Black Soil)
A trilogy novel of the lives of three generations of working class families in
the Ostrava mine region of Silesia; from the late 1880s to 1930s.

Kemenny Rad, 1956 (original 1942-1951) (Rocky Road)
Another trilogy novel of the Ostrava region, following the transformation of
peasantry to proletariat, through W.W.II and to the beginnings of socialist
Czechoslovakia in late 1940s.

NOVY, Karel

Za Hiasem Domova, 1939 (Voice of Home)
A village novel focused on the life of one landless rural worker and his family
in the Czechoslovakia of the 1930s.

OLBRACHT, Ivan (Kamil Zeman)

Anna Proletarka, 1928 (Anna the Proletarian)
A novel about a young woman who migrates from a peasant village to find work in
the city during W.W.I, her experiences in a variety of jobs under the new Czech
bourgeoisie masters of recently independent Czechoslovakia and her gradual
involvement in the working class struggles of the mid 1920s. Told not in the
deceptively simply style of a modern folk tale.

Nikola Suhaj, Loupeznik, 1933 (Nikola Suhaj, Robber, 1954)
One of the classic novels about "social bandits" set in the backward mountain
region of sub-Carpathia during the final years of the Austro-Hungarian empire and
the chaos of W.W.I. An extraordinary document of the mosaic of peoples and
cultures in a traditional refugee area, the historical layers of domination,
replacement and conflict and the intricate loyalties entailed. Focuses on the
tradition and nature of social banditry as personified in the person of Nikola
Suhaj, of what drove some to this kind of rebellion in the past, what sustained
them and of the changing historical forces which then made social banditry
untenable. A masterpiece.

Golet V Udoli, 1937 (The Bitter and the Sweet, 1967)
A collection of stories woven together as a novel; about the mosaic of peoples in
the Carpathian mountain region of eastern Czechoslovakia from the end of the
Austro-Hungarian empire and into the 1930s. Written in a brilliant folk like style
which makes Olbracht read like a progressive Isaac B. Singer.

Selected Works of Ivan Olbracht, 1956
A collection of translated extracts.

PUJMANOVA, Marie

Lide Na Krizovatce, 1937 (People at the Crossroads)
An epic novel which deals with the trajectories and lives of the opposed classes
in Czech society from the end of W.W.I to the beginning of the depression. A
roman de clef set around the factories and people in the domain of the industrialist
"Kazmar" family (a pseudonym for the Bata family). The gran bourgeoisie, state
bureaucrats, lower middle classes and factory workers during the first dozen years
of restoration Czechoslovakia.

Hra S Ohnem, 1948 (Playing With Fire)
A novel, loosely a sequel to People at the Crossroads, which deals with the
developments in central Europe, Czechoslovakia and Germany from the Reichstag Fire
of 1933 to the beginning of W.W.II. Being an account of the responses of various
individuals and classes in Czechoslovakia to the rise and consolidation of fascism
through central Europe. By one of the leading Czech socialist writers.

REZAC, Vaclav

Vetrna Setba, 1935 (Windy Place)
A novel which chronicles the lives of a Czech peasant family from before W.W.I to
the early depression years.

Nastup, 1951 (First Steps), Bitva, 1954 (Battle)
Two volumes of an uncompleted trilogy dealing with Czech village life immediately
before and during the first years of collectivization.

TILSCHOVA, Anna Marie

Haldy, 1927 (The Slag Heaps)
A populist "slice of life" novel about Czech miners during the massive industrial
expansion and union struggles of the 1920s. Detailed accounts of physical
environment, domestic lives and work, of the widely varying outlooks (progressive
and not), of the class and intra class conflicts in play.

Alma Mater, 1934 (Alma Mater)
A novel set in the medical faculty of Prague University in the 1920s and 1930s,
depicting the philistinism and class arrogance of the Czech middle class.

VANCURA, Vladislav

Pekar Jan Marhoul, 1924 (The Baker Jan Marhoul, 1960)
A novel about a much set upon small town baker, exploited and disdained by all he
deals with, who continues to honour his "obligations" despite all. A rather
bitter reversal of a Christian morality play, in which "honesty" is its own
punishment.

Pole Orne A Valecna, 1925 (Fields of Work and War)
A bitterly anti-war novel set in the Ouhrov region of manorial estates during
W.W.I, in which the martial poses of the small town and landlord ruling class is
the expectable response of congenital idiots. Vancura's sardonic talent is given
full reign in a curse on the stupidity of all military heroics.

Luk Kralovny Dorotky, 1932 (Flight to Budapest)
A novel written in local dialect about a Slovak peasant (then a discriminated
ethnic minority in Czechoslovakia) who comes to Prague and becomes an industrial
worker; and of his left wing Czech girlfriend who draws him into the political
struggles of Prague working class so that they ultimately have to flee the country.

ZAPOTOCKY, Antonin

Vstanou Novi Bojovnici, 1948 (New Fighters Will Arise), Ruda Zare Nad Kladnem,
1951 (Red Glow Over Kladno, 1954)
Two collections of revolutionary proletarian poetry memorializing the struggles of
Czechoslovak workers during the interwar years, the fascist night and the seeming
emergence of a new socialist world after 1945. A promise of the living to fallen
comrades.

SLOVAK

JILEMNICKY, Peter

Vitazny Pad, 1929 (Victorious Fall)
A lyrical novel of the beauty, yet desperate poverty and ignorance, of mountain
villages of northeastern Slovakia where the author grew up; the continuation of
mid 19th century landlord rule and backwardness quite unaffected by the liberal
rhetoric and constitution of the newly independent Czech state (whose administrators
rapidly take on the role of the previous Austro-Hungarian overlords). Also his
Pole Neorane, 1932 (Untilled Field), a novel of the stagnation
of Slovak peasant villages at the time.

Kus Cukru, 1934 (A Piece of Sugar)
Novel of Slovak mountain villages drawn into cash crop agriculture through the
spread of sugar beet crops sold to newly established sugar factory in the lowlands;
the intensification of class division among peasantry and deepening depopulation
as poorer peasants are bought out or bankrupted.

Kompaz V Nas, 1937 (The Compass Within Us, 1966)
An epic novel of Slovakian rural society; the peasantry in its various forms,

landless migrant workers, merchant money lenders, landlords and external capitalists and the changes within a single lifetime (circa 1900-1939). Historic and class forces embodied in complex individual experiences. Jilemnicky's masterpiece.

Chronicle, 1947 (Chronicle)
A novel of the 1944 uprising against the Slovakian fascist government, as experienced by an ordinary, not highly politicized peasant partizan.

KARVAS, Peter

Toto Pokolenie, 1949 (This Generation), Pokolenje V Utoku, 1959 (Generation on Attack)
Two linked novels which attempt an overview of Czechoslovakia from the early 1930s to the mid 1950s; deals with the changing nature of the component regions and classes, the trajectory of pre war Czech Republic, the fascist Hlinka regime in Slovakia, liberation and the various phases and maneuvers in socialist construction in the decade after W.W.II.

Certovao Kopytko, 1957 (The Devil's Hoof)
A collection of stories done in pseudo-folk tale style, being satiric social criticism of the assorted failings in Czechoslovakian society under socialism.

KRAL, Franco

Cesta Zarubana, 1934 (Path Blocked by Felled Trees)
A novel about the national as well as class oppression of Slovak workers in the Czech Republic during the interwar years. A widely translated work by a left Slovak worker-poet.

Stretnutie, 1945 (Encounter)
A semi-autobiographical novel of Czechoslovakia from the end of W.W.I to the end of W.W.II, including the establishment of a separate fascist state in Slovakia in 1939. A journal of struggle and exile.

LAZAROVA, Katarina

Osie Hniezdo, 1953 (Wasps Nest)
A novel which details the strength and resistance of peasant traditions to the first attempts to collectivize Slovak peasant farming; of the still prevailing social and economic backwardness and need for change, despite the errors made in collectivization.

Omyly, 1957 (Errors)
A reportage work about the excesses and errors made through both good and bad intentions during the Stalin era in Slovakia. It contrasts those injustices to the much more serious consequences seen in the nationalist uprising in Hungary of 1956, which she vehemently opposed.

MINAC, Vladimir

Smrt Chodi Po Horach, 1948 (Death Walks the Mountains)
A semi-autobiographical novel of Slovak partizans during the 1944 National Uprising. Also see his Dlhy Cas Cakania, 1959 (A Long Time to Wait), a reminiscence of Slovakia under the Hlinka regime in W.W.II.

Vcera A Zajtra, 1949 (Yesterday and Tomorrow)
A sequel to Smrt Chodi which sympathetically follows the changing and inconsistent views and actions of a Slovak partizan in the confused years immediately after liberation; the struggle with Slovak nationalism and the conflicts between socialism and more traditional peasant aims.

Modre Vlny, 1951 (Blue Waves)
A novel about the construction of a hydro electric project in a backward Slovakian mountain region in 1950.

NOVOMESKY, Laco

Svaty Za Dedinov, 1939 (The Saint Behind the Village)
A widely translated collection of near surrealistic stories about the spread of
fascism throughout Europe and the
inept but bloody-minded antics of proto-
fascist forces in Central Europe (especially in Slovakia) by the end of the
1930s. But also of those individuals who break free from the traditions of their own
backward societies to ally themselves with the international struggles for
human progress. Novemsky was considered one of the leading European poets of the
left, frequently compared with Mayakofsky, during the interwar period.

Nedel'a, 1927 (Sunday), Otvorene Okna, 1935 (Open the Window)
Two collections of poetry touching on the lives of the Slovak poor during the
interwar years, linking them with more universal forces in contention and
combining a ballad-like style with avante guarde symbolism.

Pasovanou Ceruzkou, 1948 (With a Smuggled Pencil)
A collection of anti-fascist poems written while in a Slovakian concentration camp
during W.W.II.

Stamodtial, 1964 (From Over There)
A collection of poems written while imprisoned in a forced labour camp by Stalinists
during the early 1950s; his own incredulous attempts to make sense of the absurdity
of developments, as well as later reflections and appeals that such arbitrary
power must never be allowed to re-emerge.

TARTARKA, Dominik

Farska Republika, 1948 (The Parish Republic, 1954)
A novel about life in the separate clerico-fascist Slovakian state between 1939
and the National Uprising of 1944. Revolves around the experiences and thoughts
of a Slovakian veteran of the invasion of Poland and chronicles the everyday life
among the provincial lower middle class as seen through the eyes of a school
teacher protagonist; the pomposity, stupidity, petty patriotism and deepening
brutality of the local "moral majority" and the loathing they inspire.

TAZKY, Ladislav

Amenmaria, 1963 (Amenmaria)
A massive, wide ranging novel dealing with the question of passive conformity of
many Slovaks to the Hlinka regime during W.W.II.

WEISKOPF, Franz Carl

Vor Einem Neuen Tag, 1946 (Before a New Day)
A chronicle of the class oppression and ethnic chauvinism which the Czech and
Slovak ruling classes utilized during the interwar years. Written during the
post W.W.II interregnum, it is an appeal by a veteran left exile not to allow the
forces of pre-war Czechoslovakia to re-establish themselves. It envisions a
transformation which can finally put an end to the anachronistic ethnic loyalties
which had plagued the region from time immemorial.

HUNGARY

BENJAMIN, Laszlo

Egyetlen Elet, 1956 (A Single Life)
A bitterly ironic attack on the Stalinist regime of Matyas Rakosi, which distorted and defamed the protagonists in the previous generation-long struggle for socialism in Hungary. A poetry collection by one of the leading left poets of the post war period.

CSERES, Tibor

Hideg Napok, 1964 (Cold Days)
A novel which investigates one war crime perpetrated by the Hungarian fascist regime in W.W.II; pursues the questions of guilt and innocence in universal terms.

DARVAS, Jozsef

Vizkerezttől Szilveszterig, 1935 (From Twelfth Night to New Year's Eve)
A semi-autobiographical novel of one year in the lives of poor peasants and landless workers in a depressed farm village of Hungary during the early 1930s. The mixed desperation and hopelessness in one of the most autocratically oppressive states of central Europe and a call to prepare for revolutionary struggle. In a similar vein see (Black Bread), 1934.

A Legnagyobb Magyar Falu, 1936 (Hungary's Biggest Village)
A highly regarded overview of social, economic and political conditions in Hungarian peasant villages during the 1930s. Also (The Station), 1936 and Elindult Szeptemberben, 1940 (He Started Out in September), two additional titles of a host of Darvas' reportage novels about the lives of peasants, workers, village intellectuals in rural Hungary.

Egy Parasztcsalad Törtente, 1940 (History of a Peasant Family)
A family chronicle which traces Darvas' peasant family back to the 17th century and in the process gives a history of the Hungarian peasantry as a whole.

Varos Az Ingovangon, 1945 (City on Quagmire)
A diary novel about the final year of fascist rule in Hungary, but mainly dealing with the battle for Budapest in 1944 and its liberation by the Soviet army.

Reszeg Eső, 1963 (Intoxicated Rain)
A huge novel examination of Darvas' generation, from W.W.I and the collapse of the Austro-Hungarian empire through the Hungarian Soviet Republic and its defeat by Rumanian and White armies, the counter-revolution and attempts to reimpose an 18th century manorial aristocracy, the struggles against rising fascism in the 1930s and W.W.II, the initial phase of socialist reorganization and Stalinism in Hungary, the 1956 Revolt and the developments thereafter.

DERY, Tibor

A Befejezetlen Mondat, 1947 (The Unfinished Sentence, 1962)
A remarkable novel which mixes realism and Joycean stream of consciousness techniques to capture the feeling of the twenty years (1919-1938) of struggle, hope and defeat of Hungarian people and the left in central Europe in general.

Alvilagi Jatekok, 1946 (Underworld Games)
A cycle of stories depicting ordinary Hungarians in Budapest during late 1944, with the advance of the Soviet Army and the final wave of terror unleashed by Hungarian fascist forces.

Szerelem, 1963 (Love)
A collection of philosophic and human stories which attempt to come to terms with developments in Hungary since 1945; touches on his own departure from the Communist Party, his support for the original goals of the 1956 Imre Nagy regime;

reflections on his own mistakes and those of others as well as an appreciation of the Hungary which has emerged since.

FEJES, Endre

Rozdatemento, 1962 (Generation of Rust, 1970)
A partly surrealist portrait of bureaucracy and careerism in socialist Hungary which weaves back and forth between the final days of W.W.II and the 1956 revolt. Reproduces the cliches and pomposity, chronicles the feelings and indecisive reactions of a minor government functionary who is repeatedly on the verge of becoming an emigre but who, like his cohorts, is always stopped by his own inherent caution.

GELLERI, Andor Endre

A Nagymosada, 1936 (The Laundry Works)
A semi-autobiographical and desperately anarchic novel of live in one of the poorest districts of Budapest during the late 1920s. Little recognized in his own lifetime, Gelleri's stature as an apocalyptic proletarian writer has continued to grow since his death in the early 1940s.

Szomjas Inasok, 19336 (Thirsty Apprentices), Hold Utca, 1934 (Moon Street), Kikoto, 1935 (The Harbour)
Three collections of short stories, from realistic to surrealistic, dealing with the lives of people in the poorest districts of Budapest in 1930s--displaced artizans, dyers, transport workers. A broad spectrum of desperation, grasping at life and of individual rebellion.

Villam Es Esti Tűz, 1940 (Lightening and Evening Fire)
Collection of short stories on the themes of poverty and oppression in Hungary, but from a longer term view and underlining the steps which can eventually bring about a revolutionary change.

GERGELY, Sandor

(Peace), 1924, (On the Margins of Latifundia), 1926, (Death Watch Beetle), 1929, Ember Vasar, 1930 (The Slave Market)
Four documentary novelas about the lives of the urban working class, of landless rural workers, small peasants, artizans and semi-unemployed petty middle class sectors during the Horthy and following dictatorships in Hungary of the 1920s.

(The Drums Roll), 1934
A reportage novel of one Hungarian village stagnating under the political repression and backwardness of the Hungarian landlords' regime; the mass slide into penury during the early 1930s.

Gyorgy Dozsa, 1936-1930
A trilogy of plays including Uriszek, A Nagy Tabor, Tuzes Tronus (Manour Court, The Big Camp, A Fiery Throne) about the background to and events of the Hungarian peasant rising of 1514, as revolving around its radical leader Gyorgy Dozsa.

Rögös Ut, 1955 (The Thorny Path)
A crowded novel of Hungary in the post W.W.II period; the struggle for socialism against the still potent reactionary elements, the emergence of combined dogmaticism and opportunism among   communist careerists and the cautious cynicism of many. As seen by a veteran left populist writer.

HIDAS, Antal

Marton Es Baratai, 1959 (Martin and His Friends)
A wrathful and sometimes ironic novel which portrays the lives and worlds of the Hungarian working class and lower middle class in Budapest during the late 1930s. The second volume of a semi-autobiographical trilogy.

ILLES, Bella

Eg a Tisza, 1929 (The Tisza Ablaze)
A documentary novel of the millenial hopes and struggles of the Hungarian Soviet

Republic during 1919. Set in the Tisza region and revolving around the resistance mounted by the Hungarian Red army and the mobilization of the Budapest working class to oppose the invasion of Rumanian and Allied forces; the initial successes of Hungarian revolution ending in the triumph of ultra-reactionary forces under Admiral Horthy. Possibly the best novel account of those events. (Also see Wilhelm Boehm's 1924 Imkreuzfeur Zweier Revolutionen, an autobiographic account of the German and Hungarian revolutions by the former commander of the Hungarian Red army in 1919.)

Karpati Rapzsodia, 1939-1941 (Carpathian Rhapsody, 1964)
A novel trilogy which portrays the lives, histories and interrelationships among the mosaic of peoples--Ukrainian,Jewish, German, Hungarian, Rumanian and others --in the Carpathian mountains. Landless labourers to merchant landlords from late 19th century to pre W.W.II years; the epic account of the region.

Honfoglalas, 1952-1954 (They've Come Into Their Own)
A novel trilogy of the Carpathian region of Hungary after W.W.II. The initial stages of modernization and the continuing layers of pre-capitalist social organization intermixed with the beginnings of socialist construction in an archetypical mountain refuge.

Valaszuton, 1957 (Cross Roads)
A collection of Illes writings preceding the 1956 uprising which point to the excesses and mistakes of Stalinism in Hungary but warning of the greater danger of counter-revolution.

ILLYES, Gyulla

Pusztak Nepe, 1936 (People of the Puszta, 1967)
A documentary account of the lives, culture and history of landless agricultural workers attached to the manorial estates on the central Hungarian plain during the 1930s. An amalgam of autobiographical reminiscences, oral history, fiction, sociology, all woven into a literary tour de force. Chronicles of the most oppressed sector of Hungary. Illyes was an extremely prolific left populist poet.

Egy Mondat A Zsarnoksagrol, 1956 (One Sentence of Tyranny, 1957)
A book length prose poem reviling the autocracy and seeming betrayal of revolutionary hopes by the Stalinist regimes in Hungary.

A Kegyenc, 1963 (The Minion)
A play in the form of a parable, castigating the servile and opportunist nature of Hungarian officialdom and lower echelon apparatchiks who support whatever tendency is in power.

Ebed A Kastelyban, 1962 (Evenings in Sajkod)
A collection of poems and essays which attempt to trace the humanistic streams in Hungarian socialism.

Dolt Vitorla, 1965 (With Tilted Sails)
A collection of Illyes post 1956 poetry, in which he reconciles himself with the Hungarian socialism being built as the 1956 Hungarian uprising and its suppression fades into memory.

KARINTHY, Ferenc

Man and Wife, 1956
A novel of changing personal relationships among petty bourgeoise families in Budapest in the 1950s. Told with considerable ironic flair.

KASSAK, Lajos

Angyalfold, 1926 (Angyalfold)
A reportage account of the drab and hopeless existence of workers in small town Hungary during the 1920s.

(Men Out of Work), 1930
Documentary reportage of the scope and responses to the mass unemployment ravaging Hungarian workers at the beginning of the depression.

Egy Ember Elete, 1954 (The Life of a Human)
A semi-autobiographical novel of a generation; being an account of the lives
and fates of Hungarian working people born around the turn of this century.

KONRAD, Gyorgy

A Latogato, 1969 (The Case Worker, 1974)
A humanistic narrative of a social worker dealing with the human failures and
personal tragedies which exist in a "welfare state" such as Hungary of the late
1960s. Said to be one of the best Hungarian novels of the decade.

LENGYEL, Jozsef

Visegradi Utca, 1929 (Visgradi Street)
A collage novel of the events leading up to and during the establishment of the
Hungarian Soviet Republic in 1918. Seen through the eyes of a middle aged, lower
middle class man living on an inner city street of Budapest.

Prenn Ferenc Hanyatott Elete, 1958 (The Vicissitudes of Ferenc Prenn)
An epic novel of the lives of members of the major social classes in Budapest
during W.W.I, in the short-lived Soviet Republic and through the following counter-
revolution.

Igezo, 1961 (The Spell)
A narrative of the deepening dogmatism and paranoia of the Stalinist years in
Hungary.

Elejetöl Vegig, 1963 (From Beginning to End)
A powerful anti-Stalinist account, being the reminiscences of a Hungarian communist
writer in exile during the 1920s and 1930s and his experiences during a dozen years
imprisonment in Siberian labour camps, a victim of the Stalinist purges of 1938.
A moving aspect is Lengyel's continuing loyalty to the visions of social justice
which originally led him to communism but his demand for a greater tolerance of
internal dissent. Emphasizes the illegitimacy of making "enemies" of critics.

MORICZ, Zsigmond

A Boldog Ember, 1935 (A Happy Man)
A novel in diary form which dwells on the gratuitous humiliations as well as the
poverty that were the lot of poor peasants in Hungary under the landlords regime.
Of one peasant's strivings for dignity and the increasing problems he faces
because of his struggle.

Betyar, 1937 (The Outlaw)
A novel about a poor peasant from central Hungary who cannot or will not resign
himself to the subjegation which the local squirearchy and clerics demand and who
irretrievably moves into open (individual) rebellion against the whole social
order--including the servility of many of his peasant neighbours--until he becomes
an outlaw.

Sandor Rozsa, 1940-1942 (Sandor Rozsa)
A two volume novel of a famed Hungarian peasant bandit of the 1848 rising. It
describes that revolution (which was ultimately turned to landlord advantage)
through the eyes of an armed peasantry, giving a totally different picture of the
motives and goals of the insurgents than that presented in official Hungarian
history of the time. Entails an advocacy of peasant rebellion against a
landlord regime.

NAGY, Istvan

Nincs Megallas, 1933 (Don't Stand Still), A Szomszedsag Neveben, 1938 (In the Name
of Neighbourliness), Oltyanok Unokai, 1936-1948 (The Grandchildren of Oltyan)
Two novels and an epic trilogy which deal with the lives of Hungarian and
Rumanian peasants, rural and migrant workers in Rumanian annexed Transylvania
from the turn of the century to the late 1930s. See Rumania section for a
fuller annotation.

NAGY, Lajos

Kiskunhalom, 1934 (Kiskunhalom), Harom Magyar Varos, 1936 (Three Towns in Hungary),
A Falu Alaraca, 1937 (The Mask of the Village)
Three reportage accounts of peasant village and small town life in Hungary during
the late 1930s. Filled with populist polemics and done in a zesty expose style
which was remarkably vital in central European autocracies during the interwar
years.

A Menekulö Ember, 1954 (The Fugitive)
An autobiography of Nagy's life and times as the son of the most impoverished
sector of rural working class and as a brilliant left populist writer from late
1920s to early 1950s in Hungary. Also A Lazado Ember, 1954 (Man in Revolt), a
second volume.

ORKENY, Istavan

(The Tot Family), 1966
A sardonic play about the lingering middle class sentiments of one Hungarian
family during the mid 1960s as the country enters an uncharted course of
"liberalization". By an author of socialist realist stories about contemporary
Hungarian workers.

Eheleute, 1953 (Honorable People)
A novel of the trajectories of the major components of Hungarian society from the
1930s to the early 1950s.

RIDEG, Sandor

A Tukrosszivu Huszar, 1951 (original 1943) (The Track Watchman's House)
A partly autobiographical novel of a teenaged farm worker who joins the Soviet
Hungarian revolution and has to flee the country after the triumph of the counter-
revolution. He returns later only to go into an internal sort of exile on the
mountain border with Rumania. A fragmentary account of the deepening, seemingly
unstoppable fascism spreading everywhere around him in late 1930s.

Tuzproba, 1949 (Ordeal by Fire)
A novel of migratory Hungarian workers in Rumania during W.W.II. Told in a style
combining autobiography and folk tales.

SANDOR, Kalman

(The Pillory), 1951
A novel of the White Terror instigated throughout Hungary in early 1920s after the
defeat of the Soviet Hungarian Republic.

SANTA, Ferenc

Husz Ora, 1964 (Twenty Hours)
A semi-documentary, many-faceted account of the backgrounds and responses of the
inhabitants of a Hungarian village at the beginning of the 1956 uprising; the
complex tensions of support, misunderstandings and rejection of that struggle
and of what brought it about.

Az Arulo, 1965 (The Traitor)
A novel which investigates the moral issues of loyalty to or rejection of
arbitrary political power; allegorically set in W.W.II Hungary.

SZABO, Pal

Emberek, 1929 (People of the Plains, 1932)
A documentary novel of the Hungarian peasantry and agricultural workers during
the 1920s by a leading populist author.

Bolcso (The Wedding), Lakodalom (The Cradle), Keregzteb (The Christening), 1940-
1942
A novel trilogy which deals with the all-consuming passion of a small peasant to
acquire more land and the resistance of poor peasants against the demands of
latifundists. Drawing from his own background Szabo paints an intimate and

compelling picture of the strivings for proprietorship which, under those
conditions, sets each peasant against his neighbours. Despite success, this
ultimately saps the protagonist's life of any broader purpose or meaning.
Abridged in a single volume, An Inch of Soil, 1947.

Isten Malmai, 1949 (The Mills of God)
A novel of the first steps toward socialist reorganization in the Hungarian
countryside; set in the late 1940s. Also Uj Fold, 1953 (New Land), a novel of the
changes, mistakes and resistance to but also the promise of village life in Hungary
in the early 1950s. And Nyugtalan Elet, 1955-1958 (Restless Life), an autobiography.

URBAN, Erno

(Baptism of Fire), 1955
A collection of stories dealing with problems and interpersonal conflicts which
accompany the processes of socialist transformation in the Hungarian countryside;
both the avoidable and seemingly unavoidable costs involved in difficult if
necessary social change.

VERES, Peter

Az Alfold Parasztsaga, 1936 (The Peasantry of the Great Plain), Szamadas, 1937
(Giving Account), (Outskirts of the Village), 1940, Falusi Kronika, 1941 (Village
Chronicle)
Four documentary accounts of the poverty and oppression of workers and peasants
during the interwar years in the Great Plain region of Hungary, the zone of
manorial estates and bound labour. A tapestry detailing the lives of poor, near
poor and abysmally poor rural workers on the great estates and in the intermixed
villages. Veres was a landless peasant and participant in the 1919 revolution,
a political prisoner and refugee who returned to live a sub rosa existence in
Hungary as a rural worker and writer during the 1930s. President of the National
Peasant Party in the post W.W.II period.

(Apple Orchard), 1954
A collection of stories dealing with the new opportunities, problems and only
partial adjustments of Hungarian peasants in the emerging cooperative farms, as
well as of those who leave the land to move to the cities during the early 1950s.

ZALKA, Mate

Doberdo, 1930 (Doberdo)
A semi-autobiographic novel of how a patriotic middle class man who volunteers for
the army in W.W.I and through the brutality and senselessness of that war comes to
reject the old order and capitalism in toto. Also an account of an epoch-breaking
time, the collapse of the Austro-Hungarian empire and the release of new forces
at the end of W.W.I. Zalka himself lived a frenetic life as a member of the
Soviet Red army during the Russian civil war and in Turkey, was an exile and
organizer throughout eastern Europe in the 1920s and became the "General Lukacz"
of the International Brigades in Spain. By that time he was also considered one
of the major avante guarde writers in Hungarian language.

The Planents Turn Back On Themselves, 1962 (original 1934)
A novel which combines a stream of emotions and thoughts with the external reality
of the maelstrom of events which shattered the underpinnings of the traditional
world in Hungary, central and indeed much of Europe in the dozen years since
1918, and making that brief period appear like a millenia to those who lived
through it.

ZILAHY, Lajos

Ararat, 1947 (The Dukays, 1949)
A sardonic portrait of a Hungarian petty aristocrat family from the end of the
Austro-Hungarian empire to the end of W.W.II; the world and callously backward
outlook of one of the ten thousand odd families which called themselves "The
Hungarian Nation" and which between them owned most of Hungary, until 1945. The
first volume of the trilogy, A Dukay Csalad, 1969.

RUMANIA

BARBU, Eugen

Groapa, 1957 (The Pit)
A novel about life in Bucharest immediately after W.W.II, of an interlude in
which the ruling class of the regime ancien has been ousted but where indigenous
communist organization has not been consolidated. A mixture of reminiscences
about the brutal anachronism of the past regime and the swirling opportunism
and posturing about the as yet unresolved directions Rumania will take.

Soseaua Nordulin, 1959 (The Northern Road)
An epic novel about the first phases of industrialization in Rumania during the
late 1940s and 1950s, dealing particularly with the backgrounds and life histories
of those who stream into the new industries and of the everyday lives of factory
workers under the new regime.

BOGZA, Geo

Cartea Oltuli, 1944 (Book of the River Olt), Lands of Stone, the Land of Motzi,
1954 (original 1939)
Two volumes of novelized reportage about the people, conditions and countryside
in two Rumanian regions during the late 1930s. Lands of Stone treats with the
gold mine area of mountain Transylvania, while River Olt describes a region of
poor peasants and marginal industry in lowland Rumania. Such documentary
reportage was one of the few available vehicles of protest writing during the
period and Bogza's work is said to be among the best of that genre.

Years of Darkness, 1955
A collection of translated reportage accounts of Rumania from 1934 to 1939; the
daily struggles to survive during the depression, the changing strands of
Rumanian autocracy.

Also (Man and Coal in the Jiv Valley), 1947 and (Gates of Glory), 1951, two
further reportage accounts of social conditions in Rumania. Man and Coal combines
flashbacks about life in one of the major coal mining areas in the previous
generation and the first steps of reorganization after W.W.II. Gates of Glory
touches on the amorphous, and in past defeated, struggles of Rumanian workers
told through oral accounts.

CALINESCU, George

Bietul Ionide, 1954 (Poor Ionide)
An epic novel about Rumania during the interwar years; of the stagnantly
anachronistic landlord autocracy, the exactions extracted from Rumanian occupied
Transylvania and Bulgarian territories, of the general corruption and the economic
disintegration during the 1930s with the middle classes drifting toward fascism.
The fantasies and interests which bring the country into alliance with Nazi
Germany in the invasion of Soviet Union during W.W.II and the collapse of the
whole tottering structure with the arrival of the Red Army in 1944. Described
through the eyes of a wavering, isolated and moderately democratic intellectual.

Scrinul Negru, 1960 (The Black Chest)
A sequel to Poor Ionide, portraying developments in Rumania in the years after
1944. The replacement of and struggles with the remnant bourgeoise power but also
the incorporation of members of the old professional and administrative classes
--including the narrator of the story--into the new state apparatus.

FRAY, Stefan

La Cina Din Nova Suta Sapte, 1977 (The Supper of Nine Hundred and Seven)
A historical novel of the 1907 peasant rising in Rumania. Reconstructed from war
ministry files, it chronicles the reactionary, confused, anti-semitic aspects of
the rising yet also the anti-landlor/anti-ruling class basis of it.

NAGY, Istavan

Nincs Megallas, 1933 (There Is No Stopping)
A novel of Rumanian peasants who leave their villages in 1920s and early 1930s to become workers and unemployed in the cities and towns of stagnating Rumania. Nagy was a prolific left worker-writer from Rumanian annexed (Hungarian speaking) Transylvania. The original titles here are in Hungarian.

A Szomszedsag Neveben, 1938 (The Precincts)
A documentary novel about the lives of urban and small town working class in Rumania during the mid 1930s; an anachronistic, poverty stricken country drifting in the grip of an increasingly fantasy-prone and pro-fascist ruling class.

Oltyanok Unokai, 1936-1948 (Olteanu's Grandchildren)
A novel trilogy chronicling thelives of three generations of a Rumanian peasant family from the inception of Rumanian independence from Turkish rule in the 1870s to the eve of W.W.II. A richly detailed account of class differentiation as some of the children and grandchildren become small town bourgeoisie and others landless workers and the incipient class struggle entailed. A classic of Rumanian literature.

Also (One of Thirty Years), 1954 and (At the Highest Degree of Temperature), 1955
Two novels; Thirty Years dealing with one year of the transformations which gripped Rumania in the early 1950s as caught in the reminiscences of a middle aged left intellectual. Highest Degree is a more doctrinaire Rumanian national "socialist" construction novel.

NAGY-TALAVERA, Nicholos M.

The Green Shirts and the Others; a History of Fascism in Hungary and Rumania, 1970
A personal, rambling but fascinating account of the various streams of Central European fascism (others besides Hungary and Rumania) from 1919 to 1945. As seen and experienced by a Jewish Transylvanian regional nationalist. Not a definitive study or particularly progressive, but worth reading because of its intimation of the extraordinary complexity of the interlaced peoples and ethnic loyalties in the region and the maze of anachronistically reactionary forces competing with and merging into fascism.

PETRESCU, Cezar

(Gathering Clouds), 1925
A novel about the near medieval conditions in rural society which Rumanian land-lords had taken over, little changed, from the expelled Turkish overlords. Culminating in the 1907 Rumanian peasant rising, a largely spontaneous, widespread and bloody jacquerie. Petrescu was an extremely prolific populist writer who produced some 50 volumes of short stories and reportage between 1910 and 1950s.

POPESCU, Dumitru

(Week Days), 1959
A novel which chronicles one week in the life of a collectivized Rumanian farm village; the new ways of work, the increasing urbanity and the yet co-existing peasant traditions and social conservatism, especially in domestic relations.

PREDA, Marin

Morometii, 1955 (The Morometes, 1957)
A peasant family saga, mainly chronicling the background and dissolution of small peasant farms under the impact of large capitalist farming during the 1930s.

Ferestre Intunecate, 1959 (Windows in the Darkness)
A novel dealing with the conflicting goals and views, the tensions within Rumanian farm villages during the initial period of collectivization.

REBREANU, Liviu

Ion, 1920 (Ion), Padurea Spinzuratilor, 1922 (The Forest of the Hanged, 1957)
Two novels about the squalor, misery and destruction swirling around the Rumanian

peasantry caught in the tides of W.W.I. Rebreanu was a nationalistically-inclined
peasant populist, one of the internationally best known of Rumanian writers during
the interwar period.

Rascoala, 1935 (Uprising)
A collective novel about Rumanian village life at the turn of the century and an
account of the peasant masses as "hero" during the 1907 rising.

SADOVEANU, Ion Martin (Michael Sadoveanu)

Baltagul, 1925 (The Mud Hut Dwellers, 1965)
An epic novel of the Rumanian peasantry from the last years of Turkish rule in the
mid 19th century to the eve of W.W.I; being a species of "national folk spirit
survival" saga. By a prolific and widely read "populist" writer.

Mitrea Cocor, 1953 (Mitrea Cocor, 1953)
A novel of a boy coming of age on a Kulak peasant farm during the late 1930s; of
the remnant quasi-feudal obligations, the youth's encounter with other worlds and
new ideas when he is drafted into the Rumanian army and sent into the invasion of
the Soviet Union during W.W.II. Relates his experiences in the USSR as a POW
and his return to Rumania after 1944, not as a communist or with any systematic
political outlook but with the commitment that the regime ancien has to be rooted
out if ever a decent life is to be made in his country. A simple, unaffected
account of human decency and growth away from a backward and oppressive society.
Also Anii De Ucencie, 1944 (End of the Century in Bucharest).

SAHIA, Alexandru

Revolta In Porta, 1939 (Revolt in the Port)
A slim collection of stories about the desperate poverty, oppression and the
desperate strike of dockworkers in a Rumanian Black Sea port during 1934. Also
(The Living Factory), 1933, another slim collection of stories about the lives of
casual and unemployed factory workers in Bucharest during the early 1930s. By
one of the few actual proletarian writers in Rumania during the period.

Short Stories, 1952
A translated collection of Sahia's stories written during the 1930s, including
two anti-militarist tales, "Father's Return From War" and "The Blood Soaked
Fields of Maraseti". Also see his "Rain in June" (in Jacob Steinberg's anthology,
Introduction to Rumanian Literature, 1966), a story dealing with the lot of
landless peasants in Rumania during the 1930s.

SALAMON, Erno

(On the Threshold of the Poor), 1937, (To a Poor Man's Son), 1938, (Wonderful
Destiny), 1945
Three slim collections of desperate, underground poetry dealing with the lives of
Rumanian poor, peasantry and working class during the late 1930s. By a communist
poet who died in a Rumanian forced labour camp during W.W.II.

STANCU, Zaharia

Descult, 1948 (Barefoot, 1971)
A semi-autobiographic novel about a boy from an impoverished peasant family and
covering a calamitous decade from 1907 to the final year of W.W.I in Rumania.
An amalgam of family history and that of kith and neighbours, sagacious
reminiscences of the rule of Boyars and conditions on the great landed estates,
of the fury and repression of the 1907 peasant rising and the bowed, but unbroken
bitterness which followed, ending with the teenaged protagonist's flight to seek
a new world in Bucharest. An authentic, sometimes brilliant, peasant novel. Also
his Dulai, 1952 (The Hounds), Radacinile Sint Amare, 1958 (Roots are Bitter),
Jocul Cu Moartea, 1962 (Courting Death), Padurea Nebuna, 1962 (The Crazy Forest),
a semi-autobiographical novel tetrology which paints a fresco of Rumanian
society during the first half of this century.

BULGARIA

DIMITROVA, Blaga

Journey to Oneself, 1965
A novel of a middle class professional's contradictory and changing attitudes to the "socialist reconstruction" of Bulgaria; the gradual incorporation of this sector.

DIMOV, Dimiter

Tobacco, 1951
A novel which explores the intricate personal and social differences within the Bulgarian peasantry and rural middle class, the heterogeneous tensions, the subtle differences and similarities which lead individuals either to the left or the right during the 1930s and in the war years. Revolves around the lives and decisions of two brothers from a wealthy peasant family during W.W.II, one who becomes a rich contractor-grower of export tobacco and supporter of the pro-fascist Bulgarian government and the other a left wing partizan. Possibly the most widely translated Bulgarian novel of the post 1945 period.

DJAGAROV, Georgi

The Public Prosecutor, 1969
A play which exoriates the amoral careerism and political servility operating through a public prosecutor's office in a provincial Bulgarian town during 1954, the often absurd injustice of the final Stalinist period.

DONCHEV, Anton

Time of Parting, 1965
A "historical" novel of the lives of peasant shepherds in the Rhodope mountains during the early years of Turkish rule (16th century). Their resistance to forced conversion to Islam and the survival of a Bulgarian national identity through the peasantry.

Also Awakening, 1956, Leader of the Invisible Army, 1967, and Tale of Tsar Samuel, 1969, three additional "historical" novels of Bulgarian national resistance to occupation by Byzantine Greeks and "Terrible Turks" from 15th to 18th centuries. A largely nationalist treatment by a widely translated Bulgarian author.

JAVOROV, Pejo

Goce Delcev, 1903 (Goce Delcev)
A biography of the turn-of-the-century Macedonian partizan Goce Delcev, a socialist leader of revolt against Turkish rule in a still feudal region. The Macedonian struggle of the time had international support from progressive forces and was, in a sense, one of the forerunners of later national liberation struggles.

Xajduski Kopnenija, 1908 (Dreams of a Partizan)
Memoirs of Javorov's participation in and thoughts about the Macedonian guerrilla struggle at turn-of-the-century. Also see Zakhari Stoyanov's 1913 Pages from the Autobiography of a Bulgarian Insurgent, a reworked diary of a Macedonian guerrilla leader in the first decade of this century.

KARASLAVOV, Georgi

Sporzilov, 1931 (Sporzilov)
A collective novel of a working class district in Prague of the same name during the late 20s, where Karaslavov and other Bulgarian left refugees lived as construction workers. By possibly the finest left Bulgarian novelist of the interwar period.

Die Hirtenflöte Weint, 1936 (The Shepherd's Flute Wails)
Said to be the most moving novel about the two 1923 uprisings by Bulgarian
Agrarians and Communists against the Royalist military junta. Traces the background and events of those failed risings but deals especially with the two years
of repression which scourged the country thereafter. Karaslavov was a participant
himself, escaped into exile where he lived and wrote during most of the interwar
years.

Tatul, 1938 (Tango, 1954)
Novel of the continuing reaction in Bulgaria of the mid 1930s as the upper middle
classes toy with fascist solutions and a peasantry maintains an underground
resistance.

Obikoveni Xora, 1952-1966 (Ordinary People)
An epic novel in four volumes detailing the lives and fates of members
of representative Bulgarian families from W.W.I to the mid 1950s. A novelized
social history of Bulgaria from late-established capitalism to socialism.

KONSTANTINOV, Aleko

Bai Ganyu, 1970 (original 1895)
A once extremely popular satire dealing with emerging rural capitalists during
early independence period. It reproduces the posturing, greed and general
philistinism of the class of newly rich Kulack farmers and merchants in the person
of one Bai Ganyu. Written in a style reminiscent of Mark Twain.

MANOV, Emil

(An Unauthentic Case), 1957
A novel about the injustices and arbitrary actions of the Stalinist period in
Bulgaria, but mainly about the coverup of those events, which everyone knows about,
by one provincial administration which is deeply implicated in that past.

MANTOV, Dimiter

The Wild Ones, 1972
A "historical" novel about the 1876 Bulgarian uprising against the Turkish overlords in the Turnova region; with lots of Beys, Orthodox patriarchs, colourful
haiduks, stirring deeds and assorted heroes and villains. Also see Ivan Vazov,
Under the Yoke, 1912, a once widely known "documentary" novel of the 1876 rising
which ushered in Bulgarian independence.

MILEV, Geo (Georgi Kasabov)

Grosni Prozi, 1924 (Ugly Prose)
A short collection of sketches about revolutionary Europe in the years immediately
after W.W.I; some dealing with the German revolution and the deaths of Liebknecht
and Luxemburg.

Septemvri, 1925 (September)
A book length poem in blank verse which is an evocation to the desperation of and
participants in the September 1923 rising. It is a masterpiece of revolutionary
poetry. Also see Collected Works, 1971.

POLJANOV, Dimiter (Dimiter Popov)

Morski Kapi, 1907 (Sea Drops), Zelezni Stixove, 1921 (Iron Verses)
Two collections of socialist poetry by the pioneer of Marxist writing in Bulgaria.

SMIRENSKI, Christo

Da Bede Den!, 1922 (Let There Be Light!, 1969)
A collection of revolutionary poems by a lyrical Macedonian communist poet. They
capture the desperation and millenial hopes of the times.

STAMATOV, Georgi

Isbrani Ocerci Razkazi, 1905 (Selected Sketches and Stories), Skici, 1915
(Sketches), Razkzi, 1930 (Stories)

Three collections of stories and sketches which portray and statirize many facets of Bulgarian society from the turn of the century to the 1930s. Charicatures of judges, the clergy, academics, the city gentry and rising Kulak classes, the military. By an extraordinarily prolific (over 50 volumes of collected works) and widely read populist writer.

STOJANOV, Ljudmil

Bic Bozij, 1927 (Scourge of God), Zenski Duski, 1929 (Feminine Souls)
Two collections of short stories about Bulgaria in 1920s; the chaos, the peasant struggles, the social stasis and not-so-comic-opera struttings of the military/ landlord class.

Xolera, 1935 (Cholera)
Stojanov's major novel and one of the classics of Bulgarian literature; a panorama of the poverty, anger and suppression of peasants and workers during the 1920s and early 1930s and the bumbling voracity of the Bulgarian ruling class.

STRASIMIROV, Anton

Smutno Vreme, 1899 (A Troubled Time)
A novela of the initial phase of industrialization and of the lives of displaced artizans who become the first casual industrial workers in Bulgarian cities.

Bez Pet, 1919 (Without Direction), Bena, 1921
Two linked novels about the collapse of Bulgaria during W.W.I but also of the seemingly hopeful evolution of a popular democracy and rural reform which accompanied the brief tenure of the radical Agrarian government.

Xoro, 1926 (Round Dance)
A documentary novel of the Royalist military coup which ousted the Agrarian (Peasant Party) government in 1923 and the bitter but defeated armed attempts of Agrarian party to regain control.

Robi, 1929-1930 (Slaves)
A two volume novel of the Macedonian struggle for freedom from the Turks and their local collaborators at the turn of the century. An allegory of the struggles against the Bulgarian ruling class in 1920s.

TALEV, Dimiter

The Iron Candlestick, 1964 (original 1952), The Bells of Prespa, 1966 (original 1956), Ilinden, 1953, Your Voices I Hear, 1966
Four historical novels which chronicle Bulgaria under centuries of Turkish occupation; a panorama of social conditions, cultures and intersecting interests (Bulgarian, Turkish and other) in contention. Culminates in the final struggle for national emancipation of 1870s. Talev is the most widely translated of the Bulgarian epic novelists.

VELKOW, Krum (Nikola Ikonomov)

Selo Borovo, 1949 (original 1926) (The Village of Borovo)
A novela about the turmoil and revolutionary upheavals swirling through one Bulgarian village in the 1918-1923 period; the intersecting local, national and transnational forces at work and the varying responses of villagers. Culminates in the 1923 risings.

VAPCAROV, Nikola (Nikola Yonkov Vaptzarov)

Selected Poems, 1953
A translation of some of Vaptzarov's poems written during the late 1930s and W.W.II and about the struggles of workers, peasants and partizans. Some touch on the visions of what a socialist Bulgaria would be like.

Motorni Pesni, 1940 (Motor Songs)
A collection of underground poetry which attempts to capture the personal motives in the working class resistance to deepening reaction in Bulgaria of late 1930s. In a similar vein see Xristos Raderski's 1933 Nie Sme Pravova Strana (We Are a Country of Law and Order), a collection of bitterly sardonic poetry.

YUGOSLAVIA

ADAMIC, Louis

The Native's Return, 1937
A novel of the backwardness and mid-19th century class relations in rural Croatia during the early 1930s as seen by a shocked US emigrant who returns to his native village which he left as a youth. The subservience of Kullenovo village is symbolized by the fact that it was still the source from which the Zagreb middle class recruited wet nurses (whose own infants thereby became malnourished). Marred with a certain melodrama, it contains a readable expose of "democratic" Yugoslavia under the regime ancien. Adamic was an American labour reporter.

ANDRIC, Ivo

Na Drini Cuprija, 1945 (The Bridge on the Drina, 1959)
A historical novel of Bosnia and its peoples and fate from the apogee of Ottoman power in late 16th century to the beginning of W.W.I when local Moslems have become the pawns of other external forces. Set around and in the neighbourhood of a strategic bridge crossing the Drina river which linked oriental Europe with west. The first volume of a trilogy, it is Andric's masterpiece, probably the internationally best known Yugoslav work. (Andric won the Nobel Prize for Literature in 1961.) It proceeds from a traditional
humanist position and rejects the appeals to ethnic chauvinism which flaws much Balkan national epic literature. The other major title of the trilogy is Travnicka Chronica, 1947 (Bosnian Chronicles, 1970) dealing with the deepening chaos and social anachronism of Bosnia during the first decade of the 19th century as seen by a consul of Napoleonic France in the town of Travnick, the inevitable collapse of the oriental colonialism but the seeming defeat of European liberalism as well.

Gospodjica, 1948 (The Woman From Sarajevo, 1965)
A novel about a Bosnian woman merchant and black marketeer who accumulates a small fortune through war profiteering during W.W.I. She evolves into a landlord loan shark in Sarajevo during the interwar years in Serbian-dominated Yugoslavia, a representative of the new bourgeoise. Her single weakness is to fall in love with a younger, even more rapacious fortune hunter who fleeces her like she has others.

Nove Pripovetke, 1949 (New Tales, 1966)
A collection of stories dealing with the posturings and somnolence of the newly emerged Bosnian bourgeoisie operating under the aegis of the Yugoslav Royalist regime of the 1920s and 1930s.

BULATOVIC, Miodrag

Hero on a Donkey, 1966
A novela about an inn keeper in Montenegro during W.W.II who boasts about his communist party and partizan activities to neighbours while in fact he does little more than keep a group of demoralized Italian soldiers in booze. When he finally does decide to join the partizans they send him back to his inn on a donkey and in shame he hangs himself. Intended as a satire of those Yugoslav notables of the Tito period whose be all and end all is their participation in the partizan struggle of a generation before. Stirred up quite a hornets nest.

COPIC, Branko

(The Noiseless Gunpowder), 1954
One of the major Yugoslav novels about the guerrilla war against German and a half dozen allied occupying forces during W.W.II and of the conjoined partizan struggle against the host of proto-fascist ethnic forces which arose. Portrays the tremendous suffering of the three year long struggle and sympathetically records

the realistic distrust and fears of many ordinary Yugoslavs about getting involved
in partizan activities. Describes the growing strength and ultimate victory of
the Tito forces against all odds.

(The Eighth Offensive), 1958
A novel about the post war bewilderment and adjustments of partizans from peasant
villages.to having captured state power; the overwhelming problems of rebuilding
and attempting to create a new society when they are strangers even to the former
provincial city life. Revolves around the external and internal problems which
beset and threatened the existence of a "socialist" Yugoslavia immediately after
W.W.II. Told in a humourous folk style.

COSIC, Dobrica

Daleko Je Sunce, 1951 (Far Away Is The Sun, 1963)
A documentary novel of the incredible sufferings of villagers and partizans during
W.W.II. The tenacity of Yugoslav peoples but also the Byzantine factions,
stupidities of ethnic conflict and cruelty of the struggle which involved a civil
war of Tito partizans against the Croatian Ustashi, Serbian Chetniks and assorted
other pro-fascist forces which arise during the occupation. A novel which has
grown in stature over time.

Koreni, 1954 (Roots), Deobe, 1961 (Divisions), Bajka, 1966 (A Fable), Vreme Smrti,
1975 (Time of Death)
A series of novels which constitute a social history of Yugoslavia during the
interwar years, in particular of the emergence of class struggle among Serbian
peasantry and the newly evolving industrial working class.

DJILAS, Milovan

Montenegro, 1968
A massive epic novel about Djilas' native Montenegro, a mountainous principality
(liberated from Turkish rule only in late 19th century) during and after W.W.I,
when it is incorporated into Yugoslavia. An ethnographically detailed social
history of lives, culture and internecine feuds in the guise of politics; of a
still partly pre-capitalist society into which contending imperial regimes
intrude and from which the forerunners of socialist struggle emerge. Djilas'
focus on the brutal ethnic chauvinism of the region lacks the general humanity
and balance of Andric's comparable works on Bosnia. Djilas himself was a partizan
leader and one of the four Vice Presidents of Yugoslavia in early 1950s. He rose
to international prominence as a "dissenter" through his publication of The New
Class, 1956 and Conversations With Stalin, 1961, two bitterly critical
commentaries on the oppressive party bureaucracy which arose in Yugoslavia and
Central Europe and the terrible legacy of the Stalin era.

ISAKU, Murat

Dielli E Din Rrugen E Vet, 1965 (The Sun Knows Its Orbit)
An epic novel of the Albanian-speaking region of Yugoslavia; the changes in society
during one adult lifetime, from the quasi "tribal" and semi-feudal conditions of
a mountain backland during the interwar years and the destruction of traditional
society during the partizan struggles of W.W.II. Of the overwhelming tasks of
reconstruction in the post war years when the infrastructure of a poor but
hopefully more equitable society was being laid.

JANEVSKI, Slavko

Selo Zad Sedumte Jaseni, 1937 (The Village Behind Seven Ash Trees, 1952)
A collage novel of peasant life in Macedonian Yugoslavia during the interwar years
when it was a sort of internal colony of Serbian capitalists. Done with an
emphasis on local customs and folk life by a Macedonian peasant writer.

Leb I Kamen, 1957 (Bread and a Stone)
A lyrical and undogmatic account of Yugoslav Macedonia during the initial stages
of "socialist" reorganization.

KALEB, Vjekoslav

The Beauty of the Dust, 1965
A novel of Croatia during the interwar years and of the psychopathic terror of
the Ustashi during W.W.II. The shock, exhaustion and fears of Croatian people at
the end of war followed by their cautiously rising hopes that some better and more
peaceful society is finally being created under the Tito regime.

KOSMAC, Ciril

Sreca In Kruh, 1958 (Happiness and Bread)
A collection of stories about the total physical and spiritual exhaustion, but also
the palpable relief, of people in the Slovenian region of Yugoslavia at the end of
W.W.II. Their inward looking caution but slowly growing hopes during the initial
phase of "socialist reconstruction" there.

Day in Spring, 1969
A novel of Slovenian small townspeople and farmers adjusting to, finding fault
with and coming to appreciate aspects of Yugoslav versions of socialism--which
was more or less imposed in late 1940s and 1950s.

KOVACIC, Ivan Goran

Jama, 1944 (The Pit, 1962)
An epic book length poem memorializing the murder of almost a half million Serbian
civilians by the Croatian Ustashi (nationalist) forces during W.W.II. Kovacic,
a left wing Serb, was himself murdered soon after by the Serbian (nationalist)
Chetniks.

KRLEZA, Miroslav

Hrvastska Rapsodija, 1921 (Croatian Rapsody, 1953), Hiljadu I Jedna Smrt, 1933
(A Thousand and One Deaths), Na Rubu Pameti, 1938 (On the Brink of Reason),
Banket U Blitvi, 1939 (The Banquet at Blitva)
Four novels which comprise an overview of tragically misdirected Croatian history
--an account of landlords, clerics, petty bourgeoise and peasantry--from the
Balkan Wars of early 1900s to the eve of W.W.II. Touched with a certain peasant
romanticism, the accounts contrast the relative decency of Croatian peasantry
to the reaction and fantasies of Croatian lower middle classes and the inherent
alliance of the upper class with external colonizers.

LALIC, Mihailo

Lelejska Gora, 1957 (Wailing Mountain, 1965)
A novel by a Montenegrin-Serbian writer which is considered to be one of the best
and most powerful accounts of the Yugoslav partizan war. It deals with the
experiences of and changes in a partizan organizer behind the lines, working to
recruit men and supplies and to sustain civilian morale despite the terrible
losses, privations and dangers for all involved. He is gradually forced into
lies, threats and whatever strategems will work to sustain partizan operations,
realizing at the very time that he is becoming callous and benumbed and that this
is a poor foundation for a new society. A valuable antidote to more romantic
accounts of partizan war.

Svadba, 1950 (The Wedding), Zlo Proljece, 1953 (Evil Spring), Raskid, 1955 (The
Break)
A novel trilogy about Yugoslavia in the decade after W.W.II, the problems and
hopes involved in building a new society from a shattered, divided population
faced with hostility from both capitalist and communist states.

Pramen Tame, 1970 (A Patch of Darkness), Ratna Sreca, 1973 (Fortunes of War)
Two novels about the changing lives and worlds of the Montenegrin people from the
end of W.W.II to present.

NAZOR, Vladimir

S Partizaima, 1946 (With the Partizans)
A reportage chronicle of daily life among Tito's partizan army, 1941-1944, by a

leading Croatian populist poet who joined the partizan forces when in his late sixties. Also his 1944 Pjesme Partizanke (Partizan Poems).

RACIN, Kosta

Beli Mugri, 1939 (White Dawns, 1974)
A collection of poems and tales told in a traditional Macedonian folk style; dealing with the poverty and exploitation of peasants and workers in Macedonia under the Yugoslav landlord regime of the 1930s. Racin was a member of the Macedonian Revolutionary Socialist Organization which had emerged from the struggle against Turkish occupation at the beginning of the 20th century.

VORANC, Presihov (Lovro Kuhar)

Doberdob, 1940 (Doberdob, 1952)
A novel describing the disintegration of the Austro-Hungarian empire as seen by a Slovenian conscript in the Austrian army during W.W.I who comes to recognize how he and others from all the national groups of the region have been used in their rulers' conflicts. Of his gradual move away from national and ethnic chauvinism and toward revolutionary commitment.

Pozganica, 1939 (Pozganica)
A novel which portrays the last years of the Austro-Hungarian empire and the machinations of the Slovenian ruling class at the end of W.W.I who link themselves to whichever power would defend their interests. "In his small and confined countryside he describes woodcutters, ploughmen, timbermen, their wives, their children, village priests, merchants, officials, with all their ideosyncracies, limitations, common sense, stupidities, selfishness, spitefulness and nobility, speech, curses, movements; and with an unexpected medley of human virtues."

Jamnica, 1945 (Jamnica)
A novel about life in a Slovenian peasant village which has come under control of the Royal Yugoslav regime during the 1920s. Of how the Serbian officials and entrepreneurs mount their own exactions of the region, which rapidly impoverishes the peasantry and drives even some former middle peasants into alliance with the emerging working class movement.

Nasi Mejniki, 1946 (Our Boundary Stones)
A chronicle of W.W.II and the shifting forces of resistance from 1940-1945.

ALBANIA

GJATA, Fatmir

Keneta, 1959 (The Marsh)
A novel about the attempts to reclaim a swampland region near Tirana for
agricultural production in 1946-48 despite the wiles of assorted foreign agents
and indigenous class enemies but with the help of 10,000 authentic Albanian
peasants who do the impossible. In short, an unintended satire of Stalinist
"socialist construction" literature. See Arshi Pippa's Libri I Burgut in
relation to this work.

KADARE, Ismail

The General of the Dead Army, 1969
A remarkable novel by Albania's leading writer. Deals with an Italian soldiers'
graves commission touring through Albania in the 1960s, an interchange between
past and present through the voices, memories, comments of the dead soldiers
--Albanian, Italian and others--whose graves are visited. A collage of Albanian
history from King Zog's time in 1920s, 1930s, assorted invasions and battles
between Italian, Greek, German, Serbian armies and the disparity between the goals
of ordinary soldiers on all sides and their vainglorious generals.

Oyteti I Jugut, 1964 (Southern City)
An autobiographical account of Albania from being an extraordinary anachronistic
Balkan principality of warring clans in late 1930s, the Byzantine factions and
tides of W.W.II and the triumph of the partizans and the various phases of national
reconstruction under a uniquely Stalinist regime to 1960. Also see his 1974 The
Wedding, a novela revolving around what were considered the permissible differences
of opinion within Albania of early 1970s.

MALESHOVA, Sejfulla

Vjersha, 1945 (Poems)
A slim collection of poetry written mainly in the 1930s and about rayah (ex-serf)
peasants, peasant bandits and guerrillas and even poems of the thin stratum of
Albanian proletariat, with fable-like accounts of struggles around the world
drifting into the country. Among the first communist writers in Albania,
Maleshova was later expelled from the party for "cosmopolitan tendencies".

MARKO, Petro

Hasta La Vista, 1959 (Until Then)
An autobiography describing experiences of the Spanish Civil War, in which Marko,
Memet Shehu and numbers of other Albanians fought. Spanish title of original
Albanian volume.

PIPPA, Arshi

Libri I Burgut, 1959 (The Prison Book)
A prison memoir of a liberal political prisoner in late 1940s Albania who worked
as convict labour on the drainage project recounted in Gjata's novel The Marsh.
An account of why the project was such a failure and completed only with such
effort.

SPASSE, Sterja

Afërdita, 1944
Novel of a young woman teacher in a mountain village during the late 1930s who
attempts to carry out the precepts "V Narod", bringing knowledge of the modern
world to a backward region. But she is overwhelmed and finally defeated by the
superstitions and entrenched conservatism of poor and local notables alike.

<u>Ata Nuk Ishin Vëtem</u>, 1953 (They Are Not Alone)
A "historical" novel of the last years of Turkish rule in Albania at the turn of
the century. A Turkish Bey connives to acquire village lands and soon turns the
peasants into landless labourers on his estate--evictions, local risings and the
"Terrible Turk" bogeymen theme.

STERMILLI, Haki

<u>Sikur T'isha Djale</u>, 1936 (If I Were a Boy)
A novela done in the form of a fictional reminiscence by a young peasant woman in
Albania of 1930s. Her capacities, hopes and restricted expectations, and a call
for women's emancipation.

XHUVANI, Dhimiter

<u>Tuneli</u>, 1966 (The Tunnel)
Novel of the first years of "socialist reconstruction" in Albania during late
1940s and early 1950s. It was severely criticized as revisionist.

XOXA, Jakov

<u>Lumi I Vdekur</u>, 1967 (The Dead River)
A novel of how Albanian landlords and Beys in mid 1930s divert irrigation water
from peasant plots to their own fields, leading to crop failure and peasant revolt.
The revolt is crushed but some of the peasant rebels flee into the mountains to
become the kernels of later partizan struggle. Also (The White South), 1969, a
sequel to <u>Dead River</u>, dealing with the collectivization of peasant farms and
large land holdings in the Mzeqe region after the triumph of partizan forces in
W.W.II. Some frank descriptions of the advances, mistakes, support and suspicious
caution of the peasantry.

GREECE

AKRITAS, Loukis

Neos Me Kala Systaseis, 1935 (Young Man with Excellent References)
Novel of the frayed white collar class in Athens during the stagnant late 1920s
and early 1930s; unemployment, conservatism and hopelessness.

Ho Kampos, 1936 (Valley)
A semi-documentary account of the simmering misery and frantic desperation in a
small provincial town in depression-ridden Greece on the eve of the Metaxis
dictatorship.

Ho Armatomenoi, 1947 (Men in Arms)
A reportage chronicle of the 1940 Italian-Greek war in Albania by a populist
Cypriot reporter. Said to be the most balanced treatment of this bloody squabble
between two right-wing dictatorships. The pointless suffering and the way in
which the temporary Greek victories were glorified as the triumph of "Democracy"
(under the Metaxis dictatorship).

BERATIS, Jannis (Giannes Mperates)

Hodoiporiko Tou '43, 1964 (Itinery '43)
A reportage novel written as a contemporary chronicle of the complex and bloody
struggles of left and right partizans, collaborationists, German occupiers and
civilians throughout Greece during the terrible year of 1943.

DOUKAS, Alekos

Stin Pali, Sta Neiata, 1953 (In Youthful Battle)
A novelized autobiography which is the most challenging account of Greek-Turkish
relations to appear. Details Greek life in villages and towns in Turkey during
the pre W.W.I era; the varied but relatively good relations between ordinary
Greeks and Turks and others in the mosaic of peoples (including a character like
Nazim Hikmet). Describes the rapacious trading on ethnic loyalties and fears by
both Greek and Turkish businessmen-politicos. The horrors of the Greek-Turkish
war of 1920-22, the expulsion of the entire Greek population and their lives as
unwanted refugees in Greece. The manipulations of British imperial interests in
establishing a conservative regime in power and the stagnation of Greece in the
1920s. Describes union and strike activities during the 1930s, flowing into the
Metaxis "fascist" dictatorship, W.W.II and the civil war which grew out of it.
The long drawn-out repression which followed the victory by the Royalist forces
and the final emigration of the main character (who we first met 40 years before
in Turkey) to Australia. A remarkable overview of modern Greek history from a
Marxist viewpoint.

DOXAS, Takis

(White Streets), 1938, Pikre Epoche, 1950 (Bitter Times)
Two collections of stories which revolve mainly about impoverished peasants in
decaying villages and the stagnant small towns of 1930s and 1940s which offer
neither hope nor a decent life to any of their inhabitants.

(Journeys Without Sun), 1953
A set of sketches about life in a provincial Greek town in Trace, in the form of
a novel; about the continuing poverty and stagnation in post civil war Greece.

HADZIS, Dhimitris (Dimitros Chadtzis)

Fotio, 1946 (Fire)
A documentary novel of the communist led partizan movement in Greece during W.W.II;
the terrible casualties, struggles with Greek rightist forces, support and hopes
for transforming an anachronistically backward society after the end of the war.
Written before the beginning of the Greek civil war.

To Telos Tis Mikris Mas Polis, 1963 (The End of Our Small City)
A major novel of the suppression of left and progressive elements during and after the civil war and the seemingly endless oppression of the Greek workers and poor. An epic account of a generation, rendering their inner worlds and the external realities from the early 1940s to the 1960s.

HADZOPOULOS, Konstantine (Konstantine Chatzopoulous)

Ho Pyrogos tou Akropotamou, 1915 (The Tower of Akropotamos)
A novela about life in semi-feudal Greek villages early in the century beginning to break down with capitalist penetration, the worst of both worlds. Tower of Akropotamos is said to be the first social protest novel in Greek.

Taso, Sto Skotasi, 1916 (Taso, In the Darkness)
A collection of exasperated stories about the superstitions, taboos and self-imposed ignorance which keep Greek villagers fighting and pulling each other back into the oppressed and powerless condition they are in.

IATRIDI, Julia

Ta Petrina Liontaria, 1963 (The Stone Lions)
A novel which chronicles Greece from 1922 to circa 1950, told through the eyes of a refugee girl from Greek Anatolia who is employed by a series of middle class families as a maid during thirty years. Since she is partly deaf and never gets away from work the ongoing events in Greece are told as filtered through the wiles, fears and bias of various middle class employers but with naive yet sagacious re-evaluation by the heroine. We hear the varying and changing attitudes of the Greek middle class over a generation, from moderate democrats to proto-fascists. The positions of that class from support of Metaxis during 1930s to the Royal Greek Army during the civil war and the Anglo-American military intervention in the Royalist seizure of Athens in 1944.

KAMBEROGLOU, Byron

Stom Iskio Tis Istorias, 1961-1966 (In the Shadow of History)
A three volume social history in the format of reminiscences by an aging doctor in a small town; from the mass expulsion of Greeks from Smyrna during the Greek-Turkish war of 1920s, accounts of the social conditions and growing class struggles in Greece during the inter-war years, of W.W.II and the terrible famine of 1941, of partizan activity and the emerging civil war in late 1940s. A rich and subtle account.

KASDAGLIS, Nikos

Ta Donitia Tis Mylopetras, 1955 (The Millstone's Teeth)
Novel dealing with the youthful members of the left and right wing partizans during W.W.II and the dissolution of what remaining common loyalties had existed in Greek towns.

(Shaven Heads), 1959
A protest novel dealing with the stripping away of personal dignity and the mindless obedience which the Royal Greek army attempts to drill into its peasant recruits pursuant to its own authoritarian politics.

KOSTSIAS, Kostas

O Kapnismenos Ouranos, 1957 (The Smokey City)
A richly descriptive novel of the everyday lives of ordinary Greeks, their sense of oppression and betrayal under the conservative post-civil war regime. Said to be one of the major Greek novels of that decade.

MANGLIS, Yiannis

Ee Kolasmenee Tees Thalassas, 1940 (The Damned of the Sea)
A collection of reminiscences and stories of the joys, misery and adventures of sponge fishermen in an impoverished village in the Kalymnos region during the 1930s. Marred by a certain local colour romanticism.

Taderfia Mou Ee Anthropee, 1958 (My Brothers, the People)
Collection of short stories about the Greek resistance movements during W.W.II.

MILLIEX, Tatiana

Kai Idhou Ippos, 1963 (And Behold a Green Horse)
A novel of the experience of and feelings about Greek reality during the civil
war and the following repression, as seen through the eyes of a progressive Greek
woman writer.

PANAYOTOPOULOS, I.M.

(Humble Life), 1945
A novelized account of the author's return to a poor, working class waterfront
district in the port city of Pireaus after thirty years absence; finding the
continuing poverty, spontaneous anger and frenetic joys, the gradual decay into
an urban slum. Somewhat nostalgic but rich in accounts of daily lives and
struggles for existence, with a compassionate treatment of the hopelessness which
comes to weigh down the inhabitants at middle age. Includes some bitter satire
of government agencies charged with providing aid to poor which mainly worsen
the situation through red tape.

PETRAKIS, Harry Mark

The Hour of the Bell, 1976
An unusual historical novel about the Greek wars of independence from Turkey in
1820s, in which the Greek chieftains become as brutal, rapacious and unjust as
any Turkish Pasha.

PLASKOVITS, Spyros

Thyella Kai To Fanari, 1955 (The Vineshoots)
An allegorical novel of a peasant refugee from Asia Minor and the two families he
raises in interwar Greece, who then sees his world dissolve in the struggles of
W.W.II and his sons join opposing sides in the civil war, which destroys them
and the family vineyard.

PREVELAKIS, Pantelis

Chroniko Politeis, 1938 (Chronicle of a Town)
A richly detailed reminiscence novel of Crete as it existed in 1910-1920, an
island people then dispensing with British "protection" but only slowly shaking
off the centuries of Ottoman rule and gradually re-entering the Greek mainstream.

(Forsaken Crete), 1945, (The Tree), 1948, (The First Freedom), 1949, (The City),
1950
A novel tetrology collectively known as The Cretan, being an epic social history
of Crete from the end of Turkish rule in 1866 to 1910. A somewhat nationalist
but minutely detailed account of daily lives, gradual changes and continuing
poverty and of the vendettas, oppression and rebelliousness simmering among
the Cretan people.

RITSOS, Yannis

(Tractor), 1934, (Pyramids), 1935
Two collections of revolutionary and working class poetry about Greece during the
early 1930s.

Epitaphios, 1936 (Epitaph) .
An epic poem to a mother whose son is killed in a demonstration of unemployed
workers against the Metaxis dictatorship of that period. Set to music by Mikis
Theodorakis in 1960s.

Romiosini, 1954 (Romiosini, 1969)
A collection of poems celebrating Greek resistance against fascism from the
Metaxis regime, through the Nazi occupation and against the Greek Royal army in
the civil war.

I Sonata Tou Selinophotos, 1956 (Moonlight Sonata, 1979)
A collection of strangely lush poetry revolving around the oppression but also
undying hopes of Greek working people under the right wing regime of the 1950s.
Also see Collected Poems, 1961-1964, which contain lyrical love poetry to
proletarian socialist work.

Petrinos Chronos, 1975 (Year of Stone)
Poems written originally as a political prisoner in a Royalist Greek concentration
camp in 1949-1950.

Epikairika: 1945-1969, 1976 (Timely: 1945-1969)
A collection of poems chronicling a generation of struggle in Greece from the end
of W.W.II, the defeat and repression of the left, the gradual reemergence of a
parliamentary democracy and the overthrow of the first Papandreou government by
the Greek colonels. One of some 80 collections of poetry translated into 36
languages, by a long exiled left poet.

The Fourth Dimension, 1977
A selection of Ritsos' poems written between 1939 and 1974, conveying social,
political and personal events in the life of Greece during that long and bitter
period. Contains an informative introduction by translator Rae Dalven which
provides a context of the particular poems and events.

SAMARAKIS, Adonis

(The Flaw), 1965
A novel of an anonymous, apolitic individual during the "democratic" period
preceding the colonel's regime of the 1960s who somehow seems amorphously
suspicious and is thereby drawn into a Kafkaesque net of investigations by various
arms of the security and police system, and of the inevitable repercussions which
shatter his life without any charges ever having been laid.

SOTIRIOU, Dido

Oi Nekroi Permimenoun, 1959 (The Dead Wait)
A novel of a Greek family which escapes from inland Turkey in W.W.I to Smyrna,
where the Greek army and allied merchant capitalists have dreams of annexing most
of Turkey as a Greek colony. Chronicles the defeat of the Greek army in 1922,
the Smyrna disaster, and the lives of impoverished refugees as workers in Greece
during 1920s and 1930s. Some vivid accounts of the proletarian districts of
Athens under the Metaxis dictatorship of 1936-1941 and events of W.W.II and the
partizan movement in Greece. The transformation of a petty merchant family from
Asia Minor into Greek proletarians, seen partly through their children's rejection
of past illusions and loyalties and their developing resistance to Greek
ruling class.

Matomena Homata, 1962 (Bloodied Earth)
Novel of a Greek peasant youth in pre W.W.I Turkey who becomes a bookkeeper on a
Turkish estate, leaves to work for Greek grain dealer who uses ethnic ties to
cheat all peasants, becomes involved in smuggling goods for merchants who see
W.W.I as a bonanza and is enlightened as to what is going on by a Turkish
worker. In the second half of this massive epic novel the hero escapes from a
Turkish labour battalion, is conscripted into the Greek army but is placed in a
battalion of Cretan conscripts which the Greek generals deem politically
unreliable and use as cannon fodder. Describes the behind-the-scenes infighting
between Republican and Monarchist factions during the early 1920s and the
emerging Marxist forces from the Republican ranks. Sotiriou alludes to the
relatively good relations between ordinary Turks and Greeks in pre W.W.I Anatolia
who are constantly being set against each other by their respective ethnic
leadership.

THEOTOKIS, Constantine (Konstantinos Theotokes)

(The Condemned), 1919, (The Life and Death of Karavelas), 1920
Two novels which portray Greek small town life just before and during W.W.I;
focussing on the destructive traditions and inflexible mores which harden men and
women into guardians of backwardness, unable to reshape their own lives and
suspicious of all enjoyments.

(Slaves and their Bonds), 1922
A novel which describes then contemporary Greek village culture and society in more clearly political terms; a culture which successfully coopts the poor in their own disenfranchisement. Said to be the first "socialist" novel in Greece.

TSIRKAS, Stratis

Akyvernites Politeis, 1960-1965 (Drifting Cities, 1974)
A trilogy novel dealing with the Greek partizan movement during W.W.II, the beginnings of the Greek civil war and its escalation. From the entry of the British-Royal Greek army into Athens in 1945, the mutinies in it and the more direct intervention of British and American forces. A wide ranging account of the experiences, views and goals of differing sectors drawn into the emerging struggle.

VARNALIS, Constantine Kostas

To Fos Pou Kaiei, 1923 (The Light That Burns), Sklavoi Poliorkimenoi, 1927 (The Besieged Slaves)
Two collections of prose sketches and poetry about the poverty and stagnant class misrule of Greek bourgeoise from W.W.I to the mid 1920s. Sklavoi alludes to the struggles of mankind against injustices from ancient times as mirrored in events of then contemporary Greece. Calls for an end to the religious superstitions and other myths which blind the Greek people. Varnalis was the first and one of the most eminent Greek Marxist poets.

I Alithini Apologia Tou Sokrati, 1931 (The True Apology of Socrates, 1955)
A play about the trial and death of Socrates at the hands of the slave-owning rulers of "Athenian Democracy". An allegory of Greek democracy at the beginning of the 1930s.

Eleftheros Kosmos, 1965 (Free World)
A collection of sardonic sketches and poems about the bloody hypocrisy of Greece and of the Western Democracies in general and their support of repression during the two decades since the end of W.W.II. In the intervening generation Varnalis also produced circa a dozen other collections of left socialist poetry.

Orgi Laou, 1975 (Wrath of the People)
A posthumously published collection of firey poetry by the octogenarian Cretan poet, dealing mainly with the oppression of the Greek Colonels Junta during 1967-1974.

VASSILIKOS, Vassilis

Z, 1966 (Z, 1966)
Probably the best known Greek novel of the post W.W.II period. An account of Athens in 1964 under the Greek colonels-CIA dictatorship where the letter Z, painted on walls, stands for "Zei" or "He lives", referring to the assassinated left liberal leader Lambrakis. A collage account of the popular outrage, fear, necessary caution and mass confrontations. Deals in particular with the endless series of police coverups of the murder of a leader of political opposition (modeled after Lambrakis); the disjointed denials and repression of a shaky police state, the mounting anger of Greek youth and urban working class.

The Photographs, 1968, Outside the Walls, 1970
A collage novel (Photographs)and a collection of sketches (Outside the Walls), both dealing with the progressive alienation of young Greek intellectuals and the increasingly chaotic and absurd rule of the Greco-American colonels' regime.

VENEZIS, Elias (Elias Mellos)

Aioliki Yi, 1943 (Aeolian Land, 1949)
A nostalgic novel of life in Greek Asia Minor before the Greek-Turkish war of 1920-1922; emphasizes the ordinary, decent daily relationships between Greek and Turkish "common" people. Also Oi Nikemenoi, 1955 (The Defeated), stories of the partizans during the civil war and the fate of the Greek left and working class after their defeat in late 1940s.

MIDDLE EAST AND NORTH AFRICA

Turkey
Iran
Israel
Palestine
Lebanon, Syria, Iraq
Egypt
North Africa and Sudan

TURKEY

ADIVAR, Halide Edib

Vurun Kahpeye, 1926 (Strike the Hussy)
A novel describing the tribulations of a Turkish woman teacher in a backlands
peasant village during the mid 1920s. A cabal of muktars, mullahs and assorted
village bosses feel themselves threatened by the dissemination of modern
education but are afraid to directly oppose the school because of the central
government, which at the time was willing to knock clerico-traditionalist heads
together. How the local notables incite village men and women to harass the
everyday life of the teacher and drive her into leaving. Also Conflict, 1955,
an English translation of a novel with a theme broadly similar to Strike the
Hussy.

Adivar was a pioneer Turkish woman writer, having published modern novels during
the final years of the Ottoman regime. She became a prominent middle class
proponent of Pasha Kemel Ataturk's modernization and reform programs, an advocate
for women's education and emancipation. Atesten Gomlek, 1957 (Shirt of Flame) is
a fictionalized account of the author's experiences during the Greek-Turkish
war of the early 1920s.

APAYDIN, Talip

Bozkirda Gunler, 1952 (Days on the Steppes), Sari Traktor, 1954 (The Yellow
Tractor), Karanligin Kuvveti, 1967 (The Power of Darkness)
Three reportage novels by a peasant-writer trained in one of the village institute
schools. Bozkirda and Sari deal with the daily lives, problems, characters and
changes (particularly the spread of mechanized export agriculture) in the villages
of the Polatli region during the late 1940s. Karanligin Kuvveti deals with events
surrounding Apaydin's village institute school, which an increasingly temporizing
government closed at the behest of the local mullahs and landlords who are the
"powers of darkness". Also Ortakcilar, 1964 (Sharecroppers), a family chronicle
novel about Turkish tenant farmers.

BASARAN, Mehmet

Surgunler, 1970 (Exiles)
A collection of short stories by a socialist village institute writer; set in a
Trace (European Turkey) peasant village beset by the costs of a Turkish
community development scheme and the attentions of the American Peace Corps
during the 1960s. Of how aid to village middle class drives others into ruin.

BAYKURT, Fakir

Yilanlarin Ocu, 1959 (The Snake's Revenge)
A village novel revolving around a widowed peasant woman and her son, their quest
for elemental justice from a judicial-government bureaucracy which responds only
to money or political clout. Because of the protagonists' illiteracy and lack
of powerful protectors, government judges cast an indifferent eye over the
expropriation of the peasant family's land by local landlords.

BILBASAR, Kemal

Denizin Cagirisi, 1943 (Call of the Sea)
A novel about small town life in western Turkey during the late 1930s; a region
of natural beauty and considerable economic potential but where ordinary peoples'
lives are twisted by fearful ignorance and bloody old feuds as well as by class
oppression.

Pembe Kurt, 1953 (Boll Weevil)
A novel of landlords, tenant farmers, landless labourers and others in rural

western Turkey during the late 1940s and early 1950s; of how the spread of capitalized export agriculture pushes the remaining small peasantry to the wall.

Cemo, 1967 (Cemo), Memo, 1969 (Memo)
Two novels about the continuing struggles for and tensions within social reform in Anatolia from the 1930s to the 1950s, as experienced by the two title characters. About the power of the entrenched chieftan-landlords and sheiks and of how impoverished members of ethnic minorities rally to the side of their own exploiters rather than side with the Turkish reformers. Written while Bilbasar was an active member of the Turkish Workers Party.

BUYRUKCU, Muzaffer

Korkum Parmaklari, 1959 (Fingers of Fear)
A novel about the daily lives and struggles of the working poor who live in the shantytowns which surround Istanbul during the mid 1950s.

ENIS, Resat Aygen (Enis Aygen Resat)

Despot, 1957 (Despot)
A novel of the police alliances and the rapacity of criminal gangs and drug dealers; their unchecked power over the lives of the poor in Istanbul during the 1950s.

Toprak Kokusu, 1944 (Smell of the Earth)
A somewhat melodramatic novel about a peasant family shattered and scattered by the landlord bosses of an Anatolian village, of the eventual return of one daughter who has become a successful prostitute and who, from a neighbouring town, aids striking workers on the landlord's estate and plots his extermination.

GOKCE, Enver

Panzerler Ustumuze Kalar, 1977 (Panzer Pounce on Us)
A novel about the mass struggles of Istanbul workers during the early 1970s and the use of the Turkish army to crush them. By a jailed and exiled revolutionary poet who translated Pablo Neruda's work into Turkish.

GUNTEKIN, Resat Nuri

Yesil Gece, 1928 (The Green Light)
A novel about the destructive and tenaciously reactionary religious teachers in Turkish provinces and their resistance to modernization; with the still hopeful expectation that Republican reforms would root them out.

Miskinler Tekkesi, 1946 (The Convent of the Wretched)
An early novel dealing with lives of poor ex-peasants who have migrated to the city (Izmir) and who eke out a bare existence in the growing shantytowns there.

HANCERLIOGLU, Orhan

Ekilmemis Topraklar, 1954 (Unsown Lands)
A bitterly ironic novel of the forces driving peasants out of their villages to become migratory workers. Set around an isolated village which has never felt the presence of the central government and which is dumbfounded and suspicious when, after 25 years of paper reforms, the government enters the village with a raft of "development" projects. Details the underside of what Republican populists a generation earlier had fought so hard for but which now leads to the rapid destruction of small peasant farming.

Also Insansiz Sehir, 1953 (Deserted City), Baska Dunyalar, 1962 (Other Worlds), and Buyuk Baliklar, 1958 (The Big Fish), two collections of stories and a novel about the lives of ex-peasant villagers gradually being forced to migrate in search of work, the cultural shock of being cast adrift in inhospitable worlds and the problematic lives they live there.

HIKMET, Nazim (Nazim Hikmet Ran)

Kan Konusmaz, 1936 (Blood Won't Talk, 1965)
A semi-autobiographical novel about a youth coming of age in the last days of the

Ottoman Empire, the chaos and disintegration following W.W.I, the utter
impoverishment of working people in the metropolis of Istanbul and the beginings
of class consciousness and political radicalism.

The Moscow Symphony and Other Poems, 1971 (original 1944)
An English translation of some of Hikmet's poems written in prison during W.W.II.
They deal with the effects of that conflagration on different sectors of the
Turkish people who, whether they know it or not, are part of world wide forces
in conflict.

Poems, 1954
A translation of some of Hikmet's last poems. During his lifetime Hikmet was the
internationally most prominent Turkish writer-poet, often compared with Pablo
Neruda. Themes range from conditions in Turkey to events throughout the world.

The Day Before Tomorrow, 1972, Things I Didn't Know I Loved, 1975, two
posthumously translated collections of Hikmet's poetry.

IZGU, Muzaffer

Gecekondu, 1977 (Shantytown)
A collection of stories dealing with the lives of ex-villagers and migrants
(ranging from the most benighted Turkish hillbillies to politically conscious
and cosmopolitan workers) who have wound up in the shantytowns surrounding the
major Turkish cities in the 1970s.

KARAOSMANOGLU, Yakup Kadri

Yaban, 1932 (Stranger)
A novel about the impoverished and exhausted Turkish peasantry swept along in the
maelstrom of the events following W.W.I and the Greco-Turkish war. Of their
attempts to reconstruct their lives along the lines of the status ante quo and
their inbred fear and hostility to outside (non-village) Turkish reformers of the
1920s. The as yet ephemeral effects of the Republican social reforms in the
countryside.

Ankara, 1934 (Ankara)
A novel about Pasha Kemel Ataturk's campaign to unite Turkey after the collapse
of the Ottoman Empire; the battles to drive Greek and British armies off its soil
in the early 1920s, the consolidation of an authoritarian nationalist regime and
the often stalled and much contested attempts to push through a program of
modernization and reform in the villages and towns of Turkey. By a Republican
technocrat.

KEMAL TAHIR (Kemal Tahir Demir)

Gol Insanlari, 1955 (People of the Lake)
A collection of linked short stories about poor and landless peasants from
Anatolia. Of their lives as migratory labourers in the cities, as temporary
factory workers always on the search for work, their super-exploitation through
kickback deductions, the circumventions of the legal minimum wage and benefits
payments required for permanent workers. "Guest workers" in their own country.
By a veteran, often imprisoned, left wing writer.

Sagirdere, 1952 (Sagirdere), Korduman, 1953 (Blind Mist)
Two novelas set in the late 1940s and dealing with villagers driven to migrate
seasonally to cities in search of work. Their marginal existence in shantytowns,
the increasing rootlessness of their lives and dissolution of the villages they
come from and return to.

Bozkirdaki Cekirdek, 1967 (The Seed of the Steppe)
A novel about the many faceted and cumulatively powerful results of the village
institute program during the mid 1930s to mid 1940s--a populist program of adult
education in villages which attempted to produce peasant teachers, writers,
cadres. How it roused the hostility of local mullahs, mallahs and muktars who
brought pressure to bear against an increasingly conservative national government
which largely disbanded the village institute schools after 1946. A detailed
account of the forces and interests in play and their changing alliances.

Also Kelleci Memet, 1962 (Memet Kelleci), Esir Sehrin Insanlari, 1964 (The People of Prison City), Kurt Kannu, 1969 (Law of the Wolves), three additional social realist novels about the lives of Turkish workers and peasants during the generation after W.W.II; the urbanization, industrialization and proletarianization of Turkey under anachronistically capitalist regimes and the increasingly open class struggle entailed.

KOCAGOZ, Samin

Cihan Soforu, 1954 (The World's Driver), Yilan Hikayesi, 1954 (An Endless Story) Two collections of stories largely revolving about peasant villagers who become enmeshed in migratory labour on commercial farms and in cities. Includes stories about the multifoliate effects of agricultural capitalization and mechanization, of the strategies and relations with labour contractors, of attempts to organize farm workers unions, of the desperation of marginal workers living in urban shantytowns defending their "squatters" shacks against destruction by police.

KRANIK, Orhan Veli

I am Listening to Istanbul, 1971
A posthumously translated collection of poetry ranging from love poems to proletarian and revolutionary ballads about the Turkish people from the 1930s to the 1950s. By a leading Turkish poet of that generation.

MAKAL, Mahmut
Bizim Koy, 1950 (A Village in Anatolia, 1954)
A panoramic documentary novel about the people and institutions of one supposedly typical Anatolian village during the late 1940s. Touches on the incipient decline of peasant farming and the generation of intended government reform which have barely modified age-old patterns of stasis and social oppression within the villages.

Koyumden, 1952 (From My Village)
A sequel to Bizim Koy, dealing with the cumulative effects of economic and social changes towards which the local rulers have proven resilient and cultural reaction has remained unshaken. Also treats the broadening if alienating worlds experienced by the growing numbers of villagers engaged in migratory work, influences which may one day shake out the village bosses.

Memeleketin Sahipleri, 1954 (The Masters of the Country)
A novel which arraigns folk-Islam as a tenacious force of superstition, ignorance and militant servility--the most determined opponent of the populist village institute movement and the master of the countryside.

Yer Altinda Bir Anadolu, 1968 (An Underground Anatolia)
A reportage account of Anatolian villages a generation after Bizim Koy.

NISIN, Aziz (Aziz Nesin)

Istanbul Boy, 1977
A reminiscence novel about growing up in Istanbul during the 1920s; the disparities between the official goals of the Ataturk reforms and the actual lives of Turkish working people and lower middle class in that huge metropolis. Ranges back and forth over fifty years and done with gentle but biting satire by one of the pioneers of social realist writing in Turkey.

ORHAN KEMAL (Mehmet Rasit Ogutcul)

Cemile, 1952 (Cemile)
A documentary novel set in a textile factory in a small Turkish industrial town during the late 1930s and 1940s. Written from the perspective of one of the factory workers and portraying his life and that of his friends and family. One of Orhan Kemel's twenty-eight novels.

Grev, 1954 (Strike)
A novel about a strike by Ankara textile workers who attempt to reduce their twelve hour workday and change the master-servant relations with employers. A

struggle not only for wages and working conditions but against the still potent semi-feudal attitudes carried over from village society and which some of the workers themselves support. Based partly on Orhan's experiences as a labour union activist.

72 nci Cocugu, 1958 (Cell Block 72)
Semi-fictionalized prison memoirs of left wing intellectuals and labour leaders imprisoned in a notorious political jail for their opposition to the NATO-Turkish military regime of the mid 1950s.

Bereketli Topraklar Uzerinde, 1964 (Upon the Fruitful Earth)
A wide ranging novel about the experiences and fates of migratory ex-peasant workers on the large commercial farms and as casual construction and factory workers in the Turkish cities. Their third class citizenship in both locales, without a shred of either traditional or legislative security, the super-exploitation to which they are subject.

Once Ekmek, 1968 (Bread First)
A collection of stories about Turkish working people in cities and villages during the 1960s.

PAZARKAYA, Yuksel

Oturma Izni, 1970 (Residency Permit)
A collection of stories dealing with Turkish "guest workers" in West Germany in the late 1950s and 1960s. The Turkish ghettos with their ongoing internal conflicts and the use of such workers as cheap and dirty labour in a European version of the American "bracero" system.

SABAHATTIN ALI

Kuyucakli Yusuf, 1932 (Yusuf of Kuyucak)
A novela dealing with the backwardness, the feudal and theocratic oppression and the violent blood feuds in village Turkey during the early 1930s, virtually untouched by national laws. Told through the story of a young boy, the sole survivor of a peasant family which has been wiped out by a village chief. This work was the forerunner of socialist realist novels in Turkey.

Cilli, 1936 (Freckled)
A novela about a young girl who is inexorably forced into becoming a prostitute; her frantic, brutal and ultimately fatal life in the saloon and brothel district of Izmir during the 1930s where neither hope nor inner human decency (no matter how tenacious) can survive.

Kurt Ile Kuzu, 1940 (The Wolf and the Lamb)
A novela about the total corruption, arbitrary power and unchecked brutality of the Istanbul police toward that city's working class and poor.

Yeni Dunya, 1943 (World)
A collection of some of Sabahattin's most militant stories about work and the emerging struggles in Turkish villages and cities of the time. About the alloy of traditional and new ethos among Turkish working people. Also Degirmen, 1935 (Mill), Kagni, 1936 (Oxcart), and Ses, 1936 (Voice), three collections of stories and reportage sketches of the endless varieties of poverty, injustice and back-wardness throughout Turkish society in the 1930s.

Cirkince, 1944 (A Little Ugly)
An autobiographic account of Sabahattin's youthful and idealistic beliefs about Turkish society juxtaposed to his discovery of the real Turkey in later years. Sabahattin came from Turkish Macedonia (now a part of Bulgaria), became a journalist and was one of the first socialist novelists in Turkey. Repeatedly jailed for his writing, he was killed while attempting to flee the country in 1948. Most of Sabahattin's works were reprinted in Turkey during the 1970s.

YASA, Ibrahim

Hasanoglan: The socio-economic structure of a Turkish village, 1957
A western sociological study of a "typical" Turkish village during the 1950s done

by a leftist Turkish sociologist. Deals with the bases of political and economic power within the village and their articulation with external power holders. Documents the deepening crisis of villages, their dependence upon labour migration, and portrays the lives of migratory village labourers in the shantytowns around the cities.

YASHAR KEMAL (Yasar Kemel Gokceli)

Ince Memed, 1955 (Memed, My Hawk, 1961)

The first of Yashar Kemel's novels about the impoverished shepherd peasantry of a mountain region of Anatolia in southeastern Turkey. Memed is set during the 1920s and 1930s amid the continuing tribal-feudal conditions inherited from past centuries. An extraordinarily rich and vital account of the lives of villagers, chieftains and peasant bandits with the spasmodically modernizing Turkey barely visible on the margins of that world. Yashar Kemel was a peasant youth and later migrant worker from one such Anatolian village. He received almost six years education in a village institute school before being expelled, later became a member of the Central Committee of the Turkish Workers Party and is a recurrent candidate for the Nobel Prize for Literature. Memed is probably the most widely translated Turkish novel of this generation.

The Wind From the Plain, 1963, Iron Earth, Copper Sky, 1965, The Undying Grass, 1968

An epic trilogy novel of Anatolia, revolving around the events, lives and beliefs of the members of one peasant village in the Taurus mountains; the impress of past feuds and claims, of lowland landlords, the local folk reinterpretations of Islam, its saints and alloyed reaction which nevertheless also serves to resist external exactions. The mutual aid and mutual distrust within the villages and the less-than-beneficial role of the central government--which rarely proceeds past making deals with and working through the regional landlords. Also the seasonal migration of impoverished peasants as harvest labour in the lowland commercial farms, where they come in contact with emerging full scale capitalism. Also Anatolian Tales, 1964, a collection of stories about the Anatolian peasantry and others from the 1930s to 1950s.

They Burn the Thistles, 1969

The continuing account of the peasantry of the Taurus mountains in the 1950s and of how the lowland landlords begin to reach into the mountain villages to take over that land. How money lending, foreclosure, judicial corruption, and murder are used to free peasant lands for landlord enterprise.

The Lords of Akchasz, 1974 or Murder in the Ironsmith's Market, 1979

A novel revolving around the bloody feud between two landlord families on the Chukusova Plain--one of the locales where the now wage working Anatolian villagers migrate. The profound changes wrought by mechanization and capitalization in the late 1940s and 1950s.

Kuslar Da Gitti, 1978 (The Birds Too are Gone)

A novel which evokes the shock, turmoil and daily hardships of ex-peasants along with old urban workers who are both part of the Istanbul proletariat of the 1960s. Portrays their resilience, vitality and combativeness in these new conditions.

IRAN

AFGANI, Mohammad Ali

Shuhar-i Ahu Kanum, 1962 (The Husband of Ahu Kanum)
A massive novel about the lives, culture and outlook of the reactionary sectors
of urban Iran; focused on the members of the bakers' guild in Teheran during the
1950s as they represent the artizanal-petty merchant elements linked to the
Shi'ite clergy. Dissects the ideology of Iranian working and lower middle class
reaction and is woven around the tale of a woman who sets out to keep her husband
out of the clutches of a self-liberating adventuress. About the tensions and
conflicts within this stagnant social sector. Written in prison by an army
officer who was involved in an attempt to overthrow the Shah. Said to be one of
the major Iranian novels of the past generation.

AL-E-AHMAD, Jalal

Did u Bazdid, 1945 (The Exchange of Visits)
A collection of stories which criticize clerical superstition and hypocrisy;
portray the degradation of life in city slums and denounce the social and
political oppression of the Iranian masses. Written by a left Islamic nationalist
from a clerical family.

Mudir-i Madrisa, 1958 (The School Principal, 1974)
A novel dealing with the nepotism and class favouritism which existed in the
Iranian education system during the Pahlevi regime, and of the suppression of
those teachers who wish to use the school system to improve the lot of the
Iranian poor.

'ALAVI, Buzurg (Bozorg 'Alavi)

Chamadan, 1934 (Suitcase), Varaq-Pariha-yi Zindan, 1941 (Prison Notes), Nama-ha,
1952 (Letters)
Three collections of stories and sketches (including underground and prison
memoirs) about social life and political conditions in Persia of the 1930s and
early 1940s. By a pioneer communist writer who was possibly the internationally
best known Iranian author of his generation.

Panjah-u-sa Nafar, 1942 (Fifty-three Men)
A novel about the backgrounds and prison lives of fifty-three political internees
arrested with 'Alavi in 1937 who went on to found the Tudeh (Workers) Party while
in jail. Also see his Kampfendes Iran, 1958 (Struggling Iran), an account of
the underground struggles against the CIA-Shah dictatorship in Iran during the
1950s.

Chashmhayash, 1952 (Her Eyes)
A massive novel of Iranian society from the late 1930s to the eve of the Shah
Pahlevi dictatorship in the early 1950s, as seen through the experiences and
thoughts of a group of radical Iranian intellectuals. An epic novel of a
generation.

Geschichte und Entwicklung der Modernen Persischen Literatur, 1964 (History and
Development of Modern Persian Literature)
A literary history which also provides an overview of social and political
developments in Iran from the begining of the 20th century to the 1960s.

ANSARI, Rabi

Jinayati Bashar, 1930 (Human Traffickers)
A somewhat melodramatic novel about a real-enough Iranian problem; about organized
prostitution, the vicious and compulsive nature of the enterprise, the brutal
and short lives of girls and women involved. This was a major theme in early
Iranian protest literature.

Sizda-yi Nawruz, 1932 (The Thirteenth Day of the Year)
A Kurdish novel set around the festivals of the Persian New Year during the Riza Khan period of the mid 1920s. It unfolds to show the corruption, poverty and misery of the Kurdish peasantry (in village and town) behind the scenes of the festivities.

BEHRANGI, Samad

The Little Black Fish and Other Modern Persian Stories, 1976
A collection of stories for children and allegories for adults; it describes the lives of peasants and working people in Iran under the Shah Pahlevi regime in the 1960s and contrasts their lot to that of the new middle and upper classes in an understated but biting critique.

DASHTI, Ali

Ayyami-i Mahbas, 1933 (Prison Days)
Prison memoirs and reflections by a leading radical liberal newspaper editor during the interwar (1921-1942) period. A detailed denunciation of the corrupt entrepreneurs, police and administrative lackeys and that stratum which enriched themselves in the shade of the state during the initial phase of capitalist development in Iran.

GHARIB, Shapur

The Tin Dome, 1950
A collection of short stories about the heroism of everyday life of ordinary Iranian people under conditions of backwardness, oppression and economic misery. Some powerful and bitter sketches aimed against mullahs and other clerics.

HIDAYAT, Sadiq (Sadiq Hedayat)

Hajji Aqua, 1945 (Haji Aqua)
A novel about an archtypical Iranian opportunist who manages to be on the side of every political grouping in power from Riza Shah in the late 1920s to the Allied occupation in W.W.II. Portrays the servility and calculating sychophancy inherent in a society which allows opportunism to go unchallenged.

Farda, 1946 (Tomorrow)
A novela about two Iranian workers searching for work in Teheran in the months immediately after W.W.II, a period when the Tudeh party and other left wing forces were part of the governing coalition. The protagonists' lives are little touched by those governmental developments and they are realistically pessimistic about what their futures hold.

Buf-e-kur, 1942 (The Blind Owl, 1964)
A surrealist novel about the seemingly inescapable oppression and brutality (both by the powerful and the oppressed themselves) in Iran in particular but also in the world in general. A syncretistic brew of reality and mystic escapism incorporating "universal" religious philosophies and figures past and present. Naturally hailed by literarians as the greatest novel from Iran but also praised by veteran left Iranian writers such as Buzurg 'Alavi.

JAMALZADA, Muhammad Ali

Jeki Bud, Jeki Nabud, 1922 (Once Upon a Time, 1928
A collection of stories about the lives of "common people" in Persian villages and towns during the W.W.I period. Originally serialized and written in colloquial Farsi, it was one of the first pieces of modern Iranian fiction and raised a storm of controversy in Iran because of its irreverant treatment of clerical and earthly notables. Jamalzada spent the interwar years in Europe, mainly as an official in the League of Nations International Labour Organization.

Ra-ab Nama, 1948 (The Drainage Controversy)
A novel set in the backstreets of Teheran of the time and revolving around the attempts of a group of neighbours to get a water main unplugged. Touches on the total indifference of municipal departments, the scams of building

contractors and the squabbles between neighbours themselves, who try to load the cost of repairs onto one another. Told as an exasperated satire of Iranian society.

Kuhna U Naw, 1959 (Old and New)
A collection of stories touching on a variety of social problems in Iran in the 1950s. A bemusedly tolerant sermon on the theme that it is impossible to live an honest life in a corrupt society.

KHUDADADA, Ahmad Ali

Ruz-i Siyah-i Kagar, 1926 (The Black Fate of Workers), Ruz-i Siyah-i Ra'iyat, 1927 (The Black Fate of Peasants)
Two reportage accounts which detail the oppression, corruption and exploitation under which workers and peasants live in the Iran of Riza Shah regime. Influenced by the earlier Narodnik literature of Russia, and written by a pioneer Iranian Social Revolutionary.

MAS'UD, Muhammad

Tafrihat-i Shab, 1932 (Night Diversions), Dar Talash-i Ma''ash, 1932 (In Quest of a Living), Ashrafi Makhluqat, 1934 (The Noblest of Creatures)
A trilogy novel revolving around the pervasive decay, idleness and decadence of the only recently emerged Iranian middle class. Set during the Riza Shah regime of the 1930s, it is a gloomy portrait of drunkenness, brothel-going, endemic stupidity and self-seeking by the "modern" and "educated" Iranian bourgeoisie of the period.

Gul-ha'i-ka dar Jahanam Mi-ruyad, 1942 (Flowers That Grow in Hell), Bahar-i Umr, 1944 (The Spring of Life)
A two volume novel of Iran during the interwar years, done in the form of letters by an Iranian intellectual to an ex-girlfriend in England. Describes his youth in a semi-medieval peasant village with its gradations of poverty, of the ignorance and xenophobia of the religious teachers/preachers, of the savagery of the shifting local power holders. The other theme is the exclusion of all unconnected to wealth or power and the protagonist's inability to utilize his training after returning to Iran. It touches on the deepening reaction among the Iranian bourgeoisie during the late 1930s and their drift toward an alliance with European fascism. The Allied occupation of Iran in 1942 shakes up the political rulers but does not change the basic nature of the ruling class.

NUSIN, Abdolhosein

Horus-e Sahar, 1947 (Early Crowing Cock)
A play which depicts the profiteering of merchants and industrialists in extracting the last ounce of labour from their employees but also portrays the emerging union and workers resistance in post W.W.II Iran. By a dramatist who translated and staged some of Maxim Gorky's works in Iran during that period.

Han O Digaran, 1959 (Han and the Others)
A novel which revolves around the initial organization, spasmodic growth and difficulties of the Tudeh (Workers) party in a small provincial town during the 1940s. The partly underground and sometimes quasi-legal conditions of existence, the backgrounds and hopes of the cadres, their actions and the support they sometimes mobilize. Also of the intricate and crosscutting intrigues of the local bosses and notables who are worried as much by their own class rivals as by the working class movement.

RAFFAT, Donne

The Caspian Circle, 1978
A novel which revolves around a few weeks in the life of a middle class Iranian during a trip to a resort area on the Caspian Sea in 1962. This being a framework for the collage descriptions of massive violence, smouldering revolt, police rule, corruption and daily public scandals under the "Shah of Shahs" regime.

ISRAEL

AVNERI, Uri

Israel Without Zionists, 1968

A collection of essays which propose a federated Jewish-Palestinian state in
which the interests and national identity of both are protected but in which the
apartheid and repression which have evolved in contemporary Israel are abolished.
Equally a denunciation of the radical right which was then coming to power in
Israel by a founder of the later "Peace Now" movement. Interestingly, Avneri does
not stem from the traditions of the labour Zionists but was a member of the Irgun
during the 1948 Arab-Israeli war and later an independent member of the Knesset.
Also see Arie Bober (ed.), The Other Israel, 1972, a collection of statements
issued by the Israeli Socialist Organization, an ad hoc grouping which existed
as a dissent group between 1967 and 1972, when it was broken up by the then
Labour government.

BRENNER, Yosef Haim

Breakdown and Bereavement, 1970 (original 1920)

A famous novel about the "first wave" of Jewish settlers in Palestine; a semi-
autobiographic and sometimes satiric account of the still small Jewish community
in Turkish ruled Jerusalem of circa 1911. In part it portrays the re-establishment
of an eastern European ghetto existence concentrated mainly in a few major
Palestinian towns, the assorted pilgrimage scams, the pomposity and charity ward
mentality of the directors of the Zionist settlement funds, the national chauvinism
and sectarianism within the Jewish community. At writing, Brenner still saw the
possibility of an equitable Jewish and Palestinian society emerging in the region.

ELON, Amos and HASSAN, Sana

Between Enemies, 1974

A short, somewhat hokey, juxtapositioning of views about Jewish-Arab relations
within Israel and in the region, subtitled "A compassionate dialogue between an
Israeli and an Arab". Elon later became a critic of the "excesses" of the Begin
government in its most recent invasion of Lebanon.

HANDEL, Judith

Rehov Ha-Madregot, 1954 (The Staircase Street)

A novel about the ingathering of Jewish refugees to Israel in the years immediately
after independence; the cultural shock which many immigrants face in readjusting
to a new life and the only gradually and partially changed divisions between
Oriental and Western, East and West European, rich and poor Jews. Revolves
around the courtship and marriage of two young immigrants from disparate Jewish
backgrounds whose families initially oppose the alliance. In a similar vein,
Mel Ohel, (The Bridge), 1955, a novel about a poor immigrant Yemenite family in
Israel. Of the culture shock and changes experienced by the orthodoxly
patriarchal family as a daughter refuses to accept the squalor and poverty of their
lives and goes off to work in a factory on her own. Says Reuben Wallenrod of
this genre, "At first glance these novels remind the reader of the proletarian
novels of the thirties. In the latter, class differences led to class struggle
as the only means by which the desired goal could be reached. In the Israeli
novels, however, the emphasis is mainly on cultural and traditional barriers and
the goal is reached through the unifying visions of the people."

LANGER, Felicia

With My Own Eyes, 1975

A documentary account by an Israeli woman civil rights lawyer; about her legal
defense of Israeli Arabs prosecuted for a variety of political offenses and

including documentation of the use of torture and systematic suppression of any
sort of Arab dissent mounted by Israeli police apparatus and administration.
"Grim and terrifying reading", but also of the human decency and lingering
commitment to social justice among some Israelis. Deals mainly with the post
1967 period.

MEGGED, Aharon

Ha-hai 'al ha-Meth, 1970 (The Living on the Dead, 1970)
A novel revolving around an Israeli writer who has contracted to do a biography
of a founder of the State of Israel only to discover that his subject's "heroic"
qualities are matched by unsavory features which he cannot dismiss and which are
not allowed by the official sponsors of the biography. It represents some of
the recent criticisms of the chauvinistic underpinnings of the Israeli society
even before the Begin-Irgun regime.

Ha-Hayim ha-Ketsarim, 1978 (The Short Life, 1980)
A quizzical novel about a middle aged Sabra insurance salesman and his literary
wife living their rather self centered and disengaged lives as part of the
Israeli establishment. Megged gradually introduces the environment of deepening
racism and militarism amid broad sectors of Israeli society (as well as the
historical background of Begin's Betar and other ultra-rightist groups over the
previous fifty years) through the reminiscences of some of the characters. Set
on the eve of the 1967 war which incorporated the remainder of Palestine and its
population under Israeli colonial control.

SHAHAK, Israel

The Non-Jew in the Jewish State, 1975
A collection of official Israeli policy statements, laws and administrative
decisions which document the racial-theocratic bases of Israeli law and government.
The workings of Zionism as it affects non-Jewish populations in Israel. By the
courageous chairman of the Israeli League of Human Rights. Also his Israelis
Versus Israel, 1970, a collection of dissenting articles about the deepening
racism and militarism gripping Israel and of the opposition by some Israelis.
As well, Israel Shahak and Daniel Berrigan, Arabs and Jews, 1974.

SHAHAM, Nathan (S. Katz)

Haloch Wa-Shob, 1972
A novel about a young woman from a kibbutz background who goes to London for a year
and comes to want to be accepted as herself. Recounts her gradual break with her
family's self image (i.e. pioneers dedicating their lives to establishing a
country) and her decision to live her own life, unbound from prescribed allegiances
and responses expected of her as "An Israeli". Not an especially radical theme
except when juxtaposed to the racial loyalties demanded by current western
Zionists. It may be an especially evocative theme for those hundreds of
thousands of native-born Israeli Jews who have emigrated from Israel over the last
generation.

SHAMIR, Moshe

Ha-g'bul, 1966 (The Border)
A novel revolving around reminiscences of childhood and youth in a kibbutz from
the 1920s to the war of independence in 1948. Looks back at the visions of
that earlier period and investigates the gulf between the now middle aged leftish
Sabra and both the visiting American-European Zionists and the deepening
nationalist fervour in Israel which demand allegiance to views he does not hold.

My Life with Ismael, 1970
Reminiscences of Arab-Jewish relations in Palestine/Israel during the author's
lifetime and how these have become increasingly embittered and colonial,
especially during the 1960s.

TAMMUZ, Benjamin

Ha Pardes, 1971 (The Orchard)
An allegorical novel about the long drawn out disputes relating to an apple orchard

acquired by an early Jewish settler with kinsmen among the Palestinians in 1913.
The tumult of W.W.I, the British mandate and waves of new Jewish settlement
during the interwar years. The division of the protagonist's descendents into
"Arabs" and "Jews" during the 1948 war of independence. Ends with both branches
of the original family dying out and the orchard sold for housing tracts to
contemporary Israeli suburbanites who are equally removed from the lives of both
Palestinians and the original Jewish settlers. The hostilities of past and the
co-legacy of Palestine remains unresolved. Also his novel B'Sof Ma'arab, 1966
(At the Edge of the West).

TIMERMAN, Jacobo

The Longest War - Israel in Lebanon, 1982
A volume of angry journalistic reflections about the 1982 Israeli invasion of
Lebanon, its self-righteous decimation of cities and the Palestinian population
there and its open alliance with murderous self-styled Lebanese fascist forces.
Also a shocked and contentious critique of the militarism, theocracy and ethnic
chauvinism which has swept Israel so far from its original image as a European
social democracy. By the famous left-liberal editor and political prisoner in
Argentina who was a refugee to Israel.

YEHOSHUA, Abraham B.

Mul Ha-Ye 'Aroth, 1968 (Facing the Forests)
A collection of three short novelas, the title work being about a Jewish student
of Crusader Palestine and archaeology who gets a job as a watchman over an
Israeli state forest. In the process of his work he befriends a family of
displaced Arab shepherds and later discovers that the forest covers the remains
of a destroyed Arab village whose roots go back millenia. He sets about
unearthing the history of the village but in the process the past injustices
(particularly the mass expulsion of Arab inhabitants after 1948) are rekindled,
which leads the Arab shepherd to set fire to the forest resulting in the remains
of the village being uncovered for all to see.

Bit'hillath Qayiz '70, 1972 (Begining of Summer '70)
A novel of the creeping anomie and disquiet among Israeli Sabras about the
direction their personal lives are taking in the context of an increasingly
sectarian, class divided and military-minded state. Set during a spuriously
"uneventful" moment of time. Also his Three Days and A Child, 1971, a collection
of stories about life in Israel during the late 1960s.

YIZHAR, S.

Sippure Mishor, 1964 (Stories of the Plain)
A collection of stories by a Sabra who surveys the changing ethos of Israel in
the early 1960s; the growing individualism,..callousness and rejection of past
visions for an equitable society seen through reminiscences.

Midnight Convoy, 1969
A collection of stories about the Israeli-Arab war of 1948 by a former war
correspondent; it emphasizes the unreflective toughness and self confidence of
the Israelis, touches on the degree of sympathy which some in that earlier
generation of Israeli soldiers had toward the Palestinians, but underlines the
message that Israel will take what it needs, regardless of any question of rights
or wrongs.

YUDKIN, Leon I. and TAMMUZ, B. (eds.)

Meetings With the Angel, 1973
An anthology of stories about facets of Israeli society mainly during the post
1967 period. Also see Leon Yudkin's Escape into Siege, 1974, a readable and
often revealing survey of Israeli literature since 1948, revolving around the
psychological and cultural changes in that country as charted by a dozen major
authors.

PALESTINE/PALESTINIAN

AL-ASMAR, Fouzi

To Be An Arab in Israel, 1978
An autobiography of a Palestinian growing up in British Mandated Palestine
during the 1930s and early 1940s and caught up in the first Arab-Israeli war.
Documents the massive forced exodus of Palestinians from their homes during and
following that conflict and the institutionalized inequalities facing those
remaining within the newly established Israel. Deals with becoming colonized
natives in their former homeland and touches on the gradual casting off of former
regional and internal class pretentions by Palestinians of Fouzi's generation.
Also see Sami Hadawi's Bitter Harvest - Palestine 1914-1967, 1967. Sabri Jiryis'
The Arabs in Israel, 1976, is an account based almost exclusively on Israeli
sources, which details how those Palestinians who are Israeli citizens are
juridically and administratively treated as subjegated natives.

AZZAM, Samira

Achia Saghira, 1953 (Small Things), Al-dhil Al-kabir, 1956 (The Great Shadow)
Two novelas dealing with Palestinian refugees in Lebanon and elsewhere in the
region. Portrays the lives of ordinary Palestinian men, women and children, their
everyday struggle to survive and alludes to the exploitation they face in their
"host" countries.

Wa Qissas Okhra, 1960 (And of Other Stories), Al-Insanu Was-sa'a, 1964 (Man and
the Clock)
Two collections of short stories about Palestinians in Lebanon and in the regional
diaspora "characterized by detailed reconstruction of scenes of popular life."
Combines the tension of an emerging national consciousness along with continuing
class differences among the Palestinian refugees. This quality of Azzam's work
has led another Palestinian author to claim that she was the first to write on
what could be considered "proletarian" (as distinct from merely nationalist)
themes. Azzam was also a translator of Steinbeck, Sinclair Lewis and Peal Buck
into Arabic before she died in 1967 at the age of 33.

BARAKAT, Halim

Sittat Ayyam, 1961 (Six Days)
A novela set in a small Palestinian coastal town at the begining of the Israeli-
Arab war of 1948. It focuses on the traditional Arab religious and political
leaders, their total political bankruptcy and the head-in-the-sand lassitude and
divisions which make it impossible to organize any effective defense of the town.
Alludes to what will be lost and foreshadows the expulsion of much of the Arab
population from the region.

Awdat'al Ta'ir Al Bahr, 1969 (Days of Dust, 1974)
A novel about the shock and near despair of Palestinians living in a small town
on the West Bank soon to be overrun by the Israeli army during the 1967 war.
Juxtaposes the lives, memories and smouldering hopes of Palestinian refugees
living in Beirut, driven from their home villages by Israelis some twenty years
earlier. A critical dissection of past Palestinian society and of what living in
the refugee diaspora or under Israeli military rule means. A critical
re-evaluation of traditional Palestinian (and other Arab) society, with its petty
sectional loyalties and narrow interests. Alludes to the immenent emergence of
a new Palestinian society and hope, born in defeat.

DARWISH, Mahmud

Selected Poems, 1971
A collection of poems by a leading left Palestinian poet; dealing with the martyrdom
and struggle of ordinary Palestinians and their oppression by British, Israelis
and Jordanian kings from the 1940s on.

GHAREEB, Edmund and ARURI, Naseer

Enemy of the Sun: Poetry of the Palestinian Resistance, 1970
A brief collection of Palestinian poetry about their emerging collective identity
and beginings of a liberation struggle in the 1960s.

AL-HAKEWATI THEATRE

Mahjoob, Mahjoob, 1981 (Mahjoob)
A collective play using Palestinian folk themes to portray the daily compromises
yet everyday heroism of ordinary Arab workers in the occupied West Bank after
twelve years of Israeli military rule. Of the pressures to accept defeat and a
status as colonized natives but the continuing hopes that a free Palestine will
yet emerge. Performed throughout Europe by Al Hakawati (The Storyteller), a
Palestinian theatre group from East Jerusalem.

INSTITUTE OF PALESTINE STUDIES

Tal-Al-Zaatar, 1978
A documentary account of the inhabitants of the Palestinian refugee camp of
Tal-Al-Zaatar (Beirut) which during the Lebanese civil war of 1976 was surrounded
and besieged for two months by the Christian Falangist militia. The conditions of
that siege and the massacre of the survivors after surrender make it a parallel
to the destruction of the Warsaw ghetto. A horrendous forerunner of the Israeli-
Falangist massacre of Palestinian inhabitants of Sabra and Shatila camps after the
conquest of Beirut in September 1982.

KANAFANI, Ghassan

Rijal Taht al-Shams, 1963 (Men Under the Sun, 1978)
The title novela and other short stories dealing with Palestinian refugees in the
late 1950s and early 1960s, especially the displaced peasants who have suffered
the most by the successive defeats and their attempts to survive in exile. Men
Under the Sun is the simple story of the conditions which drive three Palestinians
to risk their lives by smuggling themselves into Kuwait for the chance of a job,
and who die in the process. Kanafani indicts past and ongoing traditions in
Palestinian and Arab societies as the root of the problem and sees a solution only
through a radical transformation of Palestinian society during the recuperation of
a homeland.

Umm Sa'ad, 1969 (Umm Sa'ad)
A novel of Palestinian families who, after the obliteration of Palestine as a
political entity following the 1967 war, and their reduction to natives within a
Greater Israel, gradually change from being a defeated people to one committed to
national resistance. Both those in the refugee camps on foreign soil and those
still remaining in the West Bank find themselves in ghettos which gradually
creates a combative social transformation. Set around a Palestinian woman who is
a Gorki-like Mother figure.

SAID, Edward W.

The Question of Palestine, 1978
A book length essay on aspects of the Palestinian realities during the 20th
century. It treats the mixed ideological bases of Zionism from late 19th century
colonial roots and its evolution in an exclusionist settlers' state. He presents
Palestinians as the amalgam of indigenous people under changing colonial regimes,
the development of a national consciousness over a half century and their more
recent steps toward social transformation. Although not a history per se, Said
unearths some carefully covered up processes in Palestinian-Israeli relations.
Includes some seminal footnotes and a select annotated bibliography.

SAYIGH, Rosemary

Palestinians: From Peasants to Revolutionaries, 1979
A reportage work using oral and life history accounts; focused on the emerging
political consciousness in Palestine refugee communities around the borders of
Greater Israel since the late 1960s.

SHARQAWI, Abd al Raman al

Watani Akka, 1969 (My Home is Akka)
A play about life in a small Palestinian town of the West Bank during the early 1960s; of local-born Palestinians and recently arrived Palestinian refugees before the region was occupied by Israeli army. By a left Egyptian playwright.

TURKI, Fawaz

The Disinherited: Journal of Palestinian Exile, 1974
A chronicle of a young Palestinian and his family who, with some half million other Palestinians, were driven into exile during and after the 1948 Israeli-Arab war. Their experiences of being shuffled around in refugee camps in Syria and Lebanon, the exploitation and denigration of refugees by the established Arab (Christian and Moslem) bourgeoisie in those countries, the formation of the PLO and the gradual and circuitous evolution of a socialist outlook. Updated edition carries the story to 1974.

JORDAN

ABD AL-RAHIM, Mahmud

(The Martyr), 1948
An epic poem about the "Arab Revolt" during the mid 1930s against the British colonial program of converting Palestine into a Zionist state. Touches on the long drawn out partizan struggle which saw many of the Arab villages destroyed, over a fifth of the Arab population driven into exile and many thousands killed in campaigns which devastated Palestinian-Jordanian society. Actually written in 1936 by a Jordanian guerrilla fighter, it is a purely nationalist elegy. Also see his (Elegy of a Porter), 1946, another long poem about an Arab labourer, the dispossession of his village world and his later life and death as a "native coolie" in colonial Haifa.

SHARIF, Taufiq Abu and ZAWWATI, 'Adil (eds.)

Shi'r al-Muqawama, circa 1968 (Poetry of Resistance)
A collection of Palestinian and Jordanian poetry of resistance to the assorted colonial exactions and dispossessions by British and Israelis from the 1940s on. Includes work by Taufiq Ziyad, Samih al-Qasim and Mahmud Darwish.

LEBANON, SYRIA, IRAQ

LEBANON

ABBOUD, Maroun

A'hadith El-Qaria, 1946 (Village Stories)
A collection of sketches and stories about life in Lebanese peasant villages
during the 1930s under the French Mandate.

AWAD, Tawfiq Youssef

Al Gharif, 1939 (The Bread)
A novel about the lives of peasant villagers on the Lebanon-Syria uplands from
the last years of Ottoman rule, through the arrival of French colonialism after
W.W.I, but focused on the famines of the early 1920s which laid the bases for the
later Druze revolt against Maronite-French rulers. One of the most influential
early realist novels of the region. However by the 1970s Awad had become a
violently reactionary Lebanese "nationalist".

FAKHOURI, Omar

Al-bab Al Marcoud, 1938 (The Inscribed Portal), Adib fil-souq, 1940 (A Writer on
the March), Al-foucoul Al-arbash, 1944 (The Four Seasons)
Three volumes of combined reminiscences, reportage and political essays by a
progressive Lebanese journalist and anti-colonial activist. They touch on the
Arab struggles against Ottoman Turkish rule during W.W.I, of the initial hopes
and growing opposition to the French Mandate over Syria, the Druze revolt of
1925, the splitting off of Lebanon from Syria and the imposition of the current
colonial constitution as well as the bitter guerrilla struggle of the late 1930s.
Touch s also on Fakouri's role in the Lebanese League of Struggle against Nazism
and Fascism, against the Vichy French forces and their Lebanese Phalangist
collaborators during the early 1940s.

SYRIA

ADWAN, Mamdouh

Labudda Min Altafaseel, 1980 (Details Are of Vital Importance)
A collection of left wing poetry castigating the obfuscation and continuing
elitism of Syrian rulers as hidden behind a facade of nationalist and "left"
rhetoric.

BAKDASH, Khaled

Al-Islam Wa'l-qadiyyah Al-wataniyyah, 1948 (Islam and the National Question)
One of a number of political essays on the question of religion, nationality,
class and colonialism by the secretary of the Syrian Communist Party. For a
generation Bakdash was one of the leading left spokesmen in the Middle East, in
exile from Syria after 1964.

SAFADI, Mouta'

Hizb al Ba'ath, Ma'sat al-mawled, Ma'sat al'Nihayah, 1964 (The Ba'ath Party, the
Tragedy of its Birth and End)
A political analysis of the obscurantism and self-interested power broking in the
ruling Syrian Ba'ath party (a self styled "Arab Socialist" group). By a playwright,
poet and literary critic who came to support a Marxist view of the needs of
Syrian society.

IRAQ

ANNAWAB, Mudhaffar

Watariyat Laylia, 1976 (Nocturnal Tunes), Lilrail Wa Hamad, 1978 (For Hamad and for the Train)
Two collections of poetry which focus on the struggle of the Palestinians as symbolic of the struggles of the Iraqi and other peoples against external oppression and the betrayal and repression by the ruling classes of the respective Arab countries.

AL-BAYATI, Abdul Wahab

A Mirror for Autumn, 1974
A collection of poetry by a veteran Iraqi communist poet and playwright now in exile. They touch on a wide array of themes, including the repeated "betrayal" of the Iraqi working class and peasantry in the series of bloody military regimes which have ruled Iraq over the last two decades.

DHUL NYUN, Ayyub

La Main, La Terre et l'Eau, 1959 (Hand, Land and Water)
A novel about the Iraqi peasantry during the post W.W.II years under the King Fiesal regime. By a leading left Iraqi writer.

La Fille du Pont, 1954 (The Girl of the Bridge)
A novela about the quasi-legal labour movement and nationalist resistance which surfaced in 1948 to challenge the neo-colonial agreements which continued Anglo-American oil company hegemony over Iraq.

Stories of Vienna, 1957
A collection of stories about experiences of exile in Austria during the 1950s, reflections on past events and the ongoing developments in Iraq as they touch a committed socialist writer barred from returning to his own country.

NOURI, Abd-el Malek

Nachid Al-Ard, 1954 (Song of the Earth)
A novel which combines a simple folk tale and surrealistic elegy; revolves about a journalist who is fed up with the hypocrisy and servile opportunism of bureaucrats and the middle class in Baghdad during Fiesal's neo-colonial regime. His vision of Iraq's history, interweaving the Euphrates, its lands and peasant people, into an enduring force that will one day blossom.

TEKERLI, Fouad

Al Quindil Al Mountafiq, 1959 (The Dead Lamp)
A novel about the lives of poor Iraqi peasants during the previous generation.

Quissas Moukhtar, 1961 (Stories of Mouktar)
A collection of social realist stories about life in various sections of Iraqi society from the late 1940s to late 1950s.

ADDENDUM

A body of unseen but supposedly progressive drama by Iraqi playwrights of the 1950s and early 1960s may also be of interest. Said Mustafa's (New World), 1951 and Muneer-al-Yaseen's (Struggle in the Dark), 1957 are themes revolving around opposition to the backwardness and strictures of Islamic fundamentalism. Fuad Attikarly's (Somebody), 1954 is one of a large number of plays dealing with women's oppression in Iraq. Yousif-al Ani's (I'm Your Mother, Shakir), 1959, Nouril-deen Faris' (Rise Slaves), 1960, Abdul Bakri-al Saad's (The Arab Dawn), 1962 are calls for basic social reform after the coup which overthrew the Royalist regime in 1958. Abdul Al-Bayati's (Trial in Nisabur), 1963 is a play about the social and political residues of Iraq's autocratic and neo-colonial past as it carries over and distorts attempts to create a new society. Also Mohammed Djawahiri, a revolutionary Iraqi poet of the 1950s.

EGYPT

AWAD, Louis

Al'Anqa, Au Tarikh Hassan Miftah, 1966 (original 1949) (The Phoenix, the History of Hassan Miftah)
A novel set in neo-colonial Egypt under King Farouk during the mid to late 1940s. It portrays daily life in Cairo through the eyes of a radical but otherwise "typical" middle class Egyptian; his encounters with myriad petty corruption and structural social injustices, the teeming ignorance and decay in the Giza old quarter of that city. It touches on underground political opposition (both of the right and the left) and alludes to the impoverished Egyptian masses' glorification of and cultural proximity to the very forces which oppress them. Revolves around the social distance between the radical middle class individual and the urban poor and examines the ease with which left wing bourgeoisie gradually settle back into their class perogatives, regardless of however much they oppose the conditions which prevail in Egypt. Awad was a Coptic intellectual, a Princeton university professor, an early Marxist journalist and sometimes editor of Al Ahram whose novel was long banned in Egypt.

BADAWI, Mahmoud Al

Al Dhiab Al-Gai'a, 1960 (The Hungry Wolves)
A family chronicle set in upper Egypt and touching on the revolt of peasantry against large landholders during the first decade of the 20th century.

Al A'rag Fil Mina, 1958 (The Sweat of the Harbour), Al Araba Al-Akhira, 1961 (The Last Car)
Two novels about life in peasant villages and towns of upper Egypt during the previous generation by a journalist of village origins. Badawi was also a translator of Gorki and other Soviet authors into Arabic in the 1940s.

HUSSEIN, Mahmoud (ed.)

Class Conflict in Egypt, 1945-1970, 1973
A collection of articles surveying the components and character of the Egyptian peasantry, rural and urban working classes, their changing class consciousness, alliances and struggles from the end of W.W.II and through the various phases of proto-colonial and Nasserite Egypt.

IDRIS, Yusuf

Arkhas Layali, 1954 (The Cheapest Night's Entertainment, 1978)
Idris' most widely translated collection of short stories, dealing with the social decay and injustice in the everyday (and night) lives of people in an old quarter of Cairo. The unchanged traditions of corruption and anomie in late 1940s as recounted by a left wing doctor whose work took him into that district.

In the Eye of the Beholder: Tales of Egyptian Life, 1978
A collection of stories about Cairo life; from the petty bourgeoisie to brothel inhabitants.

Jumhuriyat Farahat, 1956 (Farahat's Republic)
A collection of sardonic stories which counterpose official government accounts and press reports about the supposed social reforms of the Nationalist programs against the typical circumventions of laws and policies on the local level. The little changed social injustices of Egypt during the early Nasser period.

Malik Al-Qutn, 1957 (The Cotton King)
A satiric protest play about the speculations and profiteering of a politically connected merchant and large landholder in Nasserite Egypt.

Al Askari Al Aswad, 1962 (The Black Policeman)
A collection of some of Idris' most bitter short stories. The title story deals

with an Egyptian policeman in the late 1940s and 1950s who sees the social
injustices around him both under King Farouk and Nasser. When he finally attempts
to protect some powerless people from a glaring case of injustice he is promptly
sacked.

Al Batal, 1957 (The Hero), A Laisa Kadhalika?, 1958 (Isn't That So?), Akhir
Al Dunya, 1961 (End of the World)
Three collections of short stories touching on the poverty, stagnation and the
lives of ordinary people of Egypt during the 1950s.
Also Al Haram, 1959 (The Sin) and Al 'Aib, 1962 (The Shame), two novels about
life in Nasserite Egypt.

MAHFOUZ, Naguib (Naguib Mahfuz)

Midaq Alley, Cairo, 1966 (original 1944)
A collective portrait of people and life in a side street of the old quarter near
the heart of Cairo during W.W.II, the alley being a central character itself.
A panorama of the traditional urban sectors of Egypt; workers, artizans, peddlers,
luftmenschen, lower middle class officials, men and women. Unstereotyped
accounts of people who combine custom-bound outlook and vital flexibility, on the
edge of the contemporary world which is as yet merely seen in glimpses.

Aulad Haratina, 1959 (Children of Our Quarter)
An account of life in an old section of Cairo during the nationalist "revolution"
of the 1950s, the continuing failings, pettiness, humanity and warmth of the
Cairo poor whose lives are very little changed by social reforms which hardly
trickle down to them. Aulad Haratina was banned during this period of heightened
class conflict within Egypt.

Bain Al-Qasrain, 1956 (Between the Two Castles), Qasr Al-Shauq, 1957 (Castle of
Shauq), Al-Sukkariyya, 1957 (The Sugar Bowl)
A massive trilogy under the general title Ath Thulathiyya (The Trilogy); follows
three generations of an Egyptian family from 1917 to 1945. Each volume named for
a different Cairo district. A document of the complex social and political
currents, of the trajectories of various sectors of the population and the changing
class lines during those formative years.

Miramar, 1967 (Miramar, 1970)
A novel which is an indictment of late Nasserite Egypt, the betrayal of social
reform and the corruption of the governing Arab Socialist Union. The protagonist
is a party member and middle echelon government administrator who comes to see
himself as the "legitimate" inheritor of the traditional perogatives of power.
Of his personal enrichment through under-the-table deals and how he and his class
impede any significant redistribution of national wealth. An autopsy of
bureaucratic opportunism triumphant, with the Egyptian workers, peasantry and
left wing parties defeated or mired in ineffectiveness. Made into a film.

Also Al-Sarab, 1948 (The Mirage), Bidaya Wa Nihaya, 1948 (Begining and End),
Al-liss Wal-Kilab, 1962 (The Robber and the Dogs), Al-Shahhadh, 1965 (The Beggar),
some of Mahfouz many other novels and collected short stories.

MUNIS, Husain

Ahlan Wa Sahlan, 1956 (Welcome)
A satirical novel set in the last years of Farouk's Egypt. It relates the
experiences of a delegation of government supporters from an upper Egypt peasant
village during their visit to Cairo to meet the leaders of the Royalist party.
The quite open corruption and self seeking they encounter, told with pseudo-naive
humour.

NAJM, Ahmad Fuad

Bayan Ham, 1976 (An Important Declaration), Ahl Baladi, 1979 (People of My Land)
Two collections of revolutionary socialist poetry which depict the poverty and
sufferings of the Egyptian peasantry and working class under a string of Egyptian
bourgeoisie regimes. Also linked to the struggles for social justice of other
peoples around the world from Cuba to Palestine. By an actual proletarian writer.

SAADAWI, Nawal-el

The Hidden Face of Eve, 1980
Subtitled "Women in the Arab World", it is a survey of the history and socio-
cultural bases of women's oppression in the Arab world and the various facets of
women's liberation over the past century. Includes a chapter on the image of
women in contemporary Arabic literature. By a leading Egyptian feminist, a
medical doctor and author of a dozen books, including the novels (The Absent One),
(A Moment of Truth) and (A Woman at Zero Point). Her conflict with the forces in
power during the Sadat period led to her exile from Egypt.

AL-SHARQAWI, Abd al-Rahman (Abd al-Rahman Al-Sharqawi)

Al Ard, 1954 (The Land, 1962)
An epic novel of the Egyptian peasantry by an "Islamic Marxist" writer. Set in
upper Egypt during the Ismail Sidqi dictatorship of the early 1930s (i.e.,
Sharqawi's childhood background), it revolves around the heterogeneous individuals
in one small peasant village; of their lives, sagacity and superstitions, and the
use of social and religious traditions in pragmatic ways to suit their current
ends. Includes fellahin, landless labourers, landlords and assorted bought-and-
paid-for petty officials, police and mullahs. A wide array of characters and
situations, including some militantly anti-clerical accounts. The aliveness of
folk myths but also of the divisions and self-destructive acts of peasantry
which flow ultimately from their powerlessness. The hidden but deep memory of
lost land and peasant revolts occasionally seeps to surface with the promise that
they will not always be quiescent.

Al Fallah, 1967 (The Peasant)
A novel of peasant Egypt set in the early 1960s. A village formerly belonging to
an Egyptian noble is involved in land reform. Alludes to the gains made under
Nasserite rural reform but also the ascendancy of a new kulak class on its way to
asserting exploitative authority over the poorer peasants, using the Arab
Socialist Union as a vehicle for its interests. Discusses the impetus created by
even the flawed agrarian reform policies and the awakening political consciousness
of the peasantry, yet details the habit of submission and defensive localism which
allows peasants to be manipulated by the new administrators.

Qulub Khaliya, 1957 (Empty Hearts)
A somewhat romantic treatment of peasant life in the late 1930s and 1940s, in
which peasant cunning and wile co-exist with honourable and supportive behaviour
toward fellow villagers. Interlaced with an xenophobic view that colonialism and
foreigners are the prime source of injustice in Egyptian society.

Al Fata Mahran, 1966 (The Lad Mahran)
A play about an Egyptian peasant turned "social" bandit during the turmoil at the
begining of the 20th century. An expansion of a folk tale told by one peasant to
another in the novel Al Ard.

Al Shawari Al Kalfiya, 1958 (The Back Streets)
A novel about the inhabitants of the back streets of Cairo in the interlude
between the overthrow of King Farouk and the Nasser regime. Deals mainly with
peasants who have come to the city to find work, their alternating resiliency and
paralysis when they leave the land and conditions they knew. A host of declasse
figures from other walks of life and a scathing rebuke of the stagnation left by
the former neo-colonial rulers of Egypt.

AL-SHATI, Bint (Bint al-Shati)

Sayyid al-Laba, 1944 (Sayyid al-Laba)
A novela about the forces which drive a woman to becoming a prostitute in order
to support herself and her child.   By a very popular feminist writer with a
melodramatic flair.

Suwar Min Hayatihinna, 1950 (Picture From Their Lives)
A collection of twenty-four stories about "emancipated" (or struggling to become
emancipated) Egyptian women; from upper middle class professionals to peasant
women, the problems and continuing restrictions they face in their lives.

SIDQI, Mohammed

Al Anfar, 1956 (The Wage Earners)
A semi-documentary novel about the everyday lives of the urban working class in Alexandria and Cairo. A not particularly left wing but supposedly authentic account written in colloquial speech by an author who was a member of Alexandria working class at age 15, a labour union official and later journalist.

Al Aydi El Khachina, 1958 (The Rough Hands)
A novel dealing with life in peasant villages of lower Egypt during and immediately after W.W.II. Of the daily rounds of agricultural labourers and tenant peasantry, their quizzical circumvention of religious maxims and their vital reinterpretations of traditional customs. The exactions by the large landlords leads to the formation of a union of agricultural workers, which is finally crushed but not before sowing the seeds of future resistance.

GENERAL ARABIC

CAMPBELL, C.G.

Told in a Marketplace, 1928
A collection of "traditional" secular Arab folk tales from the early 20th century which are strikingly different from the courtly traditions. Some of them express Moslem peasant anti-clericalism and satirize mullahs while the hodja genre tales revolve around how peasants are cheated by all and sundry. Part of a three volume series also including Tales from the Arab Tribes and From Town to Tribe. Collected by folklorist Campbell in the early to mid 1920s, from North Africa to Mesopotamia.

JOHNSON-DAVIES, Deny (ed.)

Modern Arabic Short Stories, 1967
An anthology of short stories, most written in the 1950s and 1960s, by seventeen Arabic authors from Iraq to Morocco. Includes works by Laila Baalabaki, Abdel Salam Al-Ujaili, Walid Ikhlassi, Ghassan Kanafani, Jabra Ibrahim Jabra and others.

MANZALAOUI, Mahmoud (ed.)

Arabic Writing Today: The short story, 1968
An anthology of translated short stories by leading modern Arabic writers, including some work by left wing and Marxist authors.

NORTH AFRICA AND THE SUDAN

ALGERIA

AJAR, Emile

La Vie Devant Soi, 1974 (The Life Before Him)
A novel about an Algerian from the slums of Algiers who supports the FLN during
the war of independence but who sees his hopes for dignity and a better life
disappear with the triumph of the new Algerian bureaucrat-bourgeoisie and is
forced to emigrate to France to find work. Of his life and work there as a
migrant Algerian worker.

BENSOUSSAN, Albert

Frimaldjezar, 1976 (Frimaldjesar)
A reminiscence of childhood in a poor Jewish community of Algeria in the decade
before the war of independence. Describes the mosaic of peoples in the urban
districts, the quality of life and the caste-like boundaries in which North
African Jews and non-French immigrant poor did not fit as either natives or
settlers. The world of oriental Jews in Algeria during the late colonial
period.

BOURBOUNE, Mourad

Le Mont Des Penets, 1962, Le Muezzin, 1968 (The Muezzin)
Two collage novels of the people and life in the Arab old quarters of Algiers and
Constantine during the 1940s. Conveys a feeling of the soon to be shattered but
seemingly unchanging traditional quality of these city dwellers' lives. Written
with verve and the tongue-in-cheek humour of the secular "market tale" genre.

DIB, Mohammed

La Grand Maison, 1952 (The Big House)
The first volume of the trilogy Algerie, Maison is set in a crowded tenement house
filled with families of Algerian workers and petty traders in a small town of
western Algeria during the 1930s and early 1940s. Deals with the growing distance
between the still traditional parental generation and the initial "modern"
generation of Algerian youths.

L'Incendie, 1954 (The Conflagration)
The second volume of Algerie, it deals with developments during W.W.II, the
psychological as well as political upheaval among sectors of Algerian youth and
their "fundamental" break with the quasi-colonial traditionalism which made
Algeria one of the more conservative Islamic societies.

Le Metier A Tisser, 1957 (Work of the Loom)
The final volume of the trilogy, it follows an Algerian man's transition from
youth to parenthood in a rapidly changing world, his gradual appreciation of his
own parents' views but the realization that these are inapplicable in an Algeria
where the war of independence has already begun.

La Danse Du Roi, 1972 (Dance of the King)
An allegorical novel revolving around the Algerian poor caught in the vortex of
the Algerian war and the savagery dispensed by both sides. Dib speaks for them
and for all others caught up in and maimed in wars, justified or not.

DJEBAR, Assia

Les Impatients, 1958 (The Restless)
A novel of the second class status and restricted lives of women, even those of
the modern middle class in contemporary Algeria and of the first faltering claims
for equality. The plot revolves around the attempts of a young woman to be

friends with a man of whom her family disapproves, the increasing familial restrictions she faces and her discussions of women's rights with other women. Djebar was/is one of the leading Algerian "feminist" writers.

Les Enfants Du Nouveau Monde, 1962 (Children of the New World), Les Allouettes Naives, 1967 (The Young Songbirds)
Two novels dealing with the depressed position of women in Algeria and North Africa; their sufferings and participation in the Algerian war of independence and the betrayal of their hopes for social equality in the years following independence. Both treat with the continuing submissiveness of Algerian women as well as attempts to loosen their bonds in an unregenerately patriarchal society. After constant criticism and harassment, Djebar was finally forced to leave Algeria. Also La Soif, 1957 (Thirst), a novel.

FERAOUN, Mouloud

Le Fils Du Pauvre, 1950 (Son of the Poor), La Terre et la Sang, 1953 (Earth and Blood), Les Chemins Qui Montent, 1957 (The Ascending Roads), Jours de Kabylie, 1954 (Kabylian Days)
All four works (three novels and the reportage work Kabylie) are documentary chronicles of the lives of Berber peasants in the Kabyle mountain region where Feraoun grew up. They deal with the everyday lives of Berber villagers, their poverty, internal conflicts, traditionalism, warmth and hopes. Include reflections of Feraoun's own life as an impoverished village teacher in his home region, how he gradually came to oppose French colonialism but could not bring himself to support the FLN.

Journal, 1955-1962, 1962 (Diaries, 1955-1962, 1963)
A secret diary of daily life, fears and sadness amid the increasingly brutal struggles of the Algerian war. Feraoun had fled his village and was living obscurely as a teacher in Algiers. His entries capture the polarization, the pathological and racist fantaticism in what became a multi-layered civil as well as anti-colonial war. They end on the day on which he and five fellow teachers were taken from their classroom and murdered by a squad of OAS (French fascist terrorists). Feraoun's quiet diaries have become known as among the most moving memoirs of that bloody conflict.

MAMMERI, Mouloud

Colline Oubliee, 1952 (The Forgotten Hill)
A novel set in a poor peasant village of the Kabyle mountains during the late 1930s and 1940s. Deals in part with the sense of loss and sadness felt by the first modern educated Berber generation in leaving behind the certainties of their parents' world, as well as the promises of a broader world awaiting them.

Le Sommeil du Just, 1955 (The Sleep of the Just, 1956)
A semi-autobiographical novel of a young Berber from a peasant family who manages to go to school in France (and others of his background who go as migrant labourers) on the eve of W.W.II. Their experiences as natives within France during the German occupation and the protagonist's later return to Algeria as a teacher. Of the disparities between concepts of "French justice" he has been taught and the reality of racism and colonialism in Algeria. The Algerian revolt presented as a struggle against colonialism but not against French per se. Also L'Opium et le Baton, 1965 (Opium and the Stick), a novel.

M'RABET, Fadela

La Femme Algerienne, 1964 (The Algerian Woman), Les Algeriennes, 1967 (Algerian Women)
Two non-fictional accounts about the position of Algerian women during the last generation. La Femme Algerienne deals largely with their contributions and sacrifices in the war of independence and their hopes thereafter, while Les Algeriennes deals mainly with the initial steps toward fuller equality under the first Algerian government headed by Ben Bella but the rapid reinstitution of social conservatism which accompanied the consolidation of native bureaucrat-bourgeoisie regime which followed the 1962 coup.

OUARY, Malek

Le Grain Dans La Meule, 1956 (Grist for the Mill)
A novel about village life among the Kabylia peasantry during the late colonial
period to the early 1950s.

SHARQAWI, Abd al Rahman

Masah Jamila, 1968 (The Tragedy of Jamilla)
A play about a famous heroine of the Algerian war who after independence is
pressured into assuming a cloistered life as a wife and remaining silent about
her demands of equality for Algerian women. By an Egyptian novelist who was a
journalist with the FLN during the struggle for independence.

MOROCCO

BEN BARKA, Abdelkader

El Mehdi Ben Barka, Mon Frere, 1966 (Mehdi Ben Barka, My Brother)
A brief biography of the internationally known spokesman of the Moroccan left,
the original convenor of the Tricontinental Congress, who was murdered while in
France during 1966 by the Moroccan minister of internal security (Mohammad
Ouffkir) with the aid of right wing elements within the French secret service.
Two of Mehdi Ben Barka's own published works are Problemes d'Edification du
Maroc et du Maghreb, 1959 (Educational Problems of Morocco and the Maghreb) and
Option Revolutionnaire du Maroc, 1966 (Revolutionary Option in Morocco).

CHARHADI, Driss Ben Hamed (Mohamed Choukri)

A Life Full of Holes, 1964
A fictional life history of the youth and young manhood of a poor, hard working
(and sometimes thieving) jack-of-all-trades in former Spanish Morocco, told with
tongue-in-cheek humour as a modern marketplace tale. A nominally apolitic but
deftly realist portrait of endemic callousness and exploitation, of an
indifferently repressive government, the minutae of class divisions and lives of
contemporary poor in the small towns of a backward North African society.
Touches on the lives of peasants, artizans, petty traders, government representatives, etc. and their pragmatic (sometimes cynical) personal reinterpretations
of traditional social mores. Translated by Paul Bowles.

CHOUKRI, Mohamed (Driss Ben Hamed Charhadi)

For Bread Alone, 1966
A novel about the lives of the newly urbanized ex-peasantry, the unemployed and
the lumpen proletarian elements of the growing Moroccan cities since independence.
Also see Paul Bowles' Five Eyes, compiled 1979, a collection of short stories
about facets of everyday life in Morocco during the 1970s by A. Yacoubi,
M. Mrabel, A. Boulaich, L. Layachi; with about a half of the book given over to
stories of Mohamed Choukri which continue the deft, laconic style of A Life Full
of Holes.

CHRAIBI, Driss

La Passe Simple, 1954 (Heirs of the Past)
A bitter novel about Islamic fundamentalism and the oppressive know nothingism of
religious teachers and mullahs who were an elemental part of the author's youth.

Le Boucs, 1955 (The Boucs)
An equally bitter novel about the racism, multifoliate indignities and exploitation
visited upon North African immigrant workers in France. "Boucs" being a French
racist pejorative for North Africans.

Also L'Ane, 1956 (The Ass) and La Foule, 1961 (The Mob), two other novels dealing
in part with the experience of Moroccan immigrants in France.

TUNISIA

MEMMI, Albert

Le Statue de Sal, 1953 (The Salt Statue)
An autobiographical novel of a boy growing up in the "semi-medieval" Jewish
quarter of Tunis under French colonialism in the 1930s to late 1940s. The conflict
between his visions of universality (embodied in "French culture") and the
anachronistic demands and group loyalties of his almost illiterate orthodox
parents and their community. A tale of exclusion from both the French colonial
society and the native Arab population.

La Terre Interieure, Entretiens Avec Victor Malka, 1976 (Interior Landscape,
Dialogues With Victor Malka)
Another work on the theme of Statue du Sal, dealing with life in the La Harra
quarter of Tunis during the 1940s and early 1950s as part of an Oriental Jewish
minority under French colonial rule. The rising tide of Arab nationalism
foreshadowing the later Jewish exodus from independent North African states.

ORTZEN, Len (ed.)

North African Writing, 1970
An anthology of stories and extracts by a number of leading North African writers
including Mohammed Dib, Driss Chraibi, Hacene Farouk Zehar, Ahmed Se Frioui,
Mouloud Mammeri, Mouloud Feraoun, Assia Djebar, Malek Haddad, Kateb Yacine. A
very readable introduction.

SUDAN

CHOUKRALLAH, Khogli

Le Cireur de Chaussurers, 1965 (original 1956) (Shoeshine Boy)
A semi-autobiographical novel dealing with the Sudan during the final years of
British colonial rule; the evolving political forces, alliances and emerging class
interests during the 1950s--detailing something of the daily lives of Sudanese
workers in Khartoum. Includes an account of a widespread strike of the period
by a Sudanese exile writer.

IBRAHIM, Abudallah Ali

Bashkatib Fei Iskail H, 1973 (A Functionary at Scale H)
A collection of poetry revolving around the travails and life of an impoverished
white collar clerk trying to scrape by on the lowest government pay scale in
Sudan of 1960s.

IBRAHIM, Salah Ahmed

Ghabat el-Abanus, 1969 (The Ebony Forest)
A collection of poetry revolving around the need for social liberation of the
Sudanese people beyond national independence. Also see Salah A. Ibrahim and
Ali Al Mak's (The Pettite Bourgeois), 1975, a collection of short stories about
the Sudan in the late 1960s and 1970s.

AL-MUBARAK, Khalid

Shari Al Mahatta, 1976 (Station Street), Reesh Al Naam, 1976 (Ostrich Feathers)
Two collections of Sudanese left wing poetry.

SALIH, Tayeh

The Wedding of Zein and Other Stories, 1969
Three long stories about everyday life in a north Sudanese peasant village during
the late 1950s and 1960s, an evocative idyll emphasizing the "timelessness" and
warmth of Sudan peasantry (with poverty and oppression little in evidence) but
with allusions to the proto-class self interests evident in village notables.
A quasi-reminiscence by a polished emigre author who was long a BBC script
writer in London.

AFRICA

Ethiopia and Somalia
Francophone Africa
Nigeria and Ghana
Central and East Africa
Union of South Africa
Other South African
Mozambique and Angola

ETHIOPIA AND SOMALIA

ETHIOPIA

AGONAFER, Enanu (Nagas Gabra-Maryam)

Setanna Adari, 1956 (Doxy)
A more or less realistic novel of a divorced young peasant woman who comes to
Addis Ababa and her progression through various jobs until she becomes a
prostitute. As distinct from the usual morality tales, these jobs provide her
with a substantial education and are initially as much liberating as degrading
(at least when compared to her options as a divorced woman in her native village).
Through her temporary job with an English trading company we get a view of
urbanizing and "modernizing" Ethiopia under Haile Selassie and the growing US
influence in the capital during the 1950s. While the novel ends with the
gradual dissolution of the heroine through drink and abuse, it is more the story
of the oppression of women and of one woman's attempt to escape her lot than the
standard "wages of sin" story.

ALLAMAYYAHU, Haddis

Feqer Eska Maqaber, E.C. 1955 (Love Unto the Grave)
A wide ranging protest novel of the Amharic peasantry and the landlord nobility
of Ethiopia during the late 1940s and early 1950s. A portrait of the feudal
landlords and moneylenders intertwined with totally corrupt police and judges,
of the servile and ignorant church hierarchy and the completely indifferent and
ineffective central government. About the shifta (bandit) gangs who are the
ultimate recourse of the rich when threatened. Touches on the lives of
descendents of former slaves and pariah castes of artizans who are still living
under a kind of ownerless slavery. Revolves around the doings of an Amharic
peasant who because of his own difficulties starts to organize a peasant
movement which demands rent reductions, and of the interlocking forces of
repression which this sets in motion. A leading local landholder becomes
enraged by the mainly cosmetic reform policies broached by the central government
and resorts to hiring shifta bandits to murder the peasant leader, his family and
closest followers. But events have developed so that the lesser landlords fear
that such actions may trigger a full scale peasant revolt against them. An
extensive account of the rural sociology of traditional Ethiopia. ("E.C." preceding
date refers to old Ethiopian calendar, approx. 6½ years behind western dating.)

Tarat Tarat Yamasarat, E.C. 1958 (Tales Are the Basis)
A collection of stories in traditional folk tale style; bitterly ironic and
pessimistic, alluding to the panopoly of injustice and seemingly inescapable
oppression by the feudal rulers and new merchant class of Ethiopia at the
time.

ESTIFANOS YERA-MANGESTU (Yera-Mangestu, Estifanos)

Polisenna Danna Babalagar, E.C. 1965 (Police and Judges in the Countryside)
A novel set in the final decade of the regime ancien; of the pyramiding
corruption and dissolution which sees police, local notables and landlords using
the courts to imprison not only dissidents but anyone without political protection
whom they believe they can extort money or forced labour from. Deals with a case
where local authorities protect a bandit gang for a share of the loot taken.
Despite the prevalent feudal ideology of social fixity and passivity there is a
continual flux of power throughout the society, endemic violence, assassinations
of oppressors and reprisals. But as yet no systematic attempt to overthrow the
system as such. A somewhat more melodramatic rendering of the same theme is
Mamo Weddenah's Yagabbar Leg, E.C. 1965 (Son of a Serf).

GABRA-YASUS, Afawarq (Assaffa Gabra-Maryam)

Endawattacc Qarracc, E.C. 1953 (She Went and Never Returned)
A novel-reminiscence of the Italian conquest of Ethiopia in 1935. A mixture of
melodrama and realism which follows a youth whose family has been killed in the
invasion, his experiences during wanderings throughout the country until he
manages to join a band of Ethiopian Royalist partizans. A number of other subplots
involve love affairs, accounts of the feudal lords who quickly shift to support
the Italian military regime in order to retain their holdings, the internal
divisions and backwardness of the country and the lives of ordinary people swept
away in the war. Alludes to how the feudal system was initially undermined,
with some embittered Ethiopians welcoming even the devil if he will destroy the
traditional system which has enslaved them.

GERMA, Ba'alu

Yahellina Dawal, 1974
A novel prophetically written on the eve of the overthrow of the regime ancien;
dealing with the unbearable exploitation and chaos, of the famine-stricken
regions where merchants and government officials stock pile food to sell at
maximum profits, of the rising hatred of and resistance to the Ethiopian nobility
during the late 1960s. Contains the self-justifications by assorted supporters
of the ruling class, and is formed around the dialogue between two intellectuals
debating the relative efficacy of revolutionary action versus evolutionary
reforms, pointing to events and conditions within Ethiopia as cases for their
arguments.

GUBANNA, Abbe

Alewwalladen, 1962 (I Will Not Be Born)
A novel which begins with the awakening of the hero in his beggar-mother's womb
and who, on seeing the assorted evils of Ethiopian society through her, "refuses
to be born". Nevertheless he is born and during his later life we get a roster
of exposes--of know-nothing Amharic clergy, of doctors and hospitals concerned
only with personal profit, of corrupt government officials no end, of the
bottomless indifference of the wealthy to the sufferings of the mass of
Ethiopians. As well as the inhumanity of the poor towards each other. Includes
a fantasy about a utopian cooperative farm community set up by the hero and its
demise--the impossibility of creating just social relations in an unjust society.
Ends with a military coup which after a few years turns as repressive as the
Royalist regime. The novel was banned shortly after publication. Gubanna was
one of the most prolific Ethiopian authors and his books generally revolved
around veiled exposes of social conditions.

Melkeam, Sayfa-Nabalbal, 1963 (Melkeam, Sword of Flame)
A novela which again revolves around the corruption and poverty of Ethiopian
society of the time and which has a central character expressing support for some
form of utopian "socialist" transformation.

Yapatris Lumumba Asazzan Am Wam Wat, 1964 (The Tragic Fate of Patrice Lumumba)
A play about Patrice Lumumba which ranges from events in Leopoldville at
independence to the boardrooms of multinational companies (especially Union
Minere and its role in Katanga province). Of the wheeling and dealing by UN
troops which facilitate the murder of Lumumba, and in general of a martyr caught
in the clutches of neo-colonialism aided by the worst of African puppets. Drawn
from contemporary documents and UN speeches by the leading conspirators.

Eddel Naw? Badal?, 1970
A novel dealing with the continuing quasi-feudal and new capitalist relationships
combining to create the worst of both worlds. Woven around the protagonist's
reminiscences of the Italian occupation a generation earlier and of his emerging
conclusion that the misrule and repressive exactions of the returning Ethiopian
nobility and new merchant class has become even worse than the Italian
colonialism.

Yaraggafu Ababoc, 1971
A novel which has a "Marxist" protagonist proposing that an organization based on

class struggle must be created to overthrow the regime ancien before any
significant social change can be achieved, and the views of a reformer who plunks
for gradual improvements through education and so forth. A dangerous topic to
broach in print then, even if the author ultimately comes down on the side of
evolutionary reform. A debate shortly superceded by events.

KANE, Thomas L.

Ethiopian Literature in Amharic, 1975
An excellent survey of secular Ethiopian literature (which was mainly in Amhara)
since the end of W.W.II, encompassing virtually the entire span of "modern"
writing in that country. Deals with the swath of morality tales, pulp romances
and contemporary folk tales which increasingly entail themes of dissent and quasi-
realistic portraits of life among the impoverished and disenfranchized sectors of
a voraciously anachronistic society. Kane provides the social contexts of
Ethiopian society and recent history as a background to the works discussed. He
also provides detailed plot outlines of the major titles and translated extracts.
An outstanding survey, especially since virtually none of the items listed here
have been issued in English translation.

KIDANE, Ayyala

Bunna Qagiwa, E.C. 1959 (Coffee Girl)
A novela about an initially vital and independent young woman who becomes a
prostitute in Addis Ababa and the catalogue of exploitation and brutality she
suffers at the hands of police, the hospitality industry, customers and even from
other urban poor. Supposedly one of the better accounts of that genre and a social
protest (rather than a morality tale) in that it alludes to the hypocrisy and
injustice within Ethiopian society generally.

MANAYE, Yelma

Abbaten Negarrin, E.C. 1960 (Tell Me Who My Father Is)
A novel about a prostitute as a symbol of whole classes of people who are excluded
from basic social rights and the most elemental legal protection. The trials and
tribulations of one woman, her alloyed wisdom and ignorance, vitality and despair,
as seen largely through the eyes of her school aged son.

TAKLA-HEWARYAD, Garmaccaw

Araya, 1955 (Araya)
One of the first "modern" Ethiopian novels; semi-autobiographical and historical
account mainly of the events surrounding the Italian-Ethiopian war of 1935-40.
Seen through the eyes of one of the few western-educated Ethiopians of the time,
the narrator (Araya) describes the surrealistically medieval milieu in Addis
Ababa around Emperor Haile Selassie's court in 1935, the war-like but hopelessly
anachronistic army of feudal levies which typifies the backwardness of the
country. Describes the battle of My Caw, after which the Ethiopian Empire
rapidly crumbles into its warring factions and ethnic divisions. Of the
reasonable indifference of many Ethiopian serfs and the widespread collaboration
of many feudal lords with Italian military who offer a form of indirect rule.
A chronicle which, in an understated manner, presents the fatal flaws in
Ethiopian traditional society. It details the five years of ineffective guerrilla
warfare and arrival of the British army in 1940 which reinstalls the
court of "The Lion of Judah". The regime ancien is reimposed with nothing
learned and no advances made. The story ends in 1950 with Araya (a secret
admirer of the French Revolution)as an elderly man who has given up hope of
change in Ethiopia during his lifetime but who sees the possibility of an
uncertain yet fundamental transformation within the lifetime of his son.

WARQU, Dannaccaw

Adafres, 1960 (Adafres)
A novel revolving around a western-educated, aspirantly middle class university
student (Adafres) who returns to Ethiopia to administer a largely cosmetic
program of rural development. Despite his self image as a catalyst of social

change he rapidly falls into the pattern of an indulgent opportunist. When he
attempts to do something of worth his bumbling naivety brings trouble to all who
heed him. In this, Adafres is a charicature of the educated "modern"
officialdom of the time, their complaints about the "backwardness" of the
impoverished peasantry who they are quite ready to sell out, as well as their
hidden feelings of superiority to the traditional political powers, which they
ultimately serve as much as any hireling. A biting character study set against
a background of oppression, simmering ferment and undirected revolt among the
peasantry and minority groups.

SOMALIA

FARAH, Nuruddin

From A Crooked Rib, 1970
A short novel about a "peasant" girl who migrates to Mogadishu in the 1960s, is
seduced and variously exploited in the city but responds by becoming an adept
and tough petty operator herself. Of rural innocence and powerlessness converted
into urban street wisdom, with an ending of redemption through "true" love. Told
in a quizzical folklore style by an upper class Somali emigre.

FRANCOPHONE AFRICA

SENEGAL

KANE, Cheikh Hamidou

L'Aventure Ambigue, 1961 (The Ambiguous Adventure, 1976)
A semi-autobiographical novel of a young Senegalese who goes to study in France
and there loses his faith in Islam without being able to replace it with anything
in western rationalist or political philosophy. On return to Senegal he is unable
to resurrect his previous social enthusiasms and gradually slips into a rootless
alienation.

OUSAME, Sembene

Le Dockeur Noire, 1956 (The Black Docker, 1978)
A semi-autobiographical novel about the lives and politics of African, other
immigrant and native French dockworkers in Marseilles shortly after W.W.II. The
tensions between personal, ethnic and class views, the currents of racism in French
society but also the inter-racial solidarity of the dockworkers in their union and
working class struggles.

Ousame was born into a Woloff fisherman's family, became an urban labourer in
Senegal during the late 1930s, emigrated to France as a worker and served in the
French army during W.W.II. He later worked on the Marseilles docks for a decade
where he began writing. A novelist, playwright, filmmaker and political activist,
Ousame is possibly the finest author to emerge from West Africa to date.

O Pays, Mon Beau Peuple, 1957 (Oh Country, My Beautiful People)
A novel which advocates the introduction of modern farm cooperatives among the
Senegalese peasantry. Describes one attempt in this direction which fails, due
in part to the continuing power of village chiefs and new political bosses.
Dissects the array of allegedly "richly traditional" customs which Ousame holds
must be overcome and not catered to as some sort of wonderful national heritage.

Les Bouts de Bois de Dieu, 1960 (God's Bits of Wood, 1970)
A novel about the people and forces which come into play and are transmuted by
the bitter and bloody strike by African workers attempting to unionize the Niger-
Dakar railway in 1947-48. Apart from the French colonial and company
administrators, Ousame does not focus on racial facets of the conflict.
He concentrates on the class nature of the struggle, involving African workers of
various ethnic groups, against both the French capitalist-colonialists and their
African bourgeoisie allies (who are soon to become Senegal's ruling class). God's
Bits of Wood is Ousame's most widely translated work and is one of the greatest
novels to yet appear in Africa.

Voltaique, 1962 (Voltaique)
A collection of short stories about ordinary Senegalese workers and peasants on
the eve of independence; reminiscences of youth in a backland peasant village and
life as a migrant worker in France. The implication is that social liberation of
the Senegalese people is still far distant. The title story made into a
successful film by Ousame.

Le Mandat, 1966 (The Money Order and White Genesis, 1971)
Two long stories, The Money Order being a sardonic and sadly humourous account of
a rather naive and fantasy-prone old man who comes to believe that he will receive
a large money order from his nephew in France and who is bled dry by the parasitic
schemes of his kinsmen who calculatingly manipulate "traditional customs" for just
this purpose.

Tribal Scars and Other Stories, 1970
A collection of Ousame's stories about Senegalese workers and peasants in the late
1950s and 1960s. Also Harmattan, 1969, a novel set on the eve of Senegal's
associate state/independence in 1958.

Xala, 1973 (Xala, 1979)
A sardonic novel written as a folk tale; about a voracious African trader turned
politician boss in post-independence Senegal. He is cursed by a beggar whom he
has ruined a decade earlier, and we follow his progressive ruination thereafter.

SADJI, Abdoulaye

Maimouna, 1958 (Maimouna, 1966)
A novel which revolves around a young girl from a peasant village who chaffs under
the restrictions of village life and leaves to join a married sister already
living in the metropolis of Dakar. The rounds of her daily life and search for
work in the city, the others like herself she meets. She gets pregnant, is
abandoned and has to return to the village. About everyday life in a West
African city of the mid 1950s, of youthful hopes, harsh realities and personal
tragedies in an amorphous and changing society.

MALI

GOLOGO, Mamadou

Le Rescape de L'Ethylos, 1963 (The Survivor of Ethylos)
A novel about life and political tensions in Mali on the eve of and during the
first years of independence. The initial grand visions juxtaposed to the
proliferation of seemingly insoluble economic problems. Details the effects of
these difficulties on a progressive government minister who sinks into alcoholism,
but who ultimately rededicates himself to do whatever can be done for the country.

OUOLOGUEM, Yambo

Le Devoir de Violence, 1968 (Bound to Violence, 1971)
A novel which combines realism and surrealism; deals with seven centuries of
violence, slavery, war and oppression of the Malian people both by their own kings
and by external conquerors. It sweeps back and forth between the present and past
periods of the "Naken Empire" (Mali), portraying the boundless brutality of kings,
Arabized invaders, local chiefs and also the attendent servility of the people.
An assault on both the myths of French colonialists and of the raft of Negritude
authors maundering about assorted "past glories". A powerful blending of legends,
history and fiction.

SISSOKO, Fily-Dabo

Le Passion de Djime, 1956 (The Passion of Djime), Le Savane Rouge, 1962 (The Red
Savanna)
Two lyrical portraits of village life in the Mali savanna region on the eve of
independence, told in a quiet, traditional style. They warn against sectarian
antagonisms and racial-tribal chauvinism which were to engulf so many African
states and which claimed Sissoko himself.

GUINEA

LAYE, Camara

L'Enfant Noire, 1953 (The Black Child, 1968)
A nostalgic and popular reminiscence of Laye's childhood as the son of a village
blacksmith in the 1930s, of the life and culture of Guinean villages of that
generation.

Dramouss, 1966 (Dream of Africa, 1970)
A semi-autobiographical novel about the return of a Guinean intellectual to his
homeland after a long stay in France, finding that five years of independence
under Sekou Toure's "African Socialism" had destroyed many beneficial social
traditions (as well as some traditions the country was well rid of). The
alienation, thinly disguised self-interest and amorphous fears which had come to
permeate Guinean society are juxtaposed to the limited achievements and unfulfilled
promise of independence. A Guinean emigre's account.

IVORY COAST

DADIE, Bernard B.

Climbie, 1956 (Climbie, 1977)
A novel which follows the protagonist (Climbie) from childhood in a peasant village, through the mission school system in 1930s to France. It details the forces and characters involved in the early independence movement in French West Africa between 1946 and 1951 when Dadie led the "left wing" Rassemblement Democratique Africain. Deals with a strike of government workers in the Ivory Coast during the late 1940s which was an important event in mobilizing support for independence. The movement is coopted by the emergent black bourgeoisie (organized by Felix Houphouet-Boigny) which set its stamp on the Ivory Coast to date. Written with considerable wit and verve.

KOURAMA, Ahmadou

Les Soliels des Independence, 1968 (The Suns of Independence, 1971)
A novel set in post independence Ivory Coast and depicting the wheeling and dealing of factions within the governing political party in their attempts to gain control over the chieftancy in a backlands village. Ends with the deposition of the locally admired chief by a stringer of the national party, with the ex-chief having to live a "debased" life among African workers in a distant town (and other horrors). Not so much progressive as revealing of the purely opportunist political intrigues and class chauvinism permeating a new independent African state.

CAMEROONS

BETI, Mongo

Le Roi Miracule, 1958 (King Lazarus, 1972)
A satirical novel of a Cameroonian native ruler during the 1920s who becomes Christianized and is pressured by the mission into divorcing all his wives but one. He loses the political alliances the marriages entail and then runs afoul of the French colonial authorities who pose as "protectors of African traditions" (believing that those traditions selectively applied make colonization easier). The king is dismissed and has to leave the region, but in the process he repents, converts back to his "pagan" beliefs, remarries his former wives and is ultimately reinstated by the French colonial government. A neat turnabout of the mission tract story.

Beti also wrote two other satiric novels on the underside of the mission system in Cameroons; The Poor Christ of Bomba, 1962 and Mission Terminee (Mission to Kala, 1968) both being sardonic digs at the ethnocentric colonial chauvinism entailed in the Catholic missions, by someone who rose to bourgeoise status through them.

MATIP, Benjamin

Afrique, Nous T'Ignorons, 1956 (Africa, We Don't Know You)
A novel which deals with the responses of Cameroonian villagers and local French colonials to news of the outbreak of W.W.II. The varying but complementary styles of traditionalism, ethnic tribalism and authoritarianism among both French and Cameroonians counterposed in exasperated satire.

OYONO, Ferdinand (Ferdinand Oijono)

Un Vie de Boy, 1956 (Houseboy, 1966)
A novel about a "houseboy" for a French colonial administrator of a backland Cameroon town in the late 1940s. It chronicles the narrow path between servility and dangerous truthfulness which the "boy" (allegorical of all colonized people) has to tread in his "master's" household. Through the bored deceit of the administrator's wife, he is accused of theft, is flogged and cast out of his village. Anti-colonial melodrama.

Also Le Vieux Negre et La Medaille, 1956 (The Old Negro and the Medal), a novela revolving around a Cameroonian supporter of the civilizing role of French culture and colonialism who late in life discovers the sham of this rhetoric and casts off his past allegiances to French.

CONGO (BRAZZAVILLE)

N'DEBEKA, Maxime

Soleils Neufs, 1969 (New Suns)
A collection of poetry including the poem "980,000", a satiric attack on the venality and arrogance of much of the new black ruling class in post independence Africa and their disdain for the ordinary citizens.

Le President, 1970 (The President)
A play about the sycophancy and increasing isolation of courtiers around the president of a neo-colonial African state, with an angry hint of a military coup which may purge the country of such rulers (for better or worse).

ZAIRE (BELGIAN-AMERICAN CONGO)

HEINZ, G. and DONNAY, H.

Lumumba: The Last Fifty Days, 1969
A chronicle of the last two months in the life of Patrice Lumumba, the murdered first president of Zaire. It is in effect an account of the imposition of the most blatant example of neo-colonial rule in Africa. Touches on the roles of tribal separatists, black millionaire compradores, old Belgian mining interests and new American strategic planners, foreign mercenaries and a manipulated United Nations "peace keeping" force. An almost textbook example of freedom fighting.

MUTOMBO-DIBA, Valerian

Son Excellence Boumba, 1969 (His Excellancy Bumba, 1972)
A satiric prose play about the total venality of an instant black comprador ruling class in a newly independent African country (a thinly disguised allegory of Zaire under the Mobuto-US regime). It depicts the complete indifference of that class to the deepening chaos and misery in the country as well as their ridiculous mannerisms. Told through the life of the anti-hero, a shameless but cunning careerist who betrays everyone and everything--family, friends and country--to advance himself, and so rises up through the system.

NKRUMAH, Kwame

Challenge of the Congo, 1969
An interesting if somewhat specious commentary on the overthrow of the Congo government in 1960-61 and the imposition of one of the most ruthless neo-colonial regimes in Africa. Describes the roles of Belgian and US military diplomats, the use of Western and South African mercenaries and the manipulation of Ghanaian "peace keeping" forces under UN aegis which were used to overthrow the Lumumba government. Holds that the Congo strategy was the first of a series of neo-colonialist coups which later ousted allegedly progressive African governments (including his own) in favour of comprador regimes.

MALAGASY REPUBLIC (MADAGASCAR)

RABEMANANJERA, Jasques-Jean

Antsa, 1949 (Antsa)
A collection of poems which are mainly patriotic and lyrical evocations of Madagascar, its peoples and past. Written in a prison by a nationalist poet who survived the bloody suppression of Malagasy independence by French in 1947. Also Les Boutriers del Aurore (Cobblers of the Dawn), a play on the same theme.

NIGERIA AND GHANA

NIGERIA

ACHEBE, Chinua

Things Fall Apart, 1962
A well written and in a way typical Nigerian novel, dealing with the avarice and
infectious corruption spreading among the Nigerian middle class in the years
immediately after independence. The main themes revolve around the doings and
conflicts between the newly established and aspirant sections of an emerging
bourgeoise, with ordinary working people serving merely as background.
Specifically, the novel deals with an idealistic university graduate and his
initial resistance to but gradual incorporation into a system of bribery.

Man of the People, 1965
A novel set on the eve of the first military coup in a Nigeria where corruption
and political gangsterism has become endemic and where government control over
some regions has begun to dissolve. The election fixing and injustices of one
chiefly ward boss lead a handful of young middle class dissidents into a resort
to arms, in which they are quickly killed. Also No Longer at Ease, a novel on a
comparable theme.

ALUKO, T.M.

Kinsmen and Foreman, 1966
A satiric novel revolving around the tensions between a recently returned Yoruba
engineer and a corrupt relative who oversees local public works during the early
1960s and how they relate to Yoruba villagers and townspeople of Ibadan. Aluko's
technocratic outlook is not particularly progressive or sympathetic to the
ordinary Yoruba but he does convey some of the maneuvers in play at the time.
Also One Man, One Matchet, 1964, a novel dealing with conflicts which arise over
a diseased cocoa plot and how a local politician utilizes local traditions and
maxims to derail the efforts of an expatriate and Nigerian agricultural expert
who wants to cut down trees.

EKWENSI, Cyprian

Jagua Nana, 1961
A popular Nigerian version of Zola's Nana; the life of a fading but still
influential courtesan in Lagos during the first years of independence. Some deft
descriptions of city scenes told in Lagos pidgin English and an enthusiastic
appreciation of that sprawling metropolis, mixed with folk tale-like adventures
in and charicatures of life in traditional villages. Revolves around the life
styles and dreams of newly emergent sections of the Nigerian bourgeoise. Also his
People of the City, 1955, a novel of a young man who eagerly leaves behind the
restrictions of his backlands village for the promise and freedom of city life
during the late colonial period.

Beautiful Feathers, 1966
A satiric novel of a scheming and ruthless Nigerian politican running on a
platform of Pan Africanism and his rise to power.

Survive the Peace, 1976
A sombre and more realistic novel of Ibo families at the end of the Nigerian civil
war and their attempts to pick up the pieces of their shattered lives.

IKE, Chukwuemeka

Sunset at Dawn, 1975
A roman-de-clef about the Nigerian civil war of the late 1960s as seen in the

experiences of Ibo people passing through a Biafran refugee camp. A reminiscence of that bitter struggle done in quasi-documentary style by the administrator of one such refugee camp.

IROH, Eddie

Forty-eight Guns for the General, 1977
A novel of the first year of the Nigerian civil war (1967); told as a reportage account about Biafran civilians and soldiers by a former director of Biafran Information Agency.

Toads of War, 1979
Another novel of the civil war which provides accounts of front line and guerrilla struggles by Ibo combatants but focuses on the starvation and misery of the civilian population in the Biafran enclave. The emergence of a black market millionaire class who live in luxury, profiteering in Biafran patriotism, as the bulk of the population wastes away. Told in an understated and powerful reportage style.

IYAYI, Festus

Violence, 1979
A novel which continues the account of Nigerian political corruption, but in this case from the perspective of a Nigerian worker during the early 1970s. It looks back over his personal experience of failed national opportunities; the political collapse and military coups after independence, the civil war, the oil boom oligarchy. Follows the Yoruba man and his wife as they depart from a stagnating village in early 1960s to seek work in the cities but find life among the urban poor is an inescapable trap leading to their personal dissolution. Mentions hope for some sort of "socialist" reorganization of Nigeria in a passing allusion.

SMITH, Mary

Baba of Karo, 1955
Subtitled "A life history of a Hausa woman of northern Nigeria" it covers sixty years of the life of a Hausa peasant woman from Zaria province, telling of girlhood, youth and early married life in the years before British colonial rule in circa 1905. She laconically alludes to the ever present dangers, slave raids and exactions, as well as the joys of indigenous Hausa society. Her story proceeds through a near half century lived in a quasi-feudal African Islamic society in which the British colonial apparatus is only rarely visible. In the course of her ordinary and fascinating account Baba describes that society and the changes she has seen (often for the better) to the early 1950s. A rich and realistically complex reminiscence of people and the malleable traditions of that society. An inspired and luminescent exemplar of life history.

SOYINKA, Wole

The Road, 1965
A play about people and scenes linked together by a road (i.e., the Yoruba traditions) running through towns and villages in the western region of Nigeria during the early 1960s. Alludes to the interpenetration of past and present and the spiritual requirements of future Nigerian society. Soyinka is a playwright, poet and translator of Yoruba writing as well as being possibly the most eminent Nigerian author abroad. Antithetical to social realism and given to a Menckenesque adulation of the artist as hero, Soyinka can be a cogent critic and witty gadfly.

The Interpreters, 1967
A wide ranging scatological satire of the newly emerged Nigerian ruling class in the mid 1960s; their ignorance, pettiness, venality and utter lack of vision or dignity. A particularly scathing attack on the servility and "boobocracy" of the contemporary Nigerian intelligensia. Revolves around the bosses and acquaintances of a journalist for one of the hack newspapers in Lagos. Funny and flatuent in parts.

The Man Died, 1972
Soyinka's diary and writings while imprisoned for opposing the war of attrition against Biafra. His former joie-de-vie is here transformed into a more clearly political statement which suggests that Nigeria has become an exploitative, class-based society with little relationship to any traditional conceptions of social responsibility. Touches on the repression of dissent in Nigeria during the civil war.

Season of Anomie, 1973
A novel of the internal "political" struggles and endemic strife in Nigeria on the eve of a series of military coups in mid 1960s. Also treats with the growing inter-tribal racism and attacks on Ibos throughout the country before and during the civil war. A damning account of the assorted military rulers and tribal/sectarian mobs they allowed to go unchecked.

SANDBROOK, Richard and COHEN, Robin (eds.)

The Development of an African Working Class: Studies in class formation and action, 1975
A seminal if academic compendium of articles by twelve scholars; it documents the long established presence and struggles of varied working classes throughout much of Africa from the 1890s to the 1970s and focused primarily on formerly British colonial territories, including Nigeria. Provides a useful counter to the once fashionable dogma that organized workers in Third World countries are a privileged and comprador sector of those societies. Contains an extensive bibliography on African labour union history.

GHANA

ARMAH, Ayi Kwei

The Beautyful Ones Are Not Yet Born, 1968
A novel combining allegory and realistic description of the endemic corruption wracking Ghana during the 1960s. Told by a middle echelon functionary of the national railways who stubbornly remains unbribed, despite the castigation of family and friends and the puzzled laughter of his colleagues. A quizzical investigation of the ineffectiveness of mere personal honesty in a corrupt society and also the individual alienation and social dissolution which corruption engenders. The overthrow of the Nkrumah regime changes nothing, except possibly for the worse. Also his novel Why Are We So Blest?, 1970.

AWOONOR, Kofi

This Earth My Brother, 1971
A somewhat melodramatic novel of a student lawyer who returns to find the Ghana he left five years previously in shambles and totally changed. Of his inability to gain a footing in this new/old world and his lapse into despair. Some negritude philosophizing by a member of the Ghanian intellectual establishment.

NKRUMAH, Kwame

Dark Days in Ghana, 1968
A provocative if somewhat self-interested account of the forces behind the military coup which ousted Nkrumah in 1964 (the once prestigious president of the first African country to gain independence). Deals with the class nature and exactions of the Ghanian military and bureaucratic establishment, the neo-colonialism imposed by/on this inept new ruling class and their use of negritude ideology and "Black Power" rhetoric to buttress their regime. Rather reticent about the fact that these elements first emerged under Nkrumah himself, and written before Ghana's slide into near total paralysis and bankruptcy.

CENTRAL AND EAST AFRICA

ZIMBABWE (RHODESIA)

GJERSTED, Ole and MOYO, Temba

The Organizer: Story of Temba Moyo, 1974
A fragmentary account of the background, views and underground experiences of a
ZAPU guerrilla in Zimbabwe during the late 1960s and early 1970s. One of the
"Life Histories from the Revolution" series.

LESSING, Doris

Martha Quest, 1952, A Proper Marriage, 1954, A Ripple in the Storm, 1958,
Landlocked, 1965
A tetrology of novels dealing with the rebellious young womanhood of a settler in
Rhodesia from the early 1940s to mid 1950s; the smothering quality of life in that
colonial world from the small town Victoriana to a very staid Bohemianism in
Salisbury, her growing revulsion with Rhodesian society and her drift into politics
of the white left-liberal camp before her ultimate departure for England.

MARECHERA, Dambudao

The House of Hunger, 1979
A collection of stories about a young Shona man growing up during the final years
of colonial Rhodesia, the violence of life in the African urban districts and the
increasingly random brutality of a threatened settlers regime.

SAMKANGE, Stanlake

The Mourned One, 1975
A novel revolving around the rape trial of an African man in Rhodesia of 1935, in
which the trial provides a microcosm of the colonial society at its nadir.

Year of the Uprising, 1978
A popular "history" cum novel of the last major tribal (Mashona) uprising against
European colonization in 1896-97 stemming from extended land losses to settlers.
The inter-tribal conflicts and the nature of the various colonial interests
examined from a mainly bourgeoisie Black nationalist viewpoint.

ZAMBIA (NORTHERN RHODESIA)

KAUNDA, Kenneth

Zambia Shall Be Free, 1965
A nationalist account of colonialism in Northern Rhodesia from the late 19th century
to the eve of independence. Recounts the late entry of British colonizers, the
tribal-peasant revolts, the steadily expanding land seizures and dispossession by
settlers, the growth of a massive mining-smelting complex from the first decades
of this century, the pioneer Black union movement and their struggles in the
1930s, and the evolving supra-tribal nationalism of late 1940s to 1960s. By the
first president of Zambia.

MASIYE, Andereya

Before Dawn, 1971
A novela of life in a Zambian tribal-peasant village in the 1930s and early 1940s;
everyday events and lives, including a simmering confrontation with recently
imposed hut taxes by colonial administrators (whose presence is usually not part
of villagers lives). Revolves about a village youth itching to see a wider world
who joins a British colonial regiment and is sent off to fight in Burma during
W.W.II.

MULAISHO, Dominic

The Tongue of the Dumb, 1971
A novel told partly as folk tale, partly realistically, about the struggle between
a traditional African chief and a young nationalist contender for political
leadership during the late colonial period. Europeans and the colonial structure
are only a shadowy background of villagers' lives. Portrays the poverty, sometime
hunger, self-limiting restrictions of traditional society and the potentials for
corruption by tribal chiefs.

TANZANIA

PALANGYO, Peter

Dying in the Sun, 1969
A novel about a Tanzanian man from a peasant village who has become a western-
educated professional but who, on facing the death of his father, trys to sort
out the amalgam of love and hate he has for the traditions, superstitions, support
and restrictions in his own youth and the tribal society from which he came.

RUHUMBIKA, Gabriel

Village in Uhuru, 1969
A sympathetic reportage account of what independence and the first years of
Tanzania's "path to socialism" has meant to a remote peasant village.

UGANDA

OCULI, Okello

Prostitute, 1968
A novel dealing with the life of a poor prostitute (with none of the elite
connections of Jagua Nana)in an "anonymous" East African city (Kampala). The
misery, squalor and indifference toward the poor quite unaffected by independence.
Social documentation interlaced with melodrama.

SERUMAGA, Robert

Return to the Shadows, 1969
A sardonic and somewhat surrealist novel about a Ugandan businessman and his
Sancho Panza-like servant who are caught in the absurdities of a chaotically
disorganized Ugandan military regime. Of how neither the wealthy nor poor can
find any modicum of security or normality under such conditions, leading to the
flight of both master and servant. A sophisticated though hardly progressive
work by an expatriate BBC writer, it does not/cannot imagine the holocaust later
loosed by Idi Amin.

KENYA

BARNETT, Donald and NJAMA, Karari

Mau Mau From Within, 1966
A rambling but authentic first person account of Njama's three years in the Land
Freedom Army (Mau Mau) during the early 1950s. More than anything else it
captures the disorganization, cross purposes and losses in that guerrilla struggle
and the reasons for its defeat by British forces. Njama, a Kikuyu youth from a
peasant village describes the tremendous costs borne by the civilian population
and is little given to the antics of guerrilla "field marshalls" or "spears of
the Nation". Collected and edited by sociologist Don Barnett.

KARIUKI, Joseph Mwangi

Mau Mau Detainee, 1963
An account of personal experiences in Kenya prison camps 1953-1960; it documents

the systematic brutalization and even murder of the detainees by British camp
guards. Caused a minor furore when published by Oxford University Press. (To
appreciate the hysterically racist and bloodthirsty nature of some colonials in
Kenya during the period one might consider two revealing little booklets by
Louis Leakey, Mau Mau and the Kikuyu, 1954 and Defeating Mau Mau, 1955.)

MWANGI, Meja

Kill Me Quick, 1973
A novel in "Mickey Spillane" style, but also a chilling portrait of the underside
of the Kenyan "economic miracle" in the late 1960s. The meteoric rise of an
urban lumpen proletariat, from landless ex-peasants, the squalor, poverty and
random violence of juvenile and criminal gangs in the cities.

Carcass for Hounds, 1974
A novel dealing with the last year of a Mau Mau band (and alluding to the
politically taboo figure, Dedan Kimathai) as the survivors hide in the forest
attempting to elude British patrols and Kikuyu informers. The Mau Mau treated as
a forerunner of later anti-colonial struggles in Africa and dealing with the
psychology and motives of the guerrillas.

Going Down River Road, 1976
A horrific novel of the corruption and social dissolution of urban life in Kenya
a decade after independence; the unchecked exploitation on an African road to
capitalism. The misery, brutality, disease and violence which beset the lives of
poor in Nairobi and Mombassa.

NGUGI, Wa' Thiongo (James Ngugi)

The River Between, 1965
A semi-autobiographical novel in two parts; the first about the life of a Kikuyu
peasant family immediately prior to the Mau Mau rising, and the second charting
the fear and gradual dissolution of its members as the struggle and repression
deepen. Ngugi is probably the greatest East African writer to emerge in past
generation.

A Grain of Wheat, 1968
A novel briefly touching on the Mau Mau struggle, its suppression yet the
inevitable move to independence. Focuses on the almost immediate betrayal of the
guerrilla fighters and political prisoners by the new African rulers of Kenya, but
broaches the hope that some path to African socialism can yet be found in past
traditions.

Secret Lives, 1975
A collection of stories about a Kikuyu childhood in the early 1950s but also of
the varied forms of corruption, social decay and exploitation which have followed
Kenya's independence. Ngugi himself was imprisoned for his writing and for
supporting a students strike in 1969.

Weep Not, Child, 1964
A novel of participants in the Mau Mau rising, the sacrifices and losses sustained,
and the foreboding feeling that it is in vain.

Petals of Blood, 1977
Ngugi's best known and most comprehensive novel, it incorporates most of the major
themes of his earlier writings. Focuses on the betrayal of the Kenyan peasants'
hopes with the entrenchment of the new African ruling class, the corruption and
and social dissolution. Comes to the conclusion that the platitudes about
"African Socialism" have to be dismissed and class forces mobilized if real
socialism is to be achieved in African countries.

ODINGA, Oginga

Not Yet Uhuru, 1967
An autobiography and a socio-political critique of Kenya mainly since independence
by the once leading left wing opposition figure. Alludes to the opportunism,
massive graft and landgrabbing and in general the betrayal of Kenyan peasantry and

workers by the Kenyatta-led government which overnight became the basis of a new, comprador bourgeoisie.

WACHIRA, Godwin

Ordeal in the Forest, 1967
A novel of the Mau Mau "emergency" and its effects on Kikuyu society. Revolves around four young men whose lives take drastically different paths but are all dramatically altered, for the better and the worse, by the events. The hero, initially a wastrel and troublemaker, is gradually transformed into a dedicated resistance worker. By a one time Kenyan union leader.

WACIUMA, Charity

Daughter of Mumbi, 1969
A novela about the life of a young Kikuyu girl from a family which (like the majority) did not participate in the Mau Mau struggle but who nevertheless had their lives shattered through the system of strategic hamlets and general repression used in defeating the guerrillas.

UNION OF SOUTH AFRICA

ABRAHAMS, Peter

Dark Testament, 1942
An autobiographical account of Abrahams' young manhood as a member of the
"Coloured" caste in the 1930s. He became a school teacher, journalist and finally
a member of the underground communist party of South Africa. His own hard won
achievements are counterposed to the suppression of the great mass of the non-
white population under the supposedly democratic government of Jan Smuts. Also
see Abrahams' Tell Freedom, 1954, which chronicles the struggles of white liberals
and communists and the initial left wing elements in the Coloured, Black and
Indian communities faced with the slide of South Africa into unbridled apartheid
in the years after W.W.II.

Mine Boy, 1946
A proletarian novel which describes the evolution of a young village born African
who goes to work in the gold mines of The Rand. Describes the monotony and
regimentation of barrack life, the rigours and dangers of mining, the endless
interpersonal fights and drinking bouts which ensnare the Black miners. Also of
the slowly emerging political consciousness which develops in the hero and among
a number of his compatriots, leading to their forming an underground mineworkers
union which ultimately launches one of the first African miners strikes in South
Africa. As distinct from earlier mission tracts, "proletarianization" in the
mines is not seen as a step into the abyss but one of the steps toward liberation.

The Path of Thunder, 1948
A novel of a Coloured teacher who leaves the relative openness of Captetown to
teach in an African village in the Transvaal. Describes his isolation and shock
at both the defensive hostility directed against all outsiders by the African
villagers and the naked repression of white supremacy as wielded by local Boers.

Wild Conquest, 1950
A historical novel which deals with the Boer Trek into the interior during the
mid 19th century. Treated as the response to being a colonially dominated group
themselves who wanted a free hand in fashioning their own lives (as well as
retaining their Black farm slaves). An attempt to understand what made the Boers
what they are.

A Wreath for Udomo, 1956
A novel set in a fictional colonial African country in which an African emigre
returns from a long stay in London, comes to lead a dockworkers union in a bitter
strike and emerges as a leader of the independence movement. After independence
he becomes ensnared by the expatriate capitalists and the new African bourgeoise
which springs up overnight, as well as coming into conflict with traditional
chiefly power, and is finally assassinated by one of his former supporters.
Contains a bitter sketch of George Padmore, the English "Black Nationalist" and
neo-conservative.

A Night of Their Own, 1965
A novel which deals with the relations between Blacks and East Indians in the
state of Natal during the late fifties and early 1960s, their arms-length
cooperatiion and distrust of each other in the anti-apartheid struggles of that
period. A realistic and pessimistic consideration of the forces opposing apartheid
and the power which can be mobilized against them. With a strong implication
that petitions, peaceful demonstrations and incipient interracial organizations
are ultimately ineffective against the repression of the South African regime.

ALTMAN, Phyllis

The Law of the Vultures, 1952
A protest novel about the deepening system of apartheid by a white liberal writer.

It traces the journey of a Johannesburg born African through many of the forms of racial victimization, into jail because of pass law violations and finally into an underground (but as yet non-violent) African nationalist organization.

BLOOM, Harry

Episode, 1956
A novel of the oppression which had become inherent in the fabric of South African society, as evidenced in the systematic and massive repression brought to bear against participants in peaceful protest against apartheid. Deals with the improbability that South Africa can gradually evolve into a more just society by peaceful means.

BRINK, Andre

Kennis Van Die Aand, 1974 (Looking Into Darkness)
An Afrikaans novel bitterly critical of apartheid and the all-pervasive repression and blind dogmaticism needed to enforce it. A system which dehumanizes the ruling caste as well as degrading the victims.

A Chain of Voices, 1981
A "historical" novel about a revolt of Black slaves in a Boer farm village of mid 19th century, based upon research into court records. It revolves around parallels between that earlier event and the forces set in motion in South Africa since the Soweto riots of 1970s. When promises of emancipation are withdrawn the die is cast for a struggle to the end. Counterposes Black and Boer demands which are ultimately unnegotiable.

BRUTUS, Dennis

Letters to Martha, 1968
A collection of sketches and poems in the form of letters; mainly about Brutus' underground escape from the Union of South Africa through Swaziland and Mozambique where he was siezed by Portuguese police and returned to South Africa. Also of his experiences in the Robben Island political prison.

Sirens, Knuckles and Boots, 1963
A slim collection of poems mainly about the police terror unleashed against suspected and actual political activists. Smuggled out of prison and initially published in Nigeria.

COPE, Jack

The Fair House, 1955
A novel about the 1906 Zulu uprising in South Africa, which was both the last tribal revolt and also a rising of an impoverished Zulu "peasantry". Cope deals largely with the mentality of a British army unit, recently engaged in defeating the Boers, now sent in to suppress the Zulu tribespeople.

DIKOBE, Modikwe

The Marabi Dance, 1973
A reminiscence of childhood and youth in the Black native townships of Johannesburg in the late 1930s.

DU TOIT, Bettie

Ukubamba Amadulo, 1978 (Workers' Struggles in the Textile Industry, 1978)
A popular history of the attempts to organize underground trade unions among African textile workers in South Africa from the late 1930s to the early 1970s. A remarkable catalogue of Black and white organizers and their activities as revealed through a series of capsule biographies and reportage of the union struggles and organizations which emerged. Translated from Zulu.

GORDIMER, Nadine

Burger's Daughter, 1979
A novel revolving around the reminiscences and reconsiderations of a thirtyish

Afrikaner woman, the daughter of a Bram Fischer-like character, as she travels through South Africa in the 1970s. (Bram Fischer was a member of the inner circles of the Boer Nationalist party who was revealed as a communist in the 1950s and imprisoned for life.) The novel deals with the motives and visions of a variety of South African communists and sympathizers from the 1950s to 1970s --Black, Coloured, Indian, English and Afrikaner. A generation of hope, desperation and defeat. The reminiscences are interspersed with description of the consolidated racist regime of South Africa, culminating in the Soweto riots of 1976 and the emergence of armed struggle. By a leading South African liberal writer.

GORDON, Gerald

Let the Day Perish, 1952
A novel of a light skinned Coloured man "passing for" white in South Africa of early 1950s, whose ancestry is discovered during the racial census carried out by government investigators implementing tightened pass law-apartheid regulations. The story follows the protagonist's dissolution as he is placed in the "Coloured" caste, forced to leave his home, circle of friends, job.

FIRST, Ruth

From the Barrel of a Gun, 1971
A massive yet very readable comparative history of the army coups and military regimes which had emerged during the first dozen years of post-independence Africa. Accounts of the forces and events in each case but revolving around the theme that (despite claims to the contrary) the thrust of the military takeovers were to suppress the demands of African peasants and workers in each country and to entrench the interests of one section or another of the national African bourgeoisie. First herself was an emigre South African scholar, an active member of the underground African National Congress and the chairman of the African Studies Centre of Eduardo Modlane University, Mozambique. She was assassinated by agents of the South African secret police during a UNESCO conference in Mozambique in the summer of 1982.

HUTCHINSON, Alfred

The Road to Ghana, 1960
A journalistic account of the mass opposition mounted by the African National Congress against apartheid and the Bantu Education Act during the mid to late 1950s. And of the suppression of all open opposition. Hutchinson was a leading representative of the "Coloured" supporters of the ANC; arrested for high treason he managed to escape South Africa by an underground railway which first brought him to Swaziland (see The Rainkillers) and later to Ghana.

LA GUMA, Alex

A Walk in the Night, 1962
A novel about the lives of the semi-employed Black proletariat in the "native districts" of Capetown. Portrays the total disjuncture and aversion of urban Blacks to life in the so-called "tribal" areas, their constant fear that unemployment or some other run in with the police will get them sent "back" to the "homelands" which most have never seen. Also of the intra-communal crime, drunkenness and desperation of people in the Black slums which leaves most powerless to combat the system which keeps them in that condition.

And a Three-Fold Cord, 1964
A novel about the insecurities, humiliations and constant search for a livelihood by Blacks in the Capetown slums. Focuses on the daily life of one hard pressed Black working class family struggling to survive in decency if in poverty. Written while La Guma was under house arrest for writing such works.

The Stone Country, 1966
A documentary collage of the backgrounds and prison lives of some members of the 70,000 population in South Africa's jails; of common criminals, political prisoners and the fine gradations between them.

LYTTON, David

The Freedom of the Cage, 1966
A novel which investigates the pressures and psychological cost of being part of
the dominant caste in South Africa. Revolves around an apolitic and unbalanced
(but in other ways not atypical) Afrikaner youth and his attempt to assassinate
Prime Minister Vorster in the mid 1960s.

MANDELA, Nelson

No Easy Walk to Freedom, 1968
A collection of articles, speeches and trial statements by the veteran African
National Congress leader who after the Sharpesville massacre led that organization
into underground armed struggle. Since the early 1960s Mandela has been a
prisoner in Robben Island.

MERCER, Dennis and DUKA, Norman

From Shantytown to Forest: the story of Norman Duka, 1974
A partial life history of a Black South African youth's progression from personal
opposition to apartheid to recruitment into a guerrilla unit of the African
National Congress during mid 1960s to early 1970s. One of the "Life Histories
from the Revolution" series which deal with the backgrounds, politicization and
experiences of African resistance fighters.

MODISANE, Bloke

Blame Me on History, 1963
An autobiographical account of the experiences and the range of emotions of a
forty year old Black South African writer.

MOKGATHE, Naboth

The Autobiography of an Unknown South African, 1971
A massive autobiography of a Black South African, from childhood and youth in a
small town during the 1930s, initial jobs during the 1940s and early 1950s as the
apartheid system is tightened. About Mokathe's work as a rank and file organizer
of illegal Black labour unions; of the waves of arrests and repression and his
escape from the Union of South Africa in the mid 1960s. Also contains ethnographically detailed accounts of daily lives of friends, family, neighbours and
the travails and personal joys of everyday life. Rather difficult to read but
a gold mine of information.

MPHAHLELE, Ezekiel

Man Must Live and Other Stories, 1947
A collection of stories about the   lives   and humiliations of Blacks in South
Africa during the early to mid 1940s. Mphahlele was born into a Black
proletarian family and raised in the native slums of Pretoria during the 1920s,
went to work at fourteen, later obtained a degree in education and joined the
editorial board of Sam Kahn's Drum. In the 1950s he was active in the struggles
against the Bantu Education Act, which led to his being "banned". He later
escaped the Union of South Africa to live in exile.

Down Second Avenue, 1959
A novel of life in South Africa from the late 1930s to the mid 1950s. It holds
that the forces in contention are much more complex than merely Black versus
white; there being voracious and Black exploiters of all variety as well as
militant and progressive whites, apathetic know-nothing members of all races, and
yet more intricate combinations at work. A compact survey of the shifting forces
at work over a generation and probably Mphahlele's best known book.

The Living and the Dead, 1961
A collection of stories about South Africa at the begining of the 1960s, where
the lines have hardened and the options have become increasingly few. A
pessimistic view that only armed struggle can change the situation and that such
a conflict will be long, extremely bloody and destructive. Contains some bitter

criticism of the ideology and class interests served by Negritude philosophy promoted by Black bourgeoisie in independent Africa.

In Corner B, 1967
A collection of stories about Blacks, Coloureds and others in South Africa during the early to mid 1960s, the deceptive calm as the final avenues of legal opposition are closed off.

RIVE, Richard

Emergency, 1964
A reportage novel about the March 1960 anti-Pass Law demonstrations which ended in the notorious police massacre of demonstrators in the Native Township of Sharpesville (Johannesburg). In effect, the end of non-violent mass protest and the begining of untrammeled military suppression of the non-white population. Also see Richard Rive (ed.), Modern African Prose, 1964, a collection of stories and essays by contemporary African writers and including Harry Bloom's "The Dispossessed", a story about the Coalbrook mine disaster and the toll of the mainly Black miners.

ZWELONKE, D.M.

Robben Island, 1973
An account of Zwelonke's experience in the feared South African concentration camp for political prisoners during the late 1960s. The disintegration of prisoners' wills under a regime of hunger, random and systematic terror, torture and solitary confinement.

OTHER SOUTH AFRICAN

GORDON, R.J.

Mines, Masters and Migrants: Life in a Namibian Mine Compound, 1977
An anthropological/historical account of the daily work, lives and power structure involved in resource extraction in the South African colony of Namibia. The nature and evolution of a migrant, ex-tribal African proletariat.

HUTCHINSON, Alfred

The Rainkillers, 1964
A play about the tensions between Swazi traditional society with its powerful tribal chiefs and the first few emigres and African nationalists in a Swazi village during the early 1960s. Evokes the looming presence of neighbouring South Africa with its policy of fostering traditionalist autocracies and dependencies on its periphery.

MERCER, Dennis and NDADI, Uinnia

Breaking Contract: The Story of Uinnia Ndadi, 1976
A fragmentary life history; the background, politicization and steps which led a Namibian peasant and rural worker into the SWAPO. And of experiences of partizan struggle during the early 1970s.

MOPELI-PAULUS, Attwell S.

Blanket Boy's Moon, 1953
A Xhosa novel from South Africa which mixes realism and folklore; it is the account of a young Sotho (the son of an African soldier killed in Europe during W.W.I) who grows up in the modern-traditional world of Basuto villages and the mine camps of the Union of South Africa during the 1920s and 1930s. He becomes one of the army of Basuto miners in the Rand goldfields and manages to scrabble out of the pits after some years and into the fringes of the lower middle class only to be drawn back into the world of chiefly power struggles as he becomes ensnared in a ritual murder. Discovered, he flees and his flight takes him through the various haunts of the Black and Coloured working classes in South Africa, until his capture and execution. Includes a brief account of the 1949 Black dockworkers

strike in Durban. It focuses on the continuing tug of traditional ethnic loyalties and violence among some urban Black workers of the time. Adapted and translated from Xhosa by Peter Lanham.

Lilahloane Oa Botho, 1950 (Poor Lilahloane, 1955)
Short stories about the lives of Xhosa-speaking people in village and city in the Union of South Africa during the 1940s.

NQHEKU, Albert

Arda 'Naheng Ea Maburu, 1947 (Arda in the Land of the Afrikaners)
A Basuto novela dealing with the experiences of a young villager who is recruited by a Basuto labour contractor (Thomas Mofolo?) to work on a Boer farm in South Africa, his amazement at the backward conditions which exist there (having lived without benefits of progress in a Basuto village) and the beatings, exploitation and degradation he encounteres when he tries to stand up for himself.

Tsielala, 1959 (Silence, Please!)
Another Basuto novela which describes the lives and sufferings of Basuto contract miners in the South African gold mines. It implicates and condemns the colonial authorities of the Basutoland Protectorate for permitting unchecked labour recruiting. After the independence of Basutoland/Lesotho, Nqheku's novel was banned by the chiefly Royal government as being offensive to South African employers.

PLAATJE, Sol T.

Mhudi, 1930 (Mhudi, 1978)
A Sotho novel from South Africa which is a melange of missionary romance and sometimes salient account of a group of Tswana tribespeople fleeing from the ravages of their traditional Zulu enemy, who place themselves under the protection of Boer settlers in late 19th century. It revolves around a Tswana couple a generation later who realize that they have been caught between tribal hostilities and serfdom under the Boers. By one of the pioneer Black South African writers and a founder of the African National Congress.

PLOMER, William

Ula Masondo, 1948
A Zulu novel from South Africa which follows a village-born African into the Rand mines as a contract labourer. Unlike Abrahams' novel Mine Boy (in which proletarianization is a step toward liberation) Plomer's story is about the increasing dissolution of the hero and his comrades through drink, "sin" and assorted other evils. A naturalistic mission tract but with accounts of some real enough problems.

MOZAMBIQUE AND ANGOLA

MOZAMBIQUE

CRAVEIRINHA, Jose

Karinguana Ua Karinguana, 1974 (Once Upon a Time)
A collection of Mozambique-Portuguese poetry using African oral traditions. They
memorialize the hardships of African workers and peasants and affirm the struggle
against Portuguese colonial rule by Frelimo (Mozambique Liberation Front). Two
of Craveirinha's poems on similar themes are translated into English in
Ezekiel Mphahlele (ed.), African Writing Today, 1969.

DOS SANTOS, Marcelino (Kulungano)

"Onde Estou?" (Where Am I?), "A Um Menino do Meu Pais" (To a Child of My Country),
circa 1961
Two poems which express solidarity with the travails and tribulations of blacks
in Mozambique but also evoke the struggles of black people in America (such as
Paul Robeson, Langston Hughes and Emmet Till). Dos Santos later became a
leading representative of Frelimo and vice president of Mozambique after
independence. Some additional poems can be found in Langston Hughes and
C. Reygnault (eds.), Anthologie Africaine et Malagache, 1962.

HONWANA, Luis Bernardo

Nos Matamos O Cao-Tinhosa, 1964 (We Killed Mangy Dog and Other Stories, 1972)
A collection of quietly told stories about Mozambique during the last decade of
colonial rule. The peonage and deepening oppression, the manysided and sometimes
contradictory strains of Mozambique society and its various sectors, with the
emergence of the independence struggle as background. The title story deals with
the conditions of black peasants bound to do forced labour on corporate
Portuguese plantations in early 1960s.

MALANGATANA, Valente

("My Problem With the Swamps"), ("The Miner Who Survived"), circa 1960
Two poems by a black Mozambique poet; "Swamps" touches on the lives of prostitutes,
night soil carriers, unemployed and others in Lourenco Marques, driven by class
as well as racial oppression. Written in the Creole Portuguese-English argot
which was the lingua franca of the urban poor in that major port of southern
Africa. "Miner" is about one of the army of Mozambiqueans recruited to work in
South African gold mines who survives the multifoliate spiritual and physical
casualties of that work and is a memorial to those who did not return. Also see
two poems in Uli Beier and B. Moore (eds.), Modern Poetry from Africa, 1966.

MODLANE, Eduardo

The Struggle for Mozambique, 1970
An account of the nature of Portuguese colonial society in Mozambique and the
political background to the emerging nationalist and guerrilla movement,
especially in the 1960s. By an internationally known Mozambiquean anthropologist
and an early leader of the Frelimo until his assassination by Portuguese secret
police agents in 1969. Interweaves biographical and first hand accounts of some
ordinary Frelimo partizans.

ANGOLA

CABRAL, Alexandre

Historias Do Zaire, 1965 (original 1928) (Congo Stories)
Stories describing the consolidation of Portuguese colonial control over the

Cabinda enclave (now part of Angola), covering the period 1895-1914. Told through the reminiscences of an old African watchman who has witnessed the expropriation of land and labour by colonial trading companies which act as quasi-government. By a pioneer anti-colonial Portuguese author.

CASIMIRO, Augusto

Nova Largada, 1929 (New Departure)
A novel which portrays Portuguese colonialism in Angola as experienced by the African peasantry. Details the village revolts and military repression attendent upon newly imposed land taxes which force villagers into cash economy and production for export. Set largely in northeast Angola during W.W.I period, it combines a prose account of events intermingled with the epic songs of a wandering African minstrel travelling around the region singing anti-tax songs.

DE ANDRADE, Mario C Pinto

Literatura Africana de Expressao Portuguese; Vol. 1 Poesia; Vol. 2 Prosa, 1967/68 (African Literature in the Portuguese Language, Vol. 1 Poetry, Vol. 2 Prose) Two anthologies of Portuguese African literature, dealing mainly with post W.W.II period, from the Cabo Verde Islands to Angola and Mozambique. By one of the founders of the MPLA.

DOS SANTOS LIMA, Manuel

As Sementes Da Liberdade, 1965 (The Seeds of Liberty), As Lagrimas E O Vento, 1975 (Tears and Gusts)
Two novels about the lives of ordinary Angolans caught in or committed to the armed struggle against Portuguese colonial rule. As Sementes deals with the exploitation and internal contradictions among poor Portuguese settlers in Angola who are themselves peasants under the thumb of colonial administrators and corporations but who do not oppose these exactions because they fear the native African claims on their land. As Lagrimas deals with the losses and errors as well as with the growing strength of the MPLA guerrilla movement over a dozen years of struggle. Both novels contain an undercurrent of sadness about the irretrievable losses and breaches created by the conflict. By a Portuguese-Angolan author who joined the MPLA in early 1960s and was imprisoned by Salazar forces until the liberation of Angola in 1974.

NETO, Agostinho

Sacred Hope, 1974
A collection of poems dealing with the Angolan people, their sufferings and sacrifices in the national liberation war, and the hopes for a more just society. By the leader of the MPLA and first president of independent Angola.

SOROMENHO, Castro

Terra Morta, 1949 (Dead Land)
An epic novel of colonial Angola; set in the late 1930s and portraying that world as at a dead end. Flashbacks and reminiscences by Angolan peasants and Portuguese administrators take the events back to the turn of the century when colonial rule was imposed over the interior and the sporadic tribal and anti-colonial revolts which followed. The cast includes peasants black and white, African sepoys, old traders, ex-slaves of tribal chiefs and contemporary "slaves" of contract labour systems, chiefs, priests, recent white immigrants and third generation Angolan anti-colonialists. Also deals with the ways in which colonial exactions profit a mere handful of Portuguese and help maintain the stagnation and autocracy in Portugal itself.

Viragem, 1959 (The Turn)
A rather melodramatic sequel to Terra Morta set in the late 1940s; revolves around the return to Angola of an old colonial administrator who sees all of the hopes of building an equitable society in Angola have become a hollow sham. Foreshadows the anti-colonial struggles which will shortly emerge.

VIEIRA, Jose Luandino

Luuanda, Short Stories of Angola, 1980 (original 1964)
Three stories about everyday events and life in Angola during the late 1960s and early 1970s. Told in the manner of African folk tales and involving spirits and magic as well as detailed realism, with the Angolan war of liberation as an ever present background to the events. Author was a white Angolan supporter of the MPLA.

Velhas Estorias/Vidas Novas, 1974 (Old Stories/New Lives)
A collection of short stories about individuals and conflicting interests caught up in Portugal's colonial war in Angola.

Nos, Os Do Makuluso, 1971 (Our Gang From Makuluso)
A novel which is a bitter-sad memorial to both the Portuguese peasant conscripts and the Angolan guerrilla fighters killed during the Angolan war of independence.

INDIA AND SOUTH EAST ASIA

India
Pakistan
Sri Lanka, Burma, Thailand
Viet Nam
Malaya
Indonesia
Philippines

INDIA

ABBAS, Khwaja Ahmad

Inquilab, 1955 (Inquilab, 1958)
A massive, wide ranging novel about the varied forces involved in the struggles
for Indian independence between 1919 and 1931. The account is threaded around a
maturing youth from a declining Muslim civil servant family and depicts the
growing confrontations (revolutionary as well as nationalist) in India during
those years and the protagonist's radicalization as he moves among various
political groups. His organizing journeys throughout India portray the widespread,
uncoordinated and bitter class struggles of workers and peasants, especially in
northwest India, whose interests are far removed from those of the Ghandian
Congress Party or the right wing Hindu nationalists. Underlines the protagonist's
conviction that the peasantry and Indian proletariat will have to play a decisive
role if independence is to mean anything.

Rice and Other Stories, 1947
A collection of ten short stories about supposedly representative Indian people on
the eve of independence--an Anglo-Indian servant, a Punjabi peasant mother, a
Bombay prostitute, a Bengali mill worker, etc.

Cages of Freedom and Other Stories, 1952
A collection of grim stories which include accounts of the intercommunal riots
that followed Indian independence; the seeming triumph of brutal, dirt-ignorant
sectarianism.

Black Sun and Other Stories, 1964
A series of stories ranging from the pervasive social and economic failures of
independent India to anti-imperialist struggles in the Congo and Viet Nam during
the early 1960s.

The Naxalites, 1979
An agitational "novel" cum morality play about the Naxalite peasant revolt against
landlord thugs and police in northern India during the late 1960s.

AMRITRAY

Bij, 1953 (Seed)
A Hindi novel describing the frustrations and deadend lives of lower middle class
Indian youths after independence, the gradual drift toward Marxism by some of them
and the deepening conviction that only a revolutionary solution can drag India
out of its seemingly perpetual poverty and injustice.

Hathi Ke Dant, 1956 (Elephant's Tusks)
A bitterly satiric Hindi novel which depicts the overnight switch of Zamindars (the
landowners and village political bosses) from staunch supporters of the British
Raj, which underwrote their local rule previously, to vocal supporters of the
Congress Party on independence. Depicts the scramble to retain vested interests
and line up with the new rulers of India.

ANAND, Mulk Raj

Untouchable, 1933
A novel revolving about one day in the life of an outcast sweeper in a small
Punjabi town during the late 1920s; his reminiscences, work and worries about
feeding his family. Portrays incidents of calculated indignity and callousness
which are a part of the caste system and a revelation of the physical power behind
the ideology of caste. Relates the protagonist's fantasies, failings and inner
struggles against despair in what was the first "socialist realist" novel to
appear in India. Anand is the most pre-eminent of left Indian authors, and it is
impossible to do his works justice in brief annotation.

Coolie, 1936
A novel which follows the life of a boy from a poor but rotten hill village and
his exploitation by distant kinsmen, of a different but equally oppressive stint
of bound service to a feudal landlord from which he escapes to become a labourer
in the slums of Bombay. A passage through the historic types of economic
organization existing in India, experienced at their lowest rung. All the decency,
resiliency and initiative which we originally see in the hero do not save him from
being ground down and destroyed.

Two Leaves and a Bud, 1937
A novel dealing with the trajectory of an Indian peasant family which loses its
land and migrates to work on a British-owned tea plantation in Assam. There they
find themselves in as great poverty as before, with a finely graded system of
straw bosses replacing the hierarchy of caste. Attempts to organize a union of
plantation workers are defeated following beatings and a murder by company goons,
who are protected by a British colonial court. When the protagonist's wife is
raped by one of the straw bosses the husband assassinates the plantation manager
and this triggers a brief outburst of vengeance by other workers. While
individually heroic, the clear intimation is that such acts of desperation are
only ineffective forerunners of the militant working class organization needed to
change the system.

The Village, 1939, Across Black Waters, 1940, The Sword and the Sickle, 1942
A trilogy novel which is an epic account of the Punjab from the first decade of
the century to the beginning of W.W.II; the intersecting classes, developments,
conflicts in the region. It follows a young Sikh from a peasant village who
determines to escape the strictures of village life and joins the British (Indian)
army. His experiences of events in Europe during and after the Great War place
events in the Punjab in the context of world wide forces. Relates his return to
India to find his family, kinspeople and friends scattered and changed with the
spread of commercial agriculture and the flood of people into the cities.
Portrays the multifaceted peasant and working class struggles and contradictions
which marked the Punjab in the 1920s and 1930s. Possibly Anand's greatest work.

The Big Heart, 1945
A novel about a village of artizans in South India during the early 1940s whose
livelihood is destroyed by the establishment of a nearby factory producing
copper utensils. In Anand's account, the coppersmiths (despite their pride of
work) are not committed to traditional ways of production and the associated
social relationships per se, and they recognize the ineffectiveness of the machine
wrecking they finally resort to. A study of the "class" rationality, potentially
harnessable for progressive ends, behind what seems like a purely backward and
atavistic response by Indian poor. Also see The Old Woman and the Cow, 1960 and
The Road, 1961, two other novels touching on the sometime wisdom and popular
interests entailed in seemingly "backward" social customs among peasant villagers.
Anand nevertheless underscores the necessity of cutting the Gordian knot of past
traditions and defensive peasant strategies.

Seven Summers, 1961, Morning Face, 1968
The first two volumes of Anand's autobiographic account of his life and times.

The Barbers' Trade Union and Other Stories, 1944, The Tractor and the Corn
Goddess, 1947
Two collections of stories dealing with the interpenetration of traditional and
new social relationships in India on the eve of independence; of the complex ways
in which these elements are incorporated in and affect the deeds and feelings of
individuals.

ANCHAL (Rameshvar Shukla)

Carnti Dhup, 1945 (The Sunshine of Revolution)
A Hindi novel describing the social and class struggles of Indian peasants and
workers proceeding alongside and in contradistinction to the Ghandian independence
movement during the 1930s and 1940s. Portrays the Congress Party as merely a tool
of the Indian middle and aspirant ruling classes.

Nayi Imarat, 1947 (New Building)
A novel revolving around a retrospective defense of the United Front policy
maintained by the Communist Party of India during W.W.II. Presents the contending
debates of Indian nationalists and even left workers who saw W.W.II as mainly a
conflict between British and German imperialism in which Indians had no stake.

Ulka, 1959 (Ulka)
A Hindi novel about the gradual decay and dissolution of a middle class joint
family. Juxtaposed to the domestic lives of Indian workers and poor, among whom
the joint family had already ceased to be of any real importance.

ANNADURAI, T.V.

Neethi Thevan Mayakkam, 1952 (The Seduction of the Just King)
A Tamil agitational play written to support the campaigns of the Dravidian Toilers
Party. Using a quasi-traditional folk style it portrays the Indian caste system
and the Brahmanic traditions as the codification of conquest by Hindu rulers two
millenia previously, and the major sacred text (the Ramayanna) as nothing but
ideological progaganda dressed as religion in order to ease their rule over the
Tamil speaking people.

Chandrodayam, 1943 (Rise of the Moon)
A Tamil play set in more recent times but dealing with the same theme as The
Seduction.

BANERJEE, Upendra Nath

Memoirs of a Revolutionary, 1924
An autobiographic account of the background and goals, but mainly the prison
memoirs, of a basically Indian nationalist "revolutionary". Focuses on the
conditions in and inmates of the Devil's Island prison camp established on
Andaman Islands by the British for Indian political prisoners. In a similar vein,
see Ullaskar Dutt's Twelve Years of My Prison Life, 1944.

BANNERJEE, Manik

Boatmen of the Padma, 1948
A naturalistic portrait of the lives of fishermen, boat people and others who live
and work along the Padma river in Bengal during the 1930s. Describing everyday
life, the daily struggle for subsistence, the overwhelming presence of natural
forces and the seemingly unchanging character of life stretching from distant
past to future. Also see Humayan Kabir's Men and Rivers, 1945, a novel on a
similar theme and in the same locale.

BANERJI, Vibhutibhushan

Pather Panchali, 1929 (Pather Panchali, 1968), Aranyak, 1938 (Aranyak, 1968)
Two Bengali novels which document the everyday life of caste, work, poverty, loves
and hostilities and fatalism in a small Bengal village of the 1920s. Richly
detailed in the portrayal of anonymous villagers as intricate human beings.

BHASKARAN, P.

Vayalar Garjikkunu, 1948 (Vayalar Roars)
A Malayalam epic poem which memorializes the communist led peasant uprising against
landlords and their police in the Vayalar region of Kerela during 1946. A
testimony to a sort of Naxalite movement of the 1940s. Also see The Dancer and
the Ring, 1962, a collection of poetry.

BHATTACHARAYA, Bhabani

So Many Hungers, 1947
A novel about the Bengal famine of 1942-43 as seen through the eyes of some of
the victims. Focuses on a surviving daughter of one peasant family in particular.
Describes the inaction of the British colonial and Indian state governments to
the impending and then actual deaths of over a million. Of the way in which the
starving and fleeing families are further exploited, how children were bought as

bound servants or prostitutes by other Indians, and of the manipulations of
Calcutta grain merchants who hold back stocks of grain in order to get the maximum
profits from the disaster. A powerful protest novel, although with an apolitic
conclusion.

He Who Rides the Tiger, 1954
A novel of a blacksmith in a Bengali village whose lack of subservience brings
him into conflict with the upper caste bosses of the village who finally force
him to flee to Calcutta. His search for work in the city, poverty and imprisonment
for theft, accounts of the endless daily strategies employed in order to survive
and the hero's growing hatred of the entire Indian social system.

A Goddess Named Gold, 1960
A somewhat melodramatic novel about how Indian independence has been translated
into a carnival of greed and profiteering by the assortment of landlords, entrepreneurs   and others who comprise the new ruling class. Combined with an other
wordly appeal to "return" to Ghandi's sermons of simplicity and voluntary sharing
of wealth.

CHANDAR, Krishan

I Cannot Die, a story of Bengal, 1943
A novel in which the Bengal famine is described alternately through the eyes of a
foreign consul, a wealthy Calcutta merchant and by a dying victim of the famine.

Flame and the Flower, 1951
A collection of stories translated from Urdu; they deal with events in India but
also range over the then contemporary world. One is based on a letter from an
American soldier killed in the Korean war, another is a eulogy to the Spanish
working people, one relates a train journey through north India during the
communal riots of 1947, while yet another is a story of a third generation mill
worker in Bombay. Chandar wrote twelve novels and hundreds of short stories in
Urdu.

CHATTERJI, Saratcandra

Mahes, 1921
A Bengali novel about a Muslim peasant living under the double oppression of being
a tenant farmer and member of a minority under a Hindu zamindar regime, where the
landlords, priest, village leaders and judges are all one and the same. Mahes is
the name of the family draught ox, who becomes the means through which the
zamindars stir up hatred against the Muslim minority as a way of strengthening
their own authority. Ends with the family giving up and going to Calcutta to look
for work.

CHITALE, Venu

In Transit, 1950
A novel by a Muslim woman writer which deals with the Indian independence movement
from circa 1910 to the 1940s; the various revolutionary and Ghandian strains, and
the changes wrought on a Muslim professional family who support national
independence and "progress" but see themselves gradually overwhelmed by Hindu
communalism.

DEV, Kesava

The Stories of Dev, 1940
A collection of "proletarian" stories about Kerela peasants and workers by a
prolific journalist and playwright of the Indian People's Theatre Association, the
translator of John Reed's Ten Days That Shook the World into Malayalam.

Otayilninnu, 1942 (From the Gutter)
A Malayalam novel about the conditions which force one man into becoming a rickshaw
puller, and of his short life. Set in Kerela during the 1930s and comparable to
Anand's Coolie.

DUGGAL, Katar Singh (Katar Duggal Singh)

Agg Khan Vale, 1948 (The Fire Eaters), Nawan Ghar, 1951 (New House)
Two collections of stories about the lives of an array of people, from landless
peasants to town merchants, in the author's home district of Punjab. Investigates
the social restriction and oppression both flowing from antithetical class
interests but also those self imposed by villagers on each other.

DUTT, Utpal

Charge Street, 1952
A play which "exposes" the repressive maneuvres behind the arrest of Communist
Party leaders in Bengal at the time by government officials and judges who are
afraid the Congress Party would lose the next state elections.

Angar, 1960 (Coal)
A famous Bengali play about the exploitation and deadly conditions existing in the
coal mines of Bengal. Followed a series of mine disasters there.

Teer, 1967 (Arrow)
A Bengali agitational play memorializing the Naxalite peasants in revolt against
zamindar landlord repression in north India. One of a number of Dutt's plays
evoking the tradition of armed resistance and revolt against oppressors in India.

FREEMAN, James (ed.)

Untouchable: An Indian Life History, 1979
A life history in the American social science tradition, being an account of the
caste system from the bottom. The daily life and rounds of one untouchable family
mainly from 1950 to the 1970s.

GARGI, Balwant

Loha-Kut, 1944 (Iron Smith)
A Punjabi play about a brutal blacksmith and the ultimate revolt and departure of
his wife. A rather violent Indian version of A Doll's House.

Kesoro, 1952 (Kesoro)
A Punjabi play about the roundabout ways in which some women in peasant villages
attempt to educate and liberate themselves from the near overwhelming social
restrictions which bind them.

HOSAIN, Attia

Sunlight in a Broken Column, 1961
A novel about the adolescence and young womanhood of a daughter of a Muslim family
in north India during the late 1930s and 1940s; of the love but fettering
restriction of women even in a "modern" and "progressive" middle class family.
Also Phoenix Fled and Other Stories, 1953, twelve stories mainly about Muslim
women, old and young, in traditional and untraditional roles in north India.

INDIAN PEOPLE'S THEATRE ASSOCIATION

While normally cited under individual authors, plays by members of the IPTA
included an array of agitational works utilizing a wide range of Indian traditional
and regional forms of presentation (as well as "modern" theatre). A few of the
items not mentioned elsewhere are as follows.

One of the most widely translated and performed works was Bijan Bhattacharya's
Nabanna, 1943 (Bountiful Harvest), an agitational play used to raise money for the
victims of the Bengal famine. Shahir Anand Sathe's Aklechi Goshte, 1944 (A Tale
of Wisdom) used Maharati Tamasha songs in a story attacking landlords and money
lenders. Kalicharan Pattnayak's Bhata, 1944 (Rice) is a play about the
exploitation of tenant farmers in Orissa state and how one rapacious landlord is
dealt his due desserts. Raktmati (Red Earth, circa 1946) is an agitational play
calling on the audience to smash caste and especially "untouchable" social
restrictions. Balwant Gargi's Mogha, 1954 (Water Rights), about a peasant struggle
to regain lost water rights. The collective Malayalam play, Ningalenne
Communistakki, 1952 (You Made Me a Communist), a musical using folk songs to tell

of an old man who gradually abandons his theological orthodoxy to become a
communist. More recently, the collective Bengali play Rakter Rang, 1967 (Colour
of Blood), a street theatre piece supporting the insurrectional peasantry of
Naxalbari against landlord gunmen.

ISVARAN, Manjeri

Angry Dust, 1944, Rickshawwallah Stories, 1946, No Anklet Bells for Her, 1949
Three collections of short stories originally written in Tamil; about the daily
and domestic lives of ordinary working people in the towns and cities of south
India during the 1940s.

KAMODARAN, K. (K. Damodaran)

Pattabaki, 1936 (Rental Arrears)
A very widely performed, pioneer agitational play originally in Malayalam but
translated into most major Indian languages. It deals with tenant farmers thrown
off the land by wrack-renting landlord, the organization of an anti-rent movement
as an act of desperation and the confrontation of the tenants with the various
arms of the local government in village India of mid 1930s. Ending in the
conclusion that only force will change that system.

Tears, 1937
A collection of stories about life in Kerela villages and towns during the 1930s
from a revolutionary socialist perspective.

MADGULKAR, Vyankateah

The Village Has No Walls, 1959
A novel dealing with the penetration of Indian capitalism and its allied political
forces into an isolated Maharashtra peasant village a decade after independence,
and the local conflicts which arise.

MAKAN, Tottiyute

Scavenger, 1947
A sensitive proletarian novel originally in Malayalam. Deals with the lives of
three generations of pariah "nightsoil" carriers in Kerela from the turn of the
century until the eve of independence; the poverty, overwork, humiliations and
social exclusion. The story begins with the life of the grandfather who accepts
his lot as his dharma and continues with a son who schemes and strives so that
his own son will escape both the degradations of that life and the constant
bitterness and suppressed rebellion he himself feels. Portrays psychological as
well as social pressures against an outcast trying to improve his lot. With
great sacrifice the son's son "rises" (through education) to become a very junior
white collar employee. But the grandson, unable to sustain the constant striving
necessary to maintain his position, gradually falls back into the "sweeper"
status of his grandfather. A richly descriptive account of the evanescence of
individual advancement without changing the social system.

MARKANDAYA, Kamala

Nectar in a Sieve, 1954
A novel about a peasant woman in Madras state, from the 1920s to the early 1950s.
Girlhood, marriage, the life of a low caste peasant family and the collapse of
their livelihood when a commercial tannery is established nearby and the family
loses its necessary second income as tanners. Describes their flight to Madras
in search of work, raising a family in the alien city world and the return of the
woman as a near beggar to her home village after the death of the husband in an
industrial accident. Done in the form of reminiscences.

A Handful of Rice, 1967
A novel about a member of the urban poor who manages to claw his way up into a
minor clerical position. An account of how he is gradually overwhelmed by the
continual penury, vacuity and petty indignities of his job and the upwardly mobile
aspirations of his wife. Unable to stand it anymore, he quits his job and falls

into an even deeper and inescapable poverty than when he began life as a young
worker. In a sense a companion work to Nectar in a Sieve.

NAGARAJAN, K. (K. Nagarjun)

Athawar House, 1939
A chronicle of a Marathi Brahmin family living in a small backward south Indian
town during the 1920s and 1930s, with the independence movement seeingly far
removed from local events. A detailed account of rural upper caste life of the
period, foreshadowing the conflicts and shakeup of traditional order about to
arrive.

Cold Rice, 1945
A collection of stories revolving around a Brahmin family, townspeople and local
officials, and villagers on the Coromandel coast of south India in the early
1940s. Catches the feel of a stagnant society unconcernedly sleepwalking on the
brink of social change.

Chronicles of Kedaram, 1961
A chronicle of a small south Indian town during the late 1930s; of the infighting
between the Congress Party and the arch reactionary (Hindu communalist) Justice
Party, hostilities between Muslims and Hindus and between various castes and
sects. Told with attention to the historic anachronism of these intricate
divisions and conflicts and an emphasis on the absurdity of the petty jockeying
for position in the face of the massive problems which face the entire society.

Ratinath Ki Caci, 1948 (The Aunt of Ratinath), Baba Batesernath, 1954 (Father
Batesernath), Varun Ke Bete, 1957 (Son of Varuna)
A few of Narajan's twenty odd novels written in Hindi and Marathi, dealing mainly
with everyday life in rural Bihar, one of the most backward of the Indian states.
Colloquial speech portrays views of tenant farmers, landless labourers and
lower caste Hindus--contrasted to the life styles and rhetoric of the Hindu
landlord-zamindar class whose power is ultimately based on something more
forceful than religious ideology.

Hirak Jayanti, 1962
A satiric Hindi novel which chronicles the rise of an opportunist and increasingly
corrupt local Congress Party official as a minister in the Bihar state government.

NAMBOODIRIPAD, E.M.S.

The Mahatma and the Ism, 1958
A retrospective analysis of Ghandi, the class sociology of the Ghandian movement,
the practical concommitants of its ideology--both before and after Indian
independence. By a leading Indian Marxist theoretician.

NARULA, Surinder Singh (Surinder Singh Narula)

Peo Puttar, 1946 (Father and Son)
An epic Punjabi novel about the social forces at work in the Punjab between 1896
and 1918. Revolves around an ex-British Indian army soldier, a Sikh exiled
because of his involvement with a nationalist movement, and his son who gradually
moves leftward through a welter of experiences which comprise India of the time.
British colonialism in full flower, traditional landlord autocracy and Indian
merchant capitalism, the new and old struggles of the Punjabi peasantry and the
first steps of an emerging urban working class.

Aluni Sil, 1952 (Saltless Rock)
A sequel to Peo Puttar which carries forward the account of social and political
struggles in Amritsar from 1918 to the begining of W.W.II. Revolves around the
spuriously traditional conflict over control of a Sikh temple between the merchant-
oriented priests and a group of progressive Sikhs.

Jagrata, 1948 (Vigil)
A Punjabi novel about the lives of urban factory workers in Amritsar during the
early 1930s; their anger, poverty, desperation but also their escapist fantasies.
Deals with the beginings of open class struggle, the suppression of a Sikh
revolutionary movement whose remaining activists merge with the early communists.

Din Te Dunua, 1951 (Faith of the World)
Another novel about the growth of capitalism in north India from the 1920s to
1947; the rise of an urban proletariat whose sometimes class consciousness is
alloyed with continuing ethnic, caste and other divisions. Ends on the seeming
triumph of ethnic sectarianism in the intercommunal "riots" of 1947. Also
Dil Darya, 1958 (River of the Heart), a novel revolving around the confrontation
between the policies of the Hindu communalist parties during 1947 and the
attempts of Indian communists and their organizations to head off the Muslim-
Hindu bloodletting about to erupt.

Lok Dushman, 1952 (Enemy of the People)
A novel of the continuing power of the zamindars and priests over the Punjab
peasantry; the resiliency of the landlords linked to the city capitalists since
independence and the total failure of nominal land redistribution schemes.
Similarly Jag-Biti, 1954 (Tale of the World).

Gallan Dit Rat Dian, 1966 (Talk of Day and Night)
A novel about the Indian middle classes during the 1960s, growing in power and
wealth but absolutely incapable of administering anything effectively or
beneficially. Portrays the deepening internal dissolution of India and raises
the desperate hope that collapse may ultimately result in the emergence of a
more equitable society. Also Rang Mahal, 1950 (Pleasure Palace), a novel on a
similar theme set fifteen years earlier--more optimistic in that the trajectory
of the Indian bourgeoisie is counterposed to the growing sense of inheritance in
a militant union leader.

PENDSE, S.N.

Garambicha Bapu, 1944 (The Wild Bapu of Garambi, 1968)
A lyrical Marathi novel about the squalor of peasant life barely hidden behind
the beauty and potential richness of the Konkan plateau of central India. Of the
caste barriers and landlord levies weighing down an impoverished, ex-tribal
peasantry.

Haddapar, 1951 (Outlawed)
A novel about the arbitrary injustices perpetrated by the past colonial practice
of outlawing entire tribal groups; follows the dissolution of one such "tribe"
in Maharashtra at the turn of the century.

PRASAD GUPTA, Bhairav

Ganga Maiya, 1953 (Mother Ganges)
A Hindi novel which depicts the daily and yearly struggles of peasants to survive
in a poverty stricken region of Uttar Pradesh during the late 1940s and 1950s.
The thousand and one problems of scratching a living from the land and fending
off human predators.

Mashal, 1957 (Torch)
A Hindi novel which depicts the lives of factory workers in the industrial city
of Kanpur (Uttar Pradesh). The conditions of working class life, union struggles
and political confrontations with Indian capitalism and the daily rounds of making
a living.

Sattimaiya Ka Caura, 1959
A novel about the struggles of militant unionists and communists against the
continuing sectarian, communal and caste hostilities which exist among and divide
urban workers. The multi-faceted bases and consequences of such divisions and
why they have not been overcome. Set in industrial cities of Uttar Pradesh
during the late 1950s. Prasad Gupta was a prolific working class author whose
work was translated into a number of European languages other than English.

PREMCHAND, Munshi (Dhanpat Rai Srivastava)

Maidan-e Amal, 1934 (The Field of Hope)
An Urdu novel which depicts the deepening poverty, the breakup of old relationships
of mutual aid and the increasing tensions in an intermixed Muslim and Hindu region
of north India at the time. Seen through the eyes of a journalist.

Godan, 1936 (Godan, 1957)
A classic peasant novel in Hindi. A panorama of life in Uttar Pradesh from before
W.W.I to the begining of the 1930s--farmers and peasants, moneylenders, landlords,
merchants and in general a cross section of the north Indian rural society as it
touches on the lives of the peasantry. Includes accounts of the way in which
peasants attempt to use tradition in a flexible and pragmatic manner to defend
and advance their current interests. Premchand is considered the pioneer of
social realist writing in Hindi.

A Handful of Wheat, 1955
A posthumous collection of short stories portraying village life and people in
Uttar Pradesh during the 1920s and 1930s.

PILLAI, Thakazhi S.

Rantitannazi, 1948 (Two Measures of Rice)
A Malayalam novel about the humiliations and struggles of a community of landless
labourers working in commercial rice fields of the Malabar coast. A portrait of
everyday life among the poorest in Kerela society during the early 1940s. Revolves
around a passive and fatalistic agricultural worker who rises in wrath when his
wife is raped by a local landowner, kills the landlord and triggers a brief,
bloody and unexpected jacquerie against other landlords by their serfs.

Enippatikal, 1966 (Steps in a Ladder)
A massive Malayalam novel of failed opportunities in Kerela during Pillai's life
time, from the British Raj of 1930s through the various Congress, Coalition and
Communist state governments of the 1950s and early 1960s. It focuses on the
endemic corruption, lassitude yet "flexibility" of the Indian civil service which
can adapt to and divert all reforms into administered stasis regardless of what
government is in power and regardless of what the people clearly demand.

Scavenger's Son, 1975
A novel which deals with two generations of "street sweepers" in Calcutta; of the
father's aspiration to have his son escape that life and of the impossibility of
achieving the goal despite great sacrifices. However, as distinct from earlier
novels on this theme, the son winds up proud of the value of his work and as a
union organizer fighting for better pay and job conditions for Calcutta garbage
collectors.

RAGHAV, Rangey

Gharonde, 1941 (Home)
A Hindi novel which describes the bases for but the unsuccessful attempt to organize
a peasant revolt against the web of landlords, political bosses and princely rulers
in south India during the late 1930s.

Vishad Math, 1946 (The Great Ritual)
A Hindi novel which describes the indifference of the British colonial government
to starving peasants during the Bengal famine of 1943, and their ruthless
exploitation by Indian capitalists. A Marxist treatment of a theme which has been
handled by many Indian writers.

Hazur, 1952 (Sir!)
A Hindi novel which follows the social and political developments in India from
1931 to 1951; during which the Congress Party becomes the undisguised vehicle of
the new Indian ruling class and where the alternative of a socialist revolution
to end the exploitation of India's working class and peasantry seems to become
a possibility. One of Raghav's twenty odd novels on comparable themes.

Siddha Sata Rasta, 1955 (The Direct Path)
A Hindi novel about the armed struggle for Indian independence led by sections of
the Indian Communist Party in the period immediately after W.W.II.

ROY, Manabendra N.

Memoirs, 1964
Roy was one of the most influential Asian communists during the 1920s and a leading
figure in the Comintern before his opposition to Stalin over the disastrous policy

of supporting Chinese nationalist forces. The memoirs, however, are mainly about Roy's 30 year experiences as an independent left socialist in India from the late 1920s to 1950s. Also see Letters from Prison, 1944, a running commentary on events of W.W.II as they affect the then current and future possibilities for various left wing forces throughout the world, especially in India.

SARNA, Mahinder Singh (Mahinder Singh Sarna)

Chavian Di Rut, 1959 (Season of the Choppers)
A collection of stories which depart from Sarna's account of poor and exploited people who in the past have somehow managed to retain their humanity and decency despite all odds, but who become caught by and participate in scenes of senseless and unalloyed brutality during the Hindu-Muslim intercommunal riots which flared through the Punjab in 1947.

SATARTHI, Devinder

Kung Posh, 1941, Sona Gaci, 1950 (Red Light District), Tin Boohian Vala Ghar, 1961 (The House With Three Doors)
Three collections of stories about social conditions in the Punjab during 1940s and 1950s; they utilize traditional folk tales and allegories in appeals for social reform.

SEKHON, Sant Singh (Sant Singh Sekhon)

Lahu Mitti, 1949 (Blood and Soil)
A Punjabi novel about three generations of a Punjab peasant family from 1890s to 1947. A detailed account of daily life and longer term strategies, their aspirations, tenacity and limitations. Portrays the slowly changing collage of colonialism, landlords and moneylenders, and the new Indian bourgeoisie under which peasant farming over a half century operates. Focuses on the loss of peasant farms to commercial agriculture in an irrigation project and of the emergence of a peasant movement which, although it does not significantly improve conditions, does manage to reclaim part of the lost lands. The limits of defensive strategies.

Samacar, 1948 (News), Kame Te Vodhe, 1950 (Workers and Warriors), Adhi Vat, 1954 (Midway), Nadija Pehr, 1959 (The Third Phase)
Four collections of stories about poor peasants and landless workers in rural Punjab who, despite age-old poverty and exploitation, have managed to retain a spirit of initiative and opposition to the rhetoric of "fate" and the other worldly musings of priests.

Narki,1952 (Denisons of Hell)
A play about the degeneration of family members around a rising Indian black marketeer in the post W.W.II period.

Bhoofin, 1955 (Land Gift)
A satiric play about "Saint" Vinobha Bhave's "land reform" scheme, in which reform was to be accomplished by voluntary contributions of land by landlords. Treated as a ploy by zamindars so as to stall any real land redistribution program.

Moian Sar Nain Kai, 1958 (The Dead Have No Realization)
A play about how the lassitude of Indian government is a direct and indirect outcome of two centuries of colonial rule. Also Che Ghar, 1941 (Six Houses) and Hartal, 1946 (Strike), two agitational plays produced by the Indian People's Theatre Association.

SEN, Ela

Darkening Days, 1944
Documentary reportage in the form of seven stories, mainly about women victims of the Bengal famine of 1942-1943.

SHIRURKAR, Vibhavari

Bali, 1956
A Marathi novel which exposes the exploitation of remnant tribal peoples by a

combination of Hindu landlords, backwoods entrepreneurs, upper caste politicians
and others who are otherwise engaged in calling for liberation from British rule.
Set in Maharashtra province in the late 1930s and 1940s.

SHRINAGESH, Shakuntala

The Little Black Box, 1955
A novel about a middle class woman in a T.B. sanitorium who reminisces and has
second thoughts about her life and that of other women in north India during the
first half of the 20th century. A sensitive fictional life history.

SHRIVASTVA, Shivnarayan

Dhuan Ag Aur Insan, 1960 (Smoke, Fire and Man), Subah Ka Suraj, 1970 (The Morning
Sun)
Two Hindi novels dealing with the lives of textile workers (Dhuan Ag)and
construction workers (Subah) in the industrial cities of Uttar Pradesh; their
daily domestic concerns and work, their families and friendships, political
activities and union organizing. A picture of strikes and confrontations from
the late 1950s to the late 1960s. Shrivastva stemmed from an impoverished peasant
family, became a textile worker and later a union organizer. His novels are said
to be among the more authentic accounts of contemporary working class life in
Indian cities.

SINGH, Gurdial

Marhi Da Diva, 1964 (A Lamp for the Dead)
A Punjabi novel about the deadening effects of Brahminical caste prescriptions
on the relationships of people in a small, conservative village. Of how the
budding zest for life in young is gradually extinguished to conform to the
restrictions and petty hierarchy of village society.

SINGH, Iqbal

When One Is In It, 1936
A novela by an Urdu author and organizer of Indian Progressive Writers Association.
It deals with the thoughts, fears, reminiscences of a woman worker as she stands
in the rain with 400 other job applicants for a few openings in a Bombay silk
spinning factory during the 1930s. Her sexual as well as class exploitation in
past and her inner struggles to suppress her despair and visible anger in order
to pass muster to get the job she needs to support herself and child.

SINGH, Kesar

Lehr Vadhdi Gai, 1953 (The Wave Rolled On)
A Punjabi novel about members of the "Indian National Army" (a force established
under Japanese aegis in occupied Malaya during W.W.II). The soldiers are mainly
Indian contract workers on Malayan rubber plantations and tin mines, many of whom
are politically aware and not fooled about the Japanese purposes, but who see
this as an opportunity to end British rule in India. The interplay of
contradictory goals and actions, of confusions and insights, comes tumbling down
with the defeat of Japanese imperialism. The struggle for an independent and
socially just India passes to other forces with other strategies. Alludes to the
anti-imperialist struggles which emerge throughout the region at the end of
W.W.II.

SINGH, Khuswant (Jaswant Singh Kanwal)

Train to Pakistan, 1956
A powerful novel of the intercommunal riots and massacres which took place in the
Punjab during its partition into Indian and Pakistan territories in 1947. A
despairing account of the collapse of generations of mutual aid and friendships
between Muslims and Hindus, the depravity of the massacres on both sides, the
streams of refugees fleeing their former home villages. But especially the
overnight disappearance of basic decency among many ordinary people and their
collusion in sectarian savagery.

Rat Raki Hai, 1955 (The Night is Not Yet Over)
Novel of a tenant farmers movement in the Punjab during the early 1950s which
conveys the long history of peasant-landlord struggles there. Portrays all the
narrowness, self repression and weaknesses of peasantry but also their potential
vitality.

I Shall Not Hear the Nightingale, 1959
A novel in the form of reminiscences. About a middle class Punjabi family whose
members are engaged in the Indian nationalist movement during W.W.II, their
decency and social concerns mixed with class, ethnic and sexual chauvinism.

Hani, 1961 (Mates)
A Punjabi novel revolving about two village girls who are close friends, of the
little-changed oppression of women and of the gross and subtle ways in which
traditional restrictions and caste barriers destroy personal relationships even
among those determined not to be bound by those strictures.

The Mark of Vishnu and Other Stories, 1950
A collection of stories about the mixture of promise and social injustice, human
vitality and stupidity in the Punjab on the eve of and after independence.

SINGH, Nanak

Adam Khor, 1958 (The Man-Eater)
A "sex and violence" thriller utilized as a vehicle of social criticism. Revolves
around the doings and voracity of a self-made Indian millionaire, the general web
of deceit and violence in his relationships and the murder he arranges. Involves
a disillusioned ex-policeman, combative workers, and evil battening on evil.

SINGH, Sujan

Sabh Rang, 1950 (All Colours), Narkan De Devte, 1954 (Gods in Hell), Nawan Rang,
1955 (New Colour), Manukh Pashu, 1958 (Men and Beasts), Sawal Jawab, 1962
(Questions and Answers)
Five collections of stories which deal with a wide range of social situations in
the Punjab; the hopeless stagnation, the not-so-genteel poverty of the frayed
white collar class, the exploitation of women, etc. His stories contain the
recurrent theme that oppression and poverty have not killed the humanity and
underlying strength of the oppressed and a belief in their ultimate triumph.
Ranging from calls for social reform to prescription of revolution.

SRI SRI

Sri Sri Sahityam, 1970 (Collected Works of Sri Sri) (K.V. Ramana Reddy, ed.)
The works of a remarkable Telugu poet. Poetry mainly written from the late 1930s
to early 1950s, it combines a south Indian (Andhra Pradesh) patriotism with
proletarian internationalism, romanticism with working class realism. Many of
the poems attack the escapism and apologetics of Hindu religion and social
philosophy, assault the traditions of caste and ridicule the philosophy that
"reality is an illusion". All woven together with a Narodnik celebration of the
struggles of the Telugu poor, peasants and workers.

SURVE, Narayan

Aisa Ga Mee Brahma, 1961, Maze Vidyapeeth, 1966 (My University)
Two collections of Marathi prose-poetry. They deal with the genuine heroism of
daily life among the Bombay working class--men, women and children--from their
local and immediate concerns to prosaically millenial visions. Raised on the
streets of Bombay, with no formal education, a worker since age thirteen, translated extracts indicate Surve's poetry to be of extraordinary power and humanity.

YADAV, Rajendra

Ukhare Hue Log, 1970 (The Uprooted People)
A satiric Hindi novel about the corrupt lives and unscrupulous manipulations of
Congress Party leaders who have become handmaidens of the Indian capitalist class.

The multifaceted exploitation and oppression of the Indian peasantry and working class during the 1960s and a call for mass struggle.

Shah Aur Mat (The King Checkmated), Mantra Vidh (The Enchanted), Sara Akash (The Wide Sky), 1958-1964
Three historical and socialist realist novels about the lives and struggles of Indian peasantry and workers during past ages.

YASHPAL

Dada Kamred, 1941 (Grandfather Comrade)
A semi-autobiographical novel in Hindi dealing with the underground "Hindustan Socialist Republican Army" in the late 1920s and early 1930s. The events in Punjab and throughout India which led a Punjabi left nationalist (Yashpal) to become a Marxist; of strikes and the growing labour union movement, the increasingly oppressive responses of British colonialism, the trajectory of the Indian middle class, and above all the deepening class (as distinct from national) struggle in India. A rich account of the revolutionary socialist currents in India of the time.

Deshdrohi, 1943 (Traitor)
A Hindi novel dealing with the thoughts and experiences of a Punjabi doctor who is a member of the Indian Communist Party (which though outlawed supported British imperialism against Japanese and German fascism). Debates the middle class nationalism of the Congress Party and analyses what "traitor" means, and to whom.

Divya, 1945
A historical novel set in an ancient north Indian kingdom; portrays the resistance of the bulk of the people against the initial establishment of the caste system.

Jhutha Sac: Vatan Aur Desh, 1961 (The False Truth: The Nation and the Country), Jhutha Sac: Desh Ka Bhavishya, 1967 (The False Truth: The Future of the Country)
A much translated (except into English) two volume novel in Hindi which deals with India from independence to the late 1950s. It treats with the dithering, lack of policy and self-seeking of the Congress Party which permitted the bloody inter communal riots that followed partition. Counterposed to the actions of the Indian Communist Party which is portrayed as doing what it could to defuse those conflicts. The second volume is a panoramic yet detailed account of the ingathering of all the local and regional bosses into the Congress Party, the inner quarrels, scams and pervasive corruption of this unconsolidated ruling class--as well as the growing resistance to it--from late 1940s to late 1950s.

Manushya Ke Rup, 1964 (Faces of Man), Barah Ghante, 1966, Apsara Ka Shrap, 1956 (Angel's Curse), Kyon Phesen, 1968, Sinhavlokan, 1963 (Overview)
Some of Yashpal's other novels and collected stories dealing with various facets of social and political struggle in India from the 1930s to the 1960s.

ZAHEER, Sajjad Syed

Bimar, 1941 (Sick Man)
An Urdu play widely produced by the Indian People's Theatre Association. It deals with the struggles of Indian peasants and rural labourers against landlord rent collectors and goon squads during 1940.

PAKISTAN

ALI BHUTTO, Zulfikar

The Myth of Independence, 1969
An overview of the class autocracy, unreconstructed "feudal" interests, the carryover of past colonial structures and the dominance of economic and political neo-colonialism in countries which have achieved nominal independence since W.W.II--with primary reference to Pakistan. Treats with the inability of such regimes to implement any significant economic or social reforms to rescue the bulk of their populations from increasing poverty, with an especial charge against the series of military regimes ruling Pakistan over twenty years. Although from a large landowner family, Ali Bhutto led the major mass party in Pakistan. During his brief period in power during the late 1970s he initiated the only period of democratic and economic reforms yet experienced in Pakistan. He was overthrown and executed by the ferociously reactionary and fundamentalist military regime now in power.

AZIZ AHMAD

Aisi Bulandi, Aisi Pasti, 1948 (The Shore and the Wave, 1971)
A novel of the growth of Islamic modernism and renaissance among middle class in Moslem India and their drive to create the separate state of Pakistan through partition. Touches on the contradictory pull of past ties and traditions and new hopes, the mixed interests and responses involved. It does not glimpse the downward trajectory of Pakistan in the generation since independence. A work by a leading liberal Pakistani author.

AHMAD ALI

Twilight in Delhi, 1940
A roman d'clef about the declining fortunes of a family of progressive Muslim civil servants from the first decade of the century to the 1930s; their alienation both from British colonial rule and the rising Hindu nationalism. By a left nationalist poet whose work was influential in the early years of Pakistan.

IQBAL, Muhammad

Poems of Iqbal, 1955
A collection of poetry (translated from Urdu) by one of the most influential early proponents of "Islamic socialism" during the first three decades of this century. Some bitter attacks on European colonialism and capitalism and its indigenous allies, the poems call for an Islamic revival and rededication to human justice. Occasional strains of theocratic and anti-European chauvinism may be hard to square with socialist claims.

FAIZ AHMED FAIZ

Poems by Faiz, 1971
A collection of translated Urdu poetry by the leading communist poet of Pakistan. They deal with the daily struggles for existence, the replacement of colonialism by an indigenous tyranny in Pakistan, of hopes sustained in prisons and during the seemingly ever-renewed power of reaction. A wistful style which in some ways is reminiscent of Nazim Hikmet's poetry.

SA'ADAT HASAN MANTO

Black Milk, 1955
A collection of short stories about grotesque and brutal aspects of life among variously lumpenized and quasi-illegal operators in Lahore during the first years of independence. The urban, declasse poor and fundamentalist elements juxtaposed in cinematographic form by a journalist/translator of Maxim Gorky.

SRI LANKA, BURMA, THAILAND

SRI LANKA (CEYLON)

GANESALINGAM, S., WICKRAMSINGHE, M. et al

The Colour of Tea, 1964
A collection of short stories about Ceylon by five Cingalese and five Tamil
speaking writers; the daily lives, problems and hopes of ordinary Ceylonese from
the late 1940s to the 1960s. The title story deals with continuing travails of
tea plantation workers after independence, the paper reforms and parliamentary
debates far removed from improving their living conditions.

KODITUWAKKU, Parakrama

Alut Minihek Avit, 1975 (A New Man Has Come)
A collection of poetry criticizing the strictures and authoritarian backwardness
of Ceylonese society in the 25 years since independence under various regimes.
Five of Kodituwakku's poems are translated in R. Obeyeskere and Chita Fernando's
Modern Writing From Sri Lanka, 1981.

PERERA, Karuna

Eko Math Eka Rataka, 1973 (Once Upon a Time)
A collection of wistful stories about the lives of working people and urban poor
in Ceylon during the 1960s. They draw upon the author's background and are told
as her childhood experiences.

WICKRAMASINGHE, Martin

Yuganthaya, 1949 (End of an Era), Viragaya, 1957 (Free From Desire)
Two final volumes of a trilogy which is an epic account of rural life in Ceylon
from circa W.W.I (under a little evident British colonial regime) to the first
years of independence in late 1940s. A philosophic account which examines the
initially still vital and "humane" social relationships in rural Ceylon but notes
the caste and ethnic elitism and empty religious orthodoxy of a society which
seems more stagnant than stable. Hints at the deepening inequities and anachronism
which arise during and after W.W.II. Also Snake Island, 1959, a novel on a
similar theme by the leading Ceylonese author of the previous generation.

BURMA

ORWELL, George

Burmese Days, 1934
A collection of stories about British colonial Burma during the early 1930s. From
the viewpoint of a young, dissatisfied British colonial policeman (which Orwell
was). It includes the story "On Shooting an Elephant" and provides more of an
insight into the customs of British colonial administrators than those of Burma
per se. There is an intriguing similarity between Orwell's views of Burmese
natives and some of his accounts of working class "denisons" of London slums
during his later radical phase.

MYINT, Thein Pe (Thein Pe Myinth)

What Happened in Burma, 1943
A short reportage work dealing with the Burmese independence movement and its
inception in the mid 1930s, an outgrowth of the left wing organizations of Indian
workers in Burma. Indicates the initial dalliance of Burmese anti-colonial groups
with Japanese forces but their early move to form the Anti-Fascist People's Front,
which became a major guerrilla force fighting Japanese occupation. Also his

Ashei-ga Nei-wun Htwet-thi-pama, 1960 (As Sure as the Sun Rises in the East), a novel about those developments to 1945.

Lan-za Paw-bi, 1949 (The Way Out)
A novel which covers the last months of the partizan war against Japanese occupation in 1945, the re-entry of British army and its attempts to recolonize Burma, the strengthening of the armed underground movement and its internal political debates as to which paths an independent Burma should take.

Bud-Dalin Hsaung Ba Mya, 1963 (Bu-Dalin Village)
An account of British colonial Burma in the late 1920s done through a reminiscence of Myint's home village.

Wi-thei Tha-taing Thamaing-asa, 1967 (History is Begining in the Chin Hills), Anya Pyan, 1970 (Return of Upper Burma)
Two reportage accounts of social conditions, political programs and people in different regions of Burma during the late 1950s and 1960s under the U Nu and Ne Win regimes.

MYINT, Tein Pe and MILNE, Patricia

Selected Short Stories of Thein Pe Myint, 1973
A selection of short stories in English translation by one of the leading early spokesmen for the left in Burma. Contains a brief biography of Myint and has a story ("Oil") dealing with petroleum workers in northern Burma in the 1930s, the evolution of a strike and how the union is suppressed by the colonial authorities. Also contains an account of the social concerns of the early Burmese nationalist movement and the 1936 student strike in Rangoon.

THAILAND/SIAM

DRASKAU, Jennifer (ed.)

Taw and Other Thai Stories, 1975
A collection of short stories written during the 1960s and early 1970s by six Thai writers (none of whom are particularly progressive). However, their casual descriptions of contemporary slavery and other indigeneous forms of servitude in modern Thailand do suggest the nature of that society and its "better" classes.

SRINAWK, Khamsing (Lao Khamhawn)

The Politician and Other Stories, 1973
A collection of short stories using mordant understatements to allude to the oppressive quality of life in contemporary Thailand with dry irony. They touch on the rigid caste/class system, especially in the northern region of the country, and present a peasantry (from whom Srinawk sprang) living in age old wretchedness and traditional powerlessness against exploiters old and new. He introduces the modern strata of notables hatched through their connections with the US military bases. "The Politician" and "Sales Rep for the Underworld" deal with Bangkok entrepreneurs nouveau-enriching themselves at the troughs of foreign funded "development projects".

SURANGKHANANG, E.

"The Grandmother", 1966 (in N. Cousins and F. Sionil Jose, eds., Asia P.E.N. Anthology)
A luminescent story dealing with a few days in the life of an unbemused old lady selling dumplings in a Bangkok marketplace during the early 1960s; a slice of the life and ordinary people swirling around her.

TURTON, Andrew, FAST, Jonathan, CALDWELL, Malcolm (eds.)

Thailand: The Roots of Conflict, 1978
A collection of essays which deal with the history of Siamese military regimes and social repression from 1932 on but focusing on the background and consequences of the "quasi-fascist" coup of 1976.

VIET NAM

ANH DUC

Hon Dat, 1969 (Hon Dat, 1969)
A novel about the inhabitants of the village of Hon Dat (south Viet Nam), the lives of men, women and children over the previous decade. Focuses on how they are gradually driven to revolt against the exactions of the early Diem regime and how they came to resist the punative expeditions of both the Saigon military and American troops. Also see Bui Duc Ai, The Young Woman of Sao Beach, 1962.

CONDOMINAS, Georges

We Have Eaten the Forest, 1977
A compellingly human ethnography of a Montangard tribal village in the central highlands during 1960, on the eve of the strategic hamlet system and bombing which would shatter so many such tribal peoples. By a French/Viet Namese anthropologist.

DANG TRAN CON and DOAN THI DIEM

Lamentof the Soldier's Wife, 1959
A slim collection of stories about the struggle against French colonial forces throughout Viet Nam in the late 1940s and early 1950s.

FALK, Richard, KOLKO, Gabriel, LIFTON, Robert (eds.)

Crimes of War: After Song My, 1970
An edited and condensed version of the findings of the Bertrand Russell "American War Crimes in Viet Nam Tribunal". Covers only the best documented cases and unfortunately lacks the followup of the earlier Nuremberg trials.

FALL, Bernard

Viet Nam Witness, 1953-1966, 1968
A diary-like account mainly of the post French phases of the Viet Namese war of independence. Covers the defeat of the French expeditionary army at Dien Bien Phu, the brutal intricacies in the creation of a puppet state in south Viet Nam from a cabal of private armies, mandarins and playboy emperors. Through the deepening involvement of US advisors, money and finally a half million troops, and ending on the eve of the Tet offensive which broke the will of American intervention.   .

Street Without Joy, 1964
A journalist's overview of the Viet Namese wars of independence from 1946 to 1963. Ranges throughout the country and presents summaries of reports and interviews with people from all walks of life enmeshed in the conflict. Fall was probably the most knowledgeable western reporter in Viet Nam who covered events for most of the period treated. These two titles are to stand for the vast and unsurveyable mass of reportage about that war.

FOREIGN LANGUAGES PUBLISHING HOUSE (HANOI) (ed.)

The Watchmaker of Dien Bien Phu, 1971
A collection of short stories written between 1945 and 1964 by some eleven authors. They depict various aspects and phases of the national liberation struggles against French colonialism (1945-1954) and the initial steps of reconstruction in north Viet Nam thereafter. Also issued under the editorship of Foreign Languages Publishing House, Strong Wind, 1962, a collection of stories dealing with socialist construction, especially the attempts to institute peasant cooperative and collective farming in north Viet Nam during the first six years of independence.

HO CHI MINH

Prison Diary, 1962
Some memoirs but mainly a collection of poetry written while Ho Chi Minh was imprisoned and awaiting execution by Chiang Kai Shek's forces in China during early 1940s. As well as being the leader of the Viet Namese revolution, Ho was a major poet and these poems range from strictly political themes to elegies. Also see Hoai Thanh (ed.), Days With Ho Chi Minh, being nine reminiscences by persons who worked with Ho at various stages of his life, from youth in W.W.I, through his years with the Comintern and at Yennan and through the various phases of armed struggle in Vichy and post-1945 Viet Nam.

HUU MAI

The Last Stronghold, 1963
A reportage novel about the campaign leading up to and including the seige of Dien Bien Phu in 1953 (which broke the back of the French expeditionary forces in Viet Nam). Seen through the lives of the Viet Minh soldiers and their civilian supporters and families.

HUU MAI, NGUYEN THIEN, TO HOANG et al

The Mountain Trail, 1970
A collection of stories by five Viet Namese women writers, some of whom were peasants and former partizans. Deals with the roles of women in the national liberation struggles in north and south of Viet Nam during the previous decade. Also see Xuan Vu, Vui Hein et al, Gunners Without Insignia, 1966.

HUU MAI et al

The Beacon Banner, 1964
A collection of short stories (by a different set of authors) dealing with the struggles of peasants and others in south Viet Nam during the mid to late 1950s. Of the deepening system of repression unleashed by the Saigon regime which triggers armed resistance and the drive for national reunification.

KIM LAN, TRAN KIM THACH, NGUYEN NGOC TAN

His Village, 1957
Three stories about the struggle against the reimposition of French colonialism after W.W.II. Set in disparate regions (and conditions) throughout Viet Nam and covering the years 1946 to 1954.

LE MINH KHUE et al

Distant Stars, 1976
A collection of short stories by ten authors dealing with aspects of life in north Viet Nam during the mid 1960s to early 1970s. Human accounts of what life was like under American bombardment.

NAM CAO

Chi Peo and Other Stories, 1961
A slim collection of quiet stories about the lives of ordinary Viet Namese in (relative) peace and war during the 1940s.

NGUYEN CONG HOAN

Canton Chief Ba Loses His Slippers, 1960
A collection of short stories originally written in 1937 and which satirically treat the seeming tranquility of French colonial rule in the late 1930s. Title story deals with the currents of peasant opposition to the regime of indigenous landlord/political bosses which tries to clothe itself in the garb of "Viet Namese traditions".

Impasse, 1963
A novel about the unresolved struggle for national liberation and reunification which emerged after the end of French colonial rule in north Viet Nam but with

the south falling under the control of an array of landlord powers which
coallese into the Diem regime; and the "initial" American involvement in the
conflict from 1954 to circa 1960.

NGUYEN DUY TINH et al

In the Enemy's Net, 1962
A collection of four "memoirs of the revolution" by underground communist
organizers during the 1930s and early 1940s; of political and organizational (as
well as armed) aspects of the early struggles against French, Vichy and Japanese
occupiers of Viet Nam.

NGUYEN SEN and TRUYEN TAY BAC

Stories of the North-West, 1957
A slim collection of modern folk tales from minority groups of the mountain region
in North-West Viet Nam during and after French colonial rule.

NGUYEN TI, NGUYEN SANG et al / GIAI PHONG EDITIONES

Les Bosquet Des Oiseaux, 1970 (Fury of the Birds)
A collection of twenty-six short stories by eleven resistance workers in south
Viet Nam; dealing with aspects of life under and struggle against the various
Saigon regimes and the US invader. Also La Fleur Sauvage, 1969 (Wild Flower), a
slim collection of stories by south Viet Namese resistance workers dealing with
bitter and desperate struggles of the mid 1960s. A similar collection of stories
issued by Foreign Languages Publishing House, The Fire Blazes, 1965.

PHAM NHU OANH

When the Light is Out, 1960
A novel running from the final days of combat against the French army in south
Viet Nam, through the repressive melange of Franco-American mandarins and colonels
who instituted the Saigon regime after 1954. Of the struggles against these
forces rekindled by peasant partizans during the late 1950s.

SCHELL, Jonathan

The Village of Ben Suc, 1968
A journalistic account of the people and recent history of the inhabitants of one
small village in south Viet Nam. Bled by the Boa Dai government and regional
warlords during the 1950s, involved in early peasant guerrilla insurgency, the
continuing daily rounds of farming and trying to survive, the increasing
devastation of the countryside with the arrival of American troops and the
"strategic hamlet" system. It stands for all other such villages and is written
by a western journalist with a decade of experience in Viet Nam.

VIETNAMESE STUDIES

Vietnamese Women, 1966
A special issue (Volume 10) of Vietnamese Studies dealing with facets of the lives
of Vietnamese women, old and young, from different walks of life, in the north and
south of the country since 1954. Snippets of biography and life history, writing
by and about women involved in running farms, reconstruction, the armed struggle,
political work and family life.

MALAYA

AMINURRASHID, Harun

Melihat Terang, 1953 (Seeing Clearly)
A novel about the entrenchment of neo-colonialism in the Malayan economy and
society, the class structure and conflicts which the Malay Sultanate and its
supporters were eagerly waiting to inherit from the British Raj. A protest work
from a left Islamic viewpoint. Also Dewa Lombong Minyak, 1947 (God of the Oil
Fields) and Minah Gadis Jelita, 1949 (Minah the Modern Dancing Girl), two somewhat
melodramatic novelas about Malay resource workers (Oil Fields) and the oppression
of women and prostitution (Minah) in late colonial Malaya.

BOESTAMAN, Ahmad

Hayati, 1957 (On Life)
A novel based on Boestaman's experiences in a British prison camp from 1948 to
1953; the lives of Malay and other political prisoners and the effects on his/
their families. Boestaman's wife worked as a rubber tapper on a plantation to
support their family during his imprisonment.

Kabus Pagi, 1958 (Morning Mist)
A novela about the fear and withdrawal of Malayan villagers who had previously
supported or been sympathetic toward progressive political organizations; the
effects of the repression during the Malayan Emergency. Revolving about the
isolation of a left wing Malay in his home village after years in a prison camp,
his attempts to rebuild a shattered life in a hostile social environment.

Memoir, 1972
Boestaman's autobiography which is also a personal history of the Malayan left
and progressive movement from the late 1920s to 1960s. Begining as a Malay
nationalist, he became an editor and founder of a left wing Malayan youth
movement (API) and in 1946 established the People's Party of Malaya which attempted
to unite Malay, Indian and Chinese workers and progressives in the colony. After
release from the British detention camps during the "emergency", Boestaman was
blacklisted by Malay authorities but went on to organize the political wing of
the fledgling labour union movement.

Loron Seribu Liku, 1958 (A Road With a Thousand Bends), Merangkaklah Senja
Menutup Pandangan, 1964 (Sunset Hides the Mist), Garis Hitem Membelah Langit, 1965
(A Black Line Dividing the Sky), Api Itu Masih Membara, 1967 (The Embers Still
Smoulder), Malam Tidak Berbintang, 1968 (Night Without Stars), Rumah Kaca Digegar
Gempa, 1969 (Glass House in the Earthquake)
A few of a series of novelas dealing with everyday life in Malaya from the late
1940s to the mid 1960s; about the strategic hamlet system imposed by Governor
Templer, and life in the prison camps and the pervasive fears which follow the
emergency. But mainly they are about the beauty and sadness, the ingrown
conservatism and fatalism which are part of Malayan rural life. They describe
the trappings of supposedly Islamic and traditional Malayan society as being
nothing more than the ideological vestaments of a neo-colonial bourgeoisie. They
picture everyday life in Malaya over the previous generation.

ISHAK BIN HAJI MUHAMMAD (Haji Muhammad bin Ishak)

Mencari Yang Lari, 1957 (Those Who Run Away)
A novela about the class exploitation and caste-like ethnic divisions in Malayan
society as continuations of a colonial heritage. Muhammad bin Ishak himself was
an organizer of the "All-Malaya Council of Progressive Malays, Indians and
Chinese" during the early 1950s and after his release from "preventive detention"
he helped found the Labour Party of Malaya. During the period he was blacklisted
he wrote a number of pulp novelas in the form of romances, but which contain
exposes of assorted social evils in Malayan society on the eve of independence.

A few of these are Jalan Ke Kota Baru, 1956 (Road to Kota Baru), about prostitution and women's oppression, Budek Beca, 1958 (Rickshaw Coolie), about class exploitation among Malays in a small town, Mata-Mata Suka Rela, 1959 (Volunteer Policeman), about judicial corruption among the rural notables, of how even a "patriotic" Malay policeman is blacklisted when he tries to check a blatant case of injustice.

KASSIM AHMAD

Kemaru Di Lembah, 1968 (Drought on the Meadows)
A collection of stories and poems revolving around the replacement of the British by the American Raj in Southeast Asia; mainly about the backwardness and anachronism of the Malayan political system and especially of the reaction and ignorance of Islamic fundamentalist teachers. About the exasperating alloy of individual decency and warmth but fatalistic servility which to Ahmad characterizes so much of Malayan society.

KERIS MAS, WIJAYA MALA, AWAM IL-SARKAM, ABUD SAMAL ISMAIL

Mekar Dan Segar, 1959 (Blooming and Fresh)
A collection of stories dealing with the hardship of peasants and landless plantation workers, the lives of semi-employed workers and their families. Some stories depict the know nothingism of mallams and religious teachers and the pretentions of the new government bureaucracy. Also of the tragedies and repression involved in the "Emergency Measures", the last colonial legacy to Malaya's sultans and new rulers. Also Keris Mas' Patah Tumboh, 1958, a collection of short stories on similar themes.

SAMAD SAID, A.

Salina, 1961 (Salina)
A novel which revolves around the life of a young Malay widow who migrates from an oppressive and stagnant peasant village in the 1950s to find work in Singapore. It touches on the social decay spreading through Malayan society, the poverty below the surface prosperity, and alludes to the neo-colonial mentality and entrenched self-seeking of Malay small town bosses. The main theme, however, is an account of the heroine's life and friendships in the Singapore slums which, despite its penury, retains a vitality and decency quite superior to life under petty notables in the village from which she came. Contains a host of characters --Malay, Indian, Chinese--from all classes.

SHANNON AHMAD

Protes, 1967 (Protest), Perdana, 1969 (Prime)
Two novelas which treat the web of theocratic-Sultanate rule as it is sustained by wealthy and village notables in Malaya, especially castigating the servile teachers and mean spirited mullahs who serve them. Includes accounts of the rural poor and an incipient protest movement among them, but it was the criticism of Islamic clerics that raised a storm of controversy about Shannon's books. Also his Rentong, 1965 (Burnt to Ashes) and Ranjau Sepanjang Jalan, 1966 (Stakes Along the Way),two novelas which in part portray the backwardness and half hidden rural poverty as an institutional aspect of post independence Malaya.

INDONESIA

ALISJAHBANA, Takdir S.

Lajar Terkembang, 1935 (Under Full Sail)
A novel about a middle class Indonesian woman who comes to reject the constraints imposed by her Islamic family. About her growing opposition to the confines of women's roles and her involvement in the incipient women's rights movement which culminates in the organization of a Woman's Congress in Indonesia during the late 1920s. A modestly reformist work of the time, Alisjahbana plays it safe by contrasting the heroine's rededication to her marital role with a younger sister who steams off into a supposedly unworkable "modern" arrangement with an engineer.

APIN, Rivai

Rumah Tangga, 1956 (Household)
A novela about the everyday life of an impoverished clerical worker's family struggling to survive in Jakarta during the mid 1950s. Told with sympathy and understanding by a leading left wing poet of the time. Apin's work was purged after 1965 but has been translated and resurrected in the collections of Harry Aveling. Apin also wrote the film script for the movie version of Max Havelaar.

AVELING, Harry (ed.)

From Surabaya to Armageddon: Indonesian Short Stories, 1974
A collection of translated stories including work by a number of progressive Indonesian writers and covering the period 1945 to 1965. Includes items by Rivai Apin, Klara Akustia (A.S. Dharta), M.S. Ashar and others. Accounts of Indonesian society mainly in the 1950s and early 1960s; the poverty yet hope, the steady slip into economic collapse, the deepening class struggle. Ends with the genocidal fascist coup of September 1965 in which "some 300,000 to a million 'communists' were subsequently killed and another 200,000 imprisoned."

Gestapu, 1975
A collection of translated stories by various Indonesian writers revolving about the increasing power and autocratic demands of the Indonesian army on the Sukarno government and the coups and countercoups which ushered in fascism in September 1965. Some touch on the brief resistance and destruction of progressive forces which followed.

BANDAHARO, Harahap

Dari Daerah Kehadiran Lapar Kasih, 1958 (From the Region Where Hunger and Love Dwell), Dari Rumi Merah, 1962 (From the Red Earth)
Two collections of lyrical, protest and revolutionary poetry about Indonesia in the 1950s and early 1960s; by a leading poet of the People's Cultural Institute.

IDRUS

Tjoretan Dibawah Tanah, 1949/50 (Underground Notes)
A serialized diary account of the misery prevailing in Indonesia during Japanese occupation of W.W.II (a period in which many of the later Indonesian military and nationalist leaders rose to prominence as collaborators). Also see "Surabaja", 1948, a famous story on this theme set in Indrus' home region, included in H. Aveling's From Surabaya to Armageddon.

Dengan Mata Terbuka, 1961 (With Open Eyes)
A collection of stories about Indonesia in the dozen years since independence. Idrus was also a prolific translator of French, Soviet and Czech literature.

KARTODIKROMO, Mas Marco

Rasa Merdika, Hikajat Sudjanmo, 1924 (The Spirit of Freedom, Story of Sudjanmo)
A novela of an Indonesian civil servant in the Dutch colonial government who
gradually comes to see his personal career as empty and who leaves his sinecure
to work for independence and social reform. Kartodikromo himself was a left
Islamic journalist before W.W.I, joined the Indonesian Communist Party shortly
after it was formed in 1920, worked as editor and journalist from the 1920s to
1950s. In his mid seventies, he was seized during the 1965 fascist coup and
died in Boven Digoel concentration camp shortly after.

MULTATULI (Eduard Douwes Dekker)

Max Havelaar, 1860 (Max Havelaar)
A classic anti-colonial novel castigating Dutch rule over the East Indies during
the mid 19th century. About the murderous conjunction of Dutch administrators
and native rulers and the unbearable costs this has for the Indonesian peasantry.
Ends in a desperate peasant rising, which indeed had coursed through Java a
decade before the novel was written. See Netherlands section for additional
annotation.

PANE, Sanusi

Manusia Baru, 1940 (The New Man)
A play about the problems and struggles of the Indonesian workers during the
final years of Dutch colonial rule and revolving around a strike launched by
textile workers for higher pay and better working conditions in the late 1930s.

RASUANTO, Bur

Mereka Akan Bangkit, 1963 (They Will Raise Themselves), Bumi Jang Berpeluh, 1963
(Sweating Earth)
Two collections of stories dealing with the exploitation and injustices experienced
by Indonesian workers in the plantations and mills of Sumatra during the early
1960s. In these stories, working people whether engaged in political action or
in just everyday struggles to survive, are the heroes.

Mereka Telah Bangkit, 1966 (They Have Risen)
A slim collection of "resistance poetry" produced during the brief period of
underground resistance which followed the 1965 fascist coup.

ROESTAM EFFENDI (Rustam Effendi)

Petjikan Permenungam, 1928 (Splinters of Thought)
A small collection of poems about the conditions of Indonesian peoples, their
hopes and defeats under colonialism. Roestram was a Sumatran teacher who fled
the Dutch East Indies during the repression which followed the abortive East Java
peasant rising of 1926/27. He lived in the Netherlands until 1947 and was elected
to parliament as a communist representative from a Dutch working class district
in the 1930s.

SIAGIAN, Bachtiar

Lorong Belakang, 1950 (Back Alley)
A play about the lives of urban poor in Indonesia, revolving around the theme
that the struggle for national liberation had failed as a social revolution. One
of a number of similar plays by Siagian which at the time were performed by street
theatre groups.

SIREGAR, Bakri

Djedjak Langkah, 1953 (Footprints)
A collection of stories (including "On the Edge of the Crater") about the
Indonesian war of independence of late 1940s, by one of the leading literary
figures of generation.

Sedjarah Sastera Indonesia Moderna, 1964 (History of Modern Indonesian Literature)
A Marxist literary history of Indonesian writing in its various languages, formats

and themes during this century. Siregar survived a decade in Indonesian
concentration camps but has published nothing since his release in late 1970s.

SONTAI, Utuy T.

Orang Orang Sia, 1951 (The Unfortunates)
A collection of stories about victims of social injustices and poverty in
Indonesia and of those fighting back against new/old exploiters in various ways.

Saat Yang Genting, 1957 (Crucial Moment)
An agitational play about the necessity of mounting mass actions against the
deepening poverty, endemic decay of economy and pervasive governmental corruption.
One of many similar plays which Sontai wrote and produced for the People's
Cultural Institute which include Tiga Menguak Takir, 1952 (Three Warding Off Fate)
and Awal Dan Mira, 1954 (Awal and Mira).

TOER, Pramudya Ananta

Perburan, 1950 (Pursuit)
A novela set in late 1945 and covering twenty-four hours in the life of an
Indonesian guerrilla soldier. Flashbacks relate his background and what brought
him and others into the struggle against Japanese occupation and the attempted
Dutch recolonization of Indonesia. Translated and revised by Harry Aveling as
The Fugitive, 1974, which adds historic background to the work and provides a
brief summary of events in Indonesia since the fascist coup on the tenth
anniversary of Toer's imprisonment by that regime.

Bukan Pasar Malam, 1951 (Life Is No Night Bazaar)
A more or less autobiographical journal of Toer's return home through Indonesia
after the defeat of the Dutch colonial forces. His discovery that past
friendships, family and personal ties have been irretrievably lost and shattered.

Tjerita Dari Blora, 1952 (Stories From Blora)
A collection of stories and reminiscences about life, both good and bad, in
Toer's Java village of Blora from the 1920s to 1945.

Gulat Di Djakarta, 1956 (Tales of Djakarta); Tjerita Dari Djakarta, 1957 (Stories
of Djakarta)
Two collections of stories dealing with the lives of workers and ordinary people
in Djakarta struggling to scrape by in the deepening economic stagnation and who
are victims of the venality, criminality and social decay created by the new
Indonesian merchant/political bosses.

Keluarga Gerilja, 1959 (A Guerrilla Family)
A novel about the Indonesian war of independence and its aftermath; a wide
ranging account of the suffering and social destruction arising from that drawn
out conflict. Revolves around a typical Indonesian guerrilla soldier and the
gradual dissolution of his large extended family through death, alienation,
division--representing the more general dissolution of Indonesian society. Toer's
masterpiece. Also Ditepi Kali Bekasi, 1957 (On the Banks of the Bekasi River)
and Subah, 1959 (Dawn), two works dealing with similar themes as Guerrilla Family.

A Heap of Ashes, 1975
A collection of five of Toer's short stories dealing with aspects of Indonesian
society from the eve of independence in 1948 to the social disintegration of the
country by the end of the 1950s. Translated by Harry Aveling.

WISPI, Agam

Djakarta, Oi Djakarta, 1958 (Jakarta, O Jakarta)
An epic poem portraying the conditions and intersecting classes in the tottering
megalopolis capital and a tribute to the working people of that city as everyday
heroes. Also Api 1926, 1962 (Fire of 1926), a collection of poems by Wispi and
other left Indonesian poets memorializing the 1926/27 East Java peasant risings
led by the Communist Party in an attempt to oust oppressive native rulers and
the Dutch colonial overlords; a memorial to Indonesia's revolutionary traditions
by a working class poet.

PHILIPPINES

ARGUILLA, Manuel E.

How My Brother Brought Home a Wife, 1941
A collection of stories written between 1933 and 1940 which include sketches of peasant life in the Nagrebcan region, stories of married life told with laconic humour and quietly bitter accounts of an impoverished peasantry and desperate Manila workers during the mid to late 1930s. Arguilla was an influential author of social realist stories in popular Tagalog journals of the period.

BATUNGBAKAL, Brigido C.

Pula Ang Kulay Ng Dugo, 1940 (Red Is The Colour of Blood)
A collection of stories about the lives of ordinary people and entrepreneurs in the Philippines caught up in the 1930s depression. All following titles not in English are Tagalog.

Mga Piling Katha, 1948 (Selected Short Stories)
A collection of stories about ordinary Philippinos from the late 1930s, during W.W.II and in the years immediately afterward. Includes stories about the lives of Huk guerrillas continuing the partizan battles against the still colonial Philippine Commonwealth government, told with sympathy for their cause but not support for armed struggle.

BULOSAN, Carlos

Letter From America, 1942, The Voice of Bataan, 1943, Dark People, 1944
Three short collections of sketches and reminiscences of being a tenant farmer's son and rural worker in the Philippines during 1920s and 1930s, and later a migrant worker in the US. Bulosan spent much of his life as a migrant farm worker and was recognized as a major Philippino writer only in his final years.

The Laughter of My Father, 1944
A collection of short stories about Bulosan's youth in Illoco Province during the 1920s; the corruption, the unchecked misrule of local landlords, the underside of life in the Philippines under American colonialism, told with quiet irony.

America Is In the Heart, 1946
A novel about ten years lived in the US as a Philippino migrant labourer--the racism, exploitation, spontaneous goodwill, promise and betrayal. Told with a bemused "radicalism" which sadly still wants to believe in a "real America".

FRANCISCO, Lazaro

Ilaw Sa Hilaga, 1948 (Aurora Borealis)
A novel which deals with the sell out of Philippines to American colonialism at begining of this century by the Philippino merchant capitalists. Also of the ongoing nationalist agitation against the Commonwealth home rule government in the interwar years. A reworked version of his The Country That Committed Suicide, 1932.

Maganda Pa Ang Daigdig, 1956 (The World is Still Beautiful)
A novel which depicts the devastation of Philippine rural society during W.W.II, the horrendous costs of armed resistance against the Japanese occupation.

Daluyong, 1962 (Tidal Wave)
A sequel to The World is Still Beautiful, set in late 1940s amid the peasant rebellion called the "Huk Rising". A Philippino veteran returns to a society in which "the peasant remained a slave to the tenancy system that gave rich landlords enormous wealth while peasants were mired in debts that they had inherited from their parents and would bequeath to their children." Set around a provincial town and district in Central Luzon, it depicts the vitality of the peasantry but revolves about the protagonist's rejection of both the oppressive

Philippine government and the devastating and seemingly hopeless struggle sustained by the Huks.

GONZALES, N.V.M.

Children of the Ash Covered Loam, 1954
A collection of stories about the struggles of Philippine peasant families engaged in shifting agriculture against the seeming malevolence of nature, the rapacity of landlords and the apathetic self interests of other poor peasants themselves.

A Season of Grace, 1956
A novel of the class struggle between peasant farmers and landlords on Mindoro Island. Tells the story of the "uneventful" daily lives and personal histories of a peasant couple working a hillside plot; the contest with natural calamities and forces as well as with landlord rule. Using local dialect and themes, it is said to encapsulate much of Philippine peasant life. Also The Winds of April, 1954, another novel set among the peasantry of Mindoro Island.

HERNANDEZ, Amando V.

Philipinas, 1939 (Philippines)
An epic novel of Philippine history from the time of the Spanish conquest, through the centuries of colonial rule and revolt, the struggle for national liberation in the 1890s and the American occupation, with accounts of bitter guerrilla war against American army during first decade of this century, and the continuing peasant struggles of the 1930s.

Isang Dipang Langit, 1961 (An Arm's Span of Sky)
A collection of poems and stories of political prisoners and about the continuing exploitation of the poor in Philippines of early 1950s. Written in prison.

Luha Ng Buwaya, 1963 (Crocodile Tears)
A novel which depicts the plight of the Philippine peasantry and how the landlord political boss system works; accounts of the various ways in which the peasantry have resisted and attempted to defend itself in the past.

Rice Grains, 1966
A collection of protest stories about conditions in Philippine society since the end of W.W.II. (Translated by E. San Juan.)

Mga Ibong Mandaragit, 1969 (Birds of Prey)
A novel of the neo-colonial nature of Philippine society since "independence"; the venality and corruption of the state apparatus, its total inability to do anything of value, the comprador nature of the business classes and the servile acquiescence of most intellectuals and religious leaders. Done in the form of a folk tale about a veteran who miraculously finds a treasure, decides to create a Free University for the peasantry and witnesses the repression of those peasants who go to the university and attempt to do something about their lot.

Bayang Malaya, 1970 (Free Land)
A posthumously published book length poem begining in a deceptively bucolic peasant village of Philippines in 1920s, the exactions of landlords and political bosses, the attempts at peasant organization in the 1930s. The Japanese invasion and the guerrilla resistance to them, the return of the American army and the disbanding of the guerrilla forces only to confront the same oppression that had existed previously. Migration to the city and the upsurge of labour union struggles in 1940s, the outbreak of armed class struggle in the countryside and the deepening military repression in the country. The deepening stasis, worsening conditions and the mobilization of mass struggles in the mid 1960s.

LEE, Richardo, W. VIRTUSIO, F. GARCIA, N. MIRAFLOR, D. LANDICHO

Sigwa, 1972 (Storm)
A collection of Tagalog stories by five young Philippino writers who "have clearly taken the side of the oppressed masses"; stories of class conflicts and struggle in cities and countryside during the late 1960s.

POMEROY, William

The Forest, 1963
A highly schematic account of the social bases of and the reasons for the
Hukbahlahap guerrilla movement in the late 1940s and early 1950s. By an
American advisor to the Huks (then fighting Japanese occupation) during W.W.II
who returned in 1952 to aid their struggle against the Philippine government and
was quickly imprisoned. A capsule history of earlier Philippine peasant and
guerrilla movements and additional comments on the Huk struggle in post W.W.II
period is found in Pomeroy's Guerrilla and Counter-Guerrilla Warfare, 1964.

REYES, Edgardo

Sa Kuko Ng Liwanag, 1966 (In the Claws of Light)
A novel which depicts the hopes, lives and realities of ex-peasants searching for
work in Manila of 1960s. It utilizes a love story which takes the hero in search
of his girlfriend through the shacktowns, gangster roosts, brothels and slumlord
government networks of the city. Ends with a vengeful and violent settling of
personal accounts which eliminates one vampire but which leaves everything
completely unchanged.

RIZAL, Jose

Noli Me Tangere, 1890 (The Lost Eden, 1962), El Filibusterismo, 1891 (The
Subversive, 1962)
Two novels castigating the final years of Spanish colonial rule in Philippines;
the backwardness and the racial-caste hierarchy, with some damning portraits of
the clerical reaction and the comprador nature of the Philippine upper class.
El Filibusterismo treats with the beginings of the Philippine independence
movement against Spain. Given to a florid period-piece style and certainly not
"left wing", Rizal is generally accepted as the mythic intellectual father of
Philippine independence and his writings are cited by contending later forces for
their own particular interests.

SAN JUAN, Epifano Jr.

Maliwalu, 1969
A collection of poems memorializing the site of an infamous massacre of political
dissidents by the Philippine army in the mid 1960s. Deals with that event and
the social injustices existing in the Philippines which bring individuals to
revolt.

Carlos Bulosan and the Imagination of the Class Struggle, 1972
A biography and overview of the work of Carlos Bulosan, an ex-peasant Philippine
youth who emigrated to the US in late 1930s, spent much of his adult life as a
migrant worker and "undiscovered" writer there. San Juan makes some sage comments
about the social and psychological contradictions created by this sort of
colonialism.

Introduction to Modern Pilipino Literature, 1974 (ed.)
A readable anthology of the translated poems, stories and extracts from the work
of some 25 Tagalog writers; with brief commentaries on their backgrounds and the
social and cultural conditions under which they wrote.

SANTOS, Lope K.

Banaag At Sikat, 1906 (Dawning and Daybreak)
Held to be the first realistic novel of class struggle in Tagalog, written with
the express intent of introducing Philippino workers to socialism. The vehicle is
a love story of two couples whose backgrounds and tribulations provide a panorama
of then contemporary events; the 1896 guerrilla campaign against the Spanish
colonial regime, the American occupation and the defeated 1901-1902 struggles
against American colonialism. Centers on the organization of labour unions and
their initial suppression, their reorganization in 1903 (by Santos and others),
the rapid rise of plantation agriculture and of urban factory labour, the growth
of a new Philippino bourgeoisie and the outburst of labour militancy during the

first decade of this century. All this is either woven into the story line or is discussed by the socialist union organizer who is one of the central characters of the novel. Also Faustino Aguilar's Pinaglahuan, 1907 (Engulfed by the Eclipse), a novel on a similar theme with sympathetic accounts of then contemporary socialist "agitators", labour union militancy and strikes, but focused on a melodramatic romance between a union organizer and the daughter of a factory owner.

SIKAT, Rogelio et al

Agos Sa Disyerto, 1965 (Streams in the Desert)
A collection of fifteen short stories by five young Tagalog writers (Edgardo Reyes, Eduardo Reyes, R. Ordonez, R.L. Abueg), it signaled a flood of Tagalog novels, poetry and other literature, much of it breaking with the former romantic traditions and becoming the vehicle of Philippine social protest writing. Rogelio Sikat's stories in particular deal with the abuses of landlords, the brutal and corrupt police and local governments, the oppression of peasants, etc.

TARUC, Luis

Born of the People, 1953
An autobiography by the political leader of the Hukbahlahap resistance movement during and shortly after W.W.II. Deals with the agrarian and class nature of the struggle through the backgrounds of the Huk supporters and traces its heritage to the earlier anti-colonial and peasant struggles against landlords and local caciques.

SIONEL, Jose F.

The Pretenders, 1962
A novel about the Philippine bourgeoisie after independence in 1952, its wheeling and dealing and fronting for US interests. Also about the lives of peasants, plantation workers, minority groups, ex-guerrillas, urban workers and the Philippine poor in an increasingly desperate and looted nation. Depicts the costs of the Philippines remaining a military base for US operations in Southeast Asia.

The Chief Mourner, 1968, The Balete Tree, 1972
Two novels revolving around the stagnation, poverty and monumental misuse/ mismanagement of Philippine countryside during the 1960s.

"WORKERS' THEATRE" (Anonymous)

Gintong Silahis Players; Barikada, 1971 (Barricades), an agitational play about the army seizure of the University of Philippines in 1970.

Kamayang Players; Pulang Tala, 1978 (Red Star), an agitational play about the transformation of student activists and defeated strikers into partizans during the early years of the Marcos dictatorship in 1970s.

Panday-Sining Players; Welga! Welga!, 1972 (Strike! Strike!), a play about a Manila trade union which enters a strike for circumscribed wage demands and finds itself contending with the entire system of business and political repression.

EAST ASIA

China
Korea
Japan

CHINA

AH MING-CHIH

Huo Chung, 1963 (Seeds of Flame)
A novel about the Shanghai working class between 1919 and 1927, with flashbacks
of events since the collapse of the Manchu dynasty a decade earlier. Depicts
the everyday lives and concerns of working people in an industrializing metropolis
under capitalist and quasi-colonial control, workers far removed from the
"modernist" concerns of the emerging left intelligensia. Touches on the
fustrations of an early communist organizer attempting to set up union cells in
a textile factory and the ingrained suspicion of already class conscious workers
who understand the power and complexity of the forces facing them. Of the
gathering civil war in the countryside, the upsurge of gangster armies in the
guise of traditional secret societies in the cities, the intensification of
exploitation which drives the Shanghai workers toward the communists. Portrays
the mass demonstrations and strikes of the mid 1920s and ends in the preparations
for a revolutionary seizure of power in Shanghai in 1927, which will lead to their
destruction by Chiang Kai Shek. Extracts in English translation in Chinese
Literature, Nos. 4 and 5, 1965.

Shanghai Nien-ssu Hsiao-Shih, 1946 (Twenty-four Hours in Shanghai)
A novel about life in Shanghai under Japanese occupation during the early 1940s.

AI HSUAN

Ta Chiang Feng Lei, 1965 (Storm Over the Yangtse, 1966)
An epic novel of the central Yangtse region under Japanese occupation during 1939
to 1942. A vast canvas of the dissolution of traditional Chinese society in the
countryside with the Kuomintang, local warlords and the puppet Wang Ching Wei
forces all bidding for the support of the landlord class and their private
militias--the real fundament of all past Chinese political power. The peasantry
reaches an absolute bedrock of exploitation, resulting in personal vendettas,
inchoate revolts and the appearance of a host of nativistic movements. (Sorcerers
and bandits, armed Buddhist religious orders, assorted claimants to past dynastic
thrones and a recrudescence of secret societies--all of them only half mad attempts
by people to protect themselves and find some order in the chaos.) In effect,
the disjointed components of and claimants to traditional Chinese society reemerge
in a final flurry. The Japanese army, located in the cities, serve mainly as a
catalyst to these developments. The communist underground, just begining to
penetrate the region, initially appear to the peasants as just one other of a
number of alternatives and some of the best and most audacious peasant leaders
remain with their traditional self defense organizations to the end. It
foreshadows the near future in which the communists will have gained the support
of the peasantry for a final assault on the traditional powers of China.

AI WU

Pai Lien Ch'eng Kang, 1961 (Steeled and Tempered, 1968)
A "proletarian" novel about the lives and struggles of Shanghai working class on
the eve of the 1927 rising there, with a somewhat stereotyped cast of heroes and
villains. Ai Wu was earlier a prolific author of "slice of life" accounts of
people in Kuomintang China during the 1930s and 1940s.

CHAO SHU-LI

Changes in Li Village, 1955
A novel about life in a backlands Shansi village during the war of resistance,
1937-1945. Documents the evolving resistance to Chinese warlords and landlords
as well as to Japanese invaders and depicts the social and political changes
emerging from that struggle.

Sanliwan Village, 1964
A novel about the stuttering shift of a drought-ridden village in north-central
China from peasant cooperatives to collective farming during the mid 1950s.
Details the agricultural problems of peasant farming under any system and
describes the realistic hesitations and opposition of villagers to the more
integrated farm system. Free from a cast of "cunning saboteurs" and "hidden class
enemies" which often deaden such novels. An account of the multifoliate problems
and the means used by party cadre to entice the peasantry into collective farms
but also the potential benefits of such reorganization.

CHEN JO-HSI

The Execution of Mayor Yin and Other Stories, 1978
A collection of stories about China during the "Great Proletarian Cultural
Revolution" (Maoist) period of the late 1960s in which a swath of powerful
political opportunists and levies of mainly non-working class youths intimidate
and destroy veterans of the communist movement, threaten real workers'
organizations and in general spread fear among the ordinary Chinese citizenry. A
bitter satire of the mass hysteria and dogmatic absurdities as seen through the
eyes of someone mouthing the slogans of the "cultural revolution". Allegedly
based on the experiences of the author, a Taiwanese who moved herself and her
family to China in 1966, lived through the upheaval and later became an emigre
in Canada.

CHESNEAUX, Jean

The Chinese Labour Movement, 1919-1927, 1968
A rich, massively documented history of the Chinese labour movement during its
early period of revolutionary growth. Focuses on developments in the major urban
and industrial centers but treats the many-stranded relations with peasantry,
guilds, shopkeepers and other traditional and modern social sectors, the competing
ideologies and shifting alliances. Captures the chaotic maelstrom of events and
confrontations which finally frightened the assorted warlords and right
nationalist forces into allied and separate assaults on the urban working class.
Ends with the initial defeat of organized working class in 1927 and the sorting
out of forces. Much information on the early non-communist working class
militants.

CHOU ERH-FU

Morning in Shanghai, 1964
A novel set in Shanghai during 1949 and the early 1950s, dealing with problems
encountered in transforming large scale private enterprises into state enterprises.
The aims and mistakes of the nationalization measures and the responses of owners
and managers who use an array of dodges to milk the companies dry while they still
can. Said to be a rather heavy handed account, it is one of the few here which
treat with the urban industrial scene during this transitional period.

CHOU LI-PO

The Hurricane, 1955
A novel of a Manchurian village in the late 1940s during the first years of
communist administration. About the initial phase of land redistribution and a
rather frank account of the hurricane of long pent up grievances and hatred which
is unleashed against the remaining landlords and their rent collector/strong arm
men.

Shan-Hsiang Chu-Pien, 1958 (Great Changes in a Mountain Village, 1968)
A novel about the organization of a collective farm in a small, isolated Manchurian
peasant village which was formerly limited to barely subsistence farming. Some
detailed accounts of the difficulties attendant on making this change, the honest
opposition to it with no landlords or other "class enemies" left on the scene.

CROOK, David and Isabel

Revolution in a Chinese Village: Ten Mile Inn, 1959
A sociological account of the initial changes in one north Chinese peasant village

during the late 1940s. Deals particularly with the establishment of cooperative peasant organizations and the destruction of the underlying economic power of the landlord and wealthy peasant class. Extensively based on documents.

The First Years of Yangyi Commune, 1966
Another sociological account of the forced draft transformation of peasant cooperative farming into a larger agro-industrial commune in the late 1950s. A good deal more rosey-eyed about the results and costs of that transformation than less credulous Chinese commentators a generation later were. Does not contain an epilogue by Deng Xiaoping.

HINTON, William

Iron Oxen: documentary of revolution in Chinese farming, 1970
A readable account of the people, background and problems encountered by Hinton and his Chinese co-workers while introducing mechanized farming into a north China region during the late 1940s. (Hinton being a US instructor sent to Nationalist China by UNRRA in 1947 who stayed on to train tractor operators in the liberated regions.) At times it sparkles with quick-drawn vignettes and insights interweaving technical detail and the personal responses of people. But also as exasperatingly glib and tendencious as only "technical experts" can be. Also Fanshen: documentary of revolution in a Chinese village, 1967.

HSIA CHIH-YEN

The Coldest Winter in Peking: a novel from inside China, 1978
Allegedly a set of episodic accounts about the internal struggles in Peking between varied Red Guard factions and other new and old groupings inside the communist party and the army during the early 1970s. Portrays the Byzantine intrigues, opportunistic use of dogma and hooliganism as experienced by a disillusioned former Red Guard cadre. (Possibly fabricated.)

HSIAO HUNG (Chang Nai-ying)

The Field of Life and Death and Tales of Hulan River, 1979 (original 1935, 1940)
Two novelas about civil war China by a young woman from a shattered ex-landlord family who was a refugee throughout the country most of her adult life. Field of Life and Death portrays the social restrictions, the myriad interpersonal hostilities and conflicts in a Chinese village, the multifoliate injustices only some of which stem from class oppression. Hsiao investigates the inner psychological effects on her characters and the gradual degradation of personal qualities in that world. Tales of Hulan River is a more nostalgic description of a north Manchurian peasant region, woven around the declining fortunes and ultimate disintegration of a minor landlord family during the 1930s.

HU YEBIN (Hu Yeh-pin)

Guangming Zai Womende Gianmian, 1930 (Before Us the Light)
A semi-autobiographic novel about the bloodily suppressed Shanghai general strike of May 1925. In part, a memorium to the pioneer anarcho-syndicalist militants who were central in the early union struggles of the Shanghai working class. Touches on the destruction of that earlier working class movement and the transformation of many of its remaining activists into communist supporters. She was one of the martyrs of the early proletarian writers movement.

ISAACS, Harold (ed.)

Straw Sandals, 1974
An anthology of stories and extracts by the pioneer left wing writers in China. An excellent introduction to early left nationalist, radical democratic and communist fiction from 1918 to 1933. Includes work by Lu Hsun, Kuo Mu-jo, Yu Ta-fu, Yeh Shao-chun, Ting Ling, Chiang Kuang-Tzu, Shih Yi, Hu Yeh-pin, Jou Shih, Mao Tun, Ting Chiu, Yin Fu, Tung P'ing, Cheng N'ung, Wang T'ung-chao, Ho Ku-t'ien. Ranges from the first naturalistic descriptions of rural and urban poverty or "daring investigations" of female sexuality to revolutionary proletarian tales. Isaacs (who was on the left publishing scene in China during

the 1920s) provides an informative, if somewhat tendentious, introduction which places the specific stories and authors in the context of the times. He suggests that however horrendous and unbelievable some of the accounts may seem to contemporary readers, they are not as horrendous or improbable as actual conditions were.

JIANG GUANG-TSI (Chang Kuang-Tzi)

Duan Ku Dang, 1929 (The Sansculottes)
A collection of short stories, the title story depicting Shanghai workers who supported the Nationalist forces in their Northern Expedition against regional warlords in 1926 and of how they are "betrayed" and destroyed by Chiang Kai-Shek shortly after.

Tiang Feng, 1930 (Wind Over the Fields)
A novela dealing with Chinese miners who come to support a local peasant movement struggling against landlords and warlord society during the mid 1920s. Makes the point that similar struggles between similar forces were breaking out throughout China independently and more or less spontaneously.

KOTENEV, A.

New Lamps for Old, 1931
A once influential Soviet reportage novel about the rise of factories and an industrial working class in Shanghai from circa 1900 to mid 1920s; the transformation of displaced peasants and urban coolies of a semi-feudal China into an emerging proletariat, as well as the shifting combinations of national and colonial bosses. Captures the intricate and chaotic confrontations in urban China of the period and particularly the daily lives of Shanghai workers.

KU QIU-BAI

"Warmande Yuzhong Riji", 1932 (Prison Diary)
A story/memoir about one of the initial mass actions by industrial workers in north China still under the regimes of regional warlords. Specifically about a 1923 strike of railway workers in the domain of warlord Wu Peifu. Touches on the revolutionary nationalist fervor of industrial workers as yet little effected by communist influence, describes the trajectory and bloody suppression of the strikers through the reconsiderations of two imprisoned survivors.

LAO SHE

Rickshaw, 1979 (Rickshaw Coolie, 1936)
A massive novel about the life and death of a rickshaw puller in Peking during the late 1920s and early 1930s. Valuable in that it provides a mass of ethno- graphic detail of city life in the capital of the Manchurian warlord Chang Tso Liang. The last residues of traditional dynastic China and the life of pre-modern urban workers; accounts of social structure, guilds, pre-socialist working class ideology, the urban physical environment, etc. A somewhat romantic and not especially left wing work.

LI YING-JU

Yeh-huo Ch'un-feng Tou Ku-cheng, 1961 (In an Old City)
A novel about the intrigues and struggles between the Kuomintang and communist party undergrounds in and around the city of Paoting (Hopei Province) under Japanese occupation during 1943. A semi-autobiographical account of a communist peasant organizer who attempts to coordinate rural and urban resistance. Of the practicalities and quite untheoretical considerations involved, the changing attitudes of the population and how they are drawn into the struggle despite the dangers. The heterogeneous characters retain the concerns and emotions of their previous lives (including a hatred of things traditional), the revolutionary upsurge being drawn from an indigenous magma.

In a similar vein, Szu-ma Wen-sheng, Feng-Yu Tung-Chiang, 1964 (Storm Over the Tung River), another autobiographical novel about the practical problems of

the communist underground operating in a Kuomintang-controlled region around Amoy
(south China) during mid 1940s. It also portrays the characters as stemming
fundamentally from indigenous Chinese revolutionary traditions.

LIANG PIN

Hung-chi P'u, 1958 (Keep the Red Flag Flying, 1963)
A chronicle of peasant struggles in Hopei Province under warlord domination during
the late 1920s. It depicts the amalgam of age-old personal conflicts of peasants
with an array of oppressors; it portrays the peasantry's heterogeneous and
amorphous visions which in many cases more closely approximate a "return" to a
mythical past than a revolutionary transformation. Revolves around a local
peasant who had earlier fled the region to work as a migrant worker in southern
China, then already in revolutionary turmoil. Of his return and the emergence
of a peasant movement against landlords; personal conflicts merging into mass land
seizures and finally the intervention of the troops of the regional warlord.
Drawn from events in the author's childhood.

Po Huo Chi, 1963 (Sowing the Flames)
A sequel to Red Flag in which the scattered and defeated peasant revolt makes
contact with the incipient communist organization under Li Li San and Wang Ming.
The surviving peasant rebels have become "guerrilla" bandits who initiate one of
the first revolutionary campaigns in the north (the Kaoying-Lihsien Uprising,
1929-32). Despite the presence of the CP, the uprising still draws its leaders
and goals from regional peasant society. It too is crushed, leaving behind a
nucleus of now communist partizans.

LIU CH'ING

The Builders, 1962
A novel about the initial drive to merge peasant farms into collectives during
the mid 1950s. Set in a village of the north Chinese plain, it depicts a variety
of village characters but focuses on one peasant who has supported the revolution
in the past but who is sceptical about radical theories when it comes to farming
(with good reason). He cannot bring himself to place his livelihood and the
security of his family in the hands of young cadres. Gradually both sides come to
some better understanding of the requirements and problems of collective farm
organization. All's well that bends well.

LO KUANG-PIN and YANG YI-YEN

Hung Yen, 1962 (Red Crag)
A novelized reminiscence of two communist underground organizers who are sent into
Chunking in 1948 to prepare a last minute seizure of the factories in order to
prevent them from being destroyed by the retreating Nationalists. Describes the
techniques used by the all-pervasive Kuomintang secret police and how they utilize
the flamboyance of some novice revolutionaries to capture much of the communist
underground. Concludes with a chronicle of experiences in a Chungking prison
camp which includes brief biographies of some of the inmates, both dead and
alive. Has a tribute to Liu Shao Chi, the coordinator of underground activity in
Kuomintang controlled regions and later a victim of the Maoist purges. Extracts
of Red Crag translated in Chinese Literature, No. 5-7, 1962.

LO TANG

Feng-Yu Ti LiMing, 1959 (Dawn in Wind and Rain)
A novel revolving around responses to problems encountered with the first
significant industrial complex (the Anshen steel mills in Harbin) to come under
communist control. Set in early 1948 with the Kuomintang armies still threatening
to retake the city. It supposedly touches on the degree to which communist
cadres, after the long sojourn in peasant guerrilla bases, have become removed
from a proletariat which has had to survive under warlord, Japanese and Kuomintang
occupation and which is cautious and initially suspicious of all "liberators".
Portrays the approaches of two different, both committed, communist organizers
and their relations with the mill workers, and raises the theme of "objectively
non-antagonistic" but contentious relationships of the party with the then
contemporary urban working class.

LU HSUN (Chou Shu-jen)

A Brief History of Chinese Fiction, 1959 (original 1930 edition)
A translation of Lu Hsun's literary history of pre-modern and classical Chinese
fiction which ranges back over a millenium and underscores those aspects of the
literature which depict actual social conditions and problems. (These are often
allusions interwoven through stylized novels.) It indicates the undercurrents
of protest in the pre-modern literature. Of particular interest is the
naturalistic writing which emerged in the late Manchu period, which though
generally cloaked as murder and romance thrillers, depict the social dissolution
of China under the last dynastic regime. Does not cover any modern left wing
writing.

Selected Stories of Lu Hsun, 1972
A collection of eighteen short stories by Lu Hsun including his "Diary of a
Madman" and "The Story of Ah Q". Written between 1918 and 1926, they are mainly
accounts of partly incorporated "modernism" and cultural anomie spreading among
intellectuals and sectors of the Chinese bourgeoisie during that time. A China
rending itself apart is the understated background to the stories. Although none
of Lu Hsun's works could be said to be proletarian, he was the dean
of early Chinese literary realism, a founder of the League of Left Writers in the
early 1930s and the senior spokesman of that group.

MA FENG (ed.)

I Knew All Along, 1962
A collection of stories written by ten Chinese workers and peasants; about the
Great Leap Forward which was to lay the industrial foundations of a modern China
within a decade. They present the millenial hopes of that period in the late
1950s and early 1960s but more importantly describe the types of self sufficiency
and local development projects launched, such as the "backyard" iron smelters.
This title is to stand for the host of other "socialist construction" titles
from this period.

MAO TUN (Shen Yen-ping)

Ziye, 1933 (Midnight, 1957)
A collective novel about Shanghai between the years 1923 and 1930, focused on the
industrial serfdom of textile workers in foreign and Chinese owned mills in that
city. Also treats with a host of characters from various sections of the Chinese
bourgeoisie, the increasingly radicalized youths of declining families to the
evermore rapacious wealthy businessmen who rely on a combination of gangsters,
warlords, "Nationalist" and foreign colonial forces to protect their interests.
One of the best known novels of those nightmare years.

The Lin Family Shop, 1957
A novel about a family of hard pressed small shopkeepers in China from the late
1930s to late 1940s; their patriotic and basically progressive roles during the
Japanese occupation, their bemused but fundamentally decent participation in the
travails and hopes of China during its darkest epoch. And a sympathetic account
of their uncertainties, isolation and fears.

Spring Silkworms and Other Stories, 1956
Contains the three long stories, "Spring Silkworms", "Autumn Harvest", and "Winter
Rains" (original 1936-38); linked accounts about members of peasant families
in a peaceful enclave of south China from the mid 1920s to the early 1930s.
Where the memory of the Tai Ping Rebellion is still part of everyday folk lore,
in which traditional inward looking village life is played out against a background
of national and international forces which gradually penetrate the stories as
this enclave is drawn into the vortex of struggle.

Also Rainbow, 1930, a youthful novel about the dissolution of a Chinese middle
class family; the surrounding chaos and the strivings of younger members to find
some purpose in their own lives and some direction which will lift China out of
the abyss it had fallen into during the late 1920s.

MYRDAL, Jan

Report From a Chinese Village, 1963
A set of thumbnail life histories of 32 inhabitants--old and young, women and
men, of varying backgrounds and natures--living in a north Chinese peasant village
during 1962. Interlaced with documentary material tracing the social history of
that village from the civil wars of the 1930s and 1940s through the changes which
followed the communist victory. Indicates that while only relatively limited
material improvements had been achieved there continues to be a general feeling
of having finally escaped past oppression. An undogmatic and frank account.

OU-YANG SHAN

San Chia Hsiang, 1962 (Three Family Lane)
A novel about the social ferment and rising revolutionary struggles in Canton
and Shanghai from 1921 to 1929 as experienced by three families (a former landlord,
a middle class and a skilled artizan's family) who come to live on one city street.
Peopled with a host of characters--workers, migrant peasants, sages and criminals,
traditionalist and emerging social elements--it captures the confustion, horror
and visionary hopes existing during the disintegration of traditional China.

K'u Tou, 1962 (Bitter Struggle)
A sequel to Three Family Lane which focuses on the life of a middle class youth
who, already rebellious about the injustices of the anachronistic society around
him, becomes filled with a lust for revenge against the system which kills his
fiancee in a student demonstration.   It emphasizes the personal reasons that
bring individuals into revolt, which may become transformed by a revolutionary
movement. Touches on the communist underground among the urban working class
during the late 1920s and early 1930s.

PA CHIN

The Family, 1966 (original 1931)
An adapted version of a classic modern Chinese novel. Deals with the disintegration of a traditional extended family during the 1920s, the tangled web of
personal loyalties and path taken by one young son who gradually becomes committed
to the Chinese revolution. Also see Olga Lang's Pa Chin and His Writings, 1967,
a readable survey of his life, times and extensive literary work from the early
1920s to the 1950s. Although fallen into obscurity in China during the Maoist
period, Pa Chin was one of the internationally best known Chinese writers during
the interwar years. The Family is the first volume of a trilogy novel known as
(Turbulent Stream).

SMEDLEY, Agnes and CHU TEH

The Great Road, The life and times of Chu Teh, 1956
A biography of Chu Teh, the commander of the first Red Army units; being largely
a history of the endless battles, uprisings, defeats and chaos of two decades
of armed revolutionary struggle from Wuhan in 1927, through the drawn out siege
of the initial Kiangsi Soviet, the Long March to Yennan in mid 1930s and the
struggles in north China with warlord, Kuomintang and Japanese forces in late
1930s to mid 1940s.

SNOW, Edgar

Red Star Over China, 1938
An on-the-spot journalistic account of the people, leaders and conditions in the
Chinese Soviet regions during 1936-1938 but ranging back over the previous decade
of revolutionary civil war. A once extremely influential account by an American
reporter in the John Reed tradition; may seem somewhat cavelier in retrospect.

On the Far Side of the River, 1964
A journalistic account of China's society, economy and polity in the years leading
up to, during and immediately following the stalled Great Leap Forward. Based
upon extensive interviews with Chinese leaders of the early 1960s, it is partly
their estimation of the advances and errors made in China since 1949 and Snow's
evaluation of their claims. Like most other sympathetic accounts of the time,

Snow nowhere analyses the festering nationalism which was to blossom in the Chinese Thermidor a decade later.

SNOW, Helen Foster

Women in Modern China, 1967
A study which includes biographical accounts by Chinese women; about conditions of semi-feudal bondage and the struggles for liberation from the early decades of this century to 1949 and after. Includes extracts by Ting Ling (the Chinese feminist writer of the 1930s) and first hand accounts by Chinese women factory workers, peasants and others. Describes the lives of women in socialist China and touches on the ongoing struggles for women's equality.

TIAN HAN

Meiju, 1929 (Rainy Season)
A play about a petty trader's family in Shanghai; when the father commits suicide after being ruined the mother sustains the family by going to work in a textile factory. Of their lives and growing appreciation of the tenacity of members of the Chinese working class. Also (The Death of Worker Gu Zheng Hong), 1928, a play about the Shanghai general strike of 1925.

Moonlight Sonata, 1930
Another play about the travails of Chinese workers and petty bourgeoisie in Shanghai. After Tian's murder by Chiang Kai Shek in 1931 this work was translated and performed in numerous countries abroad.

T'IEN CHUN

Village in August, 1974 (original 1935)
A documentary novel depicting the lives of people in a small Manchurian peasant village who support the (non-communist) guerrilla units fighting against the Japanese invaders during the early 1930s. Written in a colloquial style and dealing with everyday events, by a left nationalist officer of the former Chang Tso Liang army. Edgar Snow's introduction to the 1974 edition provides some necessary historical background information.

TING LING (Ding Ling)

Muqin, 1933 (Mother)
A novela by an early left feminist writer whose work has recently made a comeback in China and abroad. Mother is a tribute to Ting Ling's mother; raised in a Chinese provincial town of late Manchu China, the wife of a minor government official, she experienced the repressive strictures against Chinese women and determined to free her own daughter from them. She started a "foot-unbinding" movement, initiated education for women and organized a demonstration against hostile local authorities. About the initial struggles for women to live freer lives despite the pressures of their families, friends and officials. Untouched by western or socialist ideas, she is portrayed as one of the indigenous, rebellious mothers of China.

Sha-fei Nushi de Riji, 1929 (Diary of Miss Sophie)
A story in the form of a diary by an emancipated young Chinese woman who has broken away from her family and background and finds herself in a TB sanitorium. In a sense, a tale of what happens to a Chinese Nora after she leaves "The Doll House". The joys of some personal freedom but the stringent limitations of being alone in a world where few options are open for unattached women with no money. Ting Ling's feminist writing treated with the theme of female sexuality and desires. "Diary of Miss Sophie" translated in Harold Isaac's Straw Sandals, 1974.

Taiyang Zhaozai Sangganheshang, 1955 (The Sun Shines Over the Shangkan River)
A documentary novel set in north central China in the late 1940s. It deals with the differing streams of experience, the internal differences and the varied, sometimes contradictory purposes peasants have in aligning with the communists and assaulting the landlord system. Cast with a host of unstereotyped and realistically contentious characters who can use raunchy language and be pretty

boorish as well as heroic. She touches on both the tremendous psychological leap
forward which some men and women have made and the continuing small minded
chauvinism of others (not excluding some communist cadre). Revolves around
initiating land reform in the district and is interlaced with a strong dose of
left feminism.

Ting Ling's own life is as amazing as that of any of her characters. From a
background described in Muqin, to a teenaged writer living among anarchist
working class organizers in the 1920s, capture by Kuomintang police who murdered
her husband, escape from prison and a trek through enemy lines to join the Red
Army in Yennan in 1936, her literary disputes with Mao Tze Tung there, her
continuing radical dissent and writing which got her imprisoned in a "re-education"
centre during the 1960s, and her recent reemergence as a major author are part
of the story.

TSAO YU (Wan Chai-pao)

Thunderstorm, 1958 (original 1934)
A play about the mentality of the Chinese comprador bourgeoisie during the early
1930s; revolves around the family members of a large coal owner and his associates
who will support Chiang Kai Shek, Japanese occupation forces or anyone else who
will defend their interests and power over the Chinese workers. One of a quasi-
trilogy of plays which include (Sunrise), 1936, a study of a girl dragged into
a hellish life as an indentured prostitute, and (Wilderness), 1937, a play about
the pent up rage which ultimately leads an apolitic tenant farmer to murder his
landlord.

TU PENG-CHENG

In Days of Peace, 1965
A novel about railway building during the initial reconstruction period of early
1950s. An archetypic account which describes some of the daily work and plans in
railway rebuilding projects but peopled with a cast of "wreckers and provacateurs",
"misguided workers set straight", "cadres steeled" and so forth. This title to
serve as a representative of the host of comparable Chinese "socialist
construction" novels.

XIA YAN (Hsia Yan)

Baoshengong, 1932 (Women Slave Workers)
A play about indentured women factory workers in China at the time. About the
lives of industrial serfs who are bought and sold through the complex of money
lenders, gangster associations, industrialists and the connivance of the
Kuomintang government.

YEH TZU

Harvest, 1962
A collection of six stories about the proto-revolutionary ferment, of local
peasant revolts against landlords, tax collectors, etc. in Hunnan Province
between 1924 to 1929 and leading up to the Autumn Harvest Rising, the nominal
begining of the Chinese peasant Soviets. Based partly on the author's
reminiscences.

YON DAFU

"Chunfeng Chenzuide Wanshang", 1923 (On a Rice Wine-Drunken Evening)
A story about the life of a woman working in a cigarette factory, her
exploitation, sagacity and decency juxtaposed to the fashionable venality and
modern rapacity of her employer, a publically admired "new" bourgeoisie. One of
the earliest works of Chinese proletarian literature. Also Yin Fu, a poet and
translator of western literature, whose poems (First of May, 1929)
and (Berlin on May 1, 1929) and his story Biele Gege, 1930 (Goodbye, Older
Brother) evoke the internationalist strain in some early Chinese left wing
writing.

KOREA

AN Su-Gil

Pukkando, 1959-1967 (Northern Chientao)
A three volume historical novel chronicling the lives of four generations of a peasant family which leaves Korea amid the internal collapse of the last Korean dynasty to settle in a frontier region of Manchuria during the first decade of this century. It details their day to day lives, the changing social and political conditions over the next forty years under a variety of Korean, Chinese, Japanese and regional warlord regimes. A social history of the Pukkando region and its people, especially of the peasant struggles against assorted local exploiters and Japanese colonialism from 1910 to 1945.

BURCHETT, Wilfred and WINNINGTON, Alan

Koje Unscreened, 1953
A brief "expose" of Koje prison camp during the Korean war, where many of the North Korean POWs and a few surviving South Korean leftists were held by the American army. Of the concentration camp-like conditions and the largely unchecked terror carried out by the South Korean secret police.

CH'AE Man-Sik

T'angyu, 1938 (Turbid Waters)
A novel about the economic and social dissolution of Korea in the aftermath of the defeated revolt of 1919 and of the consolidation of Japanese colonialism in the 1920s. Revolves around the ruin of petty rice merchants by Japanese monopoly trading firms and the bankrupting of much of the Korean petty bourgeoisie. Also treats the multifoliate class and social oppression within Korean society itself, of the oppressed condition of women in particular.

CH'OE Chong-hui

In-gansa, 1960 (Man's History)
An epic novel revolving around two generations of left liberal Korean students, their struggles against the repressive regimes of their times, their brief successes and repeated defeats. Begins with a group of Korean students in Japan at the begining of the 1930s who are scattered by the deepening repression. It follows their disparate paths and fortunes through W.W.II, the Kwanju uprising against Japanese colonialism, escape into Manchuria and return to Korea after 1945--where they are torn between the North and the South. Some become involved in the amorphous "civil war" which emerged in the late 1940s on the imposition of the Syngman Rhee landlordocracy. A daughter of one of the original students joins a partizan group, survives the general destruction of the left in South Korea and emerges from prison as another generation prepares for the national student uprising which will succeed in deposing Rhee in 1960.

Chimaek, 1966 (Vein of Earth)
A novel sequel to Man's History, dealing with the continuing struggles of progressive Koreans and youths against the seemingly endless succession of repressive regimes in their country. Focuses on the culmination of the mass demonstrations which deposed Syngman Rhee with flashbacks of the history of the forces in contention. Of the short lived parliamentary period which was soon again to be crushed by a cabal of generals and KIA police colonels.

HAN Solya

Hoanghon, 1950 (Twilight)
A North Korean "proletarian" novela dealing with the desperation of Korean factory workers and landless tenant farmers during the final years of Japanese rule; of their struggles against the exploitation by both the Japanese imperialism and the Korean bourgeoisie.

LEE, Peter

Flowers of Fire, 1974
An anthology of twenty-one translated stories by Korean authors. Contains works
by some of the left populist and social realist writers of 1920s to 1950, including
stories by Kim Tongin, Hyon Chingon, An Sugil, Son Chang-sop.

PAK Kyong-su

Tongt'o, 1971 (Frozen Earth)
A novela about the son of a landless peasant who manages to become a village
teacher and wangles a job as tutor for the children of a large landlord. Despite
their contempt of him as a servant he gets one of the daughters pregnant, who he
then marries, thereby crawling up the social ladder through calculated guile.
The antithesis of a proletarian theme, this South Korean version of Room at the
Top probably captures something of the milieu during the 1960s.

SO Ki-won

Hyongmyong, 1964 (Revolution)
A historical novel about the long drawn out peasant revolt which coursed through
Korea during the last years (1905-1910) of the Korean dynasty. Told through the
stories of two brothers, one who supports the Yi landlord dynasty and the other
who joins the rebels, and both of whom ultimately become disillusioned.

Amsajido, 1958 (Amsajido)
A novel of resigned sorrow for the seemingly inescapable repression and dictatorship (of both right and left) which pervades Korean society since its independence
in 1945.

STONE, I.F.

The Hidden History of the Korean War, 1969 (original 1953)
A remarkable reportage history of the background and political bases of the
Korean war. It deals largely with events and maneuvers in the US and in Korea
from 1945 to 1953; the conversion of a long standing internal struggle into the
first battlefront of the cold war during the Truman era. Of the more or less
arbitrary installation of Syngman Rhee and the assault on the left in South Korea
ultimately resulting in the deaths of hundreds of thousands of dissidents. But
expecially about the near endless roster of coverups and fabrications, and just
plain lies perpetrated on the US and allied publics during the time. Stone was
one of the very few liberal journalists to speak out during the McCarthy era and
his account is doubly remarkable in that he himself initially believed the
government-press accounts.

TADSCHUN, I.

Nongsa, 1956 (Peasants Land)
A North Korean novel about the peasant struggles against Korean landlords and
Japanese colonizers during the 1930s and W.W.II, culminating in the first stages
of agricultural collectivization in North Korea in the late 1940s. By a North
Korean writer.

YOM Sang-Sop

Samdae, 1930 (Three Generations, 1966)
An epic novel about three generations of a Korean peasant family from the last
years of the Yi dynasty to the consolidation of Japanese colonialism. It begins
with the rigid Confucian-Mandarin society of the grandparental generation in the
first decade of the century and how this is shaken to the roots by the Tong-hak
peasant rising. The begining of Japanese colonial rule in 1910 and the effects
of the disastrous National Uprising of 1919, with its peasant, proletarian and
ruined middle class components. Deals with the mass impoverishment during the
1920s and the incipient class conscious struggles which emerge within Korea by
the late 1920s. Also (Eons Ago), 1933, a serialized quasi-sequel to Three
Generations, carrying developments into the early 1930s when the Korean left was
decimated. In a similar vein, Yi Ki-Yong's novel, (The Hometown), 1935, deals

with the disparate nationalist tendencies in Korea contending against Japanese colonialism as well as the class struggles of some Korean workers and peasants during the 1930s.

ADDENDUM: SHORT STORIES

CHO Myong-hui

"Naktong Kang", 1927 (The Naktong River)
A long story which depicts the exactions of Japanese colonialism and the abject poverty of Korean peasantry in 1920s as well as the initial steps of class struggle by some peasants and rural workers.

"Kwon To Iu Otoko", 1933 (A Man Called Kwon)
A story about the authoritarianism and narrow opportunism of teachers and small town gentry in Korea. In particular about one village boss who earns his living bootlegging and who boasts about his suppression of the local "Reds" who as yet consist of only a handful of isolated students. Cho Myong-hui was one of the founders of the Korean Proletarian Artists Federation in late 1920s.

CH'OE Sohae

"Kia Wa Sallyuk", 1924 (Starvation and Murder), "K'unmuljin Twi", 1925 (After the Flood)
Two apocalyptic stories of the daily struggles on the narrow edge of survival by the Korean poor during the 1920s and the hatred this engenders. By a left populist worker-writer who fell in the underground struggle against Japanese colonialism.

HYONG Chin-gon

"Unsu Chohu Hal", 1924 (A Lucky Day), "Halmoni Ui Chugom", 1923 (Death of a Grandmother), "Sinmunji Was Ch'olchang", 1929 (Newspapers and Iron Bars)
Three stories by a pioneer Korean social realist writer; "Lucky Day" and "Grandmother" being portraits of the human tragedy and chaos in Korea during the early 1920s, while "Iron Bars" deals with the deepening repression by Japanese colonial authorities at the end of the decade.

KIM Tong-In

"Kamdscha", 1932 (Potato)
A quietly tragic account of the misery and near starvation reigning among many Korean workers and landless peasants at the end of the 1920s. Possibly the best known and most widely translated Korean story of the interwar period by the dean of the Korean naturalist writers. Kim Tong-In wrote almost a hundred short stories in this vein during the 1920s and 1930s.

"Tscholmun Kudul", 1934 (Portrait of a Sorceress), "Pulgan-San", 1935 (The Firey Mountain)
Two serialized short novelas steeped in local Korean folklore and dealing with the poor peasantry; allegories written under Japanese censorship and hinting at the desperate need for but impossibility of social reforms under colonial rule.

YI Hyo-Sak

"Noryong Kunhae", 1929 (Coast of Russian Territory)
A story touching on the background and mixed hopes of a member of the communist underground in Korea during the late 1920s. Also Yu Chin-O, "Yojikkong", 1931 (Factory Women), a proletarian story set in an early Korean factory.

JAPAN

ARISHIMA Takeo

Kain No Matsuei, 1920 (The Last Descendent of Cain)
A novela dealing with the conditions of peasantry in the "frontier" regions of
Hokkaido in the years immediately before W.W.I. A simple, oft-repeated but well
handled story of how a tenant farmer and his family come to ruin through the
network of exploitation by landlord, money lender and government officials. An
abridged version translated in John Morrisson's Modern Japanese Fiction, 1955.

Aru Onna, 1919 (Story of a Woman)
A novela about a young woman striving for her own emancipation during a period
when Japanese women still had the legal status of wards, and of her ultimate
defeat by the economic and social strictures of that society.

FUJIMORI Seikichi

Haritsuke Mozaemon, 1926 (Crucified Mozaemon)
A novel about the rapid destruction of a man from the lower middle class who is
"forced into the depths of industrial labour" with its terrible and hazardous
working conditions, poverty and humiliations during the 1920s. A hardly
proletarian but once influential account written after Fujimori's one year stint
as a worker in a variety of Japanese factories. An already established writer,
Fujimori became a prolific contributor to left wing literary journals; two of
his stories ("The Man Who Didn't Applaud" and "Lieutenant Kusama") can be read
in English translation in Kobayashi Takiji et al, The Cannery Boat, 1933.

HAYAMA Yoshiki

Umi Ni Ikuru Hitobito, 1926 (Men Who Live on the Sea, 1934)
A novel about the lives of Japanese merchant seamen from before W.W.I to 1920;
about the working conditions and quasi-military discipline on a freighter
running between Muroran and Yokohama. Also deals with the lives of longshoremen
and others in the waterfront districts frequented by the seamen, their growing
union awareness as a means of self defense culminating in the 1919 Japanese
seamen's strike. One of the major proletarian novels of the period, written by
a former seaman and union organizer.

Hayama Yoshiki Zenshu, 1950 (Complete Works of Hayama Yoshiki)
A multi volume collection of novelas, sketches and other work which include two
once influential stories, "Inbaifu", 1928 (Prostitute) and "Idosuro Sonraku"
(Migratory Village). "Inbaifu" portrays a seaman-narrator's meeting with a
prostitute who is neither part of "a social problem" nor a character in a romantic
tragedy; his dawning realization that their mutual exploitation is not so very
different and that constructive anger rather than sympathy should be the
applicable emotion. "Idosuro Sonraku" deals with a peasant village dispossessed
of its lands, whose members become even more impoverished migratory farm
labourers.

HAYASHI Fumiko

Horoki, 1930 (Vagabond's Diary)
A picaresque novel-reminiscence of Hayashi's girlhood travelling through pre W.W.I
Japan with her peddlar mother;of her teenage life and loves, work in factories
and waitressing in noodle shops during the early 1920s. A zesty, brash account
by a proletarian feminst writer. Also her two stories, "Nakimushi Kozo", 1934
(Cry Baby) and "Inazuma", 1935 (Lightening), semi-autobiographical accounts which
depict fellow workers, marginal cafe leftists and others in Hayashi's life
during the 1920s.

Shitamachi, 1948 (Shitamachi/Tokyo, 1958)
Hayashi's major novel, being a personal account of the lives of a middle aged war

widow and her surviving friends. The battered, hungry yet tenacious vitality
among the poor and working people living in the ruins of a devastated Tokyo in
the years immediately after W.W.II.

Ukigumo, 1949 (Floating Cloud, 1957)
A novel which describes Hayashi's alienation and break with the organized left
due to its impotence during and in the years preceding W.W.II. Also a collage
of loving, unstereotyped sketches of ordinary Japanese people, especially of
working class women.

HAYASHI Fusao

Tokai Sokyokusen, 1933 (Web of the City)
A protest novel in which the face of middle class Tokyo is counterposed to the
gloomy tenements and straightened lives of semi-employed workers and their
families inhabiting the back streets of the city. Focuses on one street of
wooden tenements that runs through a ravine near the heart of Tokyo. Also the
story "Ringo", 1926 (Apples), about a group of peasant-fishermen in Hokkaido
who are cheated out of their share of a salmon catch by the owner of the fishing
vessel and how this is the last straw which sets in motion attempts to organize
a fishermen's union.

HIRABAYASHI Taeko

Seryeshitsu Nite, 1927 (In the Charity Ward)
A collection of short stories, the title story being an angry and loving account
of individual struggle for personal dignity by a middle aged woman dying in the
charity ward of a Tokyo hospital.

"Naguru", 1928 (I Hit Him)
A short story of one woman's rebellion against oppressive domestic relationships
by a major proletarian feminist writer of the period.

Hitori Yuku, 1946 (Going Alone)
An autobiography of the author's political imprisonment during the late 1930s, her
long battle with TB contracted in prison and her growing distance from the
communist party but continuing feelings of outrage and demand for human dignity
which led her into political commitment initially.

Sabaku No Hana, 1955-1957 (Flower in the Desert)
A serialized novel about a Japanese working class woman, her experiences in the
proletarian movement of the 1920s and the repression of the 1930s, the mass
slaughter of Japanese civilians during W.W.II and the protagonist's shift to a
quietism in the post war years. A roman de clef.

HIRASAWA Keishichi

Hitotsu No Senku, 1924 (One Pioneer)
A posthumously published collection of Hirasawa's agitational plays for and about
the Japanese labour movement.

Hitori To Sen-sambyaku-nin, 1954 (One Man and Thirteen Hundred People)
A collection of short stories and plays by the editor of the Labour Weekly from
1912 on, a leading syndicalist and martyr of the early Japanese labour movement,
murdered in 1923 along with a number of other union leaders by the Special
Military Police.

HIROTSU Kazuo

Yubi, 1924 (Fingers), Iki Nokoreru Mono, 1924 (Those Who Survived)
Two short novelas of the common Japanese people rising from the Great Earthquake
of 1923 and how their tenancity gave Hirotsu the strength and inspiration to
commit himself to left struggles.

Fuu Tsuyokarubeshi, 1933-34 (The Winds Will be Strong)
A serial novel of the weaknesses and trajectory of the proletarian culture
movement and its growing distance from the Japanese working class during the
deepening repression of the times.

Chimata No Rekishi, 1940 (A History in the Streets)
A novel about the daughter of the rural lower middle class who migrates to Tokyo
and runs a boarding house in the years 1900-1925, being a sort of Japanese
"Mother Courage".

Shinjitsu Was Uttaeru, 1953 (Truth Appeals), Izumi E No Michi, 1954 (Path to the
Mountains)
Two reportage works about the frame up of labour leaders by the Japanese and
American occupation government; the events surrounding the 1952 Matsukawa
Incident, in which leftist union leaders were convicted of sabotaging a rail line
by courts using blatantly doctored evidence.

HOSOI Wakizo

Kojo, 1924 (Factory)
A novela about the lives and horrendous working conditions endured by women
cotton mill workers during the early 1920s; how the industry contracted girls
from impoverished families as indentured labour and how the legal authorities
enforce these contracts.

Joko Aishi, 1954 (original 1924) (Tragedy of a Female Mill Hand)
A semi-autobiographical account of life, work and conditions among the circa one
million women and child contract workers in the textile industry of Japan. (A
longstanding scandal of industrial serfdom even within the context of Japanese
free enterprise.) Revolves around an orphaned youth sold into cotton mill
labour by his guardians at age thirteen and of his life in the plants between
1909 and 1924. Completed shortly before the author himself died (at the age of
thirty) from filibrosis, an industrial disease contracted in the mills. Also his
short story, "Aru Kikai", 1922 (A Certain Machine) which relates the dreams of
retribution by a victim of an industrial accident.

ISHIKAWA Tatsuzo

Sobo, 1935 (Poor People)
A documentary novel about poor Japanese emigrants traveling to Brazil during the
early 1930s in the steerage quarters of a steamer. A classic account of flight
from poverty to an unstated (but strongly suggested) different kind of poverty
under foreign skies.

Hikage No Mura, 1937
A novela about a northern peasant village soon to be drowned out by a hydro-
electric reservoir built to service Japan's burgeoning military-industrial
complex.

Nozumi Naki Ni Arazu, 1947 (Not Without Hope), Kaze Ni Soyogu, 1949-1951 (Reeds
Swaying in the Wind)
Two serialized novels about the devastation, exhaustion and grinding poverty in
Japan during 1945-50. Portrays the quickly reborn opportunism and rapacity of
the speculator middle class counterposed to the tenacious decency of ordinary
Japanese people from a variety of backgrounds and under the most inauspicious
conditions.

IWAFUJI Yukio

Tetsu, 1929 (Iron)
A collective novel about the horrendous working conditions in an iron foundry of
the period (by a worker-writer); of the obvious and intricate ways in which the
job affects the entire lives of the workers and their families.

KAGA Kogi (Hajime Sui)

Wata, 1950 (original 1931) (Cotton)
A semi-autobiographical novel about tenant farmers growing cotton on the Kaga
plain of northern Japan between circa 1910-1930. It portrays a boy's earliest
awareness of tenantry, the near starvation poverty of the farmers, the establishment
of cotton spinning plants in the region and the flight of peasant sons and
daughters into these factories in hopes of a livelihood. Touches on the first

sporadic resistance to landlord demands. Follows the protagonist in his migration
to the copper mines and his initial entry into the union movement, of how he
becomes a labour organizer in Osaka, and of his return home to help tenant
farmers mount a rent strike which initially fails due to the continuing
subservience of many farmers. The hero is imprisoned for his union activity
but on his release he discovers that a massive and militant peasant movement has
taken hold in his own region and elsewhere.

Kaga was a tenant farmer's son who at nine years of age was apprenticed to factory
labour; he experienced the maelstrom of hopes and defeats of the 1920s and 1930s
(part of which are recorded in Wata), was imprisoned during W.W.II, elected a
communist representative in the Japanese parliament before being purged by the
American occupation government in 1949.

KANEKO Yobun

Sentakya To Shijin, 1922 (The Laundry and the Poet)
A novela also adapted as a satiric play; about a group of laundry workers who
disinter the dirty linen of the millionaire owner of their sweat shop, parading
it, along with songs and accounts of his dirty deals and their exploitation,
before the assembled notables and guests at his sixtieth birthday party.

Jigoku, 1923 (Hell)
A novela about a drought-ridden peasant village and the exactions of landlord
demands for unpayable rents, which culminates in an incipent local peasant revolt.
Ends with the peasants, on the verge of revolt, returning to quiessance when rain
begins to fall and forgetting about the social foundations of their poverty,
thereby binding themselves to the hell that they are in.

KATAOKA Teppei

Ayasatomura Kaikyoroku, 1929 (The Heroism of Ayasato Village)
A novela about peasant-landlord struggles which emerged during the 1920s in
formerly conservative regions; of rent and tenant strikes and the use of military
police to suppress a peasantry which had formerly been one of the mainstays of
the government.

KATO Yoshizo (Kato Kazuo)

Shokko Shisu Chosasho, 1922 (Written Investigation of a Worker's Thoughts)
A sardonically humourous novela of how a naively truthful (or fed up) and
irrepressible worker in a machine factory answers an early labour management
questionnaire sent by the company. Expands on their questions and his answers
in a series of quick moving, incisive word and idea associations--scandalizing
his employers with his thoughts about priests, company loyalty, "Honest Toil",
politicians and patriotism, etc. Whereupon he is fired.

Kakushu, 1925 (Fired)
A sequel to Shokku Shisu, which follows the account of the fired worker whose
thoughts were investigated (Kato himself was fired when his employers discovered
his first published book). It sparkles with Kato's irrepressible humour and
sardonic satire, both of Japanese social institutions and of himself. For
instance, an argument with his wife who tells him he would be better off peddling
fish, while he says that she is just a woman and doesn't understand the power of
literature. Soon after Kato gave up writing and became a coolie and then a
fish peddlar.

KINOSHITA Naoe

Hi No Hashira, 1904 (Pillar of Fire, 1966)
One of the first protest novels in Japan; it combines a melodramatic romance with
a bitter personal attack on the character of Japanese militarists on the eve of
the Russo-Japanese war.

Otto No Jiyu, 1906 (A Husband's Freedom)
A melodramatic but, in its time, "daring" novel which attacks the dual standard
for men and women in Japan. A call for full civil rights for women, who then
still had the legal status of children or wards throughout their lives.

KINROSHA BUNGAKU (Workers' Literature)

Kinrosha Bangaku Senshu, 1949 (Selections from Workers' Literature)
A selection of reportage and stories from the journal Workers' Literature.
Accounts of the lives of peasants and workers in post W.W.II Japan by
K. Watanabe, G. Atsutua, Y. Hayahi, S. Inaba, K. Ozawa, K. Takemoto, K. Hamada,
C. Shoda and I. Kadowaki. They range from stories about the rise of an
aggressive new kulak farming class through the intended results of the recent
land reform program, to the use of company unionism to defeat real labour union
organization, reminiscences of the horrors of W.W.II for the Japanese working
class and stories about the still extant master-servant relations in the widespread artizanal industries.

KOBAYASHI Takiji et al

The Cannery Boat and Other Japanese Short Stories, 1933
Kobayashi's novela Cannery Boat deals with the initial bemused patriotism and
individualism of a group of fishermen-cannery workers aboard a factory ship
working in the Kamchatka fisheries during the late 1920s. The exploitation and
indifference of officers to murderously unsafe working conditions aboard ship
result in a spasmodic but growing rebelliousness among the crew. They come to
perceive the class-state forces arrayed against them when, after an incipient
strike, a Japanese naval vessel (which some hope has come to protect them)
arrests their leaders. Kobayashi himself was arrested and murdered by Japanese
police in 1933, his funeral turning into the last mass demonstration against
Japanese fascism.

The volume contains stories by six other left wing Japanese authors including
Seikichi Fujimori, "The Man Who Didn't Applaud" and "Lieutenant Kusama", Denji
Kuroshima, "Factory in the Sea", Teppei Kataoka, "Linesmen", Naoshi Tokunaga,
"The Efficiency Committee", Fusao Hayashi, "Cocoons", and Sanji Kishi, "The
Monument". They mainly revolve around union and underground political struggle
during the 1920s and early 1930s but range from Hayashi's gently moving tale of
the hidden symbols of class solidarity kept by a working class boy in a
repressively patriotic school, to Fujimori's sardonic satire, to Kishi's
desperate anger. Other works by these authors are found elsewhere in this
bibliography.

The Factory Ship and The Absentee Landlord, 1973 (translated by Frank Motofugi)
A recent translation of Kobayashi's two main novelas which captures the vitality
of the writing by utilizing the surviving original manuscripts which had been
partly censored and lost in the initial translation. Factory Ship is a re-edited
version of Cannery Boat while Absentee Landlord deals with the conditions of
tenant farmers in northern Japan during the late 1920s and a rent strike with
revolutionary overtones.

Kobayashi Takiji Zenshu, 1965 (Collected Works of Takiji Kobayashi)
A three volume collection of Kobayashi's short stories and novelas written
between 1924 and 1933.

KUBO Sakae

Noborigana, 1951 (Hillside Kiln)
A documentary novel about the lives of farmer-artizans in Hokkaido on the eve of
and during W.W.II; of their near-famish poverty due to the exactions of war and
the exactions of a chain of exploiters. The single novel by an important
translator of Soviet and international left literature. Kubo spent much of
W.W.II in a forced labour camp in Hokkaido.

KUROSHIMA Denji

Sori, 1927 (Sleigh, 1952)
An anti-militarist novela revolving around the experiences and thoughts of a squad
of Japanese soldiers during Japan's military intervention against the Soviet Union
in 1920. Of the soldiers' piecemeal destruction and their partial realization
that their rulers have as little concern for them as they do for the Siberian
peasantry. Kuroshima's work has recently been rediscovered and is considered to
be among the most seminal Japanese writing of the interwar period.

Uzumakeru Tori No Mure, 1928 (A Swirling Flock of Crows)
Another novela surveying the backgrounds and fates of a group of Japanese soldiers trapped in the wastes of Siberia, part of the sixty thousand man intervention army sent against the Soviet Union by Japanese government in 1919-1921. It plays on the emptiness of the patriotic phrases they have been fed.

Shiberia Mono, 1929 (Siberian Tales)
A collection of stories about the sufferings sustained by both the Japanese and Russian peoples through the Japanese Zaibatzu (the huge corporate monopolies) attempts to gain a foothold in Siberia by military intervention.

Also see "Dempo" (Telegram), "Ton-gun" (Pigs), "Nisen Doka" (A Copper Sen), 1925-1926, three short stories dealing with the mean spiritedness and personal tragedies among poor peasant families caused by endless penury and austerity and the lack of a few, seemingly insignificant, yen.

Bososeru Shigai, 1953 (original 1930) (Armed City, 1935)
A reportage novel about the Japanese military seizure of the Manchurian city of Tsinan in 1928. Of the sufferings caused by the Japanese invasion and of the overnight conversion of the local Chinese ruling class into an alliance with the Japanese occupation forces and against the opposition mounted by Chinese workers. Proclaims his solidarity with the Chinese working class and castigates Japanese militarism at home and abroad. The original edition was confiscated by Japanese authorities and the 1953 edition was banned by the US occupation government of Japan who during the Korean war also saw it as subversively anti-militarist. The 1953 version, under the editorship of Tsuboi Shigeji, replaces the passages cut by the original Japanese censors.

MAEDAKO Koichiro (Maedako Hiroichiro)

Santo Senkyaku, 1920 (Third Class Passage)
A semi-autobiographical novel about emigration to America by a poor Japanese youth during the first decade of this century. Maedako came from a poor peasant family, emigrated to the US in circa 1905 and worked as a farm hand, sailor, dishwasher, baker, etc. He educated himself in public libraries there and used his experiences in some of his books after return to Japan at the end of W.W.I. He became the editor of Bungei Sensei, one of the leading Marxist literary journals of the interwar period.

Daibofu Jidai, 1924 (Time of Storms)
A novel dealing with the lives of Japanese immigrant workers in the US from before W.W.I to circa 1920; accounts of the superexploitation and racism they face, of the role of the Japanese middle class abroad and of the varied attempts at union and other defensive organizations by the immigrant workers, who remain penniless and more or less powerless whatever they do.

Taigo No Kokuten, 1927 (Sunspots)
A novela dealing with the lives of left political exiles banished to Hokkaido for their activities by the pre-fascist government. Also see two long stories, "Madorosu No Mure", 1922 (Forecastle Gang), about the lives of Japanese seamen and stokers on a tramp steamer during the W.W.I period, and "Semuga", 1929 (Semuga), which sardonically counterposes the high phrases and rhetoric of official reports against the harsh realities of the exploitation of workers in the Kamchatka fisheries.

Shina, 1929 (China)
A novela championing the revolutionary left in China during the civil war which was just begining.

MAMIYA Mosuke

Aragane, 1937-1938 (Raw Metal)
A serialized documentary novel about the work and daily lives of Japanese copper miners during the mid 1930s. Describes the poverty and despair of their lives but necessarily stops short of why these conditions exist or what might be done about them. One of the last such works to appear before the defeat of Japanese fascism.

MIYAJI Karoku

Aru Shokku No Shuki, 1919 (A Worker's Notebook)
An account of the day to day life of an industrial worker (which Miyaji was)
during the frenetic phase of Japanese industrial expansion. A politically
undirected but bitter denunciation of the Dickensian exploitation involved and an
angry demand for social justice. He also wrote a number of semi-autobiographical
stories about striking and blacklisted workers during the W.W.I period;
"Kyuhaku-seru Genso", 1917 (Straightened Illusions) and "Sojo-Go", 1918 (After
the Riot).

MIYAJIMA Sukeo

Kofu, 1916 (Miner)
One of the pioneer novels about the Japanese working class by a worker-writer.
A detailed account of the lives and work of miners in the pits of Japanese
capitalism in the years immediately before and during W.W.I. Drawn partly from
Miyajima's own experiences and said to be reminiscent of Zola's Germinal in parts.

Yama No Kajiya, 1919 (Mountain Blacksmith)
A novel filled with hatred of Japanese capitalism and the servitude of Japanese
society. Not so much Marxist as proletarian anarchist. It deals with the
rising urge to revolt in a Japanese worker who has tried his hand at many jobs,
finally as a blacksmith in a mountain village. He is involved in peasant
resistance to their landlords but finally has to flee from the vengeance of the
landlords and betrayal by the peasants, who become frightened after they have
challenged the established power and look for some scapegoat. Pervaded with a
special revulsion for those oppressed people who loyally serve their oppressors.

MIYAMOTO Yuriko (Chujo Yuriko)

Mazushiki Hitobito No Mure, 1916 (Crowd of the Poor)
A youthful novel about the plight of poor farmers in northeastern Japan during
the frenetic period of industrial growth and profiteering which by 1918 led to
nation-wide hunger riots.

Nobuko, 1928 (Nobuko)
A semi-autobiographical novel about a cosmopolitan and increasingly radical
middle class woman who, despite her psychological emancipation, is everywhere
hemmed in and restricted by the traditional roles expected by her own family,
husband and friends among the liberal circles she moves in.

Banshu Heiya, 1946 (Banshu Plains, 1953)
A quiet and moving novel which conveys the chaos and devastation of Japan at the
end of W.W.II yet also the rekindled hopes of a better, more just society which
may arise from the ashes. Miyamoto's best known novel.

Fuchiso, 1947 (Purple Grass, 1954)
A collection of stories about the heroism of everyday life lived by Japanese
women amid the hunger, death and devastation wrecked by bombing raids during
W.W.II.

Futatsu No Niwa, 1947-1950 (Two Gardens)
A serialized autobiography of Myamoto's packed life, of the experiences and
responses which drew many feminists and intellectuals to communism in Japan from
the mid 1920s to the post W.W.II period. No apologies, no recantation but some
regrets. Also Dohyo, 1950 (Signpost), a novel of reflections about the previous
generation's insights and illusions and its inability to halt a state gripped
by militarism, but mainly of the contending hopes and directions in Japan
during the post war period.

MORIMURA Seiichi and SHIMOZATO Masaki

The Devil's Gluttony, 1982
A horrendous two volume reportage account which unearths the story of the
"biological" and germ warfare experiments performed on some thousands of Chinese,
Russian and Korean prisoners by a special Japanese army-medical unit in
Manchuria during W.W.II. An investigation of an especially atrocious series of

war crimes. Examines how these atrocities were covered up by both US and post war Japanese authorities, with the perpetrators exchanging their expertise in germ warfare for immunity from War Crimes prosecution and in some cases rising to prominence in major Japanese companies and government positions over the next twenty-five years. Documents the generally unreconstructed attitudes of the perpetrators and the criminal hypocrisy of the US and Japanese government agencies which shielded them.

NAGATSUKA Takashi

Earth, 1910
A long, somewhat ponderous novel about the daily lives and hardships of Japanese peasants during the late Meiji era, where the consolidation of capitalism has begun to shake the farm villages. An influential naturalistic work in its time.

NAKANISHI Inosuke

Shado Ni Mengumu Mono, 1922 (Raised in Red Soil)
A novela which deals with the exploitation of tenant farmers, their smouldering resentment and potential rebelliousness hidden beneath a surface of traditional subservience. Drawn partly from Nakanishi's own background, it is also a prophecy of the wave of rent strikes, mass demonstrations, land siezures and other peasant mass actions which burst forth in the mid 1920s.

Akatsuchi Ni Megumu Mono, 1928-29 (Sprouts in the Red Earth)
A serialized reportage novel about the multifoliate oppression of Korean peasants and workers both by Korean bosses and by the Japanese Zaibatzu (trusts). Of the disparate and bloodily suppressed resistance of Korean people to their own exploiters and Japanese colonialism. Sprouts pieces together some of Nakanishi's sketches and stories about both the Japanese and Korean peasantry while he was a reporter for the popular left journal Kaizo. Its publication led to his arrest for insulting Japanese commercial enterprises.

NAKANO Shigeharu

Kisha No Kamataki, 1937 (The Stoker)
A novel written during and touching on Nakano's imprisonment for continuing to write proletarian literature. Two of his earlier stories are "Harusaki No Kase", 1928 (Wind in Early Spring), about the police harassment which destroys the family of a worker imprisoned in the 1928 mass arrests of leftists, and "Tetsu No Hanashi", 1929 (Tetsu's Story), a tale of a peasant family driven from their village because of their son's failure to perform the rituals of the Emperor system. Details the conservative patriotism of a broad sector of the peasantry.

Goshaku No Sake, 1946 (Five Cups of Sake)
A novela about life in devastated and occupied Japan during early 1946, with the hope that a fundamental break with the past can be made.

Muragimo, 1954
An autobiographical novel about the Japanese working class and peasantry from the 1920s to the early 1950s which trys to dispense with past illusions and myths. By a communist poet-writer who was briefly an elected member of the Japanese parliament (until purged in 1949) and who attempted to ressurect the traditions of Japanese proletarian literature.

NIHON SAYOKU BUNGEIKA SORENTO (Japanese Federation of Left Writers)

Senso Ni Taisuru Senso, 1928 (War on War, 1932)
A translated anthology of anti-war and anti-militarist stories including works by N. Tateno, J. Etchu, D. Kuroshima, Y. Kaneko, K. Satumura, J. Kobori and others. They treat with the political uses of patriotism at home, militarism's alliance with capitalism and reaction in the face of workers' demands, of the suffering of Japanese peasant soldiers in overseas adventures from the 1905 war with Russia, the 1920 Siberian intervention and the incursions into China and Korea. A bitter denunciation of the human costs to both ordinary Japanese and the other peoples affected by Japanese militarism.

OSUGI Sakae

Minsu Geijutsu, 1919 (Treatise on People's Art)
A prospectus of what working class literature (and especially workers' theatre)
should be; drawn from Rolland Romain's Theatre of the People. By a leading
syndicalist organizer, editor and later a martyr of the Japanese labour movement.
Osugi along with his family was murdered by the Japanese military police in 1923.

OTA Yoka

Ama, 1934 (Woman Diver)
A proletarian feminist novel about fisherwomen in Hiroshima prefecture during the
late 1920s.

Ryuri No Kishi, 1939 (On the Vagrant Side)
A semi-autobiographical set of stories in novel form; about the experiences, doubts
and struggle of a Japanese woman for self-liberation in an extremely restrictive
and legally oppressive society. Interweaves changing personal and social
conditions in Japan from circa 1920 to late 1930s.

Skikabane No Machi, 1950 (City of Corpses)
A documentary account, powerfully restrained and brutally objective, of what the
author experienced and observed as a survivor of the US atomic bombing of
Hiroshima, August 6, 1945. Details the holocaust of that day and the continuing
deaths which followed. A work initially banned by US occupation government.

Nigen Ranru, 1951 (Human Rag)
Novel about a Japanese woman who after years of unhappiness decides to leave her
husband; of her new life with another man and how this all ends unresolved in a
flash in Hiroshima.

Han Ningen, 1954 (Half Human)
A documentary novel of people suffering the crippling after-effects and lingering
deaths of atomic poisoning. Set during the Korean war period and ending with a
powerful, unqualified pacifist protest against war.

OZAWA Kiyoshi

Machi Oba, 1946 (Town Factory)
A description of life in a tenement district of a provincial town, told through
the everyday events and language of a young worker in one of a host of family run
artizanal industries. The workers' inescapable poverty and the gradual change
of the "patriotic feelings" of the protagonist as he sees the old system of
exploitation and class privileges rising again from the ashes of Japan's defeat.

SATA Ineko (Kubokawa Ineko)

Kyarameru Kojo Kara, 1928 (From the Carmel Factory)
An influential autobiographical novel of Sata's life and experiences as a "spinning
room girl". Orphaned, she worked in the Tokyo textile plants during W.W.I (and in
candy factories) as a child labourer, became a waitress, drifted into association
with a number of anarchist writers during the early 1920s and became an early
woman working class writer herself.

Kerenai, 1936
A feminist account of Sata's married life and divorce, her sexuality and refusal
to be bound by the traditional strictures on wives.

Watakushi No Tokyo Chizu, 1947 (My Own Map of Tokyo)
A memory portrait of the then devastated and otherwise vanished Tokyo of Sata's
youth. Of the tenements, noodle shops, dark lanes and factories, open sunny
places and lost faces which she still sees in her mind's eye in travels through
bombed out Tokyo. Despite all, it speaks of an irrepressible love of life.

Kikai No Naka No Seishun, 1954 (Adolescence Among the Machines)
An expanded and more mature version of Kyarameru Kojo; a novelized account of her
friends, workmates and youth in the Tokyo factories of W.W.I as a child labourer.

Karada No Naka O Kaze Ga Fuku, 1956 (The Wind Blows Through the Body)
A novel of the trials, tribulations and joys of a single Japanese working woman
with a child in post war Japan.

SHIMAKI Kensaku (Asakura Kikwo)

Saiken, 1937 (Rehabilitation)
A "recantation novel" which left wing writers were required to produce before they
were released from prison. Shimaki managed to write this one in the accepted
style yet subtly saying that his fundamental beliefs in proletarian humanism had
not changed. Also his long story, "Rai", 1934 (Leprosy), about an imprisoned
Japanese communist in 1933. It mulls over the rationales of his former comrades
who make recantations, counterposed to four other communist prisoners doomed by
leprosy who do not, with the protagonist wavering between. Shimaki wrote a
number of stories about how progressive Japanese might survive without endorsing
a brutal system. For instance, "Reimai", 1935 (Dawn), about a community worker's
gradual absorption into the life of an Eta village.

SHIMAZAKI Toson

Hakai, 1911 (Breaking the Oath, 1976)
A novel dealing with the continued persecution of members of the Eta caste. About
the son of an Eta family who pledges his father that he will leave the locale,
pass as non-Eta and advance himself so that their descendents will not have to
bear the oppression of past generations. He finally succeeds in becoming a school
teacher but after being faced by incidents of discrimination against Eta students
he reveals his own background, breaking the oath and entering into the fight for
equal rights for Eta. But after repeated setbacks he emigrates from Japan. One
of the classics of Japanese naturalist writing.

Yoake Mae, 1934 (Before the Dawn)
A historical novel which is an account of Shimazaki's father's life as a toll
house keeper on the Tokaido Road, the main artery connecting Yedo and Osaka, from
the final years of the Tokugawa regime to 1886. It indirectly underscores Japan's
extraordinary leap from being a feudal society to the beginings of a modern
industrial society. Interweaves the changes and continuities in peoples' lives
and conveys the feeling of loss entailed, even where the transformation was
essential.

TAKEDA Taijun

Mamushi No Sue, 1947 (Generation of Vipers)
A novel of the horror felt by a traditional Japanese Buddist writer at Japan's
invasion of and atrocities committed in China during the 1930s and 1940s.
Culminates in the expulsion of the large Japanese population of Shanghai in 1945
and the seemingly unbridgeable break between Chinese and Japanese peoples.

Mori To Mizumi Mo Matsuri, 1954 (Festival of the Woods)
An "indigenista" novel about an Ainu youth who struggles to defend the culture of
his people, a segregated minority in Hokkaido who were the original inhabitants
of all the Japanese islands.

TAYAMA Katai

Ippeisotsu, 1908 (One Soldier)
A novela which revolves around the last days of a Japanese peasant conscript dying
of beri-beri in the Russo-Japanese war of 1905. An account based partly on
Tayama's own experiences in that war, from which he emerged as a vocal anti-
militarist.

TOKUNAGA Sunao

Taiyo No Nai Machi, 1929 (The Street Without Sun, 1930)
A famous documentary novel of the Tokyo working class in the mid and late 1920s.
It revolves around the lives of a group of printers (Tokunaga among them) and their
attempts to defend their union in a bitter strike crushed by the police in 1926.

It is equally about the lives of their families, neighbours and other workers who live in a typical old tenement district of Tokyo.

Shitsugyo Toshi Tokyo, 1930 (Tokyo - City of the Unemployed)
A reportage account which is a kind of sequel to Street Without Sun, documenting the despair, semi-starvation and mass unemployment of the depression struck working class in Tokyo.

Hachinen Sei (The Eight-Year System), Hataraku Ikka (A Family of Workers), Seisho No Kioku (The First Memory), Tanin No Naka (Among Strangers), 1937-1939
A series of autobiographical novelas about Tokunaga's working class childhood and young manhood in Kyushu and Tokyo during the first two decades of the century. Also his two earlier reminiscence stories, "Uma", 1925, about a work horse which is the economic mainstay and member of a family of landless tenant farmers, and "Senso Zakki", 1927 (War Miscellanea), revolving around Tokunaga's father's experiences in the Russo-Japanese war and how he is shunned by homefront patriots in his village after he returns as an anti-war veteran.

Tokyo No Katasumi, 1939 (A Corner of Tokyo)
A documentary account of the lives of the poor in one of any number of pockets of Tokyo on the eve of W.W.II.

Aloura Deri, 1948 (Sultry Sun)
A novel which continues Tokunaga's earlier accounts of the daily lives of working poor people in Tokyo; deals into the first post W.W.II years.

Shizuka-Naru Yamayama, 1950, 1954 (The Quiet Mountains)
A two volume novel depicting the struggles of Japanese workers to organize under the initially favourable period of reform under the American occupation government to 1949. The second volume deals with the political purges of left from Japanese parliament, the various strategies mobilized to crush labour unions or turn them into company associations by a hostile and resurgent conservative Japanese capitalism which had gotten the blessings of the American authorities during the Korean war. The experiences of Japanese labour during the post W.W.II years and how the cost of rebuilding a devastated Japan is again borne by workers. Also two stories about this period, "Abura-deri", 1948 (Blazing Sunshine) and "Hitotsu No Hokoku", 1949 (One Report) which touch on how post war Japanese workers, even activists, seem to be totally unaware of and uninterested in the struggles, insights and goals of the left of a generation earlier.

TSUBOI Sakae

Daikon No Ha, 1938 (Radish Leaves)
A collection of stories about the worsening living standards among what had already been a poor peasantry; of the flagrant injustices in a Japan which was gearing for a wider imperialist war. One of the few protest volumes to make it into print that late. Tsuboi came from a poor peasant family, became a migrant urban worker, wife to an anarchist intellectual and participant in a group of proletarian women writers during the late 1920s. Imprisoned in late 1930s, she moved toward the communist party. Between 1944 and her death in 1967 she wrote some 25 volumes of short stories and children's books, including Kishi Utsu Nami, 1953 (Waves Breaking on the Beach), a semi-autobiographical account of a mother and daughter in a poverty stricken fishing village.

YAMADA Seizaburo

Puroretaria Bungaku-Shi No Hito-koma, 1954-1955 (On the History of Proletarian Literature)
A history of the authors and works, the social context and political infighting involved in the various streams of Japanese left wing literature from the first decade of the century to the eve of W.W.II. A rich and oft-cited work which as well as being a history attempts to stimulate a renewed interest in and re-establish working class literature in post war Japan. Yamada, an actual proletarian writer, published a stream of warmly personal stories about Japanese workers and poor in the journals Tane-make Hito (The Sowers) and Bungei Sensen (Workers' Literature) in the 1920s and 1930s. He was one of the editorial main stays of the proletarian literature movement of that time.

SOME BIBLIOGRAPHIC SOURCES

The titles and annotations provided in the body of the present bibliography stem largely from some three hundred odd sources. They include literary histories, surveys of particular literary genres or periods, anthologies, annotated bibliographies, studies of particular authors and book reviews in uncounted issues of both literary and socio-political journals. Although some of the sources are international in scope, most revolve around writing within particular national contexts and are arranged here by country or region.
The sources cited probably account for some two-thirds of the titles dealt with in the body of the bibliography. The remaining third stem from materials so scattered as to defy practical inclusion. There is also no point in recapitulating the search through sources which ultimately proved fruitless. There were plenty.

Needless to say, I have read only a small proportion of the actual novels listed. That is not particularly unusual in the preparation of a bibliography such as this. Apart from other considerations no single compiler could be competent in the various languages entailed. Instead, I have attempted when possible to peruse at least two separate reviews or descriptions of any particular work and have occasionally combined elements of distinct reviews in the annotations. This raises some problems when two descriptions differ markedly. A good deal, but not all, of this variance is eliminated if one bypasses critical estimations of writing style, intent or "pure literary value" of the works and sticks to the bare bones of topic, setting, period and theme.
It may bear repeating that the present compilation is not a survey of necessarily the "leading" authors and works--however those might be determined--of the various national literatures per se. It is rather a brief overview of radical and working class literature around the world during the present century (mainly in the period from 1914 to 1970). Given this scope there are fairly stringent practical limits to the amount of time and space which can be allotted to the presentation of any particular body of work. Indeed, the titles listed here comprise only about a half of those initially collected for inclusion and are only a small proportion of all titles surveyed. Nevertheless, I do believe that the present bibliography does list many of the leading left-wing writers and some of their representative works, as well as re-introducing a considerable number of now rather obscure (although not necessarily inferior) works.
As anyone can see, the sources cited here hardly scratch the surface of the materials which could be surveyed to compile a more comprehensive survey. The present bibliography is not intended as a research guide for specialists. Instead it is geared for the general reader who for whatever reason may become interested in a particular country or region and be amenable to reading left wing literature in order to gain some insight into the hidden history of the times and the everyday lives of people involved. It is for readers (even some university students) who in the normal course of events are unlikely to be familiar with nor otherwise likely to encounter the themes, authors and titles presented here. The following comments on additional bibliographic sources may serve as a brief guide for the lay reader who wishes to pursue the work of some particular author, genre or topic encountered in the main entries. In most cases there are more titles of interest than could be accommodated within the confines of the biblio-graphy itself. Some of the sources, as well as a few of the dead ends to be avoided, are as follows.

For BRITAIN, P.J. Keating's (1971) The Working Classes in Victorian Fiction, which deals with a period outside the purview of the present bibliography, is a cogent survey of the various stereotypes of the British working class in 19th century fiction and touches on the quasi-realist portraits presented by the so-called Cockney school at the end of the century. Mary Eagleton and David Pierce's

(1979) <u>Attitudes to Class in the English Novel</u> pursues a similar theme from the early 19th century to the present, presents some salient criticisms and commentary, but bypasses most of the proletarian literature of the 1930s to the 1950s. Michael Wilding's (1980) <u>Political Fictions</u> is mainly a debate between the utopian and anti-utopian components in the works of some of the major British novelists of the inter-war period.

Stephan Ingle's (1979) <u>Socialist Thought in Imaginative Literature</u> is a melange of extracts and commentary about the fictional work of self-professed "socialist" writers in Britain from William Morris and G.B. Shaw to George Orwell. Some of the Fabian extracts have a certain quizzical interest. Ralph Fox's (1937) <u>The Novel and the People</u> is a posthumously published work by one of the most frenetically prolific Marxist literary critics in Britain during the 1920s and 1930s. It hardly deals with then contemporary British novels and is rather a wide ranging appreciation of the popular literature of pre-20th century Europe, revolving around the theme that the greatest novels are to be seen as embodying the popular spirit of their times.

A combative little booklet is Paul O'Flinn's (1975) <u>Them and Us in Literature,</u> a series of thumbnail sketches and critiques, mainly of those post-Edwardian Great English Writers normally foisted on students in British secondary schools. O'Flinn simply, cavalierly and audaciously appends a little of the real worlds which writers like Joseph Conrad were pontificating about and a little of the Great Men's political backgrounds in a manner which could serve to stimulate some independent thought among student readers.

Walter Allen's (1954) <u>The English Novel: A Short Critical History</u> and his (1964) <u>The Modern Novel in Britain and the United States</u> mention the existence of left-wing novels in the U.S. during the 1930s but hold that nothing comparable evolved in Britain, apart from one or two exceptional authors. John Lehmann's (1940) <u>New Writing in Europe</u> touches on the popular and progressive writers who emerged in Britain (and on the Continent) during the latter 1930s--a little book overtaken by events. In a more historical retrospective, Katherine Hoskin's (1976) <u>Literature and Participation in England During the Spanish Civil War</u> is, despite the title, a very readable social history of the left in Britain during 1936-1939 and survey of the themes of left novels, drama and non-fictional literature throughout the decade. It is quite exemplary. Jack Lindsay's (1956) <u>After the Thirties</u> is a bitter and somewhat dogmatic comparison of the wave of left novels and themes in British writing in the 1930s with the supposed return to apolitic and proctological work by British authors after W.W.II. John Lucas (ed.) (1978), <u>The 1930s: A Challenge to Orthodoxy,</u> a collection of articles by different authors, challenges the established cold war orthodoxy about what the left political and literary scene was in Britain during the 1930s. Lucas provides some seminal suggestions about the manner in which the cultural history of that decade has been rewritten and the revisions passed off as reality to a later generation. In particular, H. Gustav Klaus' article, "Socialist Fiction in the 1930s", challenges the view that such writing was limited and ephemeral by listing some seventy odd left novels in Britain during that decade. In addition there is Jurgen Enkermann's treatment of some three dozen left working class authors, "Annotated Bibliography of British Working Class Prose" in <u>Workers and Writers</u> (1975). James Gindin's (1962) <u>Post War British Fiction</u> is a zesty and uninhibited survey including the new working class writers, the pseudo-angry enfante terribles and the themes which marked British writing in the 1950s, with some cogent commentary on the changing and continuing class realities which this literature claimed to address.

In actual fact, two journals provided some of the fundamental information about left-wing British novels over the last sixty years. One is the political journal <u>Labour Monthly</u> which, from its inception in the early 1920s, is particularly good for obscure proletarian works, although it has gone through sectarian periods when it did not deal with fictional literature. <u>The Left Review</u> was an internationally influential journal from between 1934 and 1939 dealing primarily with British left literature and cultural work during that decade. The journal <u>New Left Review</u> also occasionally contains an article of interest, such as Ken Worpole's "Proletarian Expressionism" (<u>NLR</u>, No. 130, 1981), a survey of one facet of experience by British worker-writers (from the 1920s and on). <u>History</u>

Workshop, from its founding in the mid 1970s, has been an extraordinarily seminal journal. Dealing with the social and cultural history of the British working class (primarily from the early 19th century to W.W.II) it often provides some excellent accounts of little-known autobiographies, oral history and working class literature. No words of praise can do it justice.

On IRELAND, a comprehensive and balanced survey of modern Irish writing is Richard Fallis' (1977) The Irish Renaissance. It deals with Irish literature from the first decade of this century to the late 1960s, including discussion of the social and political contexts, biographical sketches and some brief synopses. Peter Costello's (1977) The Heart Grown Brutal: The Irish Revolution in Literature, 1891-1939 treats with the memoirs, novels and accounts of the Irish liberation struggles of the period. As the title suggests, it is an unsympathetic view of such struggles but does provide an exhaustive survey of the literature available; a theme central to most left-wing writing in Ireland.

For CANADA, undoubtedly the most comprehensive bibliographic sources (and one of the most exhaustive surveys of any national literature) is Carl Klinck et al three volume 1976 edition of Literary History of Canada. This work really does go a long way in mentioning all the fictional (and some non-fictional) literature in English produced in Canada from circa 1800 to 1960. It is an impressive achievement. While it presents a considerable body of literature dealing with Canadian social themes which might provide useful research material for sociologists and historians there is a virtual absence of any working class or proletarian novels. F.W. Watt provides a seminal discussion of related materials both in his section in Klinck et al (1976) and in his massive Ph.D. thesis, "Radicalism in English Canadian Literature Since Confederation" (1957, University of Toronto). It contains some interesting discussion of "radical" reportage and journal literature from late 19th and early 20th century Ontario but is stuck with a single entry (Irene Baird's 1939 Waste Heritage) as a Canadian proletarian novel. Indeed, he is forced back to considering British and American titles to exemplify the nature of such writing and into comparing Fredrick P. Grove and Morely Callaghan as the closest approximations of "radical" novelists in Canada to the end of the 1930s. Two brief attempts to survey radical Canadian literature in the 1930s themselves are a University of Toronto library pamphlet by Ruth MacKenzie (1938), "A survey of the proletarian movement in Canadian literature" and a rather vituperative little piece in Canadian Forum (May 1937), "Proletarian literature: theory and practice", by Earle Birney. After essaying the alleged themes, trends and flaws of proletarian writing in general both MacKenzie and Birney come up dry on any examples for Canada--apart from the odd short story.
    To my own surprise, I am forced to concur with F.W. Watt's conclusion that there has been little in the way of radical or working class novels published in Canada in the past. As a partial confirmation of this sad state of affairs one may consider Robert McDougall's "The dodo and the cruising auk" in Canadian Literature (1963). Or if one is sufficiently masochistic one can read the pronunciamentos of the doyens of the Canadian literary world from the early 1920s to the end of the 1940s in the cumulative issues of Canadian Author and Bookman. Watt is also probably correct when he suggests that what efforts were made along those lines flowed into journalism and writing in small left-wing magazines and newspapers scattered throughout Canada from the late 19th century on. He documents this for southern Ontario and I would attest to the talent, vitality and sagacity which crops up in some now forgotten journals in British Columbia. The one volume which so far has managed to resurrect examples of such writing is Donna Phillips' (ed.) (1979) Voices of Discord, an anthology of reportage and short stories drawn from Masses and New Frontiers, two small left journals of the 1930s. One can only hope that some publisher will at some time commission additional anthologies drawn from working class authors who wrote in comparable union and left journals. They deserve a readership wider than the handful of dust-proof researchers who presently peruse them.
    A search through the extensive writing and reportage once produced by "ethnic" language presses in Canada would also undoubtedly turn up a good deal of material worthy of translation and republication in anthology form. In that regard, R. Hann, G. and L. Kealey, and P. Warrian's (1973) Primary Sources in Canadian

Working Class History may provide a useful bibliographic introduction to the folio material. Also see the journal Canadian Ethnic Studies. Naturally all such endeavours require intensive specialist research far beyond the scope of the present survey.

A number of recent college and school surveys have canvassed past Canadian literature in an attempt to rediscover works of a radical or at least progressive nationalist tradition. These include Alice Hale and Sheila Brooks' (1976) The Depression in Canadian Literature, Paul Cappon (ed.) (1978), In Our Own House, Social Perspectives on Canadian Literature and Robin Mathews (1978), Canadian Literature: Surrender or Revolution. They do manage to add a few titles and authors to the roster by stretching their purview to include almost any work concerned with social problems in Canada. But that hardly changes the basic picture.

More than in any other national section, I have fleshed out the limited roster of more or less progressive and working class novels from Canada with The addition   of autobiographies, memoirs, reportage, informal and fairly formal histories and other basically non-fictional materials. It's a poor state of affairs.

For QUEBEC, Ben-Zion Shek's (1977) Social Realism in the French-Canadian Novel is a valuable and readable history of social realist, working class and protest novels in Quebec from the 1940s on, with a brief mention of their antecedents. It provides extensive synopses and commentary on the major novels and writers to the beginning of the 1970s, mixing sagacity with occasionally jolting patronism. Shek also provides useful bibliographic materials and footnotes. Jeanette Urbas' (1976) From Thirty Acres to Modern Times, The Story of French-Canadian Literature is a survey of Quebec writing in the last forty odd years which is geared for a junior college readership. Chapter 13, "From individual revolt to social revolution", contains a few titles of interest not discussed in Shek. For the French reader Jean-Charles Falardeau's (1967) Notre Societe et Son Roman is a sociological-historical study of more or less modern Quebec literature and society by a prolific and much cited Quebecoise scholar. Also Jean-Charles Falardeau and Fernand Dumont's (1964) Literature et Societe Canadienne-Francaises.

On AUSTRALIA, Geoffrey Dutton (ed.) (1964), The Literature of Australia, is a compact but broad-ranging survey of Australian writing from mid-19th through the 20th centuries including its surprisingly rich populist and radical traditions. A collection of articles by eighteen specialists, it provides a readable introduction. H.M. Green's (1961) A History of Australian Literature (especially Vol. 2 covering 1923 to 1950) is a politically conservative but extensive listing of the authors and works of which the reader may make his own evaluations. T. Inglis Moore's (1971) Social Patterns in Australian Literature is a quasi-anthropological commentary on supposed "deep cultural" themes in Australian literature with some provocative fragments of Australian social history. Disdainful and patronizing of working people, it nevertheless provides an interesting roster of late 19th and early 20th century populist works. Joseph Jones' (1976) Radical Cousins treats the relationship between some of the populist/socialist writers and themes in Australia and in the U.S. at the turn of the century (although in a rather cursory manner). Ian Reid's (1978) Australian Fiction and the Great Depression deals with some of the left-wing writing in that decade.

For the UNITED STATES OF AMERICA, the single most comprehensive survey of radical literature is Walter Rideout's (1956) The Radical Novel in the United States, 1900-1954. It discusses the various streams of populist, working class and progressive protest literature in that country during the first three decades of this century (usually a terra incognita in comparable accounts) as well as the more circumscribed proletarian literature of the 1930s and after. Rideout's work is somewhat short on the social and political background to the literature itself, a necessary component in the best literary histories, but he provides massive bibliographic references and touches on the format and major themes in an extensive body of material. Despite Rideout's need for occasional exculpation,

The Radical Novel in the United States is an impressive compilation, doubly so when considering the period it was written in. Those familiar with the book will recognize my debt to it. Proletarian Literature in the United States (1935), M. Gold, J. North, I. Schneider, P. Peters and A. Calmer, editors, is an anthology of prose, drama, poetry and reportage by some sixty-five contributors and provides a sample of the range of U.S. "proletarian" writing at the time. It is restricted by its almost total dismissal of all radical literature in the U.S. before 1930 and anyone outside the orbit of sympathizers with the U.S. Communist Party. Within these limits it does indicate a good deal of heterogeneity and vitality among a string of writers, from actual proletarians to middle class professionals. Daniel Aaron's (1961) Writers on the Left is a history of left-wing writers in the U.S., their causes and positions from shortly before W.W.I to immediately after W.W.II. While of interest, it deals largely with the political infighting between various groupings from a viewpoint which has been so devastatingly challenged in Britain by Lucas (1978), The 1930s: A Challenge to Orthodoxy. Moreover, Aaron provides little discussion of the novels actually written by his authors.

David Madden's (ed.) (1968) Proletarian Writers of the Thirties is a collection of fifteen review and survey articles by as many writers. Two articles by Green and Miller especially capture the combativeness of their topics and provide some long overdue criticism of the generation of detractors of anything which could be tagged with the labels "proletarian", "radical", "social realist", etc. The volume also contains accounts of a number of writers and works little treated in other surveys. Contrarywise, Harvey Swados' (1966) The American Writer and the Great Depression is an anthology of extracts from supposedly representative left wing novels written in America during the 1930s. Some of the extracts do make for interesting reading but Swados' peripathetic comments and his disparagement of writers like Steinbeck are gems of unintended self-satire, a caricature of U.S. literary cold war critics. In the same vein one may mention Gordon Milne's (1966) The American Political Novel which manages to exclude all even vaguely left-wing writing and contains the somewhat shocked introductory remark that "One can even find attacks on capitalism, at least in the depression thirties when the Marxist novel enjoyed a great vogue.... Most of the books on this topic, however, can more accurately be labelled economic rather than political novels, and thus remain outside the realm of my discussion."

Mark Van Doren's once standard literary history (1946) The American Novel, 1789-1939 provides a readable literary background and context for radical and working class novels in the U.S. although it does not treat with them per se.

For left-wing novels of the mid to late 1930s one might peruse reviews in the sometimes gallingly doctrinaire and vituperative journal, New Masses. Its successor during the late 1940s to mid 1950s, Masses and Mainstream, is a journal of a different character and calibre. It deals with assorted topics in left politics and culture, contains sometimes dogmatic but more often vital reviews of the dwindling trickle of U.S. radical writing during the period and is enlivened by the contributions of a wide range of writers and journalists which today is astounding. Unfortunately, most of the small left journals surviving in the U.S. after the 1950s, such as the Monthly Review, seem to have regarded fiction as a frivolous topic. As the reader will have noted, the present survey of U.S. radical literature ends mainly with the mid 1950s.

A large and growing body of outstanding and progressive historical writing continued to be produced in the U.S. from the late 1940s to the present, undaunted by the relative eclipse of radical fictional literature. Some of this scholarly work (such as Vernon Bruce's (1958) 1877, Year of Violence) is not only excellent social history but is written with a verve and skill which makes it as compelling as the best fiction. A survey of such historical writing in the U.S. over the past three decades would comprise a massive bibliography in its own right.

For SPANISH-SPEAKING LATIN AMERICA, Kessel Schwartz's (1971) A New History of Spanish American Fiction, volumes 1 and 2, verges on being a definitive though not exhaustive survey of the material. It outlines the history of Spanish American national literature from the late 18th century on but deals mainly with the late 19th and 20th centuries, giving brief but cogent descriptions of a host of titles

and authors. While only a part of his concern, Schwartz's presention of the
streams of populist, protest and revolutionary novels from the various countries
is remarkable (despite his obligatory condescension toward social realist writing
which he calls "public service literature"). His appreciative account of left-
wing literature from Ecuador during the last fifty years--drawn from his Ph.D.
dissertation--is particularly extensive and moving. It leads one to suspect that
similarly intensive research into the left literary traditions of other Latin
American countries might reveal a body of writing far richer than presented here.
Readers will notice my debt to Schwartz's compendium.
      John Brushwood's (1975) The Spanish American Novel: A Twentieth Century
Survey covers some of the same ground as Schwartz but provides a somewhat different
roster of writers and titles. It is rather thin on leftist works unless their
authors are otherwise eminent and is virtually void of any actual proletarian
novels. However, it does provide some items of interest not found elsewhere.
      Jean Franco's (1968) An Introduction of Spanish American Literature mentions
some of the protest and social realist writing in the major Latin American
countries from the early 1900s to the 1940s. Fernando Alegria's (1974) Historia
de la Novela Hispanoamericana is a treasure trove of additional bibliographic
material for many of the Spanish American authors listed in this present
bibliography. It concentrates on the late 19th to mid 20th centuries and is
partially in the form of extensive bibliographic notes which include titles not
listed elsewhere.
      John Brushwood's (1966) Mexico In Its Novel is an intensive treatment of the
Mexican novel from the late 19th century on, but dealing mainly with the work from
the Mexican Revolution to the early 1960s. It is clearly a labour of love and
quite superior to his continental survey, providing as it does some concise
synopses of the novels and something of the social and political conditions from
which they stemmed. Joseph Sommers' (1968) After the Storm: Landmarks of the
Modern Mexican Novel provides some additional titles of interest. One of the most
fascinating surveys of any single national literature in Latin America is Seymour
Menton's (1975) Prose Fiction of the Cuban Revolution. It provides commentary on
a mass of novels and story collections which have appeared in Cuba since 1959,
treating an array of features of socialist Cuba and accounts taking the history of
struggle back to the turn of the century. While Menton's critique is sometimes
skewed by the normal anti-socialism of American scholarship, his work is nevertheless an honest presentation of the scope of Cuban writing since the triumph of the
revolution. I am much indebted to it. Raymond Souza's (1976) Major Cuban
Novelists treats with a handful of major Cuban novelists who were established
before 1959 and of their continuing work, touching only incidently on working
class or radical themes. The quarterly Casa de las Americas is an eminent Cuban
journal of literature and culture in general which treats with progressive writing
and popular political art throughout the hemisphere. Ismael Garcia's (1964)
Historia de la Literatura Panameña is a brief survey of Panamanian literature in
the 20th century which indicates a surprising richness in social realist writing
in a country. It leaves one wondering how much more material exists elsewhere in
regions which have not yet found their literary historians. Raimundo Lazo's (1971)
La Novela Andina: Pasado y Futuro is an intensive treatment of six progressive
Andean novelists from Ecuador, Peru and Bolivia from the 1920s to the 1950s,
discussing the central themes and changing styles in their works.

      For BRAZIL, Fred P. Ellison   (1957) Brazil's New Novel suggests an absence
of social realist writing about the peasantry or working class in Brazil before
1930. It focuses on the leading half dozen Northeastern novelists of the 1930s
and 1940s, giving extensive descriptions of their major titles with something of
the social and political context of those accounts. Dorothy S. Loos' (1963) The
Naturalistic Novel of Brazil is a brief survey of certain authors and work which
emerged from the late 1870s to about the turn of the century. While interesting
they are largely outside our purview here. Luiz Pinto Ferreira's (1957-1958) two
volume Interpretacao de Leteratura Brasileria is a much cited neo-Marxist history
of Brazilian literature from its inception to the 1950s. It is not accessible to
me. Most English language surveys of Brazilian literature consulted, such as
Claude Hulet's (1976) Brazilian Literature and Modernism, fail to mention any
social realist writing apart from the Northeast writers of the 1930s. This

portrait of Brazilian writing is difficult to believe but must await further research by others.

A number of the Latin American titles cited here stem from reviews in a variety of journals. One of the most important of these is the quarterly Books Abroad (now World Literature Today), which has reviewed Latin American writing in some depth throughout the last sixty years, although from a rather cautious academic perspective. A more recent journal, Latin American Literature, deals with the more eminent authors since the 1970s. Two other journals not primarily devoted to literary matters also provided some salient reviews of titles not found elsewhere; the social science quarterly Latin American Research Review and Latin American Perspectives, a neo-left journal of contemporary social and political developments. Both of these journals contain occasional survey articles and reviews of Latin American fictional literature.

For the CARIBBEAN, Spanish language literature is here subsumed in the Latin American section and the present bibliographic sources deal mainly with the English speaking Caribbean. Of these, O.R. Dathorne's (1970) Caribbean Narrative is one of the most puzzling, being a companion work to his excellent overview of African literature, but given as much to philosophizing about Black Culture as to West Indian writing per se. It deals largely with the English speaking writers over the last two centuries but includes some of the titles and Caribbean authors in French, Dutch and Spanish as well.

Ken Ramchand's (1972) An Introduction to West Indian Literature is a college survey of the better known English language writers, mainly since the 1940s, with extensive plot synopses of and commentary on the major novels. His (1970) The West Indian Novel and Its Background is a similar but more broad ranging history, both of the writing and of its social context. Quite readable and informative. Edward Baugh (ed.) (1978), Critics on Caribbean Literature, is a collection of critical commentary on contemporary Caribbean writers and their works (that by Ngugi Wa Thiongo is especially well taken). Andrew Salkey (ed.) (1965), Island Voices: Stories from the West Indies, is a collection of extracts and stories by Caribbean writers (mainly English speaking) including some lesser known authors not generally found in other collections. Barbara Howes (ed.) (1966), From the Green Antilles: Writings of the Caribbean, is an ambitious anthology which contains translations of authors originally in French, Dutch, Spanish and English although none of the extracts or authors could be considered as radical. The journal Caribbean Studies, published in Puerto Rico between 1962 and 1978, is basically concerned with social science and politics but includes reviews and articles on writing insofar as it portrays the realities of the Caribbean regions. Possibly the most intriguing of the Caribbean literary histories is Ghislan Gouraige's (1960) Histoire de la Literature Haitienne: De L'Independence a Nous Jours, a bibliographic account of Haitian literature from 1804 to the early 1950s. He lists some 125 authors, from historians to poets, even including a few revolutionary socialist writers.

For SPAIN, Pablo Gil Casado's (1968) La Novela Social Española, 1942-1968 is possibly the most comprehensive treatment of the Spanish "social" novels of the period. Richly descriptive of the themes and exhaustive in its coverage of the titles and authors, it is a fine and appreciative literary history. Santos Sanz Villanueva's (1980) Historia de la Novela Social Española, 1942-1979 covers much the same ground as Gil Casado. Eugenio G. de Nora's three volume (in the expanded 1968 edition) La Novela Española Contemporanea surveys Spanish novels from circa 1898 to 1967, with extensive comparisons to their late 19th century forerunners. It is a more difficult to read and sometimes stilted academic classic, rather sketchy on left-wing works after 1936 but particularly useful for the naturalistic novels of the first third of the 20th century. Jose Luis Ponce de Leon's (1973) La Novela Española de la Guerra Civil is, as the title states, a study of Spanish novels about the Spanish Civil War and of its precursors in the struggles and risings in the years before 1936. It includes works written up to a generation afterwards, in Spain or in exile, and is quite useful.

Ronald Schwartz's (1976) Spain's New Wave Novelists, 1950-1974
covers part of the same ground as Gil Casado, though much less comprehensively.
It may be of use to the non-Spanish reader.

For PORTUGAL there are two works by Alexandre Pinheiro Torres, (1977) O Neo-
Realismo Literario Portugues being an account and literary criticism of neo-
realist writing in Portugal from the early 1940s to the 1960s, and (1977) O
Movimento Neo Realista Em Portugal: na sua primeira fase, a similar but more
wide ranging history of protest and neo-realist writing in Portugal from its
inception in the 1920s to the 1970s. Jose Manuel Mendes (ed.) (1975) Por Uma
Literatura de Combate is a collection of critical reviews which double as a survey
of radical socialist novels and writings in Portugal since W.W.II, most of which
are not treated in the Pinheiro Torres volumes.

On ITALY there is Sergio Pacifici's The Modern Italian Novel (1971), a
prosaic but good introduction to the neo-realist and social protest novels which
are said to have dominated Italian writing from the mid 1940s to the late 1950s.
His (1962) Guide to Contemporary Italian Literature is a more wide ranging and
cursory overview of Italian writing in the post W.W.II period, from novels to
drama and film scripts. Raleigh Trevelyan (ed.) (1967) Italian Writing Today is
a Penguin anthology with extracts of writing from the mid 1930s to the early 1960s
containing some compact bio-bibliographic notes on the major authors. Eugenio
Donadoni's (1969) A History of Italian Literature, volume 2, is part of a larger
survey and is mainly useful for the naturalistic works of the late 19th century to
circa W.W.I.
Three titles which are accessible only in Italian are Alberto Rosa's
(1965) Scrittori e Popolo, Saggio sulla letteratura populista in Italia, a survey
of the literature of peasant and urban populism in Italy from the late 19th century
to the 1950s; Elisabetta C. Vitzizzai (ed.) (1977) Il Neorealismo; anti-fascismo
e popolo nella letteratura dagli anni trenta agli anni cinquanta, a series of
articles surveying and counterposing socialist and neo-realistic writings ranged
against populism from the 1930s to the 1950s; and Ferdinand Cannon's (1974)
Letteratura e Classi Subalterne, which deals with the treatment of Italian
peasantry and working class in novels from the 1930s to 1960s. An
especially seminal article in English is Luisa Passerini's "Italian Working Class
Culture Between the Wars" in the International Journal of Oral History (February
1980).

For FRANCE one may peruse Geoffrey Brerton's (1976) A Short History of French
Literature (especially Chapter 13) or Gaeton Picon's (1974) Contemporary French
Literature, 1945 and After, a brief survey of the pre 1945 period as well as the
two decades after. Harry T. Moore's (1966) Twentieth Century French Literature to
World War II, while of some interest, excludes working class and most social
protest writing. Similarly, Dennis Saurat's (1947) Modern French Literature,
1870-1940. A comprehensive and somewhat useful general survey is P.E. Charvet's
(1967) A Literary History of France, Volume 5: The 19th and 20th Centuries,
1870-1940. Michael Ragon's (1974) Histoirie de la Litterature Proletarienne en
France (subtitled "Workers Literature, Peasants Literature and Literature of
Popular Expression") is a collage of literary history, biography, extracts and
fragments of working class culture in France from the mid 18th century on but
concentrating on the various syndicalist worker-writers of the late 19th to mid
20th centuries. It does provide a host of heterogeneous works but excludes all
socialist-realist and communist authors. An old French syndicalist, Ragon
previously compiled a booklet (1953), Histoirie de la Litterature Ouvriere. The
chapter on French working class during the inter-war years in Dimow, Dymschitz
et al (1978), Internationale Literatur des Socialistischen Realismus, outlines
some socialist realist writers and titles there but is surprisingly limited.
Lucille Becker's (1969) Louis Aragon is one of the excellent Twayne Publishers
series on leading world authors; a bio-bibliographic review of the life and work
of the best known French communist author during the last two generations.

On BELGIUM, Vernon Mallinson's (1966) Modern Belgian Literature, 1830-1960 is a brief overview of both French and Flemish literature in Belgium with some interesting if anachronistic entries dealing with the Belgian working classes. Also Jean Cultet's (1960) Bibliographe des Escrivains Francais de Belgique, 1881-1950.

For GERMANY, Harry T. Moore's (1967) Twentieth Century German Literature is a useful but fairly pedestrian survey of the major German writers to the early 1960s with relatively thin treatment of working class literature and with little on the East German writers after 1948 or with the upsurge of social protest writing in West Germany which began in the 1960s. One of the most vital accounts of West German literature during the 1960s is R. Hinton Thomas and Keith Bullivant's (1974) Literature in Upheaval. It surveys the re-emergence of social protest works and writing by and about the working class since the end of the Adenauer period. Wolfgang Rothe (ed.) (1974), Die Deutsche Literatur in der Weimarer Republik, is a collection of surveys and studies on writing in Germany between 1918 and 1933--novels, drama, poetry, "other"--with extensive bibliographic citation. It covers traditionalist works, romances, dadaistic experimentation, etc. but also gives a broad introduction to the mass of working class and socialist writing which emerged during those years (and which, as the authors say, have been systematically hidden in West Germany from 1933 to the mid 1960s). While not necessarily sympathetic and sometimes hostile to the themes or format of the earlier proletarian works, extensive bibliographic citation is presented in F. Trommler's "The political-revolutionary theatre", H. Denkler's "On the way to proletarian-revolutionary literature", and C. Rulcker's "Proletarian poetry and class consciousness". Also included is citation of East German literary surveys of this material. A single one of these East German studies is Brigette Melzwig's (1975) Deutsche Sozialistische Literatur, 1918-1945, an overview of German socialist writing during that period.
Doris and H.J. Schmitt's (eds.) (1976) Die Grossen Socialistischen Erzahler is an anthology of extracts and stories by sixteen leading German socialist and communist writers during the 1930s and 1940s. It intends to indicate the ongoing tradition of such writing in the German Democratic Republic after 1945. Theodore Huebner's (1970) The Literature of East Germany is a brief but compact account of writers and literature in the German Democratic Republic (D.D.R.) since 1945. It discusses the continuation of pre-war proletarian writing by D.D.R. authors and touches on the new generation of writers there to the mid 1960s. A very readable historical review.
Finally, a seminal article which deals with the matrix of class conscious German workers during the deluge rather than with their literature: Detlev Peukert's "Ruhr Miners Under Nazi Repression, 1933-1945", in the International Journal of Oral History (June 1980).

For AUSTRIA, one may peruse C.E. Williams' (1974) The Broken Eagle which supposedly is a study of the politics of Austrian literature from Empire to Anschluss (1918-1938) and deals with nine major Austrian writers (supposedly exemplifying the spirit of the times) but disclaims any indigenous proletarian literature. B.O. Murdoch and M.G. Ward's (1981) Studies in Modern Austrian Literature contains some accounts of the pacifist and anti-militarist literature of the inter-war period but again no specifiably working class writing. A compact survey of post W.W.II work is Alan Best and Hans Wolfschutz's (1980) Modern Austrian Writing.

For DUTCH and FLEMISH see Reinder Meijer's (1971) Literature of the Low Countries, a short history of Dutch literature, with some authors and titles from Flanders. Vernon Mallison's (1966) Modern Belgian Literature, 1830-1960 contains a few Flemish titles of interest.

For ICELAND, the main source is Stefan Einarsson's (1967) A History of Icelandic Literature, a massive and seemingly comprehensive survey of modern writing from the late 19th and 20th centuries. A somewhat conservative viewpoint, it does appreciate the social roots of Icelandic literature and provides accounts of the substantial populist and socialist writing in that country over a sixty year period.

On DENMARK, P.M. Mitchell's (1957) A History of Danish Literature is an account from the 17th century on, but dealing mainly with the second half of the 19th century to the early 1950s. It includes an extensive but far from exhaustive survey of Danish populist, radical-liberal and communist writers and their work from the turn of the 20th century on. F.J. Billeskov Jansen and P.M. Mitchell's (1964) Anthology of Danish Literature provides translated extracts of some samples of the work of a few 20th century populist writers but none from the body of Danish socialist writing. A number of extracts from the latter are found in the Elias Bredsdorff (ed.) (1974) anthology, Contemporary Danish Prose, a very readable work in its own right. Also see Fredrick Mander's (1976) Kjeld Abell.

On NORWAY, Harald Beyer's (1956) A History of Norwegian Literature is a massive study which is particularly good on the body of naturalistic literature about village and small town life produced in the last quarter of the 19th century and early 20th. It also outlines the varied socialist, proletarian, feminist, and protest writing which followed industrialization at the turn of this century and provides a good account of the shifting cultural-political milieu. Torbjorn Stoverud's (1967) Milestones of Norwegian Literature is a sketchy and unsympathetic treatment, but does mention a number of the socialist and protest writers of Norway of the 1920s and 1930s.

For SWEDEN, Alrif Gustafson's (1960) A History of Swedish Literature is a huge social and literary history which is a joy to read in its own right. Although it surveys Swedish literature from the late middle ages on the focus is mainly on the 19th to the mid 20th centuries. Gustafson provides bibliographic and biographic details of the varied peasant-proletarian "folk" writers who came to dominate Swedish writing from the mid 1920s to the 1950s, along with discussion of their social and cultural context. Bredsdorff, Elias, Mortensen, Brita, and Popperwell, Ron (1951), An Introduction to Scandinavian Literature, is an outline of Danish, Norwegian and Swedish literature from the earliest times to 1950; the final three chapters provide a cursory treatment of the naturalistic and populist writing in those three countries.

For FINLAND, one may peruse Jaakko Ahokaas' (1973) A History of Finnish Literature, a huge and exhaustive overview from earliest folk sages to the 1960s. Although Ahokaas' conservatism and near disdain for the Finnish working class makes for difficult reading, he does provide an intensive survey of the two main waves of populist and socialist literature in Finland (from 1900 to 1918 and in the 1930s to W.W.II) as well as a few titles from the post W.W.II period. He does convey the ferment and numbers of socialist writers publishing between 1900 and 1918. Richard Dauenhauer and Philip Binham (eds.) (1978), Snow in May: An Anthology of Finnish Writing, 1945-1972, provides examples of post W.W.II themes and writers in Finland (including works retrospectively dealing with the Mannerheim dictatorship before and during that war). They provide some examples of current writing about social problems but are reticent about contemporary socialist writers in Finland.

For GREECE one of the most interesting treatments of modern Greek writing is Thomas Doulis' (1977) Disaster and Fiction: Modern Greek Fiction and the Asia Minor Disaster of 1922. Despite the seemingly restricted theme (revolving around the effects of the Greek expulsion from Turkey in the early 1920s) Doulis manages to outline the social and political conditions in Greece during the 1920s and 1930s and indicates the transmutation of the Greek versus Turk theme into one of the struggle against injustice and of the oppressed against their oppressors within Greek society to the mid 1950s. Mary Gianos' (ed.) (1969) Introduction to Modern Greek Literature is an anthology of translated extracts from the late 19th century to the 1950s, which includes the work of a number of Greek populist and naturalistic writers, although no examples of proletarian novels. Linos Politis' (1973) A History of Modern Greek Literature is a massive survey of the modern Greek writers from the 1880s to the 1940s, including some social protest works and authors.   C.T. Dimaras' (1972, original 1948) A History of Modern Greek Literature deals primarily with the pre-modern period and ends in the aftermath of

W.W.I but treats with a few of the early 20th century naturalist writers. Also Edmund Keeley and Peter Bien (eds.) (1972), Modern Greek Writing.

For ALBANIA, Arshi Pipa's (1978) Albanian Literature: Social Perspectives deals with the writing since 1912 but concentrates on work since W.W.II. Skewed by the fact that Pipa is a political exile from Albania, it is an informative outline of the socio-political developments there over sixty years as conveyed in some of the literary works.

For YUGOSLAVIA, there is Antun Barac's (1977) A History of Yugoslav Literature, which attempts to survey the literature of the six republics of Yugoslavia from circa 1918 to the late 1960s. The paucity of work dealing specifically with the Yugoslav working classes until after W.W.II is rather surprising. Barac describes the literature of W.W.II and the following "socialist" period in the most exasperatingly cloying patriotic terms, making it difficult to determine just what they are about. Thoas Eekman's (1978) Thirty Years of Yugoslav Literature, 1945-1975 generally dismisses socialist-realist writing in Yugoslavia but does manage to convey the nature of some interesting and socially relevant titles.
Two provocative brief surveys are found in the Yugoslav sections of Vasa Michailovich's (ed.) (1977) White Stones and Fir Trees, an anthology of contemporary Slavic literature and in Michailovich et al (eds.) (1976) Modern Slavic Literature, volume 2.

For BULGARIA, John Colombo and Nikola Roussanoff (eds.) (1976) The Balkan Range - A Bulgarian Reader, is an anthology of extracts of Bulgarian literature from its inception, but mainly from 1876 to the 1960s. It samples the various social and political themes in Bulgarian writing in this century, provides bio-bibliographic synopses and is quite readable in its own right--including translated extracts of Geo Milev's breathtaking poem September. Vasa Michailovich et al (1977) White Stones and Fir Trees and (1976) Modern Slavic Literature also contain sections on Bulgarian writing since W.W.II. The chapter dealing with Bulgarian proletarian writing during the interwar years in Georgi Dimow, Alexander Dymschitz et al (1978) Internatinale Literatur des Socialischen Realismus, 1917-1945 is particularly seminal. A comment about this volume may be in order here. It is a collection of articles surveying (not exclusively) socialist realist writers and works in some fifteen countries during the period. The individual sections are quite uneven and outside eastern and central Europe (as well as China and Japan) the coverage is cursory. An additional limitation is that the surveys concentrate on the political struggles and groups in which the authors participated rather than on the content of their writing. Nevertheless, the Dimow and Dymschitz volume is a valuable introduction to one stream of left wing literature, as following citations indicate, and a few of the chapters are quite overwhelming.

For RUMANIA, Jacob Steinberg's (1966) Introduction of Rumanian Literature is an anthology of twenty-four leading Rumanian authors from the late 1880s to present, with some interesting background and bio-bibliographic notes. The bulk of the Rumanian titles in the bibliography listed as translated into English also stem from Twayne publishers admirable series of world literature in translation.

For HUNGARY, Tibor Klaniczay, Jozsef Szauder, Miklos Szabolcsi's (1975) A History of Hungarian Literature is a comprehensive survey of that nation's literature (mainly in the 19th and 20th centuries) including the traditional luminaries but providing extensive treatment of the working class and radical writing little mentioned elsewhere. Richly descriptive, its major flaw is a tendency to gild the lilly, finding traces of "democratic" or "progressive" concerns in almost everything. The Hungarian chapter in G. Dimow and A. Dymschitz (1978), Internationale Literatur des Socialischen Realismus, provides an extensive listing of titles during the interwar period, and tells something of the authors' lives and fates in brief biographic asides. Miklos Szabolsci and Zoltan Kenyeres' (eds.) (1964) Landmarks, an anthology of Hungarian Writing provides translated extracts from some forty-eight authors of the 1920s to 1960s but is surprisingly reticent on the topic of class struggles. Henrik Vass (ed.) (1975), Studies on the History of the Hungarian Working Class Movement, 1867-1966, is an official collection of Hungarian academic scholarship which might serve as a background. Friederick Riedl's (1969, original 1906) A History of Hungarian Literature mentions a number of interesting populist writers of the last quarter of the 19th century. Finally, Joseph Remenyi's (1964) Hungarian Writers and Literature is an archetypical emigre tract which exudes a certain unintentional self-satire; effusive about the "Magyar Soul", it finds no workers and no radical literature in Hungary before 1944 and no literature worth mentioning after that.

For CZECHOSLOVAKIA, there is M. Otruba, Z. Pesat, E. Maek, F. Burianek et al (eds.) beautifully produced (1962) The Linden Tree: an anthology of Czech and Slovak literature, 1890-1960. It includes lengthy extracts from the work of some twenty-four Czech and nineteen Slovak writers with succinct bibliographic and biographic notes on a wider range of authors as well as some social and historical background. The Czech chapter in Dimow and Dymschitz (1978) provides brief mention of a number of additional proletarian and socialist authors not found elsewhere, although it is lamentably cursory about their actual works. It also conveys something about the complex and qualified nature of Czech democracy during the inter-war years. Paul Selver's (1969, original 1929) An Anthology of Czechoslovak Literature contains no mention of proletarian writing but does provide an account of naturalist and populist writers of the 1880s to the W.W.I period. Rene Wellek's (ed.) (1963) Essays on Czech Literature, especially his "Twenty Years of Czech Literature, 1918-1938", provides some insights, particularly into the Bohemian-German radical and protest literature at the end of that period.

For POLAND, the leading work must be Czeslau Milosz's (1969) The History of Polish Literature, a rich and evocative survey of that country's literature from its inception to the early 1960s. It is especially good for the period 1890 to 1939. A Nobel Prize winning poet and somewhat reluctant emigre, Milosz manages to retain a certain historical balance and presents an intriguing and sympathetic account of the varied populist and radical writing emerging from the stagnant and repressive Polish autocracies, and the struggles against them during most of the first half of this century. It provides a useful overview of the major authors, titles and themes of post 1945 Polish writing as well, from the attempts to make sense of the internecine struggles of W.W.II, through some of the socialist construction literature and the later work. In short, a comprehensive and excellent literary history well worth reading. Julian Krzyzanowski's (1978) A History of Polish Literature is a huge tome, the final fifth of which deals with the rise of naturalism, social realism and some socialist literature from the late 19th century to 1939, with occasional references to work of the 1950s. It provides additional titles in the tradition of documentary novels of peasant and working class life in Poland during the 1920s and 1930s but is strangely reticent (considering its source) about socialist realist works. Adam Gillon and Ludwik Krzyzanowski's (1976) Introduction to Modern Polish Literature is an anthology of some fifty authors from the 1890s to the post W.W.II period and offers a handy introduction to a number of the writers noted in the body of this bibliography. Janina Hoskins' (1974) Polish Books in English, 1945-1971 is a bibliography, and Celina Wieniewska's (1968) Polish Writing Today is one of the Penguin anthology series and presents extracts from the work of younger Polish literarians.

For the SOVIET UNION, Joshua Kunitz' (1948) Russian Literature Since the Revolution is a massive anthology of stories, drama and extracts from the work of forty prominent Soviet writers in the thirty years since 1917. It emphasizes the socialist construction literature of the 1930s and the Great Patriotic War writing but is informed by an editorial orthodoxy which many will find hard to accept today. Vera Alexandrova's (1963) A History of Soviet Literature is some- what tendencious but more or less an academic survey of some two dozen major Soviet novelists and their works from the 1920s to the late 1950s, concentrating largely on the interwar years. Deming Brown's (1978) Soviet Russian Literature Since

Stalin is an extensive and wide ranging survey of the continuities and changing
themes evident in both established and new writers in the Soviet Union since 1953,
including the reconsiderations about some earlier novels. (Unlike the above
survey which provides extensive plot outlines, Brown's earlier (1959) The
Proletarian Episode in Soviet Literature deals almost exclusively with the politics
and contending groupings of Soviet "proletarian" writers during the 1920s and early
1930s with little discussion of their actual writings.) Two additional titles of
interest despite their evident antipathy are Vyacheslav Zavalishin's (1958) Early
Soviet Writers, a survey of the works by lesser known left populist, early
communist and non-party proletarian writers in the Soviet Union from 1917 to the
early 1930s, as well as Gleb Struve's (1935) Soviet Russian Literature. (Both
the above titles are a different kettle of fish from diatribes such as Marc Slonim's
Soviet Russian Literature 1917-1977, which is not only a charicature of anti-
Soviet demonology but rabidly anti-working class in the bargain.) N.N. Shneidman's
(1979) Soviet Literature in the 1970s mainly surveys the work of six major Soviet
novelists during the last two decades as representative of broader currents at
work in Soviet literature. It revolves around the emergence of a critical
realism concerned with social topics but distinct from both the strictures of
earlier "socialist realism" and the litanies of so-called dissident writers. The
introduction contains a brief but salient critique of western Sovietologists'
accounts of Soviet literature. "Multinational Soviet Literature" is a cursory but
fascinating chapter in the G. Dimow and A. Dymschitz et al volume (1978)
Internationale Literatur des Socialischen Realismus. It introduces socialist
realist writing and its forerunners among the non-Russian literatures of the Soviet
Union, by Tartar, Kirghiz, Yakut, etc. authors from the early 1920s to the mid
1940s. Soviet Literature is a monthly journal issued from 1963 to present which
combines literary criticism, memorabilia, stories and poetry, and extracts from
longer works by both major and "minor" Soviet writers of the post W.W.II period
(as well as articles about previous Russian classical literature). Although not
the sort of source one would read from stem to stern, the journal introduces the
work of lesser known authors and is particularly useful for sampling non-Russian
literature over the last thirty years which it highlights in recurrent special issues.

On TURKEY, there are two outstanding literary surveys, both of them
considerably broader than their titles suggest. Frank Stone's (1973) The Rub of
Cultures in Modern Turkey: Literary Views of Education is really an overview of
Turkish novels about the struggles and sometimes conflicting interests involved
in "modernization" from W.W.I to the 1960s, including some background to the
directed changes attempted by the so-called Kemelist "revolution". Carole
Rathbun's (1972) The Village in the Turkish Novel and Short Story, 1920-1955
deals with the entire spectrum of gradual and drastic changes, class struggles,
the reactions of various rural sectors as portrayed in Turkish novels. It
includes novels which follow rural people into urban working class contexts,
making it a rounded survey of working class and peasant writing in Turkey.
Rathbun places the novels in their social-economic context, thereby providing a
readable social history as well. The interwoven biographical data on the authors
give some understanding of how the described processes personally affect lives.
A tour de force.

For IRAN, Hassan Kamshad's (1966) Modern Persian Prose Literature is a
progressive literary history from the W.W.I era to the late 1950s and is
particularly good for the 1920s and 1930s. It is a balanced survey of writing in
Iran and in exile interwoven with some intriguing snippets of that country's
social and political history during the 20th century under an assortment of quasi-
independent/quasi-colonial regimes. It includes some titles in the longstanding
anti-mullah tradition and others directed against the Shah's regime of the late
1950s. Peter Chelkowski's chapter on Iranian writing in C.M. Kortepeter's (1971)
Modern Near East Literature and Society provides some interesting comments, if few
titles, in what otherwise is a collection quite unrelated to the present
bibliography. Jan Rypka's (1959) Iranische Literaturgeschichte is a frequently
cited but unseen Marxist literary history. The most valuable account is Bozorg
'Alavi's (1964) Geschichte und Entwicklung der Modernen Persischen Literatur, a
major literary and social history of Iran from the beginning of the 20th century

to the 1960s which concentrates on the various streams of modernist, realist and progressive writers and their works. By a veteran Iranian left-wing author and exile.

For ISRAEL, Rueben Wallenrod's (1956) The Literature of Modern Israel deals largely with Zionist literature from Palestine before the establishment of the State of Israel, along with comparable Israeli novels produced in the half dozen years after 1948. It includes a considerable number of neo-realist works which treat the settlers' world through the eyes of a variety of Labour Zionists, with their amalgam of radical concerns for justice for Jews and disdain for the native population of Palestine. Of that "social realist" genre Wallenrod says, "At first glance these novels remind the reader of the proletarian novels of the thirties. In the latter, class differences led to class struggle as the only means by which the desired goal could be reached. In the Israeli novels, however, the emphasis is mainly on cultural and traditional barriers and the goal is reached through the unifying visions of the people." Leon Yudkin's (1974) Escape into Siege, A Survey of Israeli Literature Today deals with the cultural and psychological dynamics revealed in the works of a dozen major Israeli writers since 1948. Avoiding the earlier self-congratulatory eulogies, Yudkin's survey reveals a general shift to more personalist themes, with little that could be considered as working class writing but with more troubled concern for the directions of Israeli society. Two anthologies of the   mainstream themes in recent Israel are Robert Friend's (ed.) (1977) Contemporary Israeli Literature and Dalia Rabikovitz's The New Israeli Writers. None of these really plumb the mass of Israeli writing before or after 1948 and whether or not there was some hidden radical tradition in that literature will have to be left for others to research.

For EGYPT, Hilary Kilpatrick's (1974) The Modern Egyptian Novel, a study of social criticism is a tour de force which surveys in detail a considerable number of modernist, nationalist and socialist Egyptian novels and novelists during this century. It concentrates on a relatively limited number of major writers and indicates why Egyptian writing, during much of this century, was considered the vanguard of modernist work in Arabic. For some fuller treatment of the political and social context from which some of the Egyptian novels sprang, see Mahmoud Hussein (ed.) (1973), Class Conflict in Egypt, 1945-1970, a collection of historical-political essays. A brief survey of contemporary Egyptian writing is found in "Literature of Modern Egypt" in Books Abroad (Spring 1972). Hamadi Sakkut's (1968) The Egyptian Novel, 1913-1952 provides a somewhat exasperating overview of the secular and modern (though not politically radical) writing during the regime ancien. A considerable number of additional Egyptian novelists, short story writers and others are found in the general anthologies and literary histories of modern Arabic literature listed below.

The work of writers in modern Arabic from LEBANON, SYRIA, IRAQ and PALESTINE are found in Mahmoud Manzalaoui's (ed.) (1968) Arabic Writing Today: The Short Story. It is an anthology of some thirty contemporary Arab writers, including a handful who are considered left-wing, with brief bio-bibliographic notes. R.C. Ostle (ed.) (1972), Modern Arabic Literature, is a collection of survey articles dealing with different regions and aspects of contemporary writing in Arabic. It includes a seminal article by Halim Barakat, who underlines the paucity of socialist or proletarian (as opposed to nationalist) writing in Arabic fiction to date. John Haywood's (1971) Modern Arabic Literature, part four dealing with the period 1920 to 1970, contains translated extracts of some broadly modern themes and authors.

Probably the most comprehensive survey of contemporary (circa W.W.I to the 1960s) Arabic literature is Raoul and Laura Makarius' (eds.) (1964) Anthologie de la Litterature Arabe Contemporaine. The first of its massive three volumes deals with Le Roman et la Nouvelle and covers contemporary novels and novel from throughout the Arabic speaking world. Two interesting additional volumes are Abdel Malek's (1965) Anthologie de la Litterature Arabe: Les Essais and (1970) La Pensee Politique Arabe Contemporaine, two anthologies of post W.W.II essays and political writings by Arab authors from left to right, with some interlaced bio-bibliographical materials. Finally, Walid Khalidi and Jill Khadduri's

(1974) <u>Palestine and the Arab-Israeli Conflict: an annotated bibliography</u> and <u>The Journal of Palestine Studies</u>, a quarterly published since circa 1971, contain sources for fictional and non-fictional writing about Palestinian history, society and its transformation. An intriguing if brief article by Saleem Taha al-Tikriti, "Labour Journalism in Iraq" (in <u>Iraq Today</u>, November 1, 1979), provides a sketchy outline of left and labour journals in that country from the early 1930s to the 1960s.

For NORTH AFRICA, the majorsource again is R. and L. Makarius' <u>Anthologie de la Litterature Arabe Contemporaine</u>. Len Ortzen (ed.) (1970), <u>North African Writing</u>, is an anthology of extracts from the more established writers of Morocco, Algeria and Tunisia, mainly translated from the French. Jean Dejeux's (1972) <u>Litterature Maghrebine de Langue Francaise</u> is a bibliography of North African writers from the Maghreb who have been translated into French. It suggests a richer left literature than mentioned in the above anthologies. Also Charles Bonn's (1974) <u>La Litterature Algerienne de Langue Francaise et Ses Lectures</u>. Two articles by Anne Lippert and Louis Tremaine in R.O. Priebe and Thomas Hale's (1977) <u>Artist and Audience</u> touch on a few popular Algerian playwrights and film producers working in Arabic during the 1970s.

For AFRICA SOUTH OF THE SAHARA many of the most important literature surveys have been regional or continental in scope rather than national. One main source is Vladmir Klima, Karel Ruzicka and Peter Zima's (1976) <u>Black Africa: Literature and Language</u>. It is a broad ranging and ambitious work which attempts to survey writing in both the indigenous and in the European languages. Although hardly exhaustive it does treat with most of the major writers up to the late 1960s and contains some titles of most of the major literatures and genres. Compiled by three Czech specialists in African literature, it is somewhat puzzling in that it never proceeds past an anti-colonial viewpoint and contains remarkably little appreciation of the existence of African working classes. O.R. Dathorne's (1972) <u>The Black Mind</u> (updated in 1976 as <u>African Literature in the Twentieth Century</u>) is a massive, wide ranging and often cogent treatment of the various national literatures of Africa providing titles and authors not dealt with in the Klima and Zima volume. It is clearly a labour of love, informed by Dathorne's vision of Black Nationalism which he is honest and sophisticated enough not to impress into the descriptions of the actual literature.
Eustace Palmer's (1979) <u>The Growth of the African Novel</u> is an excellent commentary in depth on the themes and work of twelve contemporary African novelists and the social-political context from which their novels sprang. It is an appreciative yet critical analysis of post-independence writing in Africa as well as an astute critique of the unreflectiveacceptance of the black bourgeoisies' visions of Africa. Palmer points to the incipient counter themes in some African literature itself and his chapters on Sembene Ousame are a joy to read. Cesmo Pietrse and Donald Munro's (1976) <u>Protest and Conflict in African Literature</u> is a collection of critical essays about African literature by African writers them- selves. Although variable, they provide welcome relief to the usual effusiveness. James Ngugi's article, "Satire in Nigeria", in particular, points to the class nature of much post-independence writing. Hans Zell and Helene Silver's (1971) <u>A Reader's Guide to African Literature</u> is an annotated listing of some 850 titles (novels, short stories, drama, poetry, and non-fiction) from some fifty African countries.
Lewis Nkosi's (1965) <u>Home and Exile</u> is a collection of a dozen critical essays by a South African writer in exile which contains a biting critique of the "Black Soul" ideology stemming   from the U.S. and then fashionable among some black African writers. Albert Gerard's (1971) <u>Four African Literatures</u> deals with writing in three major native languages of South Africa (Xhosa, Sotho, Zulu) and Amharic from Ethiopia. It is largely an account of mission influenced literatures but does provide occasionally revealing historical backgrounds. (For instance, that there was a Bantu People's Theatre in existence in Johannesburg by 1936 which performed at least one Eugene O'Neil play in Zulu.)   Emmanuel Obiechina's (1972) <u>Onitsha Market Literature</u> does what few other surveys anywhere attempt. It outlines the pulp literature and potboilers produced in Onitsha, Nigeria. While none of these titles are reproduced in the present bibliography not all of that

literature was escapist romance or moral tracts. Obiechina also drives home the point that such writing may be better known among the indigenous population than the work of some internationally read Nigerian authors.

Gerald Moser's (1969) Essays in Portuguese-African Literature is a work over-taken by events, being mainly a survey of the writings by Portuguese settlers in Angola, Mozambique and Guinea-Cabo Verde during the last generation of colonial rule. It indicates a literature often sophisticated, critical and sympathetic to the aspirations of the colonial peoples but removed from them. The bulk of the openly revolutionary authors and titles dealing with Portuguese colonial Africa listed in the body of the the bibliography are not found in Moser.

One of the most fascinating surveys of an African literature and its social-political context is Thomas Kane's (1975) Ethiopian Literature in Amharic. Despite its deceptively umpromising title, Kane provides detailed synopses of represent-ative titles, discusses their themes within the context of Amharic literature and, more importantly, within the context of the ferment and sociology of pre or proto-revolutionary Ethiopia. He allows the authors to present their evolving views and portraits but compares their fictional accounts and plots to the real Ethiopian worlds from the mid 1930s to the end of the 1960s. Since very few Amharic novels mentioned have been translated, one cannot too strongly recommend reading Kane's outstanding survey. Reidulf K. Molvaet's (1980) Tradition and Change in Ethiopia: social and cultural life as reflected in Amharic fictional literature, 1930-1974 covers much the same ground as Kane, although from a quasi-anthropological conservative viewpoint. He provides a number of additional and somewhat more recent titles but surprisingly explains away the indigenous bases of rural class and caste conflict which are shot through the novels. Neither of the these two surveys deal with the events of and the writings following the revolutionary struggles, civil war and social reorganization which have shaken Ethiopia since 1974.

The focus of the overwhelming mass of post-independence African literature has been the lives, travails and goals of various elements of the older and emerging bourgoisie. With few exceptions, African workers and peasants are either absent or appear in the background as servants, people to be led or manipulated or as other foils for the hero. Yet African miners, dockworkers, railwaymen, plantation labour, city and factory workers--with their own lives and views--have existed in significant numbers in some regions since the beginning of the century. Given the present bibliography's concerns and the general paucity of African working class literature a few non-fictional titles may provide a certain balance. Some of the untold story is raised in articles dealing with Africa in Robin Cohen, Peter Gutkind, Phyllis Brazier (eds.) (1979), Peasants and Proletarians, the struggles of third world workers. R. Cohen, P. Gutkind and Jean Copans' (eds.) (1978) African Labour History contains accounts of a quite phenomenal range of labour history throughout Africa over most of this century. Richard Sandbrook and Robin Cohen's (eds.) (1975) The Development of an African Working Class: studies in class formation and action addresses itself to the once general "wisdom" that no real African working class exists or where it does it is part of the "privileged" sectors. In addition to some cogent and well researched counter-arguments Sandbrook and Cohen include a massive and exciting bibliography providing non-fictional accounts of African working classes and their struggles throughout much of the continent.

For INDIA, one might look at K.R. Srinivasa Iyengar's (1973) Indian Writing in English, a standard compilation of the better known authors and titles from the 1930s to the early 1960s. He makes the point that while English is spoken by only a small minority of the Indian population, as many titles have been produced in that language as in all other Indian languages combined. S.C. Harrex's (1977) The Fire and the Offering: The English Language Novel of India, 1935-1970 provides a readable history and social context of English writing in India and an intensive consideration of a limited number of representative authors. His treatment of the works of Raj Mulk Anand, as they represent Marxist writing in India, is well worth reading in its own right. There is also R.S. Singh's (1977) Indian Novel in English and M.E. Derrett's (1966) The Modern Indian Novel in English which contain a few items not found elsewhere but basically exclude social realist writing.

T.C. Clark's article, "A survey of modern Bengali literature" in Edward Dimock (1967), Bengali Literature and History, is an interesting survey of the 19th century beginnings of secular writing in Bengali, in an otherwise rabidly anti-socialist tome. J.C. Ghosh's (1948) Bengali Literature and Muhammad Sadiqu's (1957) A History of Urdu Literature deal with the "traditional" secular writing in those two languages during the 19th century and, if nothing else, indirectly convey an appreciation of just how revolutionary even the mildest reformist literature of the 20th century was.

T.W. Clark's (1970) The Novel in India, Its Birth and Development is a brief outline of the origins of the novel in Bengali, Marathi, Hindi, Tamil and Urdu during the later half of the 19th into the early 20th centuries. It does contain a stimulating chapter on the early populist and later proletarian writing in Malayalam. K. Natwar-Singh's (1966) Tales From Modern India is an anthology of thirteen leading Indian authors in Bengali, Tamil, Hindi, Marathi, Telugu, Malayalam, Urdu and English. It includes works written between 1916 and 1964 and covers much of the political spectrum in India.

The single richest source was Carlo Coppola's (ed.) (1974) Marxist Influences and South Asian Literature, Volumes 1 and 2. It is a collection of twenty-four essays mainly by Indian writers and scholars about the various streams of progressive, populist and Marxist writing in India over the last half century. While some of these essays mainly represent the sort of cold war ideology one has come to expect from certain "free world" academics, others provide some excellent surveys of the social realist and left literature of particular authors or groups of authors in eight Indian languages. The articles by Surgit Singh Dulai, R.K. Kaushik, Yogendra Malik, Corinne Friend and K.A. Panikar are especially good. Two lengthy excerpt-commentaries on the Indian poets Sri Sri and Narayan Surve are truly moving.

For the PHILIPPINES, Antonio Manuud (ed.) (1967), Brown Heritage: Essays on Philippine Cultural Tradition and Literature, contains some forty odd essays on the traditional and modern literatures in Spanish, English, Tagalog and other Philippine languages over the last century. Its principal value resides in Bienvenido Lumbera's two articles on Tagalog literature, although some of the other essays do touch upon a few social protest novels in Spanish and English. Epifano San Juan Jr. (1974), Introduction of Modern Philipino Literature, is an uninhibited overview of Tagalog writing and its social context in the 20th century, mentioning the generally romantic nature of that literature in the past but discussing its change into the major vehicle of radical writing in the Philippines. It is mainly an anthology of translated extracts from the work of twenty-five Tagalog authors, novels to poetry, with some bio-bibliographic and historical annotation. Bienvenido Lumbera's article, "Philippine Literature: Old and New" in L.F. Brakel, M. Balfas et al (1976),Literaturen, is a brief, packed and altogether superb overview of the more than sixty year history of left-nationalist and revolutionary novelists, dramatists and short story writers in Tagalog, Spanish and English. Salvador P. Lopez's (1940) Literature and Society is a treatise which attempted to promulgate "proletarian literature" in the Philippines, but is bare of any existing Philippine titles. Epifano San Juan's (1978) Carlos Bulgosan and the Class Struggle is primarily a history of that emigrant Philippine writer-worker and his works in the U.S.

For INDONESIA, A. Teeuw's (1967) Modern Indonesian Literature is a massive survey of the various literary strains in the region from early in the 20th century to the mid 1960s. It is difficult to say whether the circumlocutions and difficulties of style which make this work so exasperating to read are due to problems of translation from Dutch or from more deadly flaws. In hindsight, it is probably the latter. However, Teeuw's work is unfortunately one of the only general surveys in an easily accessible language. Rosemarie Simon-Barwinkel (comp.) (1973), Chrestomathie der Modernen Indonesischen Literatur, is an anthology of extracts from the work of thirty-three Indonesian writers from the 1920s to the late 1960s. The text is in Indonesian with brief bio-bibliographic synopses of each author in German. Harry Aveling, one of the few active translators of progressive Indonesian authors into English, provides a brief overview in "Indonesian Writers and the Left" in Overland (Winter 1971). Also see

his brief introductions in (1974) From Surabaya to Armagendoon. L.F. Brakel,
M. Balfas et al (1976), Literaturen, contains an article by B. Rangkut on "Islam
and Modern Indonesian Literature", which touches on the past progressive Islamic
tradition in that country. M. Balfas' article in that same collection is a
chilling example of the fascist mentality now dominating that country. So too
A. Teeuw's second volume (1979) of Modern Indonesian Literature, which deals
mainly with Indonesian writing since the 1965 fascist coup and which includes
infuriatingly smug apologetics for the Indonesian holocaust.

For MALAYA, Li Chuan Siu's (1975) The Modern Malay Literature, 1942-1966 is
an exhaustive outline of titles and authors to the early 1970s. It includes a
number of interesting Islamic populist and a few socialist writers.

For CHINA, Harold Isaacs' (ed.) (1974) Straw Sandals is a massive anthology
of short stories and extracts from many of the early left-democratic and
revolutionary writers in China from 1918 to 1933. Most of the usually discussed
names are represented as well as some who rarely are mentioned. Isaacs (who was
in the Chinese left-literary scene in the mid 1920s) gives a moving if somewhat
querulous account of the times and the writers, while Lu Tsun provides a brief
overview   from the position of the early 1930s. It is a fine anthology.
G. Dimow and A. Dymschitz et al (eds.) (1974), Internationale Literatur des
Socialischen Realismus, 1917-1945, contains a fascinating chapter, "Development
of proletarian-revolutionary literature in China during the 1920s and 1930s",
which includes authors and works which have fallen into obscurity during the
Maoist period. It moreover provides a remarkable counterview to the image of
left Chinese struggles and writers during those early decades. A widely cited
survey is C.T. Hsia's (1961) A History of Modern Chinese Fiction, 1917-1957,
considered a comprehensive overview of the romantic and conservative as well as
progressive writing. There is also Tsi-an Hsia's (1968) The Gate of Darkness,
studies of the leftist literary movement in China which is more a study of the
politics and background of the writers' movements in the period 1918-1931 than a
survey of their actual writing.
    One of the most impressive and sympathetically critical studies of
contemporary writing in China is Joe Huang's (1970) Heroes and Villains in
Communist China, subtitled "The contemporary Chinese novel as a reflection of
life". It intensively discusses two dozen odd novels and touches on a few dozen
more as representative of more general themes and varied treatments of them.
Astute, readable and informative, it is a model for literary history. It
interweaves detailed and critical accounts of the novels with enough of the social-
historical developments in China and Chinese literature at the various times to
make sense of the works. Huang deals mainly with novels published since 1949 but
the themes cover events from the early 1920s to the mid 1960s. The Foreign
Languages Publishing House, Peking (circa 1968), Catalogue of Chinese Literature
in English, is a briefly annotated bibliography of some 150 of their titles
(novels, story collections, reportage) mainly written between the mid 1950s and
mid 1960s; they deal largely with topics surrounding the Great Leap Forward and
other antecedents of the so-called Cultural Revolution. The journal Chinese
Literature, a monthly publication of the Foreign Languages Publishing House,
Peking, is an easily available literary journal providing lengthy translated
extracts of an array of contemporary Chinese writing.
    Two valuable sources not utilized here are Kai-yu Hsu (ed.) (1980),
Literature of the People's Republic of China, a huge anthology which presents
extracts of work of some 180   Chinese writers, dramatists and poets from
1942 to the late 1970s, giving some bio-bibliographic and historical background
to the works as well. A most impressive collection. Also, Merle Goldman's (ed.)
(1977) Modern Chinese Literature in the May Fourth Era is a collection of
seventeen literary-historical essays on the political visions and social worlds
of the varied Chinese left writers during the 1920s and 1930s.

For KOREA, Kim Tong-uk and Kim Hyon's (1972) <u>Synopses of Korean Novels</u> (prepared for the South Korean U.N.E.S.C. commission) provides synopses of forty classical and forty modern novels. A handful represent the once extensive genre of populist or quasi-socialist writers in Korea. Unfortunately, no authors resident in North Korea after 1945 are mentioned and even those moderately left works of past decades are discussed in a very cautious manner. Peter Lee's (1965) <u>Korean Literature: Topics and Themes</u> is a broad survey of traditional and modern literature from circa 1910 to the mid 1950s. It includes a brief but provocative account of the early naturalist-populist and proletarian writers of the 1920s and 1930s. Lee's (1974) <u>Flowers of Fire: Twentieth Century Korean Studies</u> is an anthology of stories by eighteen Korean writers, including a few of the better known left-populist works of the inter-war years.

For JAPAN, George T. Shea's (1964) <u>Left-Wing Literature in Japan: a brief history of the proletarian movement</u> is a massive study of the various streams of radical Japanese writers and writing mainly from 1920 to the mid 1930s, with a brief synopsis of the periods immediately before and after. It documents an extraordinarily numerous and contumacious body of men and women, workers and writers. Since so much of the Japanese left literature existed only in magazine format, Shea's synopses are doubly important. Unfortunately, he deals more with the politics and membership of the contending and changing left groupings than with their literary works. Nevertheless, it is an admirable and remarkable survey. Another valuable survey is Edward Putzar's (ed.) (1973) <u>Japanese Literature: A Historical Outline</u> (originally Hisamatsu Sen'ichi et al (1960), <u>Nihon Bungaku</u>) which deals mainly with the period from the 1880s to the years immediately after W.W.II. It is especially good in its coverage of the early populist, radical-democratic and such working class literature as falls outside of Shea's purview. The Hisamatsu-Putzar volume also provides some discussion of the socio-economic conditions toward which the particular works were addressed.

Hilska Vlasta's "Early stages of Japanese proletarian literature" in H. Vlasta and Z. Vasiljevova's (1971) <u>Problems of Modern Japanese Society</u>, discusses a number of additional populist, anti-militarist, feminist and early socialist writers and their works from circa 1900 to 1920. The Japan Cultural Society/Kokusai Bunka Shinkokai (ed.) (1964) <u>Synopses of Contemporary Japanese Literature: Volume 1, 1902-1935</u> and <u>Volume 2, 1936-1955</u> are compact synopses of some particular representative work (usually a novel) of some eighty Japanese authors over a half century. It is of value for the immediate post W.W.II period. There is also Nakamura Mitsuo's (1970) <u>Contemporary Japanese Literature: Showa Period, 1926-1968</u>. John Morrison's (1955) <u>Modern Japanese Fiction</u> is a short, somewhat dated, study which still bears reading. It provides two valuable chapters on progressive and left-wing Japanese writers of the pre W.W.II period. Considering the time (late 1940s) and the country in which it was written, it was a courageous piece of scholarship.

Aakjaer, Jeppe   158
Abbas, Khwaja Ahmad   278
Abboud, Maroun   244
Abd'al-Rahim, Mahmud   243
Abell, Kjeld   158
Abrahams, Peter   269
Abramov, Fydor   174
Acevedo, Isidoro   121
Achebe, Chinua   262
Adamic, Louis   218
Adivar, Halide Edib   229
Adwan, Mamdouh   244
Afgani, Mohammad Ali   235
Agee, James   35
Agonafer, Enanu   254
Aguilar, Faustino   305
Aguilar Derpich, Juan   95
Aguilera Malta, Demetrio   80,89
Aguililla, Aracali   80
Ah Ming-Chih   306
Ahmad Ali   291
Ai Hsuan   306
Ai Wu   306
Aini, Sadriddin   174
Aitmatov, Chingiz   174
Ajar, Emile   250
Akritas, Loukis   224
Aksyonov, Vasily   174
'Alavi, Buzurg   235
Aldaraca, Bridget   75
(with E.Baker,I.Rodriguez,M.Zimmerman)
Al-e Ahmad, Jalal   235
Alegria, Ciro   95
Alegria, Fernando   98
Algren, Nelson   35
Ali Bhutto, Zulfikar   291
Alisjahbana, Takdir   299
Allamayyahu, Haddis   254
Allan, Ted   21
(with Sydney Gordon)
Allen, Jim   1
Allen, Walter   1
Allsop, Kenneth   35
Almanza, Hector Raul   68
Altman, Phyllis   269
Aluko, T.M.   262
Alvaro, Carrado   135
Amado, Jorge   106,107
Americo de Almeida, Jose   107
Ameringer, Oscar   35
Ames, Herbert   30
Aminurrashid, Harun   297
Amritray   278
An Su-gil   315
Anand, Mulk Raj   278,279
Ancal   279,280
Anda, Jose Guadalupe de   68
Andersson, Dan   165
Andreyev, Leonid   174
Andric, Ivo   218   ,
Andrzejewski, Jerzy   194
Anh Duc   294
Anker, Nini Roll   163

Annadurai, T.V.   280
Annawab, Mudhaffar   245
Ansari, Rabi   235
Aparicio Nogales, Raul   80
Apaydin. Talip   229
Apin. Rivai   299
Apitz, Bruno   142
Aragon, Louis   115
Arce, Manuel   125
Arconda, Cesar M.   121
Arderius, Joaquin   121
Ardiles Gray, Julio   101
Arenal, Humberto   80
Arevalo, Juan   73
Arguedas, Alcides   92
Arguedas. Jose Maria   95
Arguilla, Manuel E.   302
Arishima, Takeo   318
Armah, Ayi Kwei   264
Armstrong, Thomas   1
Arnow, Harriette   35
Arosev, Alekander   175
Arpino, Giovanni   135
Arraiz, Antonio   88
Arrili, Bernardo   101
Arrivi, Francisco   79
Ashleigh, Charles   36
(Al-)Asmar, Fouzi   241
Asturias, Miguel Angel   73
Attaway. William   36
Avalos, Fernando   121
Aveling, Harry   299
Avneri, Uri   238
'Awad, Louis   246
Awad, Tawfiq Youssef   244
Awoonor, Kofi   264
Azevedo, Aluisio   107
Aziz Ahmad   291
Azzam, Samira   241

Babel, Isaac   175
Bacchelli, Riccardo   135
(Al-)Badawi, Mahmoud   246
Baird, Irene   21
Bajalinow, Kasymaly   175
Bakdash, Khaled   244
Baklanov, Grigory   175
Ball, F.C.   1
Bandaharo, Harahap   299
Banerjee, Upendra   280
Banerji, Vibhutibhushan   280
Bannerjee, Manik   280
Baraka, Amiri   36
Barakat, Halim   241
Barbery Justiniano, Oscar   92
Barbu, Eugen   212
Barbusse, Henri   115
Barea. Arturo   121
Barke, James   2
Barletta, Leonidas   101
Barnet, Miguel   80
Barnett, Don   266
(with K. Njama)

Baroja, Pio   122
Barreno, Maria   130
(with Maria Horta, Maria Velho Costa)
Barrios de Chungara, Domitila   92
Basaran, Mehmet   229
Bassani, Giorgio   135
Bates, Ralph   68, 122
Battaglia, Roberto   136
Batungbakal, Brigido C.   302
(Al-)Bayati, Abdul Wahab   245
Baykurt, Fakir   229
Beals, Carleton   36
Becher, Johannes   142
Becker, Knuth   158
Behan, Brendan   16
Behrangi, Samad   236
Bell, Thomas   36
Bellanger, R.   115
Bellegrade, Dantes   112
Beleno, Joaquin   76
Beneditti, Mario   104
Benavides, Manuel   122
Ben Barka, El Mehdi   252
Benjamin, Laszlo   206
Benny, Mark   2
Bensoussan, Albert   250
Beratis, Jannis   224
Berent, Waclaw   194
Bergelson, David   175
Bergren, Myrtle,   21
Bernardi, Carlo   136
Bessal'ko, Pavel   176
Bessette, Gerard   30
Bessie, Alvah   37
Beti. Mongo   260
Bhaskaran, P.   280
Bhattacharya, Bhabani   280
Bibik, Aleksei   176
Bilbasar, Kemal   229
Binns, Archie   37
Bizzel, W.B.   37
Blais, Marie-Claire   30
Blasco Ibanez, Vicente   122
Blatchford, Robert   2
Bloom, Harry   270
Bloor, Ella Reeve   37
Blumenfeld, Simon   2
Bober, Arie   238
Bodenheim, Maxwell   37
Boestaman, Ahmad   297
Boguszewska, Helena   194
Bogza, Geo   212
Bojer, Johan   163
Bonosky, Philip   38
Boon, Louis Paul   156
Borowski, Tadeusz   194
Botelho Gonsalvez, Raul   92
Bourboune, Mourad   250
Boutron, Michel   115
Bowen, Lynne   21
Boyd, Thomas   38
Braaten, Oscar   164
Braga, Mario   130
Brand, Johanna   21

Brandao, Geraldo   107
Brandao, Raul   130
Brandys, Kazimierz   194
Braun, Andrzej   195
Brecht, Bertolt   142,143
Bredel, Willi   143
Breen, Dan   16
Bregendahl, Marie   159
Brenner, Yosef   238
Breza, Tadeusz   195
Brierly, Walter   3
Brink, Andre   270
Brissenden, Paul   38
Broadfoot, Barry   21
Brody, Katherine   38
Broniewski, Wladyslaw   195
Brown, Loyd   38
Brutus, Dennis   270
Budantsev, Sergei   176
Bui Duc Ai   294
Bulatovic, Miodrag   218
Bulosan, Carlos   302
Burchett, Wilfred   315
(with Alan Winnington)
Burke, Fielding   38
Burnet, John   3
Burton, Hester   13
Bush, Charles   38
Buyrukcu, Muzaffer   230
Buysse, Cyriel   156
Buzzi, David   80

Caballero Bonald, Jose   123
Caballero Calderon, Eduardo   86
Cabral, Alexander   130,275
Cabrera Infante, Guillermo   81
Cahan, Abraham   39
Cajar Escala, Jose   77
Caldwell, Erskine   39
Calinescu, George   212
Callado, Antonio   107
Calmer, Alan   39
Calthorpe, Mena   62
Calverton, V.F.   39
Calvino, Italo   136
Cameron, Donald S.   22
Campbell, C.G.   249
Candanedo, Cesar   77
Cantwell, Robert   39
Capek, Karel   200
Capek-Chod, Karel   200
Carco, Francis   116
Cardenal, Ernesto   75
Carias Reyes, Marcos   75
Carnelli, Maria Luisa   101
Carpentier, Alejo   81
Carranque de Rios, Andres   122
Carter, Dyson   22
Carter, Peter   13
Casey, Gavin   62
Casimiro, Augusto   276
Caso, Antonio   107
Cassola, Carlo   136

Castellanos, Rosario   68
Castelnuovo, Elias   101
Castillo, Otto Rene   73
Castro, Baltasar   98
Castro, Josue de   107
Castro, Oscar   98
Cato, Nancy   62
Caudill, Harry   39
Cayetano Carpio, Salvador   74
Cela, Camilo Jose   123
Cesbron, Gilbert   116
Cespedes, Augusto   92
Ch'ae Man-sik   315
Chamsons, Andre   116
Chandar, Krishan   281
Chaplin, Ralph   40
Chapygin, Alex   176
Chao Shu-li   306
Charhadi, Driss Ben Hamed   252
Charlier, Etienne   113
Chatterji, Saratcandra   281
Chatzis, Dimitros
  (see Dhimitris Hadziz)
Chen Jo-Hsi   307
Chesneaux, Jean   307
Chitale, Venu   281
Cho Myong-hui   317
Ch'oe Sohae   317
Chou Erh-fu   307
Chou Li-po   307
Choukrallah, Khogli   253
Choukri, Mohamed   252
Chraibi, Driss   252
Chu Teh   312
Chukovskaya, Lydia   177
Ciges Aparicio, Manuel   123
Clarke, Austin   22, 112
Claudius, Eduard   143
Coloane, Francisco   98
Coleman, McAlister   40
  (with H.S. Raushenbush)
Coleman, Terry   3
Colman, Louis   40
Colton, Samuel   40
Common, Jack   3
Coombes, B.L.   3
Condominas, Georges   294
Congrains Martin, Enrique   95
Connolly, James   16
Conroy, Jack   40
Cope, Jack   270
Copic, Branko   218
Coppard, Audrey   13
Cordell, Alexander   14
Corkery, Daniel   17
Corona Rojas, Benigno   68
Cosic, Dobrica   219
Craveirinha, Jose   275
Crook, David and Isabel   307
Cseres, Tibor   206   ,
Cunningham, William   40
Curran, Dale   41
Curtis, Jean-Louis   116

Cusack, Dymphna   62

Dabit, Eugene   116
Dabrowska, Maria   195
Dadie, Bernard   260
Dang Tran Con et al   294
Darvas, Jozsef   206
Darwish. Mahmud   241
Dash, Jack   3
Dashti, Ali   236
Davies, Rebecca   41
Davin, Dan   66
Davis, N. Brian   22
Day, Alf   62
DeAndrade, Mario C. Pinto   276
De Coster, Charles   156
Dekker, Eduard Douwes   156
Delano, Luis Enrique   98
Delany, Shelagh   4
Delius, F.C.   143
Demby, William   41
Demir, Kemal Tahir
  (see Kemal Tahir)
Denby, Charles   41
Depestre, Rene   113
Der Nister   185
Dery, Tibor   206
Desnoes, Edmundo   81
Dev, Kesava   281
Devanny, Jean   66
Devlin, Bernadette   16
Dhul Nyun, Ayyub   245
Dias de Moral, Jesus   124
Diaz Fernandez, Jose   124
Diaz Rodriguez, Jesus   81
Diaz Sanchez, Ramos   88
Diaz Ycaza, Rafael   89
Dib, Mohammed   250
Didonato, Pietro   41
Dikobe, Modikwe   270
Di Lampedusa, Giuseppe   136
Dimitova, Blaga   215
Dimov, Dimiter   215
Ditlevsen, Tove   153
Djagarov, Georgi   215
Djebar, Assia   250
Djilas, Milovan   219
Dobles, Fabian   76
Doblin, Alfred   144
Doherty, Len   4
Dolce, Danilo   137
Dombrovsky, Yury   177
Donchev, Anton   215
Dorosh, Yefim   177
Dorr, Rheta C.   41
Dorst, Tankred   144.
Dos Passos, John   41
Dos Santos, Marcelino   275
Dos Santos Lima, Manuel   276
Douglas, Jack   41
Doukas, Alekos   224
Doxas, Takis   224
Drago, Gonzalo   98

Draskau, Jennifer (ed.)   293
Drieser, Theodore et al   42
Duggal, Katar Singh   282
Dumas, Evelyn   31
Durkin, Douglas   22
Du Toit, Bettie   270
Dutt, Ullaskar   280
Dutt, Utpal   281
Duun, Olav   164
Dyson, Edward   62

Edwards Bello, Joaquin   99
Eekhoud, Georges   157
Egge, Peter   164
Ehrenburg, Ilya   116, 177
Ekwensi, Cyprian   262
Elon, Amos   238
Elsschot, William   157
Endore, Guy   113
Engelbrecht, H.C.   4
(with Haniger, F.C)
Engstrand, Stuart   42
Enis, Resat   230
Enzenberger, Hans Magnus   144
Espina, Concha   124
Estifanos Yera-Manestu   254
Evans, George Ewart   4

Fadeyev, Alexander   177, 178
Faiz Ahmed Faiz   291
Fakouri, Omar   244
Falcon, Cesar   96
Falk, Robert et al   294
Falkberget, Johan   164
Fall, Bernard   294
Fallas, Carlos Luis   76
Farah, Nuruddin   257
Farrell, James T.   42
Fast. Howard   42, 43
Fedin, Konstantin   178
Feijoo, Samuel   82
Fejes, Endre   207
Fennario, David   31
Feraoun, Mouloud   251
Fernandez, Jorge   89
Fernandez Santos, Jesus   124
Ferreira de Castro, Jose M.   108,130
Ferreira, Vergilio   131
Ferres, Antonio   124
Ferron, Jasques   31
Figgis, Darrell   16
First, Ruth   271
Flynn, Elizabeth Gurley   43
Fonseca, Manuel da   131
Fontes, Amando   108
Forrest, David   62
Forseth, Matthea   43
Forsh, Olga   178
Foster, William   43
Fox, Ralph   4
Fox, Richard   4
Franca, Oswaldo   108

Francisco, Lazaro   302
Frank, Waldo   43
Franko, Ivan   196
Fraser, Dawn   22
Fraser, Ronald   5, 124
Fray, Stefan   212
Freedman, David   44
Freeman, James   282
Freeman,Joseph   44
Frevilles, Jean   116
Fridegard, Jan   166
Fuchs, Daniel   44
Fuentes, Carlos   69
Fujimori, Seikichi   318
Furmanov, Dimitri   179
Furphy, Joseph   63

Gabra-Yasus, Afawarq   255
Gaines, Ernest   44
Galeano, Eduardo   74
Galecki, Stefan   196
Gallacher, William   5
Gallegos, Geraldo   89
Gallegos, Romulo   82, 88
Gallegos Lara, Joaquin   89
Galvez, Manuel   101
Ganesalingam, S. et al   292
Garcia Hortelano, Juan   125
Garcia Lorca, Fredrico   125
Garcia Marquez, Gabriel   86
Gargi, Balwant   282
Garner, Hugh   23
Garofalo, Jose Miguel   82
Garrett, George   5
Gelinas, Pierre   31
Gelleri, Andor Endre   207
Gelsted, Otto   159
Gergely, Sandor   207
Germa, Ba'alu   255
Ghareeb, Edmund   242
(with N. Aruri)
Gharib, Shapur   236
Gibbon, Leo Grassic   5
Gil Gilbert, Enrique   89
Giles, Barbara   44
Gjata, Fatmir   222
Gjersted, Ole   265
(with Temba Moyo)
Gladkov, Fyodor   179
Glasgow, Ellen   44
Gluchowski, Bruno   144
Godiner, S.N.   179
Goetel, Ferdinand
Gokce, Enver   230
Gold, Michael   44
Gologo, Mamadou   259
Goodman, Henry (Ed.)   45
Gonzalez, Jose Luis'   79
Gonzalez, N.V.M.   303
Gonzalez de Cascorro, Raul   82
Gordimer, Nadine   270
Gordon, Gerald   271

Gordon, R.J.   273
Gorky, Maxim   179, 180
Gorter, Herman   157
Goyanarte, Juan   102
Goytisolo, Juan   125
Graham, Margaret   45
(with Grace McDonald)
Granvina, Alfredo   104
Gravel, Pierre   32
Gray, James   23
Greenwood, Walter   5
Grieg, Nordahl   165
Grossman, Vassily   180
Grosso, Alfonso   126
Grunberg, Karl   144
Gubanna, Abbe   255
Guerrero, Jesus R.   69
Guido, Beatriz   102
Guillen, Nicolas   82
Guilloux, Louis   117
Guntekin, Resat Nuri   230
Gutierrez, Carlos Mario   104
Gutierrez, Joaquin   77
Guzman, Martin Luis   69
Guzman, Nicomedes   99

Haber, Horatius   145
Hadzis, Dhimitris   224
Hadzopoulos, Konstantine   225
Hagalin, Gudmundur   161
Hallgren, M.A.   45
Halper, Albert   45
Halward, Leslie   5
Hamilton, Patrick   6
Hamp, Pierre   117
Han Solya   315
Hancerlioglu, Orhan   230
Handel, Judith   238
Hanley, James   6
Hansen, Martin   159
Hardy, Frank   63
Hardy, George   23
Harnett, Cynthia   14
Harrison, Charles   45
Hasek, Jaroslav   200
Hauptmann, Gerhart   145
Havinghurst, Walter   46
Hayama Yoshiki   318
Hayashi Fumiko   318
Hayashi Fusao   319
Haywood, Big Bill   46
Hedenvind-Eriksson, Gustav   166
Hedges, Marion H.   46
Heineman, Margot   6
Heinz;G. and Donnay, H.   261
Hellman, Lillian
Herbert, Xavier   63
Herbst, Josephine   46
Herdal, Harald   159
Hernandez, Amado V.   303
Herrero, Juan Luis   82
Heslop, Harry   6
Hewett, Dorothy   63

Hewitt,Marsha   32
(with Claire McKay)
Heym, Stefan   46, 145, 200
Hidas, Antal   207
Hidayat,Sadiq   236
Hikmet, Nazim   230
Himiob, Nelson   88
Hinton, William   308
Hirabayashi Taiko   319
Hirasawa Keishichi   319
Hirotsu Kazuo   319
Hlasko, Marek   196
Ho Chi Minh   295
Hoar, Victor   23
Hobsbawn, Eric   7
Hochhut, Rolf   145
Holbrook, Stewart   46
Hoelz, Max   145
Holst, Henriette Roland   157
Honwana, Luis B.   275
Hora, Josef   200
Horvath, Oden von   154
Hosain, Attia   282
Hosoi Wakizo   320
Hrabal, Bohumil   200
Hsia Chih-yen   308
Hsiao Hung   308
Hu Ye-pin   308
Huanay, Julian   96
Hughes, Langston   47
Hunter, Mollie   14
Hussein, Mahmoud   246
Hutchinson, Alfred   271, 273
Hutchinson, Sidney   23
Huu Mai et al   295
Hyde, Robin   66
Hyong Chin-gon   317

Iatridi, Julia   225
Ibrahim, Abdullah Ali   253
Ibrahim, Salah Ahmed   253
Icaza, Jorge   90
Idris, Yusuf   246
Idrus   299
Igleseas, Cesar Andreu   79
Ike, Chukwuemka   262
Ilf, Ilya   180
(with Eugeni Petrov)
Illes, Bella   207
Illyes, Gyula   208
Indian Peoples Theatre Association   282
Institute of Palestine Studies   242
International Longshore and
    Warehousemens Union   24
Iqbal, Muhammad   291
Iroh, Eddie   263
Irvine, William   24
Irwin, Theodore   47
Isaku, Murat   219
Isaacs, Harold (Ed.)   308
Ishak bin Haji Muhammad   297
Ishikawa Tatsuzo   320
Iskander, Fasil   181

Isvaran, Manjeri   282
Ivanov, Vsevolod   181
Iwafuji Yukio   320
Iyayi, Festus   263
Izcaray, Jesus   126
Izgu, Muzaffer   231

Jackson, T.A.   7, 16
Jamalzada, Muhammad Ali   236
James, C.L.R.   110, 113
Jameson, Storm   7
Jandel, Ragnar   167
Janevski, Slavko   219
Jaramillo Arango, Rafael   86
Javorov, Pejo   215
Jiang Guang-tsi   309
Jilemnicky, Peter   203
Johns, Orrick   47
Johnson, Josephine   47
Johnson-Davies, Deny   249
Jonasson Ur Kotlum, Johannes   161
Jones, Glyn   7
Jones, Lewis   8
Jones, Mary Harris   47
Jonsson, Sigurjon   161
Jovine, Francisco   137
Juliao, Francisco   108
Jurado, Ramon   77

Kaatra, Kustaa   170
Kabir, Humayan   280
Kadare, Ismail   222
Kaden-Badrowski, Julius   196
Kaga Koji   320
Kahn, Kathy   47
Kaiser, George   145
Kaleb, Vjekoslav   220
Kamberoglou, Byron   225
Kamodaran, K.   283
Kanafani, Ghassan   242
Kane, Cheikh Hamidou   258
Kane, Thomas   256
Kaneko Tobun   321
Karaosmanoglu, Yakup Kadri   231
Karaslavov, Georgi   200, 215
Karinthy, Ferenc   208
Kariuki, Joseph   266
Kartodikromo, Mas Marco   300
Karvas, Peter   204
Kasdaglis, Nikos   225
Kassak, Lajos   208
Kassim, Ahmad   298
Kataoka Teppei   321
Katayev, Valentine   181
Kato Yoshizo   321
Kaunda, Kenneth   265
Kaverin, Veniamin   182
Kemal Tahir   231
Keris Mas et al   298
Kern, Alfred   47
Khudadada, Ahmad Ali   237
Kibblewhite, Liz   8
 (with Andy Rigby)

Kidane, Ayyala   256
Kielland, Alexander   165
Kim Lan et al   295
Kim Tong-In   317
Kinoshita Naoe   321
Kinrosha Bungaku   322
Kipnis, Itsik   182
Kirk, Hans   159
Kisch, Egon   201
Kjellgren, Josef   167
Knight, Rolf   24, 25
Kobayashi Takiji   322
Kocagoz, Samaim   232
Koch, Martin   167
Konetsky, Victor   182
Konrad, Gyorgy   209
Konrad, Karel   201
Konstantinov, Aleko   216
Konwicki, Tadeusz   197
Kornacki, Jerzy   194
Kornbluh, Joyce   47
Korner, Wolfgang   146
Kosmac, Ciril   220
Kotenev, A.   309
Kostsias, Kostas   225
Kourama, Ahmadou   260
Kovacic, Ivan Goran   220
Koziol, Urszula   197
Kral, Franco   204
Kramer, Ken   25
Kramer, Theodor   154
Kranik, Orhan Veli   232
Kratochvil, Jaroslav   201
Kristensen, Tom   159
Kraus, Karl   154
Krleza, Miroslav   220
Kromer, Tom   48
Kruczkowski, Leon   197
Krzywicki, Ludwik   197
Ku Qiubai   309
Kubo Sakae   322
Kulbak, Moshe   182
Kurek, Jalu   197
Kurella, Alfred   146
Kuroshima Denji   322

Laberge, Albert   32
Ladoo, Harold   110
Laguerre, Enrique   77, 78
La Guma, Alex   271
Lalic, Mihailo   220
Lambert, David   8
Lambert, Eric   63
Lamming, George   111
Lamoureux, Hemri   32
Lane, Winthrop   48
Lang, Harry   48
Lange, Dorthea   59
 (with Paul Taylor)
Langer, Felicia   238
Lanham, Edwin   48
Lao She   309

Lara, Jesus   93
Larkin, Emmet   17
Lawrence, Josephine   48
Lawson, Henry   63
Laxness, Halldor   162
Laye, Camara   259
Lazarova, Katerina   204
Le Crone, Donald   48
Le Minh Khue et al   295
Lee, John   67
Lee, Peter   316
Lee, Richardo et al   303
Leeson, Bob   14
Lehtimaki, Konrad   170
Leino, Kasimir   170
Lemelin, Roger   32
Lengyel, Jozsef   209
Leonov, Leonid   183
Lera, Angel Maria de   126
Lespes, Anthony   113
Lessing, Doris   265
LeSueur, Meridel   48
Lettau, Reinhard   147
Levi, Carlo   137
Levi, Giorgina   137
Levin, Meyer   49
Levy, Melvin   49
Lewis, Oscar   69, 82
Liang Pin   310
Li Ying-Ju   309
Libedinski, Yuri   183
Lindo, Hugo   74
Lincoln, Victoria
Lindman, Sara   167
Lindsay, Jack   8, 14
Linna, Vaino   170
Lins do Rego, Jose   109
Liu Ch'ing   310
Liversedge, Ronald   25
Livesay, Dorothy   25
Lo Kuang-Pin   310
(with Yang Yi-Yen)
Lo Tang   310
Lo-Johanason, Ivar   168
Lomboy, Reinaldo   99
London, Jack   9, 49
Lopez Nussa, Leonel   83
Lopez Pacheco, Jesus   126
Lopez Salinas, Armando   126
Lopez y Fuentes, Gregorio   70
Lora, Guillermo   94
Lu Hsun   311
Luandino   277
(see Jose Luandino Vieira)
Lumpkin, Grace   50
Lurya, Nathan   183
Lyashko, Nikola   183
Lynd, Alice and Staughton   50
Lyra, Carmen   76
Lysenko, Vera   26
Lytton, David   272

Ma Feng et al   311
McArthur, A.   9
(with H.K. Long)
McCoy, Horace   50
MacDairmid, Hugh   9
McEwan, Paul   26
McGahern, John   17
Mc Henry, Beth   50
(with Fred Myers)
Mc Intyre, John
McKay, Claude   50, 111
Macken, Walter   17
Mackenzie, Kenneth   26
MacOrlan, Pierre   117
MacPherson, C.B.   26
McWilliams, Carey   51
Madgulkar, Vyankateah   283
Madrios, Anthony   26
Maedako Koichiro   323
Magdaleno, Maurico   70
Magliore, Auguste   113
Mahfouz, Naguib   247
Mailer, Norman   51
Mais, Roger   111
Majerova, Maria   117, 201
Makal, Mahmut   232
Makan, Tottiyute   283
Malangatana, Valente   275
Malashkin, Sergei   184
Malyskin, Aleksander   184
Maleshova, Sejfulla   222
Malkiel, Theresa   51
Maloff, Peter   26
(with V.A. Sukhorev)
Maltz, Albert   51
Mammeri, Mouloud   251
Mamiya Mosuke   323
Manauta, Juan Jose   102
Manaye, Yelma   256
Mancisidor, Jose   71
Mandela, Nelson   272
Manglis, Yiannis   225
Mann, Heinrich   147
Mann, Leonard   63
Manov, Emil   216
Manto, Sa'adat Hassan   291
Mantov, Dimiter   216
Manzalaoui, Mahmoud   249
Mao Tun   311
Marchwitza, Hans   147
Marechera, Dambudao   265
Marin, Juan   100
Marin Cañas, Jose   105
Markandaya, Kamala   283
Marko, Petro   222
Marlyn, John   26
Marolta, Giuseppe   138
Marrero Aristy, Ramon   78
Marse, Juan   127
Marshall, Alan   64
Martin, David   64

Martinek, Vojtech   201
Martinez Estrada, Ezequiel   102
Martinson, Harry   168
Martinson, Moa   168
Masiye, Andereya   265
Masters, D.G.   27
Mas'ud, Muhammad   237
Mata Ordoñez, Humberto   90
Matip, Benhamin   260
Maxwell, Gavin   138
Megged, Ahron   239
Mejia Nieto, Arturo   75
Mejia Vallejo , Manuel   86
Memmi, Albert   253
Mendelsohn, Ezra   198
Mendes, Alfred   110
Mendoza, Jaime   94
Mercer, Dennis   272, 273
 (with Uinnia Ndadi)
Miguel, Maria Ester de   102
Milev, Geo   216
Miller, Arthur   51
Miller, Max   52
Milliex, Tatiana   226
Minac, Vladimir   204
Mintz, Sidney   79
Mitchell, Hannah   9
Miyajima Sukeo   324
Miyamoto Yuriko   324
Moberg, Vilhelm   169
Modesto, Juan   127
Modisane, Bloke   272
Modlane, Eduardo   275
Mokgatle, Naboth   272
Mopeli-Paulus, Attwell   273
Monteforte Toledo, Mario   74
Montenegro, Carlos   83
Montero, Gloria   27
Moore, Brian   27
Moorehouse, Hopkins   52
Mora, Fernando   127
Moravia, Alberto   138
Morcinek, Gustaw   198
Moricz, Zsigmond   209
Morris, William   9
Morrison, Arthur   10
Moscoso Puello, Francisco   78
Motley, Willard   52
Mothe, Daniel   118
Mowatt, Farley   27
Mphahlele, Ezekiel   272
M'Rabet, Fadela   251
(Al-) Mubarak, Khalid   253
Mulaisho, Dominic   266
Mulgan, John   67
Mullish, Harry   157
Multatuli   300
Mun'is, Husain   247
Muñoz, Rafael   71
Murdoch, Angus   52
Musrepow, Gabit   184
Mustafin, Gabiden   184
Mutombo-Diba, Valerian   261

Mwangi, Meja   267
Myrdal, Jan   169, 312
Myint, Thein Pe   292

Nachbar, Herbert   148
Nagarajan, K.   284
Nagatsuka Takashi   325
Nagy, Istvan   209, 213
Nagy, Lajos   210
Nagy-Talavera, Nicholas   213
Naipul, N.V.   110
Najm, Ahmad Fuad   247
Nakanishi Inosuke   325
Nakano Shigeharu   325
Nalkowska, Zofia   198
Namboodiripad, E.M.S.   284
Namora, Fernando   131
Narula, Surinder Singh   284, 285
Nascimento, Manuel do   131
Navarro, Noel   83
Nazor, Vladimir   220
N'Debeka, Maxime   261
Nearing, Scott   52
Neira, Julian   96
Neira Samanez, Hugo (ed.)   96
Nieto, Ramon   127
Nekrassov, Victor   184
Nenni, Pietro   138
Neruda, Pablo   100
Neto, Agostinho   276
Neugass, James   53
Neverov, Aleksandr   185
Newhouse, Edward   53
Nexo, Martin Andersen   160
Ngugi Wa Thiongo (James Ngugi)   267
Nguyen Cong Hoan   295
Nguyen Duy Tinh et al   296
Nguyen Sen   296
 (with Nguyen Ti, Nguyen Sang et al)
Nichols, John   53
Nihon Sayoku Bungeika Sorento   325
Nikiforov, Georgi   185
Nikitin, Nikolay   185
Nilin, Paulin   185
Nish, Cameron (ed.)   33
Nisin, Aziz (Aziz Nesin)   232
Nister (see Der Nister)   185
Nizan, Paul   118
Nizovoi, Pavel   186
Nkrumah, Kwame   261, 264
Noll, Dieter   148
Nouri, Abd el Malek   245
Novikov-Priboy, Alexey   186
Novomesky, Laco   205
Novy, Karel   202
Nqheku, Albert   274
Nuñez, Sergio   91
Nurowska, Maria   198
Nusin, Abdolhosein   237

O'Brien, Nora Connolly   17
O'Casey, Sean   17
O'Connor, Harvey   53

O'Criomhtain, Tomas   18
Oculi, Okello   266
Odinga, Oginga   267
O'Donnell, Peader   18
Odets, Clifford   54
Odulok, Taeki   186
O'Flaherty, Liam   18, 19
Ohel, Melo   238
Olbracht, Ivan (Kamil Zeman)   202
Olema Garcia, Daura   832
Olesha, Yuri   186
Oliveira, Carlos de   132
O'Malley, Ernie   19
O'Neil, Brian   19
Orhan Kemal (Mehmet Rasit Ogutcu)   232
Orkeny, Istavan   210
O'Rourke, William (ed.)   54
Ortega, Gregorio   83
Ortese, Anna Maria   138
Ortiz Hernan, Gustavo   71
Ortzen, Len   253
Orwell, George   292
Osorio Lizarazo, Jose   87
Ostenso, Martha   27
Ostrovsky, Nikolay   186
Osugi Sakae   326
Ota Yoko   326
Otero, Lisandro   84
Otero Silva, Miguel   88
Ouary, Malek   252
Ouologuem, Yambo   259
Ousame, Sembene   258
Ou-Yang Shan   312
Ovechkin, Valentin   186
Oyono, Ferdinand   260
Ozawa Kiyoshi   326
Ozores, Renato   77

Pa Chin   312
Page, Myra   54
Pagliarani, Elio   138
Pak Kyong-su   316
Pakkanen, Toivo   171
Palangyo, Peter   266
Palmer, Vance   64
Panayotopoulos, I.M.   226
Pane, Sanusi   300
Panferov, Fedor   187
Panova, Vera   187
Paolieri, Ferninando   138
Pareja Diez-Canseco, Alfredo   91
Parizeau, Alice   33
Park, Ruth   67
Parker, Edwin   54
Pärssinen, Hilja   171
Patterson, Orlando   112
Paustovsky, Konstantin   187
Pavese, Cesare   139
Payne, Robert   128
Pazarkaya, Yuksel   233
Pearson, Bill   67   ,
Pendse, S.N.   285
Peoples Autobiography of Hackney   10
Pereira, Jose Pacheco   132

Pereira Gomes, Soeiro   132
Perera, Karuna   292
Perera Sota, Hilda   84
Person, Carl E.   54
Petersen, Jan   148
Petrakis, Harry Mark   226
Petrescu, Cezar   213
Phelan, Jim   10
Pham Nhu Oanh   296
Philippes, A.   118
Phillips, Donna (ed.)   28
Pilar, Yury   188
Pillai, T. Sivasankara   286
Pilnyak, Boris   188
Piñeiro, Abelardo   84
Pinillos, Lopez   128
Pires, Jose Cardoso   132
Pitt-Rivers, Julian   128
Plaatje, Sol T.   274
Plaskovits, Spyros   226
Platonov, Andrei   188
Plievier, Theodore   148
Plomer, William   274
Plunkett, James   19
Pogodin, Nikolay   188
Poljanov, Dimiter (Dimiter Popov)   216
Poole, Ernest   54
Pomeroy, William   304
Poniatowska, Elena   71
Popescu, Dumitru Radu   213
Popp, Adeheid   149
Porta, Eliseo Salvador   104
Potrobenko, Helen   28
Poulaille, Henry   118
Prada Oropeza, Renato   94
Prasad Gupta, Bhairav   285
Pratolini, Vasco   139
Preda, Marin   213
Premchand, Munshi   285, 286
Preston, Richard   10
Prevelakis, Pantelis   226
Prevost, Jean   119
Price, Susan   15
Prichard, Katherine Susannah   64, 65
Pujmanova, Marie   202

Queiros, Rachel de   109
Quevado, Nino   128
Quinto, Jose Maria de   128

Rabemananjera, Jasques   261
Racin, Kosta   221
Raffat, Donne   237
Raghav, Rangey   286
Ramirez Velarde, Fernando   94
Ramos, Graciliano   109
Randall, Margaret   75
Raper, Arthur   54
   (with Ira Reid)
Rasuanto, Bur   300
Read, Horacio   78
Rebreanu, Liviu   213
Redol, Alves   132, 133
Redding, J. Saunders   55

Reid, Victor S.   112
Reissner, Larissa   149
Remarque, Erik Maria   149
Remy, Tristan   119
Renaud, Jacques   33
Renda, F. (ed.)   140
Requena, Andres   78
Revueltas, Jose   72
Reyes, Edgardo   304
Reyna, Ernesto   96
Reynoso, Oswaldo   96
Rezac, Vaclav   202
Ribeiro, Aquilino   133
Ribeiro, Joao Ubaldo   109
Richard, Jean Jules   33
Rideg, Sandor   210
Rintala, Paavo   171
Rios, Edmundo de los   96
Ritsos, Jannis   226
Rivarola Matto, Jose M.   105
Rive, Richard   273
Rivera, Andres   102
Rizal, Jose   304
Roa Bastos, Augusto   105
Robleto, Hernan   75
Rodero, Juan Jose   128
Rodriguez, Alberto   103
Rodriguez, Luis Felipe   84
Roestam Effendi   300
Rogoff, Harry   55
Rojas, Angel   91
Rollins, William   55
Romero, Luis   128
Ronan, Tom   65
Rosengarten, Theodore   55
Roth, Henry   55
Roumain, Jacques   113, 114
Romains, Jules   119
Romanov, Panteleimon   188
Roy, Gabrielle   34
Roy, Manabendra N.   286, 287
Rudd, Steele   65
Ruhumbika, Gabriel   266
Rusinek, Michael   198
Rutherford, Mark (William Hale)   10
Ryan, Desmond   19
Ryan, Oscar   29, 34
Ryan, Toby   28

Saadawi, Nawal-el   248
Saarikoski, Pentti   172
Sabahattin Ali   233
Sadji, Abdoulay   259
Sadoveanu, Michail (Ion Martin
  Sadoveanu)   214
Safadi, Mouta   244
Sahia, Alexandru   214
Said, Edward W.   242
Salama, Hannu   172
Salamon, Erno   214
Salazar Mallen, Ruben   72
Salih, Tayeb   253
Salo, Arvo   172

Salvador, Humberto   91
Samad Ismail, Abdul (Asmat)   298
Samad Said, A.   298
Samarakis, Adonis   227
Samkange, Stanlake   265
Samuel, Raphael   11
Sandel, Maria   169
Sandor, Kalman   210
San Juan Jr., Epifano   304
Santa, Ferenc   210
Santareno, Bernardo   133
Santos, Lope K.   304
Sarduy, Severo   84
Sarna, Mahinder Singh   287
Sassykbajew, Satkyn   189
Sata Ineko   326
Satarthi, Devinder   287
Saxton, Alexander   55
Sayigh, Rosemary   242
Schectman, Elya   189
Schell, Jonathan   296
Scherfig, Hans   160
Schilling, Wilfred   149
Schlotterbeck, Friedrich   150
Schultz, Bruno   198
Sciascia, Leonardo   140
Scorza, Manuel   97
Scott, Leroy   55
Seaver, Edwin   56
Seghers, Anna   150, 154
Sekhon, Sant Singh   287
Selvon, Samuel   110
Semenov, Sergei   189
Sen, Ela   287
Sender, Ramon J.   129
Sepulveda Leyton, Carlos   100
Serafimovich, Alexander S.   189
Serge, Victor   189
Serpa, Enrique   84
Serumaga, Robert   266
Seyfullina, Lydia   189
Shackelford, Laurel (ed.)   56
  (with Bill Weinberg)
Shahak, Israel   239
Shaham, Nathan   239
Shannon Ahmad   298
Shamir, Moshe   239
Sharif, Taufiq (ed.)   243
  (with Adil Zawwati)
(Al-)Sharqawi, Abd-al Rahman   243, 248
Sharp, Paul   28
Sharpe, Errol   28
(Al-) Shati, Bint   249
Shaw, Irwin   56
Shelest, Georgy   190
Shimaki Kensaku   327
Shimazaki Toson   327
Shirurkar, Vibhavari   287
Shishlov, Vyacheslav   190
Sholokov, Mikhail   190
Shrinagesh, Shakuntala   288
Shrivastva, Shivnarayan   288
Siagian, Bachtiar   300

Sidqi, Mohammed   248
Sieroszewski, Waclaw   199
Sikat, Rogelio et al   305
Sillanpaa, Franz   172
Sillitoe, Alan   11
Silone, Ignazio   140
Silva,Jose   134
Simonov, Konstantin   190
Sinclair, Bertrand   28
Sinclair, Upton   56, 57
Singh, Gurdial   288
Singh, Iqbal   288
Singh, Kesar   288
Singh, Khuswant   288
Singh, Nanak   289
Singh, Sujan   289
Sinkkonen, Lassi   172
Sionil, Jose   305
Siregar, Bakri   300
Sirgurthdson, Olafur   162
Sissoko, Fily-Dabo   259
Sivachov, Mikhail   191
Skjoldborg, Johan   160
Slater, Montagu   11
Slonimsky, Mikhail   191
Smedley, Agnes   57, 312
Smirenski, Xristos   216
Smith, A.E.   29
Smith, Herbert   12
Smith, Mary   263
Smith, Wessel   58
Snow, Edgar   312
Snow, Helen   313
So Ki-Won   316
Soiberg, Harry   161
Soldati, Mario   140
Soler Puig, Jose   85
Solis, Ramon   129
Sommerfeld, John   12
Sontai, Utuy   301
Soromenho, Castro   134, 276
Sotiriou, Dido   227
Soto Aparicio, Fernando   87
Soyinka, Wole   263
Spasse, Sterjo   222
Spivak, John   58
Sri Sri   289
Srinawk, Khamsing   293
Stamatov, Georgi   216
Stancu, Zaharia   214
Stavis, Barrie   58
Stead, Christina   65
Steeves, Dorothy   29
Steinbeck, John   58
Steinberg, Isaac   191
Stephansson, Stephan G.   163
Stermilli, Haki   223
Stevenson, Philip   58
Stil, Andre   119
Stivens, Dal   65
Stojanov, Ljudmil   217
Stone, I.F.   316
Stone, Louis   65

Storm, Fredrik   169
Strasimirov, Anton   217
Strati, Saverio   140
Stribling, T.S.   58
Strittmayer, Erwin   151
Suarez ,Gaston   94
Sueiro, David   129
Surangkhanang, E.   293
Surve, Narayan   289
Swankey, Ben   29
(with Jean Evans Sheils)
Syomin, Vitali   191
Szabo, Pal   210

Tadschun, I.   316
Takeda Taijun   327
Takla-Hewaryat, Germaccaw   256
Talev, Dimiter   217
Tammuz, Benjamin   239
Tangol, Nicascio   100
Tartarka, Dominik   205
Taruc, Luis   305
Tayama Katai   327
Taylor, Paul   59
Tazky, Ladislav   205
Teitelboim, Volodia   100
Terkerli, Fouad   245
Tennant, Kylie   66
Terkel, Studs   59
Terrill, Tom   59
(with Jerrold Hirsch)
Testori, Giovanni   141
Thein Pe Myint   292
Theotokis, Constantine   227
Theriault, Yves   34
Tian Han   313
T'ien Chun   313
Tihla, Hilda   172
Tijerino, Doris   75
Tilschova, A.M.   203
Timerman, Jacobo   103, 240
Ting Ling   314
Tippet, Tom   59
Todrin, Boris   154
Toer, Pramoedya Ananta   301
Tojal, Altino M. do   134
Tokunaga Sunao   327
Toller, Ernst   151
Tolstoy, Alexey   191
Trausti, Jon   163
Traven, Bruno   72
Trease, Geoffrey   15
Treece, Henry   15
Tressel, Robert   12
Trifonov, Yuri   192
Triolet, Elsa   119
Tsao Yu   314
Tsirkas, Stratis   228
Tsuboi Sakae   328
Tu Peng-Cheng   314
Tully, Jim   59
Turki, Fawaz   243
Turtianinen, Arvo   173

Unilowski, Zbigniew   199
Uppdal, Krisofer   165
Urban, Erno   211
Uribe Piedrahita, Cesar   87
Uris, Leonard   20
Urondo, Francisco   103
Uslar Pietri, Arturo   88

Vailand, Roger   120
Vallejo, Cesar   97
Valles, Jules   120
Vallieres, Pierre   34
Vancura, Vladislav   203
Van der Meersch, Maxence   120
Vapcarov, Nikola   217
Varnalis, Constantine Kostas   228
Vassilikos, Vassilis   228
Vazov, Ivan   216
Velkow, Krum   217
Venezias, Elias   228
Veres, Peter   211
Verga, Giovanni   141
Vesely, Artem   192
Viana, Javier de   104
Vieira, Jose Luandino   277
Villeneuve, Paul   34
Viñas, David   103
Viteri, Eugenia   85
Vittorini, Elio   141
Vladimov, Georgi   192
Von der Grun, Max   151
Voranc, Prezihov   221
Vorse, Mary Heaton   60

Wachira, Godwin   268
Waciuma, Charity   268
Walker, Charles   60
Wallace, Joe   29
Wallace, J.W.   66
Wallis, Keene   60
Wallraff, Gunter   152
Walsh, Jane   12
Warner, Sylvia Townsend   12
Warqu, Dannaccaw   256
Wat, Aleksander   199
Waterhouse, Keith   12
Waterman, Ray   12
Watten, Judah   66
Wayman, Tom (Ed.)   29
  (with Milton Acorn, Pat Lane,
   Clyde Warrior et al)
Weatherwax, Clara   60
Weddenah, Mamo   254
Weinert, Erich   152
Weiskopf, Franz Carl   152, 155, 205
Weiss, Peter   152
Wesker, Arnold   13
White, Howard   29
White, Walter Francis   60
Wickramasinghe, Martin   292
Williams, David   13
Williams, Eric   111
Williams, Raymond   13

Willman, Elivira   173
Wilson, Amrit   13
Wispi, Agam   301
Wittke, Carl   60
Wittlin, Jozef   199
Wolf, Christa   153
Wolf, Friedrich   153, 155
Wolfert, Ira   60
Woodward, Miguel Cossio   85
Wright, Richard   61
Wright, Richard and Endres, Robin   29

Xia Yan   314
Xhuvani, Dhimiter   223
Xoxa, Jakov   223

Yadav, Rajemdra   289
Yakovlev, Aleksander   192
Yamada Seizaburo   328
Yamakawa Ryo
Yañez, Augustin   72
Yarov, Nicolai   192
Yasa, Ibrahim   233
Yashar Kemal   234
Yashpal   290
Yeh Tzu   314
Yehoshua, Abraham   240
Yera-Mangestu, Estifanos   254

Yglesias, Jose   61
Yi Hyo-Sak   317
Yi Ki-Yong   316
Yin Fu   314
Yizhar, S.   240
Yom Sang-Sop   316
Yon Dafu   314
Yudkin, Leon I.   240
  (with B. Tammuz)
Yevdokimov, Ivan   193
Zaheer, Sajjad   290
Zalewski, Witold   199
Zalka, Mate   211
Zalygin, Sergei   193
Zapata Olivella, Manuel   87
Zapotocky, Antonim   203
Zavala Muniz, Justino   104
Zeromski, Stefan   199
Zilhay, Lajos   211
Zola, Emile   120
Zoshchenko, Mikhail   193
Zuckmayer, Carl   153
Zweig, Arnold   153
Zwelling, Marc   30
Zwelonke, D.M.   273